# Collectables

## PRICE GUIDE 2008

7
HOKY
POKY
BUCK ROGE
SOLAR SCOU
MOVIE STAR
MARCH 25c
$100,000 00
IN U. S. BONDS
GIVEN AWAY
LUCKY
NUMBERS
PAGE 16

# Collectables

## PRICE GUIDE 2008

Judith Miller
& Mark Hill

A DORLING KINDERSLEY BOOK

LONDON, NEW YORK,
MELBOURNE, MUNICH AND DELHI

A joint production from DORLING KINDERSLEY
and THE PRICE GUIDE COMPANY

THE PRICE GUIDE COMPANY LIMITED

**Publisher** Judith Miller

**Collectables Specialist** Mark Hill

**Publishing Manager** Julie Brooke

**Editors** Sara Sturgess, Carolyn Madden

**Editoral Assistants** Carolyn Malarkey, Louisa Wheeler

**Design and DTP** Ali & Tim Scrivens, TJ Graphics

**Photographers** Graham Rae, Bruce Boyajian, John McKenzie, Byron Slater, Steve Tanner, Heike Löwenstein, Andy Johnson, Adam Gault

**Indexer** Hilary Bird

**Workflow Consultant** Bob Bousfield

**Business Advisor** Nick Croydon

DORLING KINDERSLEY LIMITED

**Publisher** Jonathan Metcalf

**Managing Art Editor** Christine Keilty

**Managing Editor** Angela Wilkes

**Production Editor** Clare McLean

**Production Controller** Linda Dare

**Production Manager** Joanna Bull



First published in Great Britain in 2007 by
Dorling Kindersley Limited
80 Strand, London WC2R 0RL

A Penguin Company

The Price Guide Company (UK) Ltd
Studio 21, Waterside
44–48 Wharf Road
London N1 7UX
info@thepriceguidecompany.com

2 4 6 8 10 9 7 5 3 1



A CIP catalogue record for this book is available from the British Library.

ISBN: 978 1 4053 2217 1

Printed and bound in Singapore by Star Standard

Discover more at

**www.dk.com**

# CONTENTS

# LIST OF CONSULTANTS

## Books

**Roddy Newlands**
Bloomsbury Auctions, London

## Ceramics

**Beth Adams**
Alfie's Antiques Market, London

**Judith Miller**
The Price Guide Company (UK) Ltd

**Richard Wallis**
richardwallisantiks.com

## Coins, Banknotes & Bonds

**Rick Coleman**
Bloomsbury Auctions, London

## Comics

**Phil Shrimpton**
phil-comics.com

## Compacts

**Sara Hughes**
http://mysite.wanadoo-members.co.uk/sara_compacts

## Chess & Games

**Luke Honey**
Bloomsbury Auctions, London

## Glass

**Ashmore & Burgess**
ashmoreandburgess.com

**Dr Graham Cooley**
Private Collector

**Michelle Guzy**
No Pink Carpet

**Mark Hill**
markhillpublishing.com

**Marcus Newhall**
sklounion.com

## Inuit Art

**Duncan McLean**
Waddington's, Toronto

## Posters

**Patrick Bogue**
onslows.co.uk

## Sci-Fi, Sixties & Seventies

**Sasha Keen**
neetstuff.com

## Teddy Bears

**Leanda Harwood & Peter Woodcock**
leandaharwood.co.uk

## Watches

**Mark Laino**
Mark of Time, Philadelphia, USA

We are also very grateful to our friends and experts who gave us so much help and support - Beverley Adams of Beverley London, James Bassam of T.W. Gaze & Sons, Rich Bertoia of Bertoia Auctions, Richard Caton and Alexander Crum Ewing of Bloomsbury Auctions, Gary Grant, Jeanette Hayhurst, Gary Hendy, Andrew Hilton of Special Auction Services, Geoffrey Robinson at Alfie's Antiques Market, and Ron & Ann Wheeler of Artius Glass.

# WHAT'S HOT

As I'm sure most of you will agree, collecting quickly becomes an obsession. Nevertheless, it's a highly enjoyable and rewarding obsession, so you won't hear me complaining! And I know I'm not the only one who has been bitten by the collecting bug. Car boot sales and antiques fairs and markets have become among the most popular places to spend Sundays. Whatever the season or weather, the internet also provides us with an enormously varied market, 24 hours a day. Homes all over the country proudly display treasures found on days out or days in, and never before has collecting been such a popular pastime.

## WEARABLE WONDERS

Collecting changes with fashion, and fashion changes collecting. Over the past year I have noticed a strong growth in interest in vintage wristwatches. Led by major names from Switzerland, such as Rolex and Blancpain, men across the world have begun to pay more attention to what was once deemed a functional item of which only one was needed. Almost like women and their handbags, many are now building collections of fine timepieces to suit different occasions. But it's not just the most expensive examples that seem to be attracting increasing levels of interest. Watches in styles that are typical of the period they were produced in, regardless of the maker, are also proving very popular. It's the 'style statement' that appeals, with the timeless elegance of the 1950s and the chunky look of the 1960s and '70s being particularly popular. If this is twinned with a well-known maker and a fine quality mechanism, so much the better. Time will tell if this fashion lasts, but with men paying more attention to their appearances and accessories generally, the countdown to further price rises has already clearly begun.

▲ 1940s 'apple juice' bakelite bangle, with reversed carved and filled goldfish design. **Worth £800-1,200 ROX**

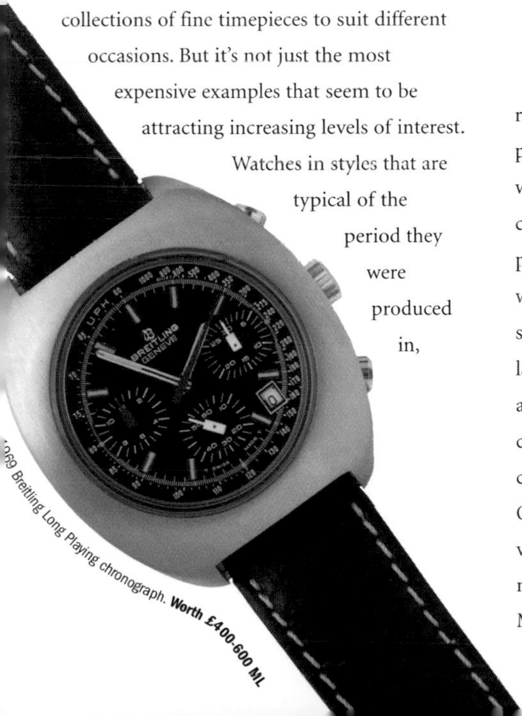


1969 Breitling Long Playing chronograph. **Worth £400-600 ML**

Of course, women have paid close attention to vintage styles for some years now. One of the most desirable markets is still costume jewellery. Making a statement is as important as ever, and

A 1950s fabric and bead cornflower handbag. **Worth £100-150 CRIS**

the chunky, bright and cheerful designs produced in Bakelite and other plastics from the 1920s to the 1950s continue to rise in value and desirability. They seem to be as popular today as they were with women during the Great Depression of the 1930s, when they brought affordable cheer during a time of immense difficulty and change – much like today's world.

Although the best names such as Trifari and Stanley Hagler continue to attract the best prices, I've noticed a surge in interest and values for unsigned pieces. Here, as with watches, the 'look' and style is everything. If a piece has instant eye appeal, colour and the all-important sparkle factor, it's sure to find a ready buyer. My advice is to snap up the best pieces now, as they are already becoming much harder to find.

A 1950s unsigned glass brooch. **Worth. £50-60 PC**

## NECESSARY ACCESSORIES

Researchers have found that the average British woman spends over £30,000 on shoes and over £15,000 on handbags throughout her lifetime. A third are said to spend well in excess of those figures.

Often following the lead of models and celebrities such as Kate Moss and Keira Knightley, I know that part of these vast sums is being invested in vintage pieces. The 1950s and 60s are still the most popular decades, partly due to the affordability of most of the pieces, but also due to the variety of designs available, and their great wearability. Although the major names in fashion will always attract the most attention, canny buyers look for more affordable pieces by lesser names that strongly represent the look of these decades in terms of style. As many are

A pair of 1960s striped silk shoes by Rhythm Step. **Worth £25-35 NOR**

A Dartington Glass Kingfisher blue FT65 vase. **Worth £60-80 GC**

bought to be used, pieces in unworn condition, or those that were looked after well, tend to fetch the highest prices. Vintage examples are also often used by today's designers as inspiration – your boot sale bargain might just end up revamped on a catwalk next year!

Also, having seen the attention being paid to today's top designs and re-editions of much-loved classics, such as Chanel's limited edition 2.55 bags, I am convinced that these will become the collectables of tomorrow. As fashions change, it's always worth keeping an eye on celebrity magazines to try to spot 'the next big thing'.

## GREAT GLASS

In fact, 'What's the next big thing?' is the question my collectables specialist Mark Hill and I are most frequently asked. If we knew for sure, we certainly wouldn't be telling everyone about it quite yet! However, one area that we are sure fits the bill is 20th century glass.

Usually deemed the poor relation to ceramics in terms of popularity, the last few years have seen a marked change. The Whitefriars phenomenon was an early testament to this. Geoffrey Baxter's designs produced in the 1970s, that were once worth under £20, began to fetch increasingly higher prices around five years ago. They reached a high point over the past two years, with rumours of a unique red 'Banjo' vase fetching over £5,000 last year.

The key here is research, and the knowledge and understanding it generates. Just as Baxter's designs for Whitefriars were re-appraised in the context of 20th century glass design and decorative arts, so the work of others is now being addressed. Two particularly hot areas must be Chance Glass, and Frank Thrower's designs for Dartington Glass. Typical designs such as Thrower's textured range produced in Scandinavian-inspired colours, and Chance Glass'

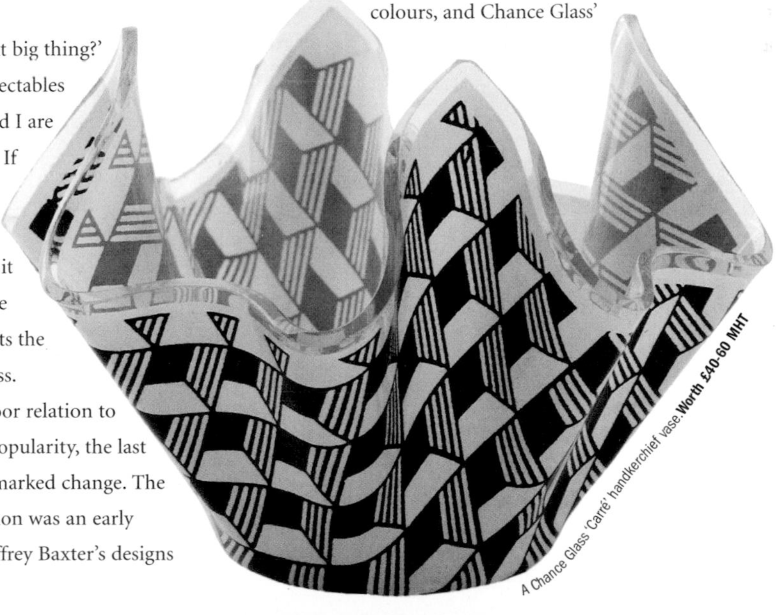

A Chance Glass 'Carré' handkerchief vase. **Worth £40-60 MHT**

handkerchief vases have been showing considerable increases in both interest and value, mainly due to new research and public exhibitions. They also look both appealing and very much of their time.

Glass is, of course, a fantastically visual medium that offers so much. Nothing pleases me more than seeing my small collection of Whitefriars glass glowing in the early morning sun when I come downstairs to make coffee.

These changes in the glass collecting world are also representative of one of the factors that make the collectables market so interesting and vibrant to me. As new information is unearthed, and a design is attributed or re-attributed, a little more of the incredibly varied history of the decorative arts is recorded.

A 1950s Italian handpainted ceramic vase. **Worth £70-100 GC**

A T. G. Green Cornishware 'Icing Sugar' storage *jar*. **Worth £80-120 GA**

## CLASSIC CERAMICS

Of course, for many reasons including a lack of original information or records, some areas take more time to research. It may even be that very little will ever be found out about them. But, despite this, examples continue to fetch strong prices. Here the key is the immediate visual appeal of the piece. One area that fulfills all of these criteria is Italian ceramics of the 1950s-60s. Very little is known about the makers and designers behind these cheerful and often quirky pieces, but their period appeal and has led to a growth in prices over the past year. Most are decorated in the bright colours typical of the Mediterranean, but it is those with well-executed designs that are typical of the era, that are proving to be the most popular. Having said this, it's not all about new areas, and I have been delighted to learn about the return of some old friends. Established collecting areas such as Cornishware have seen

A Transformers 'Optimus Prime' toy. **Worth £30-40 NOR**

a recent surge in interest too. Country styles have been popular for years now, and few ceramics reflect this area better than Cornishware, and indeed its very different cousin – Chintzware.

## TIMELESS TOYS

The appeal of the country look shows that nostalgia is an important driver in the collectables market. We're all guilty of harking back to simpler days, perhaps when we were children. And in today's increasingly threatening world, who can blame us? As a result, toys have long been established collecting areas. However, much like fashion, areas change and develop rapidly. As successive generations grow up and become thirty-somethings with incomes, many begin to collect the toys of their youth. Over the past few years, 1980s toys have become more popular. Transformers are an excellent example, and I have seen interest rise on both sides of the Atlantic for these memorable toys. I'm sure many have rushed home to raid their old toy box in the attic. That is, unless their parents haven't got there first!

However, there's one stylish young lady who has continued to remain in fashion – Barbie. The past year has seen her popularity reach new heights, with a Barbie No.1 fetching over £2,500 at auction.

All this goes to show that despite fashion often changing exactly what we may collect, there's one thing that fashion never changes – and that's collecting itself.

Judith Miller.

A Barbie 'Miss America' doll, by Mattel, with original clothes. **Worth £20-30 BH**

# HOW TO USE THIS BOOK

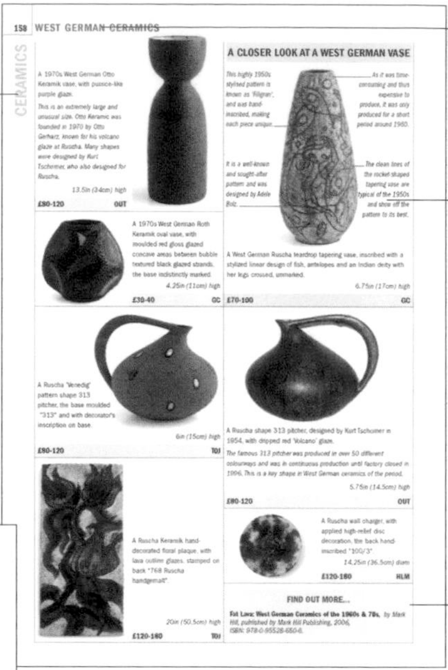


**Category Heading**
Indicates the general category as listed in the table of contents on pp.5–6.

**Subcategory Heading**
Indicates the subcategory of the main category heading and describes the general contents of the page.

**A Closer Look at...**
Here, we highlight particularly interesting items or show identifying features, pointing out rare or desirable qualities.

**Find out more...**
To help you seek further information, these boxes list websites, books, and museums where you can find out more.

A Ruscha shape 313 pitcher, designed by Kurt Tschomer in 1954, with dripped red 'Volcano' glaze.

*The famous 313 pitcher was produced in over 50 different colourways and was in continuous production until factory closed in 1996. This is a key shape in West German ceramics of the period.*

*5.75in (14.5cm) high*

**£80-120** **OUT**

**The Caption**
Describes the item and can include the maker, model, year of manufacture, size and condition.

**The Price Guide**
All prices are shown in ranges and give you a "ball park" figure close to what you should expect to pay for a similar item. The great joy of collectables is that there is not a recommended retail price. The price given is not necessarily that which a dealer will pay you. As a general rule, expect to receive approximately 30-50 per cent less. When selling, pay attention to the dealer or auction house specialist to understand why this may be, and consider that they have to run a business as well as make a living. When buying, listen again. Condition, market forces and location of the place of sale will all affect a price. If no price is available, the letters NPA will be used.

**Collectors' Notes**
Provides background information on the designer, factory or make of the piece or style in question.

**The Object**
All collectables are shown in full colour, which is a vital aid to identification and valuation.

**The Source Code**
The image is credited to its source with a code. See the "Key to Illustrations" on pp.576-580 for a full listing of dealers and auction houses.

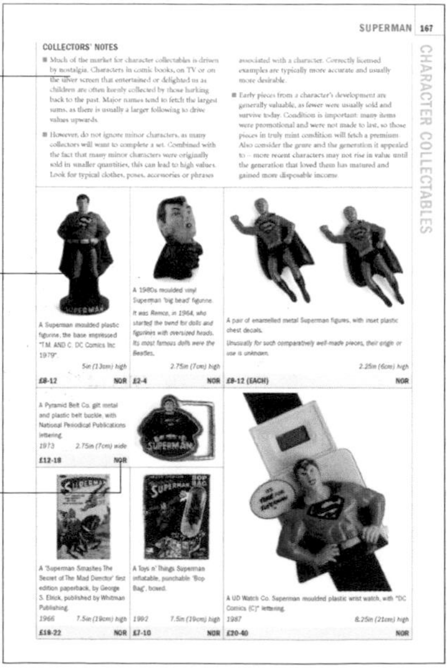

## COLLECTORS' NOTES

- The value and desirability of advertising memorabilia is based primarily on the brand, followed by the type of item and the date it was made. Larger brands often have strong followings, and the increased competition leads to higher values. Colourful pieces displaying the typical hallmarks of a brand, such as a character or logo, are likely to be sought-after. The style of a piece, including the logo, font and colours used, can often help with dating.
- Signs, shop display boards and packaging are popular types, with tin signs and tins often being worth the most. Huntley & Palmers are perhaps the most famous and collected name, particularly for their novelty shaped tins of the early to mid-20th century. Also consider items that would have been thrown away, as although they were initially made in large quantities, fewer will have survived today. Condition is also important as these items were often made to be used, but were not necessarily made to last – and as a result a premium will be paid for items in mint condition.

A William Crawford & Sons Ltd shaped and lithograph printed biscuit tin, in the form of a Georgian style tea caddy.

*1925* *6in (15.5cm) wide*

**£60-80** **SS**

A Huntley and Palmers 'creel' biscuit tin, in the shape of an angel's fishing basket, marked "Regd. No. 486204" near base on back.

*c1907*

**£120-180** **DN**

A W. & R. Jacob & Co. Ltd. 'Coronation Coach' biscuit tin, with tinplate wheels, the removable roof with crown-shaped knop.

*Tins with moveable parts, and those that could be played with as toys, are often found damaged, or were broken and thrown away at the time. As such, surviving examples are often scarce and desirable. The Royal connection also adds to the desirability of this tin.*

*c1936*

**£120-180** **DN**

A Lifeguard 'Extra Lustre Car Polish' can, with printed exterior.

*1959* *6.25in (16cm) high*

**£15-20** **DH**

A 'Black & White Scotch Whisky' advertising perfume bottle, by The English Perfumery Co.

*c1930* *3.25in (8cm) high*

**£15-20** **DH**

An Edwards Brilliantine 'Uzon' sample bottle.

*c1900* *2in (5cm) high*

**£20-30** **DH**

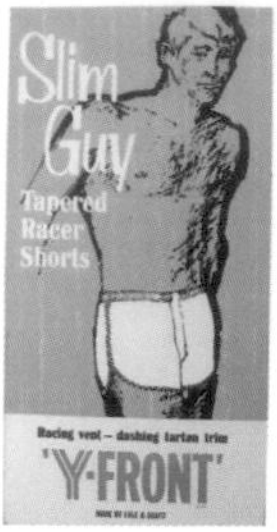

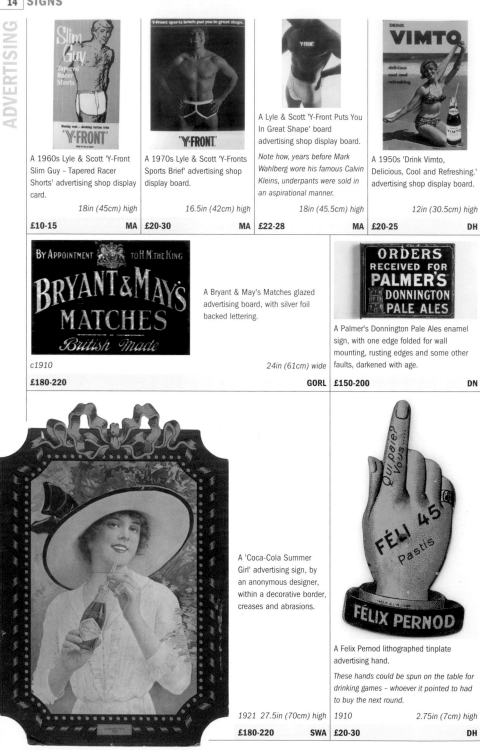

A 1960s Lyle & Scott 'Y-Front Slim Guy – Tapered Racer Shorts' advertising shop display card.

*18in (45cm) high*

**£10-15** **MA**

A 1970s Lyle & Scott 'Y-Fronts Sports Brief' advertising shop display board.

*16.5in (42cm) high*

**£20-30** **MA**

A Lyle & Scott 'Y-Front Puts You In Great Shape' board advertising shop display board.

*Note how, years before Mark Wahlberg wore his famous Calvin Kleins, underpants were sold in an aspirational manner.*

*18in (45.5cm) high*

**£22-28** **MA**

A 1950s 'Drink Vimto, Delicious, Cool and Refreshing.' advertising shop display board.

*12in (30.5cm) high*

**£20-25** **DH**

A Bryant & May's Matches glazed advertising board, with silver foil backed lettering.

*c1910* *24in (61cm) wide*

**£180-220** **GORL**

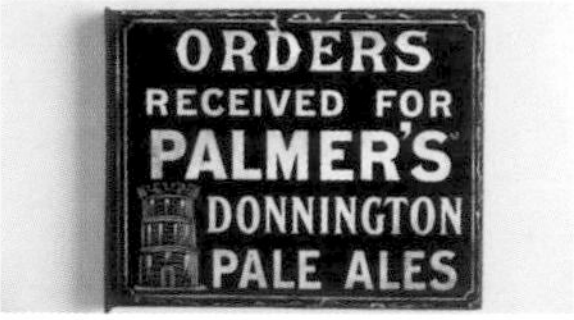


A Palmer's Donnington Pale Ales enamel sign, with one edge folded for wall mounting, rusting edges and some other faults, darkened with age.

**£150-200** **DN**

A 'Coca-Cola Summer Girl' advertising sign, by an anonymous designer, within a decorative border, creases and abrasions.

*1921 27.5in (70cm) high*

**£180-220** **SWA**

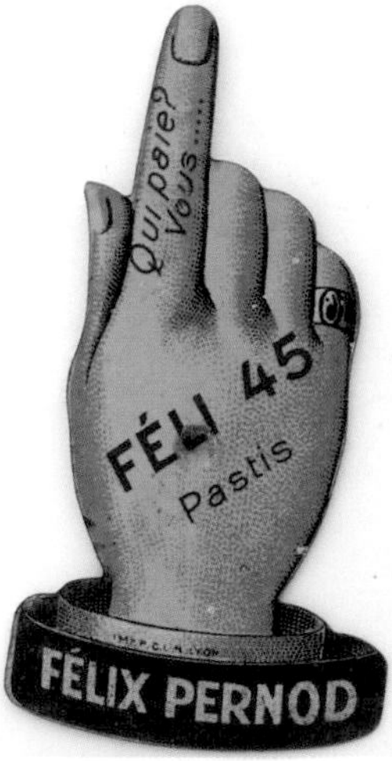


A Felix Pernod lithographed tinplate advertising hand.

*These hands could be spun on the table for drinking games – whoever it pointed to had to buy the next round.*

*1910* *2.75in (7cm) high*

**£20-30** **DH**

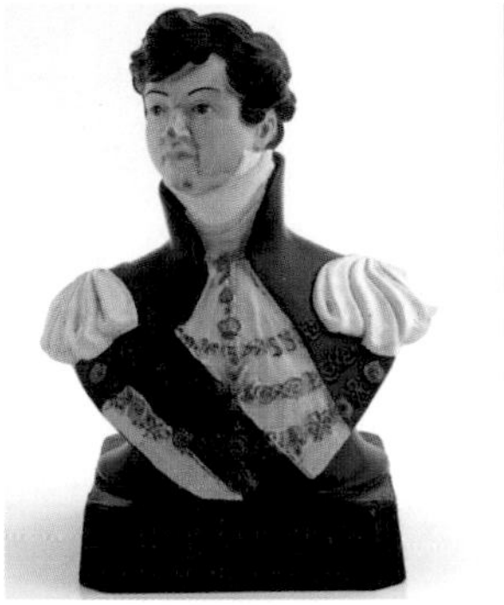

A 1950s King George IV Old Scotch Whisky advertising figure.

*8.5in (22cm) high*

**£50-70** **DH**

A Horner 'Dainty Dinah' Toffee shop display, in a glass sweet jar.

*The Dainty Dinah brand was introduced in 1914, examples from before 1918 generally show Dinah with a parasol.*

*c1930* *10.5in (26.5cm) high*

**£100-150** **DH**

A WWI advertising brass tank, for metal manufacturers McKechnie, Birmingham.

*c1914* *3in (7.5cm) long*

**£70-90** **DH**

A 1960s 'Queen Anne Rare Scotch Whisky' lithographed tin advertising tray.

*13.5in (34.5cm) wide*

**£15-20** **DH**

A Dewar's Whiskey lithographed tin advertising tray.

*The quality of printing is excellent on this example, hence the higher price.*

*c1910* *16in (40.5cm) long*

**£80-120** **DH**

A 1930s Essolube advertising pocket penknife.

*3in (7.5cm) high*

**£35-45** **DH**

A Fry's Chocolate tinplate fold-up advertising ruler, with printed design, some damage.

*c1905* *12in (30.5cm) long*

**£70-100** **DH**

An early 20thC Bryant & May's box of unused braided cigar lights.

*Box 2.5in (6.5cm) wide*

**£25-35** **GAZE**

A 1920s Joseph Fray Ltd Bentley 4.5 litre nickel-plated mascot, with horizontal wings, accent lines around the edge of the 'B', original threaded mounting stud.

*This is the larger of the two sizes available in the 1920s, and was used on 4.5 and 6.5 litre cars.*

*3.5in (9cm) high*

**£400-600** **TCA**

A cold-painted bronze parrot car mascot, on a brass plinth.

*4.5in (11.5cm) high*

**£150-200** **GORL**

A Boyce Moto Meter 'Universal' type temperature gauge, with an intact glass tube, black scale plate and chamfered glass.

*8in (20cm) wide*

**£80-120** **TCA**

A Bugatti Owners Club 'Prescott' table top trophy, fashioned as a Bugatti radiator grill, upon a circular base with four protrusions inscribed "June 1966 First Class", "July 1966 First Class", "R. Rose".

*c1966* *8in (20cm) high*

**£180-220** **BIG**

A 1920s French Charles Paillet plated car mascot, depicting a rodeo rider, lacks horse's tail and reins.

*Paillet (1871-1937) was a notable French sculptor known for his 'Animalièr style animal bronzes.*

*4.25in (10.5cm) high*

**£1,800-2,200** **L&T**

A 1920s Augustine & Emile LeJeune cold-painted bronze 'Felix' car mascot, stamped "Felix AEL Copyright".

*Felix mascots predate Mickey Mouse mascots by around a decade. Examples of this Mascot are very rare and attract interest from both mascot collectors and Felix fans. LeJeune were also one of the most famous, high quality mascot makers.*

*3.25in (8cm) high*

**£650-750** **DIM**

An American 'Studebaker Driver's Club Inc.' printed felt pennant.

*18in (45.5cm) wide*

**£15-25** **LDE**

An American 'Souvenir of Indianapolis' large printed blue felt pennant.

*29.25in (74cm) long*

**£70-90** **LDE**

A 1950's Mobil Pegasus chequered flag, with the red Mobil Pegasus logo in the centre, minor tears and stains.

*35in (89cm) wide*

**£180-220** **AGI**

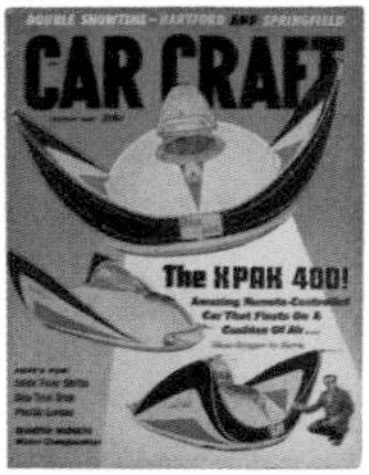


'Car Craft' magazine, March 1961.

*The cover with futuristic cars is desirable. The value of these magazines depends on such factors, and also the desirability of the car, engine and driver in any internal features. The whackier the conversion, the better.*

*10.75in (27.5cm) high*

**£15-25** **NOR**

A 1970's 9ct gold Rolls-Royce key ring, the engine grill fob suspended from a sprung key ring, hallmarked for Birmingham 1975.

*1975*

**£250-350** **HAMG**

'Car Craft' magazine, August 1960, with 'Starbird's Wild ... Dream Custom' cover story and artwork.

*10.75in (27.5cm) high*

**£15-25** **NOR**

A small oil can, with brass fittings and copper spout, in very good condition.

*4.5in (11.5cm) high*

**£40-60** **MUR**

A 1960s large scale '66 Ford Mustang, with battery-powered motor and lights.

*This well detailed and well-made scale model was probably made for an American Ford showroom.*

*16in (40.5cm) wide*

**£180-220** **W&W**

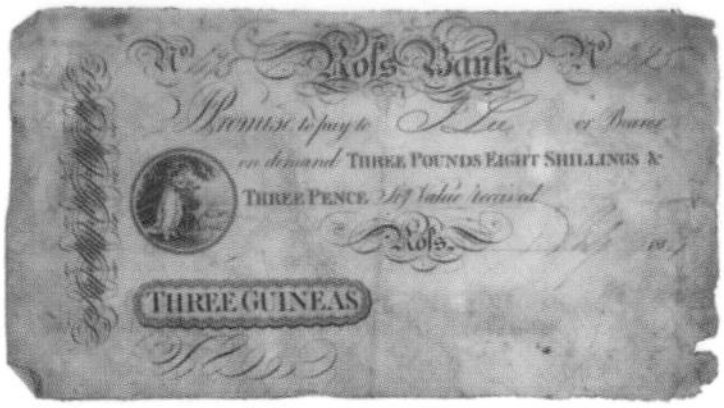


An unissued Irish Ross Bank three guineas note, dated 1 July 1814, black on white with maiden resting on anchor.

*As this is not signed, it was not issued.*

*1814*

**£180-220** **BLO**

An Irish Ross Bank four Guineas note, no.174, dated 1st September 1814, issued and signed by Peter Roe, black on white with maiden resting on anchor left side.

*1814*

**£150-250** **BLO**

An Andover Old Bank one pound bank note, serial number 12174, dated 5th October 1825, issued to Joseph Wakeford, William Wakeford and Robert Wakeford.

*1825* *8in (20cm) wide*

**£180-220** **WW**

An Irish Galway Bank six shillings note, no.A/1938, issued to Walter Joyce and Mark Lynch on 12th July 1804, black on white with two coats-of-arms on left.

*1804*

**£800-1,200** **BLO**

A Bahamian George VI five pounds note.

*This note is rare in this very fine, uncirculated condition.*

*1940*

**£350-450** **BLO**

A Northern Ireland Ulster Bank Limited fifty pounds note, no.2314, hand-signed by J.R.Williams and dated 1st March 1941, in fine condition.

*1941*

**£150-200** **BLO**

An Irish Central Bank of Ireland twenty pounds notes, no.80X 052691, dated 24.3.1976, in extremely fine condition.

*1976*

**£70-100** **BLO**

A British, Bradbury Wilkinson purple advertising note, with Nelson at right.

**£70-100** **BLO**

## COLLECTORS' NOTES

- Belt buckles have become enormously collectable over the past few decades. Most focus on military examples or more modern buckles that celebrate music, advertising companies such as John Deere or simply those that are fashionable. However, there are a large number of buckles dating from before the 1960s that are currently largely ignored by many collectors.
- Perhaps the earliest area for collecting is the Art Nouveau period from the late 19th century to the early 20th century. Many of these are made from silver or copper, and are often decorated by hand. Sinuous, curving, naturally inspired motifs are typical. Learn makers' marks and look for well-known makers.
- The Art Deco period of the 1920s and '30s also provides plenty of scope for collecting. Here, the design is important again, with geometric patterns and bright colours or a bold combination of black and silver being popular. Good quality plastics also peaked in popularity at this time. Look for typical forms and the bright colours associated with the age.
- In general, look for designs that represent the prevalent style of the period the buckle was made in. Precious metals such as silver are likely to raise the value considerably, as is the addition of any hand-applied work such as hand engraving or enamelling. Be aware that many buckles were made in two pieces. If only one survives, the price should be adjusted accordingly as it can be hard to find a matching replacement.
- After considering the style and marks, examine a buckle closely for damage. As they were functional items, many have become worn or damaged through use. Chips to the enamel and lost 'stones' reduce value, and it can be hard to find replacements of the right size and colour. Although the presence of the original belt adds interest, it rarely adds to value unless it too is well made and an intrinsic part of the overall design.

A rare American Kerr & Co. silver-plated belt buckle, in the form of coiled cobras, with an inset central ruby red rhinestone.

*Snakes were a popular motif at the end of the 19thC and turn of the 20thC. Vintage examples are much sought-after today.*

*c1900-05* *5in (12.75cm) wide*

**£250-300** **CGPC**

An American Art Nouveau Kerr & Co. vermeil double peacock motif belt buckle, set with ruby glass cabochons.

*Vermeil is the term used to describe a gold finish on sterling silver.*

*c1900-05* *3.5in (9cm) wide*

**£250-300** **CGPC**

An English Art Nouveau W.H. Haeler silver two-piece buckle, with Birmingham hallmarks for "W.H.H."

*1902* *3.75in (9.5cm) wide*

**£120-180** **DN**

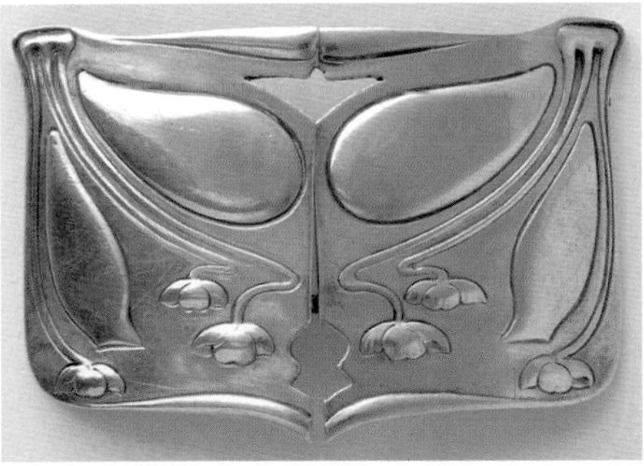

A William Hutton & Sons Art Nouveau silver two-piece belt buckle, of shaped outline, embellished with slightly lobed panels flanked by stylized lilies, with maker's mark and hallmark for London.

*1902* *3.5in (8.5cm) wide*

**£180-220** **DN**

An early 1900s American Art Nouveau silver metal floral and foliate belt buckle, on a black fabric belt.

*2.25in (6cm) high*

**£25-35** **NOR**

An American vermeil belt buckle, unsigned, with scrolling acanthus forms and selective enamelling.

*c1905* *3in (7.5cm) wide*

**£150-200** **CGPC**

An early 1900s American oval sterling belt buckle, set with 'French paste' stones.

*Paste is the term used to describe glass with a high lead content that has been cut to resemble real precious stones.*

*3.5in (9cm) diam*

**£100-150** **NOR**

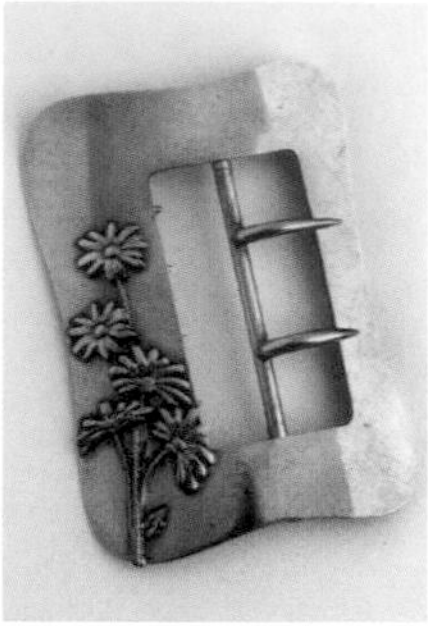

An American Howard & Co. sterling silver belt buckle, with applied sterling silver floral design.

*The style and simplicity of the design recall Japanese designs, which were popular when this buckle was made.*

*c1885-1900 3in (8.5cm) high*

**£60-90** **CGPC**

An early 1900s American sterling silver belt buckle, with engraved floral and lined pattern, the reverse stamped "Sterling".

*4in (10cm) wide*

**£60-90** **NOR**

A 1930s Art Deco cast silver metal and black Bakelite belt buckle, set with paste stones and mounted on a black silk belt.

*The large stones and geometric shape are in imitation of diamond and platinum 'cocktail' jewellery that was popular during the 1920s and '30s.*

*2.25in (6cm) wide*

**£20-30** **NOR**

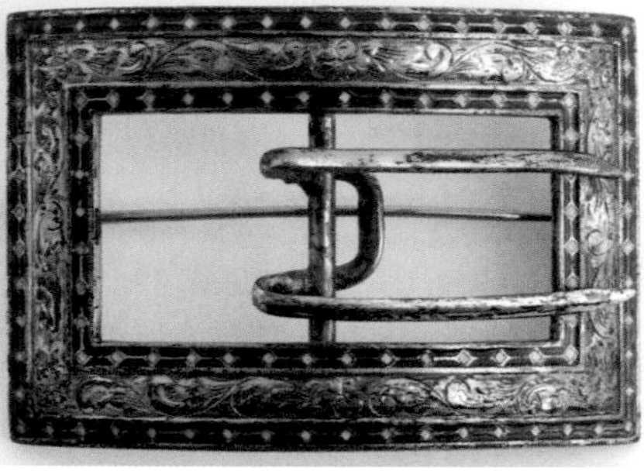

An American Kerr & Co. hand-engraved sterling silver belt buckle, with an enamelled border.

*The third pin seen in the middle of the buckle allows it to be worn as a brooch. This is a later addition.*

*c1905 3in (7.5cm) wide*

**£150-200** **CGPC**

An Art Deco silver metal belt buckle, with diamond and dimple design, some pitting to the surface.

*3.25in (8cm) wide*

**£15-20** **NOR**

An Art Deco gold-tone metal monkey and rope curl belt buckle, with paper label for "La Mode".

*3.5in (9cm) wide*

**£20-30** **NOR**

An Art Deco engraved and painted mother-of-pearl disc belt buckle.

*2.5in (6.5cm) diam*

**£25-35** **NOR**

An unsigned American belt buckle, of hammered copper comprising rectangular and circular forms, the centre with an inlaid shell.

*c1910* *4.25in (10.75cm) wide*

**£80-120** **CGPC**

A 1930s Art Deco brass belt buckle, inset with faceted coloured glass 'stones'.

*The bright colours of the glass and the geometric and stepped design are all typical of the Art Deco movement.*

*3.5in (9cm) wide*

**£50-70** **NOR**

A 1930s hammered brass belt buckle, with inset faux coral glass and overlaid filigree.

*Note the strong influence of Pre-Colombian and Mexican jewellery.*

*5in (13cm) wide*

**£40-50** **NOR**

An early 20thC pressed brass filigree belt buckle, set with faceted coloured glass 'stones'.

*5in (12.5cm) wide*

**£40-50** **NOR**

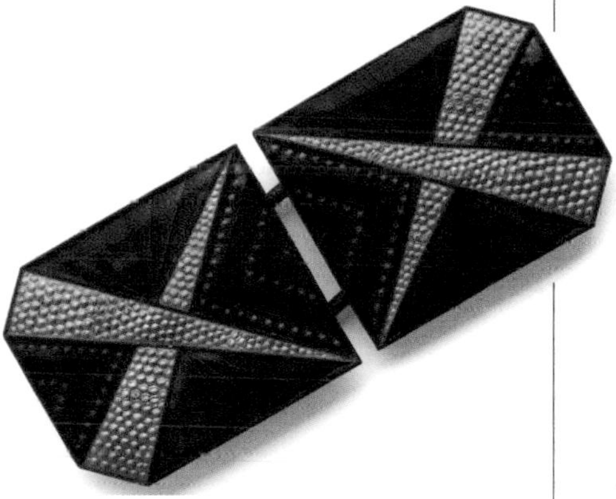

An Art Deco burgundy enamelled cast metal belt buckle.

*2.5in (6.5cm) wide*

**£20-30** **NOR**

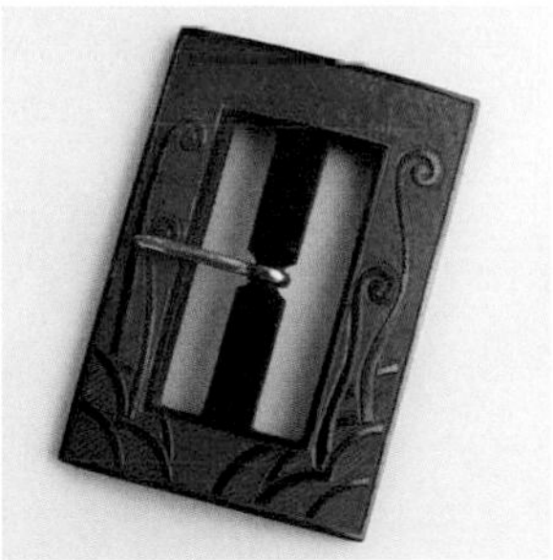

A 1930s Art Deco plastic belt buckle, with carved decoration.

*3.25in (8cm) high*

**£20-30** **JBC**

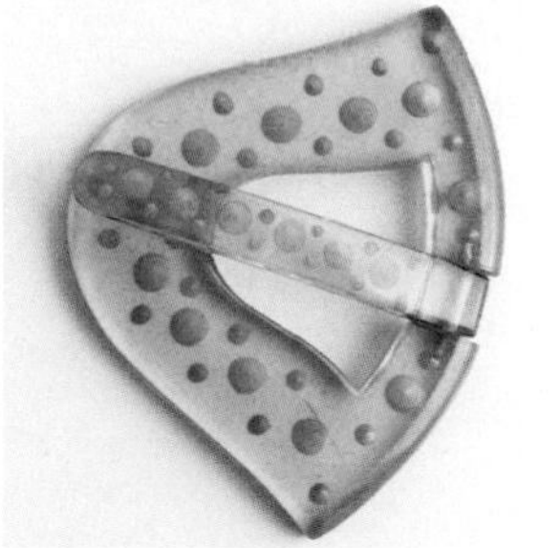

A 1930s yellow cast Lucite belt buckle, with carved 'bubble' decoration.

*2.75in (7cm) wide*

**£15-20** **JBC**

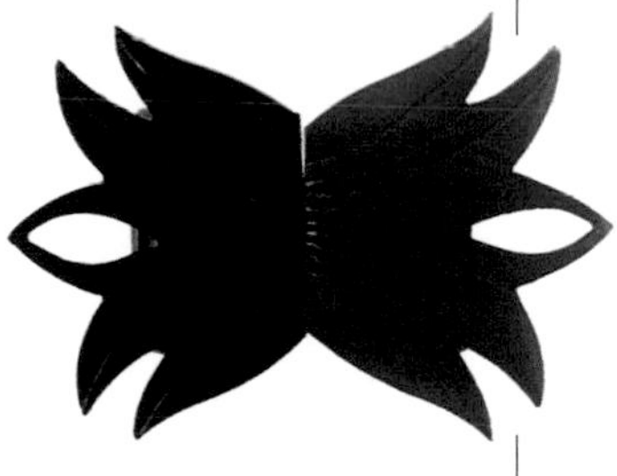

A 1930s Art Deco belt buckle, of mirror-image stylized leaves in black and amber-red bakelite.

*3.5in (9cm) wide*

**£40-50** **ABAA**

A French 'Hurtu' bicycles advertising poster, for the Exposition Universelle in 1889, printed by Charles Verneau, Paris, some tears.

*1889* *53.5in (137.5cm) high*

**£600-1,000** **LOZ**

'Moi Aussi, J'ai Une Peugeot' (I have a Peugeot too) French advertising poster, printed by Gaillard, Paris, a small hole at the top of the image, and a tear on the left.

*23.75in (60.5cm) high*

**£300-500** **LOZ**

'7 Raisons Pour Acheter un vélo-moteur Alcyon...' French advertising poster, printed by Gaillard of Paris and Amiens, in good condition.

*The poster gives seven reasons to buy a part-motorised Alycon bicycle including not requiring a driving licence or a garage, avoiding taxes, and a minimal purchase cost.*

*24in (61cm) high*

**£400-600** **LOZ**

A rare American bicycling paper-on-linen printed poster, with tin bars at the top and bottom, "Copyrighted 1884", printed by Donaldson Brothers, Five Points, NY.

*1884* *28.25in (72cm) high*

**£400-600** **SOTT**

A 'Bicycling' transfer-printed and painted nursery plate, with moulded border and scene depicting George IV and a large lady riding a boneshaker entitled "A Visit from Richmond to Carlton House", hairline crack.

*Inspiration for this caricature may well have come from George IV's friendship with the ample Lady Conyngham which was the subject of a cartoon by Heath, published on the 28th March, 1824.*

*c1825* *6.5in (16.5cm) diam*

**£400-500** **SAS**

An unusual 'Bicycling' nursery plate, the border moulded with flowers and foliage, the centre printed with a boneshaker ridden by a hatted gentleman.

*c1820* *6.25in (15.5cm) diam*

**£600-700** **SAS**

A French mechanical hand-propelled tricycle horse, cast-iron head and wooden body in original colour, leather saddle with velvet seat, rococo-style cast-iron panel, steel wheels, missing tail, complete and working condition.

*c1880*

**£500-600** **ATK**

## COLLECTORS' NOTES

- True first editions are from the first print run of the first edition of a book. A 'first edition' may then have subsequent printing runs, and later editions may be changed in some way, such as errors being corrected. Therefore numbers of 'firsts' are limited and value rises as desirability increases.
- Famous, iconic titles will always be prized, but a classic title published at the height of an author's career will often be worth less than an early or less well-received work, partly as fewer first edition copies of the earlier work will have been printed.
- To identify a first edition, look for the number '1' in the series of numbers on the copyright page. Some publishers state clearly that a book is a first edition, and some use a sequence of letters – learn how to recognise the different styles. Always check that the publishing date and copyright date match, and check the original publishing date in a reference book. Book club editions tend to be ignored by many collectors.
- Authors' signatures add value to a first edition, particularly if it is a limited or special edition. The smaller the edition and the more renowned the title, the higher the price is likely to be. Dedications are less desirable, unless the recipient is famous in their own right, or connected to the author in some way.
- There are many consistently popular authors such as Ian Fleming and Agatha Christie, but fashion plays a large role in value. Some first editions can rise in value if the book is made into a film and proves successful. Look out for signed first edition copies by up-and-coming authors, particularly those nominated for major prizes.
- Always consider condition. Dust wrappers (or dust jackets) should be clean, unfaded and undamaged and values of modern titles can fall by over 50 per cent without them. However, damage to older examples can often be restored. Also look inside to make sure the book is complete, and has not been damaged or defaced.
- Paperback books from the 1930s-60s are generally collected for the design of the cover, rather than for their content. As they were inexpensive and not made to last, some titles can be rare. Condition plays an important part in value. Gangster, crime, and science fiction are popular categories. Look out for books by Ben Sarto, Hank Janson and cover artwork typical of this 'pulp fiction' genre.

G.K. Chesterton, "Greybeards at Play", first edition, first issue, with illustrations by the author, published by Brimley Johnson.

*This is the author's first title and is comparatively scarce.*

*1900*

**£180-220** **BLO**

G.K. Chesterton, "The Napoleon of Notting Hill", first edition, inscribed by the author and with illustrations by William Graham Robertson, published by John Lane Co. at The Bodley Head Press.

*1904*

**£200-250** **BLO**

G.K. Chesterton, "The Innocence of Father Brown", first edition, published by Cassell.

*This is more commonly found bound in red cloth with gilt lettering.*

*1911*

**£350-450** **BLO**

### A CLOSER LOOK AT "THE MASTER & MAGARITA"

*The book tells the story of the Devil (Woland) and his strange associates visiting Moscow and the ensuing chaos caused to a Russian writer and life in Moscow.*

*Bulgakov started writing it in 1928 and, after destroying one draft due to fear of it being banned or censored and subsequent reprisals, it was finished by his wife from 1940, after his death in that same year.*

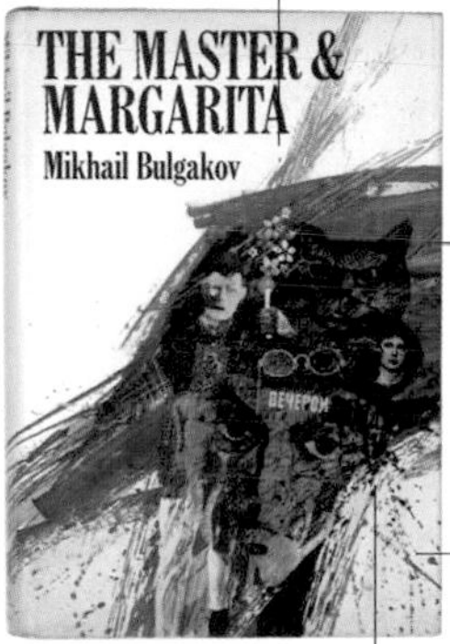


*It was first published in an edited form across issues of the Moscow magazine, with the complete version only being published in Russian in 1973, six years after this edition was published in English.*

*The story is actually a criticism of the stifling bureaucratic rule of the atheistic Soviet leadership, and also covers themes of good and evil, and love and sensuality.*

Mikhail Bulgakov, "The Master & Margarita", first English edition, published by Collins & Harvill Press.

*1967*

**£180-220** **BLO**

Agatha Christie, "The Body in the Library", first edition, published by Collins in 1942

**£500-600** **BLO**

Arthur C. Clarke, "Childhood's End, first English edition, published by Sidgwick & Jackson.

*Clarke is more famous for his science fiction stories, however, early in his career he was fascinated by psychics and the paranormal.*

*1954*

**£350-450** **BLO**

Hal Clement (Harry Clement Stubbs), "Mission of Gravity", first edition, signed by author, published by Garden City, New York.

*The signature reads '"Hal Clement" (Harry C Stubbs)'.*

*1954*

**£280-320** **BLO**

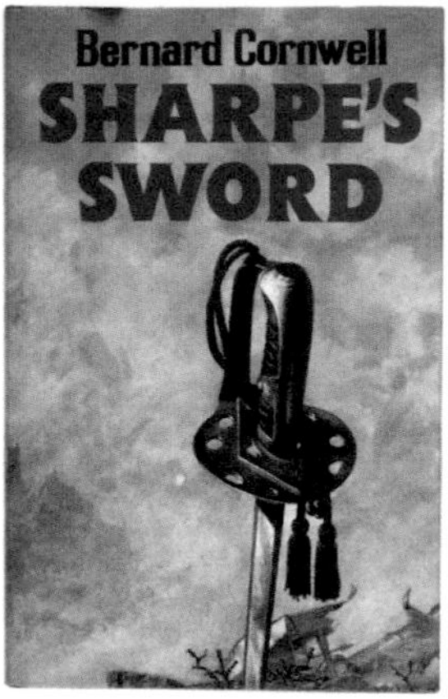


Bernard Cornwell, "Sharpe's Sword", first edition, signed by the author, published by Collins.

*This is a scarce first edition of the fourth in the Sharpe series.*

*1983*

**£650-750** **BLO**

Bernard Cornwell, "Sharpe's Eagle", first English edition, original cloth, dust jacket, published by Collins.

*This is the first book in the series covering the military life of the heroic Richard Sharpe. The series has proved immensely popular, captivating adults and children alike, resulting in a large following.*

*1981*

**£350-450** **BLO**

Bernard Cornwell, "Sharpe's Enemy", first edition, published by Collins.

*1984*

**£280-320** **BLO**

Bernard Cornwell, "Sharpe's Honour", first edition, published by Collins.

*1985*

**£220-280** **BLO**

Don DeLillo, "Americana", first American edition, signed by the author, published by Houghton Mifflin Co.

*A version of the same book without the author's signature could be worth less than half of this example.*

*1971*

**£450-550** **BLO**

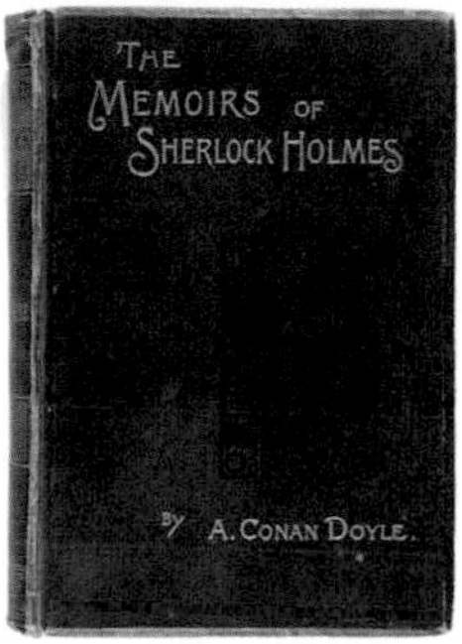


Sir Arthur Conan Doyle, "The Memoirs of Sherlock Holmes", first edition, published by George Newnes, with wear to the cloth covered boards.

*1894*

**£250-350** **BLO**

## A CLOSER LOOK AT A T.S. ELIOT BOOK

*This book is from a limited edition of 600. Five days later an 'ordinary' edition of 2,000 was produced.*

*It is a first edition and was printed by the Curwen Press.*

*It was originally sold with a clear 'glassine' dust wrapper and a hard slipcase, had these been present it could be worth over twice as much.*

*Each limited edition copy was signed by T.S. Eliot.*

T.S. Eliot, "Ash-Wednesday", published by Fountain Press & Faber.

*1930*

**£280-320** **BLO**

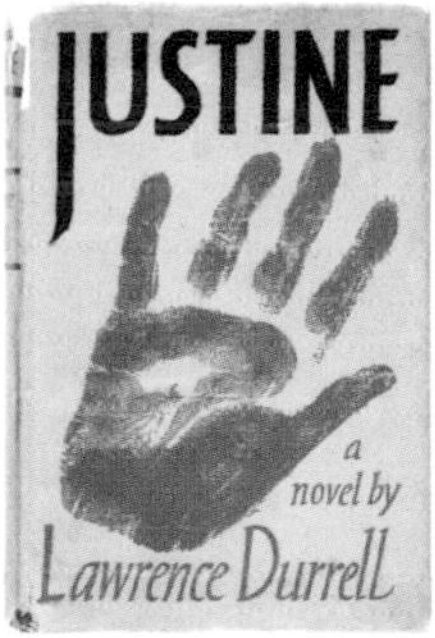


Lawrence Durrell, "Justine", first edition, published by Faber.

*1957*

**£180-220** **BLO**

William Faulkner, "The Wild Palms", first English edition, published by Chatto & Windus.

*1939*

**£180-220** **BLO**

Jasper Fforde, "Something Rotten", first edition, published by Hodder & Stoughton, signed by the author.

*2004*

**£15-20** **BIB**

Ian Fleming, "Dr. No", first edition, second state, published by Cape.

*1958*

**£150-200** **BLO**

Ian Fleming, "Goldfinger", first edition, published by Cape.

*This example is signed by Honor Blackman, who played Pussy Galore in the 1964 film version, which adds to to its desirability. A copy without the signature would be worth about £300-500.*

*1959*

**£800-1,000** **BLO**

Richard Ford, "A Piece of My Heart", first edition, published by Harper & Row.

*This is the author's first book, and is also an inscribed presentation copy. Despite growing up in Mississippi, this is Ford's only novel set in the South.*

*1976*

**£200-300** **BLO**

## A CLOSER LOOK AT "A FAREWELL TO ARMS"

*This version is the first issue of the first edition without the legal disclaimer in the early pages.*

*It retains its dust wrapper, which is rare, even though it is restored.*

*Look out for the first issue of the first UK edition published by Jonathan Cape where 'serious' is misspelt in line 28 of page 66, as this is also valuable, often fetching up to quarter of this value.*

*The most valuable version of this book is the first edition signed by Hemingway with clear 'glassine' dustwrapper and slip case, of which only 510 were produced - it can fetch over twice this value.*

Ernest Hemingway, "A Farewell to Arms", first edition, first issue, published by Scribner, New York.

*1929*

**£2,000-3,000** **BLO**

Robert Heinlein, "The Puppet Masters", first English edition, published by Museum Press.

*The first US edition dates from 1951 and was published by Doubleday. It is usually more valuable and can fetch up to twice as much as the first English edition in mint condition.*

*1953*

**£150-200** **BLO**

Ernest Hemingway, "The Old Man and the Sea", first American edition, published by Scribner, New York.

*1952*

**£400-500** **BLO**

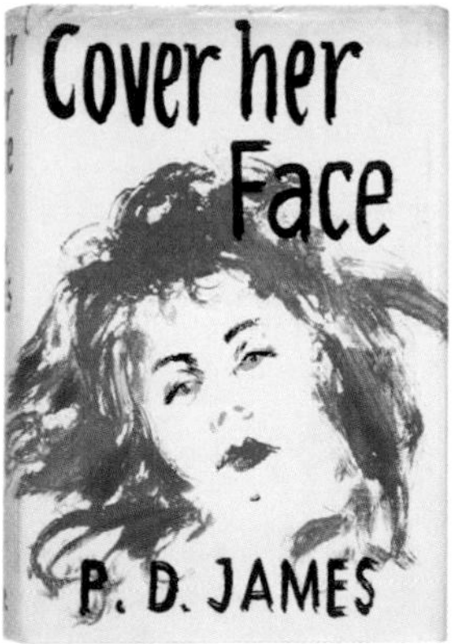


P.D. James, "Cover Her Face", first edition, published by Faber.

*This is the first novel from James' series covering the detective Adam Dalgleish, much of which has been televised, increasing interest.*

*1962*

**£800-1,200** **BLO**

P.D. James, "The Black Tower", first edition, published by Faber.

*1975*

**£80-120** **BLO**

Captain W.E. Johns, "Biggles and the Noble Lord", first edition, published by Brockhampton Press.

*1969*

**£120-180** **BLO**

C.H.B. Kitchin, "Crime at Christmas", first edition, published by Hogarth Press.

*1934*

**£1,200-1,800** **BLO**

## A CLOSER LOOK AT A JOHN LE CARRÉ BOOK

*It is is first novel, introducing Le Carré's famous Cold War spy character George Smiley.*

*This book is particularly scarce signed.*

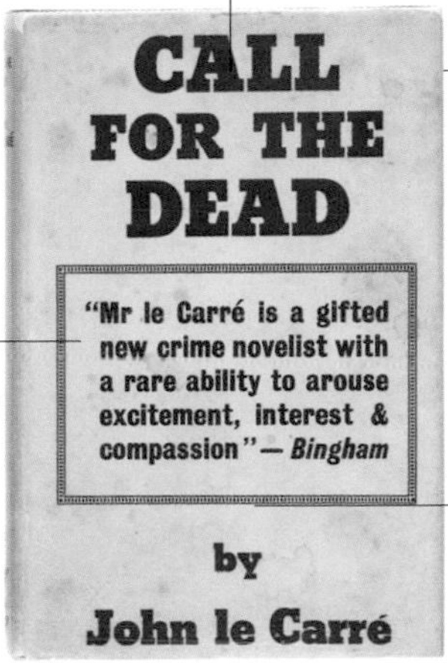


*Le Carré has signed this example with both his pseudonym (John Le Carré) and real name (David John Moore Cornwell), which adds value and interest.*

*A letter from Cornwell accompanying the book is dated 2002, showing that was signed that year, rather than earlier which would have been preferable to some collectors.*

John Le Carré, "Call for the Dead", first edition, published by Gollancz.

*1961*

**£3,000-4,000** **BLO**

John Le Carré, "The Spy Who Came in From the Cold", first edition, published by Gollancz.

*1963*

**£1,000-1,500** **BLO**

John Le Carré, "The Looking-Glass War" first edition, signed with the author's real name and pseudonym, published by Heinemann.

*1965*

**£1,000-1,500** **BLO**

Harper Lee, "To Kill a Mockingbird", first English Book Society Choice edition, with author's signature.

*1960*

**£60-80** **BLO**

C.S. Lewis, "The Lion, The Witch and the Wardrobe", ex-library first edition, with dust jacket from fifth impression, published by Bles.

*1950*

**£350-450** **BLO**

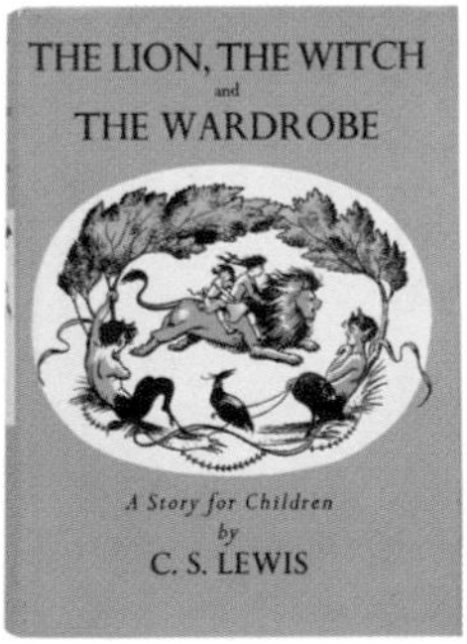


Ian McEwan, "First Love, Last Rites", first edition, published by Cape.

*This is the author's first book, and this UK first edition is usually worth over three times the value of the first US edition published in the same year.*

*1975*

**£300-400** **BLO**

Alan Moore & David Lloyd, "V for Vendetta", first hardcover edition, first printing, with mylar dust jacket, in mint condition.

*The first edition of this cult graphic novel is hard to find and leapt in value after the release of the film in 2006.*

*1990* *10.5in (26.5cm) high*

**£150-250** **NOR**

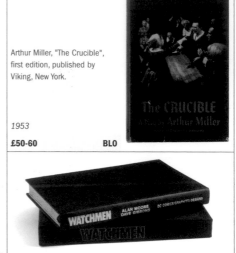

Arthur Miller, "The Crucible", first edition, published by Viking, New York.

*1953*

**£50-60** **BLO**

Alan Moore & Dave Gibbons, "Watchmen", first hardback edition, published by D.C. Comics & Graphitti Designs, with slip cover.

*1987* *10.75in (27.5cm) high*

**£100-150** **NOR**

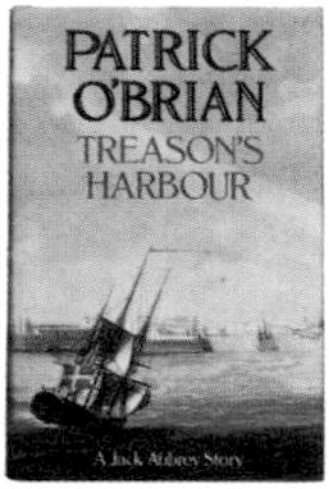


Patrick O'Brian, "Treason's Harbour", first edition, first issue, published by Collins

*1983*

**£500-600** **BLO**

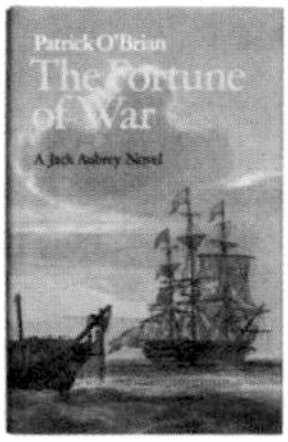


Patrick O'Brian, "The Fortunes of War", first edition, original boards, dust jacket, published by Collins.

*1979*

**£220-280** **BLO**

Patrick O'Brian, "Men-of-War", first edition, with some colour plates, published by Collins.

*1974*

**£120-180** **BLO**

Patrick O'Brian, "H.M.S. Surprise", first edition, original boards and dust jacket, published by Collins.

*1973*

**£500-600** **BLO**

Patrick O'Brian, "Post Captain", first edition, original boards, dust jacket, published by Collins.

*1972*

**£300-400** **BLO**

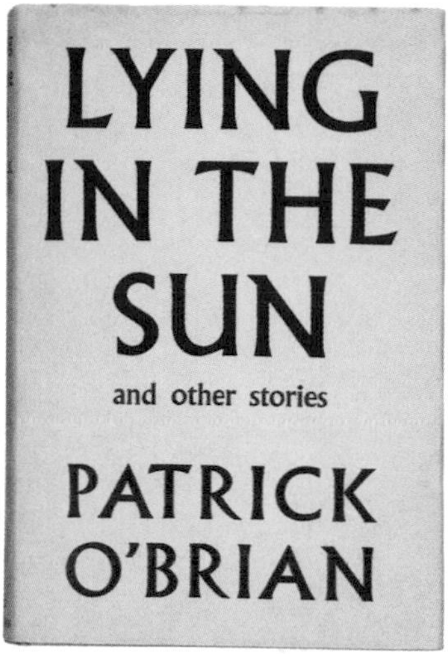


Patrick O'Brian, "Lying in the Sun and Other Stories", first edition, with original cloth and dust jacket, published by Hart Davis.

*This collection of short stories was published in the US the year before with slightly different contents as "The Walker and Other Stories".*

*1956*

**£550-650** **BLO**

## A CLOSER LOOK AT "LUSTRA"

*This book is from the limited edition first impression of only 200 copies - each is numbered inside with an orange stamp.*

*Due to the suppression of D.H.Lawrence's "The Rainbow" the year before, the more complete content in this version (itself lacking four poems) was only available by request and limited to these 200 copies.*

*The more common second impression of this edition contains nine fewer poems again, and is usually worth under around half the value of this rarer edition.*

*It retains its clear 'glassine' dustwrapper.*

Ezra Pound, "Lustra", first edition, privately published by Elkin Matthews.

*The frontispiece is a reproduction of a photograph of Ezra Pound by Alvin Langdon Coburn, with a tissue protection leaf.*

*1916*

**£1,000-1,500** **BLO**

Patrick O'Brian, "H.M.S. Surprise", first edition, published by Collins.

*1973*

**£200-300** **BLO**

Flann O'Brien, "The Third Policeman", first edition, published by McGibbon & Kee.

*1967*

**£200-300** **BLO**

Tim O'Brien, "If I Die in a Combat Zone", first English edition, published by Calder & Boyars.

*1973*

**£70-100** **BLO**

Peter O'Donnell, "Modesty Blaise", first edition, dust jacket, published by Souvenir Press.

*1965*

**£150-200** **BLO**

Philip Pullman, "The Subtle Knife", first edition, dust jacket, printed by Scholastic.

*1997*

**£150-250** **BLO**

## A CLOSER LOOK AT "NORTHERN LIGHTS"

*This is the first book in Pullman's increasingly popular 'His Dark Materials' trilogy, which has risen in desirability and value partly due to interest in such stories largely created by J.K. Rowling's 'Harry Potter' series, although this book was released earlier.*

*Many examples went to libraries and were stamped with ownership details and worn through use over time - this example is in excellent condition.*

Philip Pullman, "Northern Lights", first edition, dust jacket, Carnegie Medal sticker.

*1995*

*It was recently voted third in the BBC's poll of all time best books and won the Carnegie Medal for children's fiction in 1995, as indicated by the gold sticker on the cover.*

*The US edition and the film version of this book are known as The Golden Compass.*

*The very rare and desirable first issue of the first edition lists the publisher's address as being on Pratt Street, and can fetch up to £5,000.*

**£800-1,200** **BLO**

Ian Rankin, "Let it Bleed", first edition, published by Orion.

*1995*

**£300-400** **BLO**

Ian Rankin, "Strip Jack", first edition, published by Orion.

*1982*

**£400-500** **BLO**

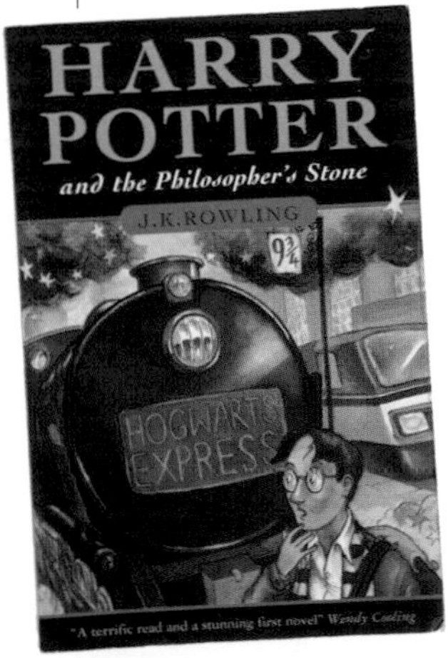


J.K. Rowling, "Harry Potter and the Philosopher's Stone", first paperback edition, with original pictorial cover, published by Bloomsbury.

*The first UK issue of this first edition paperback is the rarest variation of this title. Reputedly only 200 copies were printed, and it can fetch over £2,000.*

*1997*

**£800-1,200** **BLO**

J.K. Rowling, "Harry Potter and the Half-Blood Prince", first edition, signed by author, with original dust jacket.

*This signed book is accompanied by a letter from Rowling's personal assistant, on J.K. Rowling headed paper, confirming that Rowling signed and donated the item for an auction.*

*2005*

**£1,500-2,000** **BLO**

Salman Rushdie, "Midnight's Children", first American edition, signed by the author, with original dust jacket, published by Alfred Knopf.

*1981*

**£450-550** BLO

## A CLOSER LOOK AT A J.K. ROWLING BOOK

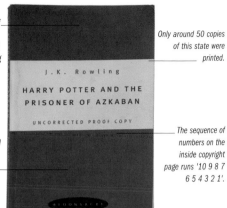

*This uncorrected proof copy is the very first state of the book, and is incomplete including having a '?' on the dedication page and some extra text.*

*The purple covers are different from the final book and indicate clearly what it is.*

*Only around 50 copies of this state were printed.*

*The sequence of numbers on the inside copyright page runs '10 9 8 7 6 5 4 3 2 1'.*

J. K. Rowling, "Harry Potter and the Prisoner of Azkaban", uncorrected proof copy, published by Bloomsbury.

*1999*

**£1,800-2,200** BLO

Paul Theroux, "Waldo", first English edition, published by The Bodley Head Press.

*This is the author's first novel.*

*1968*

**£80-120** BLO

Edgar Wallace, "The Stretelli Case and other Mystery Stories", first edition, published by International Fiction Library, Cleveland.

*This collection of short stories was never published in the UK in this form.*

*1930*

**£70-90** PB

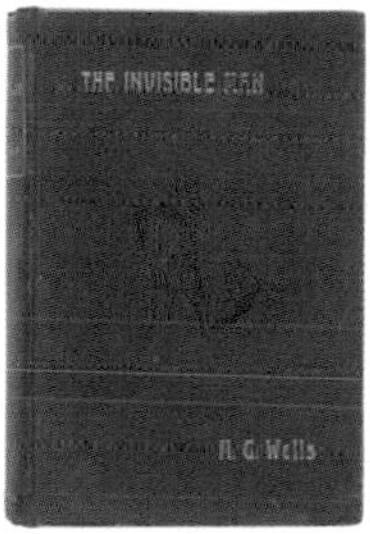


H. G. Wells,"The Invisible Man", first edition, ownership bookplate of Alfred Wynne Corrie, published by Pearson.

*Major Alfred Wynne Corrie married Mrs Charlotte Cotton, a landowner from near Oswestry, Shropshire, in 1886 and inherited the Park Hall estate upon her death in 1913.*

*1897*

**£250-350** BLO

Henry Williamson, "Tarka the Otter", first trade edition, published in London & New York.

*1927*

**£220-280** BLO

Tennessee Williams, "A Street Car Named Desire", first edition, published by New Directions, with upper cover damage.

*1947*

**£100-150** BLO

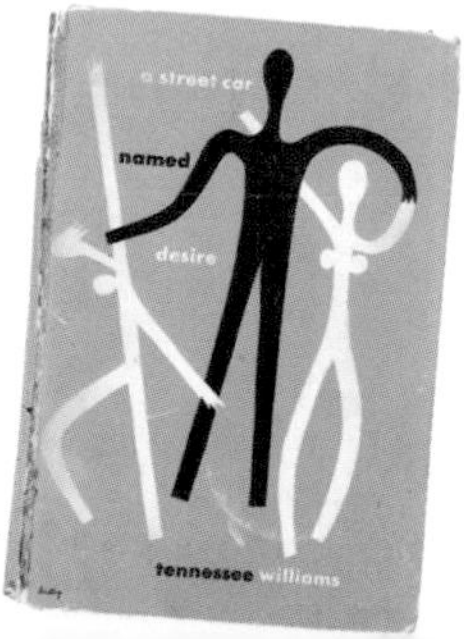

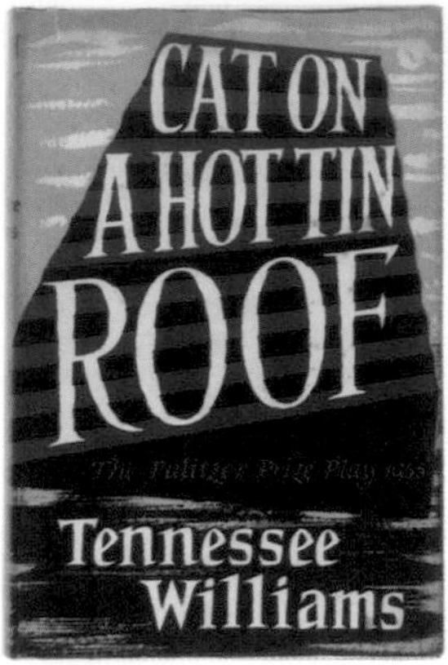


Tennessee Williams "Cat on a Hot Tin Roof", first English edition, published by Secker & Warburg.

*1956*

**£20-40** **BLO**

## A CLOSER LOOK AT "KEW GARDENS"

*This version was produced as a limited edition of 500 copies.*

*It contains 'decorations' by Vanessa Bell, who was Virginia's sister and a leading member of London's artistic and literary Bloomsbury Group.*

*It is signed by both the author and Vanessa Bell.*

*It retains its original dust wrapper, also designed by Bell.*

Virginia Woolf, "Kew Gardens", signed by author and artist, printed by the Hogarth Press.

*1927*

**£2,500-3,500** **BLO**

A. N. Wilson, "The Sweets of Pimlico", first edition, published by Secker & Warburg, London.

*This was the author's first book.*

*1977*

**£180-220** **PB**

Jeanette Winterson, "Sexing the Cherry", first edition, presentation copy signed by the author on the title page, published by Bloomsbury, London.

*1989*

**£80-120** **PB**

P.G. Wodehouse, "Lord Emsworth and Others", first edition, first issue, original cloth and dust jacket, published by Robert & Jenkins.

*1937*

**£550-650** **BLO**

P. G. Wodehouse, "Psmith Journalist", published by A. & C. Black, with half-title, frontispiece and 11 plates from drawings by T.M.R. Whitwell.

*1915*

**£350-450** **BLO**

Virginia Woolf, "Monday or Tuesday", first edition, published by the Hogarth Press.

*This is one of only 1,000 first edition copies. The cover design and woodcut illustrations inside are by Vanessa Bell.*

*1921*

**£400-500** **BLO**

Hank Janson, "Baby, Don't Dare Squeal", published by S.D. Frances, distributed by Gaywood Press Ltd.

*Janson's paperbacks are particularly collectable, especially with 'ravished dame' covers by Reginald Heade, as here.*

**£30-40** **PCC**

John Erskine, "Helen of Troy", second (December) printing of the first paperback edition, published by Popular Library.

*The cover artwork is by Rudolph Belarski (1900-83), who was a popular pulp/paperback cover artist and whose work for the Popular Library was particularly influential. His style used dramatic and unusual perspectives and proportions, such as the angle of the architrave on the building behind, which has been altered to make it more angular, and the slightly odd proportions of Helen's body. This cover also caused a scandal when released as Helen's nipples are clearly visible through her dress.*

*1948*

**£25-35** **NOR**

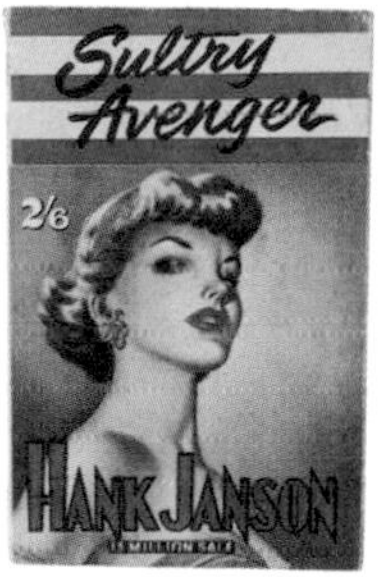


Hank Janson, "Sultry Avenger", published by Alexander Moring Ltd.

*1959*

**£5-8** **PCC**

Erie Stanley Gardener, "Perry Mason Solves The Case Of The Crooked Candle", Pocket Book, published by Cassell & Company, first published in 1947.

*1952*

**£5-8** **PCC**

Jim Thompson, "King Blood", published by Sphere Books.

*1954*

**£50-80** **ZDB**

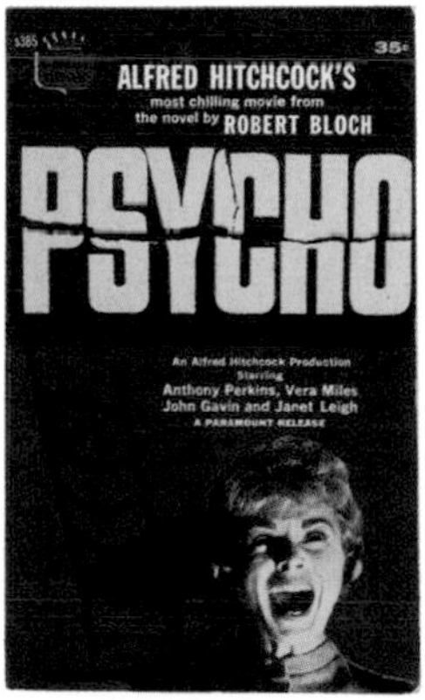


Robert Bloch, "Psycho", first paperback edition, movie tie-in published by Crest Books, July 1960.

**£40-50** **NOR**

William Irish, "Marihuana" paperback, published by Dell Books.

*William Irish was the pseudonym of Cornell Woolrich, who also used the name 'George Hopley'. Outwardly, this famous cover criticises drug use with the menace of the man, the unconscious lady and the sub-title, which reads "A cheap and evil girl sets a hopped-up killer against a city". However, the 'ravished dame' in her low cut dress would have added a contrasting titillating salaciousness.*

*1951*

**£70-100** **NOR**

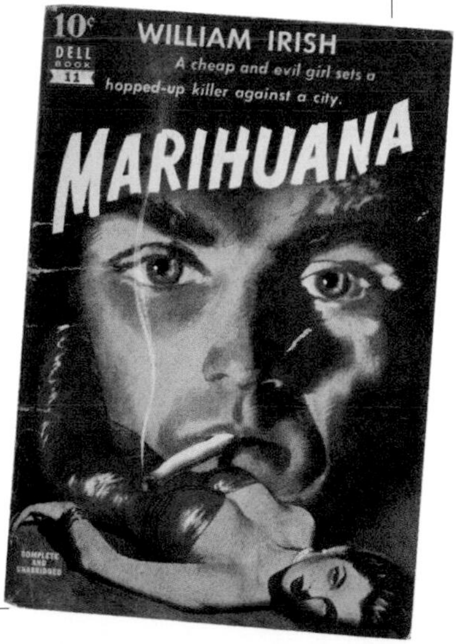

## COLLECTORS' NOTES

- The crimped metal cap securing carbonated drinks was invented by Irish-born American William Painter (1838-1906) in 1891. Known as the 'Crown Cap', it was successfully patented in 1892 and solved the many problems in sealing bottles economically, reliably and securely. Made from steel, early examples used cork as a sealant. Today, plastic is used.
- Although Painter initially suggested prising the top off with a knife or corkscrew, he also developed the first recognisable metal opener, which was patented in February 1894. Another American, Alfred Bernadin, had patented a bar-mounted opener in 1893, and over the following years many new shapes were issued.
- Some carry registered design numbers for 1923, 1924 or 1936, dates after which indicate that previous patents have expired.
- The style of a company's logo, or an event, can help to date an opener. A square hole larger than the usual aperture for hanging the opener up is often know as a 'Prest-O-Lite' hole. It was used for operating the valve on gas-powered car headlights before electricity took over in the early 1930s. Consider condition, as serious dents, wear and rust reduce value.
- Most carry advertising logos or wording, typically for beer or soft drinks companies, but also for events. Figural or other novelty shapes are often the most desirable and valuable. The presence of a well-known brand can widen appeal amongst different collectors.

An American 'Have A Coke' Coca-Cola' cast iron bottle opener.

*This is the most common Coca-Cola bottle opener found.*

*3.5in (9cm) long*

**£2-5** **BB**

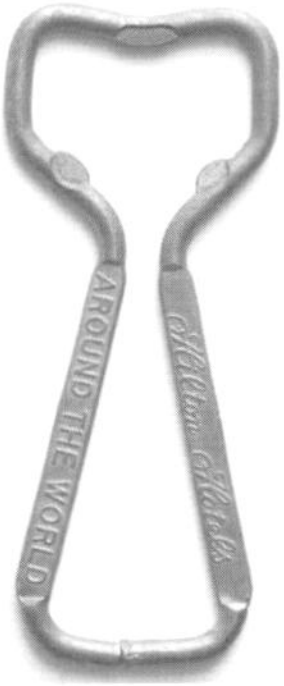


A Hilton Hotels 'Around The World' cast iron bottle opener.

*3.5in (9cm) long*

**£4-5** **BB**

An American 'Drink Booth's Beverages Try Booth's Cola' cast iron bottle opener.

*3.5in (9cm) long*

**£18-22** **BB**

A French 'Perrier' cast iron bottle opener.

*3.5in (9cm) long*

**£10-15** **BB**

An American 'Braun's Old Settler Rye Bread' cast iron bottle opener, some rust.

*3.5in (9cm) long*

**£4-7** **BB**

An 'Apollinaris' mineral water cast iron bottle opener, with rusting and moulded registered number 702661 for 1923.

*Apollinaris is a German brand launched in 1852, and is known as 'The Queen of Mineral Waters'.*

**£3-4** **BB**

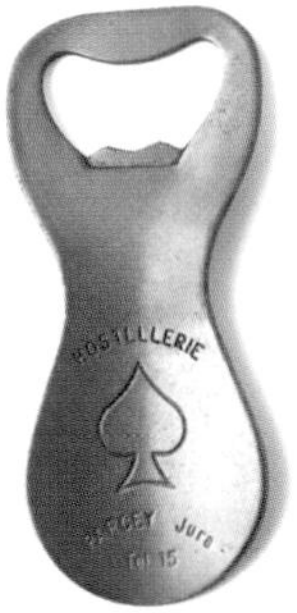


A French 'Hostellerie Parcey Jura' bottle opener.

*Produced for a French hotel, the word 'Hostellerie' has been misspelt.*

*3.5in (9cm) high*

**£18-22** **BB**

An American 'White Rock Water & Ginger Ale' cast iron opener.

*White Rock adopted Psyche as its logo in 1893, after buying a painting of her by Paul Thumann.*

*3.5in (9cm) long*

**£18-22** **BB**

An Italian Bilora Radix 35mm small camera for 24x24 film on rapid cassettes, with original tin box.

*The addition of the original tin box virtually triples the value of the camera on its own.*

*c1947-51*

**£50-80** **OACC**

A Russian Kiev IIIA camera, in working order.

*The Russians copied many Western camera styles and designs, particularly the immensely successful Leica and most are of low value compared to the original camera. This is a copy of a Contax.*

*c1967*

**£30-60** **COLC**

A Bakelite Kodak Baby Brownie box camera, with original card box.

*Thousands of 'box brownies' were made, and most are worth much less than this example, which retains its scarce Art Deco style card box. It was designed by Frank Brownell for Eastman Kodak in 1900, and named after a cartoon character. Aimed at those who wanted to take photographs simply and cheaply, it brought photography to the masses.*

*c1935*

**£10-15** **OACC**

An Eastman Kodak no.1A Pocket Kodak rollfilm camera, the body with brown fabric covering.

*Brown is scarcer than the much more common black version, which can be worth up to £20. Look out for grey, blue, red or green coverings, as these are similarly, if not more, desirable.*

*c1930*

**£50-70** **COLC**

A Kodak Disc 4000 camera, in near mint condition and with its original box.

*Disc cameras were produced during the early 1980s, but were not successful. The format did not last beyond the decade, and film discs stopped being manufactured in 1998. Prices are currently very low and they are not difficult to find. Look out for special promotional models, which can be worth more.*

*1982-84*

**£15-20** **COLC**

An Eastman Kodak Stereo Camera, with Kodak Anaston 3.5/35mm dual lenses and lens caps.

**£100-150** **ATK**

A Japanese Konishiroka Kogaku 'Rokuoh-Sha' machine-gun camera, with Hexaar 4.5/75mm lens, in original wooden box with accessories and spare parts.

*These large and heavy machine gun-shaped cameras were used for training Japanese machine gunners during WWII. They are rare, particularly with their original cases, viewfinders and accessories.*

*1943*

**£1,000-1,500** **ATK**

A Leica Model IC camera, with black top and base plate, and Leitz Elmar 3.5/50mm lens.

*This was the first Leica camera produced with an interchangeable lens. 2,995 units in black were produced according to the Leitz archives.*

*1931*

**£300-400** **COLC**

A Nikon 'S' 35mm camera, in excellent condition.

*This was the second model that Nikon produced.*

*c1952*

**£500-600** **COLC**

A Japanese Panon 'Panorama-Camera Widelux F6B' panorama camera, for 24x59mm on 35mm film, with maker's case.

*1975*

**£280-320** **ATK**

A German Berning & Co. 'Robot Star' camera, with Xenon 1/4/40mm lens.

*1952*

**£150-200** **ATK**

A 1980s Chinese Seagull 35mm rollfilm camera, with flip-down front and lens with bellows.

*This is a copy of a German Zeiss Ikon Super Ikonta of the 1950s.*

**£50-70** **COLC**

A Baby Ikonta 'Ikomat', with flop-down front, bellows and rare 3.5 Tessar lens.

*This camera usually comes with a Novar lens, which is worth less.*

*c1935*

**£160-200** **COLC**

A German Zeiss Ikon 'Kolibri' camera, with Tessar f 3.5/55mm lens, in part of a maker's leather case.

**£100-150** **EG**

## COLLECTORS' NOTES

- Beatrix Potter (1866-1943) published her first book 'The Tale of Peter Rabbit' in 1902 and wrote a total of 23 books, which have been loved by children even since. In 1947, Beswick modeller Arthur Gredington created the first figure based on Potter's drawings, 'Jemima Puddleduck', at the suggestion of Lucy Beswick, following her visit to Potter's Lake District home.
- Following the success of this figure, a collection of ten figures was released in 1948 and today, these earliest examples are among the most valuable. In 1969 Beswick was acquired by Royal Doulton and the production process was reassessed, resulting in a number of changes to the backstamp and design of existing figures.
- The main indicator to value is the backstamp, which has gone through a number of, sometimes confusing, changes. The earliest Beswick gold-coloured backstamp, referred to here as BP-1, was in use between 1948 and 1954 and had the wording 'Beswick England' in a circle and then, later, in parallel lines. In 1955 this was changed to the wording in an oval, referred to here as BP-2. The gold-coloured lettering was replaced with brown in 1972 and the backstamp has the wording in a simple line arrangement. This is referred to as BP-3 and is one of the most commonly found versions today.
- In 1989 the figures were briefly made under the Royal Albert name, which is also part of Royal Doulton group, these are known as BP-4. The Beswick name reappeared in 1993, but now included the name Royal Doulton, which continues from BP-5 onwards. The early gold backstamps, (BP-1 and BP-2) are by far the most desirable so it is advisable to acquaint yourself with the many variations. Also look for the variations in design and colourways that have appeared over time, a specialist guide will help.

A Beswick Beatrix Potter 'Amiable Guinea Pig' figurine, no.2061, modelled by Albert Hallam, with BP-2 backstamp.

*1967-72* *3.5in (9cm) high*

**£220-280** **PSA**

A Beswick Beatrix Potter 'Anna Maria' figurine, no.1851, modelled by Albert Hallam, with BP-2 backstamp.

*1963-72* *3in (7.5cm) high*

**£180-220** **PSA**

## A CLOSER LOOK AT A BEATRIX POTTER FIGURINE

*Benjamin Bunny was produced in a range of versions and variations with a wide range of values, the earliest, such as this, are the most sought-after.*

*This is the first version of this figure with the shoes sticking out as well as the ears, which are not visible here.*

*A version with a brown jacket was also produced and tends to be worth the same as an equivalent green-jacketed version.*

*The gold backstamp can be identified by 'Beswick England' in an oval. They tend to be popular with collectors.*

A Beswick Beatrix Potter 'Benjamin Bunny' figurine, no.1105, modelled by Arthur Gredington, with green jacket, shoes and ears out, and with BP-2 backstamp.

*1955-72* *4in (10cm) high*

**£150-200** **PSA**

A Beswick Beatrix Potter 'Appley Dapply' figurine, no.2333/1, modelled by Albert Hallam, first version with brown mouse and bottle out and BP-3 backstamp.

**£80-120** **CHEF**

A Royal Albert Beatrix Potter 'Benjamin Ate a Lettuce Leaf' figurine, no.3317, modelled Martyn Alcock, with BP-6a backstamp.

*By the time the BP-6 backstamp was introduced, both Beswick and Royal Albert were owned by Royal Doulton. The name appeared from on Beatrix Potter figurines from 1989 until 1998 when it was dropped, however Beswick backstamps were in use concurrently.*

*1992-98* *4.75in (12cm) high*

**£45-55** **OACC**

A Beswick Beatrix Potter 'Cecily Parsley' figurine, no.1941/1, modelled by Arthur Gredington, version one with head down and bright blue dress, with BP-3 backstamp.

*1973-85* *4in (10cm) high*

**£28-32** **CHEF**

A Beswick Beatrix Potter 'Cousin Ribby' figurine, no.2284, modelled by Albert Hallam, with BP-3b backstamp.

*1974-85* *3.5in (9cm) high*

**£35-45** **PSA**

A Beswick Beatrix Potter 'Duchess' figurine, no.2601, modelled by Graham Tongue, version two holding pie, with BP-3b backstamp, boxed.

*This is a desirable figure, the earlier version with the dog holding flowers rather than a pie is even rarer and can be worth four times as much.*

*1979-82* *4in (10cm) high*

**£120-180** **PSA**

A Beswick Beatrix Potter 'Fierce Bad Rabbit' figurine, no.2586/1, modelled by David Lyttleton, version one with feet out, with BP-3b backstamp.

*1977-88* *4.75in (12cm) high*

**£100-150** **CHEF**

A Beswick Beatrix Potter 'Flopsy, Mopsy and Cottontail' figurine, no.1274, modelled by Arthur Gredington, with BP-3 backstamp.

*1973-88* *2.5in (6.5cm) high*

**£35-45** **CHEF**

A Beswick Beatrix Potter 'Foxy Whiskered Gentleman' figurine, no.1277/1, modelled by Arthur Gredington. with BP-2 backstamp.

*1955-72*

**£80-120** **CHEF**

A Beswick Beatrix Potter 'Ginger' figurine, no.2559, modelled by David Lyttleton, with BP3b backstamp.

*The colour of the green jacket does vary but the value is the same.*

*1976-82* *3.75in (9.5cm) high*

**£220-280** **PSA**

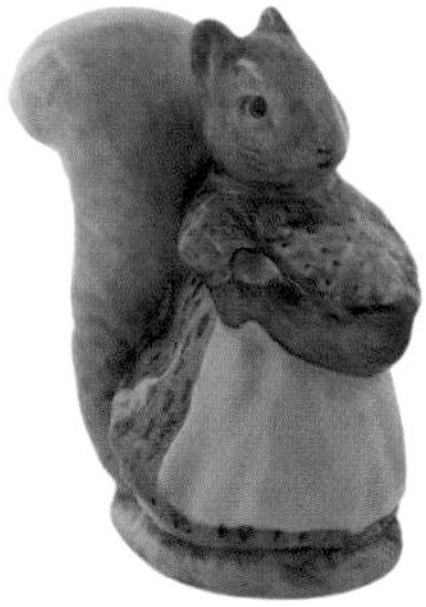

A Beswick Beatrix Potter 'Goody Tiptoes' figurine, no.1675, modelled by Arthur Gredington, with BP-3 backstamp.

*1973-88* *3.5in (9cm) high*

**£25-35** **CHEF**

A Beswick Beatrix Potter 'Hunca Munca' figurine, no.1198, style one, modelled by Arthur Gredington.

*1951-2000* *2.75in (7cm) high*

**£30-40** **AOY**

A Beswick Beatrix Potter 'Jemima Puddle-Duck' figurine, no.1092/1, version one, modelled by Arthur Gredington, with backstamp BP3b.

*1974-85* *4.75in (12cm) high*

**£22-28** **PSA**

A Beswick Beatrix Potter 'Johnny Townmouse Eating Corn' figurine, no.3931, modelled by Martyn Alcock, with backstamp BP10a, boxed.

*2000-2002* *3.75in (9.5cm) high*

**£25-35** **PSA**

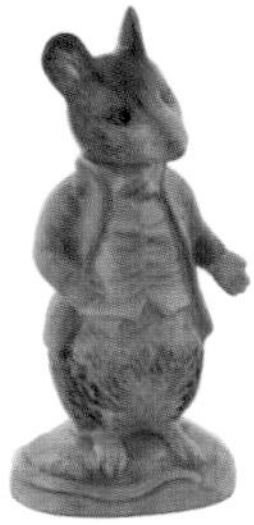

A Beswick Beatrix Potter 'Johnny Town-Mouse' figurine, no.1276, modelled by Arthur Gredington, with BP-2 backstamp.

*1955-72* *3.5in (9cm) high*

**£50-80** **CHEF**

A Beswick Beatrix Potter 'Lady Mouse' figurine, no.1183, modelled by Arthur Gredington, with BP-3 backstamp.

*1973-88* *4in (10cm) high*

**£40-60** **CHEF**

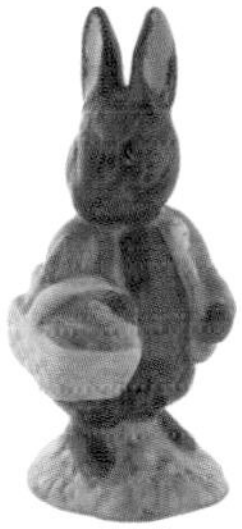

A Beswick Beatrix Potter 'Little Black Rabbit' figurine, no.2585, modelled by David Lyttleton, with BP-3 backstamp.

*1977-88* *4.5in (11.5cm) high*

**£28-32** **CHEF**

A Beswick Beatrix Potter 'Little Pig Robinson' figurine, no.1104/1, modelled by Arthur Gredington, first version with striped outfit and with BP-3 backstamp.

*1973-74* *4in (10cm) high*

**£50-70** **CHEF**

A Beswick Beatrix Potter 'Miss Moppet' figurine, no.1275/1, modelled by Arthur Greddington, with BP-3b backstamp.

*1978-85* *3in (7.5cm) high*

**£35-45** **PSA**

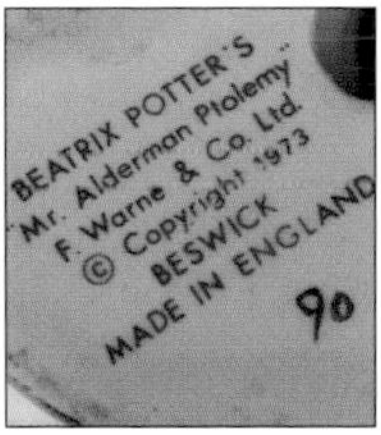


A Beswick Beatrix Potter's 'Mr Alderman Ptolemy' figurine, no.2424, modelled by Graham Tongue, with BP-3b backstamp.

*The detail shows the second all-brown backstamp used – the first was introduced in 1973 and omitted the copyright date. It is a relatively common backstamp being used on 63 figures for over 10 years.*

*1974-85* *3.5in (9cm) high*

**£30-40** **CHEF**

A Beswick Beatrix Potter 'Mr Benjamin Bunny' figurine, no.1940/1, modelled by Arthur Gredington, with dark maroon jacket and pipe out, with BP-2 backstamp.

*1965-72* *4.25in (11cm)*

**£180-220** **PSA**

A Beswick Beatrix Potter 'Mr Benjamin Bunny And Peter Rabbit' figurine, no.2509, modelled by Alan Maslankowski, with BP-3b backstamp.

*1975-85* *4in (10cm) high*

**£70-100** **PSA**

A Beswick Beatrix Potter 'Mr Jeremy Fisher' figurine, no.1157/1, modelled by Arthur Gredington, first variation with spotted legs and BP-2 backstamp.

*1955-72* *3in (7.5cm) high*

**£100-150** **CHEF**

A Beswick Beatrix Potter 'Mrs Flopsy Bunny', no.1942, modelled by Arthur Gredington, with BP-3 backstamp.

*1973-85* *4in (10cm) high*

**£50-70** **CHEF**

A Beswick Beatrix Potter 'Mrs Rabbit' figurine, no. 1200/1, modelled by Arthur Gredington, with lilac dress and umbrella out, with BP-2 backstamp.

*With this backstamp the pink and lilac versions are worth the same.*

*1955-72* *4.25in (11cm) high*

**£120-180** **PSA**

A Beswick Beatrix Potter 'Mrs Rabbit And Bunnies' figurine, no. 2543, modelled by David Lyttleton, with BP3b backstamp.

*1976-85* *3.75in (9.5cm) high*

**£30-40** **PSA**

A Beswick Beatrix Potter 'Mrs Tiggy Winkle Takes Tea' figure, no. 2877, modelled by David Lyttleton, with BP-3b backstamp.

*1985* *3.25in (8.5cm) high*

**£30-50** **PSA**

A Beswick Beatrix Potter 'Mrs Tittlemouse' figurine, no.1103, modelled by Arthur Gredington, style one without white apron and with BP-2 backstamp.

*1955-72* *3.5in (9cm) high*

**£120-180** **CHEF**

A Beswick Beatrix Potter 'Old Mr Brown' figurine, no.1796, modelled by Albert Hallam, with brown owl and BP-3 backstamp.

*1973-85* *3.25in (8.5cm) high*

**£22-28** **CHEF**

A Beswick Beatrix Potter 'The Old Woman Who Lived In A Shoe' figurine, no.1545, modelled by Colin Melbourne, with BP-2 backstamp.

*1959-72* *2.45in (7cm) high*

**£50-70** **PSA**

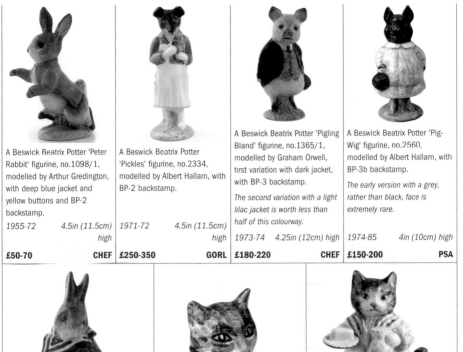

A Beswick Beatrix Potter 'Peter Rabbit' figurine, no.1098/1, modelled by Arthur Gredington, with deep blue jacket and yellow buttons and BP-2 backstamp.

*1955-72 4.5in (11.5cm) high*

**£50-70 CHEF**

A Beswick Beatrix Potter 'Pickles' figurine, no.2334, modelled by Albert Hallam, with BP-2 backstamp.

*1971-72 4.5in (11.5cm) high*

**£250-350 GORL**

A Beswick Beatrix Potter 'Pigling Bland' figurine, no.1365/1, modelled by Graham Orwell, first variation with dark jacket, with BP-3 backstamp.

*The second variation with a light lilac jacket is worth less than half of this colourway.*

*1973-74 4.25in (12cm) high*

**£180-220 CHEF**

A Beswick Beatrix Potter 'Pig-Wig' figurine, no.2560, modelled by Albert Hallam, with BP-3b backstamp.

*The early version with a grey, rather than black, face is extremely rare.*

*1974-85 4in (10cm) high*

**£150-200 PSA**

A Beswick Beatrix Potter 'Poorly Peter Rabbit' figurine, no.2560, modelled by David Lyttleton, with BP-3 backstamp.

*1976-88 3.75in (9.5cm) high*

**£40-60 CHEF**

A Beswick Beatrix Potter 'Simpkin' figurine, no. 2508, modelled by Alan Maslankowski, with BP3b backstamp.

*'Simpkin' was only produced with this backstamp. It is a hard figure to find.*

*1975-83 4in (10cm) high*

**£300-400 PSA**

A Beswick Beatrix Potter 'Ribby' figurine, no.1199, modelled by Arthur Gredington, with BP-3 backstamp.

*1973-88 3.25in (8.5cm) high*

**£40-60 OACC**

A Beswick Beatrix Potter 'Sally Henny Penny' figurine, no.2452, modelled by Albert Hallam, with BP-3 backstamp.

*1974-88 4in (10cm) high*

**£25-35 CHEF**

A Beswick Beatrix Potter 'Sir Isaac Newton' figurine, no.2425, modelled by Graham Tongue, with BP3b backstamp.

*1973-84 3.75in (9.5cm) high*

**£150-200 PSA**

A Beswick Beatrix Potter 'Susan' figure, no.2716, modelled by David Lyttleton, with BP-3b backstamp.

*Look for the version with the BP-6a which was only produced in 1989 as it can be worth six times are much.*

*1983-85* *4in (10cm) high*

**£200-300** **PSA**

A Beswick Beatrix Potter 'Squirrel Nutkin' figurine, no.1102/1, modelled by Arthur Gredington, with golden-brown squirrel and green apple, and with BP-3 backstamp.

*The reddish-brown squirrel, holding a brown/green apple is earlier and more desirable.*

*1980-88* *3.75in (9.5cm) high*

**£40-60** **CHEF**

A Beswick Beatrix Potter 'Tabitha Twitchett' figurine, no.1676, modelled by Arthur Gredington, with BP-3b backstamp.

*The earlier version, also found in with the BP-3b backstamp has a blue striped top and is worth about double this one. Earlier versions are also marked "Tabitha Twitchit".*

*1974 3.5in (9cm) high*

**£40-60** **PSA**

A Beswick Beatrix Potter 'Tabitha Twitchit And Miss Moppet' figurine, no.2544, modelled by David Lyttleton, with BP-3b backstamp.

*1976-85* *3.5in (9cm) high*

**£50-70** **PSA**

A Beswick Beatrix Potter 'Tailor of Gloucester' figurine, no.1108, modelled by Arthur Gredington, with BP-2 backstamp.

*1955-72* *3.5in (9cm) high*

**£60-70** **CHEF**

A Beswick Beatrix Potter 'Timmy Willie from Johnny Town-Mouse' figurine, no.1109, modelled by Arthur Gredington, with BP-3 backstamp mark.

*1973-88* *2.5in (6.5cm) high*

**£100-150** **CHEF**

A Beswick Beatrix Potter 'Timmy Tiptoes' figurine, no.1101/, modelled by Arthur Gredington, first variation with red jacket, with BP-2 backstamp.

*The variation with a pink jacket is slightly more desirable.*

*1955-72*

**£60-80** **CHEF**

A Beswick Beatrix Potter 'Tom Kitten' figurine, no. 3405/2, by Martyn Alcock, version two with gold buttons, BP9c stamp.

*This was sold as a pair with Jeremy Fisher.*

*1994-97* *5.25in (13.5cm) high*

**£22-28** **PSA**

A Beswick Beatrix Potter 'Tommy Brock' figurine, no. 1348/3, by Graham Orwell, backstamp BP3b, version two.

*Version one is worth at least twice as much.*

*1974-85* *3.5in (9cm) high*

**£25-35** **PSA**

**FIND OUT MORE...**

**Beswick Collectables,** *Hank Corley and J. Callows, published by The Charlton Press, 9th Edition, 2005.*

## COLLECTORS' NOTES

- Founded in Loughton, Staffordshire in 1894, the Beswick Pottery began to produce the animal figurines for which they are so well known around 1900. By the 1930s, they had become a major part of their production. In 1969, the factory was sold to Royal Doulton, and production of both companies' animal figures was merged under the Doulton name in 1989, before adopting the Beswick name once again in 1999. In 2002, the factory closed.
- Collectors tend to focus on one type of animal, with cattle currently being one of the most desirable types. Large, visually impressive bulls can fetch high values and, although generally less valuable, cows and calves are also popular. The work of the modeller Arthur Gredington, who joined in 1939, is sought-after. However, do not ignore the work of others such as Graham Tongue and particularly Colin Melbourne.
- Look out for variations in colours, types of glaze and the precise form. 'Rocking Horse Grey' is usually more valuable than brown, and matte glazes are often more valuable than glossy glazes. Limited editions, and those mounted on plinths are also worth looking out for as their values can be higher. Prices have risen over the past few years since the factory's closure, and still remain strong.

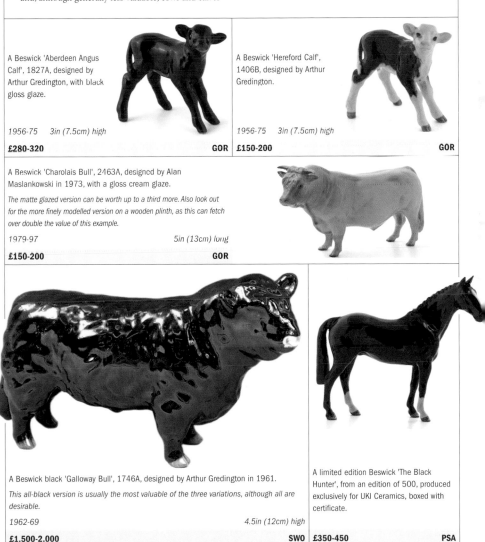

A Beswick 'Aberdeen Angus Calf', 1827A, designed by Arthur Gredington, with black gloss glaze.

*1956-75* *3in (7.5cm) high*

**£280-320** **GOR**

A Beswick 'Hereford Calf', 1406B, designed by Arthur Gredington.

*1956-75* *3in (7.5cm) high*

**£150-200** **GOR**

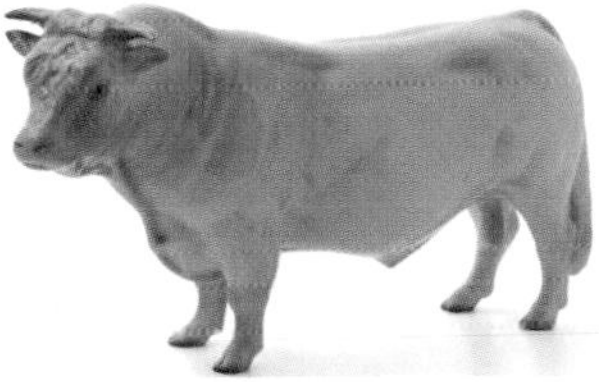

A Beswick 'Charolais Bull', 2463A, designed by Alan Maslankowski in 1973, with a gloss cream glaze.

*The matte glazed version can be worth up to a third more. Also look out for the more finely modelled version on a wooden plinth, as this can fetch over double the value of this example.*

*1979-97* *5in (13cm) long*

**£150-200** **GOR**

A Beswick black 'Galloway Bull', 1746A, designed by Arthur Gredington in 1961.

*This all-black version is usually the most valuable of the three variations, although all are desirable.*

*1962-69* *4.5in (12cm) high*

**£1,500-2,000** **SWO**

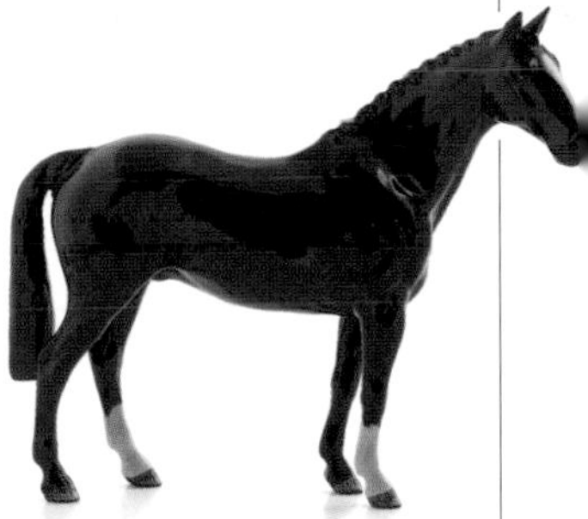

A limited edition Beswick 'The Black Hunter', from an edition of 500, produced exclusively for UKI Ceramics, boxed with certificate.

**£350-450** **PSA**

A Beswick 'Cantering Shire Horse', 975, designed by Arthur Gredington, in 'rocking horse grey' glaze.

*c1944-62* *8.75in (22cm) high*

**£220-280** **BIG**

A Beswick 'Old English Sheepdog' advertising figurine for Dulux Paints, designed by Mr. Mortimer.

*These are often found in poor condition with chips and cracks as they were often used as doorstops, and were generally not cared for when displayed in hardware shops.*

*1964-70* *12.5in (32cm) high*

**£400-500** **NEA**

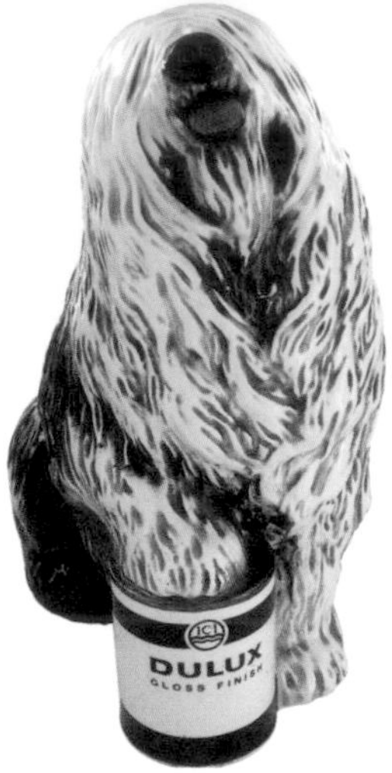

A Beswick 'Game Cock', 2059, designed by Arthur Gredington.

*The tail feathers and beak are prone to damage, so inspect all examples carefully.*

*1966-75* *9.5in (24cm) high*

**£350-450** **BIG**

A Beswick 'Kestrel', 2316, designed by Graham Tongue.

*Unusually, the gloss version tends to be worth slightly more than the matte glazed version.*

*1970-89* *6.75in (17cm) high*

**£70-100** **BIG**

A Beswick 'King Eider Duck', designed by Colin Melbourne, from the Peter Scott Wildfowl Series.

*Conservationist and ornithologist Scott founded the renowned Severn Wildfowl Trust at Slimbridge in 1948, and was also a co-founder of the World Wildlife Fund.*

*1958-71* *4in (10cm) high*

**£60-90** **BIG**

A Beswick 'Girl With A Hat' wall face mask, 380, the back with impressed marks.

*Face masks are popular, particularly highly stylized examples from the 1930s, and those by Goldscheider.*

*8.75in (22.5cm) high*

**£150-200** **WW**

A Beswick 'Sam Weller' character teapot, 1369, designed by Arthur Gredington, from the Dickens series.

*1955-73* *7in (17.5cm) high*

**£70-100** **BAD**

## COLLECTORS' NOTES

- Unlike most studio potteries, which tend to be in rural areas, Briglin Pottery was founded in Baker Street, central London, in June 1948. The name was taken from the forenames of the two founders – Brigitte Appleby and Eileen Lewenstein. In 1959, it moved to Mayfair, London, and Lewenstein left.
- The company became known for attractive and functional handmade and hand-decorated pottery after the modern Scandinavian style, which was offered at affordable prices. The works became fashionable and were exhibited and sold at leading department stores Heal's and Peter Jones, as well as other stores across the UK.
- The colour of the underlying clay is was exposed, with wax resist and sgrafitto processes being used to create the patterns. Designs tend to be based around the natural world, focusing on country flowers and foliage. Glazes tend to be muted, adding to the earthy, countryside feel. Forms are simple and show off the patterns well.
- Fashions changed during the 1980s and, despite thirty years of continued popularity, the pottery closed in 1990. Kitchenware and novelty, animal forms tend to be less popular, with decorative pieces being the most desirable. Look out for well-designed, harmonious combinations of glazed and unglazed areas, or pieces that are covered in a glaze. Large pieces and theatrical figurines currently fetch the highest sums.

A Briglin cylinder vase, with wax resist and sgraffito design of stylized round flowers.

*7.5in (19cm) high*

**£100-150** **GC**

A Briglin beige and brown glazed vase, with scored patterns and flower design.

*7.75in (19.5cm) high*

**£30-40** **GC**

A Briglin cylinder vase, with wax resist and sgrafitto leaf design and a glossy creamy-blue glaze.

*5in (13cm) high*

**£30-40** **GC**

A 1970s Briglin green glazed, with brown petalled flowers and scored patterns.

*8in (20cm) high*

**£30-40** **GC**

A Briglin blue/grey glazed vase, with seeding flower pattern.

*7.25in (18.5cm) high*

**£50-70** **GC**

A Briglin tapering vase, with cream glaze and copper oxide, wax resist and sgraffito decoration of a thistle.

*7.75in (19.5cm) high*

**£60-80** **GC**

A Briglin tall waisted vase, hand-painted with a branch of leaves.

*Unusually, this vase has no sgrafitto decoration, and uses the cobalt oxide glaze all over.*

*10in (25.5cm) high*

**£70-90** **GC**

A Briglin waisted vase, with sgraffito wheat sheaves inscribed through a glossy cream glaze, stamped "Briglin".

*7.5in (19cm) high*

**£60-80** **GC**

A Briglin vase, with cobalt oxide and creamy glazed stylized flower decoration, stamped "Briglin".

*5in (13cm) high*

**£30-40** **GC**

A Briglin vase, with painted blue-grey petals, brown sgrafitto flowers and brown bands.

*6.5in (16.5cm) high*

**£50-80** **GC**

A Briglin cylindrical flower pot, with grey-blue glaze and sgrafitto circular and banded design.

*5.5in (14cm) high*

**£40-60** **GC**

A Briglin footed flower pot holder, with sgrafitto and wax-resist decoration.

**£15-20** **OACC**

A Briglin bowl, with sgrafitto banded and leaf decoration, highlighted with black glaze, with a creamy-brown background glaze.

*7.5in (19cm) diam*

**£30-40** **GC**

## A CLOSER LOOK AT A BRIGLIN VASE

*Unlike much Briglin pottery, this piece is exceptionally large and, with its small opening, is purely decorative rather than functional.*

*The design was scratched into the body and then a creamy glaze was applied. The glaze was then wiped off, remaining only in the scratches.*

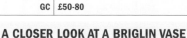

*The form, colour and sgrafitto (scratched) decoration recalls tribal pots.*

*It as likely to have been made for an exhibition or special commission, perhaps by Eileen Lewenstein, who left Briglin in 1959 to found her own studio pottery.*

A fine and large Briglin vase, with sgrafitto design and green wiped-away glaze, stamped "Briglin".

*9.75in (25cm) high*

**£400-600** **GC**

A Briglin spherical vase, with a sgrafitto and black painted design of a band of leaves.

4.25in (10.5cm) high

**£30-40** **GC**

A Briglin brown baluster vase, with glossy cream glazed band and sgrafitto swirls.

*This is an unusual pattern, form and colourway for Briglin.*

7.25in (18.5cm) high

**£70-100** **GC**

A Briglin lamp base, with manganese oxide and wax resist tree design, and a creamy glaze.

*The style of the trees recalls designs by Clarice Cliff.*

6.25in (16cm) high

**£60-80** **GC**

A Briglin stylized cat money box, with hand-painted design, inscribed "Briglin".

*This is formed and decorated after ceramicists Susan and Richard Parkinson, whose works have become highly popular today. In 1959, Richard Parkinson designed a series of figurines of theatrical personalities decorated in green and black on white, which were made by Briglin. Thus, it is likely that the influence came from here.*

7.5in (19cm) high

**£70-90** **GC**

A Briglin cat figure, with brown painted and sgaffito decoration.

4.75in (12cm) high

**£50-70** **GC**

A very rare and large Briglin 'Viking King' figure, handmade and hand-decorated, with an all over creamy glaze, stamped "Briglin".

*This large piece would have been time-consuming to construct, so was likely to have been made for a special commission or event, such as an exhibition.*

18in (45.5cm) high

**£800-1,000** **GC**

## FIND OUT MORE...

**Briglin Pottery 1948-1990**, *by Anthea Arnold, published by Briglin Books, 2002.*

## COLLECTORS' NOTES

- Bunnykins were the brainchild of Barbara Vernon, daughter of Cuthbert Bailey, the manager of Royal Doulton's Stoke-on-Trent factory. The young nun had used drawings of a family of rabbits to entertain her class at convent school. Her father saw their potential as a range of nurserywares, which was launched in 1934. Six figurines, possibly modelled by Charles Noke, were then introduced in 1938, although they were somewhat different in appearance to Vernon's original drawings. Production was interrupted by WWII, and these early, prewar examples are rare today.
- Royal Doulton took over Beswick in 1969 and, encouraged by Beswick's success with their Beatrix Potter range, the Bunnykins figures were resurrected and the range extended in 1972, being remodelled by Albert Hallam. Harry Sales became responsible for and modernised the range in 1980, introducing contemporary themes such as space travel, rock-and-roll and the 1984 Los Angeles Olympics.
- Nearly 300 figures have been released so far, with more added and retired yearly. A number of backstamps have been used over the years, but do not affect value greatly. Limited editions issued in small numbers, models produced for short periods of time and prewar models tend to the most desirable and valuable.

A special edition Royal Doulton 'Statue of Liberty' Bunnykins figure, DB198, designed by Caroline Dadd, from an edition of 3,000 produced exclusively for Pascoe & Co., from the American Heritage series, boxed.

*1999* *5in (12.5cm) high*

**£45-55** **PSA**

A Royal Doulton 'Billie & Buntie Bunnykins Sleigh Ride' figure, DB4, designed by Walter Hayward.

*1972-97* *3.25in (8.5cm)*

**£18-22** **PSA**

A Royal Doulton 'Bogey Bunnykins' figure, DB32, designed by Harry Sales.

*1984-92* *4in (10cm) high*

**£50-70** **PSA**

A special edition Royal Doulton 'Boy Skater Bunnykins' figure, DB187, designed by Graham Tongue, from an edition of 2,500 produced exclusively for Colonial House of Collectables in a new colourway, boxed.

*1998* *4in (10cm) high*

**£28-32** **PSA**

A Royal Doulton 'Boy Skater Bunnykins' figure, DB152, designed by Graham Tongue.

*1995-98* *4.75in (11cm) high*

**£18-22** **PSA**

A Royal Doulton 'Brownie Bunnykins' figure, DB61, designed by Graham Tongue.

*1987-93* *4in (10cm) high*

**£70-80** **PSA**

A Royal Doulton 'Collector Bunnykins' figure, DB54, designed by Harry Sales, produced exclusively for the Royal Doulton International Collectors Club.

*1987* *4.25in (11cm)*

**£250-350** **PSA**

A Royal Doulton 'Cook Bunnykins' figure, DB85, designed by Graham Tongue.

*1990-94* *4.25in (11cm) high*

**£50-80** **PSA**

A Royal Doulton 'Daisy Bunnykins Spring Time' figure, DB7, based on a design by Walter Hayward.

*1972-83* *3.5in (9cm) high*

**£70-100** **PSA**

A Royal Doulton 'Family Photograph Bunnykins', DB1, based on a design by Walter Hayward.

*1972-88* *4.5in (11.5cm) high*

**£50-80** **PSA**

A Royal Doulton 'Fisherman Bunnykins' figure, DB84, designed by Graham Tongue.

*1990-93* *4.25in (11cm) high*

**£55-65** **PSA**

A Royal Doulton 'Hallowe'en Bunnykins' figure, DB132, designed by Graham Tongue.

*1993-97* *3.25in (12.5cm) high*

**£28-32** **PSA**

A Royal Doulton 'Home Run Bunnykins' figure, DB43, designed by Harry Sales, boxed.

*1986-93* *4.25in (12.5cm)*

**£50-70** **PSA**

A Royal Doulton 'Ice-cream Seller Bunnykins' figure, DB82, designed by Graham Tongue.

*1990-93* *4.5in (12cm) high*

**£80-120** **PSA**

A limited edition Royal Doulton 'Banjo Player Bunnykins' figure, DB182, designed by Kimberley Curtis, from an edition of 2,500, from the Jazz Band series.

*1999* *5in (12.5cm) high*

**£60-80** **PSA**

A Royal Doulton 'Clarinet Playing Bunnykins' figure, DB184, designed by Kimberley Curtis, from an edition of 2,500 from the Jazz Band series, boxed with certificate.

*1999* *5in (12.5cm) high*

**£40-60** **PSA**

A limited edition Royal Doulton 'Jester Bunnykins' figure, DB161, designed by Denise Andrews, from an edition of 1,500 produced exclusively for UKI Ceramics.

*1995* *4.5in (12cm) high*

**£120-180** **PSA**

A Royal Doulton 'Jogging Bunnykins' figure, DB22, designed by Harry Sales.

*1983-89* *2.5in (6.5cm) high*

**£45-55** **PSA**

A special edition Royal Doulton 'Joker Bunnykins' figure, DB171, designed by Denise Andrews, from an edition of 2,500 produced exclusively for UKI Ceramics boxed.

*1997* *5in (12.5cm) high*

**£60-80** **PSA**

A Royal Doulton 'Knockout Bunnykins' figure, DB30, designed by Harry Sales, with Jubilee backstamp, boxed.

*1984-88* *4.25in (12.5cm)*

**£120-180** **PSA**

A Royal Doulton 'Mr Bunnykins At The Easter Parade' figure, DB18, designed by Harry Sales, boxed.

*1982-93* *5in (12.5cm)*

**£50-80** **PSA**

A Royal Doulton 'Mr Bunnykins Autumn Days' figure, DB5, based on a design by Walter Hayward, underglaze chip to ear.

*1972-82* *4in (10cm) high*

**£70-100** **PSA**

A Royal Doulton 'Mrs Bunnykins At The Easter Parade' figure, DB19, designed by Harry Sales, boxed.

*This figure was also the special event figure in 1986 with model no. DB52. The special event version can be worth over ten times as much.*

*1982-96* *4.5in (12cm) high*

**£35-45** **PSA**

A Royal Doulton 'Mrs Bunnykins Clean Sweep' figure, DB6, based on a design by Walter Hayward.

*1972-91* *4in (10cm) high*

**£50-70** **PSA**

A Royal Doulton 'Olympic Bunnykins' figure, DB28A, designed by Harry Sales, with 1984 Jubilee backstamp.

*The DB28B variation has a green and gold colourway and was produced for the 1984 Jubilee only. It can be worth over three times as much as this colourway.*

*1984-88* *3.75in (9.5cm) high*

**£50-80** **PSA**

A Royal Doulton 'Drummer Bunnykins' figure, DB26A, by Harry Sales, 1st variation for the 50th anniversary, style one from the Oompah Band series.

*The standard version was produced between 1984-1990 and is worth about the same.*

*1984* *3.5in (9cm) high*

**£45-55** **PSA**

A Royal Doulton 'Paperboy Bunnykins' figure, DB77, designed by Graham Tongue, boxed.

*1989-93* *4in (10cm) high*

**£70-100** **PSA**

A Royal Doulton 'Partners in Collecting' Bunnykins figure, DB151, designed by Walter Hayward, boxed.

*Produced exclusively for the Royal Doulton International Collectors Club 15th anniversary in this colourway.*

*1999* *3in (7.5cm) high*

**£60-80** **PSA**

A limited edition of 250 Royal Doulton 'Harry The Herald' Bunnykins figure, DB95, 2nd variation, by Harry Sales, Royal Family series, for UKI Ceramics.

*The 3rd variation, DB115, edition of 300 for 1991 Collectors Weekend can fetch double.*

*1990* *3.5in (9cm) high*

**£200-300** **PSA**

A limited edition Royal Doulton 'King John' Bunnykins figure, DB91, second variation, designed by Harry Sales, from the Royal Family series.

*This colourway was produced exclusively for UKI Ceramics in a limited edition of 250. The standard version is red, blue and yellow and is worth about a quarter of this version. Special editions were produced for each of the five members of the Royal Family series.*

*1990* *4in (10cm) high*

**£220-280** **PSA**

A Royal Doulton 'Prince Frederick' Bunnykins figure, DB48, designed by Harry Sales, 1st version, from the Bunnykins Royal Family Series, boxed.

*1986-90* *3.5in (9cm) high*

**£50-70** **PSA**

A limited edition Royal Doulton 'Prince Frederick' Bunnykins figure, DB94, 2nd variation, by Harry Sales, edition of 250, Royal Family series, for UKI.

*1990* *3.5in (9cm) high*

**£200-300** **PSA**

A limited edition Royal Doulton 'Princess Beatrice' Bunnykins figure, DB93, second variation, designed by Harry Sales, from an edition of 250 from the Royal Family series produced exclusively for UKI Ceramics.

*1990* *3.5in (9cm) high*

**£200-300** **PSA**

A limited edition Royal Doulton 'Queen Sophia' Bunnykins figure, DB92, second variation, designed by Harry Sales, from an edition of 250 from the Royal Family series produced exclusively for UKI Ceramics.

*1990* *4.5in (12cm) high*

**£220-280** **PSA**

A special edition Royal Doulton 'Santa's Little Helper" Bunnykins figure, DB192, designed by Graham Tongue, from an edition of 2,500 produced exclusively for Pascoe & Co., boxed.

*1999* *3.5in (9cm) high*

**£25-35** **PSA**

## A CLOSER LOOK AT A BUNNYKINS FIGURE

*The Santa figure, DB17, was produced between 1981 and 1996 in the red and white colourway, it can be worth less than a tenth of this one.*

*Besides the different model number, this can also be differentiated by the hole in the ear for hanging the piece.*

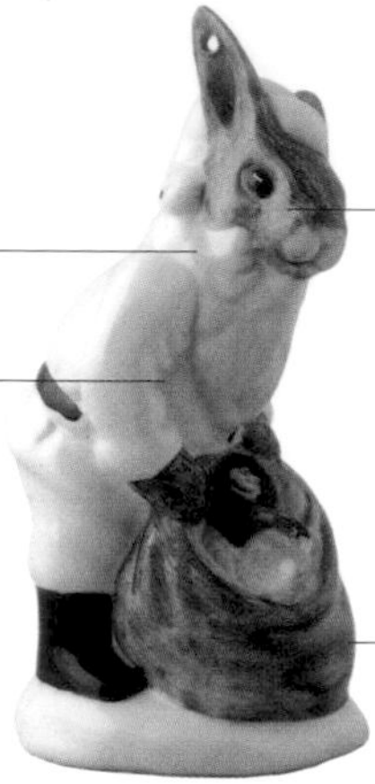

*The figure is usually a more traditional red and white colourway, but some unpainted examples, such as this, do exist.*

*A music box also featured this figure and was produced between 1984 and 1991. The value is about a third of this.*

A limited edition Royal Doulton 'Santa Bunnykins Happy Christmas' Christmas tree ornament, DB62, designed by Harry Sales, unpainted, from an edition of 1,551.

*1987* *3.75in (12.5cm) high*

**£120-180** **PSA**

A Royal Doulton '60th Anniversary Bunnykins' figure, DB137, designed by Graham Tongue, boxed.

*1994* *4.5in (12cm) high*

**£22-28** **PSA**

A Royal Doulton 'Tally Ho! Bunnykins' figure, DB78, based on a design by Walter Hayward, with a special edition special colourway.

*This shape was first released in 1973 as 'Tally Ho Bunnykins' DB12 and is of a similar value to this version.*

*1988* *4in (10cm) high*

**£80-120** **PSA**

A Royal Doulton 'William Bunnykins' figure, DB69, based on a design by Walter Hayward, boxed.

*1988-93* *4in (10cm) high*

**£50-80** **PSA**

A limited edition Royal Doulton 'Fortune Teller Bunnykins' toby jug, D7157, designed by Kimberley Curtis, from an edition of 1,500 produced exclusively for UKI Ceramics.

*1999* *5.5in (12.5cm) high*

**£90-100** **PSA**

A Royal Doulton 'Happy Birthday Bunnykins' music box, DB36, designed by Harry Sales, playing "Happy Birthday To You".

*1984-91* *7in (18cm) high*

**£80-120** **PSA**

### FIND OUT MORE...

**Royal Doulton Collectables,** *by Jean Dale & Louise Irvine, published by Charlton Press, 4th edition, 2006.*

A 1930s Carlton Ware 'New Anemone' vase, no.4245, with painted marks to base.

*6in (16cm) high*

**£180-220** **WW**

Left: A Carlton Ware 'Floral Comets' pattern baluster vase and cover, no.3422, printed and painted factory marks to base.

*9in (23cm) high*

**£80-120** **L&T**

Right: A Carlton Ware 'Floral Comets' pattern cylindrical vase, no.3422, with flaring rim, printed and painted factory marks to base.

*8in (20.5cm) high*

**£1,000-1,500** **L&T**

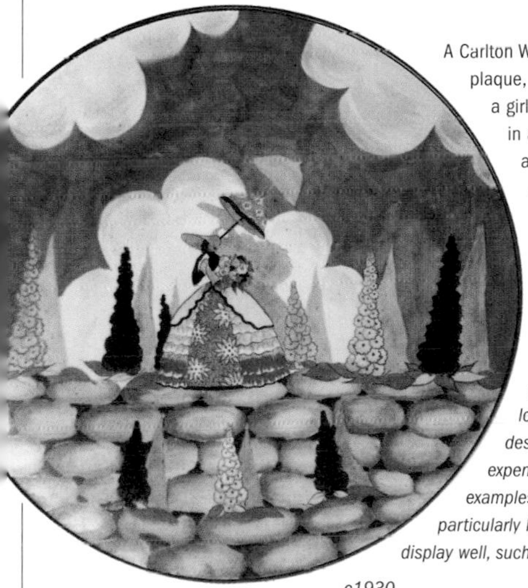

A Carlton Ware 'Handcraft' wall plaque, no.1908, painted with a girl in a crinoline walking in a garden, with printed and painted factory marks to base.

*The hand-decorated 'Handcraft' range was released in 1929 with a subtler palette and charming rural scenes or flower patterns. It required less work than the lustre designs, and was less expensive. Nevertheless, examples are desirable today, particularly large pieces that display well, such as this charger.*

*c1930* *15.5in (39cm) diam*

**£1,000-1,500** **L&T**

A 1930s Carlton ware 'Handcraft' butter dish and cover.

*5.5in (14cm) wide*

**£50-70** **BAD**

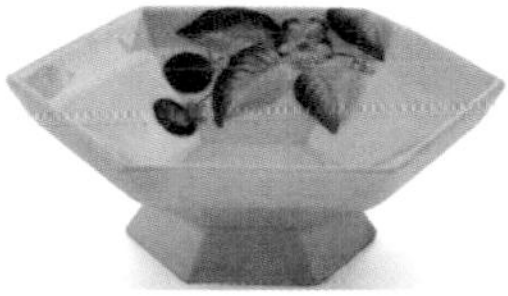

A Carlton ware 'Blackberry' pattern hexagonal bowl,from the Fruit range.

*c1930* *5in (12.5cm) wide*

**£40-60** **BAD**

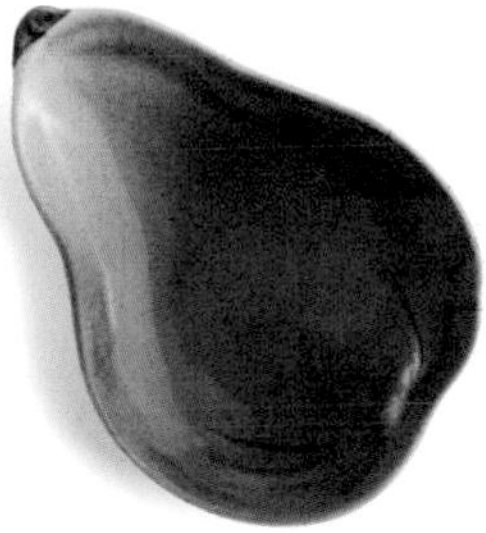

A 1950s-60s Carlton ware 'Pear' pattern dish, from the Fruit range.

*5in (12.5cm) long*

**£22-28** **BAD**

A 1950s/60s Carlton ware 'Apple' teapot, from the Fruit range.

**£80-120** **BAD**

## COLLECTORS' NOTES

- Character jugs have their roots in toby jugs, which have been made since the 18th century. The first character jug was made in the early 1930s in the form of 'John Barleycorn', the personification of barley, and is popularly ascribed to Charles Noke, the Royal Doulton, Burslem art director.
- A toby jug has a full body, either seated or standing, distinguishing it from a character jug, which features the head (and sometimes shoulders) only. Many popular designs are based on real or fictional characters from history, such as political or literary figures.
- One of Doulton's most sought-after designs is a white two-handled Winston Churchill jug, which was withdrawn after complaints that it was not a good likeness. This jug is not to be confused with the best selling Churchill jug by Harry Fenton, which is readily available in three sizes.
- Colour variations add to a jug's value, as some colours were in limited supply during the war. Rarer examples are hotly sought-after, as are mugs that were made in smaller quantities or limited editions. The popularity of a character will also affect the value, particularly if it crosses over into other areas of collecting such as sports and politics.
- Handles became more of a decorative element of the design in the 1950s, and began to say more about the character. For example, musical figures such as Chopin feature their musical instrument, and Captain Hook, a crocodile.
- Character jugs are easy to look after due to their robust nature and good quality glaze. However, rims and handles can be vulnerable. If a jug does get damaged, they can usually be repaired by professionals leaving chips or cracks 'invisible'.

A Royal Doulton 'Athos' small character jug, D6452, designed by Max Henk, from the Characters from Literature series.

*A table lighter version was produced and is worth around four times as much.*

*1956-91 3.75in (9.5cm) high*

**£40-50 PSA**

A Royal Doulton 'Auld Mac' musical large character jug, D5889, designed by Harry Fenton, with printed marks.

*The Thorens movement plays 'The Campbells are Coming'. The version without a musical movement was made until 1986 and is worth about half this version.*

*1938-39 6.25in (16cm) high*

**£200-300 CHEF**

A Royal Doulton 'Auld Mac' large character jug, D5823, designed by Harry Fenton.

*1937-86 6in (15cm) high*

**£35-45 CLV**

A Royal Doulton 'Captain Hook' small character jug, D6601, designed by Max Henk and David B. Biggs, style one with crocodile handle.

*The hatless style two is less desirable despite having been in production in 1994 only.*

*1965-71 4in (10cm) high*

**£150-200 PSA**

A Royal doulton 'Falstaff' large character jug, D6287, designed by Harry Fenton, from the Characters from Literature series, green printed marks.

*1950-95 6.25in (16cm) high*

**£35-45 LFA**

A Royal Doulton 'Gulliver' small character jug, D6563, designed by David B. Biggs, small glaze fault.

*1962-67 4in (10cm) high*

**£120-180 PSA**

A Royal Doulton 'Mad Hatter' small character jug, D6602, designed by Max Henk, from the Alice in Wonderland series, first variation with red bow-tie.

*The second variation with a yellow bowtie was only produced in a small limited edition and is worth about double this version.*

*1965-83* *3.75in (9.5cm) high*

**£50-70** **PSA**

A Royal Doulton 'The Mikado' miniature character jug, D6525, designed by Max Henk.

*1960-69* *2.5in (6.5cm) high*

**£180-220** **PSA**

A Royal Doulton 'Old King Cole' small character jug, D6037, designed by Harry Fenton, second variation with orange crown.

*The first variation with a yellow crown was only made from 1938-39 and can be worth over 10 times as much.*

*1939-60* *3.5in (9cm) high*

**£50-80** **PSA**

A Royal Doulton 'Robin Hood' large character jug, D6205, designed by Harry Fenton, style one lacking feather in cap and with plain handle.

*1947-60* *6.25in (16cm) high*

**£50-80** **L&T**

A Royal Doulton 'Robinson Crusoe' miniature character jug, D6546, designed by Max Henk, from the Characters in Literature series.

*1960-82* *2.75in (7cm) high*

**£30-40** **PSA**

A Royal Doulton 'Sancho Pança' large character jug, D6456, designed by Geoff Blower, from the Characters from Literature series.

*1957-83* *6.5in (16.5cm) high*

**£40-60** **PSA**

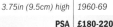

A Royal Doulton 'Tony Weller' musical character jug, D5888, designed by Leslie Harradine and Harry Fenton, from the Charles Dickens' Characters series, repaired damages.

*The Tony Weller jug was used as the basis for a number of derivatives including this musical jug, a sugar bowl, bust, bookend and napkin ring. They were generally only made for a few years making them desirable today.*

*1937-39* *6.5in (16cm) high*

**£150-200** **WW**

A Royal Doulton 'Ugly Duchess' small character jug, D6603, designed by Max Henk, from the Alice in Wonderland series.

*1965-73* *3.5in (9cm) high*

**£150-200** **PSA**

A Royal Doulton 'Catherine Parr' miniature character jug, D6752, designed by Michael Abberley, from the King Henry and His Six Wives series, style one with handle formed from a bible and pulpit.

*1987-89* *2.5in (6.5cm) high*

**£80-120** **PSA**

A limited edition Royal Doulton 'Charlie Chaplin' large character jug, D6949, designed by William K. Harper, from an edition of 5,000, style one with walking cane handle, with certificate.

*1993* *7.25in (18.5cm) high*

**£100-150** **PSA**

A Royal Doulton 'Chopin' large character jug, D7030, designed by Stanley James Taylor, from the Great Composers series, boxed.

*1996-2000* *7in (18cm) high*

**£60-90** **PSA**

A Royal Doulton 'John Doulton' small character jug, D6656, designed by Eric Griffiths, from the RDICC series, first variation with clock face reading 8 o'clock.

*On examples from the first year of production, Big Ben shows a time of 8 o'clock, and from 1981 onwards, it shows a time of 2 o'clock. The first variation is more desirable.*

*1980* *4.25in (11cm) high*

**£50-80** **PSA**

A Royal Doulton 'John Peel' small character jug, D5731, designed by Harry Fenton, second variation with orange riding crop handle.

*3.5in (9cm) high*

**£35-45** **PSA**

A limited edition Royal Doulton 'Queen Victoria' character jug, D6788, designed by Stanley James Taylor, from an edition of 3,000 specially commissioned by The Guild of Specialist China & Glass retailers, style one with sceptre handle, second variation with red jewels in sceptre.

*All the styles and colour variations are of approximately the same value.*

*1988* *7.25in (18.5cm) high*

**£70-100** **GAZE**

A Royal Doulton 'Sam Johnson' small character jug, D6296, designed by Harry Fenton.

*1950-60* *3.25in (8.5cm) high*

**£70-90** **PSA**

A limited edition Royal Doulton 'Sir Walter Raleigh' large character jug, D7169, designed by Robert Tabbenor, from an edition of 1,000, character jug of the year, with box and certificate.

*2002* *7in (18cm) high*

**£100-150** **PSA**

A Royal Doulton 'Winston Churchill' character jug, D6907, designed by Stanley James Taylor, style one with bulldog handle, Character Jug of the Year.

*1992* *7in (18cm) high*

**£120-180** **PSA**

## A CLOSER LOOK AT A CHARACTER JUG

*Three styles of Clown character jug were produced by Doulton between 1937 and 1995.*

*This form was introduced in 1937. The colour variation with black hair is the rarest, only one example is known.*

*This is the most common colour variation of style one, the other colourways can be worth three times as much.*

*This is style one, without a hat. Style two has a hat and is styled as a more modern clown.*

*Later examples are worth less than 50 per cent of this version.*

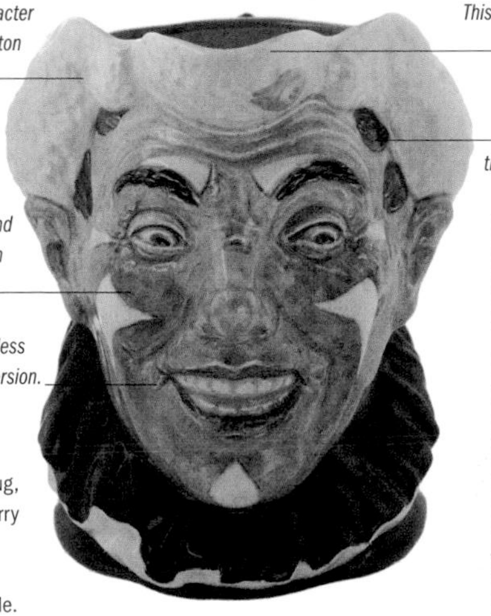

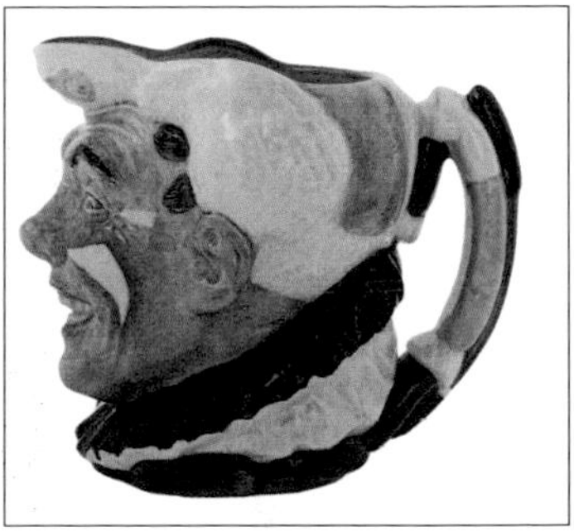

A Royal Doulton 'The Clown' large character jug, D6322, designed by Harry Fenton, style one, third variation with white hair and multicoloured handle.

*1951-55* *7.5in (19cm) high*

**£400-500** **WW**

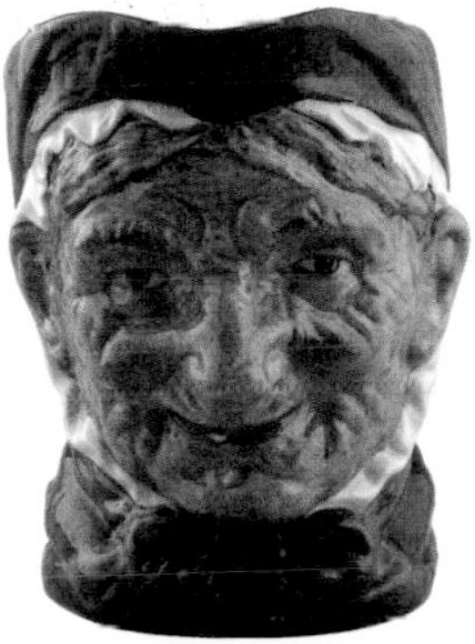

A Royal Doulton 'Farmer John' large character jug, D5788, designed by Charles Noke, style two.

*Unknown-1960*

**£40-60** **DN**

A Royal Doulton 'Gladiator' miniature character jug, D6556, designed by Max Henk.

*1961-67* *7.75in (19.5cm) high*

**£180-220** **PSA**

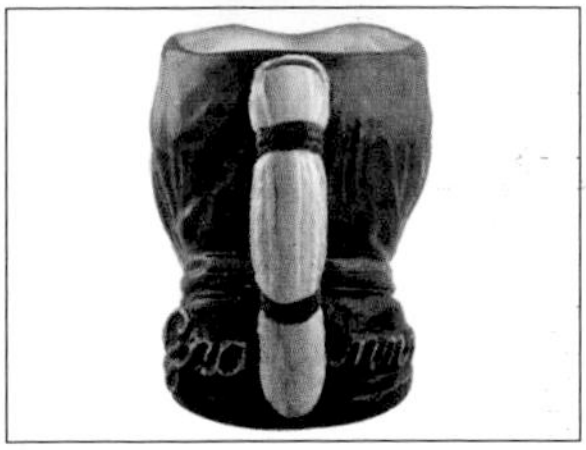

A Royal Doulton 'Granny' large character jug, D5521, designed by Harry Fenton, second variation with one tooth showing.

*The first variation with no teeth showing was made from 1935-41 and is rare in both sizes.*

*1941-83* *6.25in (16cm) high*

**£35-45** **CLV**

A limited edition Royal Doulton 'Great Britain's Britannia' small character jug, D7107, designed by William K. Harper, from an edition of 1,997 commissioned by the Travers Stanley Collection, with box and certificate.

*1997* *4.25in (11cm) high*

**£40-60** **PSA**

A Doulton 'Honest Measure' small character jug, D6108, designed by Harry Fenton.

*1939-91* *4.25in (11cm) high*

**£45-55** **PSA**

A Royal Doulton 'Jarge' small character jug, D6295, designed by Harry Fenton.

*1950-60* *3.5in (9cm) high*

**£80-120** **PSA**

A Royal Doulton 'Lobster Man' small character jug, D6620, designed by David B. Biggs, first variation with white jersey.

*1968-91* *3.75in (9.5cm) high*

**£35-45** **PSA**

A Royal Doulton 'Mine Host' large character jug, D6468, designed by Max Henk.

*1958-82* *7in (18cm) high*

**£40-60** **GORL**

A rare Royal Doulton blue 'Pearly Boy' small character jug, unnumbered, designed by Harry Fenton, first variation with brown hat and blue coat.

*There are five colourway variations of this jug, all of which are sought-after. This is one of the rarest, superceeded only by the all-white glaze variation.*

*1947-Unknown* *3.5in (9cm) high*

**£1,200-1,800** **PSA**

A Royal Doulton 'Pearly Queen' small character jug, D6843, designed by Stanley James Taylor, from the London Collection series.

*1987-91* *3.5in (9cm) high*

**£40-60** **PSA**

A Royal Doulton 'Punch And Judy Man' small character jug, D6593, designed by David B. Biggs.

*1964-69* *3.5in (9cm) high*

**£180-220** **PSA**

A Royal Doulton 'Regency Beau' small character jug, D6562, designed by David B. Biggs.

*1962-67* *4.25in (11cm) high*

**£250-350** **PSA**

A Royal Doulton 'The Viking' miniature character jug, D6526, designed by Max Henk.

*1960-75* *2.5in (6.5cm) high*

**£70-90** **PSA**

An Ashtead Potter's Guild 'Lloyd George' character jug, designed by Percy Metcalfe, glazed overall in lavender blue, numbered "298-1000", printed marks.

*Political figures are a popular choice to be turned into character jugs.*

*7.5in (19cm) high*

**£150-200** **CHEF**

A limited edition Carlton Ware 'The Pigeon Fancier' character jug, from an edition of 500.

**£30-50** **GAZE**

A Lancaster's 'Neville Chamberlain' earthenware small character jug.

*3in (7.5cm) high*

**£60-70** **H&G**

A SylvaC 'George Bernard Shaw' cellulose painted character jug, stamped "3279".

*6in (15.5cm) high*

**£50-80** **MCOL**

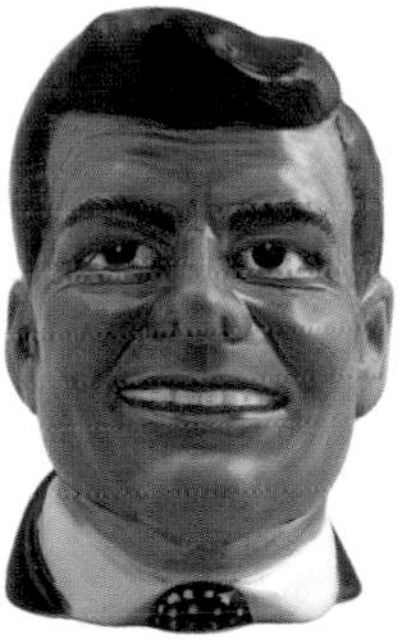

A 1960s SylvaC 'John F. Kennedy' character jug, stamped "2899".

*6.25in (16cm) high*

**£50-70** **MCOL**

A 1970s SylvaC 'Maid Marion' character jug, stamped "5117".

*7in (18cm) high*

**£40-60** **MCOL**

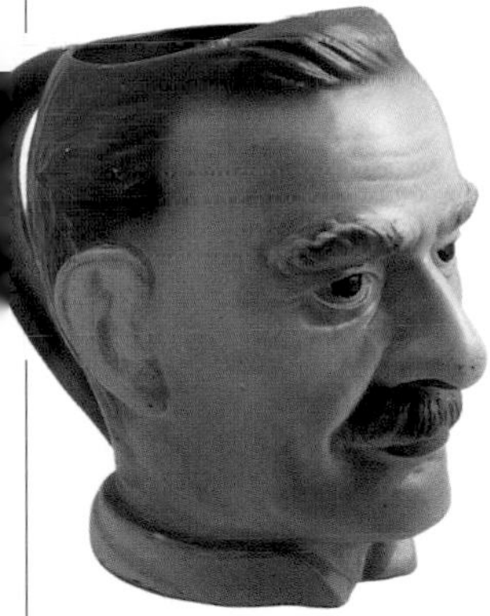

A SylvaC 'Neville Chamberlain' cellulose painted character jug, stamped "1463".

*6.5in (16.5cm) high*

**£80-120** **MCOL**

A 1970s SylvaC 'Robin Hood' character jug, stamped "5114".

*6.25in (16cm) high*

**£40-60** **MCOL**

A 1960s SylvaC 'Uncle Sam' character jug, stamped "2888".

*6.75in (17cm) high*

**£50-80** **MCOL**

**FIND OUT MORE...**

**Royal Doulton Jugs**, *by Jean Dale, ninth edition published by Charlton Press, November 2005.*

## COLLECTORS' NOTES

- Clarice Cliff's ceramics designs, produced at A.J. Wilkinson in Burslem, Staffordshire, have become mainstays on the collecting scene. Cliff (1899-1972) first began working in the Potteries in 1912, before moving to A.J. Wilkinson in 1916. In 1925 her managing director, lover and future husband, Colley Shorter, gave Cliff her own studio at the Newport Pottery.
- Cliff is best known for her 'Bizarre' range, produced from 1928, which initially comprised defective blank wares hand-painted with colourful, geometric designs. Their obviously hand-painted nature, combined with the cheerful colours and designs was revolutionary and also highly fashionable, capturing the spirit of the new Art Deco movement.
- The 'Fantasque' range was also launched in 1928, and over time both ranges grew more elaborate, abstract and bold. By 1935, both ranges had been phased out as tastes had begun to change. After WWII, she continued to produce new designs but these were never as popular, or arguably as successful, as her pre-war designs.
- Today, these earlier pieces produced during the height of her geometric phase from 1928-c1935 tend to be the most desirable. Longer running ranges, such as 'Crocus', may not necessarily be rare, but still have a strong following. Learn to recognise patterns and look out for variations, as these can be rare and valuable.
- In general, look out for the combination of a geometric shape and geometric or modern pattern. Chargers, jugs and large vases display the pattern well and have great visual appeal, so tend to be the most valuable. Orange tends to be a common colour; blue and purple tend to be less common. Damage can affect value considerably, so examine a piece carefully.

A Clarice Cliff Fantasque Bizarre 'Blue Autumn' pattern side plate.

*1930-34* *7in (18cm) diam*

**£280-320** **GHOU**

A Clarice Cliff Fantasque Bizarre 'Green Autumn' pattern two-handled grapefruit bowl.

*1930-34* *6.75in (17cm) wide*

**£220-280** **NEA**

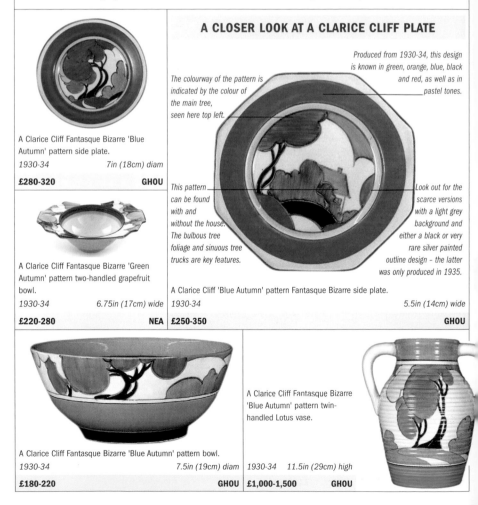

### A CLOSER LOOK AT A CLARICE CLIFF PLATE

*Produced from 1930-34, this design is known in green, orange, blue, black and red, as well as in pastel tones.*

*The colourway of the pattern is indicated by the colour of the main tree, seen here top left.*

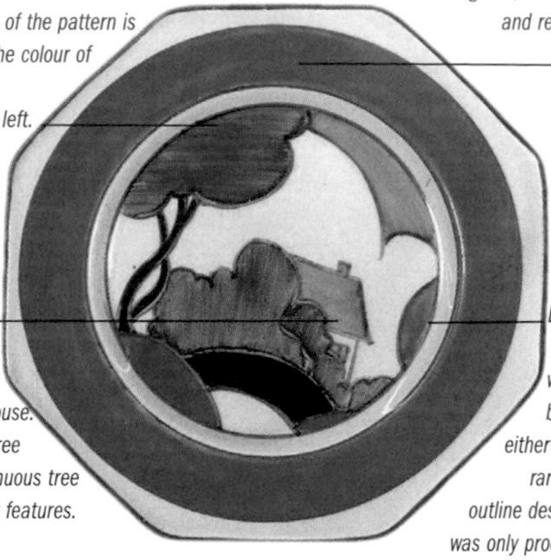

*This pattern can be found with and without the house. The bulbous tree foliage and sinuous tree trucks are key features.*

*Look out for the scarce versions with a light grey background and either a black or very rare silver painted outline design - the latter was only produced in 1935.*

A Clarice Cliff 'Blue Autumn' pattern Fantasque Bizarre side plate.

*1930-34* *5.5in (14cm) wide*

**£250-350** **GHOU**

A Clarice Cliff Fantasque Bizarre 'Blue Autumn' pattern bowl.

*1930-34* *7.5in (19cm) diam*

**£180-220** **GHOU**

A Clarice Cliff Fantasque Bizarre 'Blue Autumn' pattern twin-handled Lotus vase.

*1930-34* *11.5in (29cm) high*

**£1,000-1,500** **GHOU**

A Clarice Cliff Fantasque 'Melon' pattern vase, shape 358.

*1930* *8in (20cm) high*

**£700-900** **GHOU**

## A CLOSER LOOK AT A CLARICE CLIFF VASE

*Melon was introduced in early 1930. It can be found in green, red, orange and pastel colourways, and with orange, pastel or red bands.*

*Rather than being outlined in black, as with many other patterns, the elements are outlined in brown, giving less emphasis to outlines and more to colour.*

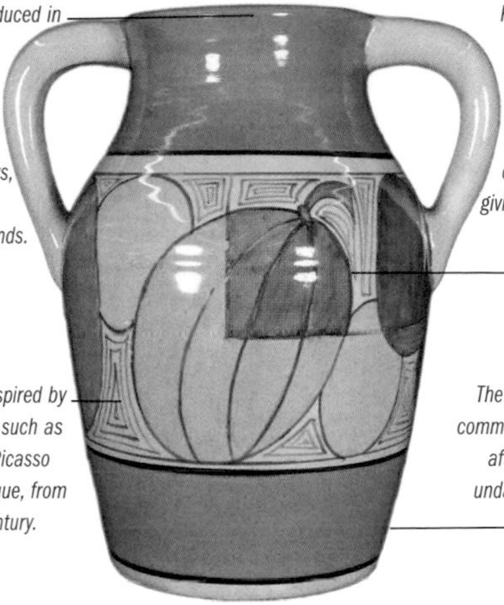

*The style was inspired by Cubist paintings such as those by Pablo Picasso and George Braque, from earlier in the century.*

*The Lotus vase is not common and is sought-after, particularly in undamaged condition as here.*

A Clarice Cliff Fantasque Bizarre 'Melon' pattern twin-handled Lotus vase.

*1930* *11.5in (29cm) high*

**£1,500-2,000** **GHOU**

A Clarice Cliff Fantasque 'Melon' pattern vase, shape 362.

*1930* *8in (20cm) high*

**£750-850** **GHOU**

A Clarice Cliff Fantasque 'Melon' pattern vase, shape 373.

*1930* *7in (18cm) high*

**£800-1,200** **GHOU**

A Clarice Cliff Fantasque Bizarre 'Melon' pattern vase, shape 342.

*1930* *8in (20cm) high*

**£750-850** **GHOU**

A Clarice Cliff Fantasque Bizarre 'Melon' pattern Drum preserve pot base, lacks lid.

*1930* *3in (7.5cm) high*

**£120-180** **GHOU**

A Clarice Cliff Fantasque Bizarre 'Melon' pattern stepped candlestick, shape 391, lacks factory marks.

*Candlesticks are not a commonly found Clarice Cliff form. The stepped design is typically Art Deco. Examine the corners carefully for damage.*

*1930* *3.5in (9cm) high*

**£250-350** **GHOU**

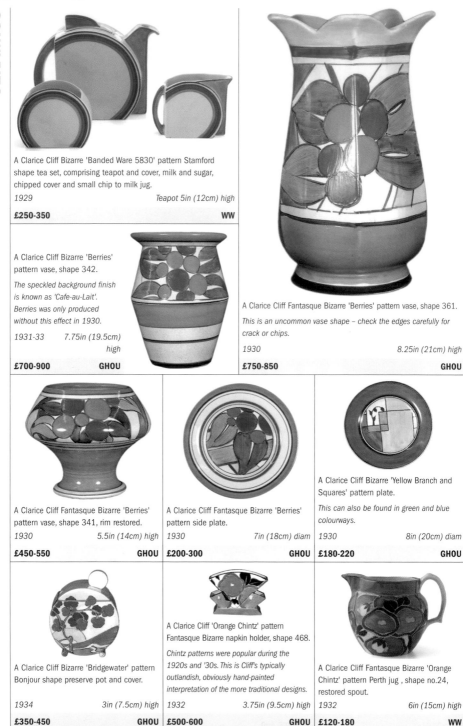

A Clarice Cliff Bizarre 'Banded Ware 5830' pattern Stamford shape tea set, comprising teapot and cover, milk and sugar, chipped cover and small chip to milk jug.

*1929* *Teapot 5in (12cm) high*

**£250-350** **WW**

A Clarice Cliff Bizarre 'Berries' pattern vase, shape 342.

*The speckled background finish is known as 'Cafe-au-Lait'. Berries was only produced without this effect in 1930.*

*1931-33* *7.75in (19.5cm) high*

**£700-900** **GHOU**

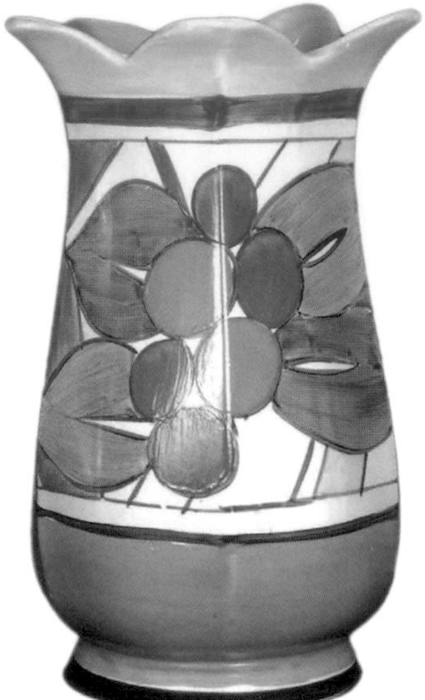

A Clarice Cliff Fantasque Bizarre 'Berries' pattern vase, shape 361.

*This is an uncommon vase shape - check the edges carefully for crack or chips.*

*1930* *8.25in (21cm) high*

**£750-850** **GHOU**

A Clarice Cliff Fantasque Bizarre 'Berries' pattern vase, shape 341, rim restored.

*1930* *5.5in (14cm) high*

**£450-550** **GHOU**

A Clarice Cliff Fantasque Bizarre 'Berries' pattern side plate.

*1930* *7in (18cm) diam*

**£200-300** **GHOU**

A Clarice Cliff Bizarre 'Yellow Branch and Squares' pattern plate.

*This can also be found in green and blue colourways.*

*1930* *8in (20cm) diam*

**£180-220** **GHOU**

A Clarice Cliff Bizarre 'Bridgewater' pattern Bonjour shape preserve pot and cover.

*1934* *3in (7.5cm) high*

**£350-450** **GHOU**

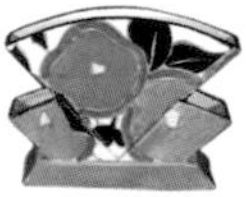

A Clarice Cliff 'Orange Chintz' pattern Fantasque Bizarre napkin holder, shape 468.

*Chintz patterns were popular during the 1920s and '30s. This is Cliff's typically outlandish, obviously hand-painted interpretation of the more traditional designs.*

*1932* *3.75in (9.5cm) high*

**£500-600** **GHOU**

A Clarice Cliff Fantasque Bizarre 'Orange Chintz' pattern Perth jug , shape no.24, restored spout.

*1932* *6in (15cm) high*

**£120-180** **WW**

A Clarice Cliff Fantasque Bizarre 'Blue Chintz' pattern Drum preserve pot and cover.

*1932* *3in (7.5cm) high*

**£280-320** **GHOU**

A Clarice Cliff Bizarre 'Autumn Crocus' pattern vase, shape 186.

*1928-63* *6in (15cm) high*

**£350-450** **GHOU**

A Clarice Cliff Bizarre 'Autumn Crocus' pattern jardinière.

*1928-63* *8in (20cm) high*

**£400-500** **GHOU**

## A CLOSER LOOK AT A CLARICE CLIFF BOWL

*This geometric Art Deco form is very popular, particularly when the pattern is similarly geometric.*

*It was part of the Conical range introduced in May 1929, and originally known as 'Odilon'.*

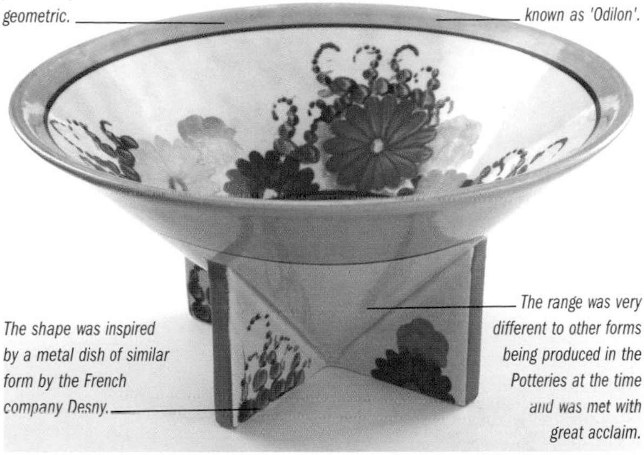

*The shape was inspired by a metal dish of similar form by the French company Desny.*

*The range was very different to other forms being produced in the Potteries at the time and was met with great acclaim.*

A Clarice Cliff Bizarre 'Gayday' (variant) conical bowl, shape 383.

*1930* *7.75 (19.5cm) diam*

**£450-550** **NEA**

A Clarice Cliff Bizarre 'Crocus' pattern part washset, comprising a ewer, basin, chamberpot and a toothbrush mug.

*1928-63* *Ewer 10in (25cm) high*

**£650-750** **L&T**

A Clarice Cliff Bizarre 'Gibraltar' pattern Stamford shape tea-for-two set, comprising a teapot and cover, milk jug, sugar basin, side plate and two conical cups and saucers.

*1933*

**£4,500-5,500** **GHOU**

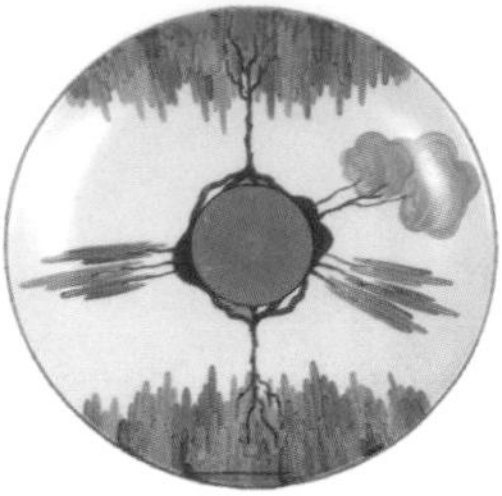

A Clarice Cliff 'Latona Tree' pattern Bizarre wall charger.

*1929-30* *13in (33cm) diam*

**£550-650** **GHOU**

A rare Clarice Cliff Fantasque 'New Fruit' pattern Lotus jug.

*Fakes of these highly sought-after jugs are often seen - one clue is to check the handle. If it is hollow, perhaps with a hole at the base, it is a fake - all original Clarice Cliff Lotus jugs have solid handles.*

*1931* *11.5in (29cm) high*

**£2,200-2,800** **GHOU**

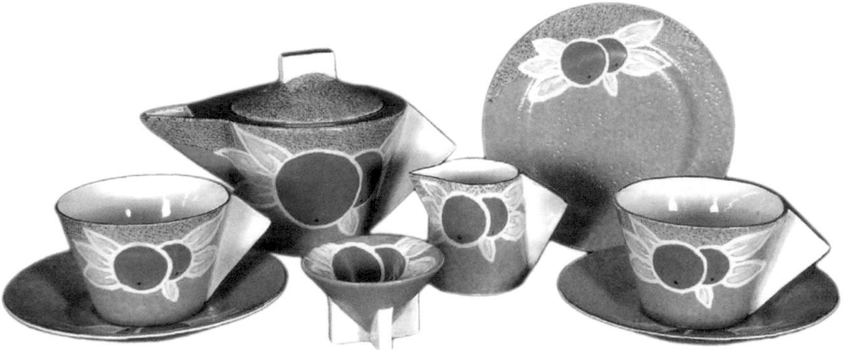

A Clarice Cliff Bizarre 'Nuage' pattern Conical shape tea-for-two set, comprising teapot and cover, milk jug, sugar basin, two cups and saucers and a side plate, faint hairline to the milk jug.

*This pattern was produced in a number of different colours and with two pattern variations showing either fruit (as here) or flowers.*

*1932*

**£1,500-2,000** **GHOU**

A Clarice Cliff Fantasque Bizarre 'Oranges' pattern candlestick, shape 310.

*1932* *3in (7.5cm) high*

**£250-350** **GHOU**

A Clarice Cliff 'Original Bizarre' sabot.

*1928-29* *6in (15cm) long*

**£300-400** **GHOU**

A Clarice Cliff 'Original Bizarre' vase, shape 186.

*1928-29* *7in (18cm) high*

**£400-500** **GHOU**

A Clarice Cliff 'Original Bizarre' vase, shape 186-1, printed gold backstamp.

*1928* *8.5in (21.5cm) h*

**£400-500** **GHOU**

A Clarice Cliff Bizarre 'Patina Coastal Tree' pattern Stamford shape tea-for-two set, comprising a teapot and cover, two cups and saucers, milk jug and sugar bowl, restored milk jug spout, printed marks.

*1932*

**£800-1,000** SWO

A Clarice Cliff Bizarre 'Red Picasso Flower' pattern Drum preserve pot and cover, minor chip to the rim.

*1930* *3in (7.5cm) high*

**£400-500** GHOU

A Clarice Cliff Bizarre 'Orange Picasso Flower' pattern plate.

*1930* *9in (23cm) diam*

**£280-320** GHOU

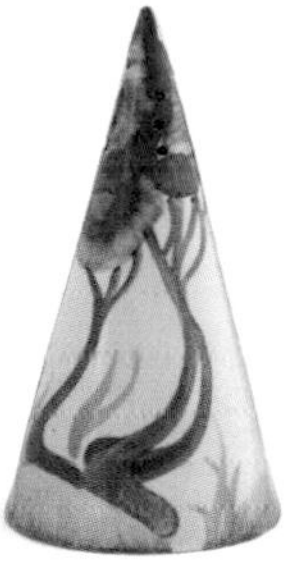

A Clarice Cliff Bizarre 'Rhodanthe' pattern conical sugar sifter.

*1934* *5.5in (14cm) high*

**£200-300** WW

A Clarice Cliff Fantasque 'Green Secrets' pattern sugar sifter, with an electro-plated cover, shape 478.

*1933-37* *6.5in (16.5cm) high*

**£300-500** GHOU

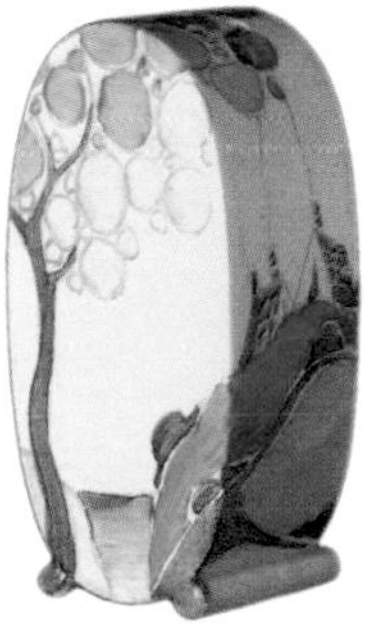

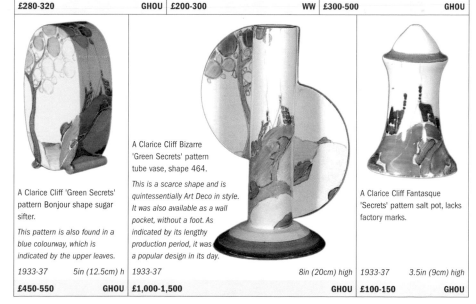

A Clarice Cliff 'Green Secrets' pattern Bonjour shape sugar sifter.

*This pattern is also found in a blue colourway, which is indicated by the upper leaves.*

*1933-37* *5in (12.5cm) h*

**£450-550** GHOU

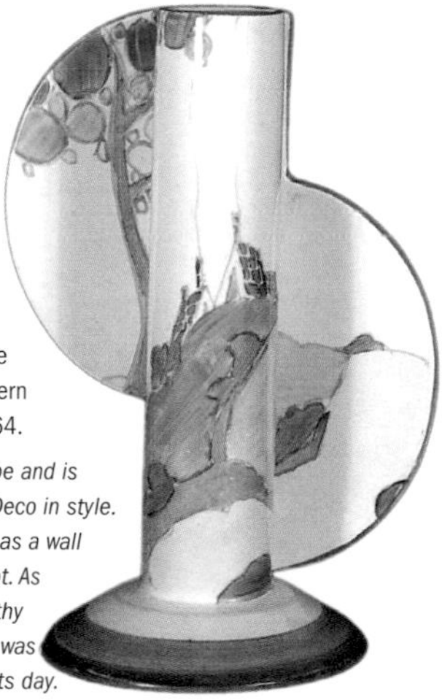

A Clarice Cliff Bizarre 'Green Secrets' pattern tube vase, shape 464.

*This is a scarce shape and is quintessentially Art Deco in style. It was also available as a wall pocket, without a foot. As indicated by its lengthy production period, it was a popular design in its day.*

*1933-37* *8in (20cm) high*

**£1,000-1,500** GHOU

A Clarice Cliff Fantasque 'Secrets' pattern salt pot, lacks factory marks.

*1933-37* *3.5in (9cm) high*

**£100-150** GHOU

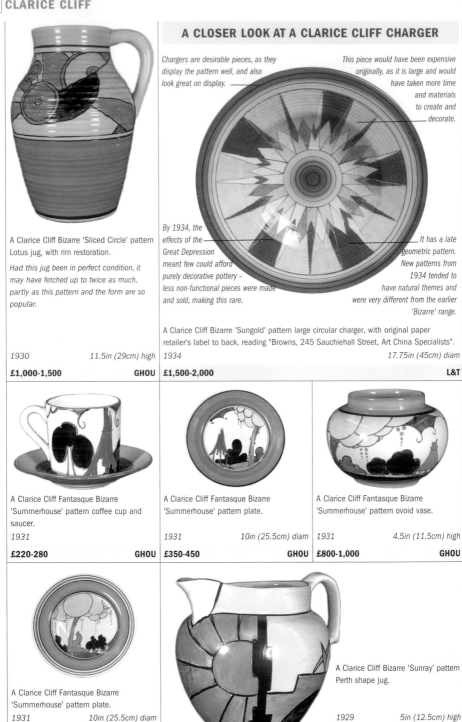

A Clarice Cliff Bizarre 'Sliced Circle' pattern Lotus jug, with rim restoration.

*Had this jug been in perfect condition, it may have fetched up to twice as much, partly as this pattern and the form are so popular.*

*1930* *11.5in (29cm) high*

**£1,000-1,500** **GHOU**

## A CLOSER LOOK AT A CLARICE CLIFF CHARGER

*Chargers are desirable pieces, as they display the pattern well, and also look great on display.*

*This piece would have been expensive originally, as it is large and would have taken more time and materials to create and decorate.*

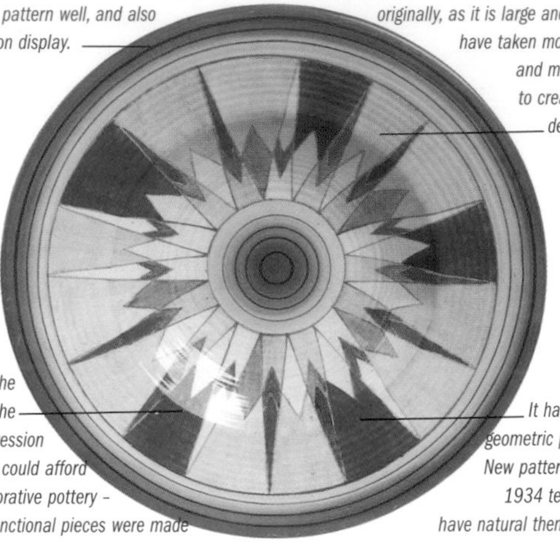

*By 1934, the effects of the Great Depression meant few could afford purely decorative pottery – less non-functional pieces were made and sold, making this rare.*

*It has a late geometric pattern. New patterns from 1934 tended to have natural themes and were very different from the earlier 'Bizarre' range.*

A Clarice Cliff Bizarre 'Sungold' pattern large circular charger, with original paper retailer's label to back, reading "Browns, 245 Sauchiehall Street, Art China Specialists".

*1934* *17.75in (45cm) diam*

**£1,500-2,000** **L&T**

A Clarice Cliff Fantasque Bizarre 'Summerhouse' pattern coffee cup and saucer.

*1931*

**£220-280** **GHOU**

A Clarice Cliff Fantasque Bizarre 'Summerhouse' pattern plate.

*1931* *10in (25.5cm) diam*

**£350-450** **GHOU**

A Clarice Cliff Fantasque Bizarre 'Summerhouse' pattern ovoid vase.

*1931* *4.5in (11.5cm) high*

**£800-1,000** **GHOU**

A Clarice Cliff Fantasque Bizarre 'Summerhouse' pattern plate.

*1931* *10in (25.5cm) diam*

**£350-450** **GHOU**

A Clarice Cliff Bizarre 'Sunray' pattern Perth shape jug.

*1929* *5in (12.5cm) high*

**£800-1,000** **GHOU**

A Clarice Cliff Bizarre 'Sunray' pattern vase, shape 358.

*This pattern is meant to represent a stylised skyscraper, a sunburst and a bridge with birds in flight above it – the first two being typical motifs of the Art Deco movement.*

*1929* *8in (20cm) high*

**£1,500-2,000** **GHOU**

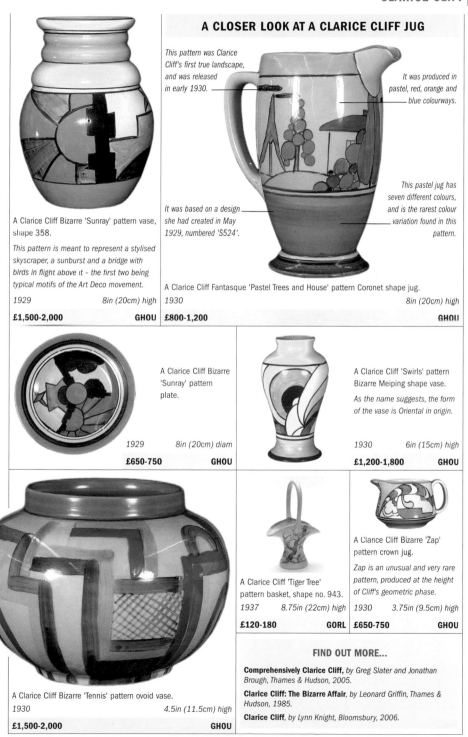

## A CLOSER LOOK AT A CLARICE CLIFF JUG

*This pattern was Clarice Cliff's first true landscape, and was released in early 1930.*

*It was produced in pastel, red, orange and blue colourways.*

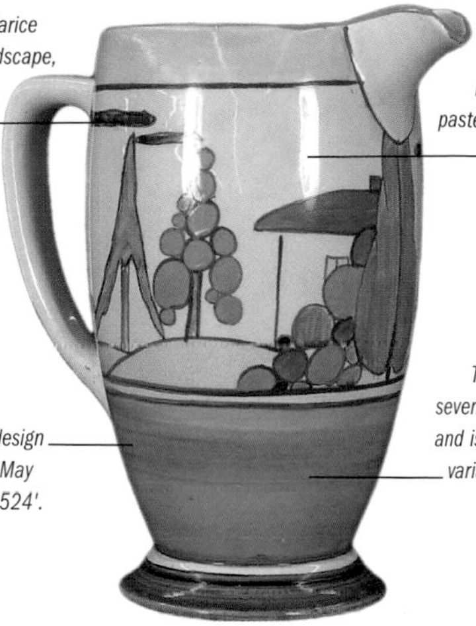

*It was based on a design she had created in May 1929, numbered 'S524'.*

*This pastel jug has seven different colours, and is the rarest colour variation found in this pattern.*

A Clarice Cliff Fantasque 'Pastel Trees and House' pattern Coronet shape jug.

*1930* *8in (20cm) high*

**£800-1,200** **GHOU**

A Clarice Cliff Bizarre 'Sunray' pattern plate.

*1929* *8in (20cm) diam*

**£650-750** **GHOU**

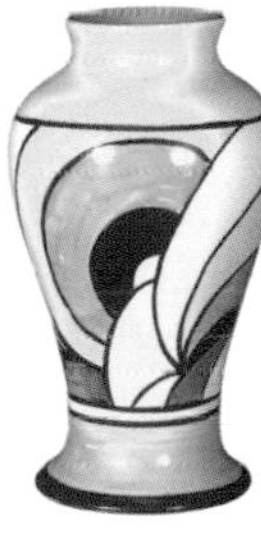

A Clarice Cliff 'Swirls' pattern Bizarre Meiping shape vase.

*As the name suggests, the form of the vase is Oriental in origin.*

*1930* *6in (15cm) high*

**£1,200-1,800** **GHOU**

A Clarice Cliff Bizarre 'Tennis' pattern ovoid vase.

*1930* *4.5in (11.5cm) high*

**£1,500-2,000** **GHOU**

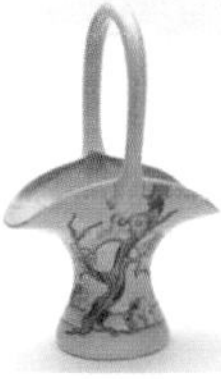

A Clarice Cliff 'Tiger Tree' pattern basket, shape no. 943.

*1937* *8.75in (22cm) high*

**£120-180** **GORL**

A Clarice Cliff Bizarre 'Zap' pattern crown jug.

*Zap is an unusual and very rare pattern, produced at the height of Cliff's geometric phase.*

*1930* *3.75in (9.5cm) high*

**£650-750** **GHOU**

### FIND OUT MORE...

**Comprehensively Clarice Cliff,** *by Greg Slater and Jonathan Brough, Thames & Hudson, 2005.*

**Clarice Cliff: The Bizarre Affair,** *by Leonard Griffin, Thames & Hudson, 1985.*

**Clarice Cliff,** *by Lynn Knight, Bloomsbury, 2006.*

## COLLECTORS' NOTES

- Cornishware was introduced by the T.G. Green pottery, in Church Gresley, Derbyshire, during the 1920s. It is made by spraying the body with blue liquid clay (slip) and then lightly carving away bands on a lathe to reveal the underlying colour, before firing and glazing. Popularity peaked in the 1940s and '50s and declined in the 1980s. In the late 1990s and again early this century, prices peaked again on the secondary market – particularly for rare pieces.
- Although the design has been copied, only T.G. Green's production is widely and seriously collected. Storage or 'household' jars are one of the most popular forms, although most collectors like to build up a set. Beware of fakes – most authentic storage jars use a black T.G. Green shield-shaped mark or a green church mark. Stamps are the best way to help date a piece to a period.
- In 1987, the company was sold to Cloverleaf, who incorporated its name into marks. In 2001, it was sold again to Masons Cash & Co. who continue to make it today. It is primarily pieces produced from the late 1920s until the 1970s that are of interest.
- The work of Royal College of Art graduate Judith Onions, who redesigned shapes from 1966-c1968, is becoming increasingly sought-after. Her forms are more modern, with clean lines approaching the geometric. She also designed the 'target' brand mark that was used throughout the late 1960s until 1980.
- Although Cornishware is best loved in its hallmark blue and white, it was produced in other colours from the 1960s onwards. These include the popular yellow and white, green, and an increasingly desirable black and white. Red is perhaps the rarest colour, only being used on a test range.

A T.G. Green Cornishware 'Candied-Peel' storage jar.

*2.5in (6.5cm) high*

**£100-150** **GA**

A T. G. Green Cornishware 'Currants' storage jar.

*5in (12.5cm) high*

**£40-60** **GA**

A T. G. Green Cornishware 'Flour' storage jar.

*7in (17.5cm) high*

**£50-70** **GA**

A T. G. Green Cornishware 'Ginger' storage jar.

*2.5in (6.5cm) high*

**£70-100** **GA**

A T. G. Green Cornishware 'Icing Sugar' storage jar.

*5.5in (14cm) high*

**£80-120** **GA**

A T. G. Green Cornishware 'Loaf Sugar' storage jar.

*5in (12.5cm) high*

**£70-100** **GA**

A T. G. Green Cornishware 'Nutmegs' storage jar.

*2.5in (6.5cm) high*

**£50-80** **GA**

A T. G. Green Cornishware 'Rice' storage jar.

*4in (10cm) high*

**£50-70** **GA**

## A CLOSER LOOK AT A CORNISHWARE STORAGE JAR

*Storage jars are one of the most recognisable, varied and collectable of the Cornishware range.*

*Look out for unusual or expensive ingredients, or terms used in foreign countries as here, as it is likely less were made, possibly making them rare today.*

*Beware of fakes, which often have a green shield T.G. Green stamp. Also run your fingers over the wording, as originals are totally smooth and under the glaze.*

*The diameters of jars vary widely, and not all lids will fit another jar, so measure a jar carefully if you are buying a replacement.*

A T. G. Green Cornishware 'Meal' storage jar.

*7in (17.5cm) high*

**£300-400** **GA**

A T. G. Green Cornishware 'Graduated Milk Jug', with quantities printed to interior.

*4.75in (12cm) high*

**£50-70** **GA**

A Cloverleaf (T. G. Green) Cornishware teapot, with combined 'Cloverleaf' and T. G. Green stamp to base.

*Cloverleaf marks indicate a piece made from 1987-2001. Four numbers under a mark indicate the month and year of manufacture, but these may not always appear. This teapot shape was designed by Judith Onions.*

*5in (12.5cm) high*

**£30-40** **GA**

A T. G. Green Cornishware 'Dreadnought' jug.

*4.5in (11.5cm) high*

**£30-50** **GA**

A T. G. Green Cornishware mug.

*3.5in (9cm) diam*

**£7-10** **GA**

A T. G. Green Cornishware 'Milk Horn' beaker.

*4in (10cm) high*

**£35-45** **GA**

A T.G. Green Cornishware sugar sifter.

*5.5in (14cm) high*

**£40-60** **GA**

A T. G. Green Cornishware 'Vinegar' bottle, lacks white ceramic and cork stopper.

*7.25in (18.5cm) high*

**£70-100** **GA**

A T. G. Green Cornishware salt box, with wooden lid.

*Although this is an earlier piece, Cloverleaf also used wooden lids and stoppers during the late 1990s.*

*4.5in (11.5cm) high*

**£80-100** **GA**

A Cloverleaf (T.G. Green) Cornishware 'Olive Oil' bottle, made for the Cornishware Collectors' Club, lacks stopper.

*The Cornishware Collectors' Club existed from the late 1990s-2002 and released a number of limited edition shapes. The presence of the limited edition card, if one was issued for that shape, adds desirability.*

*c2000* *7.25in (18.5cm) high*

**£40-60** **GA**

A Cornishware rolling pin.

*Rolling pins with five blue stripes and blue handles can be seen in T.G. Green's 1934, 1955 & 1957 Cornishware catalogues - in the 1960 catalogue it is plain white with blue handles.*

*Barrel 9.75in (24.5cm) long*

**£70-100** **GA**

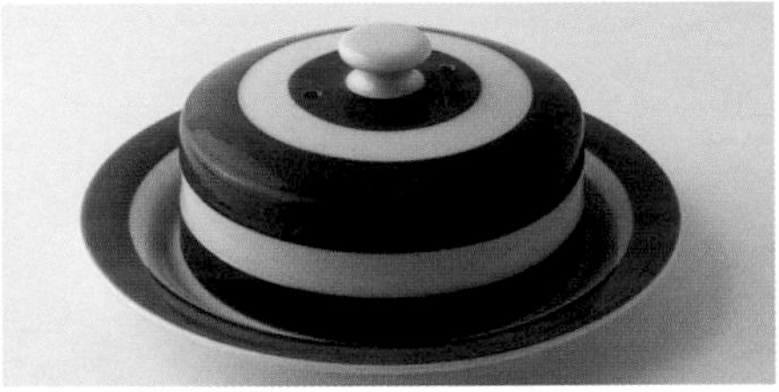

A T. G. Green Cornishware cheese dish.

*8.5in (21.5cm) wide*

**£40-60** **GA**

A T. G. Green Cornishware dinner plate.

*As flatwares such as plates cannot be easily rotated on a lathe, they are not covered with blue slip and cut: instead the blue lines are sprayed on where desired.*

*9in (22.5cm) diam*

**£15-20** **GA**

A 1960s T. G. Green yellow and white Cornishware tea plate.

6.5in (16.5cm) diam

**£8-10** **GA**

A 1960s T. G. Green Cornishware yellow and white 'Covered Butter Dish'.

*The clean, angled lines and simple knob show this form was designed by Judith Onions.*

5.5in (14cm) wide

**£40-60** **GA**

Two 1960s T.G. Green yellow and white Cornishware egg cups.

2in (5cm) diam

**£7-10 (EACH)** **GA**

A 1990s T.G Green Cornishware 'Country Road Green' banded cafetière, made for the Australian market.

*Country Road Green range was produced for the Australian retailer 'Country Road' in the 1990s. Do not confuse this with the darker, deeper green known as 'Teal' that was introduced as part of the standard range in 1996.*

7.5in (19cm) high

**£70-100** **GA**

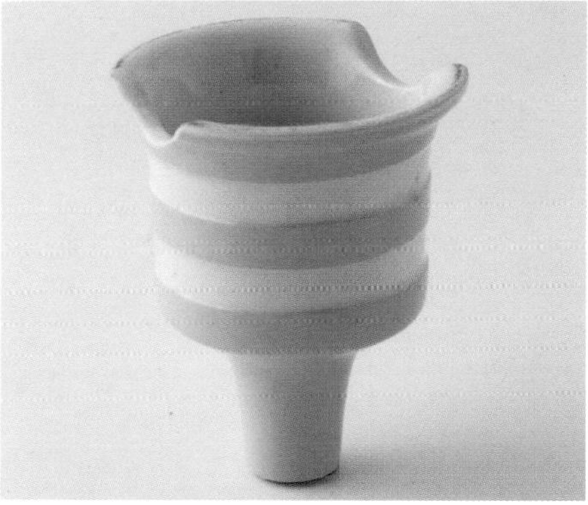

A Cloverleaf T.G. Green yellow and white Cornishware funnel, made for the Cornishware Collectors' Club.

c2000 3.25in (8.5cm) high

**£50-80** **GA**

A 1960s T. G. Green Cornishware 'Polo' tea pot.

*Polo was first made in the 1930s and reintroduced in 1957. From 1958, it was also produced in pink. This teapot was part of a range of tablewares re-introduced to attract some of the 'modern' market catered for by factories such as Midwinter.*

6.5in (16.5cm) high

**£30-40** **GA**

A 1950s T. G. Green 'Club Hunt' teapot.

*This complex design, produced for only a few years in the 1950s, used stencils to mask out the design. After the body has been sprayed with blue slip, the stencil was removed, leaving the design in white. Although not strictly Cornishware, it is still of interest to collectors.*

c1956 4.25in (10.5cm) high

**£70-100** **GA**

## COLLECTORS' NOTES

- Cups and saucers are collected to be both displayed and used. Different cups and saucers can be combined to great visual effect, even with a mix of patterns and dates, and are known as 'harlequin sets'. Most of these were made from the late 19th century to the early 20th century as parts of dinner or tea services. These sets can be excellent value for money today as they are largely considered unfashionable, and have been replaced by mass-produced modern examples from chain stores.
- Many examples have hand-painted details, such as flowers and gilt highlighting, a fact that surprises many bearing in mind the skill and time required to decorate them. Prices range from as little as a few pounds to more than £200 for the finest examples from specialist dealers, although large or part sets can often be bought at auction for as little as £50.
- Consider the maker, pattern, and quality and method of execution. Prestigious, well-known makers such as Coalport, Royal Doulton and Minton will often fetch higher prices. Well-painted, finely detailed patterns will also be more valuable, and will usually fetch more than similar transfer-printed patterns of the period. Look closely for brush strokes, rich colours and designs, and appealing shaped forms.
- Many of the more highly decorated examples, particularly those that are also decorated on the inside of the cup, were intended primarily for display and are often known as 'cabinet cups'. Always examine all pieces closely, ensuring that the saucer matches the cup, and that the pattern and the gilding are not worn or scratched.

A William Alsager Adderley cup and saucer, pattern no.5165, with dark blue flowers and gilt highlights on a light blue ground.

*c1910-20*

**£30-50** **MH**

A John Aynsley cup and saucer, with hand-painted and transfer-printed garland pattern, pink panels and gilt rim.

*c1900*

**£30-50** **MH**

A John Aynsley cup and saucer, decorated with pink roses and garlands of leaves on a white ground with pink panels, and gilt highlights.

*c1900*

**£50-80** **MH**

A Belleek 'Tridacna' coffee cup and saucer, the base printed with the sixth green mark.

*Tridacna refers to the moulded, almost basket-weave pattern that is popular with collectors. The sixth mark was used from 1965-80.*

*1965-80*

*Saucer 4.5in (11.5cm) diam*

**£50-70** **OACC**

A Brown-Westhead & Moore cup and saucer, with painted flowers in panels on a grey/beige ground with gilt highlights, the cup interior also with gilt highlights.

**£60-80** **MH**

A Coalport porcelain cup and saucer, painted with flowers in panels on a strong green background, with gilt highlights.

*c1830*

**£60-90** **MH**

A Susie Cooper 'Graduated Black Bands' cup and saucer.

*The severity of the Art Deco black lines is reduced by the bright green interior. The use of such contrasting colours is another typical Art Deco feature. This pattern, numbered E/501, can be found with different bright colours.*

*c1933* *Cup 2in (5.5cm) high*

**£50-70** **SCG**

## A CLOSER LOOK AT A SUSIE COOPER CUP & SAUCER

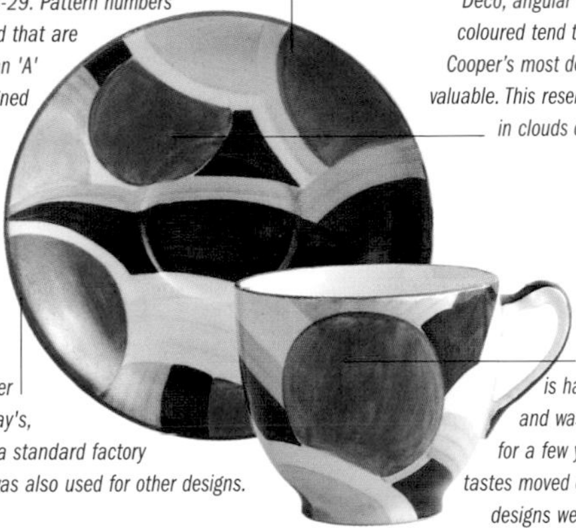

*Susie Cooper produced designs at A.E. Gray & Co. Ltd from 1923-29. Pattern numbers from the period that are prefixed with an 'A' were not designed by Cooper.*

*Designs that are strongly Art Deco, angular and brightly coloured tend to be among Cooper's most desirable and valuable. This resembles a sun in clouds or over hills.*

*Like most of her designs for Gray's, this is use on a standard factory shape,which was also used for other designs.*

*The pattern is hand-painted, and was only made for a few years before tastes moved on, and new designs were released.*

A Gray's Pottery cup and saucer, designed by Susie Cooper, with hand-painted geometric pattern.

*1928* *Saucer 5.5in (14cm) diam*

**£200-250** **SCG**

A Crown Derby blue and white porcelain cup and saucer, with blue transfer-printed Oriental pattern, gilt rim and details.

*This sort of decoration is unusual for this period, when modern forms and patterns by those such as Midwinter had begun to emerge. However, it does show that even into the 1950s, public tastes were still quite conservative and traditional, with long-established names such as Crown Derby still appealing to that market.*

*c1950*

**£30-50** **MH**

A Crown Staffordshire cup, saucer and plate, with sprigs of hand coloured flowers on a white ground, and cobalt blue panels highlighted with gilt hatched and scrolling designs.

*Sets such as these are known as 'Trio' sets, and are often used for afternoon tea.*

*c1906*

**£60-80** **MH**

A Davenport cup and saucer, pattern no. 356, with hand-painted gilt leaf, trellis and stylized cloud designs on a burgundy ground, the saucer with central gilt stylized flower.

*The patterns, particularly the cloud design, are based on historic Oriental examples.*

*c1860*

**£80-120** **MH**

A C.J. Mason cup and saucer, decorated with panels containing hand-coloured and transfer-printed Oriental scenes, and blue panels with stylized leaf gilt highlights.

*c1835-45*

**£70-100** **MH**

A Minton cup and saucer, decorated with hand-painted flowers including roses and pansies on a white ground, and with scalloped edge gilt rim.

*c1910*

**£60-80** **MH**

A Minton cup and saucer, pattern no. G599, decorated with a hand-coloured and transfer-printed pattern of wild flowers, and with painted butterfly shaped handle.

*c1860*

**£120-180** **MH**

A Minton cup and saucer, with hand-coloured band of roses in lozenges, surround with cerulean blue bands and with gilt highlights.

*c1863*

**£30-50** **MH**

A 1930s Wedgwood matte green tea cup and saucer, designed by Keith Murray.

*This is typical of architect Murray's designs for Wedgwood in terms of the muted colour, the lack of any surface pattern and the simple moulded designs.*

*Saucer 5in (12.5cm) diam*

**£40-60** **SCG**

An 'Old Paris' cup and saucer, decorated with panels of hand-painted bouquets within gilt scrolling frames, the cup with gilding to inside rim.

*'Old Paris' (or Vieux Paris), is the name given to porcelain made in and around Paris from the 1770s-1880s. The development of the factories is tied closely with that of Sevrès. Many examples were brought to the US by French immigrants and importers, many of whom were based in and around New Orleans. Most are unmarked, and styles vary from Neo-Classical to Rococo Revival. The use of gilt and hand-painted motifs is also typical. Most examples found today date from the mid-late 19thC, with 18thC examples usually being more valuable.*

*c1870* *Saucer 6in (15cm) diam*

**£40-50** **BH**

A Noritake 'Progression' cup and saucer, with transfer-printed pattern, the base with printed marks.

*Saucer 5.5in (14cm)*

**£10-15** **CHS**

An 'Old Paris' cup and saucer, decorated with panels of hand-painted bouquets within gilt scrolling frames, the cup with unusual feet.

*Cup 4in (10cm) high*

**£40-50** **BH**

An 'Old Paris' cup and saucer, decorated with pink and white panels of hand-painted bouquets within gilt scrolling frames, the cup with unusual feet.

*Cup 3in (7.5cm) high*

**£40-50** **BH**

A John Rose Coalport cup and saucer, decorated with panels of hand-painted birds and floral sprays, within gilt frames on a cobalt blue ground decorated with gilt stylized floral and scrolling motifs.

*John Rose was the founder of Coalport, in 1796. The gilded cobalt blue ground around colourful flowers is typical of Coalport's style.*

*c1815*

**£150-250** **MH**

A 1940s Osbourne cup and saucer, decorated with a transfer-printed pattern of pansies and vines.

*The all-over pattern is similar to Chintzware of the 1930s and would appeal to Chintz collectors. The conical shape of the cup very similar to some of Shelley's more desirable forms and is typical of their Art Deco shapes.*

**£30-50** **MH**

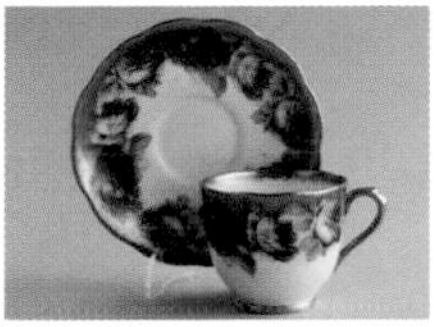

A Royal Albert cup and saucer, pattern no.1341, decorated with a band of large hand-painted roses and heavy gilt rim.

**£25-35** **MH**

A Shelley 'Marguerite' chintz cup and saucer.

*Chintzware was inspired by Indian textiles from the 19thC and peaked in popularity during the 1920s-30s and 1950s. Patterns are transfer-printed, and cover the surface. Royal Winton was a major producer, but Shelley also produced a number of designs.*

*1945* *2.5in (6.5cm) high*

**£60-80** **RH**

A Shelley cup and saucer, decorated with hand-coloured roses and pansies on a white ground, with a scalloped, light blue edged rim.

**£35-45** **MH**

A Spode cup and saucer, decorated with hand-painted floral sprays on a white ground within scrolling gilt borders on a blue ground, with scalloped edge, the cup with fancy handle.

*c1827-30*

**£100-150** **MH**

A Spode porcelain cup and saucer, decorated with hand coloured flowers within alternating panels of cobalt blue and white grounds, heavily highlighted with gilt stylized leaf patterns and outlines.

*The pattern echoes the popular Japanese Imari palette and designs.*

*c1815*

**£180-220** **MH**

An early 19thC Neo-Classical style cabinet cup and saucer, decorated with a stylized floral design on a brown ground, with gilt highlights and winged handle.

**£220-280** **BRI**

## COLLECTORS' NOTES

- Denby was founded as The Bourne Pottery by William Bourne in 1806, in Denby, Derbyshire. Production initially focused on utilitarian salt-glazed stoneware, including bottles. Kitchenware became more important from the end of the 19thC, with decorative items only representing a small percentage of production.
- During the early 20thC, the production of decorative wares expanded with the introduction of new glazes and the employment of designers. New 'art pottery' ranges included 'Danesby Ware' of the 1920s, and 'Electric Blue' and 'Orient Ware' of the 1930s.
- Along with Donald Gilbert, one of the most important designers was Albert Colledge (1891-1972), whose son Glyn Colledge (1922-2000) came to dominate postwar Denby design. One of his first ranges was 'Glyn Ware', introduced from 1948-50, which set the standard for his hand-painted, natural designs.
- 'Freestone' and 'Burlington' were also successful, with both Glyn and Albert often working together on designs. 'Glynbourne', in production from 1960, was one of Glyn's most successful and long-lived ranges. As each form was handmade and each pattern was hand-painted, each piece is effectively unique.
- Kenneth Clark (b.1922) is a similarly influential name. A Modernist industrial designer and an experienced potter, he was responsible for popular, yet austere, lines such as 'Classic' and the similar 'Cotswold' and 'Gourmet'. The latter designs used a resist tape to reveal the colour of the clay, against a subtle cream glaze and contrasting black line.
- 'Glyn Ware' and 'Glynbourne' are amongst the most popular and collected ranges today. Look for pieces signed by Glyn Colledge, particularly where the signature is inscribed, rather than stamped. Well-painted, large examples tend to be the most valuable, as do decorative items rather than functional kitchenwares.

An early 1950s Denby 'Glyn Ware' jug, designed by Glyn Colledge, with hand-painted stylized leaf pattern, with signature mark to base.

*5in (12.5cm) high*

**£10-15** **GAZE**

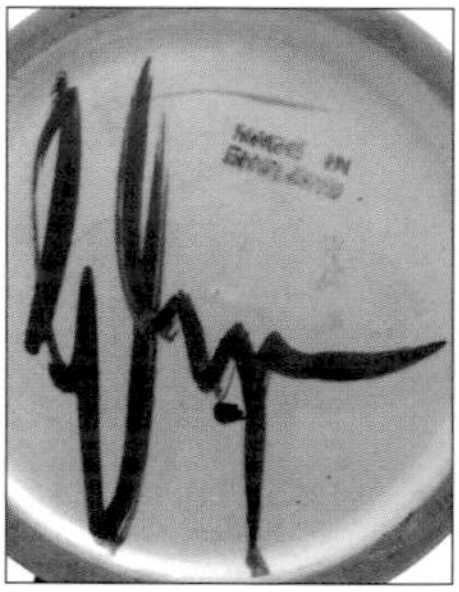

An early 1950s Denby 'Glyn Ware' hand-painted Hunting Beaker, designed by Glyn Colledge, with signature painted to base.

*This style of signature was used for a decade from c1948. Signatures were applied during the immediate postwar period to identify pieces as studio pottery, thus avoiding a punitive purchase tax.*

*5.5in (14cm) high*

**£12-18** **GAZE**

A mid-1950s Denby 'New Glyn Ware' flared oval section vase, designed by Glyn Colledge, with hand-painted pattern.

*6in (15cm) high*

**£80-120** **GC**

A mid-1950s Denby Pottery 'Cretonne' range vase, designed by Glyn Colledge, with hand-painted floral pattern.

*9in (22.75cm) high*

**£100-150** **GGRT**

A Denby 'Cretonne' vase, designed by Glyn Colledge, with hand-painted stylised floral and foliate pattern.

*This pattern, introduced in the mid-1950s, can be found in different colour combinations including blue and pink. The bright colours and stylization are typically 1950s.*

*8in (20.5cm) high*

**£150-200** **GC**

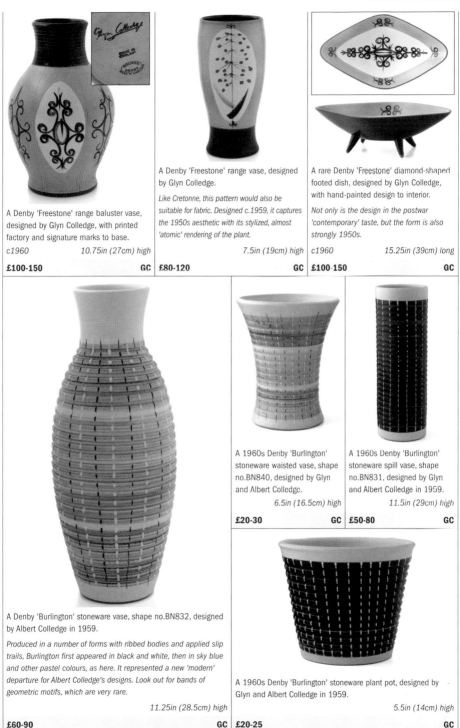

A Denby 'Freestone' range baluster vase, designed by Glyn Colledge, with printed factory and signature marks to base.

*c1960* *10.75in (27cm) high*

**£100-150** **GC**

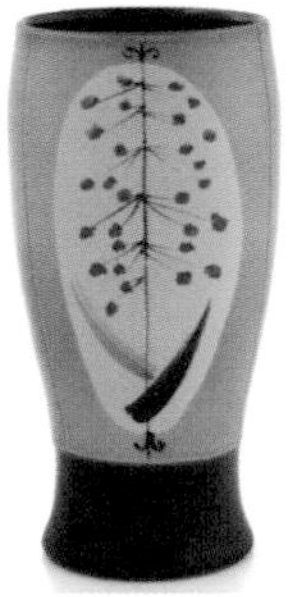

A Denby 'Freestone' range vase, designed by Glyn Colledge.

*Like Cretonne, this pattern would also be suitable for fabric. Designed c.1959, it captures the 1950s aesthetic with its stylized, almost 'atomic' rendering of the plant.*

*7.5in (19cm) high*

**£80-120** **GC**

A rare Denby 'Freestone' diamond-shaped footed dish, designed by Glyn Colledge, with hand-painted design to interior.

*Not only is the design in the postwar 'contemporary' taste, but the form is also strongly 1950s.*

*c1960* *15.25in (39cm) long*

**£100-150** **GC**

A Denby 'Burlington' stoneware vase, shape no.BN832, designed by Albert Colledge in 1959.

*Produced in a number of forms with ribbed bodies and applied slip trails, Burlington first appeared in black and white, then in sky blue and other pastel colours, as here. It represented a new 'modern' departure for Albert Colledge's designs. Look out for bands of geometric motifs, which are very rare.*

*11.25in (28.5cm) high*

**£60-90** **GC**

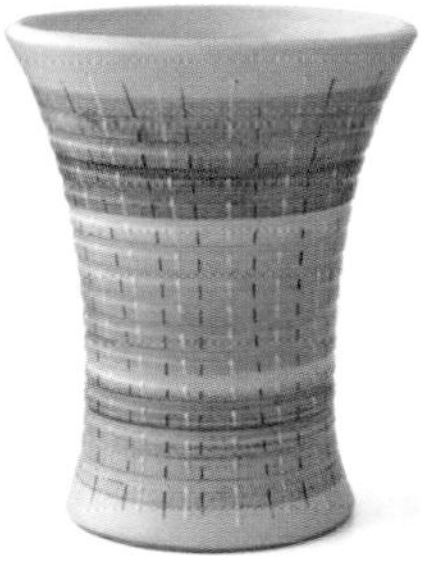

A 1960s Denby 'Burlington' stoneware waisted vase, shape no.BN840, designed by Glyn and Albert Colledge.

*6.5in (16.5cm) high*

**£20-30** **GC**

A 1960s Denby 'Burlington' stoneware spill vase, shape no.BN831, designed by Glyn and Albert Colledge in 1959.

*11.5in (29cm) high*

**£50-80** **GC**

A 1960s Denby 'Burlington' stoneware plant pot, designed by Glyn and Albert Colledge in 1959.

*5.5in (14cm) high*

**£20-25** **GC**

A 1970s Denby 'Glynbourne' vase, shape no.GB869, designed by Glyn Colledge, with hand-painted stylized folate and floral pattern.

*6.5in (17cm) high*

**£60-80** **GC**

A 1970s Denby 'Glynbourne' baluster vase, shape no.865, designed by Glyn Colledge, with hand-painted leaf pattern, the base with rectangular "Denby Made in England" ink stamp.

*8.75in (22cm) high*

**£70-100** **GC**

A 1960s Denby 'Glynbourne' large vase, designed by Glyn Colledge, with stylized leaf pattern, the base with printed oval and signature marks.

*12in (30.5cm) high*

**£100-150** **GC**

A 1960s Denby 'Glynbourne' vase, shape no. GB870, designed by Glyn Colledge, with hand-painted stylized foliate decoration.

*8in (20cm) high*

**£60-80** **GC**

A 1960s Denby 'Glynbourne' jug vase, designed by Glyn Colledge, with hand-painted stylized leaf pattern, with printed signature and oval factory marks.

*These brown and very dark grey/black tones are comparatively unusual in this range.*

*12in (30.5cm) high*

**£150-200** **GC**

A 1970s Denby 'Glynbourne' jug vase, shape no.GB861, designed by Glyn Colledge, with hand-painted leaf pattern, and rectangular "Denby Made in England" ink stamp.

*13.25in (33.5cm) high*

**£80-120** **GC**

A 1960s Denby 'Glynbourne' jug, shape no.GB871, designed by Glyn Colledge, with hand-painted stylized leaf pattern.

*9in (23cm) high*

**£70-100** **GC**

A Denby 'Flamstead' baluster vase, shape no.353, designed by Glyn Colledge.

*9.25in (23.5cm) high*

**£80-120** **GC**

A Denby 'Flamstead' jug vase, shape no.FS356, designed by Glyn Colledge.

*12.5in (32cm) high*

**£100-150** **GC**

A Denby 'Flamstead' globular jug vase, shape no.FS354, designed by Glyn Colledge.

*Note the extravagant line of the strap-like handle.*

*6.5in (16.5cm) high*

**£40-60** **GC**

A Denby 'Flamstead' small tray or ashtray, shape no.FS360, designed by Glyn Colledge.

*5.75in (14.5cm) diam*

**£15-20** **GC**

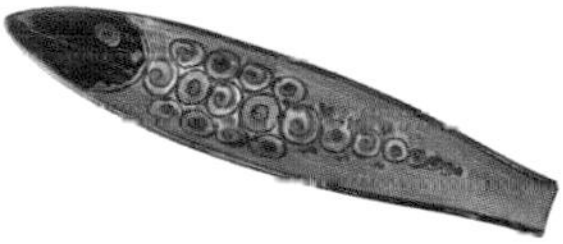

A Denby 'Flamstead' stoneware fish-shaped tray, shape no.FS36, designed by Glyn Colledge.

*Flamstead was named after John Flamstead, the first Astronomer Royal, and first released in late 1966. It features three rows of sgrafitto circles with glossy glazed interiors, and tube-lined white outlines.*

*15.75in (40cm) long*

**£70-100** **GC**

A 1980s Denby 'Savannah' range squat globe vase, designed by Glyn Colledge, with hand-painted swirled pattern, the base impressed "93".

*9.5in (24cm) diam*

**£60-80** **GC**

A 1980s Denby 'Savannah' range baluster vase, designed by Glyn Colledge, with hand-painted swirled pattern and fluted bands.

*13.75in (35cm) high*

**£80-120** **GC**

A 1980s Denby 'Savannah' range waisted vase, designed by Glyn Colledge, with hand-painted swirled pattern and fluted rings.

*9.5in (24cm) high*

**£60-80** **GC**

A 1980s Denby 'Savannah' range charger, designed by Glyn Colledge, with handpainted swirled pattern and fluted rings.

*Savannah was introduced in 1978, and was the last of Colledge's decorative 'art pottery' ranges.*

*12.5in (32cm) diam*

**£60-80** **GC**

A 1950s Denby 'Cotswold' range medium stoneware Windrush vase, shape no.C.D.811., designed by Kenneth Clark.

*6.25in (16cm) high*

**£40-60** **GC**

A 1950s-60s Denby 'Cotswold' range large Windrush vase, shape no. C.D.811, designed by Kenneth Clark.

*8.5in (21.5cm) high*

**£70-100** **GC**

A 1950s Denby 'Cotswold' range Broadway plant pot, shape no.C.D.814, designed by Kenneth Clark.

*5.75in (14.5cm) high*

**£30-40** **GC**

A 1950s Denby 'Cotswold' range Broadway plant pot, shape no.C.D.814, designed by Kenneth Clark.

*4.75in (12cm) high*

**£20-30** **GC**

A 1950s Denby 'Cotswold' range stoneware Chedworth bowl, shape no.C.D.816., designed by Kenneth Clark.

*4.5in (11.5cm) high*

**£30-40** **GC**

A 1950s Denby 'Cotswold' stoneware Stowe vase, shape no.C.D.813., designed by Kenneth Clark.

*10in (25.5cm) high*

**£70-100** **GC**

A 1950s Denby 'Cotswold' range stoneware Birdlip jug, shape no.C.D.812., designed by Kenneth Clark.

*6in (15.5cm) high*

**£30-40** **GC**

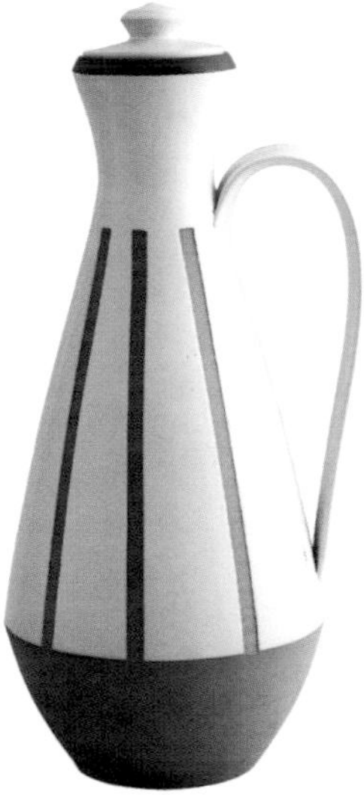

A late 1950s-early 1960s Denby 'Gourmet' pattern jug with stopper, designed by Kenneth Clark.

*Cookware and tableware in this design is known as 'Gourmet', and was introduced in 1957, before the Cotswold range of decorative wares.*

*12.5in (31.75cm) high*

**£150-200** **GGRT**

A 1960s Denby 'Classic' range vase, designed by Kenneth Clark.

*The austere 'Classic Ware' range was designed after 1957 and released in 1960.*

*8.75in (22cm) high*

**£70-100** **GC**

A Denby 'Classic' range vase, designed by Kenneth Clark.

*8in (20.25cm) high*

**£100-150** **GGRT**

A 1960s Denby 'Classic' range large plant pot, designed by Kenneth Clark.

*7.75in (19.5cm) high*

**£70-100** **GC**

A 1960s Denby 'Classic' range medium flower pot, designed by Kenneth Clark.

*5.75in (14.5cm) high*

**£30-50** **GC**

A 1960s Denby 'Classic' range bowl, designed by Kenneth Clark.

*8.25in (21cm) diam*

**£50-80** **GC**

A 1970s Denby 'Minaret' vase, shape no.801, designed by David Yorath, with hand-painted banded decoration, the base with decorator's mark "ACP".

*Minaret was designed by David Yorath and was inspired by Middle Eastern and Persian patterns. The Hopwoods state that the monogram on the base stands for the paintress Audrey Cole-Parker, who was responsible for much of the handpainting. The simple, cylindrical forms display the patterns well.*

*7in (17.5cm) high*

**£40-60** **GC**

A 1970s Denby 'Minaret' vase, shape no.804, designed by David Yorath, with hand-painted banded decoration, the base with decorator's mark "R.W".

*Blue is a less commonly seen colour variation.*

*11.25in (28.5cm) high*

**£70-100** **GC**

A Denby 'Potters Wheel' lidded pot, designed by David Yorath in 1973.

*The central ring can be found in yellow, green, blue or a 'rust' red.*

**£7-10** **MTS**

**FIND OUT MORE...**

**Denby Pottery 1809-1997**, *by Irene & Gordon Hopwood, published by Richard Dennis, 1997.*

## COLLECTORS' NOTES

- Royal Doulton first made decorative figurines under George Tinworth from the mid-1880s, at the Lambeth studio. Modeller Charles Noke joined Doulton from the Worcester factory in 1899 and soon produced a range of vellum figures. Noke felt that a range of figurines would be popular with the public, as Staffordshire figures had been in the 19thC. Noke commissioned a range of designs from well-known sculptors that could be reproduced on a small scale, in 1909. By 1912 a small collection had formed and the first figurine, 'Darling', by Charles Vyse was released. It was given the model number HN1, the HN standing for Harry Nixon who was in charge of the painting department. The HN numbering system is still in use today.
- Today there are over 4,000 figurines, although not all are unique as different colourways were often given their own number. Given the huge range available to a collector, many choose to concentrate on one area. A number of talented artists have produced designs for Doulton over the years and many base their collections around one designer. Popular names include Leslie Harradine, famous for his 'Fair Ladies', as is Margaret 'Peggy' Davies, and of course Charles Noke himself.
- Others prefer to collect by subject matter, such as the Fair Ladies range, studies of children or characters from history, the world of entertainment or literature.
- Value tends to be dictated by condition,desirability and availability. Some figurines have been in production for over 50 years and are easy to come by, in these cases, examples in less than perfect condition can be worth less than half. Look for rare colourways or variations. A specialist guide will help to identify them as well as keeping you up to date with current collecting trends.

A Royal Doulton 'Pantalettes' figurine, HN1362, designed by Leslie Harradine, style two.

*1929-38* *7.75in (19.5cm) high*

**£120-180** **L&T**

A Royal Doulton 'Hillary' figurine, HN2335, designed by Margaret Davies.

*1967-81 7.25in (18.5cm) high*

**£35-45** **L&T**

A Royal Doulton 'Melanie' figurine, HN2271, designed by Margaret Davies.

*1965-81 7.75in (19.5cm) high*

**£45-55** **L&T**

A Royal Doulton 'Autumn Breezes' figurine, HN1913, designed by Leslie Harradine, style one.

*Autumn Breezes is another commonly found figure which was in production between 1939 and 1998. This is one of the least valuable colourways.*

*1939-71* *7.5in (19cm) high*

**£50-70** **L&T**

A Royal Doulton 'Premiere' figurine, HN2343, designed by Margaret Davies.

*This figurine was in production between 1969 and 1979. At some point the design was changed so the the figure's right hand was no longer holding the cloak, but was instead resting on it. This is the first version, although both are worth the same amount.*

*Intro. 1969* *7.75in (19.5cm) high*

**£80-120** **PSA**

A Royal Doulton 'Simone' figurine, HN2378, designed by Margaret Davies.

*1971-81* *7.5in (19cm) high*

**£40-50** **L&T**

A Royal Doulton 'Veneta' figurine, HN2722, designed by William Harper.

*1974-81* *8in (20cm) high*

**£30-40** **L&T**

A Royal Doulton 'Loretta' figurine, HN2337, designed by Margaret Davies.

*1961-81* *7.75in (19.5cm) high*

**£28-32** **L&T**

A Royal Doulton 'Top o' the Hill' figurine, HN1834, designed by Leslie Harradine, style one.

*This is the most common colourway for this popular figure.*

*Intro. 1937* *7in (18cm) high*

**£40-60** **L&T**

A Royal Doulton 'Sweet Anne' figurine, HN1496, designed by Leslie Harradine, style one.

*1932-67* *7in (18cm) high*

**£70-90** **L&T**

A Royal Doulton 'Judith' figurine, HN2089, designed by Leslie Harradine.

*1952-59* *7in (18cm) high*

**£80-120** **L&T**

A Royal Doulton 'Honey' figurine, HN1909, designed by Leslie Harradine.

*The red and blue, and red versions are at least twice as valuable as this colourway.*

*1939-49* *7in (18cm) high*

**£120-180** **PSA**

A miniature Royal Doulton 'Paisley Shawl' figurine, M4, designed by Leslie Harradine.

*1932-45* *4in (10cm) high*

**£80-120** **JN**

A Royal Doulton 'Noelle' figurine, HN2179, by Margaret Davies.

*1957-67* *7in (17.5cm)*

**£150-200** **DN**

A Royal Doulton 'The Ermine Coat' figurine, HN1981, designed by Leslie Harradine.

*1945-67* *7in (18cm) high*

**£100-150** **PSA**

A Royal Doulton figure 'Mantilla' figurine, HN2712, designed by Eric Griffiths, from the Haute Ensemble series.

*The similar HN3192 was released to commemorate Expo 92 in a limited edition of 1,992, and is worth the same amount.*

*1974-79* *11.75in (29cm)*

**£120-180** **L&T**

A Royal Doulton 'Columbine' figurine, HN2738, designed by D. Tootle.

*This is the pair to the 'Harlequin' figurine on p88.*

*Intro. 1982* *12.5in (31.5cm) high*

**£750-850** **PSA**

## A CLOSER LOOK AT A ROYAL DOULTON LAMP BASE

*Despite being customised into a table lamp base, this example is very sought-after. It would be worth more in original condition.*

*Another colourway was produced under HN1473 for the same period and has the same value.*

*This figurine was only made for six years, before the outbreak of WWII.*

*Unlike most 'Fair Lady' figurines, this figure is seated rather than standing.*

A Royal Doulton 'Dreamland' figurine, HN1481, designed by Leslie Harradine, mounted on a wooden base incorporating lamp fitments.

*1931-37* *6.25in (16cm) long*

**£1,800-2,200** **DN**

A Royal Doulton 'Marietta' figurine, HN1446, designed by Leslie Harradine, damaged base.

*1931-40* *8.25in (21cm) high*

**£350-450** **WW**

A Royal Doulton 'Angela' figurine, HN1204, designed by Leslie Harradine, style one, extensively restored.

*This desirable figurine was also known as Fanny. A blue variation was released two years after this colourway and is slightly more valuable. Had this example not been restored it could have been worth much more.*

*1926-40* *7.25in (18.5cm)*

**£280-320** **GORL**

A Royal Doulton 'Lady From Williamsburg' figurine, HN2228, designed by Margaret Davies, from the Figures of Williamsburg series.

*1960-83* *6in (15cm) high*

**£70-100** **PSA**

A Royal Doulton 'Pensive Moments' figurine, HN2704, designed by Margaret Davies.

*1975-81* *5in (12.5cm) high*

**£35-45** **L&T**

A Royal Doulton 'Memories' figurine, HN2030, designed by Leslie Harradine.

*The three earlier versions, discontinued in 1949 can be worth between 30 and 50 per cent more.*

*1949-59* *6in (15cm) high*

**£80-120** **L&T**

A Royal Doulton 'Belle o' the Ball' figurine, HN1997, designed by Roy Asplin.

*1947-79* *8.5in (21.5cm)*

**£180-220** **PSA**

A Royal Doulton 'Lorna' figurine, HN2311, designed by Margaret Davies.

*1965-85* *8.5in (21.5cm) high*

**£50-80** **PSA**

A Royal Doulton 'Bethany' figurine, HN4326, designed by Valerie Annand, from the Chelsea series.

*2001-03* *8.5in (21.5cm) high*

**£50-80** **PSA**

## A CLOSER LOOK AT A ROYAL DOULTON FIGURINE

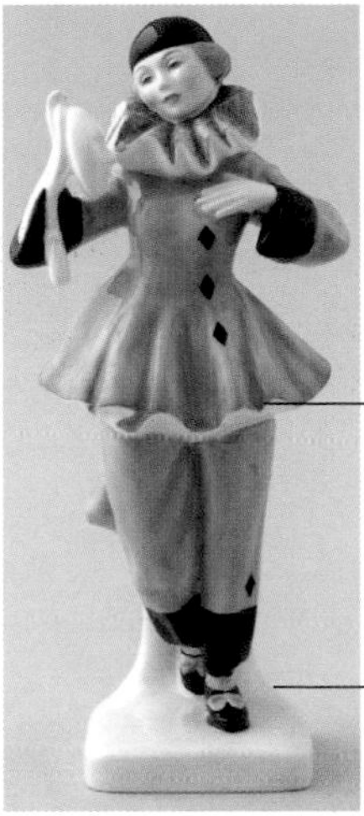

*This figurine is based on a model first released as HN656 in 1923.*

*Four other variations were produced, the last, HN1271, was discontinued in 1938.*

*This later reissue is worth about one tenth of the earlier example.*

*Despite being a modern figurine, the small edition number makes this sought-after.*

A limited edition Royal Doulton 'The Mask' figurine, HN4141, designed by Leslie Harradine, modelled by William Harper, commissioned by Lawleys By Post, from an edition of 1,500.

*1999* *10in (25.5cm) high*

**£150-200** **PSA**

A Royal Doulton 'A Winter's Walk' figurine, HN3052, designed by Adrian Hughes, from the Reflections series.

*1988-95* *12.25in (31cm)*

**£50-70** **L&T**

A Royal Doulton 'Strolling' figurine, HN3073, designed by Adrian Hughes, from the Reflections series.

*1987-95* *13.5in (34.5cm)*

**£50-70** **L&T**

A Royal Doulton 'Enigma' figurine, HN3110, designed by Robert Jefferson, from the Reflection series.

*1987-95* *12.75in (32cm)*

**£50-70** **L&T**

A rare Royal Doulton 'Spring' figure, HN1827, designed by Richard Garbe RA, restored.

*Richard Garbe was Professor of Sculpture at the Royal College of Art when he was invited by Charles Noke to design several pieces for Doulton. This figure, like a number of others by Garbe, was also produced in an all white limited edition which is most sought-after today. The ivory carving that this figure is based on can be seen at the Victoria & Albert Museum, London. This is a very desirable figure but the restoration has reduced the value of this example.*

*1937-49* *21in (53.3cm) high*

**£1,200-1,800** **PSA**

A Royal Doulton miniature 'Robin' figurine, M38, designed by Leslie Harradine.

*1933-1945* *2.5in (6.5cm)*

**£250-350** **PSA**

A limited edition Royal Doulton 'Faith' figurine, HN3082, designed by Eric Griffiths, from the NSPCC Charity series in an edition of 9,500 commissioned by Lawleys By Post.

*1986* *8.5in (21.5cm)*

**£40-50** **L&T**

A limited edition Royal Doulton 'Hope' figurine, HN3061, designed by Stan Mitchell, from the NSPCC Charity series in an edition of 9,500 commissioned by Lawleys By Post.

*This is the most desirable of the three NSPCC Charity figures produced and also the earliest.*

*1984* *8.25in (21cm)*

**£65-75** **L&T**

## A CLOSER LOOK AT A MINIATURE FIGURINE

*The 'M' series of miniature figures were introduced in 1932, although small scale Dickens figures had been produced previously.*

*Despite their reduced size, the level of detail is extremely high.*

*Most of the 'Fair Lady' miniatures were scaled down versions of full-size Leslie Harradine figurines.*

*Rising production costs meant that the Fair Ladies 'M' range was discontinued in 1949, making them hard to find today.*

A rare Royal Doulton 'Erminie' miniature figurine, M40, designed by Leslie Harradine.

*1933-1945* *4in (10cm) high*

**£450-550** **PSA**

A limited edition Royal Doulton 'Hope' figurine, HN3087, designed by Eric Griffiths, from the NSPCC Charity series in an edition of 9,500 commissioned by Lawleys By Post.

*'Grown-up' versions of these characters were produced in 1999 for a breast cancer charity series.*

*1987* *8.5in (21.5cm) high*

**£55-65** **L&T**

A Royal Doulton 'Georgina' figurine, HN2377, designed by Margaret Davies, style one, from the Kate Greenaway series.

*1981-86* *7.25in (18.5cm) high*

**£60-80** **L&T**

A Royal Doulton 'Francine' figurine, HN2422 designed by John Bromley.

*This figure was in production from 1972 until 1981. At some point the design was changed so the the bird's tail was moulded into the girl's hand rather than sticking out as in this version. Both versions are worth the same amount.*

*Intro. 1972* *5in (12.5cm) high*

**£40-50** **L&T**

A Royal Doulton 'Miss Muffet' figurine, HN1936, designed by Leslie Harradine.

*The green version, discontinued 15 years before this colourway, is worth nearly twice as much.*

*1940-67* *5.5in (14cm) high*

**£70-100** **PSA**

A Royal Doulton 'Tom' figurine, HN2864, designed by Margaret Davies, from the Kate Greenaway series.

*This is one of the more sought-after Kate Greenaway figures, together with the only other boy figure in the series, James.*

*1978-81* *5.75in (14.5cm) high*

**£80-120** **L&T**

A Royal Doulton 'Sleepy Darling' figurine, HN2953, designed by Pauline Parsons, from the RDICC series.

*1981* *7.25in (18.5cm) high*

**£40-50** **L&T**

A Royal Doulton 'Little Boy Blue' figurine, HN2062, designed by Leslie Harradine, from the Nursery Rhymes series one.

*1950-73* *5.5in (14cm) high*

**£45-55** **L&T**

A Royal Doulton 'Off To School' figurine, HN3768, designed by Nada Pedley.

*1996-98* *5.5in (14cm) high*

**£100-150** **PSA**

A Royal Doulton 'River Boy' figurine, HN2128, designed by Margaret Davies.

*1962-75* *4in (10cm) high*

**£45-55** **L&T**

A Royal Doulton 'Baby Bunting' figurine, HN2108, designed by Margaret Davies.

*1953-59* *5.25in (13.5cm) high*

**£80-120** **L&T**

A Royal Doulton 'Sleepyhead' figurine, HN2114, designed by Margaret Davies.

*This scarce figure was only made for a short period of time.*

*1953-55* *5in (12.5cm) high*

**£700-900** **L&T**

A Royal Doulton 'Willy-Won't-He' figurine, HN1561, designed by Leslie Harradine.

*This is the most desirable version of this figurine.*

*1933-49* *5.75in (14cm) high*

**£220-280** **L&T**

A Royal Doulton 'Hold Tight' figurine, HN3298, designed by Adrian Hughes.

*1990-93* *8.5in (21.5cm)*

**£120-180** **L&T**

A Royal Doulton 'Captain MacHeath' figurine, HN464, designed by Leslie Harradine, from the Beggar's Opera series, minor restoration.

*1921-49 7in (18cm) high*

**£220-280 PSA**

A miniature Royal Doulton 'Falstaff' figurine, HN3236, designed by Charles Noke and remodelled by R. Tabbenor, style three.

*Falstaff was first released as a full size figure in 1923 and appears in three different styles. Perhaps unsurprisingly, this smaller, later example is the least desirable.*

*1989-90 in (10cm) high*

**£35-45 PSA**

A Royal Doulton 'Harlequin' figurine, HN2737, designed by Douglas Tootle, style two.

*This figure is a pair with the 'Columbine' figurine seen on page 84.*

*Intro. 1982 13in (33cm) high*

**£800-1,000 PSA**

A Royal Doulton 'Mr Pickwick' earthenware figurine, HN2099, designed by Leslie Harradine, style three from the third Dickens series, restored legs.

*1952-67 7.5in (19cm) high*

**£80-120 WW**

A Royal Doulton 'Little Lord Fauntleroy' figurine, HN2972, designed by Adrian Hughes, from the Characters from Children's Literature series, second.

*Seconds have a score mark or hole through the Doulton mark.*

*1982-85 6.25in (15.9cm) high*

**£45-55 PSA**

A Royal Doulton 'Barliman Butterbur' figurine, HN2923, designed by David Lyttleton, from the 'Middle Earth' series.

*This series was inspired by J.R.R. Tolkien's 'The Lord Of The Rings' series. Values for these figures have escalated in recent years due to the huge success of the 'Rings' film trilogy by Peter Jackson.*

*1982-84 5.25in (13.3cm) high*

**£300-400 PSA**

A Royal Doulton 'Grossmith's Tsing Ihang Perfume of Thibet' earthenware figurine, HN582, by an unknown designer.

*1923-Unknown 11.5in (29cm) high*

**£450-550 L&T**

A Royal Doulton Kate Greenaway 'Sophie' figurine, HN2833, designed by Margaret Davies, from the Kate Greenaway series, minor scratches to glaze.

*1977-87 6in (15cm) high*

**£50-70 PSA**

A Royal Doulton 'Alice' figurine, HN2158, designed by Margaret Davies.

*1960-81 5in (12.5cm) high*

**£30-40 L&T**

A Royal Doulton 'Christopher Columbus' figure, HN3392, by Alan Maslankowski, from an edition of 1,492, boxed with certificate.

*This edition celebrates the anniversary of Columbus' discovery of America.*

*1992* *12in (30.5cm) high*

**£350-450** **PSA**

A Royal Doulton 'Guy Fawkes' figurine, HN3271, designed by Charles Noke, from the Miniatures series.

*Doulton reintroduced miniature figures in 1988 with character figures, such as this one, introduced a year later. The characters proved unpopular and were soon withdrawn. Given their short production span, these small figures could become sought-after in the future.*

*1989-91* *4in (10cm) high*

**£60-80** **PSA**

A Royal Doulton 'Pied Piper' figurine, HN2102, style one, designed by Leslie Harradine.

*Look for the Pied Piper figure HN1215, produced between 1926 and 1938, as it is worth over five times more than this later version.*

*1953-76* *8.5in (21.5cm)*

**£150-200** **L&T**

A Royal Doulton 'The Captain' figurine, HN2260, designed by Mary Nicholl, from the Sea Characters series.

*1965-82* *9.5in (24cm) high*

**£150-200** **PSA**

A Royal Doulton 'Old King Cole' figurine, HN2217, designed by Margaret Davies.

*1963-67* *6.5in (16.5cm) high*

**£150-200** **L&T**

A Royal Doulton 'The Mermaid' figurine, HN97, designed by Harry Tittensor.

*1918-36* *7in (18cm) high*

**£200-300** **L&T**

A Royal Doulton 'Omar Khayyam' earthenware figurine, HN2247, designed by Mary Nicholl.

*1965-83* *6.25in (16cm)*

**£120-180** **CLV**

A Royal Doulton 'Bluebeard' figurine, HN2105, designed by Leslie Harradine, style two.

*The earlier version, HN1528, produced between 1932 and 1949, is twice as valuable.*

*1953-92* *11in (28cm) high*

**£150-200** **PSA**

A limited edition Royal Doulton 'Grace Darling' figure, HN3089, designed by E.J. Griffiths, commissioned by 'Lawleys By Post' and from an edition of 9,500.

*1987* *9in (23cm) high*

**£150-200** **PSA**

A Royal Doulton 'A Jester' figurine, HN1702, designed by Charles Noke.

*The Jester is a popular character for Royal Doulton figures and has been in production from 1915 in a number of variations. Most are sought-after, particularly the very early versions.*

*1935-49* *10in (25.5cm)*

**£350-450** **L&T**

## A CLOSER LOOK AT A PRESTIGE FIGURINE

*In the early 1950s Doulton introduced a limited Prestige range of large format figurines.*

*This, 'King Charles' and 'The Moor', all designed by Noke, were three of the first to be remodelled to a very high standard from existing figurines.*

*Despite their very long production runs, they are only issued in very small amounts each year.*

*The limited production, handsome subject matters and larger than average size makes the Prestige range highly sought-after.*

A Royal Doulton 'Jack Point' Prestige figurine, HN2080, designed by Charles Noke.

*The original figurine, HN404, was introduced in 1920 and can be worth nearly twice as much.*

*1952-Current* *16.25in (40.5cm) high*

**£1,000-1,500** **L&T**

A Royal Doulton 'King Charles' Prestige figurine, HN2084, designed by Charles Noke and Harry Tittensor.

*1952-92* *17in (43cm) high*

**£700-900** **PSA**

A Royal Doulton 'The Moor' Prestige figurine, HN2082, designed by Charles Noke.

*1952-Present* *17in (43cm)*

**£800-1,200** **PSA**

A Royal Doulton 'The Jovial Monk' figurine, HN2144, designed by Margaret Davies.

*1954-76* *7.75in (19.5cm)*

**£80-120** **L&T**

A Royal Doulton 'In The Stocks' figurine, HN2163, designed by Mary Nicholl, style two.

*1955-59* *5.75in (14.5cm)*

**£350-450** **PSA**

A Royal Doulton 'The Potter' figurine, HN1493, designed by Charles Noke.

*1932-92* *7in (18cm) high*

**£180-220** **PSA**

A Royal Doulton 'The Mendicant' earthenware figurine, HN1365, designed by Leslie Harradine, damage to one hand.

*1929-69* *8in (20cm) high*

**£50-80** **PSA**

A Royal Doulton 'The Cobbler' figurine, 'HN 1705', designed by Charles Noke, style three.

*The green and brown version, HN1706, was produced for a further 20 years after this colourway was discontinued. It is worth about 60 per cent of this example.*

*1935-49* *8.5in (21cm) high*

**£250-350** **L&T**

A rare Royal Doulton 'The Snake Charmer' figure, HN1317, by an unknown designer, hairline crack.

*1929-38* *4in (10cm) high*

**£800-1,000** **PSA**

A Royal Doulton 'The Carpet Seller' figurine, HN1464A, style one with closed hand, designed by Leslie Harradine.

*At some point the design of this figure was changed so that the figure's right hand was closed, as in this example. The material was also changed from earthenware to porcelain. The earlier version is worth nearly twice as much.*

*Unknown-1969* *9.5in (23.5cm)*

**£200-300** **L&T**

A Royal Doulton 'The Balloon Man' figurine, HN1954, designed by Leslie Harradine.

*1940-Present* *7.75in (19.5cm)*

**£80-120** **CHEF**

A Royal Doulton 'The Auctioneer' figurine, HN2988, designed by Robert Tabbenor.

*This figure was made exclusively for the Royal Doulton International Collectors Club.*

*1986* *8.5in (21.5cm) high*

**£150-200** **PSA**

A Royal Doulton 'Town Crier' earthenware figurine, HN2119, designed by Margaret Davies, style one.

*1953-76* *8in (20.5cm) high*

**£180-220** **DN**

A Royal Doulton 'The Jersey Milkmaid' figurine, HN2057, designed by Leslie Harradine, style one.

*Style two has a green, white and brown colourway and is known as 'The Milkmaid', HN2057A. It's worth slightly less than this version.*

*1950-59* *6.5in (16.5cm) high*

**£100-150** **L&T**

A Royal Doulton 'Country Lass' figurine, HN 1991A, designed by Leslie Harradine.

*This is the slightly less desirable colourway. HN 1991, known as 'Market Day' is earlier and more sought-after.*

*1975-81* *7.25in (18.5cm) high*

**£80-120** **L&T**

A Royal Doulton 'The Apple Maid' figurine, HN 2160, designed by Leslie Harradine.

*1957-62* *6.5in (16.5cm) high*

**£150-200** **L&T**

A rare Royal Doulton 'All A Blooming' figurine, by Leslie Harradine.

*This un-numbered figure is a colour variation of HN1466 produced between 1931 and 1938. This and the other colour variation HN1457 are both desirable.*

*c1931* *6.25in (16cm)*

**£1,000-1,500** **DN**

A Royal Doulton 'Old Balloon Seller' figurine, HN1315, designed by Leslie Harradine.

*This is a particularly common figure, in production for nearly 70 years. Older figures, or those with unusual backstamps can be worth slightly more.*

*1929-98* *7.5in (19cm) high*

**£50-60** **L&T**

A Royal Doulton 'Fortune Teller' earthenware figurine, HN2159, designed by Leslie Harradine.

*1955-67* *6.5in (16.5cm) high*

**£150-200** **L&T**

A Royal Doulton 'Schoolmarm' figurine, HN2223, designed by Margaret Davies.

*1958-81* *6.75in (17cm) high*

**£120-180** **L&T**

A Royal Doulton 'The Mask Seller' figurine, HN2103, designed by Leslie Harradine, boxed.

*1953-1995* *8.5in (21.5cm) high*

**£70-100** **D**

**FIND OUT MORE...**

**The Charlton Standard Catalogue of Royal Doulton Figurines,** *by Jean Dale, 11th edition, 2006*

A Royal Doulton 'Penguins' flambé figure, HN103, printed mark to base.

*1913-c1946* *6in (15cm) high*

**£180-220** **JN**

A Royal Doulton 'Rhinoceros (lying)' veined flambé large figure, no.615, designed by Leslie Harradine, with printed mark to base and initials "A.M.".

*During the 1890s, Charles Noke and John Slater had tried, without success, to imitate the desirable Chinese sang-de-boeuf glazes. The problem was solved by Bernard Moore and Cuthbert Bailey in around 1902-04, who then launched the glaze at the 1904 St Louis World's Fair. Today, the rich varied glaze is highly sought-after, particularly on animals.*

*c1973-96* *9.75in (25cm) high*

**£500-600** **JN**

A Royal Doulton 'Elephant With Trunk Down' flambé figure, HN181, designed by Charles Noke, with impressed date.

*1932* *4.25in (11cm) high*

**£220-280** **PSA**

A Royal Doulton 'Bulldog Standing' small figure, HN1044, designed by Frederick Daws.

*1931-68* *8.5cm (3.25in) high*

**£80-120** **PSA**

A Royal Doulton 'Bulldog (Old Bill)' figure, HN146, with moulded helmet and haversack.

*Look out for this model in the Titanian glaze, which is extremely rare and may fetch up to three times the value of this khaki version with a bronze helmet. The Titanian glaze was developed by Charles Noke and released in 1915 – it can be recognised from its varied smoky grey/steel blue colours.*

*1918-25* *6.5in ( 16.5cm) high*

**£350-450** **BRI**

A Royal Doulton figure of a night heron, painted in colours, impressed and incised marks for Harry Simeon and Florrie Jones.

*6in (15cm) high*

**£600-700** **L&T**

A Royal Doulton Lambeth stoneware ring tray, modelled as a large billed bird seated on a stump issuing from a blue water-like flanged base, impressed mark and numerals "11497" to base.

*4.25in (11cm) high*

**£250-350** **BONS**

A Royal Doulton Lambeth stoneware trinket dish, with a figurine of a koala clutching a short tree trunk, the base with impressed and incised marks.

*4.25in (11cm) high*

**£200-300** **L&T**

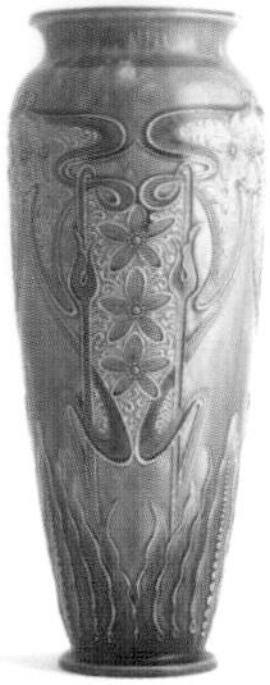

A tall Royal Doulton vase, decorated by Eliza Simmance, with blue flowers and stylized leaves on a green and cobalt flambé ground, the base with Lambeth stamp, artist's signature, and "BN ROO 454", and two grinding chips.

*17.25in (44cm) high*

**£750-850** **DRA**

A pair of Doulton Lambeth stoneware vases, decorated by Florence Barlow, using the pâte-sur-pâte technique with parrots and budgerigars on branches against a textured ground, the base with incised and impressed marks.

*13.75in (35cm) high*

**£1,200-1,800** **L&T**

A pair of Doulton Lambeth stoneware vases, decorated by Hannah Barlow, with an incised frieze of grazing goats, the bases with incised and impressed marks, the rims restored.

*12.25in (31cm) high*

**£700-900** **L&T**

A rare Doulton Lambeth stoneware group, by George Tinworth, modelled with frogs and mice leaping a fence upon an oval base, impressed monogram and factory marks.

*4.5in (11.5cm) high*

**£3,500-4,500** **GHOU**

## A CLOSER LOOK AT A PAIR OF DOULTON VASES

*An original pair of vases such as these is worth more.*

*The Art Nouveau style decoration is appealing and was executed by Florence Barlow, who is an important decorator well-known for her bird designs.*

*They are large and make a strong visual impression, and one that is typical of Doulton stonewares of the period.*

*Barlow has used the 'pâte-sur-pâte' technique, in use from 1878-c1906, to build up layers of coloured glazes to give prominence to certain areas, in this case the birds and their feathers.*

A pair of Doulton Lambeth stoneware vases, of shouldered baluster form, decorated with birds on branches and with panels of flowers, the base with incised and impressed marks.

*16.25in (41cm) high*

**£1,500-2,000** **L&T**

A Royal Doulton Flambé gourd-shaped vase, painted by Charles Noke, with Royal Doulton stamp "Noke" and "Flambe" and "FM".

*7.5in (19cm) high*

**£300-400** **DRA**

A Royal Doulton stoneware moon flask, designed by Harry Simeon, from the Toby Wares series, the front with a low relief Toby, the reverse showing his back, the rim with a silver collar with Birmingham hallmarks for 1936.

*This range was introduced in the 1920s and was popular.*

*c1936*

**£550-650** **JN**

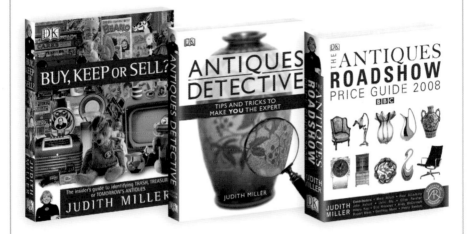

## COLLECTORS' NOTES

- Fairings take their name from the fact that most were given away as prizes at fairgrounds. They were also sold as inexpensive decorative objects, inspired by more costly figures by makers such as Meissen. They were popular with the British working classes from the mid-19th century until WWI, and were made primarily in Germany from a white soft paste porcelain. Sizes vary from 3in (7.5cm) high to around 5in (12.5cm) high.
- As they were mass-produced, the quality of the modelling varies, but it is generally comparatively simple. Fairings are often divided up into different themes, and collectors tend to focus on one. One of the most popular themes are the 'bed chamber' fairings that were often risqué for the period, with marital scenes, courtship, or other cheeky 'seaside' humour.
- Look out for marks on the base, as these can help with identifying a maker. Conta & Boehme was the largest and most prolific, and used a mark of a shield with an arm holding a dagger. It also numbered its pieces from the 1870s onwards. Numbers run from 2850 to 2899 and from 3300 to 3385. Not all pieces are marked.
- Earlier examples tend to be of higher quality, with finer modelling and painting. Colours tend to be eye-catching and bright, particularly on those produced from c1890 onwards. The more salacious and amusing the subject, the more attention it is likely to attract. Animal subjects are also sought-after due to their wide appeal. Some fairings are rarer than others, so it is best to buy a reference book to learn how to spot them.
- Beware of fakes and reproductions, which have become more commonplace as prices for authentic examples have risen. Reproductions often have two small holes on the base, and if a number is used, it begins with an 18. Colours tend to be very bright and poorly applied, with badly applied gilt highlights. Always examine fairings for signs of damage or restoration.

A 'Two different views' group figure fairing.

*4.74in (12cm) high*

**£280-320** **LC**

A Conta & Boehme 'Checkmate', an illicit kiss' fairing.

*c1870* *4in (10cm) high*

**£80-120** **LC**

An 'If you please, Sir' fairing.

*The glass on the table has been restored.*

**£180-220** **SAS**

A 'Cancan' dancing subject fairing.

*This is a scarce and desirable fairing with a good sense of movement and a fun theme.*

*c1870* *3.75in (9.5cm) high*

**£550-650** **SAS**

A 'Welsh Tea Party' group figure fairing.

*4.75in (12cm) high*

**£30-40** **LC**

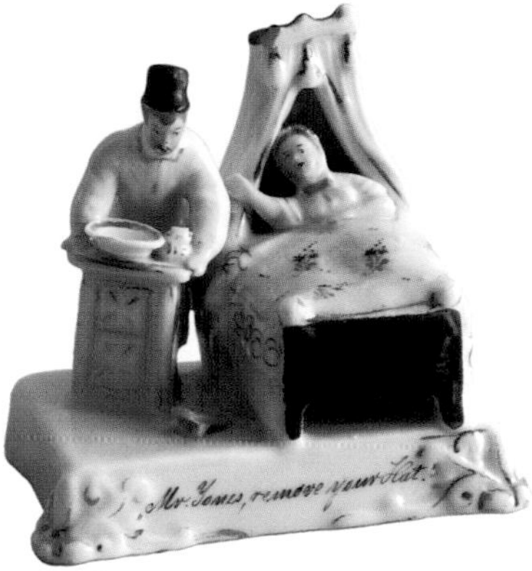


A 'Mr Jones, remove your hat' bedchamber subject fairing.

*The use of black script lettering shows this is an early example.*

*3.5in (9cm) high*

**£80-120** **LC**

A 'Shall we sleep first, or.....?' bedchamber subject fairing.

*3.25in (8cm) high*

**£25-35** **LC**

A Conta & Boehme 'Three o'clock in the morning' bedchamber subject fairing.

*2.75in (7.25cm) high*

**£50-70** **LC**

A 'Married for money' bedchamber subject fairing.

**£60-80** **LC**

A Conta & Boehme 'Returning at one o'clock in the morning' bedchamber subject fairing.

*This is not a mother beating a child but is instead a wife beating her husband for getting back late.*

*c1880*

**£40-60** **LC**

A Conta & Boehme 'The last in bed to put out the light' bedchamber subject fairing.

*This is one of the most popular fairings produced by Conta & Boehme.*

*3.25in (8cm) high*

**£50-70** **LC**

A 'Twelve months after marriage' bedchamber subject fairing.

*Rather than having a salacious subject, this highlights the responsibilities of having a child. This example is in very good condition with bright colours.*

*4in (10cm) high*

**£100-150** **LC**

A 'Taking a beating' bedchamber subject fairing, untitled.

*3.5in (9cm) high*

**£40-60** **LC**

An 'Alone at last' bedchamber subject fairing.

*On authentic examples, the couple face the viewer when seen from the front. On many fakes, they have their backs to the viewer.*

*c1890* *3.75in (9.5cm) high*

**£80-120** **LC**

A 'Kiss me quick' butler and maid fairing.

*The colours on fairings can vary widely, examples are known where the butler is wearing a green coat, and the ochre painted screen here is highlighted with gilt lines.*

*3.5in (9cm) high*

**£60-80** **SAS**

A 'Wedding night, undressing by the fire' fairing.

*3.5in (9cm) high*

**£40-60** **LC**

A 'Who is coming?' dressing room subject fairing.

*3.75in (9.5cm) high*

**£40-60** **LC**

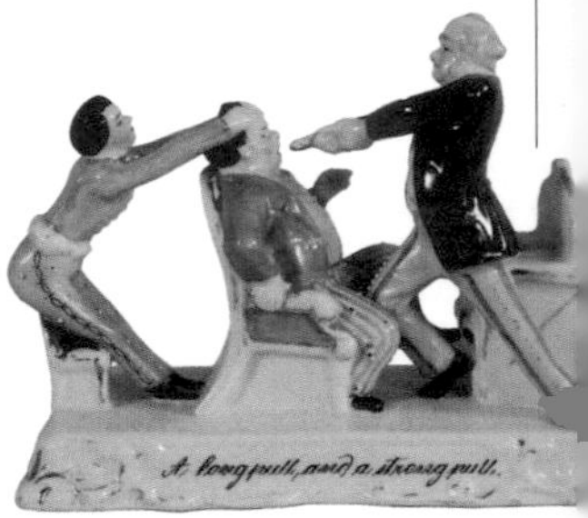

An 'A long pull, and a strong pull' fairing.

**£280-320** **SAS**

A 'Did you ring, Sir?' bath tub scene fairing, the caption in capitals.

*Conta & Boehme did not use capital letters for the entire caption on its fairings, probably indicating that this example was made in England.*

*3.25in (8cm) high*

**£70-100** **LC**

A rare Vienna-style fairing, untitled, depicting two ladies whispering, well-painted and gilded.

**£150-250** SAS

A Conta & Boehme 'Taking the Cream' fairing, with impressed marks.

*c1870* *3.5in (9cm) high*

**£120-180** LC

A rare 'Je t'aime tant' Vienna-style fairing.

**£300-400** SAS

A 'The last match' figure subject fairing, with tethered pig.

*5.25in (13cm) high*

**£70-100** LC

A 'Please Sir, what would you charge to Christin my doll' figure group fairing.

*4in (10cm) high*

**£220-280** LC

## A CLOSER LOOK AT A FAIRING

*At first glance, this looks like a typical Victorian theme of indulgence and naughtiness.*

*Although some of the colours are worn, it is in good condition and the colours are still bright*

*Looking closer, the drunk is being led home by the Grim Reaper and a spirit, both dressed as undertakers.*

*It is a very rare fairing and is desirable due to its moralistic theme.*

A 'Seeing Him Home' fairing.

**£600-700** SAS

An 'Oysters, Sir' fish stall subject fairing.

*4in (10cm) high*

**£150-200** **LC**

A 'Favourable opportunity' carriage and ladies fairing.

**£280-320** **SAS**

An 'English neutrality 1870-71 attending the sick' fairing.

**£500-600** **SAS**

An 'A Dangerous Encounter' cyclists subject fairing.

*This is a rare fairing and also appeals to collectors of bicycling memorabilia, hence the higher price. As the bone shaker was only introduced in 1865, such fairings can be dated to after this date.*

*3.25in (8.5cm) high*

**£550-650** **LC**

A 'Where are you going to, my pretty maid' subject fairing, with begging dog and barrel, the barrel acting as a spill holder.

*4.5in (11.5cm) high*

**£120-180** **LC**

## A CLOSER LOOK AT A FAIRING

*This fairing commemorates the fact that England did not enter the Franco-Prussian war, remaining neutral.*

*Political themed fairings are sought-after and scarcer than other categories such as more amusing or appealing 'bedchamber' fairings.*

*The fence, head and top hat are particularly prone to damage –they are not damaged on this example.*

*There are other fairings to collect with the same theme, such as the one at the top this page.*

An 'English neutrality 1870 attending the wounded' fairing.

**£600-700** **SAS**

An 'A spicey Bit' fairing.

*4.5in (11cm) high*

**£150-200** **LC**

A 'Good Templars' cats at the tea urn fairing.

*c1880* *3.5in (8.5cm) high*

**£150-200** **LC**

A 'Five o'clock tea' cats at the tea table fairing.

*3.5in (9cm) high*

**£150-200** **LC**

An 'A Present From Rothesy' fairing, restored.

*Despite being restored, this macabre fairing is both scarce and desirable. It has also been dedicated as a seaside souvenir, even though the town's name is misspelt.*

**£250-350** **SAS**

A child on a goat lidded box fairing, painted in bright colours.

*4.75in (12cm) high*

**£80-120** **LC**

A bedchamber subject lidded box fairing, showing a child dressing on a bed.

*4.5in (11cm) high*

**£60-80** **LC**

A wheelbarrow trinket dish fairing, in the form of a pensive girl sitting on a wheelbarrow with floral decoration.

*5in (13cm) long*

**£60-80** **LC**

A mantelpiece and fireplace subject fairing.

*A small mirror was intended to be fitted into the frame, into which the small child is looking.*

*4in (10cm) high*

**£50-70** **LC**

### FIND OUT MORE...

**Victorian Fairings & Their Values**, *by Margaret Anderson, published by Lyle Publications, 1975.*

**Victorian China Fairings** *–The Collectors' Guide, by D.H. Jordan, published by The Antique Collectors' Club, 2003.*

## COLLECTORS' NOTES

- Hummel figurines were first produced by Goebel in 1935, with the charming boy and girl characters being based on drawings of children by the nun, Sister Berta Hummel. Over 500 different figurines have been released, and many of the first 46 designs modelled by Arthur Moeller are still in production today.
- Early figurines tend to be worth the most, as do larger examples measuring over six inches high. Although it is not usually possible to date a figurine to a precise year (except for some modern editions), look at the style of the mark on the base to date a figurine to a period. 'Crown' marks are usually the earliest and were used from 1936-50, but a black printed Crown mark with the words 'Goebel' and 'Germany' date from 1991-2000.
- Marks comprising a bee in a 'V' shape are more commonly seen, and date from 1940-c1980. The larger the bee is, the earlier the piece will be. Later, the bee became more stylized and smaller in size. Dates given here relate to the use of a mark on that particular piece, not the dates the model was produced between.
- All authentic Hummel figurines are marked with one of Goebel's marks – be wary of any figurines that are not marked as poor quality copies produced in the Far East are frequently seen. The impressed number is the mould or model number. Look out for unusual variations, particularly in the colour of clothing or slight mould variations, as these can be worth more.
- The bisque chips easily, so be careful when moving Hummel around, particularly on display shelves. Also always examine a piece thoroughly before buying it to ensure that it is not damaged. Be aware that many characters were produced for long periods of time, and some are still in production today, so check the company's current catalogues to see which are.

A Hummel 'Village Boy' figure, no.51/2/0, with crazing to glaze.

*Note the difference in size between these two figurines. Look out for an early, rare variation of the 4inch size with a blue jacket and yellow handkerchief, as this can be worth over ten times more.*

*1964-72* *5in (12.5cm) high*

**£20-30** **AAC**

A Hummel 'Village Boy' figure, no.51/3/0.

*1972-79* *4in (10cm) high*

**£15-20** **AAC**

A Hummel 'Little Gardener' figure, no.74, with glaze crazing to base.

*1958-72* *4.25in (11cm) high*

**£20-30** **AAC**

A Hummel 'Little Fiddler' figure, no.2.

*c1972-79* *5in (12.5cm)*

**£65-75** **OACC**

A Hummel 'Merry Wanderer' figure, no.11/2/0, damaged.

*1958-72* *4.25in (11cm) high*

**£8-12** **AAC**

A Hummel 'Skier Doll' figure, no.1722, with Goebel medal, signed "Hummel".

*1958-72* *11in (28cm) high*

**£40-50** **AAC**

A Hummel 'Heavenly Angel' figure, no.21/0/I/2, minor base crazing.

*1972-79* *6in (15cm) high*

**£30-50** **AAC**

A Hummel 'Doll Bath' figure, no.319, crazing to base and bathtub water.

*Designed by Gerhard Skrobek in 1956, this figure was not released until 1962. Look out for early examples with the 'full bee' mark as these are rare and can command prices of over 50 per cent more than later examples.*

*1962-72* *5.25in (13.5cm) high*

**£30-50** **AAC**

## A CLOSER LOOK AT A HUMMEL FIGURE

*This is a complex figurine with many protrusions, so check examples carefully for cracks, chips or other losses.*

*Its companion piece has a girl clinging to the tree and is known as 'Out of Danger'.*

*It was designed by Arthur Moeller in 1936. It was produced in one size only at around 6.5in high, and was also later produced as a lamp.*

*Variations are known with open rather than downcast eyes as here. These are earlier, but are usually worth about the same.*

A Hummel 'Culprits' figurine, no.56/A.

*6.5in (16.5cm) high*

**£100-170** **MAC**

A Hummel 'Good Friends' figure, no.182, with 'full bee' mark to base.

*c1946-59* *4in (10cm) high*

**£80-120** **GCA**

A Hummel 'Happy Pastime' figure, no.69.

*c1936-96* *3.25in (8.5cm) high*

**£70-90** **GCA**

A Hummel 'Joyous News' figure, no.27/III.

*1979-91* *4.75in (12cm) high*

**£60-80** **AAC**

A Hummel 'Friends' figure, no.136/I, with incised circle, marked "Western Germany" in black.

*1957-60* *5in (12.5cm) high*

**£45-55** **AAC**

A Hummel 'Prayer Before Battle' figure, no.20, base crazing.

*1958-72* *4.25in (11cm) high*

**£30-40** **AAC**

## COLLECTORS' NOTES

- Brightly coloured with an enormous variety of designs, and available at many different price levels, it is perhaps not surprising that Italian ceramics have become more popular over the past three years. Many also fit into the prevailing 'retro-modern' style of interior decoration.
- Makers and designers such as Guido Gambone (1909-69) and Marcello Fantoni (b.1915) are at the top end, with prices typically fetching from £100 into the thousands. Their designs display bright or earthy colours, glazes applied in a painterly manner, rough surfaces and a combination of modern and ancient forms.
- More affordable are the vast numbers of vases produced by currently unknown Italian factories that are simply marked with a model or design number and 'Italy'. Prices range from a few pounds up to around £50, with a very few fetching over £100. Many of these were sold inexpensively as souvenirs to the increasing number of tourists from the 1950s onwards.
- The main indicator to value is the quality of the design and how it is executed. Look for well-painted, detailed designs in typical, bright 'sun-soaked' Italian colours. However, do not ignore the whimsical or more outrageous designs, as these have great novelty appeal. Large pieces also command a premium.
- Many of these vases were distributed by Raymor in the US and by Hutchison & Sons, amongst others, in the UK and some retain retailers' labels. Examples with better executed designs and of a higher quality were generally retailed by such companies. Always examine a piece closely, and even tap it gently, to check for any damage as this will reduce value dramatically, particularly on those by unknown makers.

An Italian Fantoni for Raymor bulbous vase, with hand-painted red band over yellow drips, with painted marks to base.

*6.75in (17.5cm) high*

**£120-180** **HLM**

An Italian Raymor double gourd vase, with vertical dripped brown and orange streaks, painted "Italy 1054 Raymor" on the base.

*10.75in (27.5cm) high*

**£80-120** **HLM**

An Italian Raymor vase, with thin neck, with yellow, blue and brown 'lava' glazed band, the base painted "Italy 974 Raymor" on the base.

*The 'lava' effect, textured glazes with their different, graduated colours, are particularly desirable.*

*10.75in (27.5cm) high*

**£150-200** **HLM**

An Italian mottled green and yellow striped hand-painted vase, the base painted "Made in Italy".

*6in (15cm) high*

**£20-30** **GC**

An Italian hand-painted vase, with panels of stylized flowers and trellis pattern, the base painted "Italy 7449".

*7.25in (18.5cm) high*

**£20-30** **GC**

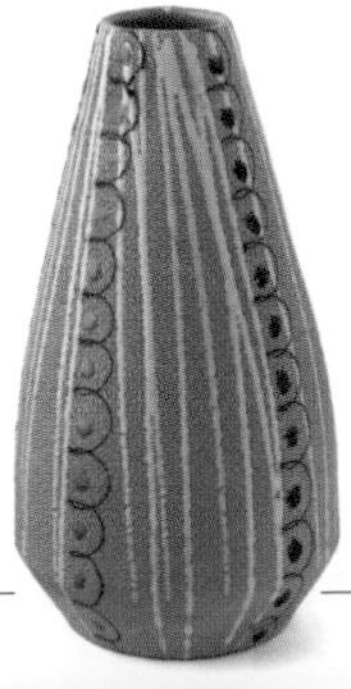

An Italian hand-painted vase, with tube-lined white lines, and blue and red dots on a textured light blue ground, the base painted "Italy 6679".

*These pastel bases are typical of these ceramics and can be found in pastel blue, pink or yellow.*

*9in (23cm) high*

**£30-40** **GC**

An Italian red and cream glazed small vase, with sgrafitto pattern of a deer amidst leaves, the base painted "6941 Italy".

*6in (15cm) high*

**£30-40** **GC**

An Italian hand-decorated vase, with a stylized fish and octopus against brown lines, unmarked.

*This was extremely thinly moulded, and has a very light weight.*

*8.5in (21.5cm) high*

**£30-50** **GC**

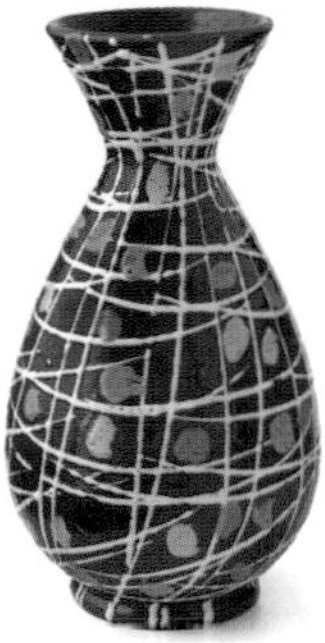

An Italian baluster vase, hand-decorated with tube-lined white lines and printed multicoloured dots, the base painted, "120 Italy".

*8in (20.5cm) high*

**£30-50** **GC**

An Italian cylindrical footed vase, hand-decorated with linear and diamond patterns, the base painted "H63/77 Italy".

*12.25in (31cm) high*

**£30-40** **GC**

An Italian vase, with wide aqua glazed band inscribed with a stylized group of women, the brown areas with sgrafitto lines, the base painted "Italy B923".

*8.5in (21.5cm) high*

**£30-50** **GC**

A 1960s-70s Italian square section vase, with textured orange and yellow banded finish, painted "Italy 900".

*13in (33cm) high*

**£20-30** **MTS**

## A CLOSER LOOK AT AN ITALIAN VASE

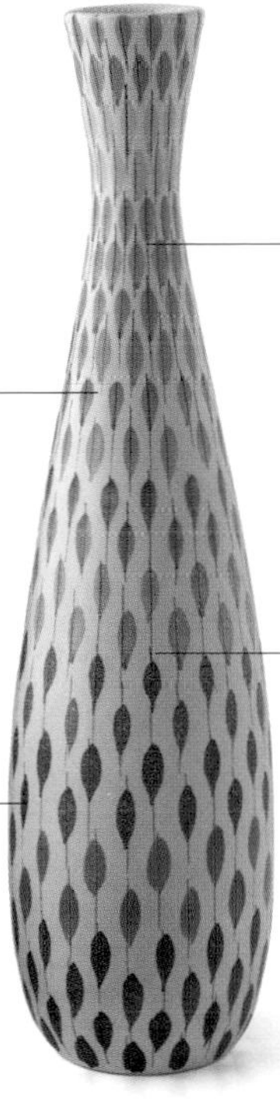

*The colours and pattern recall Stig Lindberg's landmark faïence wares designed for Gustavsberg from the late 1940-50s.*

*This is extremely well-decorated, with a graduated colour design that would have taken time and skill to produce.*

*A label on the base is a rare survivor and indicates it was sold by Raymor – the "BIT" wording may indicate the piece was produced by Bitossi.*

*It is also a large size, with a well-proportioned form.*

A 1950s Italian hand-decorated attenuated vase, with graduated multicoloured leaf-like shapes linked by lines, the base with Raymor label "Raymor 'B/115/BIT" and painted "B115 Italy".

*18in (46cm) high*

**£150-200** **GC**

An Italian hand-decorated tapering vase, with a 'dainty lady' to the front and floral pattern on the reverse.

*The flower mark on the base may indicate a factory or range. Stylized stylish ladies are commonly found on Italian vases of the late 1950s and '60s.*

*10in (25.5cm) high*

**£80-120** **GC**

A 1950s Italian tapering vase, hand-decorated with an Italian gentleman seated in the countryside, the base painted with "V4 5/A Italy".

*This vase also has the same single flower mark on the base as the vase on left. The design is also in the same style and shares a similar sense of 'carefree whimsy'.*

*6in (15.5cm) high*

**£80-100** **GC**

An Italian vase, hand-decorated with a pattern of a goat's head with foliage and a baluster urn to the reverse, of sgrafitto black lines and a white glaze over a pink textured ground, the base marked "5252 Italy".

*5.75in (14.5cm) high*

**£20-30** **GC**

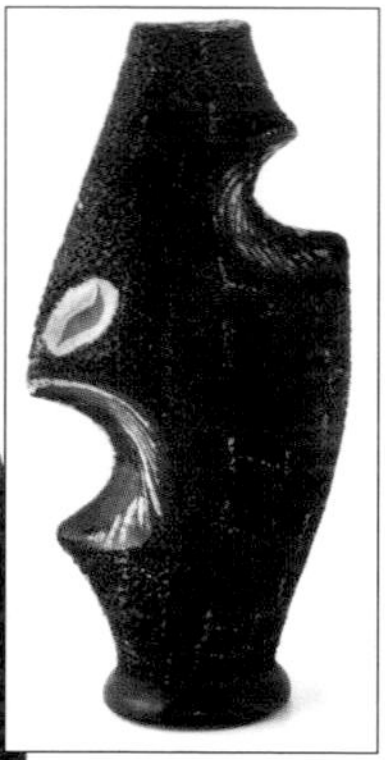

An Italian asymmetric vase, hand-painted with a stylized animal's face on a textured black painted ground, unmarked.

*Seen from the side this vase form is very 1950s. Even though the crazy design may look as if it was added by an amateur later, the textured background and these colours are found on many other Italian ceramics of the period. Beauty is certainly in the eye of the beholder!*

*12in (30.5cm) high*

**£40-60** **MHC**

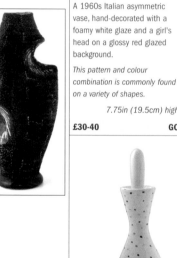

A 1960s Italian asymmetric vase, hand-decorated with a foamy white glaze and a girl's head on a glossy red glazed background.

*This pattern and colour combination is commonly found on a variety of shapes.*

*7.75in (19.5cm) high*

**£30-40** **GC**

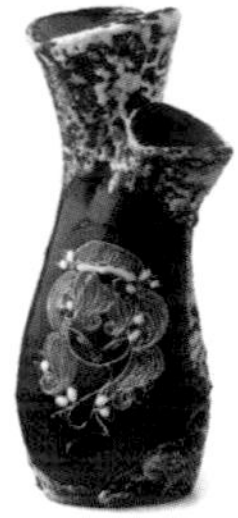

An Italian Raymor ceramic decanter and six glasses, with hand-painted black and gold polka dot pattern, the base painted "Italy 808/B".

*12.5in (32cm) high*

**£50-80** **HLM**

## COLLECTORS' NOTES

- After the end of WWII, the allies occupied Japan. In order to help the country regenerate and rebuild its economy, Japan was allowed to export its ceramics and other items providing that it was clearly marked. This rule was in place from 1947 until April 1952. Only the marks 'Occupied Japan' and 'Made in Occupied Japan' guarantee that a piece was made and exported during this short period. It is these marks that serious collectors look for and all pieces shown here bear one of these authentic marks.

- Ceramics made up the vast majority of objects, most of them functional kitchenware or dinnerware, but many decorative items, such as vases and figurines, were also exported. Items made from celluloid and transfer-printed tinplate, such as toys, were also exported. Most pieces are stamped on the base with printed marks in red, but beware of fakes. The marks on glazed ceramics are always under the glaze.

- Ceramics were produced in moulds on a factory production line process and then decorated in colour by hand. Key indicators to value include the type, shape and size of the object and how well it is painted. The detail of the object is also important. A more finely detailed, well-painted example is always going to be more desirable than one that is not so well painted or modelled.

- Many were based on existing European or American forms or styles that were already desirable. This took advantage of an existing market and allowed many to buy into a look at a more affordable price. Condition is also very important. Unglazed bisque should be clean and is generally an off-white colour. Chips and glued repairs reduce value considerably as collectors only seek out pieces in undamaged condition, unless a piece is exceptionally rare. Always examine delicate protruding parts for signs of repair.

A pair of 'Made In Occupied Japan' mantelpiece figurines, each with male lute player and seated lady, with hand-painted detailing.

*These are often found as lamp bases, and exact style and form differ widely, as does the value. This is a comparatively appealing pair, loosely based on fine 19thC Meissen porcelain from Germany.*

*6in (15cm) high*

**£40-50 (pair)** **TOA**

A Paulux 'Made in Occupied Japan' hand-painted seated lady figurine, with gilt highlights.

*5.75in (14.5cm) high*

**£18-22** **TOA**

A Paulux 'Made in Occupied Japan' hand-painted bisque flower holder, with a lady leading a swan shaped-carriage.

*6.75in (17cm) high*

**£60-90** **TOA**

A Lenwile Ardalt 'Made in Occupied Japan' 'Fallen Skater' hand-painted bisque figurine, also painted "2350" on the base.

*This figurine is hard to find in perfect condition as the legs, skate blades and particularly the delicate fingers are usually broken in some way or repaired.*

*5.5in (14cm) wide*

**£50-80** **TOA**

A pair of fine quality Andrea 'Made in Occupied Japan' hand-painted ceramic mantelpiece busts, marked "23/66" on the base.

*As well as being an unusual shape, both the moulded details and the painting on these busts is comparatively fine, hence their higher value.*

*9.75in (25cm) high*

**£180-220** **TOA**

A rare pair of 'Made in Occupied Japan' historical hand-painted ceramic figurines.

*8in (20cm) high*

**£50-80** **TOA**

## A CLOSER LOOK AT A PAIR OF FIGURINES

*These figures are direct copies of those made by Florence of California, a highly successful company founded by Florence Ward in Pasadena, California, in 1942. It is known for its desirable and decorative historical or literary figurines.*

*They appealed to those looking for a more affordable alternative to the sought-after 18thC and 19thC figurines by notable factories such as Meissen and Derby.*

*The poses, hand-painting and moulded details are comparatively finer than other Japanese examples, and include textured areas, gilt highlights and well-painted faces.*

*They are in excellent condition with no damage or wear to the paint. They lack the wooden bases on which they would have been mounted for sale, although this does not affect the value.*

A pair of Royal Sealy 'Made in Occupied Japan' hand-painted ceramic figurines of a Victorian or early 20thC couple, with gilt highlights.

*9.5in (24cm) high*

**£40-60** **TOA**

A 'Made in Occupied Japan' hand-painted ceramic figurine of Little Bo Peep, with her shepherdess' crook.

*As with the figurines above, this is a direct copy of a figurine designed and made by Florence of California.*

*6.25in (16cm) high*

**£15-25** **TOA**

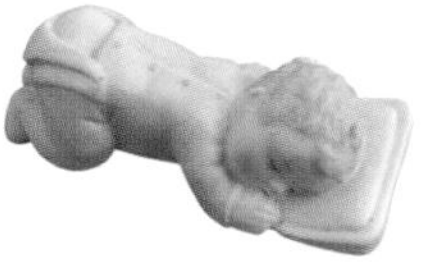

A 'Made in Occupied Japan' hand-painted bisque sleeping baby, painted "434" on the base.

*4.75in (12cm) long*

**£12-18** **TOA**

A 'Made in Occupied Japan' hand-painted bisque figurine, of a small boy playing a fiddle.

*Popular figurines made in the US were not the only target for post war Japanese manufacturers. This charming boy is a copy of German factory Goebel's 'Little Fiddler' Hummel figure, designed for Goebel by Arthur Moeller in 1935 and still in production today. Other children figures from the 'American Children's Series' are more valuable and can be worth up to £80.*

*4.75in (12cm) high*

**£12-18** **TOA**

A 'Made in Occupied Japan' hand-painted bisque figurine, of a seated baby with his hands held aloft.

*As with the Hummel figurine to the left, this is a copy of German doll and ceramic maker Heubach's range of 'Piano Babies'. Although this is a finely moulded and painted example, with a good facial expression, better examples closer to the high quality associated with Heubach can be found.*

*5in (12.5cm) high*

**£50-80** **TOA**

A U.C.A.G.CO China 'Made in Occupied Japan' hand-painted bisque Bacchanalian putto figurine, with grapes and cup.

*U.C.A.G.CO stands for United China & Glass Company, which was a distributor of china and glassware based in New Orleans and New York. Their agent S. Stolaroff signed the first contract allowing Japanese imports into the US. During the 1950s, they were one of the biggest importers of Japanese ceramics.*

*6in (15cm) high*

**£25-30** **TOA**

A 'Made in Occupied Japan' hand-painted bisque 'Uncle Sam' figurine.

*4.25in (11cm) high*

**£25-30** **TOA**

A 'Made in Occupied Japan' hand-painted ceramic Mickey Mouse figurine, playing a bassoon.

*Mickey Mouse was a popular character for the Japanese to copy. Most were not licensed by Walt Disney, hence he can look very different to the real Mickey Mouse, as here. Note the mark on the base, which is typical of 'Made In Occupied Japan' pieces. If there is more space between the words, it is likely to be a later reproduction.*

*3.25in (8cm) high*

**£40-60** **TOA**

A Lenwile China Ardalt 'Made in Occupied Japan' hand-painted ceramic clown, printed "6141" on the base.

*5in (12.5cm) high*

**£25-30** **TOA**

A 1950s 'Made in Occupied Japan' hand-painted ceramic tribesman figurine.

*This figurine crosses two collecting areas – Occupied Japan and Black Americana.*

*4.75in (12cm) high*

**£22-28** **TOA**

A 'Made In Occupied Japan' hand-painted bisque humourous monkey figurine.

*The 'fur' on this example is made using small flakes of the ceramic, giving a rough texture. Although it has been used for centuries, this technique is commonly found on early to mid-20thC German bisque 'snow baby' novelty figurines.*

*4in (10cm) high*

**£15-20** **TOA**

A 'Made in Occupied Japan' hand-painted ceramic standing 'business-turtle', with cane, monocle, hat and briefcase.

*4.25in (10.5cm) high*

**£18-22** **TOA**

A pair of 'Made in Occupied Japan' turkey-shaped salt and pepper shakers.

*These would also appeal to collectors of Thanksgiving holiday memorabilia.*

*2.5in (6.5cm) high*

**£10-12** **TOA**

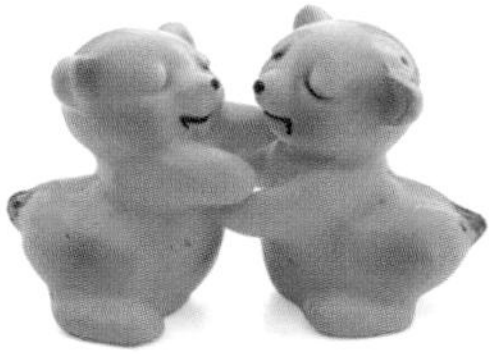

A pair of 'Made In Occupied Japan' bear shaped salt and pepper shakers.

*The form, colour and particularly the closed eyes of these shakers indicate US maker Shawnee was the inspiration. However, Shawnee are better known for their pigs and cookie jars.*

*2.5in (6.5cm) high*

**£8-12** **TOA**

A 'Made in Occupied Japan' recumbent duck figure.

*This is likely to be an un-licensed version of Donald Duck's girlfriend Daisy Duck, who made her debut in 1937.*

*4.25in (10.5cm) long*

**£18-22** **TOA**

A 'Made in Occupied Japan' hand-painted ceramic 'Mexican' liquor bottle.

*Liquor bottles are a popular area for collectors. They can be found in a wide variety of novelty shapes. Colourful and humourous shapes and recognisable characters are sought-after, as are finely painted or moulded examples. The original contents does not add to the value.*

*6in (15cm) high*

**£25-35** **TOA**

A 'Made in Occupied Japan' hand-painted ceramic bassoon-player liquor bottle.

*5in (13cm) high*

**£20-30** **TOA**

A 'Made in Occupied Japan' hand-painted ceramic centaur-shaped liquor bottle.

*4in (10cm) high*

**£25-35** **TOA**

A 'Made in Occupied Japan' hand-painted seated satyr-shaped liquor bottle.

*Classical forms related to Greek and Roman Bacchanalian festivals, such as putti and satyrs are typical for liquor bottles.*

*4in (10cm) high*

**£28-32** **TOA**

A 'Made in Occupied Japan' hand-painted liquor bottle in the form of a Scottie dog and yellow puppy.

*Dogs are one of the most common shapes for liquor bottles. The Scottie dog is the most popular and desirable breed to be featured, with examples usually being more valuable.*

*3.25in (8cm) high*

**£25-30** **TOA**

A 'Made in Occupied Japan' hand-painted ceramic liquor bottle, in the form of a Scottie dog and sorrowful looking puppy.

*3.25in (8cm) high*

**£25-30** **TOA**

A 'Made in Occupied Japan' hand-painted ceramic liquor bottle, in the form of a squirrel holding a nut.

*4in (10cm) high*

**£25-30** **TOA**

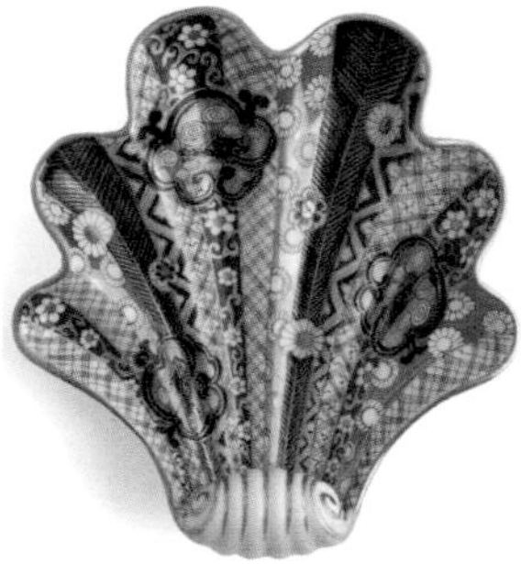

A Hokutosha 'Made in Occupied Japan' acanthus leaf-shaped dish, hand-painted in the Imari-style with gilt highlights.

*9.5in (24cm) long*

**£20-25** **TOA**

## A CLOSER LOOK AT A 'MADE IN OCCUPIED' JAPAN VASE

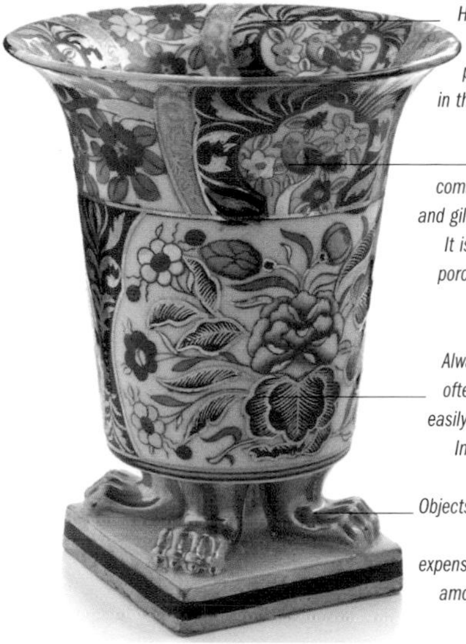

*Hokutosha are well-known for their Imari-style patterns, but also produced other historical patterns in the style of Delft and Crown Derby.*

*Imari can recognised by the combination of a cobalt blue, iron red and gilt highlights, and floral patterning. It is named after a type of Japanese porcelain made at Arita and exported from the port of Imari.*

*Always look closely at the gilt as it is often thinly applied and so can wear easily, particularly on protruding parts. Intact, original gilt increases value.*

*Objects like this vase are slightly harder as they would have been more expensive at the time. This is due to the amount of hand-painting required for the complex pattern.*

A Hokutosha 'Made in Occupied Japan' Neoclassical style planter vase on square base, decorated with an Imari-style pattern and with gilded lion claw feet.

*8in (20.5cm) high*

**£40-60** **TOA**

A pair of 'Made in Occupied Japan' baluster vases, decorated with high relief applied dragon's heads.

*The dragon is a sacred beast in Japanese mythology, and is often depicted flying through clouds clutching the 'tama' or sacred pearl in its claw.*

*6in (15.5cm) high*

**£60-90** **TOA**

A Lenwile China Ardalt 'Made in Occupied Japan' lidded box, in the style of a copy of Wedgwood green Jasperware, with marks to base.

*6.75in (17cm) diam*

**£50-80** **TOA**

A 'Made in Occupied Japan' Capodimonte-style lidded dish, with printed 'TM' monogram to base.

*Capodimonte was founded in Naples, Italy, in 1743. It is known for its heavily moulded and brightly coloured wares. This copy is a scarce pattern and shape, with most of the gilding still intact and undamaged.*

*8in (20cm) high*

**£80-120** **TOA**

A 'Made in Occupied Japan' hand-painted bisque 'Memento Mori' stamp dispenser.

*'Memento mori' are moralistic images or objects that remind us we are mortal, despite what we may learn, gain or achieve.*

*3.75in (9.5cm) high*

**£30-40** **TOA**

A 'Made in Occupied Japan' hand-painted bisque 'Who Left This Behind?' combined match and cigarette holder and ashtray, in the form of a black boy and a washing line with hanging clothes.

*2.5in (6.5cm) high*

**£10-15** **TOA**

## COLLECTORS' NOTES

- The Midwinter Pottery was founded in Burslem, Stoke-on-Trent, Staffordshire in 1910 by William Robinson Midwinter. Tableware and nursery ware dominated production, with the prevalent Art Deco style being used from the mid-1920s-30s when the company had expanded to employ over 700 staff.
- In 1946, William's son Roy joined the company and worked his way up to become Managing Director. He then began to revitalise the company, particularly after visiting the Festival of Britain exhibition in 1951 and a trip to the US in 1952, where he was influenced by the modern forms and designs of US ceramics designers such as Eva Zeisel, Raymond Loewy and Russel Wright.
- The result was the 'Stylecraft' range, released in 1953. Patterns were supplied by the designer Jessie Tait, who was also influenced by current trends in the ceramics and design industries. Using bright, cheerful colours, patterns were abstract or based on natural themes, and were aimed at young buyers. Some represented changes in taste and habits, from the wider range of food available to the rise in foreign holiday travel.
- Designs could be applied by hand or transfer, or by a combination of the two. The 'Fashion' shape range appeared in 1955, followed by the 'Fine' range in 1962 and other new shapes and patterns. The Midwinter factory closed in 1987.
- Larger pieces and teapots, more complex items or those produced for short periods, are usually the most valuable. Dinner plates, and even teacups and saucers, are typically more common as they were originally made and bought in larger quantities. As they were made to be used, damage or wear is not uncommon, so examine pieces carefully before buying.
- Pattern also counts towards value, and collectors tend to prefer the more modern, abstract and colourful patterns of the late 1950s and 60s that typify Midwinter's designs at this time. Jessie Tait's work also attracts a wide following, as do designs by Terence Conran and Hugh Casson, to a lesser extent. More desirable patterns such as 'Caribbean', 'Zambesi', 'Primavera' and 'Chequers' will typically fetch a higher price than some of the more traditional floral patterns.

A Midwinter Fashion shape transfer-printed 'Alpine Pink' pattern plate, by an unknown designer.

*This pattern was also produced in blue.*

*Introduced 1960* *6in (15.5cm) diam*

**£3-6** **FFM**

A Midwinter Fashion shape printed and hand-painted 'Cannes' pattern plate, designed by Sir Hugh Casson.

*This is a later version of the 1954 'Riviera' pattern, and was available into the 1970s.*

*Introduced 1960* *8.5in (22cm) diam*

**£10-20** **FFM**

A Midwinter Fashion shape printed and hand-painted 'Capri' pattern TV cup and plate, designed by Jessie Tait.

*This was also produced as the 'Bolero' pattern using bright yellow and turquoise.*

*1955* *Plate 8.5in (22cm) diam*

**£30-45** **FFM**

A rare Midwinter Fashion shape printed and hand-painted yellow 'Caribbean' pattern buffet or TV plate, designed by Jessie Tait.

*This was the first pattern made with the new Murray Curvex printing method, which increased the rate of production dramatically.*

*Introduced 1955* *12.25in (31cm) diam*

**£75-85** **FFM**

A Midwinter Fashion shape transfer-printed and hand-painted 'Caribbean' pattern plate, designed by Jessie Tait.

*Introduced 1955* *9.5in (24.5cm) diam*

**£80-120** **GGRT**

## A CLOSER LOOK AT A MIDWINTER DISH

*Conran based this design on a textile pattern he had produced for David Whitehead in 1951, and which had featured at the Festival of Britain.*

*On hollowware examples, the body was originally grey, but was changed to yellow, perhaps as grey made food look unappealing.*

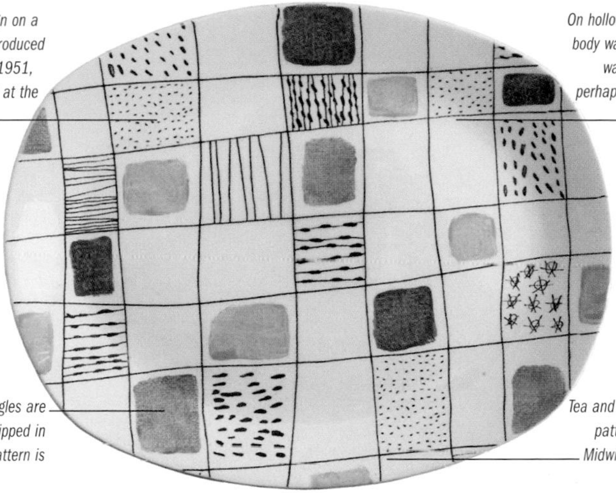

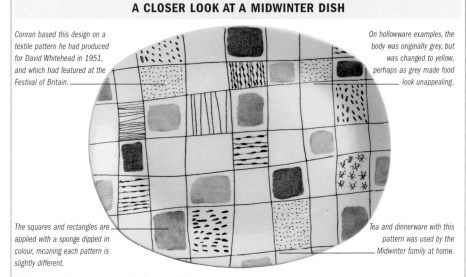

*The squares and rectangles are applied with a sponge dipped in colour, meaning each pattern is slightly different.*

*Tea and dinnerware with this pattern was used by the Midwinter family at home.*

A Midwinter Fashion shape painted and sponged 'Chequers' pattern oval platter, designed by Terence Conran.

*Introduced 1957* *13.75in (35cm) wide*

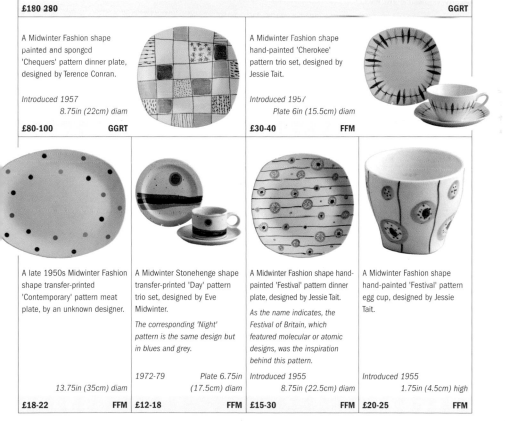

**£180-280** **GGRT**

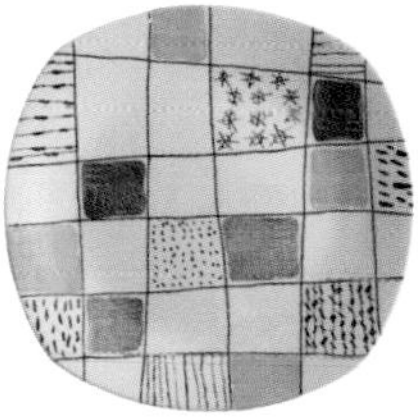

A Midwinter Fashion shape painted and sponged 'Chequers' pattern dinner plate, designed by Terence Conran.

*Introduced 1957*
*8.75in (22cm) diam*

**£80-100** **GGRT**

A Midwinter Fashion shape hand-painted 'Cherokee' pattern trio set, designed by Jessie Tait.

*Introduced 1957*
*Plate 6in (15.5cm) diam*

**£30-40** **FFM**

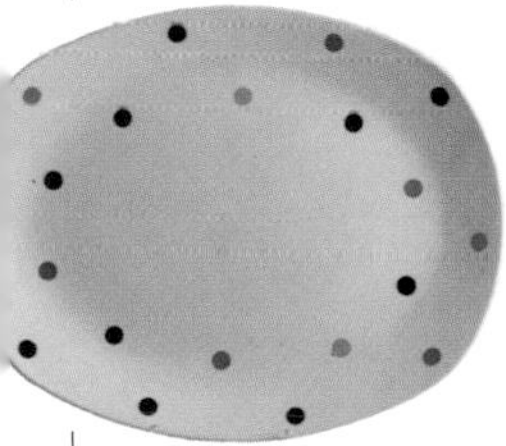

A late 1950s Midwinter Fashion shape transfer-printed 'Contemporary' pattern meat plate, by an unknown designer.

*13.75in (35cm) diam*

**£18-22** **FFM**

A Midwinter Stonehenge shape transfer-printed 'Day' pattern trio set, designed by Eve Midwinter.

*The corresponding 'Night' pattern is the same design but in blues and grey.*

*1972-79* *Plate 6.75in (17.5cm) diam*

**£12-18** **FFM**

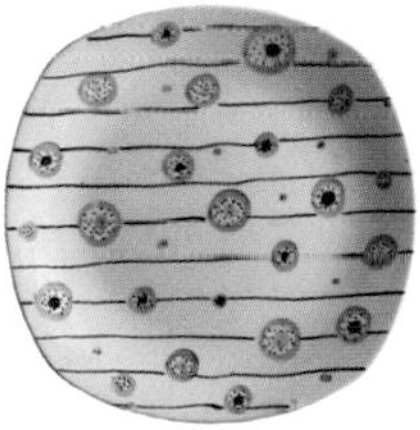

A Midwinter Fashion shape hand-painted 'Festival' pattern dinner plate, designed by Jessie Tait.

*As the name indicates, the Festival of Britain, which featured molecular or atomic designs, was the inspiration behind this pattern.*

*Introduced 1955*
*8.75in (22.5cm) diam*

**£15-30** **FFM**

A Midwinter Fashion shape hand-painted 'Festival' pattern egg cup, designed by Jessie Tait.

*Introduced 1955*
*1.75in (4.5cm) high*

**£20-25** **FFM**

Two Midwinter Fashion shape hand-painted 'Festival' pattern milk or water jugs, designed by Jessie Tait.

*1955* *Larger 5.25in (13.5cm) high*

**£30-50 PAIR** **FFM**

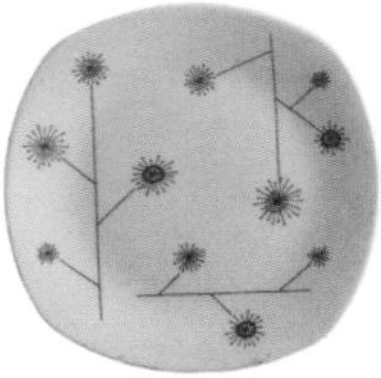

A Midwinter Fashion shape transfer-printed and hand-coloured 'Flower Mist' pattern plate, designed by Jessie Tait.

*This design can be found on Stylecraft Hotelwares bearing marks for Weatherby, Staffordshire, and also on some German porcelain of the period.*

*Introduced 1956* *8.5in (22cm) diam*

**£20-30** **FFM**

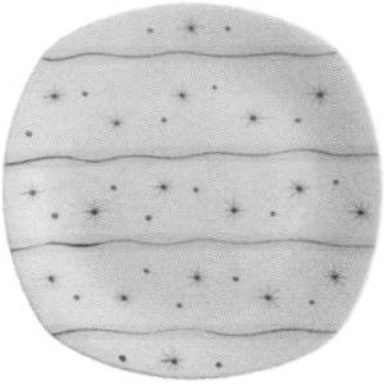

A late 1950s Midwinter Fashion shape hand-painted 'Hollywood' pattern plate, designed by Jessie Tait.

*Check the design carefully as the Elstree pattern is virtually identical, but has turquoise instead of grey stars.*

*9.5in (24.5cm) wide*

**£60-80** **GGRT**

A Midwinter Fashion shape hand-painted 'Hollywood' pattern sugar bowl, designed by Jessie Tait.

*c1957* *2in (5cm) high*

**£12-18** **FFM**

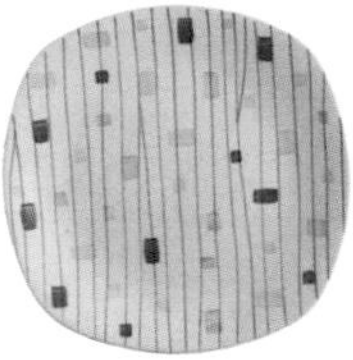

A late 1950s Midwinter Fashion shape hand-painted 'Magic Moments' pattern plate, designed by Jessie Tait.

*This pattern was not available on every shape and was not produced in large quantities.*

*9.5in (24.5cm) wide*

**£90-120** **GGRT**

A Midwinter Fashion shape transfer-printed 'Magnolia' pattern plate, designed by John Russell.

*Taken from one of Russell's paintings, this pattern was aimed to appeal to more conservative, traditional customers, widening the appeal of the modern shape.*

*c1955* *6in (15.5cm) diam*

**£3-5** **FFM**

A Midwinter Fashion shape transfer-printed 'Melody' pattern trio set, designed by Terence Conran.

*Introduced 1958*

*Plate 6in (15.5cm) diam*

**£35-45** **FFM**

A Midwinter Stylecraft shape printed and hand-painted 'Ming Tree' pattern platter, designed by Jessie Tait.

*This is also found in the Fashion range in dark blue or black.*

*Introduced 1953*

*12in (30.5cm) wide*

**£20-30** **FFM**

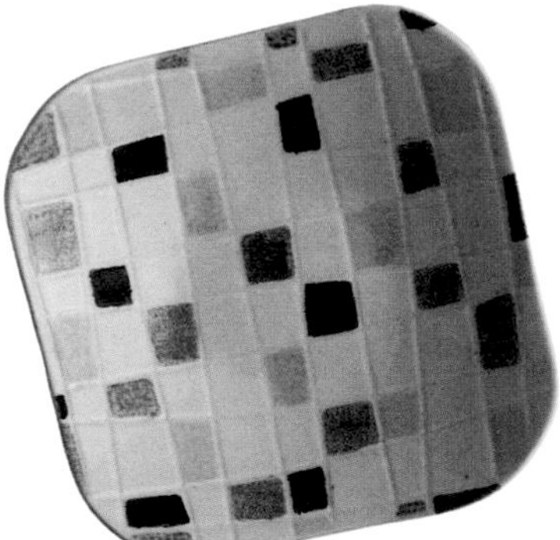

A Midwinter Fashion shape incised and sponged 'Mosaic' pattern dish, designed by Jessie Tait.

*This is unusual for Midwinter as it has an incised grid pattern, rather than an entirely flat surface.*

*Introduced 1960* *7.75in (19.5cm) wide*

**£100-120** **GGRT**

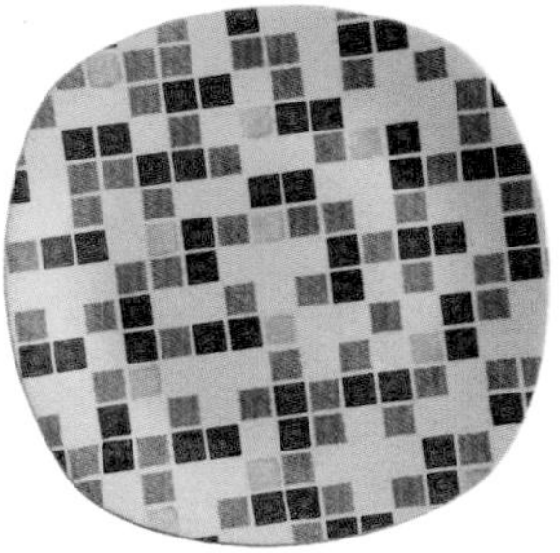

A Midwinter Fashion shape transfer-printed and sponged 'Patio' pattern plate, designed by Jessie Tait.

*Introduced c1959* *9.5in (24cm) diam*

**£70-90** **GGRT**

## A CLOSER LOOK AT A MIDWINTER DISH

*This is a highly sought-after pattern today. Tait was inspired by a visit to London's Tate Gallery to see contemporary ceramic designs.*

*The TV plate, with its recessed sections for different foods, is a rare shape.*

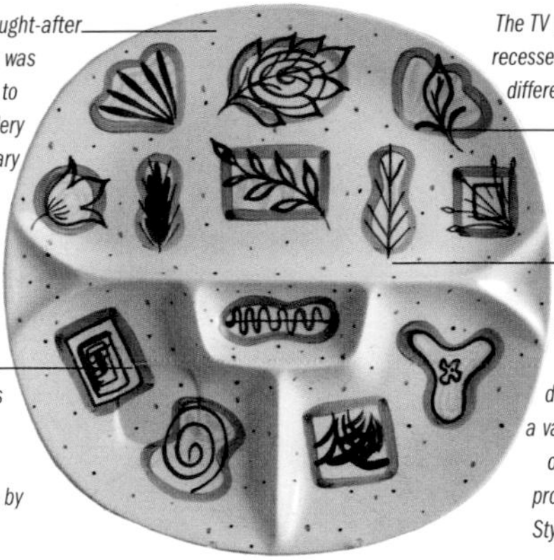

*There is a recess for a cup, which is missing from this example. This has reduced the value by around 25%.*

*Combining 1950s polka dots, amoeba and organic designs, this is a variation of the original design produced on the Stylecraft range.*

A rare Midwinter Fashion shape printed and hand-painted 'Primavera' TV dinner pattern plate, designed by Jessie Tait.

*Surprisingly, this pattern was initially unpopular with the public and only became popular after London department store Heal's stocked it.*

*Introduced 1954* *12.5in (32cm) diam*

**£40-60** **FFM**

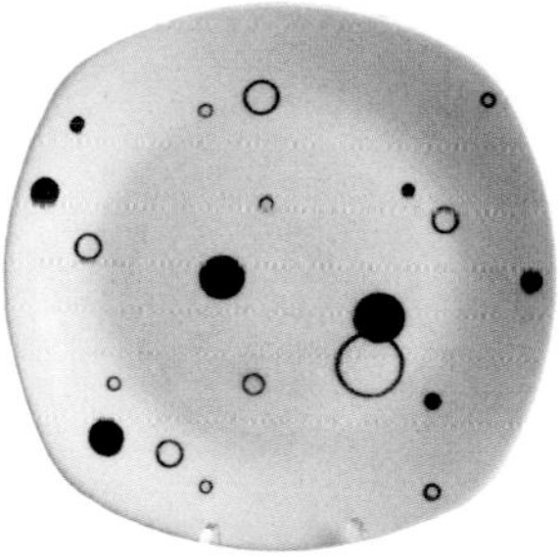

A Midwinter Fashion shape transfer-printed 'Pierrot' pattern plate, designed by Jessie Tait.

*Introduced 1955* *6.25in (16cm) diam*

**£25-35** **FFM**

A Midwinter Fashion shape transfer-printed 'Plant Life' pattern trio set, designed by Terence Conran.

*The colours show that this is the later version of the original 1954 design.*

*c1960* *Plate 6in (15cm) diam*

**£40-50** **FFM**

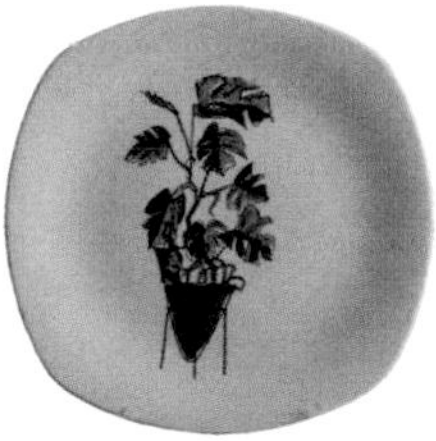

A Midwinter Fashion shape 'Plant Life' transfer-printed pattern plate, designed by Terence Conran.

*This showed the new 'fashion' for exotic houseplants amongst the young and also featured Conran's own design for a plant holder.*

*Introduced 1956* *7.75in (19.5cm) diam*

**£18-30** **FFM**

A Midwinter Fashion shape hand-painted 'Primavera' pattern TV set plate, designed by Jessie Tait, originally with tea cup.

*Introduced 1955* *8.5in (22cm) diam*

**£15-20** **FFM**

A Midwinter Stylecraft shape hand-painted 'Primavera' pattern plate, designed by Jessie Tait.

*This pattern was also used on the later Fashion range, but in a simpler form and with different colours.*

*Introduced 1954* *9.5in (24.5cm) diam*

**£20-35** **FFM**

A Midwinter Fashion shape transfer-printed 'Quite Contrary' pattern plate, designed by Jessie Tait.

*This is one of the more common patterns found.*

*Introduced 1959* *6in 15.5cm) diam*

**£5-8** **FFM**

A Midwinter Fashion shape printed and hand-coloured 'Saladware' pattern tea plate, designed by Terence Conran.

*This pattern was inspired by a 1955 design by Piero Fornasetti, where the fruit and vegetables had faces. Later examples from the 1960s used pastel colours.*

*Introduced 1955* *6in (15.5cm) diam*

**£12-25** **FFM**

A Midwinter Fashion shape transfer-printed and sponged yellow 'Savanna' pattern plate, designed by Jessie Tait.

*Introduced 1956* *9.5in (24.5cm) diam*

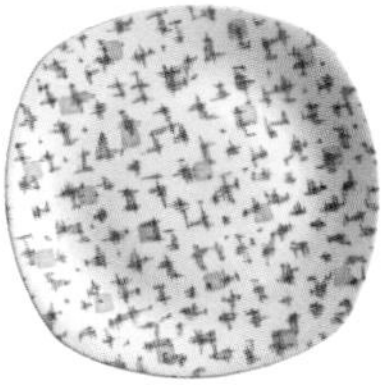

**£18-25** **FFM**

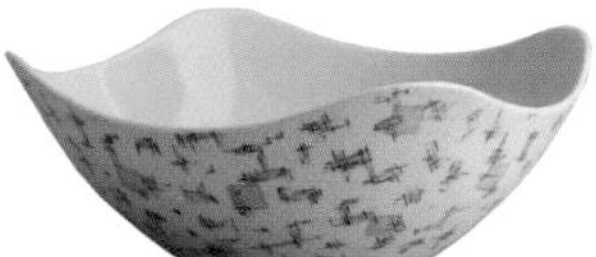

A Midwinter Fashion shape transfer-printed and sponged 'Savanna' pattern bowl, designed by Jessie Tait.

*Examples of this pattern with a turquoise interior indicates production for export to Canada.*

*Introduced 1956* *10in (25.5cm) diam*

**£80-120** **GGRT**

A Midwinter Fine shape transfer-printed 'Sienna' pattern milk jug and sugar bowl, designed by Jessie Tait.

*This was one of the most popular patterns on the Fine shape and can usually be found easily today.*

*1962-78* *Bowl 2.25in (5.5cm) high*

**£8-10** **FFM**

## A CLOSER LOOK AT A MIDWINTER VASE

*These rare studio range vases were designed by Jessie Tait and influenced by her return to the potter's wheel at the Burslem College of Art.*

*Ten modern, angular shapes are known, decorated in a number of different patterns, most of them tube-lined or decorated by hand.*

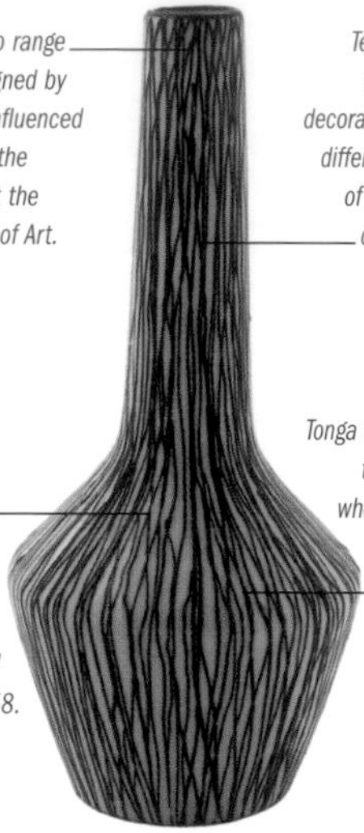

*The vases were produced from 1956-60, and appeared in the 'Pottery & Glass' magazine in 1958.*

*Tonga was later extended to the entire range, where it was transfer-printed onto the Fashion shape.*

A Midwinter small 'Tonga' pattern F201 shape studio range vase, designed by Jessie Tait.

*c1956* *6.75in (17.5cm) high*

**£80-120** **GGRT**

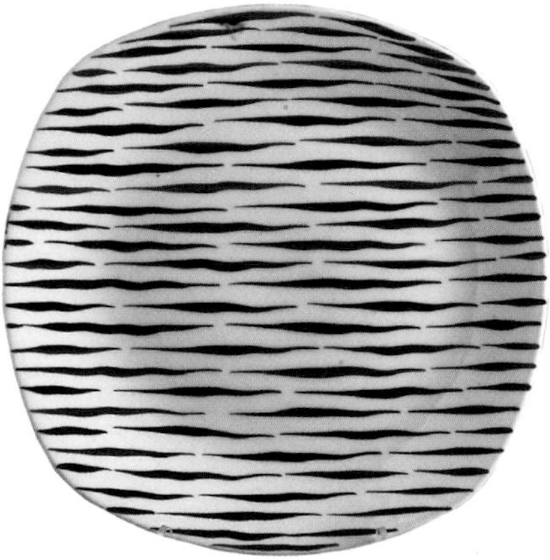

A Midwinter Fashion shape hand-painted 'Zambesi' pattern plate, designed by Jessie Tait.

*This immensely popular tribal art and Op Art inspired pattern was widely copied by other manufacturers, including Beswick. Hollowware, such as teapots, are also have red rims or handles.*

*Introduced 1956* *8.5in (22cm) diam*

**£10-20** **FFM**

### FIND OUT MORE...

**Midwinter Pottery**, *by Steven Jenkins, published by Richard Dennis, 2003.*

## COLLECTORS' NOTES

- Designer William Moorcroft (1982-45) began working at James Macintyre's Staffordshire ceramics factory in 1898. His first major designs were the 'Aurelian' and 'Florian' ranges, with their often symmetrical and Moorish inspired floral and foliate designs, which exemplify the prevalent Art Nouveau style in ceramics.
- Moorcroft split from Macintyre's in 1912, founding his own company with backing from retailer Liberty, who had sold his designs for Macintyre's with great success. His success grew, with the company being awarded the Royal Warrant in 1929. Stylized floral designs executed in a tube-lined process with rich and deep glazed colours became the company's hallmarks.
- Tube-lining uses liquid clay piped on to the surface of the body forming enclosed 'cells' that are then filled with liquid glaze. William died in 1945 and his son Walter took over and continued many of his father's designs, as well as introducing his own designs. On these pages, the designer of the pattern is shown, and date ranges refer to the range's production dates.
- Early ranges, including 'Florian', 'Claremont' and 'Eventide', and limited production ranges, tend to be the most valuable. However, more modern and even contemporary ranges designed by artists including Sally Tuffin and Rachel Bishop are becoming hotly sought-after. Look out for large pieces and limited editions in particular.
- Pieces can be dated to a period from the shape, size, pattern, colours and type of marks on the base. Damage affects value considerably, so inspect pieces very carefully. Patterns produced for long periods of time tend to be the least valuable, particularly if in small sizes.

A Moorcroft 'Anemone' pattern ginger jar and cover, the tube-lined decoration on a shaded blue and green ground, impressed and painted initials, paper label.

*6.25in (16cm) high*

**£180-220** **NEA**

A modern Moorcroft 'Anemone' pattern vase, with a green ground, the base stamped "Moorcroft Made In England" on the base and signed "WM" in green slip by the artist.

*The original pattern was redesigned in 1989 by Walter Moorcroft after his retirement in 1987.*

*2000* *10.25in (26cm) high*

**£150-200** **BEL**

A Moorcroft 'Burdock' pattern baluster vase, designed by Philip Gibson, from the 'Herb Series', with graduated cream and purple ground, with impressed and painted marks to base.

*1999* *6in (15.5cm) high*

**£150-200** **AAC**

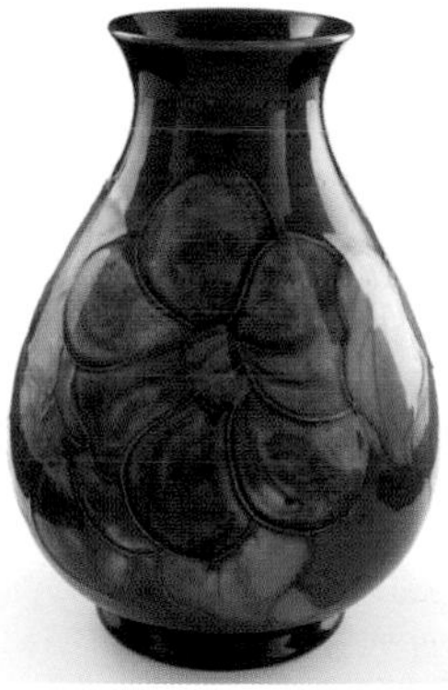

A Moorcroft 'Clematis' pattern baluster vase, with a blue and green ground, designed by William Moorcroft, with impressed and painted signature marks and paper label.

*The design was produced by Walter Moorcroft in 1939 drawing from the flowers in his garden. After WWII, it was developed into a range.*

*1946-83* *8.25in (21cm) high*

**£450-550** **NEA**

A Moorcroft 'Clematis' pattern ovoid vase, designed by William Moorcroft, with a graduated blue ground.

*5.25in (13.5cm)high*

**£200-300** **GORL**

A Moorcroft 'Columbine' pattern bowl, with a green ground, designed by Walter Moorcroft, with factory marks and paper label to base, flaw to rim.

*This was Walter Moorcroft's first independent design, and was inspired by flowers in his garden. Some pieces were made from 1947, but the full range only appeared in the 1980s, initially with a blue ground.*

*5in (12.5cm) diam*

**£50-70** **FRE**

A Moorcroft 'Eventide' pattern vase, designed by William Moorcroft, with a circular hammered pewter foot stamped "Tudric, Moorcroft, 01359".

*Pewter mounts and this mark were used on items initially sold by Liberty and, later, other retailers such as Connell in Cheapside, London. The mounts were made by Haseler.*

*c1916-23* *7.5in (19cm) high*

**£700-1,000** **GHOU**

## A CLOSER LOOK AT A MOORCROFT VASE

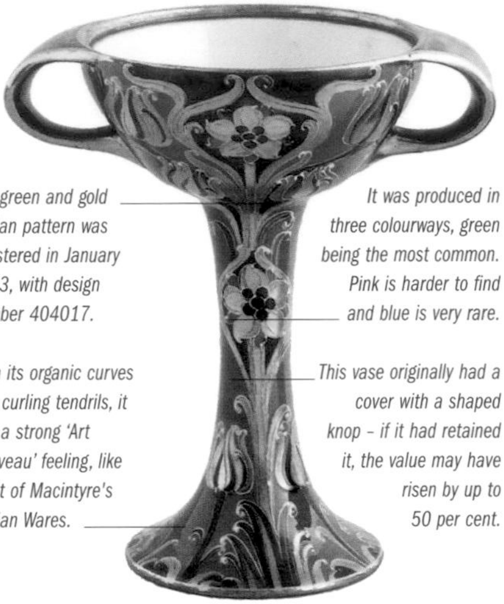

*The green and gold Florian pattern was registered in January 1903, with design number 404017.*

*With its organic curves and curling tendrils, it has a strong 'Art Nouveau' feeling, like most of Macintyre's Florian Wares.*

*It was produced in three colourways, green being the most common. Pink is harder to find and blue is very rare.*

*This vase originally had a cover with a shaped knop - if it had retained it, the value may have risen by up to 50 per cent.*

A Moorcroft Macintyre green and gold Florian Ware double handled vase, designed by William Moorcroft, with factory marks to base.

*c1905* *7in (18cm) high*

**£700-900** **GORL**

A Moorcroft 'Hibiscus' pattern baluster vase, designed by Walter Moorcroft, the base with impressed and painted initials and paper label.

*Intro. 1949 10in (25.5cm)*

**£350-450** **NEA**

A Moorcroft 'Hibiscus' pattern ovoid vase, designed by Walter Moorcroft, with a graduated yellow and green ground and factory marks to base.

*7.25in (18.5cm) high*

**£180-220** **GORL**

A pair of Moorcroft 'Hibiscus' pattern miniature candlesticks, designed by Walter Moorcroft, with green and blue shaded ground.

*3.5in (9cm) high*

**£180-220** **MAX**

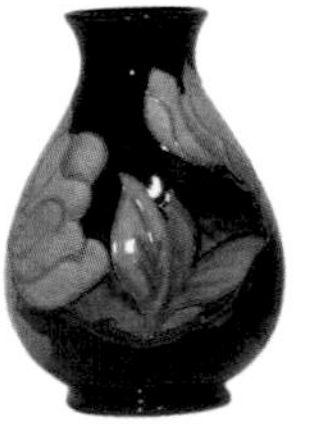

A 1980s Moorcroft ' Magnolia' pattern baluster vase, designed by Walter Moorcroft, with a blue ground, the base with impressed and painted marks.

*8.5in (21.5cm) high*

**£180-220** **MAX**

A Moorcroft 'Orchid' pattern ovoid jug, designed by William Moorcroft, with a mottled blue ground and loop handle, with impressed and painted initial marks and paper label.

*8.25in (21cm) high*

**£500-600** **NEA**

A Moorcroft 'Orchid' pattern small baluster vase, with a deep blue ground, facsimile signature and "Potter to HM The Queen" marks.

*1937-72* *4in (10cm) high*

**£180-220** **GORL**

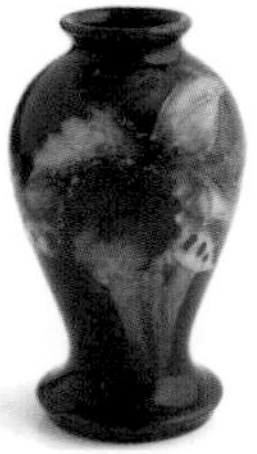

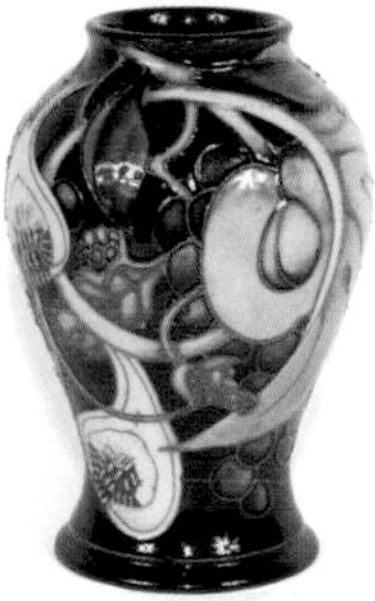

A modern Moorcroft 'Queen's Choice' pattern vase, designed by Emma Bossons, on a blue ground, the base with factory and decorator's marks.

*2000* *6.25in (16cm) high*

**£120-180** **BEL**

A Moorcroft 'Seadrift' pattern tall vase, designed by Rachel Bishop, with graduated cream and blue ground, the base with impressed printed and painted marks and signed by Rachel Bishop.

*2001* *8in (20cm) high*

**£150-200** **AAC**

A Moorcroft 'Trout' pattern squat vase, designed by Philip Gibson in 1999, with two trout chasing a dragonfly, the base with factory marks, decorator's mark "I.B", "Copyrighted in 98" and a black "GP" stamp.

*c1999* *8in (20cm) wide*

**£280-320** **BEL**

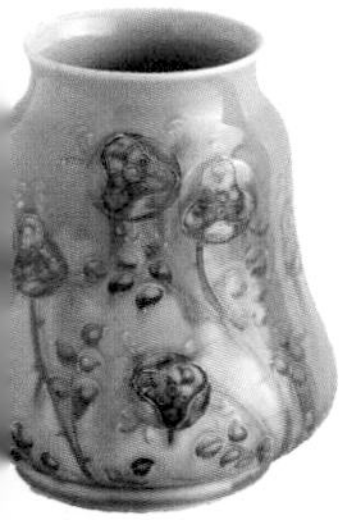

A Moorcroft 'Tudor Rose' pattern vase, designed by William Moorcroft, with waisted form and a turquoise ground, the base with printed marks and registered no. 431157 for 1904, crack to rim.

*Registered in 1904, this design is rare in turquoise and is more commonly found in green. Liberty, who retailed the design initially, devised the name.*

*c1905* *8in (20cm) high*

**£1,200-1,800** **GORL**

A limited edition Moorcroft 'South Pacific' pattern vase, designed by Sian Leeper, from an edition of 300, decorated with a turtle, jellyfish, seahorse, fish and other marine life.

*14.5in (37cm) high*

**£500-600** **GORL**

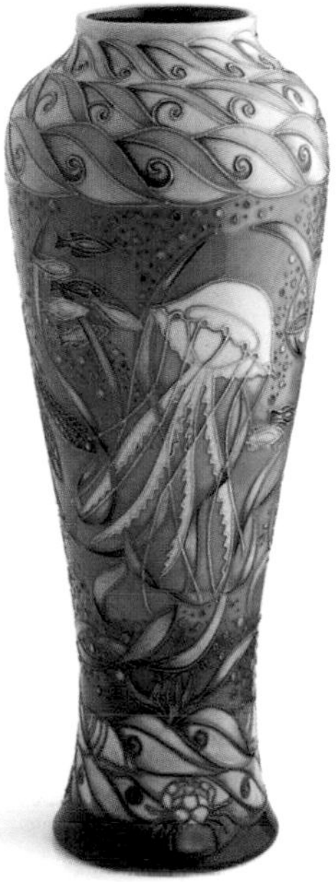

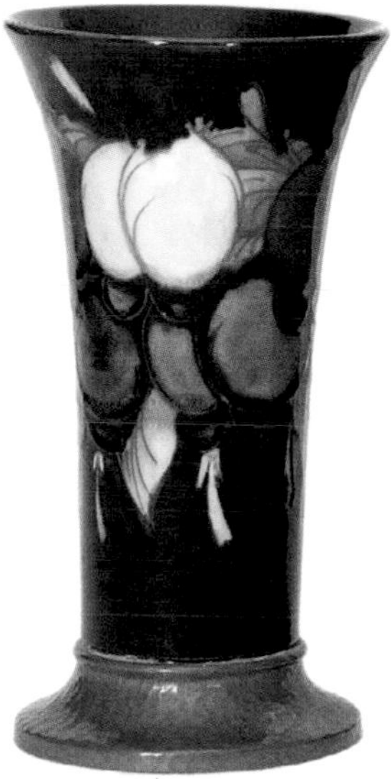

A Moorcroft 'Wisteria' pattern flared vase, designed by William Moorcroft, model 01310/6, with a blue ground and a planished pewter mount stamped "Tudric, Moorcroft, 01310".

*c1916-23* *6.5in (16.5cm) high*

**£550-650** **GHOU**

### FIND OUT MORE...

**Moorcroft**, *by Paul Atterbury, published by Richard Dennis, 1998.*

## COLLECTORS' NOTES

- In 1921, the Carter & Co. Pottery in Poole, England acquired a subsidiary pottery that became known as Carter, Stabler & Adams. Known from early on as the 'Poole Pottery', the company soon became well known for its decorative wares.
- During the 1920s and 1930s, Truda Carter was a key designer. She produced patterns in a strongly modern, Art Deco style that was typified by stylised flowers and leaves, and geometric patterns. All pieces were hand thrown and hand-decorated.
- After the war, the company continued to be at the forefront of modern designs with their 'Contemporary' range. Designed by Alfred Burgess Read, simple geometric or curving linear patterns were set against plain colours. Where used, foliate designs were even more stylised and repeated, being set against plain white backgrounds.
- Read worked closely with thrower Guy Sydenham over shapes, and decorator Ruth Pavely over designs. Although some pre-war shapes were used, new, curving shapes were introduced. Many designs were influenced by Scandinavian designs of the period by those designers such as Stig Lindberg.
- In 1958, Robert Jefferson became the resident designer. Together with Sydenham and designer Tony Morris, he devised the Delphis range, which bridged the gap between commercial wares and increasingly fashionable studio pottery.
- Oranges, reds and bright greens and swirling abstract designs that typify the period are hallmarks of the range. The range has become extremely popular with collectors today. In 1966, the Craft Section of the pottery was founded, to produce unique studio pottery pieces and help create other decorative ranges.
- These included the Aegean, Ionian and Atlantis ranges, which have darker palettes and used a range of decorating techniques. In 2006, the pottery closed, but interest in their 20thC designs continues to increase.

A 1950s Poole Pottery 'PRB' pattern peanut-shaped freeform vase, shape no.701, designed by Guy Sydenham and Alfred Read, the base marked "Poole England 701".

*12.5in (32cm) high*

**£200-300** **GAZE**

A 1950s Poole Pottery 'Contemporary' range 'PQB' pattern vase, shape no.337, probably designed by John Adams, decorated by Gwen Haskins, the base with impressed and printed marks.

*9.75in (25cm) high*

**£180-220** **GAZE**

A 1950s Poole Pottery 'Contemporary' range 'YFT' pattern vase, shape no.687, decorated by Gwen Haskins and Jean Cockram, the base with printed, painted and impressed marks.

*6.75in (17cm) high*

**£60-80** **GAZE**

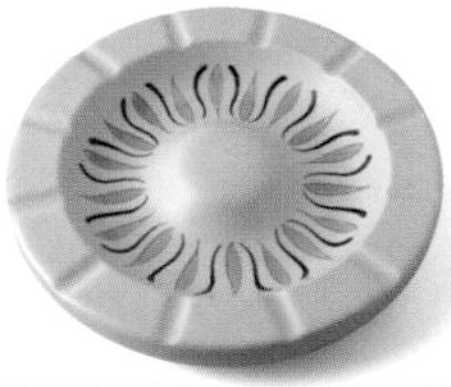

A Poole Pottery Freeform 'UFT' pattern club ashtray, shape no.217, the pattern designed by Ruth Pavely, the shape designed by Guy Sydenham.

*1956-57* *10in (25.5cm) diam*

**£80-150** **KCS**

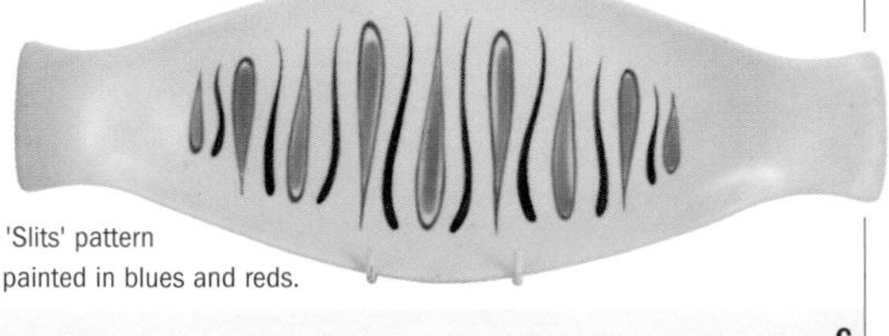

A 1950s Poole Pottery 'Slits' pattern shaped dish, painted in blues and reds.

**£35-45** **C**

## A CLOSER LOOK AT A DELPHIS BOWL

*This bowl is decorated with a mis-shapen 'alien' head, a typical feature of Cutler's work.*

*Cutler worked for Poole Pottery from 1969-76 and used a 'CC' monogram from 1970 - in 1976 she married and used a 'CK' monogram.*

*The mottling is undesirable and reduces the value.*

*This is typical of the Delphis range with its new palette of bright colours, and abstract, unique design.*

A Poole Pottery 'Delphis' bowl, shape no.89, painted by Carol Cutler.

*1969-75* *9in (23cm) wide*

**£80-120** **KCS**

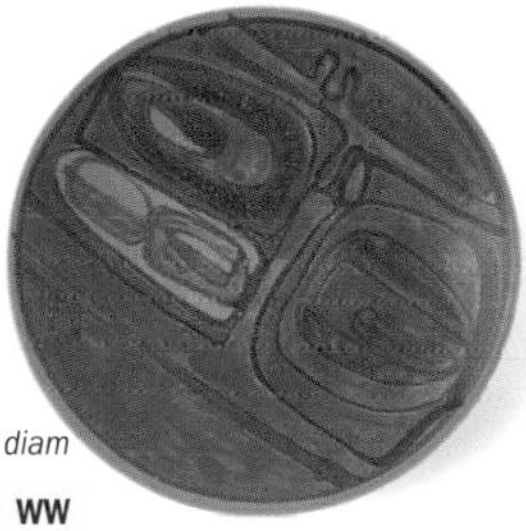

A Poole Pottery Delphis plate, decorated with a geometric design, the base with printed and painted marks.

*10.5in (26.5cm) diam*

**£180-220** **WW**

A Poole Pottery Delphis dish, decorated by Ann Godfrey, with textured, bubbled glaze.

*Ann Godfrey only used the 'A' mark during 1967, although she worked at Poole from 1965-70.*

*1967* *8in (20.5cm) diam*

**£60-80** **GAZE**

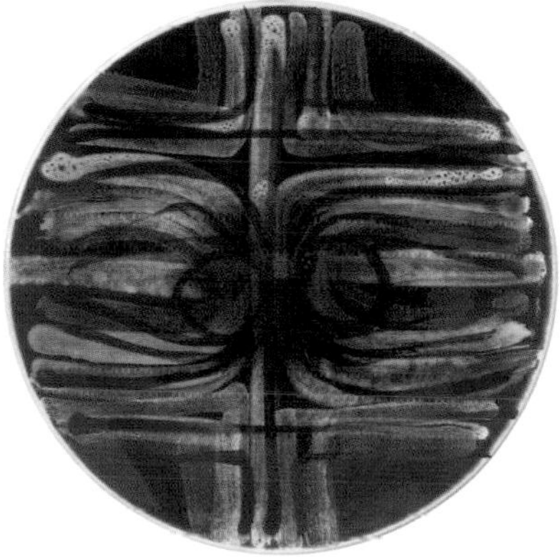

A Poole Pottery Delphis shape no.3 plate, painted by Geraldine O'Meara.

*1966* *8in (20cm) diam*

**£75-85** **KCS**

A Poole Pottery Delphis shape no.57 dish, painted by Carol Cutler.

*10.5in (26.5cm) diam*

**£60-80** **GAZE**

A Poole Pottery Delphis shape no.86 fruit dish, painted by Angela Wyburgh.

*Wyburgh used a 'II.' mark in 1968 only. Her work is increasingly desirable and values are rising.*

*1968* *5in (13cm) diam*

**£15-20** **GAZE**

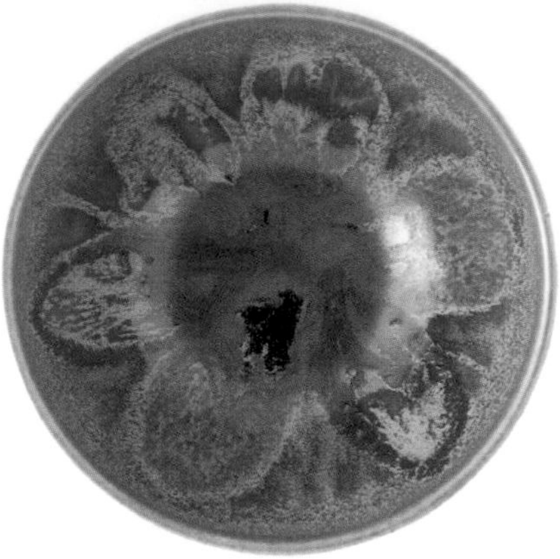

A Poole Pottery 'Delphis' bowl, painted by Thelma Bush, in metallic colours.

*The use of metallic paints was usually limited to Studio pieces. Thelma Bush trained at the Bournemouth and Poole Colleges of Art and worked for Poole Pottery from 1966-68.*

*5in (12.5cm) wide*

**£60-80** **KCS**

A Poole Pottery Delphis charger, painted by Sally Merch, with textured decoration.

*1968-69* *14in (35.5cm) diam*

**£100-150** **KCS**

A Poole Pottery Delphis shape no.49 dish, painted by Shirley Campbell.

*1968* *5in (12.5cm) diam*

**£40-60** **KCS**

A 1960s Poole Pottery Delphis plate, painted by Patricia Wells.

*8in (20cm) diam*

**£75-85** **KCS**

A late 1970s Poole Pottery Delphis footed bowl, shape no.40.

*This is an unusual shape.*

*10.5in (26.5cm) diam*

**£150-200** **KCS**

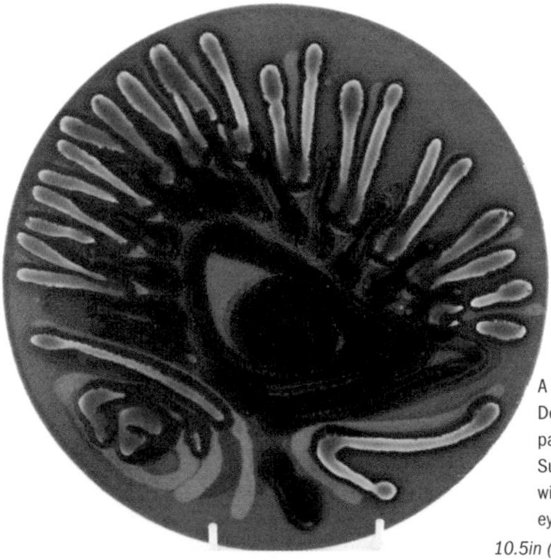

A Poole pottery Delphis dish, painted by Susan Allen, with an abstract eye design.

*10.5in (26.5cm) diam*

**£180-220** **C**

A Poole Pottery 'Delphis' range spear shaped dish, painted by for Cynthia Bennett, with hand-painted design and marked with artist's monogram.

*17.25in (44cm) long*

**£35-45** **GAZE**

A Poole Aegean 'Yachts' pattern shallow dish, designed by Leslie Elsden.

c1973 10.5in (27cm) diam

**£22-28** **GAZE**

## A CLOSER LOOK AT AN AEGEAN VASE

*This is an unusual form, with the waisted band appearing towards the base. It is usually found nearer the top on vases numbered with the same shape number.*

*It uses the sgrafitto technique, but also hints at the 'silhouette' technique with its coloured forms over a black ground.*

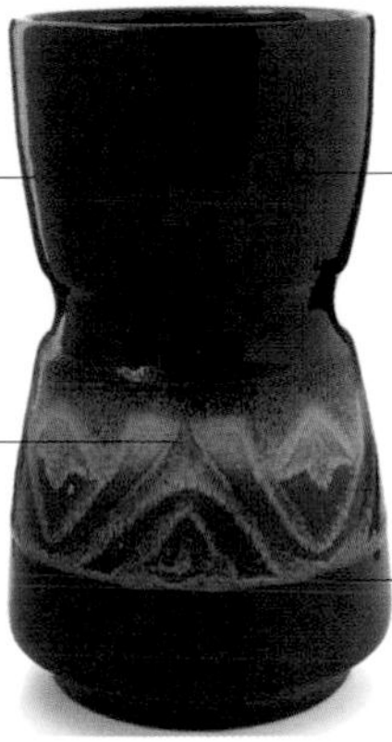

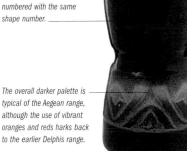

*The overall darker palette is typical of the Aegean range, although the use of vibrant oranges and reds harks back to the earlier Delphis range.*

*Aegean was introduced in 1970 on 22 standard shapes and was produced until 1980.*

A 1970s Poole Pottery 'Aegean' vase, shape no.84, with sgraffito decoration, indistinct painter's mark.

9.25in (23.5cm) high

**£120-150** **KCS**

A Poole Aegean charger, depicting a stylized sailor against the sea and a ship, the reverse printed "54" and with decorator's mark.

*This pattern was designed by Leslie Elsden, who developed much of the Aegean line.*

20.5in (52cm) diam

**£120-180** **GAZE**

A rare Poole Pottery Aegean 'Yacht' pattern shape no.3 plate, designed by Leslie Elsden and painted by Carolyn Willis, with sgraffito decoration.

1972-79 8in (20cm) diam

**£60-80** **KCS**

A 1970s Poole Pottery Aegean shape no.3 plate, the back stamped "Aegean".

*Despite looking very similar to the Delphis range, the rarely seen stamp on the base indicates this is from the Aegean range.*

8in (20cm) diam

**£60-80** **KCS**

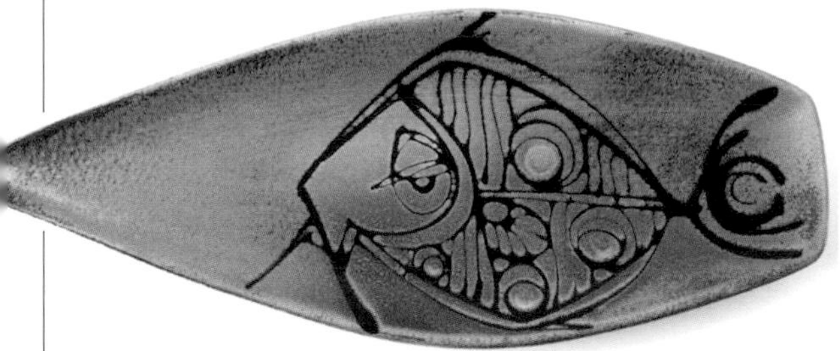

A 1970s Poole Pottery Aegean spear-shaped dish, painted with a stylized 'Silhouette' fish design, the back stamped "82".

17.5in (44.5cm) long

**£40-50** **GAZE**

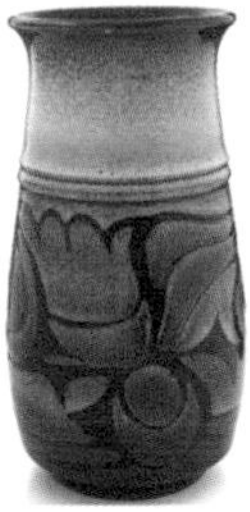

A 1970s Poole Pottery 'Aegean' shape no.84 vase, with silhouette and sgraffito decoration, indistinct painter's mark.

9in (23cm) high

**£80-120** **KCS**

A 1930s Poole pottery fish, shape no.334, finished in a pink glaze.

*8in (20cm) high*

**£120-180** **C**

A Poole Studio Pottery bear on a plinth, finished in a glossy blue glaze.

*This bear was inspired by Poole's 1930s animal figures. A leaping deer and an elephant on a plinth were also made.*

*1996* *8in (20cm) high*

**£50-70** **KCS**

A limited edition Poole Pottery 'Dolphin Blue' glazed seated rabbit figure, from an edition of 500.

*This is one of four rabbit poses produced in this range, the standing figure is the most desirable.*

*4in (10cm) high*

**£40-60** **KCS**

A Poole Pottery 'Dolphin Blue' glazed badger figure, designed by Barbara Linley Adams.

*Badger figurines can be found in four poses.*

*1989-90* *7in (18cm) long*

**£60-70** **KCS**

A rare Poole Pottery 'Dolphin Blue' glazed stoat figure, designed by Barbara Linley Adams.

*This model was only produced for one year.*

*1990* *6.75in (17cm) high*

**£70-90** **KCS**

A late 1970s/early 1980s Poole Pottery thrush on stump stoneware figure, designed by Barbara Linley Adams, signed on the base.

*Linley Adams trained at the Slade and Central School of Art and is an internationally renowned sculptor. As well as animal figurines, she also designed a series of animal plates.*

*7in (18cm) high*

**£120-180** **KCS**

A Poole Pottery small fawn figure on stand, shape no.772, designed by Barbara Linley Adams.

*1979-89* *5in (12.5cm) wide*

**£30-40** **KCS**

A Poole Pottery large model of a seated tabby cat, designed by Barbara Linley Adams.

**£250-350** **C**

## COLLECTORS' NOTES

- The Portmeirion Pottery was founded by Susan Williams-Ellis (b.1918), daughter of Sir Clough Williams-Ellis, architect and creator of Portmeirion village in North Wales. Trained in pottery under Bernard and David Leach, book illustration by Graham Sutherland and modelling by Henry Moore, she initially became a designer, working in illustration, textiles and wall murals.
- Her father asked her to run the Portmeirion gift shop in the mid-1950s, for which she developed designs that were produced by pottery-decorating company A.E. Gray & Co. Ltd. These early designs, based on black and white prints and spatter lustre ware, were successful and Williams-Ellis and her husband acquired Gray's in 1960. As their success grew, they also acquired Kirkhams Ltd, a company which manufactured white ceramic bodies, allowing them to control all aspects of production.
- Designs were screen- or transfer-printed, and hand-painted, until the release of her landmark moulded 'Totem' design in 1963. This met with great success and the style was later adapted into the 'Jupiter' and 'Cypher' patterns. All were produced in many colours, with the low relief moulded motifs showing in lighter tones. Other transfer-printed patterns, such as 'Tivoli' and 'Magic Garden' show her interest in textile design.
- From 1972, the company's production has been dominated by the popular 'Botanic Garden' range. Early and rare patterns such as 'Malachite' and 'Moss Agate', and key shapes such as 'Serif', tend to be the most desirable, and often the most valuable. Ranges that were highly successful, such as 'Totem', will generally be more commonly found today and as such are usually less valuable. Damage reduces value considerably, particularly on more common designs.

A Portmeirion Potteries Meridian shape transfer-printed 'Botanic Garden - Citron' dinner plate.

*When it was introduced, this pattern was available in 28 different species-based designs, based on 19thC botanical prints found in reference books.*

*Introduced 1972 7.25in (18.5cm) diam*

**£20-25 FFM**

A Portmeirion Potteries Meridian shape transfer-printed 'Botanic Garden - Night-Flowering Cactus' pattern dinner plate.

*Introduced 1972 8.25in (21cm) diam*

**£15-25 FFM**

A Portmeirion Potteries Serif shape 'Cypher' pattern coffee pot.

*Introduced 1963 11.75in (30cm) high*

**£20-25 FFM**

A Portmeirion Pottery 'Dolphin' pattern tea storage jar.

*This was the second design produced by Williams-Ellis for Portmeirion and was based on an engraving designed by her. Early examples were decorated with spattered bands of a lustre glaze.*

*Introduced 1960 6.5in (16.5cm) wide*

**£100-150 CHS**

A 1960s Portmeirion Potteries transfer-printed 'Greek Key' pattern sugar or flour sifter.

*Although white was the earliest colour, other colours such as yellow, purple and orange are more desirable.*

*6.5in (16.5cm) high*

**£20-25 FFM**

A Portmeirion Potteries Cylinder shape 'Greek Key' pattern coffee pot.

*1968-70s 13in (33cm) high*

**£25-35 FFM**

A Portmeirion Pottery 'Greek Key' pattern mug.

*5in (12.5cm) high*

**£15-20 CHS**

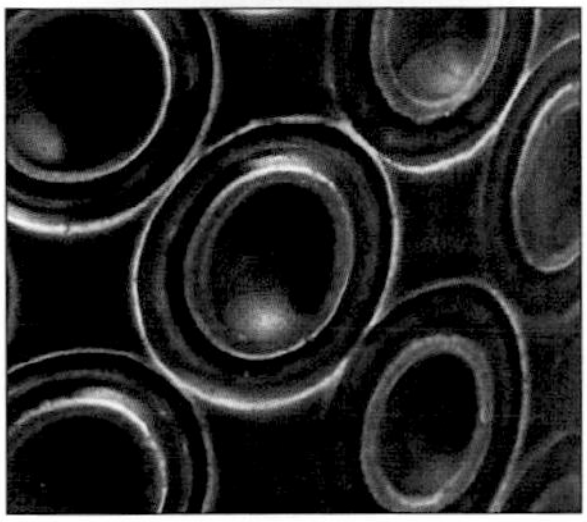

A Portmeirion Potteries Petrol Blue Serif shape 'Jupiter' pattern tureen with lid.

*The Petrol Blue was prone to fading when it came into contact with washing-up liquid, which at the time of the range's production was acidic, making strongly coloured examples scarce today.*

*Introduced 1964* *9in (23cm) wide*

**£20-30** **FFM**

## A CLOSER LOOK AT A PORTMEIRION JAR

*Moss Agate was an early pattern for the company, introduced c1961.*

*It was mainly applied to decorative pieces such as urns, boxes and storage jars.*

*Its 'cameo' effect gilt designs were costly to produce, meaning it was both expensive at the time and only produced for a few years – making it rare today.*

*It was designed by co-founder Susan Williams Ellis, using designs from an 18thC geological book.*

A Grays Pottery for Portmeirion 'Moss Agate' pattern jar.

*c1962* *3.75in (9.5cm) high*

**£300-400** **GGRT**

A Portmeirion Potteries Serif shape transfer-printed 'Magic City' pattern coffee cup and saucer.

*1966 to c1978*

*Saucer: 5in (13cm) diam*

**£5-8** **FFM**

A Portmeirion Potteries transfer-printed 'Monte Sol' pattern storage jar.

*Introduced 1966*

*6.25in (16cm) high*

**£20-25** **FFM**

A Portmeirion Potteries transfer-printed 'Pantomime' pattern plate.

*The characters shown were adapted from prints of Benjamin Pollock's Theatre Drawings. They were produced in other colours, including black and white.*

*Introduced 1966* *10in (25.5cm) diam*

**£30-40** **FFM**

A Portmeirion Potteries transfer-printed 'Sailing Ships' pattern wall plate.

*Introduced 1966* *8in (20.5cm) diam*

**£10-15** **FFM**

A Portmeirion Potteries Cylinder shape transfer-printed 'Velocipedes' pattern plate.

*These patterns were inspired by a 1920s article on the development of the cycle in The Strand magazine.*

*Introduced 1966* *7.25in (18.5cm) diam*

**£8-10** **FFM**

A Portmeirion Potteries Kings shape screen-printed 'Talisman' pattern cigarette box.

*Introduced 1962* *5.25in (13.5cm) wide*

**£20-30** **FFM**

A Portmeirion Potteries screen-printed 'Talisman' pattern storage jar.

*Introduced 1962* *6.25in (16cm) high*

**£15-25** **FFM**

A Portmeirion Potteries screen-printed 'Talisman' pattern jug.

*Introduced 1962* *7in (17.5cm) high*

**£15-25** **FFM**

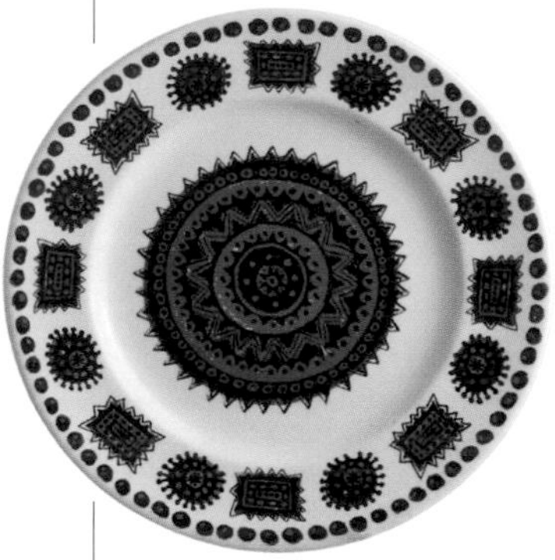

A Portmeirion Potteries screen-printed 'Talisman' pattern dinner plate.

*Introduced 1962* *10in (25.5cm) diam*

**£8-12** **FFM**

A Portmeirion Potteries 'Talisman' pattern mixing bowl.

*Talisman was the first screen-printed pattern produced by Portmeirion, due to Williams-Ellis' dissatisfaction with the quality of transfer-printing.*

*Introduced 1962* *11in (28cm) diam*

**£20-30** **FFM**

A Portmeirion Potteries 'Tivoli' pattern herb jar.

*This was inspired by a visit to the Tivoli gardens in Copenhagen, Denmark. Originally intended to be in brighter colours, it was Williams-Ellis' Sales Director Frank Thrower (later Designer at Dartington Glass) who persuaded her to use a more sober palette.*

*Introduced 1964* *4.25in (10.5cm) high*

**£8-12** **FFM**

A Portmeirion Potteries white Cylinder shape 'Totem' pattern coffee pot.

*This pattern was reintroduced in 2002.*

*1963-c1976* *13in (33cm) high*

**£20-30** **FFM**

Two Portmeirion Potteries 'Totem' pattern soup goblets, with matte white and olive green glazes.

*Introduced 1963* *Tallest 5in (12.5cm) high*

**£15-20 EACH** **FFM**

A Portmeirion Potteries cobalt blue 'Totem' pattern meat plate.

*1963-c1976* *5.75in (14.5cm) diam*

**£20-35** **FFM**

**FIND OUT MORE...**

**Portmeirion Pottery,** *by Steven Jenkins and Stephen McKay, published by Richard Dennis, 2000.*

A Rosenthal vase, designed by Hans Balimann, with transfer-printed gold design, some restoration, the base with printed marks and signature.

*c1960* *9.75in (25cm) high*

**£60-80** **TCM**

A Rosenthal Netter tall yellow cylinder vase, with rough surface and bright onion-shaped patterns, the base painted "Made in Italy" and with company range label.

*11.75in (30cm) high*

**£80-120** **HLM**

An Italian Rosenthal Netter brown globe vase, with multicoloured hand-painted bands, painted "Made In Italy" on the base, with a label.

*5.75in (14.5cm) high*

**£50-70** **HLM**

A 1980s Rosenthal stylized seated cat figurine, designed by Otmark Alt, model no.1139/29, painted in colours, with factory marks to the base.

*Alt has worked for Rosenthal since 1978. This is typical of his brightly coloured work that is also often a caricature of human emotion.*

*11.5in (29cm) high*

**£500-600** **HERR**

A 1970s Rosenthal Studio Line vase, designed by Björn Wiinblad, with white matte and glazed body with moulded abstract bird motifs.

**£30-50** **MHT**

A Rosenthal lidded box, designed by Björn Wiinblad, with 'We're all fishing for the perfect design' transfer printed caption and fishing scene.

*6in (15cm) wide*

**£20-30** **GAZE**

A Rosenthal figurine of a young girl dressed as a Spanish senorita, designed by Claire Weiss, factory marks to base.

*9.25in (23.5cm) high*

**£220-280** **JN**

A limited edition late 1960s Rosenthal Studio Line wall plaque, designed by Victor Vasarely, with marks to base and original certificate.

*Victor Vasarely (1908-97) worked for Rosenthal from 1964.*

*16in (40.5cm) high*

**£600-700** **HERR**

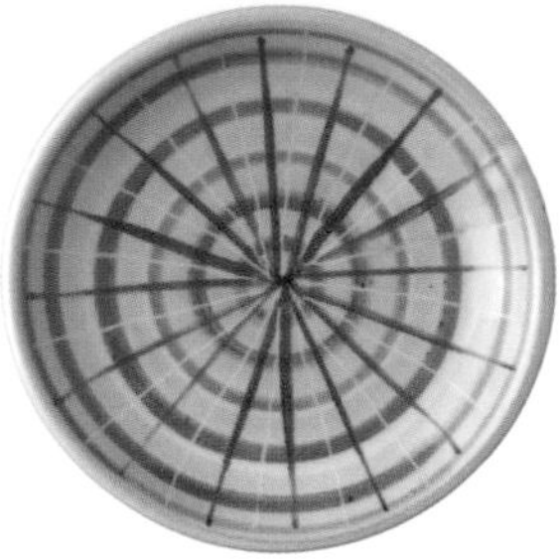

A Rye Pottery pin or butter dish, with hand-painted yellow and blue circular pattern and black stylized star.

*3.25in (8.5cm) diam*

**£30-40** **GAZE**

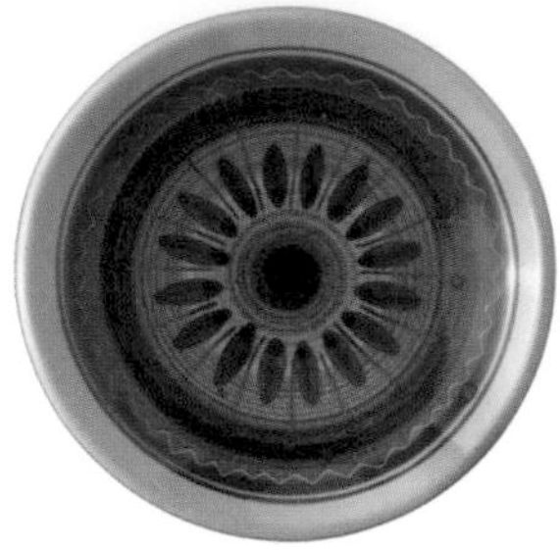

A Rye Pottery pin or butter dish, with hand-painted blue, pink and red circles and stylized flower motif, with blue centre.

*3.25in (8cm) diam*

**£25-35** **GAZE**

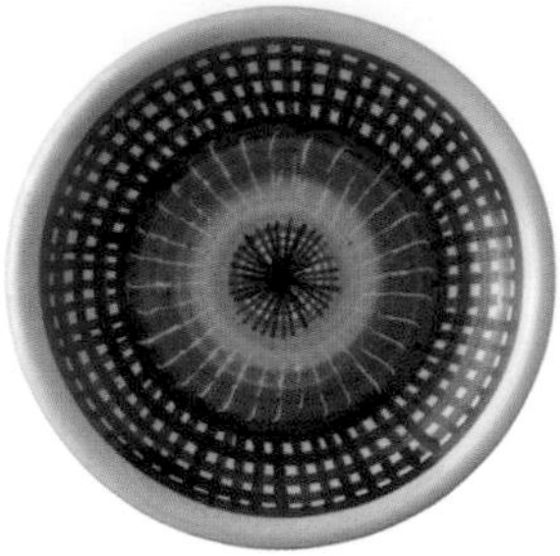

A Rye Pottery pin or butter dish, hand-painted with black lines and a stylized star pattern.

*3.25in (8.5cm) diam*

**£20-30** **GAZE**

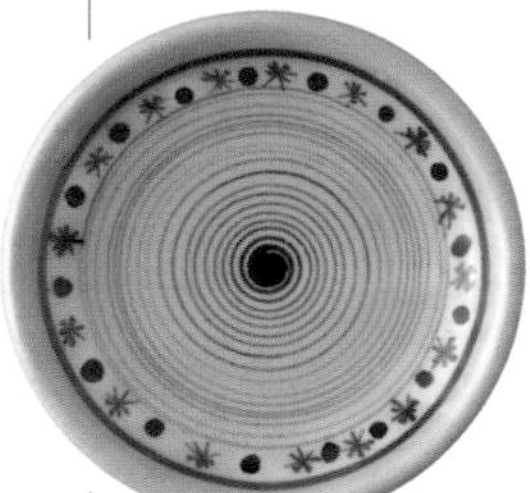

A Rye Pottery pin or patter dish, hand-painted with concentric circles and star-and-dot motifs.

*3.25in (8.5cm) diam*

**£25-35** **GAZE**

A Rye Pottery elliptical bowl, hand-painted with coloured stripes and thin black lines, the base impressed "R".

*2.25in (5.5cm) high*

**£30-50** **GAZE**

A Rye Pottery elliptical bowl, hand-painted with stars and red dots, the base impressed "D".

*The impressed 'D' indicates that David Sharp threw this particular piece. Pottery has been produced in and around Rye since the Middle Ages, but much of today's interest is in the pottery designed and made by David Sharp from 1956 into the 1960s. The town has had many potters and potteries, including 'The Monastery', set up by Sharp's business partner George Gray, and Dennis Townsend's 'Iden Pottery'. Values are steadily creeping up again after peaking and then falling a couple of years ago.*

*2.25in (5.5cm) high*

**£40-60** **GAZE**

A Rye Pottery cylindrical vase, hand-painted with green dots on yellow squares and purple bands, the base impressed "D".

*4in (10cm) high*

**£30-40** **GAZE**

A Rye Pottery tapered footed vase, hand-painted with alternating black lines and yellow and black chevrons, the base impressed "D".

*3.25in (8.5cm) high*

**£30-50** **GAZE**

A Rye Pottery 'Mosaic' tankard, with hand-painted multicoloured hatched design, and green bands, unmarked.

*5.5in (14cm) high*

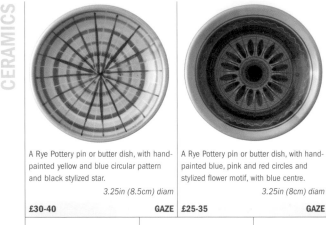

**£40-60** **GAZE**

## COLLECTORS' NOTES

- Post-war developments in Scandinavian ceramic design set the tone for much of the production not only in Scandinavia throughout the late 20thC, but also across the world. Leading factories such as Rorstrand, Gustavsberg, Royal Copenhagen and Arabia employed designers such as Wilhelm Käge, Stig Lindberg, Gunnar Nylund and Kaj Franck to produce designs for ceramics that are modern, and often refer to the natural environment and handmade crafts.
- Value is primarily indicated by the factory and designer, with major names such as those listed above tending to fetch higher prices. Consider form, glaze and size carefully, as these will also have a bearing on value. Particularly noteworthy are the influential faïence designs produced by Stig Lindberg for Gustavsberg from the late 1940s onwards. Tableware is generally more affordable than hand-decorated art ceramics.
- Smaller factories such as Upsala Ekeby, Saxbo and Palshus can offer a more affordable entry point for new collectors. The haresfur glazes used by Per Linnemann-Schmidt at Palshus are particularly sought after. Look for typical hallmarks of this period of design, such as clean-lined modern forms, or highly stylised natural or other motifs. Colours can vary from earthy, strong colours to jaunty, bright and colourful designs, the latter typically used for tableware.
- Marks on the base will often help identify a factory and designer, although it is worth consulting reference books and visiting museum collections to build up an 'eye' for a particular designer's work. Away from factory production, studio ceramics are also rising in terms of desirability and value, partly as many experimental designs influenced later styles. Names such as Arne Bang, Conny Walther and Bode Willumsen are worth looking out for.

A Swedish Rorstrand studio pottery (atelje) vase, glazed with brown and dark grey bands, designed by Inger Persson, with painted marks to base.

*Persson (b.1936) worked for Rorstrand from 1959-71 before setting up her own studio. In 1969, she won the gold medal at Faenza.*

*10.5in (26.5cm) high*

**£40-60** **GAZE**

A Swedish Rorstrand studio pottery (atelje) earthenware vase, designed by Drejar Gruppen.

*7.5in (19cm) high*

**£30-40** **GAZE**

A Swedish Rorstrand stoneware vase, designed by Drejar Gruppen.

*8.5in (21.5cm) high*

**£40-60** **GAZE**

A Swedish Rorstrand stoneware pot, designed by Drejar Gruppen.

*6in (15cm) high*

**£40-60** **GAZE**

A Swedish Rorstrand ochre glazed waisted stoneware vase, designed by Gunnar Nylund.

*10.25in (26cm) high*

**£30-50** **GAZE**

A Swedish Rorstrand large vase, with blue glaze over-studded decoration, designed by Gunnar Nylund.

*12.25in (31cm) high*

**£60-90** **GAZE**

A Swedish Rorstrand green glazed vase incised with wavy lines, designed by Gunnar Nylund.

*10.75in (27.3cm)*

**£150-200** **ADE**

A Swedish Rorstrand 'Havana' range vase, designed by Carl-Harry Stålhane.

*Not only is the moulded pattern inspired by tribal and ancient art forms, but the form is reminiscent of African tribal head rests.*

*9.75in (25cm) high*

**£40-60** **GAZE**

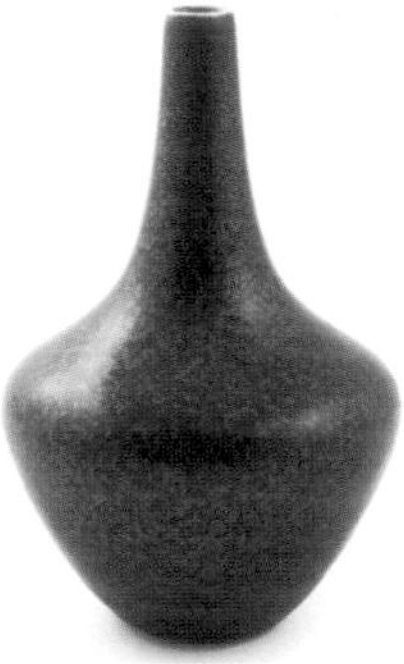

A Swedish Rorstrand vase, with speckled black glaze, designed by Carl-Harry Stålhane.

*6.25in (16cm) high*

**£150-200** **RWA**

A Swedish Rorstrand heart-shaped shallow dish with a graduated blue glaze with brown edges, designed by Gunnar Nylund.

*9in (22.5cm) long*

**£40-60** **GAZE**

## A CLOSER LOOK AT A MINIATURE VASE

*Miniature vases and bowls are highly sought-after by collectors and have high values considering their small size.*

*They were made by a number of factories - look out for those by Gustavsberg, particularly examples by Stig Lindberg.*

*The base is marked with Stålhane's monogram, showing he designed and probably made it.*

*Miniature pieces are often glazed with high quality, interesting and subtly varied glazes that cannot be found on other, larger pieces.*

A Swedish Rorstrand miniature stoneware vase, in a graduated orange-brown tri-colour glaze, handmade by Carl-Harry Stålhane.

*4.25in (11cm) high*

**£80-120** **GAZE**

A 1960s Swedish Rorstrand leaf dish, glazed in red and glossy cream, with incised veins, possibly designed by Gunnar Nylund.

*Leaf shapes are typical of the inspiration from nature that many Scandinavian designers drew on at this time. Perhaps the best known are those by Stig Lindberg for Gustavsberg.*

*11in (28cm) wide*

**£70-100** **MHT**

A Swedish Rorstrand 'Lavende' hand-painted charger, impressed "3561" and with decorator's mark.

*13.75in (35cm) diam*

**£12-18** **GAZE**

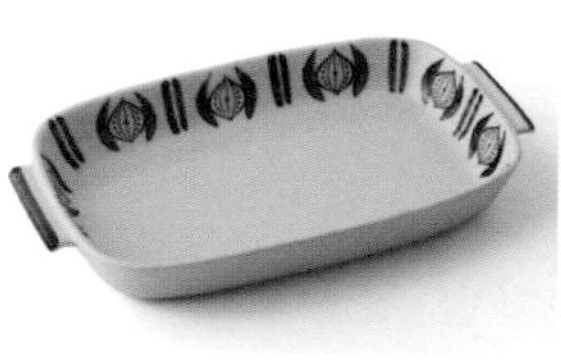

A 1950s Swedish Rorstrand 'Delikat' printed and hand-painted vase, designed by Marianne Westmann.

*Many Scandinavian ceramics produced at this time had patterns that were interchangeable, so people could mix and match between ranges and colourways.*

**£40-60** **MHT**

A set of three Swedish Rorstrand cups and saucers, with various printed patterns.

*c1965*

**£35-45** **MHT**

## A CLOSER LOOK AT A RORSTRAND STOAT

*Gunnar Nylund's range of animal figures is very rare, and also highly collectable.*

*It is marked as factory second quality but there appears to be only some pimples in the glaze, and no other flaws.*

*Here he combines an understanding of the elegance of natural form with a high quality, subtle glaze that itself recalls the natural environment.*

*Gunnar Nylund was highly influential, as Art Director at Rorstrand from 1931-58, and then working for glass maker Strömbergshyttan and Danish ceramics maker Nymølle.*

A rare 1950s Swedish Rorstrand stoat figure, by Gunnar Nylund, with brown shiny and matt glazes, marked to base with incised "R" with three crowns, and "GN".

*9in (23cm) long*

**£120-180** **RWA**

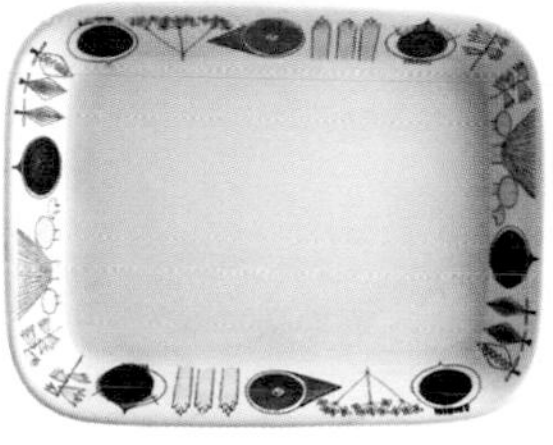

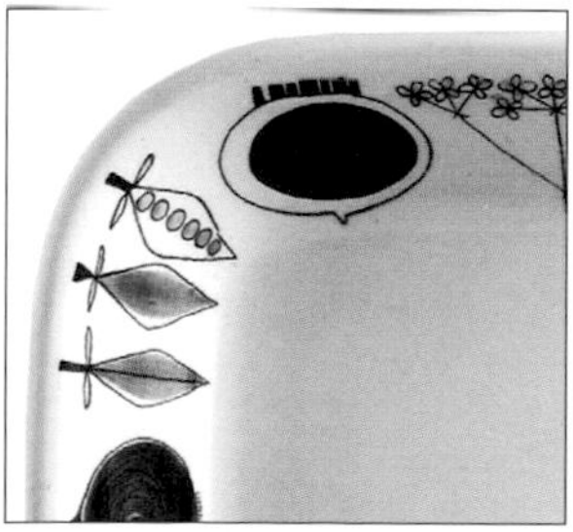

A Rorstrand Sweden 'Picknick' pattern serving dish, designed by Marianne Westmann, printed and hand-painted.

*c1960* *14.25in (36cm) wide*

**£30-50** **FFM**

A Rorstrand Sweden 'Picknick' pattern tureen with lid, designed by Marianne Westmann, printed and hand-painted.

*This popular range was printed with black outlines and then hand-decorated with colours. Finally, a solid colour lid was added. It was designed in 1956 and produced until 1969 in various patterns.*

*8.75in (22cm) high*

**£40-60** **FFM**

A Swedish Gustavsberg faïence dish, with a hand-painted striped and oval pattern, designed by Stig Lindberg.

*10.25in (26cm) wide*

**£250-300** **GGRT**

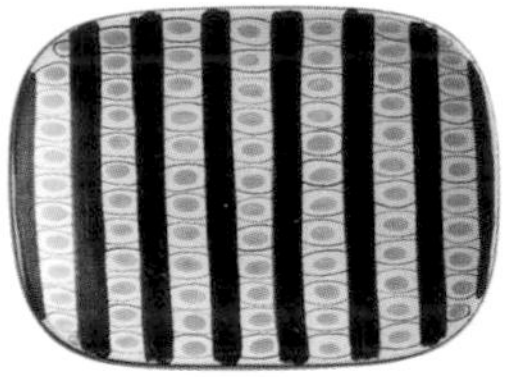

A Swedish Gustavsberg faïence dish, designed by Stig Lindberg, with a hand-painted striped and oval pattern.

*10in (25cm) wide*

**£250-300** **GGRT**

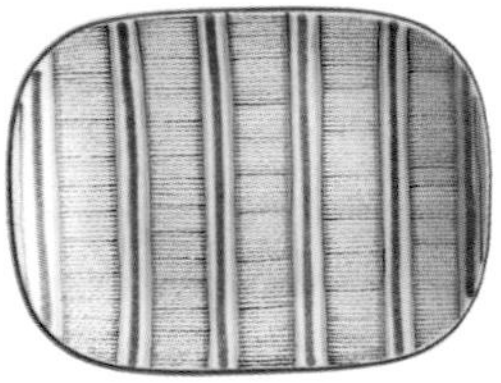

A Swedish Gustavsberg oblong platter, designed by Stig Lindberg, with a hand-painted striped and dragged pattern, with original trade labels to base.

*12.75in (32.5cm) long*

**£300-400** **GGRT**

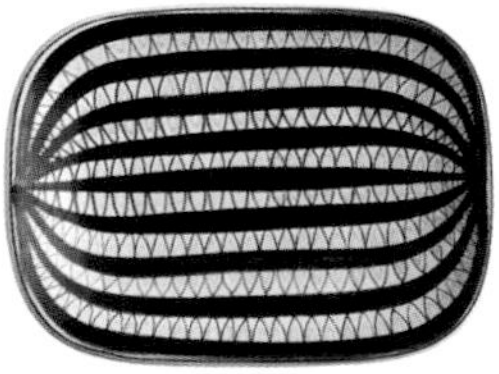

A Swedish Gustavsberg ovoid bowl, designed by Stig Lindberg, with a hand-painted blue and white striped and zig-zag pattern, with original trade labels to base.

*10.5in (26.5cm) wide*

**£200-300** **GGRT**

## A CLOSER LOOK AT A GUSTAVSBERG PLATTER

*Faïence is the term used to describe tin-glazed earthenware.*

*Gustavsberg's pieces took a truly Modern look at natural themes in terms of their form and decoration.*

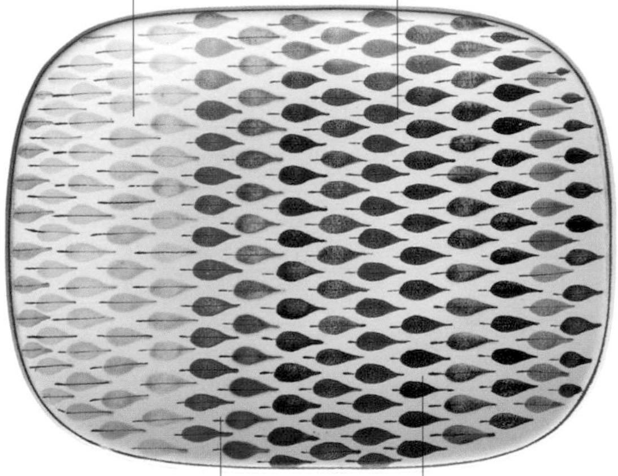

*Designed and produced from 1942 onwards, these ceramics were highly influential, inspiring factories such as Rye and Poole Pottery in the UK, as well as other Scandinavian factories.*

*Brightly coloured and extremely appealing, they anticipated the 'Op Art' movement championed by Bridget Riley by nearly a decade.*

A Swedish Gustavsberg faïence oblong platter, with hand-painted teardrop design, designed by Stig Lindberg.

*12.5in (31.5cm) wide*

**£300-500** **GGRT**

A Swedish Gustavsberg freeform bowl, designed by Stig Lindberg, with a blue and white striped and dash pattern, with original trade labels to base.

*Note the form, which is like a curling leaf.*

*10.5in (26.5cm) wide*

**£280-320** **GGRT**

A Swedish Gustavsberg round dish, designed by Stig Lindberg, with a hand-painted blue and yellow lattice pattern.

*8in (20.5cm) wide*

**£150-200** **GGRT**

A Swedish Gustavsberg dish, designed by Stig Lindberg, with a blue and yellow lattice pattern.

*8in (20.5cm) wide*

**£150-200** **GGRT**

A Swedish Gustavsberg vase, designed by Stig Lindberg, of melon shape with pink stripes and scalloped collar.

*c1940-50* *8.5in (21.5cm) wide*

**£300-400** **GGRT**

A Swedish Gustavsberg hand-painted baluster vase, decorated by Maja Snis and designed by Stig Lindberg, with bands of brown and green dots in circles.

*The painted marks on the base indicate that it was designed by Stig Lindberg (the hand) and decorated by Maja Snis (the fish).*

*10.5in (26.5cm) high*

**£300-400** **GC**

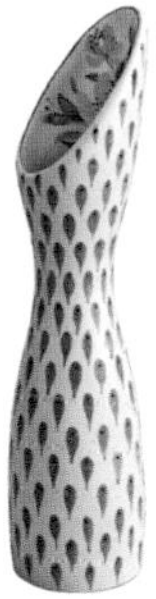

A Swedish Gustavsberg vase, designed by Stig Lindberg, hand-painted with a yellow and blue teardrop pattern.

*Although the form and pattern on the exterior are very modern, there are somewhat more traditional flowers painted on the inside of the neck. The multi-coloured teardrop pattern can be found on a range of shapes.*

*c1950* *11.75in (30cm) wide*

**£200-250** **GGRT**

A Swedish Gustavsberg 'Pelle' figurine, designed by Lisa Larson, the base painted "Pelle Sweden L.L".

*Larson is better known for her popular 'Kennel' series of dog figurines.*

*1962-79* *7in (18cm) high*

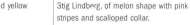

**£60-100** **RWA**

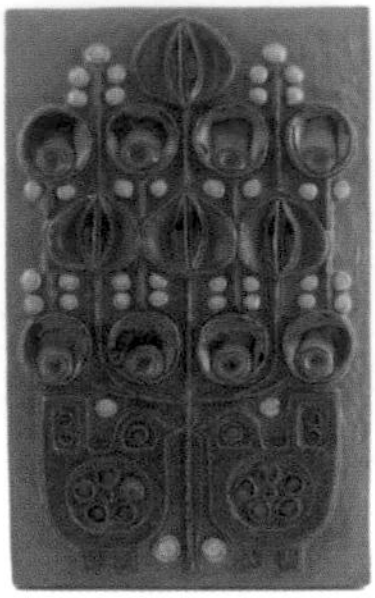

A Danish Michael Andersen wall plaque, designed by Marianne Starck, with low relief birds and tree design in brown and blue glazes.

*c1970s* *13.25in (34cm) high*

**£80-100** **RWA**

A pair of Danish Michael Andersen giraffes, glazed in yellow, brown and black, with fish mark to base and "Michael Andersen & Son, Ronne, Dänemark".

*12.75in (32cm) high*

**£40-60** **WDL**

A 1950s Danish Michael Andersen & Sons deer figure, designed by Peter Hald, marked to base with impressed underglaze three fish in shield mark, incised "Hald" and written "Hald".

*5.25in (16cm) high*

**£60-100** **RWA**

A Finish Arabia blue and white printed coffee cup and saucer.

**£3-5** **GAZE**

A Finnish Arabia pottery oviform vase, impressed factory marks, the base inscribed "JM".

*15.5in (39cm) high*

**£180-220** **DN**

A Finnish Arabia studio vase, with hand-painted blue rectangular design with black lines.

*10.25in (26cm) high*

**£30-40** **GAZE**

## A CLOSER LOOK AT A PAIR OF CREAM BOTTLES

*The Modernist angularity based on geometric forms is typical of Kaj Franck's designs.*

*These were designed from 1950-55 as part of the 'Kilta' range, launched in 1952, which was intended to be simple to produce and inexpensive.*

*He designed similar forms during the 1950s for glass company Nuutajärvi Nöstjo.*

*These particular forms were not put into large scale production, and can be quite hard to find.*

A pair of Finnish Arabia cream bottles with cork stoppers, shape MM, designed by Kaj Frank, with a dark brown glaze.

*5.5in (14cm) high*

**£35-45** **GAZE**

A 1920s Danish Bing & Grøndahl squat stoneware vase, designed by Gunnar Nylund, with impressed factory mark, "Model Nylund" and number 3227 to base.

*5in (13cm) high*

**£120-180** **RWA**

A Danish Aluminia 'Carlsberg' commemorative plate, the plate crested with a crown and leaves in blue and brown above a square tower, painted and impressed mark to base.

*1908* *10in (25.5cm) wide*

**£35-45** **JN**

A Danish Royal Copenhagen large 'Fajance' vase, designed by Johanne Gerber, with monogram and marked "Royal Copenhagen Denmark", numbered "805" over "3259".

*8.75in (22cm) high*

**£70-100** **FD**

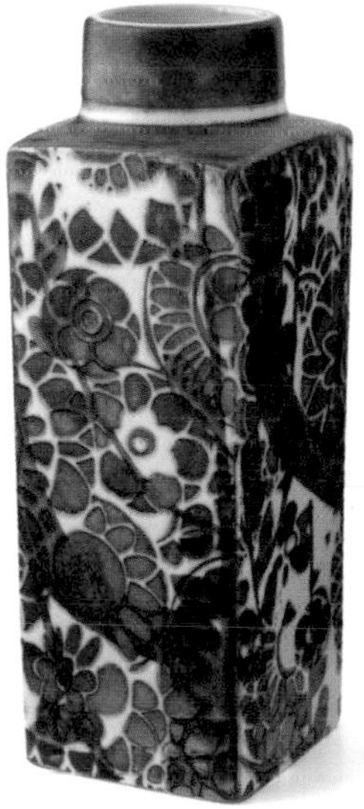

A 1970s Danish Royal Copenhagen 'Baca' vase, by Johanne Gerber, with factory, model and decorator's marks on base.

*8.75in (22cm) high*

**£60-80** **GC**

A Norwegian Figgjo Fajanse 12-piece 'Lotte' dinner service, designed by Turi Gramstad-Oliver, hand-painted and silk-screen printed.

*Gramstad-Oliver (b.1938) worked for Figgjo Fajanse from 1960-80, and also produced its Market, Astrid and Tor Viking services.*

*Pot: 9in (23cm) wide*

**£60-80** **GAZE**

A 1950s Norwegian Figgjo Flint ashtray, with screen-printed decoration of tribesmen.

*5.5in (24cm) wide*

**£18-22** **GROB**

A set of six Swedish Ganiopta small storage jars, with printed and painted designs and rosewood tops.

*3in (7.5cm) high*

**£22-28** **GAZE**

A Danish Palshus lamp base, designed by Per Linnemann-Schmidt, with blue-grey haresfur glaze.

*13.25in (34cm) high*

**£100-150** **RWA**

A Danish Palshus large flared bottle vase, designed by Per Linnemann-Schmidt, the base inscribed "1179/2".

*13.5in (34.5cm) high*

**£100-150** **GAZE**

A Danish Palshus 'Torpedo' vase, with blue haresfur glaze, designed by Per Linnemann-Schmidt.

*c1950s 8.5in (22cm) high*

**£180-200** **RWA**

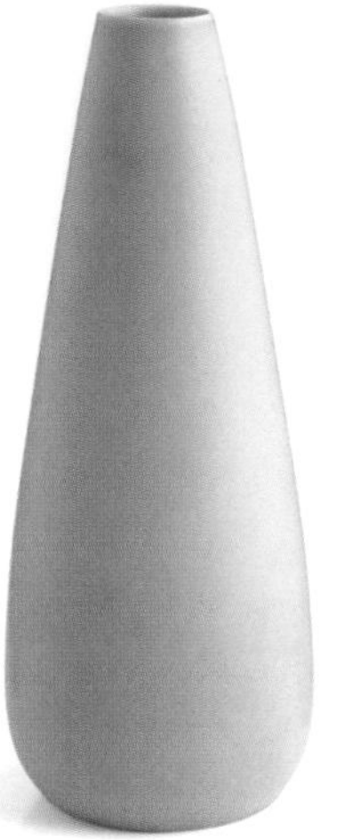

A rare 1950s Danish Palshus tapered stoneware vase, designed by Per Linnemann-Schmidt, with beige haresfur glaze, marked to base with incised "Palshus Denmark", "PL-S" and "1126/2".

*Haresfur glazes are known for their soft and subtly varying streaked colours, often in bold tones. Blue is one of the more desirable colours, and this light beige is rare.*

*9in (23cm) high*

**£200-300** **RWA**

A Norwegian Stavangerflint oval platter, with transfer-printed and painted decoration.

*13.25in (33.5cm) long*

**£12-18** **GAZE**

A large Danish Søholm Stentoj dish, dated.

*1961 14.25in (36.5cm) diam*

**£50-80** **GAZE**

A 1950s Swedish Upsala Ekeby chamotte stoneware dish, designed by Mari Simmulson, marked "UE", "4062" and "Mari S".

*To achieve its characteristic rough texture, chamotte clay is fired, smashed and mixed with more chamotte, worked and then refired.*

*7.75in (20cm) wide*

**£70-100** **ADE**

A Swedish Upsala Ekeby vase, probably designed by Mari Simmulson, with sgraffito decoration.

*Estonian Mari Summulson worked for Gustavsberg from 1945-49, and then Upsala Ekeby from 1949-72.*

*9.75in (24.5cm)*

**£10-15** **GAZE**

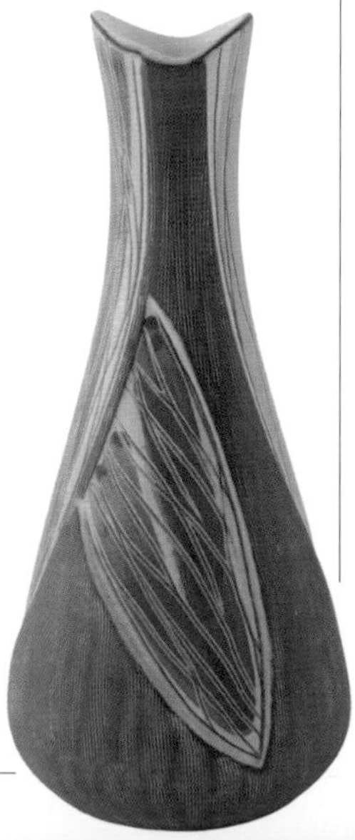

A Danish Arne Bang stoneware vase, with ribbed (cog) design.

*c1930s-40s* *3.25in (8cm) high*

**£60-80** **RWA**

A 1930s-40s Danish Arne Bang studio bowl, with a speckled blue glaze and ribbed decoration.

*Arne Bang (1901-83) was the brother of renowned Danish glass and ceramics Jacob Bang, who is most notable for his Modernist designs for Holmegaard & Kastrup. Arne opened his first studio in 1932. He won many prizes and was a major influence on Scandinavian ceramic design. His forms are typically simple and Modernist, and ribs and lightly textured, sober glazes were hallmarks of his designs. Natural motifs can also be found.*

*7.5in (19cm) diam*

**£120-160** **RWA**

A 1930s-40s Danish Arne Bang workshop fluted edge bowl, marked to base with painted "AB" and pattern number "108".

*4.5in (11.5cm) diam*

**£50-80** **RWA**

A 1930s-40s Danish Arne Bang workshop vase, with brown and beige glaze.

*5in (12.5cm) high*

**£80-120** **RWA**

A 1930s/40s Danish Arne Bang workshop fawn figurine, with a mottled brown glaze, marked to base with painted "AB" and pattern number "16".

*5in (12.5cm) high*

**£80-120** **RWA**

A Danish Jeppe Hagedorn-Olsen studio oblong dish, with rough applied clay decoration, thick brown, fawn and grey-blue high-glazes, marked to base with incised full signature with "M.G.S. 84".

*Interest in Scandinavian studio ceramics is increasing. Due to the way they are made, each piece is unique, with many influencing designs in the 1960s and '70s. Interest in Hagedorn-Olsen, and his abstract designs, is increasing.*

*1984* *6.5in (26.5cm) wide*

**£60-100** **RWA**

A Danish 1950s-60s Eigil Hinchisen studio vase.

*5.25in (13.5cm) high*

**£70-100** **RWA**

A 1960s Danish Jørgen Mogensen studio vase, with relief decoration of faces and symbols in brown and fawn glazes, marked to base with painted "F051" and "JM" monogram with label.

*7.75in (19.5cm) high*

**£120-180** **RWA**

A 1950s/60s Danish Finn Lynggaard studio stoneware bottle vase, in brown glaze with ring of exposed body at base, marked to base with impressed Lynggaard studio mark and painted signature.

*The size of this piece, at over 15 inches, is particularly notable.*

*15.5in (39.5cm) high*

**£200-250** **RWA**

A Carl-Harry Stålhane design studio dish, brushed glaze decoration.

*10.75in (27.5cm) diam*

**£25-35** **GAZE**

A ceramic sculpture of a robot, possibly Swedish, impressed "Bergsten".

*6in (15cm) high*

**£60-80** **TCM**

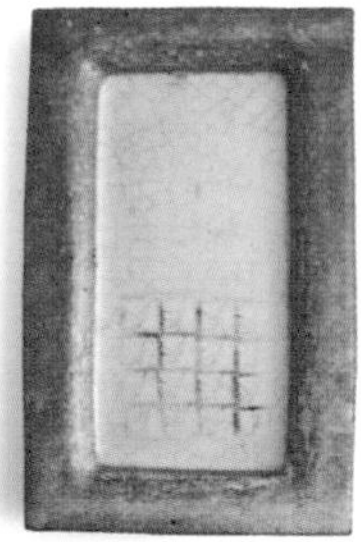

A 1960s Danish Conny Walther studio oblong tray, with blue-grey mottled glaze on edge and grey glaze to recessed centre, marked to base with impressed "CW" and original retailer's label for Meyers of Esbjerg Denmark.

*12in (30.5cm) long*

**£70-100** **RWA**

A 1930s Danish Bode Willumsen studio vase, with shiny green-brown glaze, marked to base incised indistinct "BW" studio mark.

*6.25in (16cm) high*

**£120-180** **RWA**

A 1960s Danish Conny Walther studio large squat chamotte earthenware vase, with a thick grey-blue glaze running down to base, very light crazing all over glaze, marked to the base impressed "CW Conny Walther" studio mark.

*4.5in (11cm) high*

**£120-180** **RWA**

## FIND OUT MORE...

**Scandinavian Ceramics & Glass in the Twentieth Century**, *by Jennifer Opie, published by V&A Publications, 2001.*

**Scandinavian Design**, *by Charlotte & Peter Fiell, published by Taschen, 2002.*

## COLLECTORS' NOTES

- Strehla was founded in 1828 and takes its name from the town it was established in, north west of Meissen and Dresden in Saxony, Germany. Like most ceramics factories, it produced a wide range of functional wares, tablewares and decorative pieces. Under Communist rule from the 1950s to the 1980s, the company produced decorative ceramics similar to those produced on the other side of the Iron Curtain.
- From the late 1960s and 70s one of hallmarks of Strehla's decorative pieces was the use of a 'lava' type glaze that is tube-lined onto the surface to form a design or pattern. This typically contrasts strongly against less textured or flat, glossy or matte glazes. Generally speaking, Strehla designs are more conservative and lack the whacky, highly experimental edge of West German designs.
- All pieces were moulded on a production line basis and decorated by hand, as indicated by the base stamp 'Handgemalt' (hand-decorated). Many elements also found in West German designs, such as decorative handles with no intended function and cubic or exaggerated forms, are also found in Strehla's designs. The goblet vase form, however, is more typically associated with Strehla.
- Arguably, the success of many designs varies widely, as does the quality, with later pieces tending to be of poorer quality. Many pieces are marked for export to the West, and it is likely that a fair proportion of pieces made were exported, although examples tend to be less easily found today than those by West German makers.

An East German Strehla goblet, with tube-lined black lava, and orange and red glossy glazed swirls, the base with "Made in GDR" ink stamp, and impressed "7285".

*9in (23cm) high*

**£20-30** **GC**

An East German Strehla goblet vase, with matte black lava tube-lined stylized floral patterns and glossy yellow glaze, the base stamped "Foreign".

*7.25in (18.5cm) high*

**£20-25** **GC**

An East German Strehla vase, with orange and mottled brown glazes, the base "Strehla" ink stamp and impressed "7232".

*8in (20cm) high*

**£20-25** **GC**

An East German Strehla vase, with glossy graduated blue glaze and matte black lava tubelined decoration, the base with "Strehla made in GDR" ink stamp.

*8.25in (21cm) high*

**£20-30** **GC**

An East German Strehla waisted vase, with green glazes and matte black lava tube-lined foliate design, the base impressed "23".

*11.5in (29.5cm) high*

**£20-25** **GC**

An East German Strehla torpedo vase, with dripped and tube-lined blue glaze over red, the base with "Strehla Handgemalt" ink stamp.

*This is very close to many of the colours and dripping glazes used by West German makers such as Scheurich.*

*10.75in (27cm) high*

**£30-40** **GC**

An East German Strehla cylinder vase, with tube-lined green decoration over a yellow ground.

*5.5in (14cm) high*

**£20-30** **GC**

An East German Strehla jug vase, with tube-lined black lava glaze banded and circle design over a blue glaze, the base with "Strehla Keramik Import handgemalt" black ink stamp.

*7in (18cm) high*

**£30-40** **GC**

An East German Strehla jug vase, with hand-painted green and yellow flowers on a mottled creamy ground, the base impressed "Strehla GDR 9013".

*5.75in (14.5cm) high*

**£15-20** **GC**

An East German Strehla bulbous jug vase, with brown lava tubelined pattern and glossy yellow glaze on a matte creamy glaze ground, the base impressed "9017 Strehla GDR".

*6in (15.5cm) high*

**£15-20** **GC**

An East German Strehla squat globe vase, with rough lava type brown glaze and glossy blue glaze over a cream glazed ground, the base impressed "1421 Strehla GDR".

*6in (15.5cm) high*

**£20-30** **GC**

An East German Strehla cube vase, with matte creamy-beige lava glaze over a glossy red glaze, the base impressed "Strehla 1300".

*Rectangular or cubic ceramic vases with small openings seem to have been a European post war preoccupation - West German, East German and Italian factories made examples in a variety of designs.*

*6.75in (17cm) high*

**£25-30** **GC**

An East German Strehla vase, with tube-line black lava glaze leaf design, the base with "Strehla Made in GDR" ink stamp.

*6in (15cm) high*

**£15-25** **GC**

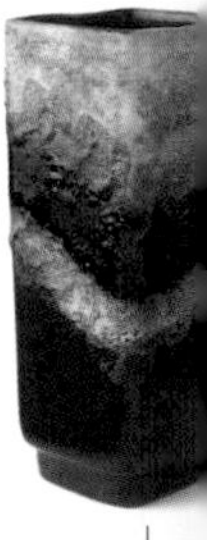

An East German Strehla vase, with foamy, glossy glazes with white "Strehla" ink stamp and indistinct number.

*Note the similarity to Dumler & Breiden's 'Lava' range, designed by Rudolf Kugler.*

*6.75in (17cm) high*

**£35-45** **GC**

## FIND OUT MORE...

**Keramik der 50er Jahre**, *by Dr Horst Makus, published by Arnoldsche, 2006 (German language).*

## COLLECTORS' NOTES

- Studio pottery is the term applied to pottery made either by the owner of the pottery, or by others under his direct guidance or supervision. Pieces are unique by their handmade or hand-decorated nature, and can be purely decorative, or have a functional and decorative role. Although there were some 19thC practitioners, studio pottery primarily began during the early 20thC, booming in the post-war period.
- The earliest and most influential figures are generally the most collected, and their work is typically the most valuable. These names include Bernard Leach, Shoji Hamada, Lucie Rie and Hans Coper. The Leach family were particularly influential, having taught a great many important potters, many of whom went on to teach others.
- Although work by these names may fetch hundreds, and frequently thousands, of pounds, the work of other less well-known potters is more affordable. Many of these are arguably 'yet to be discovered' or re-appraised by collectors. Look for quality in terms of form, glaze, overall design and novelty. Forerunners of, or those that typify, a movement or a period look, will often be a good bet.
- Always examine a pot closely for marks, as these can help identify the potter. Invest in a reference book on the seals and marks used by potters, as some may have not been correctly recognised by the seller. Learn about the lives, works and styles of the key potters, where they worked and who they trained. Always examine pieces for flaws and damage as these reduce value.

A Bernard Leach stoneware glazed vase, minor glaze flaw to the shoulder, with impressed seal marks.

*7.5in (19cm) high*

**£800-1,000** **GHOU**

A Bernard Leach vase, with sliced facets and overall tenmoku glaze.

*Tenmoku is the deep brown-to-black Oriental style glaze that appears light brown where it is thinnest, such as on rims and patterns.*

*c1960* *5.5in (14.5cm) high*

**£800-1,000** **ADE**

A Leach Pottery, St Ives small porcelain vase, by Bernard Leach, decorated with random patches of tenmoku glaze parting in places to reveal the white body beneath, with impressed seal marks.

*This tiny piece was reputedly a favourite of Leach's, and sat for many years on the mantelpiece of his flat in Barneloft, St. Ives.*

*2.25in (5.5cm) high*

**£600-800** **JN**

A rare Leach Pottery, St Ives raku bowl, by Bernard Leach, painted in blue, green and brown with a bunch of grapes, with impressed St Ives seal mark, some restoration to rim.

*A similar bowl, made in Tokyo c1914, is in the Hitomi Museum in Japan.*

*4.5in (11.5cm) diam*

**£350-450** **JN**

A David Leach small jug, with linear pattern on a mottled grey glaze, and impressed seal.

*7.75in (19.5cm) high*

**£280-320** **GAZE**

A Lowerdown Pottery jug, with brown glaze and impressed seal.

*This is one of the seals David Leach used at Lowerdown after 1956.*

*11.5in (29cm) high*

**£300-500** **GAZE**

## A CLOSER LOOK AT A DAVID LEACH VASE

*David Leach (1911-2005) was Bernard Leach's son and worked in his father's tradition, producing functional and decorative wares to great acclaim.*

*This form was frequently used by Leach and is based on Oriental designs - this example is unusually large.*

*The simple, yet boldly executed foliate design is again typical of Leach.*

*Leach worked with celadon, tenmoku, and flecked dolomite glazes, which gave subtle browns, greens, blues, greys and an oatmeal colour.*

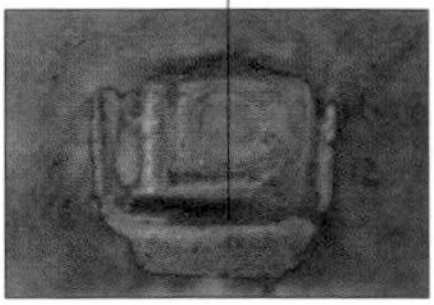

A very large David Leach vase, with stylized brown ilmenite glaze foliate design on a slate blue glaze, with impressed seal.

*13.5in (34cm) high*

**£800-1,000** **GAZE**

A Lowerdown Pottery stoneware vase, decorated with wave patterns and covered with a streaked and mottled beige and tenmoku glaze, seal mark.

**£80-120** **JN**

A Lowerdown Pottery fluted bowl, by David Leach, covered in a tin glaze, with impressed seal mark.

*3.5in (9cm) diam*

**£100-150** **WW**

A David Leach large pedestal bowl, with oxblood glaze and impressed seal mark.

*This impressed seal is another mark David Leach used at Lowerdown.*

*12.5in (31.5cm) diam*

**£400-600** **GAZE**

A David Leach stoneware charger, comb-decorated with a stylized willow tree under tenmoku glaze, with impressed "DL" seal.

*13.5in (34cm) diam*

**£400-600** **WW**

A David Leach butter dish and cover, with impressed "DL" seal.

**£60-80** **GAZE**

A Janet Leach circular footed bowl, with creamy glaze and impressed "JL" seal.

*4.5in (11.5cm) diam*

**£350-450** **JN**

A Janet Leach stoneware square section dish, painted with tenmoku cross motif, impressed with the "JL" and St Ives seals.

*6in (15cm) wide*

**£150-200** **WW**

A Janet Leach bottle vase, with creamy glaze and brown stripe.

*Janet Leach (1918-97) is known for her bottles and surprising, almost randomly applied streaks or patches of glazes, that add great movement. Despite marrying Bernard Leach in 1956, she pursued her own aesthetic and working methods.*

*c1970* *7.75in (20cm) high*

**£350-400** **ADE**

A rare Leach Pottery, St. Ives slipware cylindrical jar and cover, by Shoji Hamada, sgraffito decorated with simple stylized foliage against white slip beneath a honey glaze, with impressed artist and pottery seal marks, some chipping.

*c1921-23* *4in (10cm) high*

**£1,200-1,800** **JN**

A Leach Pottery, St Ives stoneware bottle vase, by Shigeyoshi Ichino, covered with a tenmoku glaze, with impressed seal marks.

*1969* *8.5in (21.5cm) high*

**£180-220** **JN**

A Leach Pottery, St Ives stoneware bottle vase, by Shigeyoshi Ichino, of squared oviform, with hakeme and painted dark brown decoration, with impressed seal marks.

*Shigeyoshi Ichino (b.1947) was born into a family of potters in the Tamba region of Japan, known for its potting tradition. He trained as a potter there, and met Janet Leach in 1954 when she was studying Japanese pottery. In 1969, he brought his experience to the Leach pottery in St Ives while working there for a year, before travelling around Europe and returning to Japan.*

*1969* *7.25in (18.5cm) high*

**£200-300** **JN**

A Winchcombe Pottery jug, by Sidney Tustin, with brown glaze and cream slip details, with impressed seals for Winchcombe and Sidney Tustin.

*The mark on the left is Tustin's personal seal, the mark on the right the Winchcombe seal. Tustin (b.1914) joined Winchcombe aged 13, and remained there until his retirement in 1978, having reputedly made over a million pots.*

*7.75in (19.5cm) high*

**£100-150** **GAZE**

## A CLOSER LOOK AT A WINCHCOMBE POTTERY JUG

*Michael Cardew (1901-83) was arguably Bernard Leach's most important and influential student, and founded the Winchcombe Pottery in 1926.*

*He was also influenced by Shoji Hamada. He was drawn to traditional English slip glazes and decoration, as seen on this jug.*

*He ran Winchcombe until 1939, when he embarked on influential travels in Africa - in 1944, he sold it to potter Ray Finch.*

*The left-hand mark is the Winchcombe Pottery seal, which was also used by other potters, and the mark on the right is his personal seal.*

A Winchcombe Pottery slip-decorated red earthenware jug, by Michael Cardew, with sgrafitto designs and impressed seals for Winchcombe and Michael Cardew.

*1927-39* *7.5in (19cm) high*

**£350-450** **GAZE**

A Winchcombe Pottery small oil jug and stopper, by Sidney Tustin, with impressed seals for Winchcombe and "ST".

*5.5in (14cm) high*

**£25-35** **GAZE**

A Winchcombe Pottery large double-handled casserole dish and lid, with impressed seal to base.

*Cardew also used dark glazes, but was not as interested in Oriental forms as Bernard Leach.*

*6.5in (16.5cm) diam*

**£80-120** **GAZE**

A Winchcombe Pottery bowl, by Michael Cardew, slip decorated to the interior with a chevron and grid motif, the exterior with chevrons, in brown on an ochre ground, with impressed seal marks, hairline crack.

*10.25in (26cm) diam*

**£200-250** **WW**

A Winchcombe Pottery plate, by Sidney Tustin, with brushed brown abstract decoration and impressed seal marks.

*c1950* *9in (23cm) wide*

**£100-150** **MHT**

An Ambleside flower pot, with blue sgraffito design and brown bands, inscribed "Ambleside SJ" on base.

*1948-66* *4.25in (10.5cm) high*

**£20-30** **GC**

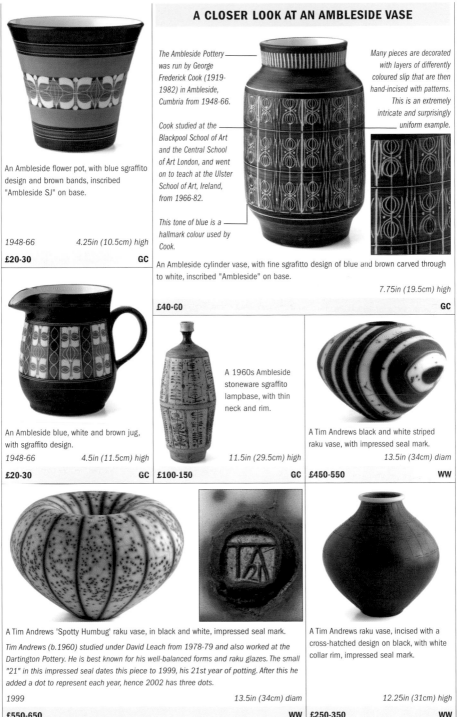

## A CLOSER LOOK AT AN AMBLESIDE VASE

*The Ambleside Pottery was run by George Frederick Cook (1919-1982) in Ambleside, Cumbria from 1948-66.*

*Cook studied at the Blackpool School of Art and the Central School of Art London, and went on to teach at the Ulster School of Art, Ireland, from 1966-82.*

*This tone of blue is a hallmark colour used by Cook.*

*Many pieces are decorated with layers of differently coloured slip that are then hand-incised with patterns. This is an extremely intricate and surprisingly uniform example.*

An Ambleside cylinder vase, with fine sgrafitto design of blue and brown carved through to white, inscribed "Ambleside" on base.

*7.75in (19.5cm) high*

**£40-60** **GC**

An Ambleside blue, white and brown jug, with sgraffito design.

*1948-66* *4.5in (11.5cm) high*

**£20-30** **GC**

A 1960s Ambleside stoneware sgraffito lampbase, with thin neck and rim.

*11.5in (29.5cm) high*

**£100-150** **GC**

A Tim Andrews black and white striped raku vase, with impressed seal mark.

*13.5in (34cm) diam*

**£450-550** **WW**

A Tim Andrews 'Spotty Humbug' raku vase, in black and white, impressed seal mark.

*Tim Andrews (b.1960) studied under David Leach from 1978-79 and also worked at the Dartington Pottery. He is best known for his well-balanced forms and raku glazes. The small "21" in this impressed seal dates this piece to 1999, his 21st year of potting. After this he added a dot to represent each year, hence 2002 has three dots.*

*1999* *13.5in (34cm) diam*

**£550-650** **WW**

A Tim Andrews raku vase, incised with a cross-hatched design on black, with white collar rim, impressed seal mark.

*12.25in (31cm) high*

**£250-350** **WW**

A very large Celtic Pottery moulded lampbase, with hand-painted cockerel or phoenix design and gilt label to base.

*This piece is exceptionally large, and the pattern is typical of Celtic designs.*

*18in (46cm) high*

**£200-250** **GC**

An Aviemore Pottery vase, with blue and cream glaze with band of linear design, marked to base.

*5.75in (14.5cm) high*

**£100-150** **MHT**

An Alan Caiger-Smith punch pot, with a white glaze and brown designs, signed.

*Caiger-Smith (b.1930) founded Aldermaston Pottery in 1955 and is known for his tin-glazed functional wares.*

*10.25in (25.5cm) high*

**£250-350** **SWO**

A Compton Pottery mug, modelled in low relief with St Nicholas on a Pilgrim's Way, unmarked, glaze nicks.

*4.5in (11.5cm) high*

**£120-180** **WW**

A Gordon Cooke large pebble-form vase, with impressed seal.

*Since 1998, Cooke has also made pottery for interior and garden plants. The drainage hole in the bottom of this pot may signify that it could be planted up.*

*10.75in (27cm) long*

**£150-200** **GC**

A Waistel Cooper stoneware vase, of tapering form with flaring rim, sgraffito decorated with vertical stripes in shades of brown and ochre, the base painted "Waistel", restored rim.

*Cooper (1921-2003) is widely collected for his unusual forms and textured surfaces.*

*9.25in (23.5cm) high*

**£350-450** **WW**

A Crowan Pottery low bowl, by Harry Davis, with unglazed rim, and impressed "CP" seal.

*6in (15.5cm) diam*

**£15-20** **GROB**

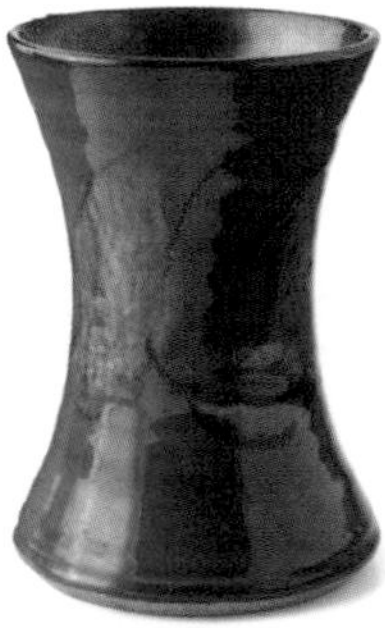

A Fosters Pottery, Redruth vase, with orange glaze and hand-painted abstract oval design.

*Note the similarity to Poole's popular Delphis colours and patterns. Fosters also made oven-to-tableware.*

*5.5in (14cm) high*

**£7-10** **GAZE**

A large Iden Pottery lampbase, with moulded star-shaped pattern and lustrous brownish-green glaze.

*13.75in (35cm) high*

**£70-100** **GC**

## A CLOSER LOOK AT A CAROL MCNICOLL BOWL

*McNicoll's designs often imitate or hint at other materials - here a patchwork quilt is suggested.*

*This attention to the process of creation and the decorative nature of the piece mean this becomes more than just a functional bowl.*

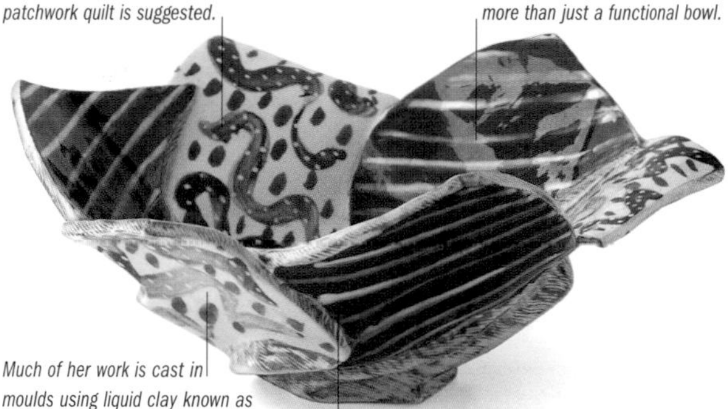

*Much of her work is cast in moulds using liquid clay known as 'slip', even though it often looks like it has been assembled from separate parts.*

*These factors combine with the strong colours and vibrant pattern to add a strong Postmodern feel to McNicoll's work.*

A 1980s Carol McNicoll glazed and hand-painted bowl, with inscribed signature.

*17.25in (44cm) wide*

**£350-450** **GAZE**

An 'Island Pottery' tenmoku and rust red glazed vase, with monogram and paper label to base.

*A vase this size would have taken great skill to pot on a wheel.*

*15.25in (39cm) high*

**£60-80** **GROB**

An Eric Leaper square form vase, with a red and orange decoration on a green ground, incised signature to base.

*6in (15cm) high*

**£35-45** **JN**

An Eric Leaper model of a bull, decorated in green and brown.

*3.25in (8.5cm) high*

**£50-70** **JN**

An Eric Leaper bulbous vase, with a green and brown slip glaze, incised signature to base.

*Eric Leaper (1921-2002) is known for his contrasting, brightly coloured glazes that are at the opposite end of the spectrum to those used by most of his contemporaries.*

*4.75in (12cm) high*

**£80-120** **JN**

A pair of Eric Leaper swan-shaped table salts, with red and brown glazes.

*3.75in (9.5cm) high*

**£100-150** **JN**

## A CLOSER LOOK AT A KATHERINE PLEYDELL-BOUVERIE VASE

*Katherine Pleydell-Bouverie (1895-1985), also known as 'Beano', studied under Bernard Leach from 1924-25 and also met Shoji Hamada.*

*Her forms are simple yet strong, and often based on Oriental examples.*

*She became renowned for her ash glazes, which were highly influential.*

*She founded her first pottery at her family estate in Coleshill, Berkshire in 1925, moving to Kilmington Manor in Wiltshire in 1946. Her mark is a combination of her initials.*

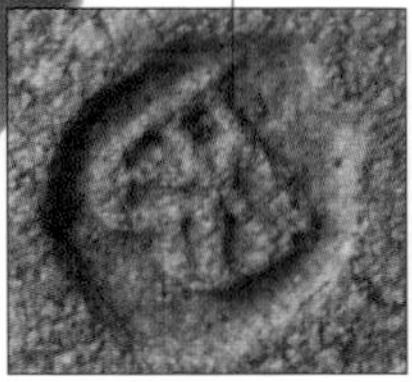

A Katherine Pleydell-Bouverie bulbous stoneware vase, with impressed seal.

*6in (15.5cm) high*

**£350-450** **GAZE**

A Geoffrey Maund 'Sugar' sifter, with hand-painted design.

*The Maund Pottery produced tablewares and piggy banks, decorated with stylised patterns in bright colours.*

*5in (12.5cm) high*

**£22-28** **BAD**

A Promenade Pottery of Brighton slip-cast charger, screen-printed decoration and incised marks.

*There is a Postmodern feel to this piece: not surprising given that the pottery operated for about 20 years around the 1980s.*

*15in (38.5cm) diam*

**£50-80** **WW**

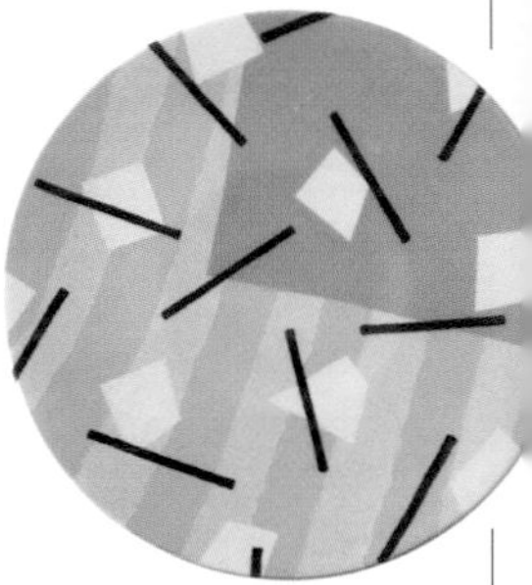

A 1980s-90s Phil Rogers stoneware vase, with incised decoration of simplified grass stems beneath a streaked olive-brown glaze, impressed potter's and Marston Pottery seal marks.

*12in (30.5cm) high*

**£220-280** **JN**

A Phil Rogers stoneware vase, incised with simple tree motif, glazed to the foot with a pale sand glaze, impressed seal mark.

*10.75in (27cm) high*

**£150-200** **WW**

A Phil Rogers 'Tenmoku and Nuka' glazed press-moulded stoneware vase, with moulded initials.

*Phil Rogers (b.1952) opened his first pottery in Wales in 1977 and the Marston Pottery in 1984. He is known for his ash glazes, salt glazes and reduced stoneware.*

*7in (18cm) high*

**£180-220** **GAZE**

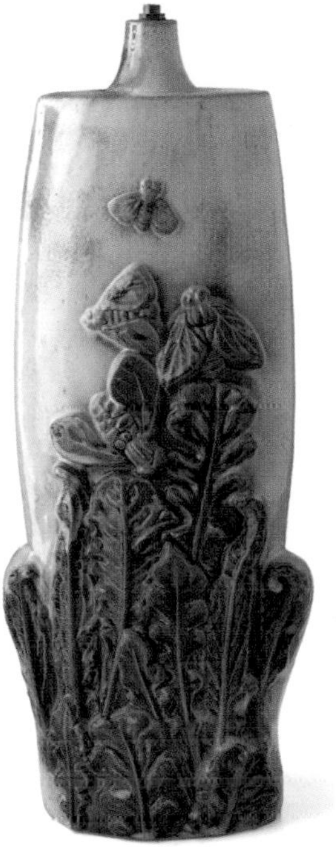

A Bernard Rooke large lamp base, with foliage and butterfly moulded motifs, incised "BR".

*Lampbases are among the most common objects found by Rooke (b.1938).*

*23.25in (59cm) high*

**£120-180** **GAZE**

A Bernard Rooke vase, with grey-green and green glazes, unmarked.

*This is typical of Bernard Rooke's heavy, stylized geometric forms that make much of the rough surface and colour of the clay, combined with muted glazes.*

*12.25in (31cm) high*

**£50-80** **GAZE**

A Bernard Rooke vase, with butterfly and reed moulded motifs and glazed in browny-green, blue and white, incised "BR".

*7.5in (19cm) high*

**£50-80** **GAZE**

A lampbase, possibly by Bernard Rooke, unsigned.

*The fine detail resembles a stylised Viking.*

*10.25in (26cm) high*

**£100-150** **GC**

A Bernard Rooke biscuit jar, with applied leaf and frog motifs and bamboo handle, incised "BR".

*7in (18cm) high*

**£40-60** **GAZE**

A Duncan Ross stoneware vase, decorated with the terra-sigilatta technique, incised "DR" mark.

*Terra-sigilatta uses an outer layer of glossy red/orange slip. Ross is known for his complex arrangements using combinations of many layers of slip, resists and inlaid decoration.*

*6.75in (17cm) high*

**£350-450** **JN**

A Shelf Pottery squat vase, with two handles and 'dentcd' motif with moulded squares and blobs, brown glazed interior.

*6in (15.5cm) high*

**£20-30** **GC**

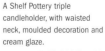

A Shelf Pottery triple candleholder, with waisted neck, moulded decoration and cream glaze.

*5.75in (14.5cm) high*

**£20-30** **GC**

An early Tremaen rectangular slab vase, with moulded relief runic pattern and green glaze.

*Although Tremaen's founder Peter Ellery went his own way, note the similarities to Troika pottery.*

*8.75in (22cm) high*

**£80-100** **GC**

## A CLOSER LOOK AT A CHARLES VYSE VASE

*Charles Vyse (1882-1971) is considered a key, early figure in the development of studio pottery in the UK.*

*He produced a range of figurines as well as 'art pottery', which was strongly influenced by Chinese forms and glazes.*

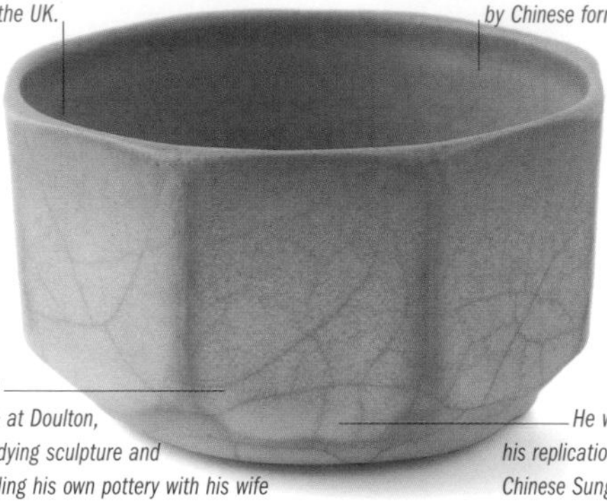

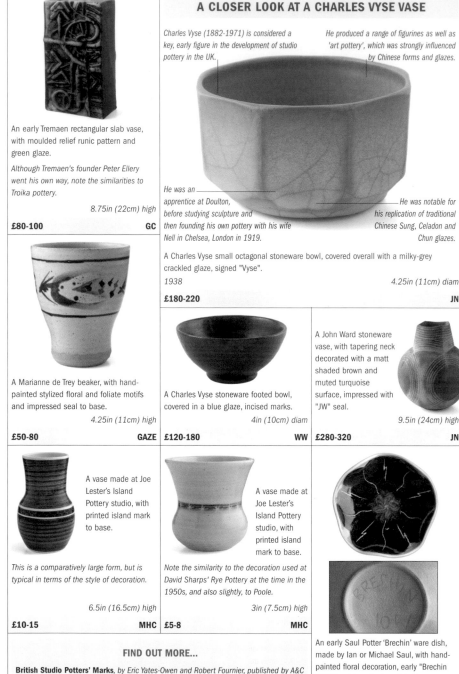

*He was an apprentice at Doulton, before studying sculpture and then founding his own pottery with his wife Nell in Chelsea, London in 1919.*

*He was notable for his replication of traditional Chinese Sung, Celadon and Chun glazes.*

A Charles Vyse small octagonal stoneware bowl, covered overall with a milky-grey crackled glaze, signed "Vyse".

*1938* *4.25in (11cm) diam*

**£180-220** **JN**

A Marianne de Trey beaker, with hand-painted stylized floral and foliate motifs and impressed seal to base.

*4.25in (11cm) high*

**£50-80** **GAZE**

A Charles Vyse stoneware footed bowl, covered in a blue glaze, incised marks.

*4in (10cm) diam*

**£120-180** **WW**

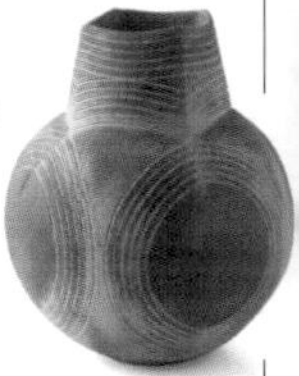

A John Ward stoneware vase, with tapering neck decorated with a matt shaded brown and muted turquoise surface, impressed with "JW" seal.

*9.5in (24cm) high*

**£280-320** **JN**

A vase made at Joe Lester's Island Pottery studio, with printed island mark to base.

*This is a comparatively large form, but is typical in terms of the style of decoration.*

*6.5in (16.5cm) high*

**£10-15** **MHC**

A vase made at Joe Lester's Island Pottery studio, with printed island mark to base.

*Note the similarity to the decoration used at David Sharps' Rye Pottery at the time in the 1950s, and also slightly, to Poole.*

*3in (7.5cm) high*

**£5-8** **MHC**

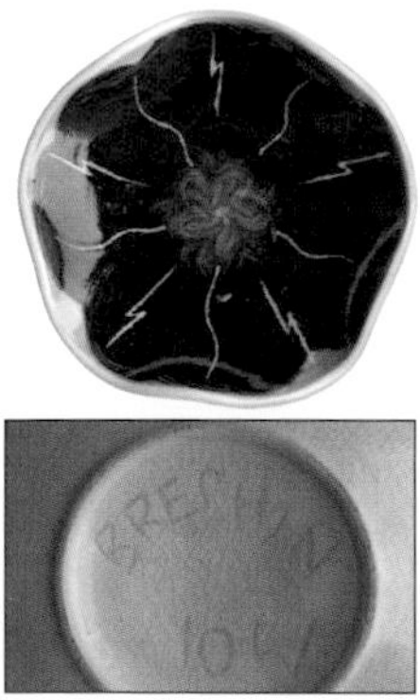

An early Saul Potter 'Brechin' ware dish, made by Ian or Michael Saul, with hand-painted floral decoration, early "Brechin IOW" hand-inscribed mark to base.

*4.5in (11.5cm) diam*

**£5-8** **MHC**

### FIND OUT MORE...

**British Studio Potters' Marks**, *by Eric Yates-Owen and Robert Fournier, published by A&C Black, 2005.*

**Ten Thousand Years of Pottery**, *by Emmanuel Cooper, published by The British Museum Press, 2000.*

## COLLECTORS' NOTES

- The Troika Pottery was founded in St Ives, Cornwall in 1963 by painter Lesley Illsley, potter Benny Sirota and architect Jan Thompson. Many of the first wares were functional, including tiles, teapots and mugs, and had a shiny glaze. The renowned geometric, matte textured designs were not developed until the mid-1970s.
- In 1970, the pottery expanded and moved to Newlyn, and production grew. Look on the base for painted marks that can help identify when a piece was made – early examples can be highly desirable. A 'trident' shaped mark dates from before 1967, and the word 'St Ives' was used until 1970. The word 'Newlyn' was never used.
- Decorators also applied a monogram – the work of some decorators can be more prized than others. Consider the date, shape, size and pattern. Large 'wheel', 'anvil' and 'chimney' vases are typical of the pottery and are generally desirable. 'Coffin' and cylinder vases are more common.
- After the success of the 1970s, the pottery closed in 1983. Look for pieces with visually appealing geometric patterns in typical Troika colours. Check the body for cracks and chips, as these devalue a piece. Values seem to have reached a plateau recently, so now could be a good time to build up a collection.

A Troika Pottery dish square, with bronze glaze roundel, painted mark "Troika Cornwall England" and artist's monogram.

*5in (12.5cm) wide*

**£180-220** **WW**

A late 1960s Troika Pottery white square dish, decorated by Sylvia Valance, the interior with a with blue circle.

*Valance was Head Decorator from 1967-69.*

*4.5in (11.5cm) wide*

**£180-220** **JN**

A Troika Pottery bronze glazed square ashtray, decorated by Penny Black.

*c1970 4.5in (11.5cm) wide*

**£120-180** **JN**

An early Troika Pottery blue square slab vase, with a glazed stylized flower pattern.

*The shiny glaze and design indicate that this was probably made before 1970, when the factory was in St Ives.*

*c1967 4.5in (11.5cm) high*

**£150-200** **JN**

## A CLOSER LOOK AT A TROIKA PLAQUE

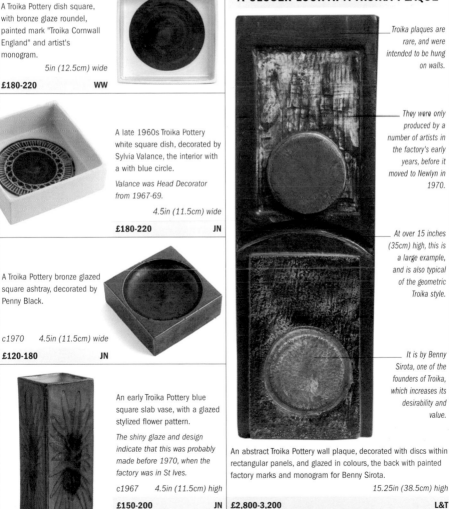

*Troika plaques are rare, and were intended to be hung on walls.*

*They were only produced by a number of artists in the factory's early years, before it moved to Newlyn in 1970.*

*At over 15 inches (35cm) high, this is a large example, and is also typical of the geometric Troika style.*

*It is by Benny Sirota, one of the founders of Troika, which increases its desirability and value.*

An abstract Troika Pottery wall plaque, decorated with discs within rectangular panels, and glazed in colours, the back with painted factory marks and monogram for Benny Sirota.

*15.25in (38.5cm) high*

**£2,800-3,200** **L&T**

A Troika Pottery lamp base, decorated by Alison Brigden, of cube form and two sides with incised geometric designs, marked "Troika AB Cornwall".

*1976-83* *11in (28cm) high overall*

**£220-280** **SWO**

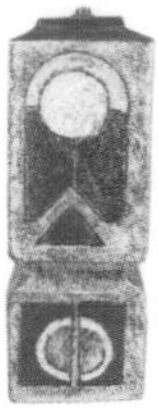

A Troika Pottery rectangular table lamp, decorated by Simone Kilburn, with incised and moulded geometric designs, the base painted "Troika SK Cornwall".

*1975-77* *12.25in (31cm) high*

**£280-320** **SWO**

A Troika Pottery 'chimney' vase, decorated to one side with rough textured geometric designs, the base painted "Troika Cornwall" and with "NIP" unidentified decorators' initials.

*c1975* *8in (20cm) high*

**£250-350** **NEA**

A 1970s Troika pottery lamp base, with stylized circles, signed to base, small chips.

*10.25in (26cm) high*

**£100-200** **JN**

A Troika Pottery mask, decorated by Alison Bridgen, modelled in relief to both sides with a stylized mask, the neck forming the stepped base, the base with painted marks and with "AB" artist's monogram.

*Troika's impressive masks are rare and highly desirable, and have been known to sell for over £2,000. However, prices have plateaued in recent months and many have become more affordable. This late example is cracked, which seriously affects its value.*

*1977-83* *9.75in (25cm) high*

**£550-650** **L&T**

A Troika Pottery mask, modelled with geometric faces in shades of ochre and blue, the base painted "Troika Cornwall" and with "CC" monogram for an unidentified decorator, small chip to foot rim.

*Masks have two sides, the back usually being far less detailed than the front. The simplicity of the reverse of this mask, which appears to be winking, is extremely appealing.*

*10in (25.5cm) high*

**£700-800** **WW**

A Troika Pottery double blue and white egg cup and stand.

**£180-220** **JN**

### FIND OUT MORE...

**Troika Ceramics of Cornwall**, *by George Perrott, published by Gemini Publications Ltd, 2004.*

## COLLECTORS' NOTES

- Although West German ceramics from the 1950s and early 1960s have been a recognised collecting field for some years, their later, funkier 1960s and 70s cousins have largely been ignored. Over the past few years, this has begun to change and the area is now growing rapidly in popularity.
- Much research is still to be done, and the lack of official company records, which were not kept or were destroyed, makes it hard to identify pieces. Handling as many definitely identified pieces, preferably with labels, is the best way of learning. The maker and a period of manufacture can be identified from considering the shape, colour of clay used, colour and type of glaze and the marks on the base.
- The most desirable designs are known as 'fat lava' by collectors and are brightly coloured with thick, dripped and cratered textured glazes that look like molten or dried lava, or the moon's surface. Many of these were complex to produce and have not been repeated. Shapes that were typical of their time are also desirable. Simple, glossy glazes in dull colours on simply moulded bodies are less desirable.
- Many of the more sought-after 'wild' glazes were only produced in limited numbers, the 'tamer' designs were exported widely in much larger numbers. Size is important: large floor-standing vases were sold in smaller quantities at the time, so are rarer today. Many collectors collect by shape, glaze or company.
- Always buy in the best condition possible, as many examples can still be found on the market. Most companies closed, or discontinued their decorative ranges, from the mid-1970s to the early 1990s as tastes changed, and less expensive imports from the Far East swamped the market.

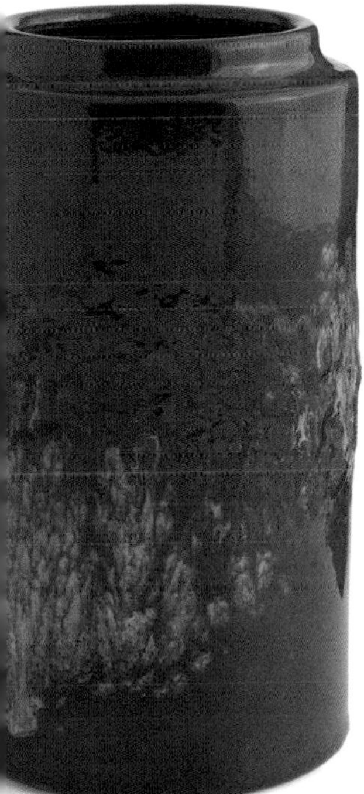

A West German Scheurich cylindrical vase, with yellow and orange-red dripped glaze, leaving central bubble textured black band, the base moulded "203-18 W.Germany".

*7in (18cm) high*

**£20-30** **GC**

A West German Scheurich tapering vase, with glossy light blue and cream drip effect glaze, the base moulded "203-26 W.Germany".

*10.25in (26cm) high*

**£20-30** **GC**

A 1970s West German Scheurich vase, with double brown lava bands and white foamy glaze swirl, the base moulded "205-26 W.Germany".

*10.5in (26.5cm) high*

**£15-25** **L**

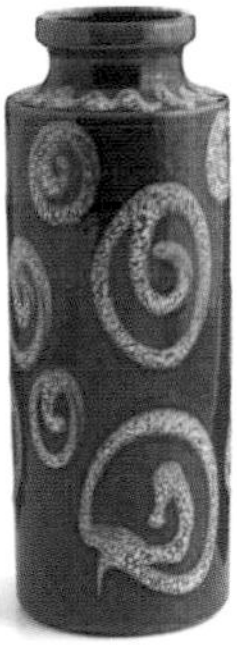

A West German Scheurich cylinder vase, with green-tinted cream-speckled swirls painted over a glossy bottle green ground, the base moulded "203-26 W.Germany".

*10.5in (27cm) high*

**£25-35** **GC**

A West German Scheurich floor vase, with alternating graduated bands of brown, cream and sage green glaze, the base moulded "553-38 W.Germany".

*15in (38cm) high*

**£30-40** **GC**

A West German Scheurich orange and brown glazed vase, inscribed "W. Germany" and "284-47".

*18.75in (47.5cm) high*

**£40-60** **GAZE**

## A CLOSER LOOK AT A WEST GERMAN FLOOR VASE

*The 270 form has a strong 1950s style, with its angled handle and rim and tapered body.*

*The form was probably designed by Hans Siery, a key designer at Scheurich from the 1950s onwards who was responsible for the popular and similarly shaped 271 jug.*

*The style of the design and glaze dates it to the early 1960s - the beige pumice glaze has been cut through with slices and painted in colours.*

*The base is moulded 'Foreign' indicating that it was made for export to English-speaking countries - Scheurich exported many thousands of their ceramics.*

A West German Scheurich floor jug vase, possibly designed by Hans Siery, with coloured 'slices' and pumice glaze, the base moulded "Foreign 270 50".

*19.75in (50cm) high*

**£80-120** **OUT**

A West German Scheurich vase, brown ground with red and orange bands, the base moulded "216-20 W Germany".

*8.25in (21cm) high*

**£20-30** **FD**

A West German Scheurich cylinder vase, with ribbed lip and moulded banded stylised floral pattern, the base moulded "289-27 W.Germany".

*This is typical of the types of vases that were exported in huge numbers by West German makers.*

*10.75in (27cm) high*

**£10-15** **MHC**

A West German Scheurich 'flame' pattern vase, with sliced orange streak and cream lava glaze over a black ground, the base moulded "401-18 W.Germany".

*7.25in (18.5cm) high*

**£30-40** **TCM**

A West German Scheurich 'flame' vase, with a grey and blue lava glaze and sliced orange pattern, the base moulded "238-18 W.Germany".

*This colour combination is unusual.*

*7in (18cm) high*

**£50-80** **GC**

A West German Scheurich small vase, with glossy dripped white glaze over green, the interior glazed in bright blue, the base moulded "550-10 W.Germany".

*4in (10cm) high*

**£3-5** **MHC**

A West German jug vase with handle, with painted, dragged and dripped bands of glossy green and yellow glaze on a glossy brown ground, the base moulded "426-47 W.Germany".

*18.25in (46.5cm) high*

**£60-80** **GC**

A 1950s West German Bay Keramik handpainted jug vase, marked "246-35" to base, with original silver foil label.

*13.5in (34.5cm) high*

**£35-45** **MA**

A West German Carstens 'Ankara' pattern vase, with gunmetal grey glaze over a speckled matte blue glaze, the base moulded "W.Germany 1236-23".

*This sought-after glaze combination was applied partly using a stencil. Designed by Scholtis, it can be found with different geometric motifs. A red colour variation is extremely rare.*

*9in (23cm) high*

**£50-70** **GC**

A West German Dümler & Breiden floor vase, the base impressed with the "DB" motif and "1062/47 Germany".

*This is a typical combination of glazes for the company, incorporating the beige dripped lava, smoother beige and glittering copper glazes.*

*18in (46cm) high*

**£100-150** **OUT**

A West German Dümler & Breiden cylinder vase, with slightly textured cream glaze finished with a black powder speckled finish, and central dark green band painted with orange circular motifs in alternating blue and green squares, with yellow gloss glazed interior, indistinctly marked.

*7in (18cm) high*

**£20-25** **GC**

A West German Dümler & Breiden baluster vase, with slightly textured cream glaze finished with a black powder speckled finish, and central dark green band painted with circular motifs in squares, with yellow gloss glazed interior, the base impressed "118 25 Germany".

*10.25in (26cm) high*

**£20-30** **GC**

A West German Dümler & Breiden vase, with central band of red 'lava' trails on a matte blue ground between two lightly textured matte cream areas, the base impressed "108/20 Germany".

*8in (20.5cm) high*

**£35-45** **GC**

A West German Dümler & Breiden waisted tapering vase, with black line-and-dot dripped pattern over a graduated blue ground, the base impressed "1021 25 Germany".

*9.75in (25cm) high*

**£30-40** **GC**

A 1970s West German Otto Keramik vase, with pumice-like purple glaze.

*This is an extremely large size and unusual shape. Otto Keramik was founded in 1970 by glaze technician Otto Gerharz, who was known for his 'Vulcano' glaze at Ruscha. Many shapes were designed by Kurt Tschörner, who also designed for Ruscha.*

*13.5in (34cm) high*

**£80-120** **OUT**

A 1970s West German Roth Keramik oval vase, with moulded red gloss glazed concave areas between bubble textured black glazed areas, the base indistinctly marked.

*4.25in (11cm) high*

**£30-40** **GC**

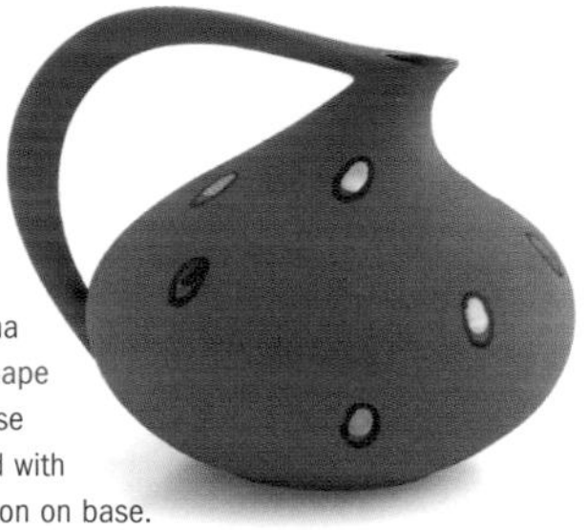

A late 1950s Ruscha 'Venedig' pattern shape 313 pitcher, the base moulded "313" and with decorator's inscription on base.

*6in (15cm) high*

**£80-120** **TOJ**

A Ruscha Keramik hand-decorated floral wall plaque, with lava tubelined glazes, stamped on back "768 Ruscha handgemalt".

*Wall plaques were widely produced by West German ceramics factories during the 1970s.*

*20in (50.5cm) high*

**£120-180** **TOJ**

## A CLOSER LOOK AT A WEST GERMAN VASE

*This highly 1950s stylised pattern is known as 'Filigran', and was hand-inscribed, making each piece unique.*

*As it was time-consuming and thus expensive to produce, it was only produced for a short period around 1960.*

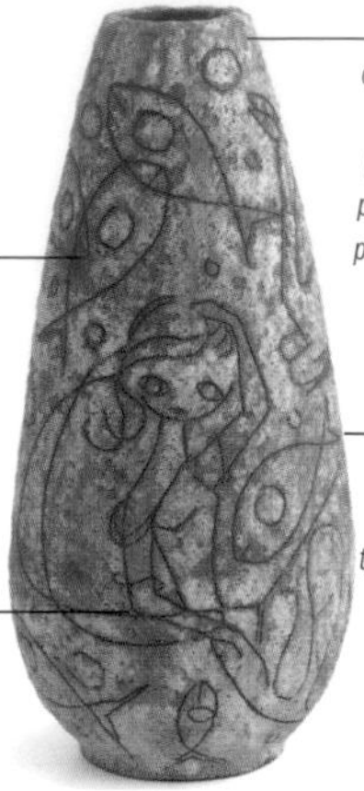

*It is a well-known and sought-after pattern and was designed by Adele Bolz.*

*The clean lines of the rocket-shaped tapering vase are typical of the 1950s and show off the pattern to its best.*

A West German Ruscha teardrop tapering vase, inscribed with a stylized linear design of fish, antelopes and an Indian deity with her legs crossed, unmarked.

*6.75in (17cm) high*

**£70-100** **GC**

A Ruscha shape 313 pitcher, designed by Kurt Tschörner in 1954, with dripped red and green 'Vulcano' glaze.

*The famous 313 pitcher was produced with over 50 different glazes and was in continuous production until the factory closed in 1996. This is a key shape in West German ceramics of the period.*

*5.75in (14.5cm) high*

**£80-120** **OUT**

A Ruscha wall charger, with applied high-relief disc decoration, the back hand-inscribed "100/3".

*14.25in (36.5cm) diam*

**£120-180** **HLM**

### FIND OUT MORE...

**Fat Lava: West German Ceramics of the 1960s & 70s,** *by Mark Hill, published by www.markhillpublishing.com, 2006, ISBN: 978-0-95528-650-6.*

A large Amphora Pottery vase, decorated in silver lustre, with flower heads, printed mark.

*Amphora was founded in 1892 in Turn-Teplitz, Bohemia (now the Czech Republic). Around the turn of the 20thC, the pottery gained a reputation for its Art Nouveau ceramics, many of which were designed by either Paul Dachsel or Eduard Stellmacher. When Dachsel and Stellmacher left in 1903 and 1904 respectively, the quality of design and manufacture arguably began to wane. Nevertheless, the company's output has been recently re-appraised, and prices are rising.*

*15.5in (38.5cm) high*

**£180-220** **WW**

## A CLOSER LOOK AT A BURSLEY VASE

*Bursley Ware was produced by Bursley Ltd, run by Harry Wood. Charlotte Rhead worked there from 1922-26 and from 1942 until her death in 1947.*

*This is pattern number 'TL5', and dates from her second period of working for Wood. Many of her designs were not produced until after 1952 and were sold until c1960.*

*The design is typical of Rhead's work, being applied by tube-lining, a process where liquid clay is trailed onto the body and the colours then hand-painted on the inside each section.*

*Compared to Clarice Cliff, Rhead's designs are under-appreciated and possibly under-valued.*

A Bursley Ware vase, designed by Charlotte Rhead, with tube-lined decoration of stylized flowers and fruit, printed marks.

*This pattern is listed in a 1954 catalogue, and is usually found in browns and beiges.*

*8.25in (21cm) high*

**£100-150** **DN**

A Bing & Grøndahl 'Woman with Fish' porcelain figure, no.2233HN.

*8.25in (21cm) high*

**£120-180** **AAC**

A C.H. Brannam green glazed pottery vase, with dragon handles, decorated with a bird and flower to each side, incised to base "C H Brannam, Barum".

*c1903* *16.5in (42cm) high*

**£220-280** **SWO**

A Bursley Ware tapering jug, designed by Charlotte Rhead, decorated with colourful flowers and leaves, signed on base, chipped.

*11.25in (28.5cm) high*

**£150-250** **JN**

A Bursley Ware tapering jug, designed by Charlotte Rhead, decorated with colourful leaves and flowers, with signature to base, chipped.

*11.25in (28.5cm) high*

**£100-150** **JN**

A pair of Bursley Ware 'Amstel' candlesticks, two small chips to one drip pan.

*12in (30.5cm) high*

**£250-350** **GHOU**

A Coalport 'Sandringham' pattern twin-handled urn and cover, the crimson ground profusely decorated.

*10.5in (26.5cm) high*

**£100-150** **SAS**

## A CLOSER LOOK AT A CROWN DEVON JUG

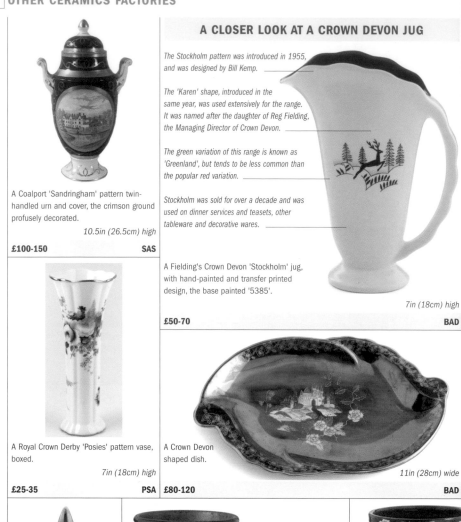

*The Stockholm pattern was introduced in 1955, and was designed by Bill Kemp.*

*The 'Karen' shape, introduced in the same year, was used extensively for the range. It was named after the daughter of Reg Fielding, the Managing Director of Crown Devon.*

*The green variation of this range is known as 'Greenland', but tends to be less common than the popular red variation.*

*Stockholm was sold for over a decade and was used on dinner services and teasets, other tableware and decorative wares.*

A Fielding's Crown Devon 'Stockholm' jug, with hand-painted and transfer printed design, the base painted '5385'.

*7in (18cm) high*

**£50-70** **BAD**

A Royal Crown Derby 'Posies' pattern vase, boxed.

*7in (18cm) high*

**£25-35** **PSA**

A Crown Devon shaped dish.

*11in (28cm) wide*

**£80-120** **BAD**

A 1960s English Ducor lidded pot, with gilt knop.

*5in (12.5cm) high*

**£7-10** **MTS**

A 1930s Etruscan Ware vase, with hand-painted geometric design over a yellow ground, the base stamped in black "Etruscan Ware made in England", and impressed "129".

*This decorative treatment employs no overglaze, leaving the painted surface exposed to potential damage.*

*8.5in (22cm) high*

**£30-40** **GC**

A small Foley Intarsio jardinière, designed by Frederick Rhead, transfer-printed and painted in colours with a frieze of geese with floral bands above and below, factory marks and numbered "3147".

*4.25in (11cm) high*

**£220-280** **JN**

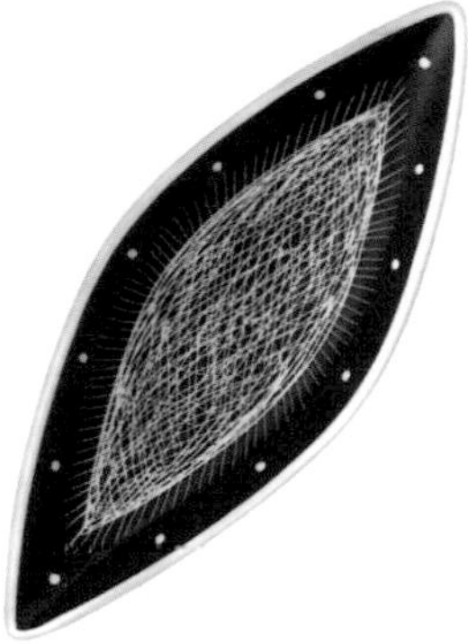

A 1950s Foley Bone China dish, designed by Hazel Thrupston, with sgraffito hatched design.

*6.in (15.5cm) long*

**£10-15** **BB**

A rare Goldscheider wall mask, with original label to lower neck.

*1925-28 11.5in (29cm)*

**£800-1,200** **SCG**

A small W.H. Goss tyg, decorated in colours with the 'Trusty Servant' and heraldic shields.

*2in (5cm) high*

**£60-80** **SAS**

A Dutch Schoonhoven factory Gouda 'Festin' pattern baluster vase, the base painted "120 Festin Schoonhoven Holland +" on base.

*Schoonhoven was founded in 1920 by Tijs Visser, Tijs Volker and Kornelis Prins after the Plateelbakkerij De Rozenboom was closed in the same year. Corel is one of their most commonly found patterns. The company is still producing Gouda style art pottery today.*

*9.25in (23.5cm) high*

**£70-90** **GC**

A W.H. Goss cruet, the egg shaped condiments decorated in colours with the 'Trusty Servant' and emblems of Winchester.

*4.5in (11cm) high*

**£120-180** **SAS**

A Dutch Schoonhoven factory Gouda 'Festin' pattern small faceted bottle, painted "104 Festin Schoonhoven Holland +" on base.

*6in (15cm) high*

**£30-40** **GC**

A Dutch Flora factory Royal Gouda 'Tokio' pattern vase, painted "916 Tokio Flora Gouda Holland" on base.

*6.75in (17cm) high*

**£40-60** **GC**

A Koninklijke factory Gouda 'Marion' pattern tapered cylindrical vase, painted with a two-colour leaf design, the base with crown mark and "4841 Marion Koninklijke Gouda Royal Holland" marks.

*5.5in (14cm) high*

**£30-40** **GC**

A T.G. Green 'Pork Dripping' storage jar, with target mark.

**£10-15** **MTS**

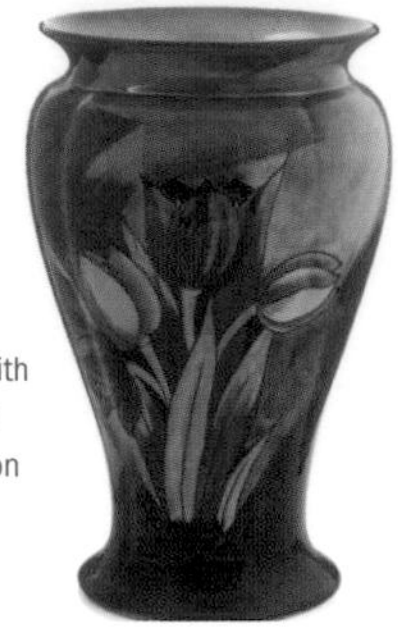

An H. & K. Tunstall Art Deco vase, with hand-painted tulip design on a graduated glossy brown ground.

*The unicorn mark over 'H. & K. Tunstall' was used by Hollinshead and Kirkham Ltd, who operated from 1876-1956.*

*8.75in (22cm) high*

**£100-150** **BAD**

A Sampson Hancock Art Deco 'Ivoryware' hand-painted candleholder.

*4.25in (11cm) wide*

**£18-22** **BAD**

A Hornsea Pottery Slipware tall vase, the base stamped with mould number "85", designed in 1963.

*This is the tallest vase made in this range.*

*1963* *13.5in (34.5cm) high*

**£100-150** **AGR**

A Hornsea Pottery Studio Craft jardinière, designed by John Clappison, model no.384, from the 'Home Decor' range, the base with printed marks.

*13.75in (35cm) wide*

**£150-200** **WW**

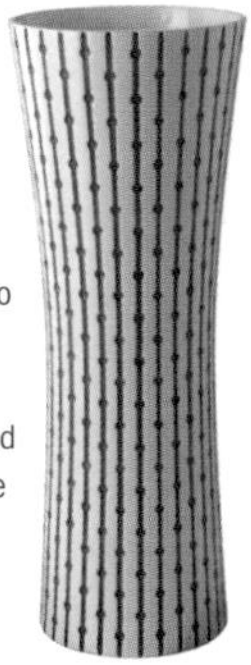

A Hornsea Pottery Studio Craft vase, designed by John Clappison, of slender waisted form and incised with vertical pale pink lines and dots.

**£70-90** **DN**

A 1960s Hornsea Studio Craft 'Home Decor' range dish, designed by John Clappison from 1960-62, in the form of a Viking longboat.

*11in (28cm) long*

**£50-70** **MHT**

A Japanese Holt Howard hand-painted cat shaped string holder, with "Japanese Holt Howard 1958" printed to base.

*Holt Howard was an American ceramics designer and distributor. His lady head vases and small spice and sauce jars are highly collectable.*

*c1958* *5in (13cm) wide*

**£15-25** **TM**

A Kingston Pottery of Hull vase, with green glaze with dripped brown and white glazes vase, the base impressed "KP698".

*8in (20.5cm) high*

**£30-40** **GC**

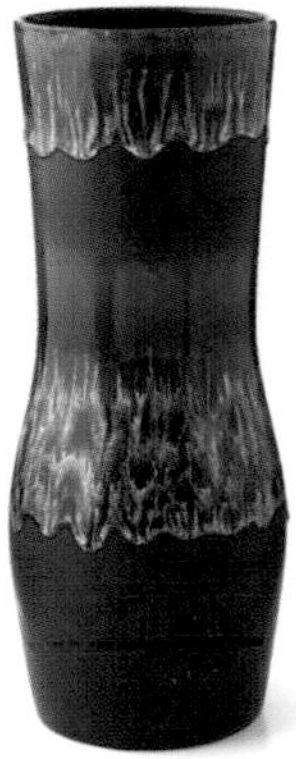

A large Kingston Pottery of Hull waisted vase, with brown and green graduated glaze, with dripped white glaze, the base impressed "KP74".

*12.25in (31cm) high*

**£50-80** **GC**

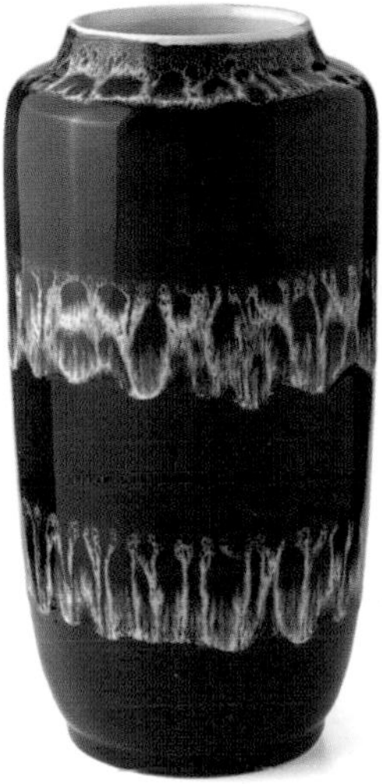

A large Kingston Pottery of Hull vase, with burgundy banded and foamy white glaze design, indistinct marks.

*Little is known about the Kingston Pottery, although it is likely that the ceramics on this page were designed during the early 1970s. Their similarities to West German 'Fat Lava' ceramics is striking, this form is almost identical to Scheurich's model 517 vase. It is also interesting to consider Ireland's 'Kilrush' ceramics for the same reason. The Kingston Pottery is known to have also produced character jugs and a range of animal figurines.*

*10.75in (27.5cm) high*

**£50-80** **GC**

A Kingston Pottery of Hull tall baluster vase, with brown and green graduated glazes and dripped foamy white glaze, the base impressed "KP39 No3".

*10.25in (26cm) high*

**£30-50** **GC**

An L. & Sons Ltd Hanley chintz jam pot, with 'EPNS' lid, on four ball feet.

*4in (10cm) wide*

**£30-40** **BAD**

A Lenci pottery figure of a young girl sitting on a wall, with black hair and wearing a floral dress, and shoes, Turin factory marks and dated 1932.

*1932* *5in (13cm) high*

**£350-450** **JN**

Two Theodore Haviland Limoges porcelain frog shaped pepper pots, designed by Edouard Marcel Sando, with factory and designer marks.

*1.75in (4.5cm) high*

**£180-220** **JN**

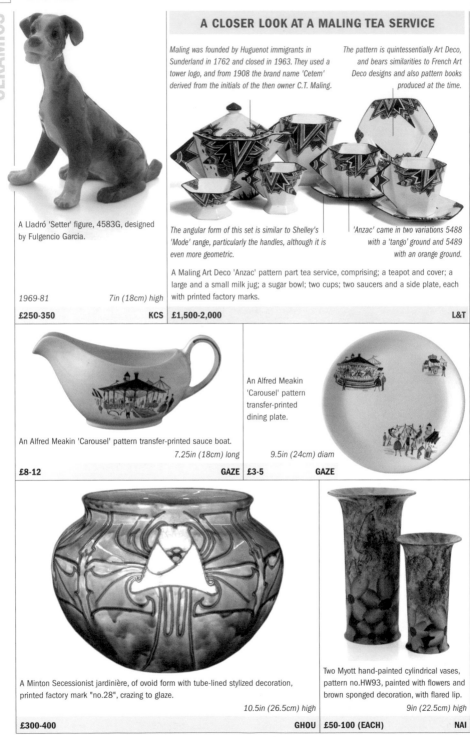

A Lladró 'Setter' figure, 4583G, designed by Fulgencio Garcia.

*1969-81* *7in (18cm) high*

**£250-350** **KCS**

## A CLOSER LOOK AT A MALING TEA SERVICE

*Maling was founded by Huguenot immigrants in Sunderland in 1762 and closed in 1963. They used a tower logo, and from 1908 the brand name 'Cetem' derived from the initials of the then owner C.T. Maling.*

*The pattern is quintessentially Art Deco, and bears similarities to French Art Deco designs and also pattern books produced at the time.*

*The angular form of this set is similar to Shelley's 'Mode' range, particularly the handles, although it is even more geometric.*

*'Anzac' came in two variations 5488 with a 'tango' ground and 5489 with an orange ground.*

A Maling Art Deco 'Anzac' pattern part tea service, comprising; a teapot and cover; a large and a small milk jug; a sugar bowl; two cups; two saucers and a side plate, each with printed factory marks.

**£1,500-2,000** **L&T**

An Alfred Meakin 'Carousel' pattern transfer-printed sauce boat.

*7.25in (18cm) long*

**£8-12** **GAZE**

An Alfred Meakin 'Carousel' pattern transfer-printed dining plate.

*9.5in (24cm) diam*

**£3-5** **GAZE**

A Minton Secessionist jardinière, of ovoid form with tube-lined stylized decoration, printed factory mark "no.28", crazing to glaze.

*10.5in (26.5cm) high*

**£300-400** **GHOU**

Two Myott hand-painted cylindrical vases, pattern no.HW93, painted with flowers and brown sponged decoration, with flared lip.

*9in (22.5cm) high*

**£50-100 (EACH)** **NAI**

A Myott hand-painted medium Trumpet jug, pattern no.P9635.

*7.75in (19.5cm) high*

**£80-100** **NAI**

A Myott hand-painted large Trumpet jug, pattern no.P9640.

*9in (22.5cm) high*

**£100-150** **NAI**

A Myott hand-painted Doric lemonade jug, pattern no.H8286.

*The Doric shape is quite common and was produced with a range of patterns. As with the 'pinchtop' jugs, a collection can be formed relatively inexpensively.*

*6.25in (16cm) high*

**£60-80** **NAI**

A Myott hand-painted Diamond vase, pattern no.8660.

*Myott, Son & Co. Ltd was founded in 1898 and produced Art Deco style, hand-painted ceramics during the late 1920s and '30s. A factory fire in 1949 destroyed all records and little information is now known. The charm of their hand-painted scenes makes them increasingly collectable. Although this is a desirable shape, look out for the 'Wedge', 'Owl' and 'Cone' shapes. See the 'DK Collectables Price Guide 2006' by Judith Miller & Mark Hill for more information.*

*6in (15.5cm) high*

**£100-150** **NAI**

A Lord Nelson Pottery printed 'Brown Soft Sugar' storage jar.

*Lord Nelson Pottery was one of the brand names use by Elijah Cotton Ltd, based in Hanley, Stoke-on-Trent.*

*7.75in (19.5cm) high*

**£7-10** **MTS**

A Lord Nelson Pottery printed 'Caster Sugar' storage jar.

*Look out for more unusual or expensive ingredients, as jars for commonly bought ingredients are usually more common.*

*7.75in (19.5cm) high*

**£10-15** **MTS**

A 1930s Hanley New Hall Boumier Ware bowl, decorated with a green lustre glaze and floral border, together with a similar oval dish

**£50-80** **BIG**

A Price Kensington apple sauce jar, with moulded and hand painted decoration.

*4.75in (12cm) high*

**£15-25** **MTS**

A 1930s Sadler racing car teapot, decorated with Mabel Lucie Attwell pixies and animals, with female driver, silver lustre and green highlights, painted signature and impressed registered marks "820236".

*The Mabel Lucie Attwell characters make this a very rare example. This teapot is more commonly found in plain yellow, and green with black highlights, in which case the value is usually around £40-70, depending on condition.*

*9in (23cm) wide*

**£450-550** **NEA**

A Dutch van Woerden hand-thrown vase, with hand-painted mottled grey glaze and original paper label.

*Note the similarity to some of Scheurich's shapes. This was made at a time when West German pottery was flooding into Holland and competing against local potters such as Van Woerden.*

*7.5in (19cm) high*

**£15-20** **MHC**

A 19thC Staffordshire wall pocket, probably by Wilshaw & Robinson, modelled as a spray of tulips, naturalistically coloured in yellow and purple, inscribed "WNR", registration number 110914.

*11in (28cm) high*

**£120-180** **NEA**

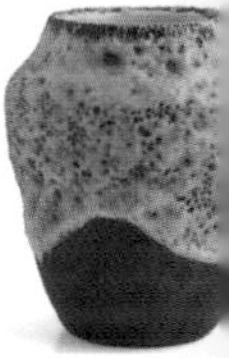

A Dutch De Steenuil studio pottery vase, with dripped white 'lava' salt glaze on a brown textured body, the base with an impressed mark of a stylized owl.

*De Steenuil (the owl) was a small Dutch pottery founded by H.J. Goosen in 1947. Most work has dripped 'lava' type salt and other glazes, and was sold to florists. The pottery closed in 1997, and examples of Goosen's work can be seen today in the Rijswick Museum.*

*4.75in  (12cm) high*

**£10-15** **MHC**

An Austrian cylinder vase, with three bands of matte and gloss textured glaze, the base impressed "Austria".

*This was probably made by Carstens.*

*7.75in (19.5cm) high*

**£40-60** **GC**

A pair of French Art Deco pottery vases, decorated with panels of colourful florets and geometric gold and silver lustre bands, and turquoise glaze grounds.

*Even though the maker is not known, the strongly Art Deco form and pattern, and their visual appeal make these desirable.*

*9.75in (25cm) high*

**£250-350** **JN**

## COLLECTORS' NOTES

- Much of the market for character collectables is driven by nostalgia. Characters in comic books, on TV or on the silver screen that entertained or delighted us as children are often keenly collected by those harking back to the past. Major names tend to fetch the largest sums, as there is usually a larger following to drive values upwards.
- However, do not ignore minor characters, as many collectors will want to complete a set. Combined with the fact that many minor characters were originally sold in smaller quantities, this can lead to high values. Look for typical clothes, poses, accessories or phrases associated with a character. Correctly licensed examples are typically more accurate and usually more desirable.
- Early pieces from a character's development are generally valuable, as fewer were usually sold and survive today. Condition is important: many items were promotional and were not made to last, so those pieces in truly mint condition will fetch a premium. Also consider the genre and the generation it appealed to – more recent characters may not rise in value until the generation that loved them has matured and gained more disposable income.

A Superman moulded plastic figurine, the base impressed "T.M. AND C. DC Comics Inc 1979".

*5in (13cm) high*

**£8-12** **NOR**

A 1980s moulded vinyl Superman 'big head' figurine.

*It was Remco, in 1964, who started the trend for dolls and figurines with oversized heads. Its most famous dolls were the Beatles.*

*2.75in (7cm) high*

**£2-4** **NOR**

A pair of enamelled metal Superman figures, with inset plastic chest decals.

*Unusually for such comparatively well-made pieces, their origin or use is unknown.*

*2.25in (6cm) high*

**£8-12 (EACH)** **NOR**

A Pyramid Belt Co. gilt metal and plastic belt buckle, with National Periodical Publications lettering.

*1973* *2.75in (7cm) wide*

**£12-18** **NOR**

A 'Superman Smashes The Secret of The Mad Director' first edition paperback, by George S. Elrick, published by Whitman Publishing.

*1966* *7.5in (19cm) high*

**£18-22** **NOR**

A Toys n' Things Superman inflatable, punchable 'Bop Bag', boxed.

*1992* *7.5in (19cm) high*

**£7-10** **NOR**

A UD Watch Co. Superman moulded plastic wrist watch, with "DC Comics (C)" lettering.

*1987* *8.25in (21cm) high*

**£20-40** **NOR**

A 1970s plastic faux leather Superman child's belt, with "(C) DC Comic Inc 1978" lettering.

*1978* *26.25in (66.5cm) long*

**£8-12** **NOR**

A 1980s Superman badge.

*1.75in (4.5cm) diam*

**£1-2** **NOR**

A Staffordshire Potteries 'Kiln Craft' Superman transfer-printed mug.

*This was available at the time that the first Superman movie was released.*

*c1978* *3.5in (9cm) high*

**£7-10** **MTS**

An A.P.C. Superman 204-piece jigsaw puzzle, complete, with original box.

*c1974* *5.5in (14cm) high*

**£7-10** **BH**

A Russell Mfg Co. set of Superman colouring-in playing cards.

*3.5in (9cm) high*

**£4-6** **NOR**

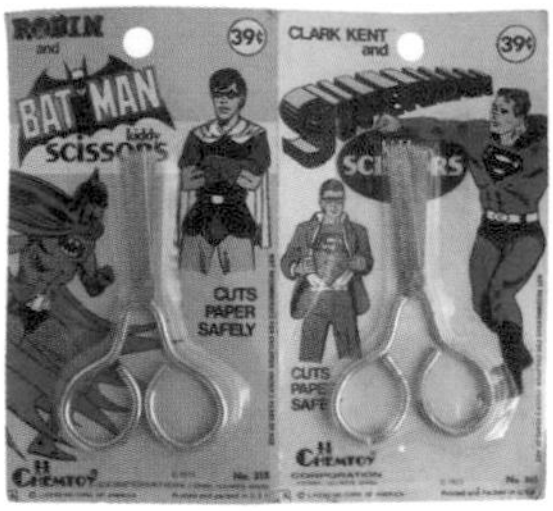


A Chemtoy Corp. pair of Batman and Superman carded metal scissors.

*As with most character collectables of this type, it is the card that is of interest. These otherwise unmarked scissors would have been inexpensive and the vast majority were opened, ruining the artwork.*

*c1973* *6.75in (17cm) high*

**£15-25** **NOR**

## A CLOSER LOOK AT A SUPERMAN FIGURE

*Toy Biz's DC Comics figurines were deemed poorly made by many buyers - the paint work was comparatively poor and a magnet inside Superman rattled.*

*As there had not been a Superman figurine for some years, the character sold relatively well despite the poorer quality.*

*Superman did not sell as well as other characters such as Batman - furthermore, this example is mint and unopened, which makes it doubly rare.*

*It is also complete with its original 'Kryptonite' ring, which was usually lost - rings are popular collectables.*

A 1990s Toy Biz Superman figurine, mint and unopened with card and Kryptonite ring.

*Toy Biz was awarded the DC Comic character license in 1989, after Kenner's 'Super Powers' line closed.*

*9.75in (25cm) high*

**£35-45** **NOR**

A Toy Biz Wonder Woman action figure.

*Although visually very similar to Kenner's version, Toy Biz' version is chunkier and shorter and has no peg hole in her foot.*

*4.25in (10.5cm) high*

**£4-6** **NOR**

A 1980s Wonder Woman pocket mirror.

*Will the new Wonderwoman film slated for 2009 mean that Diana will once again spin her Lasso of Truth and clink her indestructible bracelets together to rapturous applause?*

*3.25in (8cm) high*

**£2-3** **NOR**

An American G.E.C. electrical Wonder Woman plug nightlight, mint and boxed.

*1979 Card 6in (15cm) high*

**£8-12** **NOR**

A Mego World's Greatest Superheroes range 'The Penguin' dressed action figure, in complete, dressed condition.

*Mego's The Penguin, with his characterful face, was released in 1974 and was sold into the early 1980s. Surprisingly, he did not come with his umbrella, or indeed any accessory.*

*8.25in (21cm) high*

**£20-40** **NOR**

A Ralstons Natural Honey Nut Flavour 'Batman' cereal box, unopened, with free Batman plastic money bank promotion.

*1989 11in (28cm) high*

**£8-12** **NOR**

A Robin, The Boy Wonder screen-printed glass, with licensing wording.

*Boy Wonder items are often scarcer than those for Batman, as people preferred to buy pieces relating to the main character.*

*5in (13cm) high*

**£15-20** **NOR**

A 44-card set of Topps Batman 'Red Bat' series cards, printed with "1966 ©National Periodical Publications Ltd".

*1966 3.75in (9.5cm) wide*

**£10-15** **NOR**

A Captain Marvel 'Shazam' 7-Eleven promotional plastic slurpee cup.

*As the Captain Marvel name was owned by Marvel, DC Comics used the 'Shazam' trademark for their version.*

*1973 5.25in (13.5cm) high*

**£6-9** **BH**

A box of four Automatic Toy Co. lithographed tinplate 'Captain Marvel Racing Cars' clockwork toys, each with rubber tyres.

*This box would most probably have been displayed on a shop counter, rather than intended for sale as a 'boxed set'.*

*c1947 Each 4in (10cm) long*

**£550-650 BER**

A 'Captain Midnight' Ovaltine Shake-Up mug and cover, made for Wander Co. of Chicago.

*Ovaltine's far from cosy Captain Midnight character first aired on a Chicago radio station in 1938, and appeared on TV from 1954-56.*

*5in (12.5cm) high*

**£10-15 BH**

A 1980s Super Ted foam rubber bendy toy, by Petalcraft.

*Super Ted first aired in the UK in 1982, and bears many similarities to Captain Marvel, including the use of a magic word to transform. In 1992, he was revived in the US.*

*9.5in (24cm) high*

**£10-15 DIM**

A Popeye hand-painted figure, with two holes - possibly lacking cans of spinach, impressed "KFS Inc 1980".

*10.75in (27cm) high*

**£8-12 KNK**

A pair of Popeye and Olive Oyl poseable figures, by Broncho.

*c1978 6.5in (16.5cm) high*

**£15-25 RBC**

A J. Chein lithographed tinplate clockwork walking Popeye carrying parrot cages.

*8.5in (21.5cm) high*

**£180-220 BER**

A Japanese Linemar lithographed tinplate clockwork 'Popeye Roller Skater', with Popeye carrying a plate of spinach in one hand and wearing silk trousers.

*6.5in (16.5cm) high*

**£400-500 BER**

A Marx lithographed tinplate clockwork 'Popeye The Pilot' plane, lacks pipe.

*8in (20cm) wide*

**£600-800 BER**

A box of four Transogram Company 'Popeye's Big Fleet' wooden ships, each with a celluloid sail transfer-printed with Popeye in a different pose.

*Each 4in (10cm) long*

**£180-220 BER**

## A CLOSER LOOK AT A BUCK ROGERS BOOK

*This was part of the Solar Scouts membership pack offered as a promotion with Cream of Wheat cereal, who sponsored the radio show from 1935-1936.*

*The radio program was accompanied by a great many premiums and promotional toys from different sponsors - Solar Scout memorabilia is amongst the most desirable.*

*This booklet is extremely rare as many were worn through, damaged, defaced or lost - this example is in near mint condition with bright colours.*

*The interior shows 'secret information', which includes the other promotional items available such as a 'Repeller Ray Ring', leather helmet and a child's playsuit.*

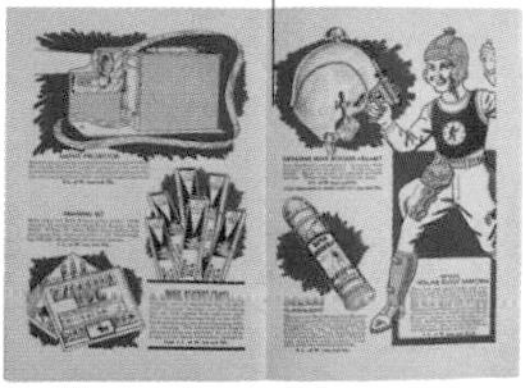

A 'Buck Rogers Solar Scouts' membership booklet, with equipment, Special Secrets of The Solar Scouts, etc.

*Buck Rogers first appeared in a comic strip in 1929, aired on radio from 1932-47, and first appeared on screen in 1939. Most will remember his more recent incarnation on TV from 1979-81, with Gil Gerard as Buck.*

*1936* *7.75in (19.5cm) high*

**£300-400** **LDE**

A Buck Rogers 'Solar Scouts' moulded brass pin, printed on back "To My Solar Scouts Pal" with stamped Buck Rogers signature.

*This was also offered as part of the 'Cream of Wheat' promotion, but is not as rare or desirable as the 'Repeller Ray Ring', which in top condition can fetch over £1,000.*

*1936* *1.5in (4cm) high*

**£50-70** **LDE**

A Sylvania Electric Products 'Buck Rogers Space Ranger Kit', with several card kits which can be folded and assembled into numerous Buck Rogers props from the popular comic book.

*This was also a promotional item, given away with a television. It included a large number of items essential for a space adventurer, such as an Atomic Space Rocket, Space Ranger Helmet, Disintegrator and even an Interplanetary Space Phone.*

*1952*

**£40-60** **BER**

A Pelham Puppets Collectors Series Thunderbirds 'Virgil' puppet, lacks box.

*1992*

**£35-45** **RBC**

A Pelham Puppets Collectors Series Thunderbirds 'Parker' puppet, lacks box.

*Not being one of the Tracey brothers, Parker was less popular among buyers, so tends to be harder to find. These were intended more as collectors' display pieces than toys. A second edition was released in 1999, using the same moulds and the Pelham brand name.*

*1992*

**£70-100** **RBC**

A Chinese Thinkway Toys 'Buzz Lightyear' poseable, speaking action figure.

*When 'Toy Story' was released in 1995, Buzz's popularity was so great that toy shops became virtual battle grounds in the lead-up to Christmas 1996. The manufacturer thought Woody would be the more popular toy and produced more Woody than Buzz figures.*

*1995-99* *11.75in (30cm) high*

**£8-12** **NOR**

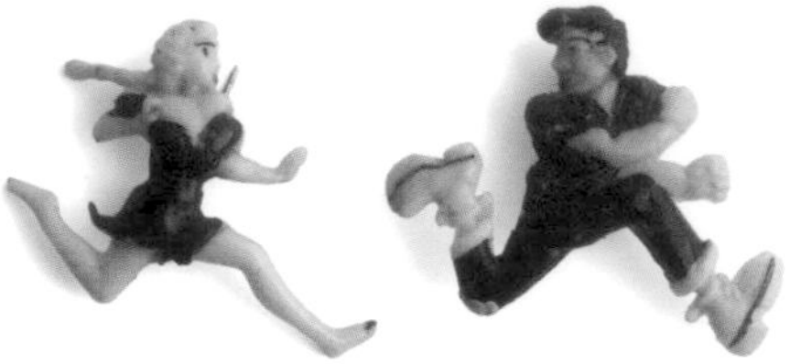

A pair of 1940s Daisy Mae and Li'l Abner painted celluloid pins.

*These delicate pins are rare on three counts. All the protruding parts have survived intact, with little wear to the paint, and they are very hard to find in a pair.*

*1.5in (4cm) high*

**£70-100** **LDE**

A 1920s Alfred E. Neuman 'Me, Worry?' postcard.

*5.5in (14cm) high*

**£8-12** **LDE**

A late 20thC 'Completely MAD' promotional pin, the reverse reading "To Order Call 1-800-343 9204".

*2.5in (6.5cm) diam*

**£30-40** **LDE**

A 1920s 'Alfred E. Neuman' painted plaster plaque, impressed "C A.E.N."

*Alfred E. Neuman is the fictional mascot of EC Publications' Mad magazine with the catchphrase "What, Me Worry?" He first appeared on a cover in November 1954 but the image had been in circulation much earlier.*

*6in (15cm) high*

**£40-60** **LDE**

A 1950s Chad Valley Andy Pandy hand puppet, with moulded vinyl head and fabric body.

*9in (23cm) high*

**£20-30** **RBC**

A 1930s 'Orphan Annie' transfer-printed mug, made for The Wander Co., Chicago, Makers of Ovaltine.

*3.25in (8cm) high*

**£10-15** **BH**

A 'Swing With Archie' pin, marked "1971 Archie Comic Publications Inc".

*1971* *3in (7.5cm) diam*

**£20-30** **LDE**

An Asterix plastic figure.

*2.25in (5.5cm) high*

**£8-12** **RBC**

A 1930s printed velvet Dismal Desmond soft toy, together with two small posters for 'A Howling Success', the new song and two shop display cards.

*Designed by Richard Ellett, Dismal Desmond was one of the most popular character toys in the UK during the 1920s, and was the mascot for the England cricket team in 1926. He was produced until the start of WWII and was reproduced during the 1980s and 1990s.*

*First 8.75in (22cm) long*

**£70-100** **BONC**

## A CLOSER LOOK AT A PIN

*This pin was made by Coro, a highly collectable costume jewellery maker.*

*It is extremely rare in any condition - this example only has a few chips to the black enamelling.*

*It was first advertised in Women's Wear Daily magazine in October 1937, with Bergen's phrase "My Diminutive Little Chum Enters Jewellery"*

*The tab at the bottom moves Charlie's mouth up and down, as on the real ventriloquist's dummy.*

A Coro 'Charlie McCarthy' enamelled and gold-plated cast metal pin, the back marked "Pat. 2038343 Mf'd under exclusive license from Edgar Bergen and Charlie McCarthy Inc".

*1in (3cm) high*

**£50-70** **LDE**

An Obelix plastic figure.

*2.25in (5.5cm) high*

**£8-12** **RBC**

A 1970s hard plastic Basil Brush figural night light.

*11in (28cm) high*

**£35-45** **MTS**

A Betty Boo brass and enamel pin.

*1.5in (4cm) high*

**£35-45** **LDE**

A Charlic McCarthy card figure, marked "Patent Applied for Ketterlinus Phila and NY".

*20.75in (53cm) high*

**£40-60** **TM**

A Louis Marx lithographed tinplate 'Charlie McCarthy Benzine Mobile' clockwork toy, in very good condition.

*7.5in (19cm) long*

**£100-150** **BER**

## A CLOSER LOOK AT A FELIX FIGURE

*This Felix was made by Schoenhut, an American company renowned for its wooden toys.*

*Schoenhut made him in a number of different sizes, the largest at 8in high is the rarest and can fetch over £350.*

*There is also a special 24in-high display version, which is exceptionally rare and could fetch considerably more.*

*It is in excellent condition, retaining the ears, nose, chest transfer and even the copyright transfer on the bottom of its foot.*

A small elastic-strung, jointed wood Felix the Cat figurine, with black painted leather ears, 'FELIX' transfer to stomach and "Felix (C)1922, 1924 by Pat Sullivan Pat June 23, 1925" transfer to foot.

*c1925* *4in (10cm) high*

**£80-120** **PWE**

An early 1920s straw-filled, wire-limbed felt Felix toy.

*Even though he is possibly homemade, earlier examples of Felix tend to look more 'scary'. Later on in his life, he became rounder and more friendly, losing his toothy grin.*

*13.75in (35cm) high*

**£70-100** **DIM**

A Born To Play 'Grommett' soft toy, with plastic rain coat and so'wester and handkerchief on stick.

*1989* *13.5in (34.5cm) high*

**£12-18** **RBC**

A 1970s boxed 'Happy Herman' figure, by Larami Corp.

*Larami Corp. was known during the 1970s for its inexpensive TV and character tie-in toys, typically found in grocery stores. This rather unsavoury character seems to have no tie-in however.*

*7.25in (18.5cm) high*

**£15-20** **NOR**

A 1970s Far Eastern plastic figure, probably Larami Corp.

*This figurine uses the same head as the one to the left, showing how companies recycled expensive moulds for different toys.*

*5.25in (13.5cm) high*

**£15-25** **NOR**

An NBC Howdy Doody doll, or child's ventriloquist's dummy, with moving mouth.

*1973* *25.25in (64cm) high*

**£40-50** **MG**

A 1950s Howdy Doody child's umbrella, with celluloid head.

*This is a rare survivor, with a complete and intact head and printed umbrella cover.*

*19in (48cm) long*

**£70-100** **MG**

A Howdy Doody Colouring Book, in mint and uncoloured condition.

*1954* *10.75in (27.5cm) high*

**£3-5** **BH**

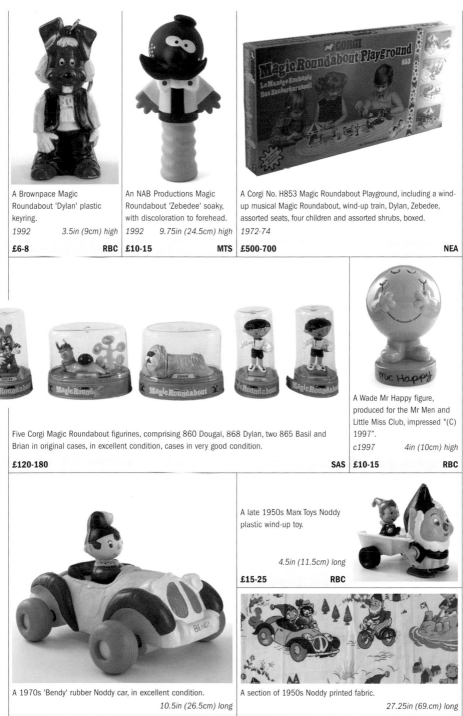

A Brownpace Magic Roundabout 'Dylan' plastic keyring.

*1992* *3.5in (9cm) high*

**£6-8** **RBC**

An NAB Productions Magic Roundabout 'Zebedee' soaky, with discoloration to forehead.

*1992* *9.75in (24.5cm) high*

**£10-15** **MTS**

A Corgi No. H853 Magic Roundabout Playground, including a wind-up musical Magic Roundabout, wind-up train, Dylan, Zebedee, assorted seats, four children and assorted shrubs, boxed.

*1972-74*

**£500-700** **NEA**

Five Corgi Magic Roundabout figurines, comprising 860 Dougal, 868 Dylan, two 865 Basil and Brian in original cases, in excellent condition, cases in very good condition.

**£120-180** **SAS**

A Wade Mr Happy figure, produced for the Mr Men and Little Miss Club, impressed "(C) 1997".

*c1997* *4in (10cm) high*

**£10-15** **RBC**

A 1970s 'Bendy' rubber Noddy car, in excellent condition.

*10.5in (26.5cm) long*

**£30-40** **RBC**

A late 1950s Marx Toys Noddy plastic wind-up toy.

*4.5in (11.5cm) long*

**£15-25** **RBC**

A section of 1950s Noddy printed fabric.

*27.25in (69.cm) long*

**£20-30** **MA**

A 1970s Noddy painted rubber figurine.

*5in (13cm) high*

**£7-10** **MA**

A Gabrielle Designs Paddington Bear soft toy, dressed in a felt hat, coat, and Wellington boots.

*19.5in (49.5cm) high*

**£40-50** **F**

A Louis Marx lithographed tinplate 'Porky Pig' clockwork toy, in very good condition.

*8.5in (21.5cm) high*

**£150-200** **BER**

A 1960s Chad Valley Sooty hand puppet.

*Many thousands of these hand puppets were sold, and the condition matters greatly for value. Items need to be in original, clean state to fetch this price.*

**£25-35** **RBC**

A 1970s Pedigree Great Uncle Bulgaria (Bulgaria Coburg Womble) stuffed toy, complete with spectacles, blanket and pipe cleaner walking stick.

*In the two original stop-motion TV series that aired in 1973 and 1975, Great Uncle Bulgaria's tartan was green and blue. In 1998, Elizabeth's Beresford's characters were acquired by a Canadian company who transformed them into an animated series.*

*10in (25.5cm) high*

**£20-30** **RBC**

A Pedigree 'Madame Cholet' Wombles soft toy, with hat and apron.

*7in (18cm) high*

**£15-20** **RBC**

A 1990s Wombles fur-covered plastic figure.

*7in (18cm) high*

**£7-10** **RBC**

A 1970s The Wombles 'Great Uncle Bulgaria' shaped soap, boxed, by Bellair Cosmetics of Cheshire.

*Box 4.25in (10.5cm) high*

**£5-7** **MTS**

A Worzel Gummidge handpuppet, with plastic head and fabric body.

*Living scarecrow Worzel Gummidge was played in the popular 1979-81 TV series by Jon Pertwee, who more famously played the third incarnation of Doctor Who from 1970-74.*

*c1980 10.5in (26.5cm) high*

**£30-40** **RBC**

## COLLECTORS' NOTES

- Metal chocolate moulds were widely used from the late 1800s, reaching their height of popularity during the 1920s and 1930s. Germany was a centre of production, but molds were also made in France and the US. Metal chocolate moulds were replaced by less costly plastic moulds in the 1950s.
- Makers included H.Walter of Berlin, Sommet of Paris and Eppelsheimer of New York. Many examples carry stamped numbers which were used in the ordering process to indicate a catalogue number. Although many moulds do not have maker's names, their style, manufacture and position of the catalogue number can help to identify makers.
- A variety of symbols were used by the different makers. Sommet, for example, used a stylised fish and Eppelsheimer, a spinning top. Marked, and particularly dated, examples are more desirable in general. Materials can also indicate date of manufacture. Tin-plated copper was used until the late 1890s, when it was largely replaced by tin-plated steel (the most commonly found material). Later examples used nickel-plated steel and nickel silver and have a shiny silvery appearance.
- Moulds by German maker Reiche are particularly popular. Founded in 1870, the company produced over 50,000 designs. T.C Weygandt of New York imported Reiche moulds from 1885 until 1939, when WWII broke out. The factory re-opened in Communist East Germany in 1950 after the original plant was destroyed in the war. It closed in 1972.
- Large moulds and fine detailing attract higher prices. Unusual details or forms can add value. Clips are rarely original as they were interchanged many times during use.

A French Sommet chocolate and one litre ice cream mould, no. 1417, in the form of a cockerel.

*The presence of a pull off lid on the base shows this is also an ice cream mould. It is stamped with a stylised fish showing it was made by Sommet and also has a '49' in a diamond stamping, dating it precisely.*

*1949* *10.5in (27cm) high*

**£150-200** **DF**

An unmarked cockerel hugging a chicken chocolate mould, no. 6537.

*3.5in (9cm) high*

**£50-100** **DF**

A chicken in a basket chocolate mould, no. 6558.

*Makers' numbers and marks are often worn away by the clips being pulled on and off.*

*3.75in (9.5cm) high*

**£20-30** **DF**

An American Eppelsheimer dressed chick mould, no. 8037.

*5in (12.5cm) high*

**£40-60** **DF**

A German Anton Reiche cockerel, chicken, and chick chocolate mould, with date mark and agency copyright wording "Ohne Unsere Genehmigung Darf Dieses Muster Anderen Nicht Unterbrietet Werden" and "George Diltoer Agent Generale Berchem Bruxelles".

*1933* *6in (15cm) long*

**£40-60** **DF**

A French Letang Fils pelican chocolate mould, no. 3611.

*8in (20cm) high*

**£140-160** **DF**

A penguin chocolate mould, no. 4270, stamped "F.Q". or "F.O". on the base.

*4.75in (12cm) high*

**£50-80** **DF**

An unmarked elephant chocolate mould, with raised trunk.

*A raised trunk was meant to bring or indicate good luck.*

*8.5in (21.5cm) wide*

**£100-150** **DF**

A German Walter chocolate mould of a dromedary.

*2.25in (6cm) high*

**£40-60** **DF**

A 1930s French Letang Fils fish chocolate mould.

*The remarkable condition of this mould can be explained by the fact that many Letang moulds, made just before WWII, languished in a warehouse during the war. They were distributed later, during the 1940s and 1950s, but many were not used.*

*12.5in (31.5cm) long*

**£70-100** **DF**

## A CLOSER LOOK AT A CHOCOLATE MOULD

*It is lacking one of its two separate ears – if it were complete, its value could be around £5,000.*

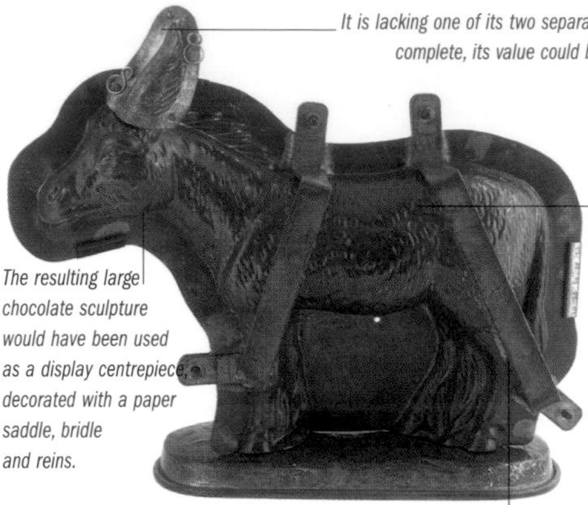

*The resulting large chocolate sculpture would have been used as a display centrepiece, decorated with a paper saddle, bridle and reins.*

*These support brackets are unusual for Reiche, being more commonly associated with French maker Letang.*

*Weighing in at over 11kg, this chocoholics' dream would also have been dressed with chocolate baskets filled with individual chocolates.*

A large German Anton Reiche donkey chocolate mould.

*16.5in (42cm) high*

**£3,000-4,000** **DF**

A postwar American T.C. Weygandt Scottie dog nickel-plated chocolate mould, no.383.

*Weingandt was originally an importer for German maker Anton Reiche. After the war, it also made its own moulds, but these do not have the sharpness and detail of Reiche's originals.*

*4.75in (12cm) high*

**£35-45** **DF**

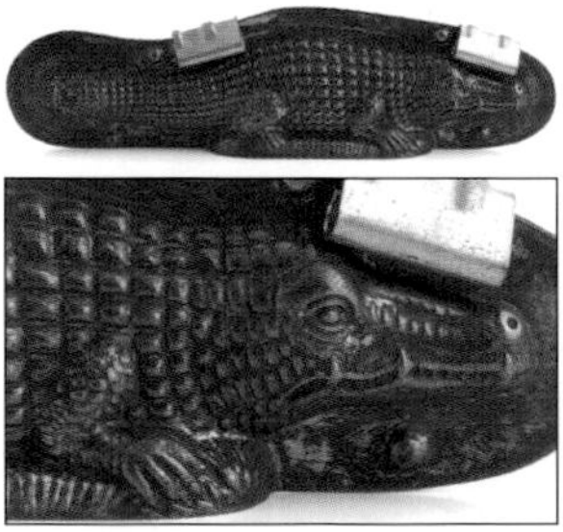

A German Anton Reiche crocodile chocolate mould, no. SB1156.

*8in (20.5cm) long*

**£120-180** **DF**

A postwar Dutch Vormenfabriek dog nickel-plated chocolate mould, no. 16164, stamped "JKV Tilburg".

*4.25in (11cm) high*

**£15-20** **DF**

An unmarked frog chocolate mould, no. 8435.

*3.5in (9cm) long*

**£60-90** **DF**

A French Letang Fils Santa chocolate mould, with clasped hands and long coat, no. 2040.

*6.5in (16.5cm) high*

**£40-60** **DF**

An American nickel-plated Santa chocolate mould, no. 1042.

*This more rounded form is the other most common form for Santa to take, and is more American in style.*

*8in (20.5cm) high*

**£180-220** **DF**

## A CLOSER LOOK AT A CHOCOLATE MOULD

This size of mould, at over 13 inches high, is very rare - most were half this size.
This specific type of Santa is usually found without the teddy and horse, just holding the lantern
This tall, long-coated style is one of the most typical forms for Santa. Values vary depending on the maker, as well as how much and what he is holding.
This is one of only a few examples of this type known to collectors, making him extremely rare.

A German Anton Reiche Santa chocolate mould, no. 13133.

*13.75in (35cm) high*

**£1,200-1,800** **DF**

A German Anton Reiche 'postcard' chocolate mould, with Santa and children in front of a Christmas tree, no. 522.

*Rectangular 'postcard' molds are highly collectable. Values vary depending on the maker, size, image shown and level of detail in the image. This is a highly detailed example by a known maker in a sought-after theme.*

*7in (17.5cm) high*

**£350-450** **DF**

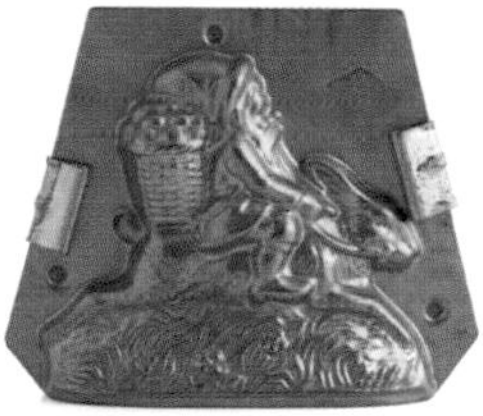

A postwar BM nickel silver chocolate mould of Santa on a running rabbit, stamped "34 Solid Nickel Silver".

*4.25in (11cm) high*

**£250-300** **DF**

A German Walter Santa on a motorbike chocolate mould, numbered inside "9599".

*Walter was the only company to stamp its mould numbers on the inside.*

*4.25in (10.5cm) wide*

**£80-120** **DF**

A German Anton Reiche angel chocolate mould, no. 13053.

*5.25in (13cm) high*

**£70-100** **DF**

A French Letang Fils angel chocolate mould.

*This example and the near identical example on the left show how often makers copied each other. However, the finishing on the Letang is not as fine, note the badly cut 'overlap' on the middle left corner. The detail is also less fine than on Reiche's example.*

*4.75in (12cm) high*

**£60-90** **DF**

A large French Letang Fils turkey chocolate mould, unmarked, no. 274.

*7.5in (19cm) high*

**£200-300** **DF**

A small unmarked turkey chocolate mould.

*4.5in (11.5cm) high*

**£25-35** **DF**

A German Anton Reiche witch on a broomstick chocolate mould, no. 22167S, marked and imported into the US by T.C Weygandt.

*6.25in (16cm) high*

**£150-200** **DF**

A German three-piece turkey chocolate mould, stamped "Germany" and "93".

*It is rare to find a chocolate mould with three pieces as here.*

*8in (20cm) high*

**£350-450** **DF**

A German Anton Reiche Halloween 'scaredy cat' chocolate mould, dated and stamped no. 17473.

*Note the clips, which are clearly not original. This does not affect the value as clips were never original, being interchanged many time over by the chocolatiers as they used the molds.*

*1930* *3.5in (9cm) long*

**£70-100** **DF**

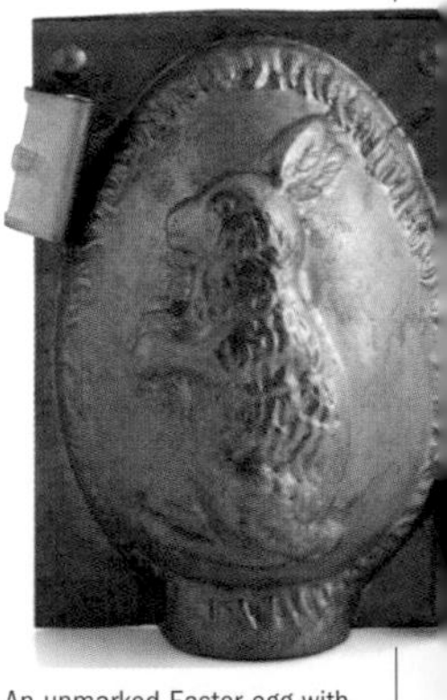

An unmarked Easter egg with rabbit chocolate mould.

*4.5in (11.5cm) high*

**£50-80** **DF**

A Belgian car chocolate mould, stamped "Cer ... ernard S.A. Bruxelles".

*5.25in (13.5cm) long*

**£40-60** **DF**

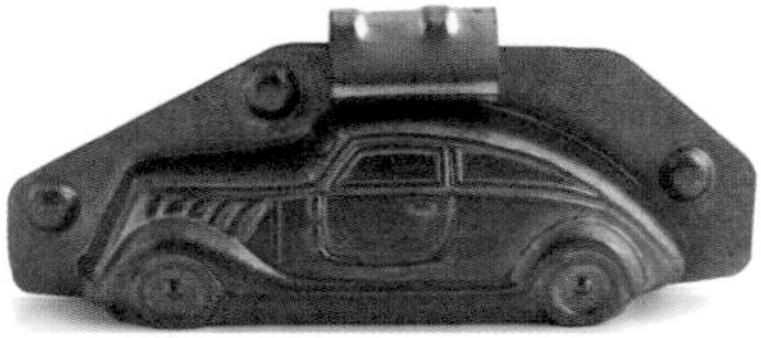

A German small car chocolate mould, stamped "Made in Berlin Germany".

*4.25in (10.5cm) long*

**£20-30** **DF**

An unmarked German chocolate mould of an armored car.

*4in (10cm) long*

**£40-60** **DF**

A German postwar nickel-plated tractor chocolate mould, imported and stamped by "E. Hahn Buffalo N.Y." and "Made in Germany".

*4.75in (12cm) long*

**£20-30** **DF**

A rare German F.W. Kutzscher of Schwarzenberg Zeppelin chocolate mould, no. 5551.

*Due to its quality, this mould was once thought to have been made by Walter or Anton Reiche, but a recently discovered catalogue has now identified it as being by short-lived maker Kutzcher. The Zeppelin is also a desirable form and it is very well detailed, adding to its desirability.*

*9in (23cm) wide*

**£200-250** **DF**

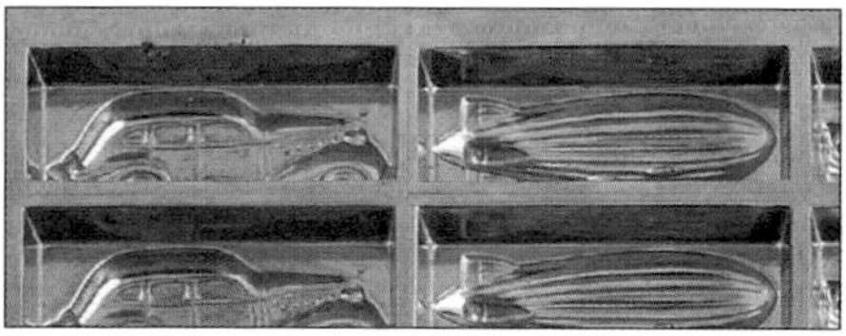

A German Anton Reiche flat chocolate mould of various modes of transport, no. 29907-10, with T.C. Weygandt importers and date stamps.

*The maker, date, large size and form make this a desirable and valuable mould. It would have been used to create 48 individual flat-backed chocolates and includes a desirable Zeppelin.*

*1934* *16.5in (42cm) long*

**£150-200** **DF**

A postwar Dutch Vormenfabriek kettle chocolate mould, no. 16014, also marked with retailer's stamp for "Jos Boyen Bruxelles".

*23.5in (60cm) high*

**£20-30** **DF**

A pre-war German Walter coffee grinder nickel-plated chocolate mould, no. 9574.

*Unusually for Walter, the number is stamped outside. The use of nickel shows that the mould was in use before the war.*

*2.25in (6cm) high*

**£40-60** **DF**

A German Anton Reiche shop scales chocolate mould, no. 28409, with date stamp.

*1935* *3.75in (9.5cm) high*

**£30-50** **DF**

An unmarked very large and heavy key chocolate mould.

*It is the size as well as the unusual shape that make this so valuable - a smaller 6in example may fetch around $70-100.*

*16.25in (41cm) long*

**£120-180** **DF**

An American Eppelsheimer shell chocolate mould, no. 7470.

*7.75in (19.5cm) long*

**£70-100** **DF**

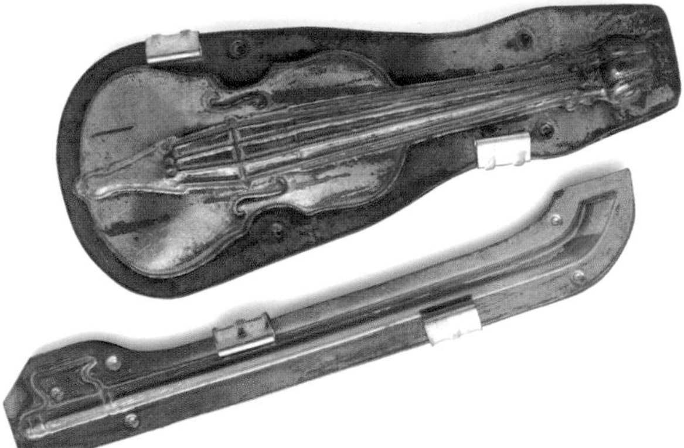

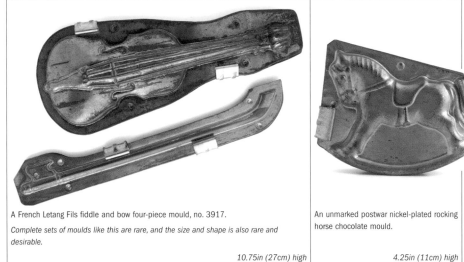

A French Letang Fils fiddle and bow four-piece mould, no. 3917.

*Complete sets of moulds like this are rare, and the size and shape is also rare and desirable.*

*10.75in (27cm) high*

**£120-180** **DF**

An unmarked postwar nickel-plated rocking horse chocolate mould.

*4.25in (11cm) high*

**£30-50** **DF**

A Dutch De Smedt Willebroek teddy bear chocolate mould, no. 16159.

*5.25in (13.5cm) high*

**£30-50** **DF**

A postwar Dutch Vormannfabriek teddy bear nickel-plated chocolate mould, no. 16055.

*4.25in (10.5cm) high*

**£30-50** **DF**

An unmarked German teddy bear chocolate mould, no. 23989, with hinged clips.

*The teddy bear is a highly collectable subject and so can fetch high prices, even for simpler, later moulds. This example is valuable because it is finely detailed, is in a different and charming pose and is more three-dimensional than others.*

*4in (10cm) high*

**£250-350** **DF**

An unmarked defecating monk chocolate mould, stamped "43".

*As well as being aimed at children, some subjects appealed to adults. A series of unusual, sometimes bizarre, subjects can be found and are highly collectable among today's collectors.*

*4.5in (11.5cm) high*

**£22-28** **DF**

A German Laur ... 'Paul on the Pot' chocolate mould, no. 13055, with oval maker's stamp.

*4.25in (11cm) high*

**£20-30** **DF**

A postwar Hansel & Gretel nickel chocolate mould, no. 2597, also stamped "121".

*5.25in (13.5cm) high*

**£50-80** **DF**

A French Sommet tin-plated copper horse and jockey chocolate mould, no. 1811.

*Sommet moulds are typified by overlapping edges.*

*9.5in (24cm) high*

**£250-350** **DF**

## COLLECTORS' NOTES

- Due to the vast range of coins produced in different countries, during different time periods and across different denominations, most collectors choose to focus on one country, date period or type of coin. Coin collectors are known as numismatists, however, bank notes, bonds and share certificates can also be added to the wider collecting area.
- If a coin is early, it is not necessarily valuable. A rare 20th century coin can be worth more than a more common Roman coin. Nevertheless, dates are important considerations as regards the amount of coins minted in a year, or the first year a type of coin was produced, so always pay close attention. Also consider denomination, the higher the value of a coin, the rarer it may be, as fewer are likely to have been made.
- Beware of facsimile coins, which are not necessarily made to deceive but to allow collectors to add a representation of a certain rare or valuable coin to their collections. In general, do not clean coins, as collectors tend to prefer them with their original patina, built up over time. Cleaning can reduce a coins value by up to 90 per cent.
- Condition is of vital importance to collectors and value, and it would be a good idea to familiarise yourself with the different terms used and the appearances of coins in different level of condition. Handle coins as little as possible, and store them in special plastic albums or cases.

A tetradrachm of Alexandria, Ptolemaic Kingdom, minted by Ptolemy II Philadelphia (285-246BC), diademned bust of Ptolemy I right, the reverse with eagle with closed wings, monogram to left, obverse slightly offcentre, in extremely fine condition.

**£550-650** **BLO**

A Bactrian Kingdom tetradrachm, minted by Eukratides I, bust right wearing crested helmet, the reverse with The Dioskouri on horseback right, "NP" monogram to left, in about extremely fine condition.

*171-145BC*

**£350-450** **BLO**

A Byzantine Empire gold solidus of Constantinople, minted by Constans II (AD641-668), the obverse with facing busts of Constans and Constantine IV, the reverse with "Victoria AVGV", cross potent on steps between Heraclius and Tiberius, in about extremely fine condition.

**£250-350** **BLO**

A Ptolemaic Kingdom tetradrachm of Paphos mint, minted by Ptolemy VI, "LK" in field indicating year 20, in very fine condition with attractive grey tones.

*180-145BC*

**£120-180** **BLO**

A Roman denarius, minted by Tiberius (AD14-37), the reverse with pontif maxim, Livia seated, good to very fine condition.

*This coin is commonly referred to as the 'Tribute Penny of the Bible' and is believed to be the penny referred to by Christ in Matthew 22:20-21. Variations are known with different chair legs, an example with plain, straight chair legs is said to be the earliest.*

**£80-120** **BLO**

A Syrian silver tetradrachm, minted under Seleukos II, diademed head right, the reverse with Apollo left holding arrow, in good to very fine condition.

*246-226BC*

**£320-380** **BLO**

A scarce 2ndCBC Thracian gold stater, Callitis, posthumous type, the reverse with Athena enthroned, trident in exergue, "PHA" monogram to left, in extremely fine condition.

**£600-700** **BLO**

A scarce type 4a crown, of Tower mint under Parliament, minted by Charles I, foreshortened horse, mid-grey tones, in very fine condition, noting weak areas of strike around King's head.

*1625-49*

**£800-1,200** **BLO**

A cartwheel twopence, minted by George III (1767-1820), in extremely fine condition, noting some edge bruising.

*Around 15 per cent of the original red lustre remains, which is a scarce feature.*

*1797*

**£80-120** **BLO**

A halfcrown, minted by Edward VII (1902-10), virtually mint state, light obverse marks.

*1910*

**£220-280** **BLO**

## A CLOSER LOOK AT A BRITISH COIN

*This is from a series of milled silver and gold coins designed by Thomas Simons and produced on Peter Blondeau's machines - the sixpence is the rarest.*

*They are known as 'Tanner's Dies' sixpences as John Tanner, the Royal Mint's chief engraver, produced copies of the original dies in 1738, after they had been acquired by the Royal Mint.*

*The bust is that of Oliver Cromwell, Lord Protector, who first ordered his bust to appear on coins in 1656. Coins with his bust are scarce.*

*Made from Tanner's dies, this is an excellent, detailed strike with appealing toning and is perhaps the best example to have come to the market in recent years.*

An extremely rare 'Tanner's Dies' sixpence, virtually as struck with charcoal, blue and gold tones, contained in a Professional Coin Grading Service slab and graded "PR65".

*1658*

**£7,000-9,000** **BLO**

A 'young head' shilling, minted by Victoria (1837-1901), in about as struck condition with full radiant lustre, light obverse friction.

*'Young head' refers to the youthful appearance of Queen Victoria. The 'old head' bust was introduced in 1893 and was used until her death in 1901.*

*1845*

**£220-280** **BLO**

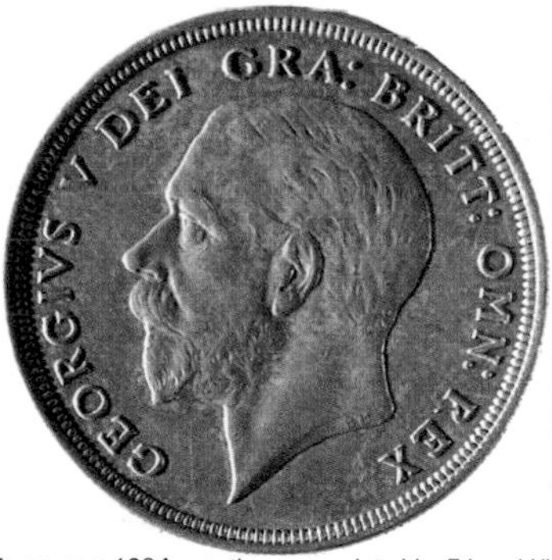

A very rare 1934 wreath crown, minted by Edward VII (1902-10), in about as struck condition, the reverse with proof-like fields.

*Keep your eyes peeled - only 932 crowns were struck in this year, making them very rare today.*

*1934*

**£2,500-3,000** **BLO**

An American Liberty dollar, with obverse engraved "R.v.B, 5IX.1903", coin fair, scarce as a love token.

*Unengraved, the value may rise to £1,000.*

*1799*

**£200-300** **BLO**

An American capped bust quarter, slight staining, in good very fine condition.

*1825*

**£400-500** **BLO**

An extremely fine American trade dollar.

*This was the first year Trade Dollars were produced. Poorer quality Chinese copies are being made today, which are lighter in weight.*

*1874* *27.22 grams*

**£70-100** **BLO**

An American five dollars Half Eagle, in about as struck condition with full lustre, light abrasion to obverse.

*Circulated versions of this coin are generally worth only the value of the metal as they are much more common than high grade condition coins, which themselves are not too hard to find.*

*1899*

**£150-200** **BLO**

An American twenty dollars Double Eagle, in good very fine condition, lightly polished.

*6,256,699 examples of this coin were minted. As such, it can be quite easily found in mint condition.*

*1904*

**£400-500** **BLO**

An emergency issue dollar, with small oval countermark and bust of George III on a Mexico 8 Reales 1795 FM, coin and mark about extremely fine.

*Emergency dollars were coins from other countries that were seized and restruck as British currency to solve the short fall of Crowns caused by a shortage of silver. Similar hexagonal countermarks are rarer and can double the value.*

*1795*

**£280-320** **BLO**

A scarce Lima, Peru mint of eight Reales, in good very fine condition, toned.

*1824*

**£80-120** **BLO**

A Freiberg, German City States, kreuzgroschen, minted by Frederick the Bellicose (1386-93), in good to very fine condition.

*1382*

**£35-45** **BLO**

## A CLOSER LOOK AT AN AUSTRALIAN SOVEREIGN

*The discovery of gold in Australia in 1851 led to the creation of Australian gold coins. This was uncontrolled and could have destabilised the official currency.*

*This coin is from the first run of 21,000, and as such was the first authorised and official Australian gold currency.*

*To prevent this, the Bank of England founded the Sydney Mint, which opened in 1855 and became the first mint to produce a British sovereign outside the UK.*

*It is generally found in poorer circulated condition. Examples in very fine or better condition are rare.*

An Australian first-type Sydney mint sovereign, in about very fine condition.

*Interestingly this coin was also the first to have a portrait of Victoria different to that used in London. In 2005, a 150th anniversary commemorative coin was issued by the Australian Mint.*

1855

**£1,800-2,200** **BLO**

A German five reichmarks, from the Weimar Republic, in about as struck condition, noting some friction to high points.

*1927*

**£150-200** **BLO**

A scarce 1914 Australian florin, with 'H' date mark denoting it was struck by the Heaton Mint, Birmingham, in good condition.

*1914 (H)*

**£40-60** **BLO**

An Indian Princely States gold mohur, in very fine condition.

*c1770*

**£100-150** **BLO**

A Mombassa Imperial British East Africa Company rupee, uncirculated, noting slight contact marks.

*1884*

**£70-90** **BLO**

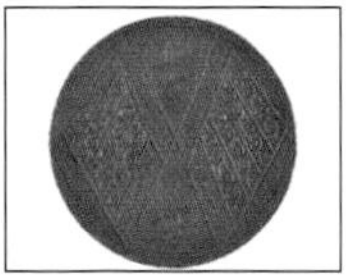

A Chinese sar (tael), from Sinkiang, the reverse with flags with arabesques in four stripes, in good fine to very fine condition with weakly struck obverse.

*c1912*

**£80-120** **BLO**

## COLLECTORS' NOTES

- Interest in British comics continues to rise, fuelled by nostalgia and a lively trade on the Internet. Although not reaching the giddy heights of some US superhero titles, the market is growing and solidifying.
- One of the main publishers in the UK was, and still is, Dundee-based D.C. Thomson, who were responsible for titles including The Beano, The Dandy, The Wizard, The Hotspur and Victor, all of which can be sought-after today. Other titles to look for include the Eagle, running from 1950 to 1969 and featuring the ever-popular Dan Dare. While comics aimed at girls are of less interest, the market is growing along with prices.
- Given the quality of the paper these comics were printed on, examples in good condition, with no tears or annotations, are the most sought-after. Look for issues that retains their promotional gifts as they were usually removed to be played with and then thrown away.

"Adventure", no.1321, May 13, 1950, published by D.C. Thomson & Co. Ltd.

*A story paper as rather than a comic, Adventure ran from 1921 to 1961 and was one of D.C. Thomson's 'Big Five'*

**£3-4** **PCOM**

"The Beano", no.407, May 6, 1950, published by D.C. Thomson & Co. Ltd., with Biffo the Bear cover story.

*Biffo the Bear was the cover star from 1948 until 1974, after which Dennis the Menace took over. Pre-1950 issues are scarce.*

**£8-12** **PCOM**

"The Beano Book", published by D.C. Thomson & Co. Ltd., limited edition reprint of the first Beano Book published in 1940, in an edition of 2,000.

*A copy of the 1940 original Beano Book could be worth around £3,000 in very good condition.*

*2004*

**£80-100** **PCOM**

"The Beano", no. 1066, December 22, 1962, Christmas edition, published by D.C. Thomson & Co. Ltd.

**£10-15** **PCOM**

"Beryl the Peril", 1959 annual, published by D.C. Thomson & Co. Ltd.

*Beryl the Peril appeared in Topper comics from its inception in February 1953. She gained her own annual in 1959, which were published bi-annually with the Dennis the Menace annuals until 1977, after which there were three further annuals in 1981, 1987 and 1988.*

*1959*

**£50-65** **PCOM**

"The Broons", October 2006, published by D.C. Thomson & Co. Ltd. and Aurum Press, reprint of the 1939 annual.

*A copy of the original 1939 annual has made £4,000 at auction.*

*2006*

**£10-15** **PCOM**

"Bunty", January 24, 1959, published by D.C. Thomson & Co. Ltd.

*1959*

**£3-5** **BPAL**

"The Dandy", no.121, March 23, 1940, published by D.C. Thomson & Co. Ltd., with Korky the Cat cover story.

*Early Dandy comics contained a propaganda strip called 'Addie & Hermy, The Nasty Nazis' for morale boosting. The pair were the brunt of many a war time prank.*

*1940*

**£25-45** **PCOM**

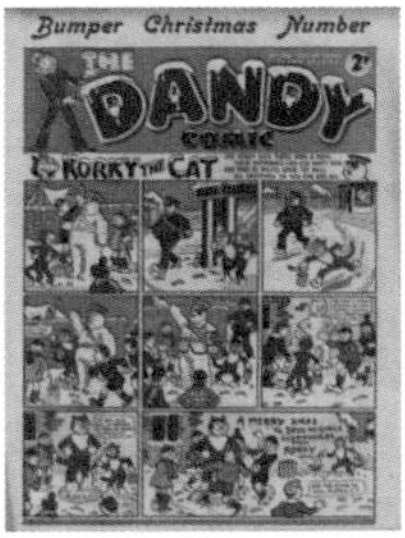


"The Dandy", no.159, December 14, 1940, published by D.C. Thomson & Co. Ltd., with Korky the Cat cover story.

*The Dandy was reduced in both page number and dimensions during WWII due to paper shortages.*

*1940*

**£20-30** **PCOM**

"The Dandy", no.326, August 31, 1946, published by D.C. Thomson & Co. Ltd., with Korky the Cat cover story.

*Print runs during WWII and immediately afterwards were low due to paper shortages. Korky the Cat was The Dandy cover star from no.1 (1937) through to the 1980s.*

*1946*

**£15-25** **PCOM**

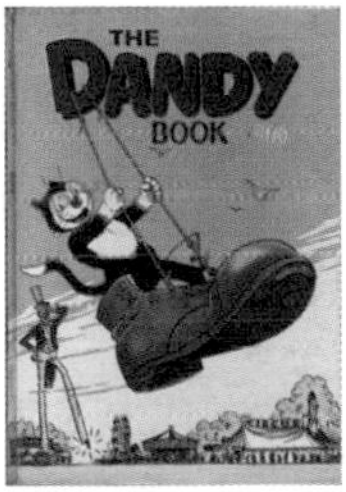


"The Dandy Book", 1966 annual, published by D.C. Thomson & Co. Ltd.

*Dandy comics had laminated covers from 1961 and examples without cracks to the laminated spine groove are very hard to find.*

*1966*

**£25-35** **PCOM**

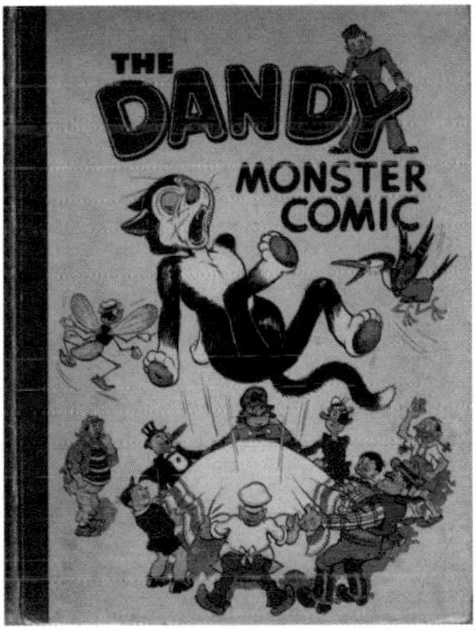


"The Dandy Monster Comic", 1947 annual, published by D.C. Thomson & Co. Ltd.

*The Dandy Monster annuals are sought-after. The name changed to The Dandy Book in 1952.*

*1947*

**£250-350** **PCOM**

"The Dandy Summer Special", 1966 annual, published by D.C. Thomson & Co. Ltd.

*The Summer Special was a large format comic which often had a classic British seaside scene on its front and rear cover story. 1960s issues are scarce.*

*1966*

**£30-50** **PCOM**

A Dandy Thunderbang promotional gift, produced by D.C. Thomson & Co. Ltd.

*This cardboard 'banger' was one of a number of promotional gifts given away with The Dandy. This is from a 1960 issue and is hard to find today.*

*c1960*

**£15-20** **PCOM**

"Eagle", vol.3, no.10, June 13, 1952, published by Hulton Press, with Dan Dare cover story.

*1952*

**£3-5** **PCOM**

"The Hotspur", no.687, January 7, 1950, published by D.C. Thomson & Co. Ltd.

*1950*

**£6-8** **BPAL**

"The Hotspur", no.874, August 8, 1953, published by D.C. Thomson & Co. Ltd., with dramatic one-shot cover.

*Hotspur was another of Thomson's 'Big Five' boys comics. It first appeared in 1933 and ran until the 1980s.*

*1953*

**£2-3** **PCOM**

## A CLOSER LOOK AT AN OOR WULLIE COMIC

*Oor Wullie is a Scottish institution, the speech bubbles being written in such a style that they are spoken with the accent.*

*First appearing in The Sunday Post Fun Section in 1936, Oor Wullie had his own bi-yearly annual from 1940*

*The Summer Fun Specials were produced during the 1980s, and are surprisingly scarce.*

*A number of characters from The Broons have crossed over to Oor Wullie and The Broon annual is printed in between this one.*

"Oor Wullie Summer Fun Special", 1987 annual, published by D.C. Thomson & Co. Ltd.

*1987*

**£10-15** **PCOM**

"The Magic Comic", no. 30, February 10, 1940, published by D.C. Thomson & Co. Ltd.

*Magic began in 1940 and ran for only 80 issues until it's demise in 1941 due to paper shortages. Some of the characters, including Koko the Pup, were transferred to The Beano and Magic-Beano annuals were produced between 1943 and 1950. Given the short print run of this title, it is sought-after today.*

*1940*

**£50-100** **PCOM**

"The Magic-Beano Book", 1950 annual, published by D.C. Thomson & Co. Ltd.

*All issues of this title are hard to find, particularly those printed during WWII.*

*1950*

**£150-250** **PCOM**

"Rainbow", no.1474, April 29, 1944.

*1944*

**£15-25** **VM**

"The Rover Book For Boys", 1958 annual, published by D.C. Thomson & Co. Ltd., in fine condition.

*1958*

**£20-30** **PCOM**

"The Rover", no.1494, February 13, 1954, published by D.C. Thomson & Co. Ltd.

*1954*

**£2-3** **PCOM**

"Sparky", no.11, April 3, 1965, published by D.C. Thomson & Co. Ltd.

*Sparky ran from 1965 until 1977 when it merged with Topper.*

*1965*

**£5-8** **PCOM**

"TV Century 21", no.1, January 23, "2065", published by Century 21 Productions.

*This first issue was released in 1965, but was dated at 2065 as if it were reporting the current news of that time. From issue 165 'Century' was dropped from the title. In 1969 it became "TV21 & Joe 90" until 1971 when it merged with Valiant. The comic featured stories about Gerry Anderson characters such as Captain Scarlet, Thunderbirds, Fireball XL5 and Stingray.*

*1965*

**£15-25** **PCOM**

"Wham!", no.1, June 20, 1964, published by Odhams Press.

*Wham! was created by Leo Baxendale, a former D.C. Thomson artist best known for his work on The Bash Street Kids. It ran for 187 issues before merging with Pow! in 1968.*

*1964*

**£20-30** **PCOM**

## A CLOSER LOOK AT A RUPERT ANNUAL

*Rupert Bear has featured in the Daily Express for over 80 years, and has had his own annual every year since 1936.*

*In the 1960s, 'Magic Paintings' were included in the annuals, in which readers could apply water with a paint brush to the pages and colour would 'magically' appear.*

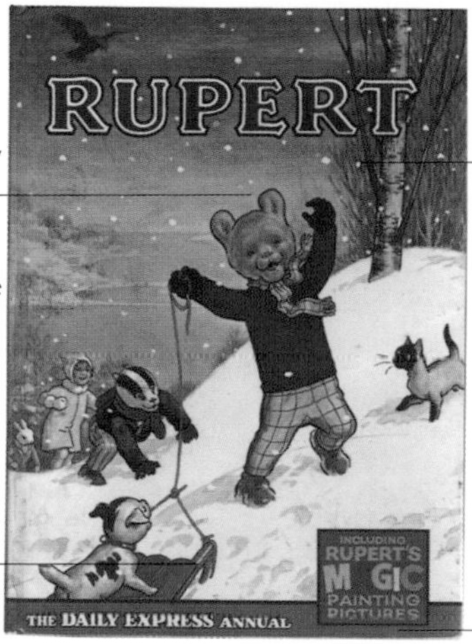


*Early 1960s annuals in excellent condition can be worth over £200.*

*It is hard to find copies where the 'Magic Painting' hasn't been painted over. If this example had been in mint condition with the Magic Paintings untouched, then the value would be £100-150.*

"Rupert", 1967 annual, published by the Daily Express.

*1967*

**£15-25** **PCOM**

"The Victor for Boys Summer Special", 1970 annual, published by D.C. Thomson & Co. Ltd.

*The Victor ran until the 1990s with an annual each Christmas from 1964, and a Summer Special each year from 1967.*

*1970*

**£7-10** **PCOM**

"Victor", no.1099, March 13, 1982, published by D.C. Thomson & Co. Ltd.

*1982*

**£2-3** **BPAL**

"The Wizard", no.1484, July 24, 1954, published by D.C. Thomson & Co. Ltd.

*1954*

**£2-3** **PCOM**

"The Wizard", no.1821, January 7, 1961, published by D.C. Thomson & Co. Ltd.

*1961*

**£5-6** **BPAL**

## COLLECTORS' NOTES

- Collecting vintage comics first became popular during the 1960s when the first conventions were organised, and had become an established field by the 1970s. Since then the market has grown steadily and comics are traded almost as stocks and shares. While mainstream characters such as Spiderman and Superman will always be popular, more minor characters are affected by changing trends, often influenced by spin-off blockbuster movies.
- While many automatically think of superheroes when it comes to comics, horror comics are also a very popular collecting area. The heyday for these titles was the 1950s, when superheroes were in decline. The two publishers best known for horror comics are E.C. Comics run by William Gaines and Star Publications owned by L.B. Cole. The lurid covers, combined with shocking storylines inside were hugely popular with teenage boys, but less so with the Comic Code Authority ruling of 1954, which saw the end of horror comics and changed the comic industry as a whole.
- Condition is vital as comics are often damaged and worn when read. Early comics and pulp magazines were not made to last, being printed on inexpensive paper. The paper darkens with age and its colour affects the value. Look for doodles and scrawlings by previous owners, detached or missing covers, tears and lost pages or areas. Restoration is possible and is considered necessary on some rarer titles.

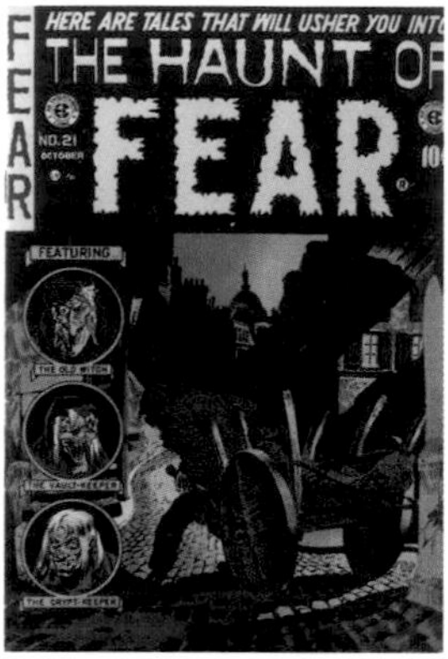


"The Haunt of Fear", no.21, October 1953, published by E.C. Comics, with cover artwork by Graham Ingels, in near mint condition (9.2), with white pages.

*1953*

**£400-500** MC

"The Vault of Horror", no.15, October/November 1950, published by E.C. Comics, with cover artwork by Johnny Craig, near mint condition (9.4).

*Although numbered 15, this is the fourth issue of the Vault of Horror title, it was known as War Against Crime from issues 1-11. The first issue with this title, numbered 12, is very scarce and can be worth over five times are much. This example is in particularly fine condition.*

*1950*

**£1,000-1,500** MC

"The Haunt of Fear", no.27, September/October 1954, published by E.C. Comics, with cover artwork by Graham Ingels, in near mint condition (9.2).

*1954*

**£400-500** MC

"The Vault of Horror", no.19, June/July 1951, published by E.C. Comics, with cover artwork by Johnny Craig, in near mint condition (9.4).

*1951*

**£500-600** MC

"The Vault of Horror", no.23, February/March 1952, published by E.C. Comics, with cover artwork by Johnny Craig, in near mint condition (9.4), with off-white to white pages.

*1952*

**£700-1,000** MC

"Walt Disney's Comics and Stories", no.240, September 1960, published by Gold Key.

*1960*

**£2-3** **MC**

"Walt Disney's Mickey Mouse", no.191, January 1979, published by Whitman.

*1979*

**£1-2** **MC**

"Walt Disney's Mickey Mouse", no.65, May 1959, published by Dell.

*1959*

**£1-2** **MC**

"Walt Disney's Super Goof - The Thief of Zanzipar", no.1, October 1965, published by Gold Key.

*1965*

**£2-3** **MC**

"Looney Tunes", no. 192, October, 1957, published by Dell.

*1957*

**£2-3** **MC**

"Bugs Bunny", no.203, December 1978, published by Whitman.

*1978*

**£1-2** **MC**

"Tom and Jerry", no.230, June 1966, published by Dell.

*1966*

**£1-2** **MC**

"Tweety & Sylvester", no.1, November 1963, published by Warner Bros. Pictures Inc.

*1963*

**£2-3** **MC**

"Classics Illustrated - Frankenstein", no.25, edition 6A, with 15¢ cover price, originally issued in 1945.

*A first edition of this title could be worth 25 times this later edition.*

**£15-25** **NOR**

## A CLOSER LOOK AT A CLASSIC COMICS ILLUSTRATED

*Classic Comics Illustrated was started by Albert Lewis Kanter (1897-1973) in 1941 for Elliot Publishing. After three issues he started his own publishing company called Gilberton Publications.*

*In 1967 the company was sold to Twin Circle publisher Patrick Frawley who released two new titles before turning his attention to foreign sales and reprints for four years.*

*There are at least 22 variations and reprints of this title alone, this, the first, is the most desirable. Late versions can be worth as little as a few pounds.*

*Given the huge number of foreign editions and reprints available for each issue, the market for Classic Illustrated can be confusing to a new collector. Investing in a specialist guide will help you identify the different editions.*

"Classic Comics Illustrated - The Three Musketeers", no.1, October 1941, published by Elliott Publications, in very fine condition (8.5).

*1941*

**£7,500-8,500** **MC**

A Watchman limited collectors' series badge set, released by DC Comics, packaging marked "1986 DC Comics Inc".

*Given the huge popularity of the Watchman limited run comic book series, there is very little official merchandise connected with it. This controversial badge set was released by DC Comics as a 'promotional' item, rather than merchandising, meaning writer Alan Moore and artist Dave Gibbons were not eligible for royalties from its sale. This increased the friction between DC and Moore, who refused to be connected with any further merchandise causing DC to cancel plans for a hardcover edition and action figures to commemorate the 15th anniversary of the title.*

*c2000* *11.5in (26cm) high*

**£50-60** **NOR**

"Mad", no.24, July 1955, published by E.C. Comics, with ballpoint pen annotations to cover.

*This was the first issue of Mad to be produced as a magazine rather than a comic. It was thought this was to circumvent the Comic Authority Code of 1954 but was in fact because editor Harvey Kurtzman had received an offer from the rival publishers of Pageant magazine and E.C. publisher Bill Gaines had to upgrade Mad to a more prestigious magazine to retain the title.*

*1955*

**£30-40** **NOR**

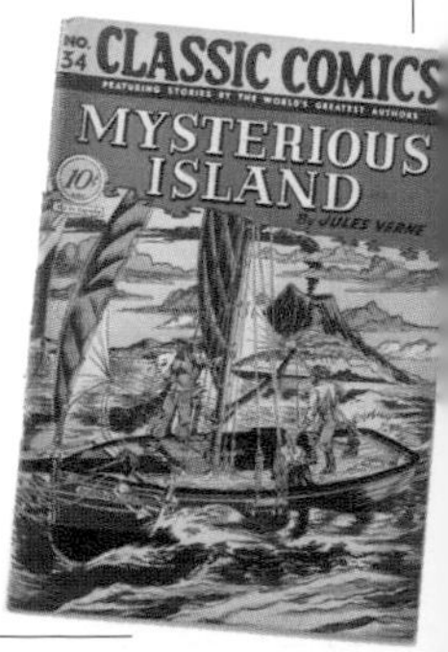


"Classic Comics Illustrated - Mysterious Island", no.34, February 1947, published by Gilberton Publishing.

*This the last issue to carry the name "Classic Comics Illustrated". The next issue, "The Last Days of Pompeii", was titled Classics Illustrated.*

*1947*

**£80-120** **NOR**

"Captain Future, Wizard of Science", no.2, Spring 1940, written by Edmond Hamilton and published by Thrilling Publications.

*Captain Future was initially conceived by Mort Weisinger of Thrilling Publications. Writer Edmond Hamilton took the character and fleshed him out as a dashing scientist-cum-adventurer.*

*1940* *9.75in (25cm) high*

**£70-100** **NOR**

"Captain Future, Wizard of Science", no.3, Summer 1940, written by Edmond Hamilton and published by Thrilling Publications, set on Neptune.

*This cover, highlighting Joan Randall's prominent curves, was considered quite shocking at the time.*

*1940*

**£70-100** **NOR**

"Captain Future, Man of Tomorrow", no.7, Summer 1941, written by Edmond Hamilton and published by Thrilling Publications, set on Mars.

*1941*

**£60-80** **NOR**

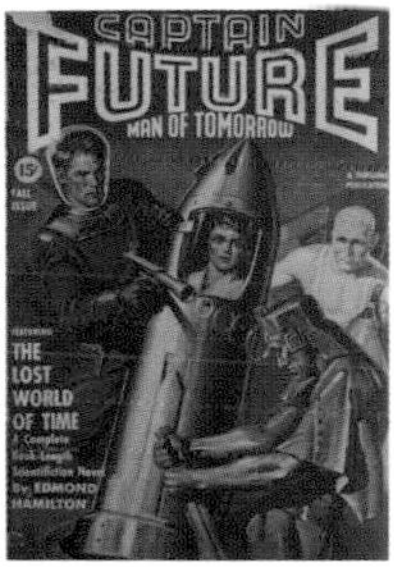


"Captain Future, Man of Tomorrow", no.8, Autumn 1941, written by Edmond Hamilton and published by Thrilling Publications, set on Venus.

*1941*

**£50-70** **NOR**

"Captain Future, Man of Tomorrow", no.9, Winter 1942, written by Edmond Hamilton and published by Thrilling Publications, set on the moon.

*1942*

**£40-60** **NOR**

"Captain Future, Man of Tomorrow", no.11, Summer 1942, written by Edmond Hamilton and published by Thrilling Publications.

*1942*

**£35-45** **NOR**

**FIND OUT MORE...**

**The Overstreet Comic Book Price Guide**, *37th edition, by Robert M. Overstreet, published by Gemstone Publishing, 2007.*

"Captain Future, Man of Tomorrow", no.15, Summer 1943, written by "Brett Sterling" and published by Thrilling Publications.

*When Ed Hamilton was drafted, the final four stories were published under the house name "Brett Sterling". Joseph Samachson was responsible for two of them and Hamilton himself wrote this one under the house name.*

*1943*

**£35-45** **NOR**

## COLLECTORS' NOTES

- Clothes by the major fashion labels known across the world tend to fetch the highest values when it comes to mid-late 20th century vintage clothes. Look for classic names who led key trends, such as Dior, Chanel, Pucci, Yves Saint Laurent and Vivienne Westwood. Nevertheless, many of these values are a fraction of the original cost, particularly as regards unique or specially commissioned couture pieces.
- Aim to buy pieces that represent the designer and their signature styles, or that reflect the style of the period, in terms of look, fit, colour and material. Examine labels closely to ensure they have not been added, and get to know the different types of labels a designer or company used. 'Diffusion' ranges were usually labelled differently to higher end ranges.
- Also always consider quality. Pieces by notable designers will typically be made from good quality materials and will have fine quality tailoring, stitching and construction. These guidelines of adhering to the style of a period and looking for quality also apply to pieces by lesser designers, or those bearing no names at all. Most of these can be found more easily and at lower prices, and are eminently wearable.
- The 1950s-70s have long been the most collectable decades, and the 'vintage' look from this period has now become part of mainstream fashion. However, the Edwardian 'dandy' look and the gaudy styles of the 1980s have affected fashion recently. Keep an eye on fashion magazines and clothes worn by famous models to spot the 'next big thing'.

A 1960s-70s Norman Norell pale taupe wool jersey chemise day dress, with Peter Pan collar, three patch pockets and silk lining.

*American fashion designer Norman Norell (1900-72) won five prestigious Coty awards for his 1940s-60s designs, some of which were used in films. His clean-lined and well-proportioned look was particularly popular during the 1960s, when he challenged the dominance of Parisian haute couture in New York. The company that bears his name still continues to produce designs today.*

**£70-100** **FRE**

A 1960s-70s Norman Norell camel wool jersey chemise day dress, with pussycat bow collar, button-up top, two pockets and silk lining.

**£60-90** **FRE**

A 1960s-70s Norman Norell cream wool jersey chemise day dress, buttoned at the top half, with patch pockets at the hip, self-belt and silk lining.

**£70-100** **FRE**

A 1970s Pauline Trigère silk day dress, with abstract green and blue printed 'jungle' design on a black background, with high pleated scoop neckline, natural waist and long sleeves with rhinestone button cuffs.

**£80-120** **FRE**

A 1970s Pauline Trigère wool and mohair winter shift dress, with cyan and white printed leaf design, with zippers at wrists and a matching necktie.

*Pauline Trigère (1909-2002) was born in France, but moved to New York at the age of 25. She was assistant director at Hattie Carnegie and went on to design costume jewellery to accompany her closely cut designs produced under her own name from 1942. She is credited with introducing removable scarves on dresses.*

**£70-100** **FRE**

A late 1960s Henri Bendel full-length black sheer polka dot dress, with extra long split belled-sleeves, labelled "Henri Bendel Limited Editions Made in England".

**£80-120** **FRE**

A late 1960s Henri Bendel salmon metallic crochet halterneck jumpsuit, lined with acetate and labelled "Henri Bendel Limited Editions Made in England".

**£70-100** **FRE**

A 1960s Pucci Saks 5th Avenue printed silk dress and matching belt.

*In terms of its form, this is a classic dress style for Pucci. The brightly coloured geometric design is also typical of his style. Also look out for his boldly curving, Art Nouveau inspired patterns.*

**£300-500** **S&T**

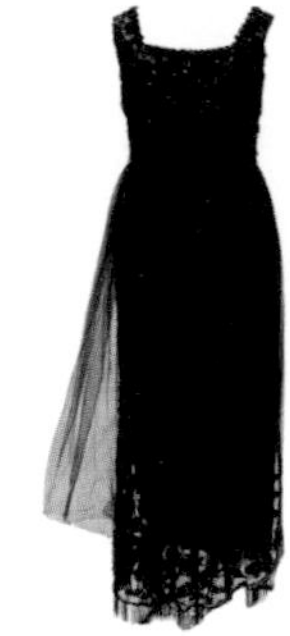

A 1920s black tulle and sequinned evening dress.

*Size 8/10*

**£180-220** **VV**

A 1930s navy crepe dress, with print bodice.

*Size 12*

**£40-50** **VV**

A 1980s printed polyester shirt, by Pant Man.

*Although the material used would make this uncomfortable to wear in Summer, the colours and computer pixel inspired pattern are typical of the 1980s.*

**£5-6** **BR**

A yellow bowling shirt, by Da Vinci.

*Look out for classic 1950s bowling shirts bearing the names of teams, towns or companies, as these can be worth more than double this example, particularly if they have added details such as differently coloured trims.*

**£25-35** **BR**

An American Boy Scouts of America cotton shirt, with applied embroidered award badges and "Official Blouse" label.

*Sold in vintage clothing shops in many countries, the colour, 'military' look and 'skinny' fit has become popular with many following the current trend for clothing with a slim and closely fitted profile.*

**£10-15** **BR**

An American men's printed cotton Army jacket.

**£10-15** **BR**

A red T-shirt, with Snoopy and Woodstock transfer decoration to front.

**£7-10** **BR**

## COLLECTORS' NOTES

- Handbags are no longer just an essential accessory, but have also become a must-have fashion statement, and hot collectable. Today, fashion designers release new collections many times per year, and the latest look is immediately copied by popular chain stores. Many designers look to the past for inspiration, choosing bags that summed up the changing styles of the 20th century.
- When collecting vintage handbags, consider the maker, designer, style and date of the bag, as well as the materials used and the quality of its manufacture. A well-made bag designed by a renowned designer or notable maker that sums up the styles of its age is more likely to be desirable to a collector and thus of a higher value.
- Certain fine materials such as snakeskin and kid leather will often command a premium over other materials. These, combined with fine quality construction with good stitching and detailing, will usually indicate a good manufacturer. Beadwork bags with intricate patterns in many colours can be very valuable, particularly if early in date, but avoid examples with bead loss as this is extremely difficult to repair.
- Names are important and can apply in different ways. The maker and designer of a bag are important to value, but also look out for bags that were sold by retailers in prestigious locations such as central London and New York. Bags that sum up the prevalent style of the day will nearly always be of more interest to collectors and those who follow a 'retro' look in fashion.
- Always consider condition, examining the finish, corners, linings and fittings for signs of wear. A collector will always want a bag in the best condition possible, and the growing number of 'fashionistas' who buy vintage bags to use will also aim to buy examples that are not damaged.
- Online auction sites such as eBay, vintage fashion shops and charity shops are ideal places to look for pieces to start a collection with – but always keep an eye on fashion magazines, models and celebrities to try and spot the 'next big thing'.

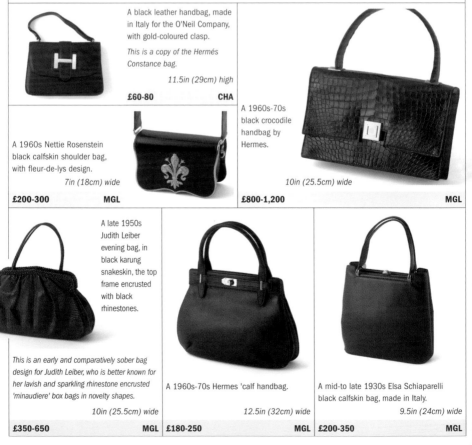

A black leather handbag, made in Italy for the O'Neil Company, with gold-coloured clasp.

*This is a copy of the Hermés Constance bag.*

*11.5in (29cm) high*

**£60-80** **CHA**

A 1960s-70s black crocodile handbag by Hermes.

*10in (25.5cm) wide*

**£800-1,200** **MGL**

A 1960s Nettie Rosenstein black calfskin shoulder bag, with fleur-de-lys design.

*7in (18cm) wide*

**£200-300** **MGL**

A late 1950s Judith Leiber evening bag, in black karung snakeskin, the top frame encrusted with black rhinestones.

*This is an early and comparatively sober bag design for Judith Leiber, who is better known for her lavish and sparkling rhinestone encrusted 'minaudiere' box bags in novelty shapes.*

*10in (25.5cm) wide*

**£350-650** **MGL**

A 1960s-70s Hermes 'calf handbag.

*12.5in (32cm) wide*

**£180-250** **MGL**

A mid-to late 1930s Elsa Schiaparelli black calfskin bag, made in Italy.

*9.5in (24cm) wide*

**£200-350** **MGL**

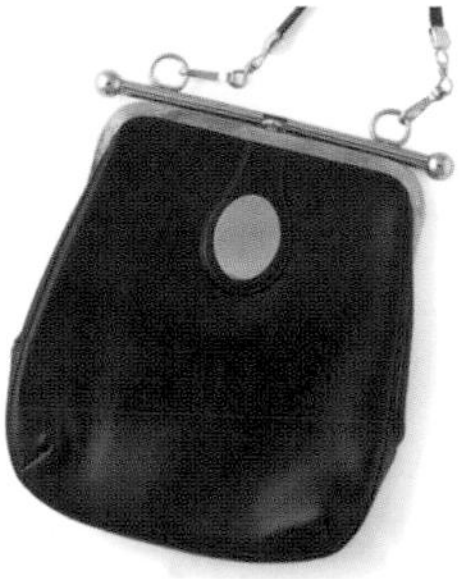

A 1960s black leather handbag, of unusual shape, with a metal frame.

*10.5in (26.5cm) high*

**£15-25** **CHA**

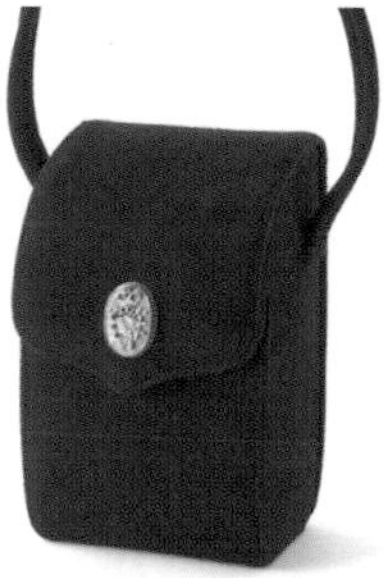

A 1950-60s Nettie Rosenstein dark brown suede box purse, with design on the clasp, made in Florence, Italy.

*5in (13cm) wide*

**£150-250** **MGL**

A 1960s Ingber patent leather oblong clutch, with black and white striped lining.

*18.5in (47cm) wide*

**£80-120** **MGL**

A 1950s Nettie Rosenstein pumpkin-tan pettled grain handbag, of unusual design and shape, made in Florence, Italy.

*10.5in (26.5cm) wide*

**£200-350** **MGL**

A 1960s American Lena red pebbled leather handbag, with a curved form.

*13in (33cm) wide*

**£80-120** **MGL**

A 1950s Nettie Rosenstein chocolate brown structured fabric purse, made in Florence, Italy.

*10.5in (26.5cm) wide*

**£150-250** **MGL**

A 1940s python-skin clutch bag, with black bakelite catch and attached carrying handle.

**£30-50** **PC**

## A CLOSER LOOK AT A HANDBAG

*This handbag follows the 'Surrealist' movement and brings to mind artworks by Salvador Dali.*

*Anne-Marie of Paris is known for her range of 'surreal' handbags, including a clock, a piano and a ship.*

*Look out for her black buckskin 'Ice Bucket' bag, shaped like an ice bucket with a bottle of champagne inside, which was given to VIP guests at the Ritz, as it can be worth over £2,000.*

*It is made from white kid leather, a fine quality and very soft material - it is also found in black suede.*

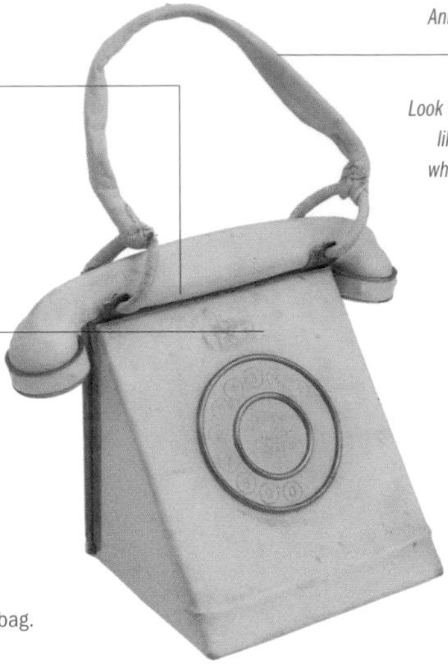

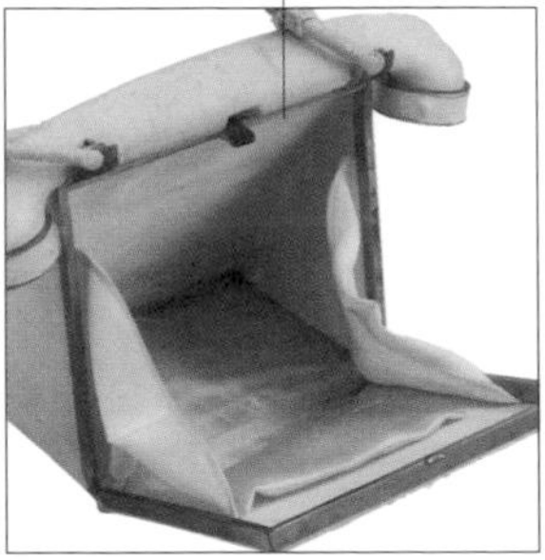

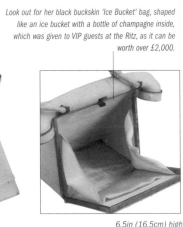

An extremely rare 1940s French Anne-Marie of Paris white kid leather telephone handbag.

*6.5in (16.5cm) high*

**£1,500-2,000** **RG**

A 1940s-50s American Milch brown leather accordion handbag.

*Milch are known for their innovatively structured handbags.*

*12in (30.5cm) wide*

**£100-150** **MGL**

A 1970s Judith Leiber bone-coloured karung snakeskin handbag.

*A karung is a type of water snake that produced a small, tight skin which is often used on handbags and shoes.*

*8.5in (21.5cm) wide*

**£150-200** **MGL**

A tooled and coloured leather clutch bag, lined with beige moiré.

*c1929* *9in (23cm) wide*

**£15-20** **AAC**

A 1960s Paco Rabanne black leather and silver aluminium disc bag.

*This bag lacks a label, although the branding has been stamped into the metal, ensuring its authenticity.*

*10.5in (26.5cm) wide*

**£600-1,000** **MGL**

## A CLOSER LOOK AT A POODLE HANDBAG

*The poodle became a fashion statement during the 1950s as people looked to Paris for its fashions and style.*

*The entire bag is made from tiny pearlescent beads on threads, which were hand-woven into the form in Japan.*

*Although other companies made similar bags, those by Walborg are the most sought-after for their originality and quality.*

*Look out for the earlier black version from the 1940s, which is even rarer, and also a seated cat, which is rarer still.*

A very rare Walborg beaded poodle purse, in very good condition. *c1955*

*13.5in (34cm) high*

**£1,000-1,500** **RG**

A late 1950s Enid Collins beaded bucket bag, with butterfly motif.

*Bags by Enid Collins of Texas have become immensely collectable over the past five years. Look out for her hallmark features of bold designs, inset rhinestones and faux pearls. Her wooden box bags are particularly sought-after. If her full name cannot be found, look for a lower case 'ec'.*

*13in (33cm) wide*

**£70-100** **SM**

A 1940s French Pierre Marot hand-beaded evening purse, with tambour embroidery flowers, beaded frame and clasp, gilt snake chain handles, and black satin lining, in mint condition.

*10.25in (26cm) wide*

**£220-240** **RG**

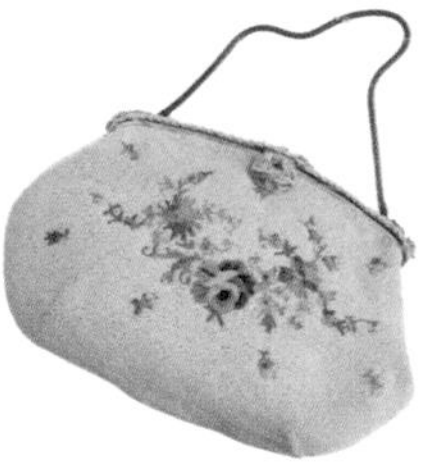

A 1950s French hand-beaded evening purse with tambour embroidery, beaded frame and clasp, snake chain handle and cream satin lining, un-used.

*8.25in (21cm) wide*

**£150-180** **RG**

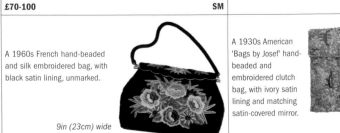

A 1960s French hand-beaded and silk embroidered bag, with black satin lining, unmarked.

*9in (23cm) wide*

**£120-140** **RG**

A 1930s American 'Bags by Josef' hand-beaded and embroidered clutch bag, with ivory satin lining and matching satin-covered mirror.

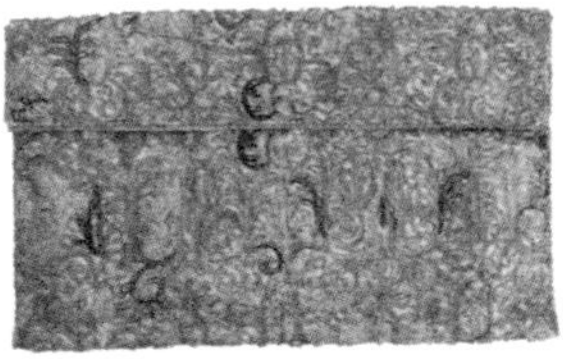

*9in (23cm) wide*

**£70-90**

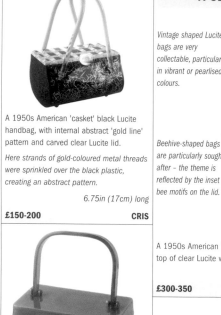

A 1950s American 'casket' black Lucite handbag, with internal abstract 'gold line' pattern and carved clear Lucite lid.

*Here strands of gold-coloured metal threads were sprinkled over the black plastic, creating an abstract pattern.*

*6.75in (17cm) long*

**£150-200** **CRIS**

## A CLOSER LOOK AT A LUCITE HANDBAG

*Vintage shaped Lucite bags are very collectable, particularly in vibrant or pearlised colours.*

*This bag is in excellent condition, with no crazing to the plastic.*

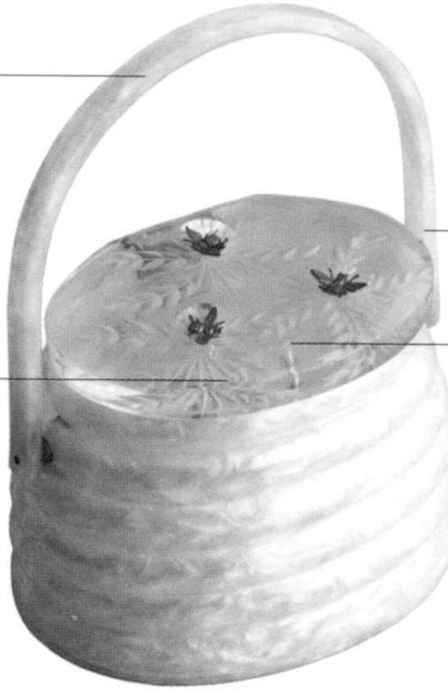

*The lid is also carved with flower and leaf motifs.*

*Beehive-shaped bags are particularly sought-after – the theme is reflected by the inset bee motifs on the lid.*

A 1950s American 'beehive' handbag, the body of ribbed and pearlized white Lucite, the top of clear Lucite with inset gold-plated bee motifs.

*5.5in (14cm) high excluding handle*

**£300-350** **CRIS**

An American Myles Originals amber Lucite box bag, with rigid handle.

*8.75in (22cm) high*

**£100-150** **MG**

A French petit point needlework bag, with a white metal frame and catch set with pearlised panels.

*c1900* *6in (15cm) wide*

**£200-250** **ATL**

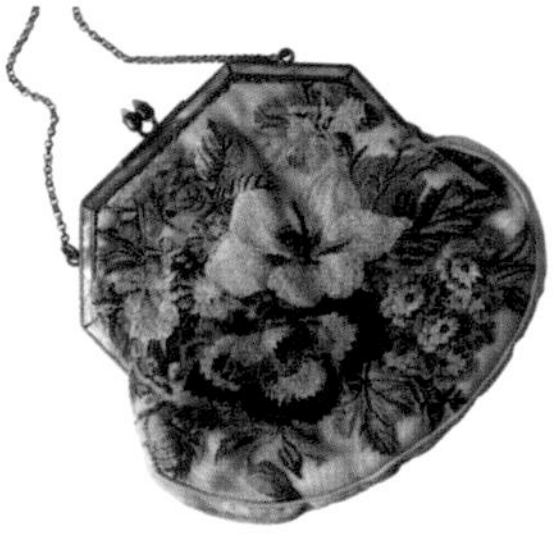

A North American Indian embroidered felt purse.

*1880* *6in (15cm) wide*

**00-150** **ATL**

A 1930s American silk 'duffle' handbag, with a striped pattern with embroidered flowers and a carved ivorine clasp of an oriental figure.

*Ivorine was an early plastic made to imitate ivory. Ivory was an expensive, luxury material and needed to be carved, which required time and skill, whereas Ivorine could simply be moulded. It is distinguishable from ivory by its rows of parallel lines and uniform colour.*

*8in (20.5cm) wide*

**£400-500** **CRIS**

A late 1950s Italian Nettie Rosenstein tapestry bag with applied glass beads and satin lining, with minor bead loss.

*9.5in (24cm) wide*

**£400-500** **MGL**

A 1960s Italian Nettie Rosenstein large tapestry and sculpted chenille bag, with satin lining and metal frame.

*13in (33cm) wide*

**£250-400** **MGL**

An Italian Nettie Rosenstein black and red Kelly-style handbag, with black stamped flower design on red velvet, with fitted interior.

*Rosenstein began her career as a milliner, turning to fashion in the 1930s. She is perhaps best known for her costume jewellery designs, which were first made to compliment her fashion designs. Her handbags are of fine quality and were made in Florence, Italy.*

*c1960* *10.25in (26cm) wide*

**£250-400** **MGL**

A 1950s Italian Nettie Rosenstein lynx fur handbag, with leather lining.

*13.5in (43.5cm) wide*

**£400-600** **MGL**

A late 1950s American Bienen-Davis evening bag, covered with metallic tapestry with gold, silver and black threads on a black background.

*7.75in (19.5cm) wide*

**£50-80** **MGL**

A 1950s Chinese Mr Jonas woven wicker handbag, with cut-felt Scottie dogs covered with clear vinyl, with label to the coloured fabric interior.

*This bag would appeal to a collector of Scottie dogs as much as to a handbag collector. Scottie dogs were popular motifs during the 1930s and '50s, partly due to personalities and celebrities including Shirley Temple, and Presidents Eisenhower and Roosevelt owning examples of the breed.* *See pages 441-444 for more Scottie Dogs.*

*12.25in (31cm) wide*

**£40-60** **ROX**

A 1950s American Source-Bag of New York cornflower motif handbag, with brass frame, black plastic handle and body, one side with covered with white cloth, fine yellow beads and amber cabochon cornflowers.

*10.5in (27cm) high*

**£100-150** **CRIS**

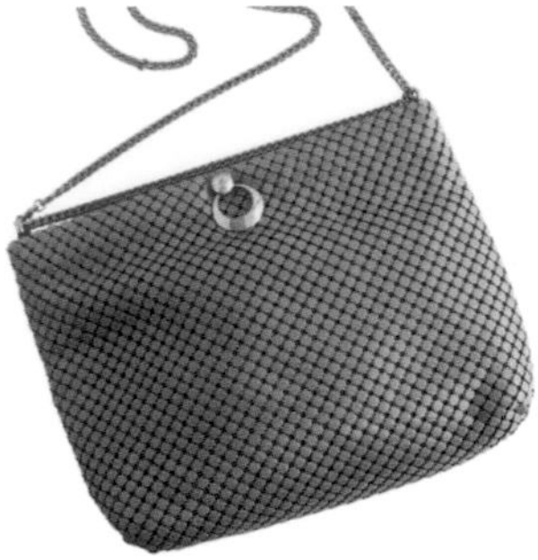

A 1970s Whiting & Davis gold-tone mesh purse, with a matching metal clasp and chain.

*Whiting & Davis is the best known maker of metal mesh handbags, and has operated since 1876 and before the 1920s the bags were produced by hand. During the 1930s they collaborated with designers such as Elsa Schiaparelli and Paul Poiret. Look for brightly coloured examples with Art Deco style forms and patterns, as these tend to be the most valuable. All their bags are marked with a label, helping with identification. The bags went out of fashion during the 1950s, but their sparkle ensured a popular comeback in the disco era of the 1970s and '80s.*

*10in (25.5cm) wide*

**£50-70** **MILLB**

## A CLOSER LOOK AT A HANDBAG

*After WWII, fashions became more frivolous and less formal, with cheerful and fun animal-themed bags becoming popular.*

*Vintage examples in excellent condition like this one are highly sought-after as so many were worn through use.*

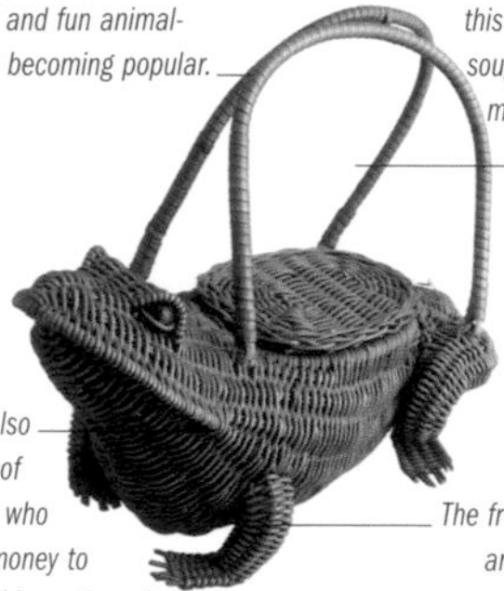

*The 1950s also saw the rise of the teenager who had pocket money to spend on fashion - these bags were an enormous hit.*

*The frog is a popular animal with wide appeal.*

A late 1950s American green frog basketwork handbag.

*14in (36cm) long*

**£350-400** **CRIS**

A clutch bag, by Bags by Josef of New York, the fabric body woven from gilt thread and topped with scrolling gold-tone wire set with red, green, blue and yellow glass beads.

*This maker is not to be confused with Joseff of Hollywood who is better known for his stunning costume jewellery, which was favoured by various celebrities of his age and which used a gold-coloured metal known as 'Russian gold'. For examples, see pages 210-225.*

*9.75in (25cm) wide*

**£500-600** **RITZ**

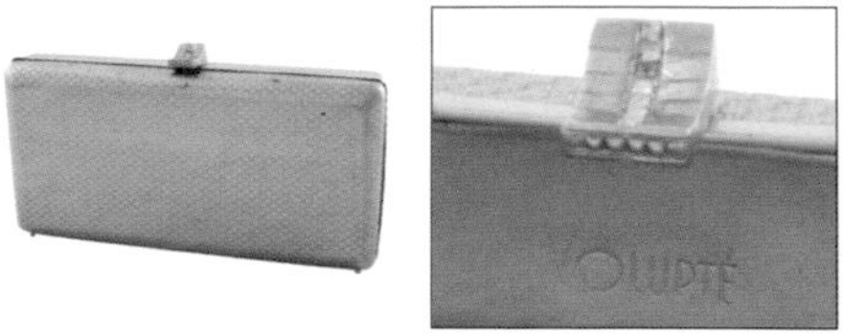

A 1950s Volupté metal case bag, with pink interior, retailed by Bergdorf Goodman.

*Always look inside a handbag to see if it is marked as the name can make a difference to the value. Volupté are more notable for their powder compacts. For examples of these, please see pages 414-420.*

*7.75in (19.5cm) wide*

**£35-45** **FAN**

A 1950s rigid handbag, with velvet-covered exterior, brass strips and plastic lid.

*11.5in (29cm) high*

**£40-60** **AAC**

A 1960s Ingber black and white polka dot plastic handbag, with double handles and black and white striped lining.

*11in (28cm) wide*

**£40-80** **MGL**

A 1950s/1960s umbrella-shaped child's handbag, with drawstring fastening and wooden handle.

*This novelty form is typical of this period, but surviving examples are scarce and desirable. The small size suggests it was made for a child.*

*13.75in (35cm) high*

**£20-30** **NOR**

### FIND OUT MORE...

**Handbags**, *by Judith Miller, published by DK, 2006.*

## COLLECTORS' NOTES

- Shoes have become as popular as handbags, vying for ever-more space in women's wardrobes. As with vintage costume, vintage shoes are bought both to build collections with and to wear, giving an individual look to an outfit.
- Examples from before, and from the first few decades of, the 20th century tend to be collected for display rather than use due to the small sizes available and their delicate nature. Shoes from the early 19th century and before can be very rare, particularly if finely made. Some of today's designers also use these historic examples as inspiration for their new designs.
- Shoes and boots from the 1950s-70s tend to be generally the most popular, following the vogue for retro styles in fashion. The 1970s are currently a 'hot' area, with typical examples that follow the Disco look and original platforms being highly sought after.
- Look out for key designer or retailer's names, and styles that are typical of a period in terms of form, colour and any decoration. Shoes that launched or led a particular trend or style will nearly always be sought after. Bright colours, unusual detailing, and fine quality materials and construction are good factors.
- Condition is also very important. Stains may be removed and scuffed leather treated, but tears, broken heels and customisation may be harder to rectify. If a shoe is very worn through use, it will have less appeal. A pair of shoes in truly mint condition is more preferable, but will command a premium.
- Also look for matching handbags and original boxes, as these will add value. Shoes with important celebrity connections, such as the purple Vivienne Westwood boots worn by Naomi Campbell when she fell over on the catwalk in 1993, will also be of interest.

A pair of 1930s black fabric 'Cushion-Step Arch Shoe' shoes, with cut leather-on-leather panels.

*These comparatively hard to find shoes take the style of 18thC footware.*

*8.75in (22cm) long*

**£40-50** **NOR**

A pair of 1940s Mackey Starr of New York suede platform high heeled shoes, decorated with multicoloured metal studs.

*8.25in (21cm) long*

**£100-150** **NOR**

A pair of 1940s Wilshire Originals cream and green leather wedge platform shoes.

*9in (23cm) long*

**£100-150** **NOR**

A pair of 1940s Dickerson 'The Archlock Shoe' shoes, wedge balanced, and made of open weave mesh fabric, unworn with original Dolly Preston box.

*9in (22.5cm) long*

**£20-30** **NOR**

A pair of 1940s Blum Store, Philadelphia real crocodile high heeled shoes, with original 'Chandler's French Room Originals' card box.

*8.75in (22cm) long*

**£40-60** **NOR**

A pair of 1940s French 'Tres Biens Par Les Hommes d'Or' black suede wedge high heeled shoes, the straps set with with faux pearls, cut steel and rhinestones.

*8.75in (22cm) long*

**£50-80** **NOR**

A pair of 1950s Catalano grey leather studded shoes, by Catalano.

*9.5in (24cm) long*

**£30-40** **NOR**

A pair of 1950s leather shoes, with printed black squiggles and pink interior.

*8in (20cm) long*

**£20-30** **NOR**

A pair of 1940s-50s Cinderella beaded heels.

*Bead work such as this is usually hand-made and the finer the detail, the more desirable it will be. Always examine beaded items carefully for wear or damage as it is very hard to repair. With their matching beaded bag, the value of these shoes leaps up to over £120.*

*8.25in (21cm) high*

**£50-80** **NOR**

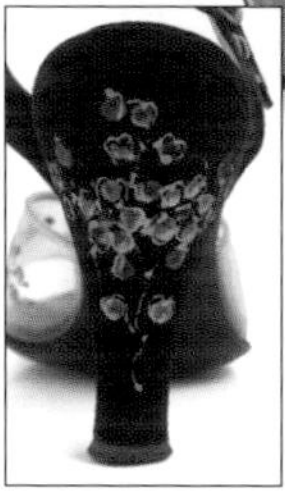

A pair of 1950s handmade Delagardo shoes, with hand-painted flowers on a felt and plastic front.

*The heels are covered with black velvet, which has also been hand-painted.*

*7.5in (19cm) long*

**£50-80** **NOR**

A pair of 1950s-60s Rhythm Step pink, purple and orange striped silk covered shoes.

*9.75in (25cm) long*

**£25-35** **NOR**

A pair of 1950s red leather and pony skin heels.

*11in (28cm) long*

**£15-25** **NOR**

A pair of Schiaparelli green silk shoes, the toes set with rhinestones.

*As well as the inset rhinestones and fine overall quality, the name of renowned fashion designer Elsa Schiaparelli makes these as valuable as they are.*

*c1958* *9.75in (25cm) long*

**£50-80** **NOR**

A pair of 1960s Saigonese Gucc 'Kim Thank' gold, white and black tartan hand-painted wooden heels, with suedette straps with inset plastic beads and sequins, with original box.

*The original box adds value, as does the amusingly misspelt attempt at copying famous brand 'Gucci'.*

*8.75in (22cm) long*

**£25-35** **NOR**

A pair of 1970s Fashion Right brown, yellow and orange leather buckled 'Mary Jane' shoes, in mint, unworn condition.

*9in (22.5cm) long*

**£25-35** **NOR**

A pair of 1970s yellow and black leather platform shoes, with indented heel backs.

*10.75in (27cm) long*

**£70-100** **NOR**

A pair of 1970s Minikin blue and white leather platform shoes.

*9.75in (24.5cm) long*

**£30-50** **NOR**

A pair of 1970s-80s leopard print pony skin Giorgio Brutini boots, with zip fastening.

*11in (28cm) long*

**£50-80** **NOR**

A pair of 1960s-70s Jack Rogers purple suede boots, with inset silvery balls and applied silk stars.

*With fashion veering increasingly towards making an individual statement, these fantabulous Disco-era boots would most likely be bought to be worn.*

*16.25in (41cm) high*

**£100-150** **NOR**

## A CLOSER LOOK AT A PAIR OF SHOES

*This style of 'slide' shoe was introduced by Charles Cole, father of shoemaker Kenneth Cole, who founded El Greco in 1978.*

*A popular TV advertising campaign featuring women in various states of undress, running around a college dormitory in the shoes. Over 14 million pairs were sold from 1978-81.*

*The Candie's style shot to fame when Olivia Newton-John wore a similar pair for the final 'transformation' scene in the 1978 film 'Grease'.*

*The style was copied, but El Greco are the original and most collectible name. This pair is also in mint, unworn condition.*

A pair of 1970s Italian El Greco 'Chicklet Candies', in mint, unworn condition, new-old stock.

*9in (23cm) long*

**£25-35** **NOR**

A 'Patch' burgundy advertising baseball cap, with applied patch and embroidered oak leaves to the bill.

*Although the trucker style baseball cap seems to have fallen out of favour among fashionistas, there are plenty who still appreciate their variety, colour and comfortable ease.*

**£4-5** **BR**

A 'Gerry's Automotive' red advertising baseball cap.

**£3-5** **BR**

A 'Delta Air Charters' blue advertising baseball cap.

**£4-5** **BR**

A Canadian Krystal Cap Co. Ltd grey and brown tweed hat, with fur lining, size large.

**£8-12** **BR**

A blue and green 'Nova Scotia' tartan cap, by Easter Hats & Caps.

*The official Nova Scotia tartan was adopted in 1955.*

**£5-6** **BR**

A 1950s American Eva Mae Modes ladies printed green, gold and blue hat.

**£4-5** **BR**

An American Lanning beige cotton corduroy cowboy hat, with band and feathers, size medium.

**£10-14** **BR**

A blue denim cowboy hat, by Lanning, with braided band and feather decoration, size medium.

*Plenty of parents have said 'if you want to get ahead, get a hat', and hats have certainly returned to fashion once again. Although baseball caps and knitted beanies are without doubt the most common styles worn, smarter and more idiosyncratic looks are also increasing in popularity. Much of this return to popularity has been due to models, celebrities and pop stars, like Pete Doherty, being routinely seen wearing hats.*

**£12-18** **BR**

An Anson Sterling Silver tie pin and cufflinks boxed set, with cultured pearls and stamped "Anson, Sterling".

*Anson were as prolific as Swank, and are just as collectable.*

**£30-40** **BB**

A pair of 1950s Swank embossed Sterling silver 'Marlin' fish cufflinks, in original retailer's box.

*Cufflinks 1in (2.5cm) wide*

**£50-70** **CVS**

A pair of early 1970s faceted plastic and gold coloured cufflinks.

*0.75in (2cm) diam*

**£8-12** **DTC**

A pair of 1950s American plated base metal cufflinks, with pink plastic cabochon stones.

*Cufflinks don't need to be serious. Retro styles are immensely popular and have been increasing value over the past few years, particularly if they represent the style of the period or are eye-catching and unusual.*

*1.5in (4cm) wide*

**£25-35** **CVS**

A pair of 1950s plated metal 'Artist's Palette' cufflinks and a tie pin.

*2in (5cm) wide*

**£40-60** **CVS**

A pair of oval silver gilt cufflinks, enamelled in red, sky blue and green in a harlequin design, with belcher link connections, Birmingham hallmarks.

*1998*

**£60-80** **F**

A pair of 1970s Tiffany sterling silver cufflinks, with polychrome enamel flags.

*Fine quality materials, construction and decoration combined with a timeless design and renowned name are factors that typically make cufflinks valuable.*

*0.75in (2.25cm) diam*

**£350-500** **RBRG**

A pair of 1950s Swank gold-plated and plastic 'Eiffel Tower' cufflinks.

*0.75in (2cm) high*

**£50-70** **CVS**

A pair of Unger Bros. Sterling silver owl's head cufflinks, set with amber and dark brown glass cabochon eyes.

*Unger Bros are a well-known and sought-after American silversmiths. Cufflinks by them are not common, and these are of typically very fine quality.*

*1904-5* *0.5in (1.5cm) diam*

**£350-400** **CGPC**

## COLLECTORS' NOTES

- The recent reappraisal, and subsequent enormous growth in the popularity, of costume jewellery has led to some considerable rises in value. Much of this has applied to signed pieces, with makers such as Trifari, Miriam Haskell, Coro, Joseff of Hollywood and Dior leading the pack.
- Although these pieces can often be recognised from their style and appearance, it is always best to examine the back carefully for names, as designs were copied, and influenced others.
- However, many people buy to wear, and unsigned pieces, where the manufacturer is not known, can be an affordable way to get the look without the cost of buying a signed piece. Look out, in particular, for unsigned sterling pieces from the 1930s and '40s, as these are often the best in design and manufacture, and show the highest percentage increase in value.
- Examine a piece closely, looking for signs of quality in the setting, the 'stones' themselves, and the design. Designs that would have taken considerable skill or long periods of time to manufacture are among the most valuable. Pieces by Miriam Haskell and Stanley Hagler are good examples.
- Also look for missing stones as although many can be replaced, less common examples such as specially produced baroque faux-pearls and Murano glass beads favoured by some makers, cannot. Size, shape and the exact shade of a colour can also make matching a replacement hard.
- Nevertheless, it is often the 'look' that is the most important aspect – if it has that 'sparkle appeal' it is likely to be popular. Styles worn by Hollywood film stars, and popular models and celebrities will command a premium.

A Trifari gold-plated 'Jelly Belly' chick-in-egg pin, with pavé-set clear rhinestone head, coral cabochon eyes and grey Lucite body.

*Trifari is well known for its 'Jelly Belly' pins, inset with clear Lucite stomachs. Earlier examples from the 1930s-40s, those in amusing and appealing forms and rare animals tend to fetch higher prices.*

*2in (5cm) long*

**£550-650** **TR**

A 1940s Trifari gold-plated sterling silver 'Jelly Belly' fly pin, with grey Lucite belly and clear rhinestones.

*3in (7.5cm) long*

**£450-550** **TR**

A 1940s Trifari gold-plated sterling silver 'Jelly Belly' crab pin, with grey Lucite body and clear rhinestone highlights.

*3in (7.5cm) wide*

**£450-500** **TR**

A 1940s Trifari sterling silver and gold-plated bird on a branch pin, with inset rhinestones.

*2.5in (6.5cm) long*

**£100-150** **RG**

A 1930s Trifari rhodium-plated winged insect pin, with round and teardrop emerald-green cabochons, black, yellow and red enamelling and clear rhinestones.

*1.5in (4cm) long*

**£80-120** **ROX**

A 1950s Trifari gold-plated snake brooch and earrings, with glass simulated ruby and emeralds.

*brooch 2.75in (7cm) long*

**£100-150** **RG**

A 1930s Trifari rhodium-plated floral pin, with trailing leaves, large blue glass baguettes forming the petals, and clear rhinestones.

*3.25in (8cm) long*

**£120-180** **ROX**

A 1940s Trifari rhodium-plated floral pin, with sapphire navette and amethyst-blue rhinestones.

*3.5in (9cm) long*

**£100-150** **ROX**

A 1930s large Trifari flower pin, with yellow, green and orange enamel and clear rhinestones.

*Trifari was founded in New York in 1918, it is still in operation today, owned by Liz Claibourne. The fine quality of the enamelling and the attention to design details, such as the curling petals and the rhinestone-lined curving leaves, make this pin so valuable and make Trifari so appealing.*

*4in (10cm) long*

**£250-350** **ROX**

A 1950s Trifari gold-plated leaf pin, with pinkish-red, navy blue, emerald-green and clear rhinestones.

*2.75in (7cm) long*

**£70-90** **RG**

A 1940s Trifari gold-plated sterling silver bow-and-fruit pin, with large emerald green and small clear rhinestones.

*2.25in (6cm) long*

**£80-120** **RG**

A Trifari partridge in a pear tree pin, with green, blue and gold enamelled details.

*2in (5cm) long*

**£30-40** **ROX**

## A CLOSER LOOK AT A TRIFARI PIN

*This pin is made up of two separate halves, each of which is a separate pin - Coro was best known for this style.*

*It is made from gold-plated sterling silver, known as vermeil, rather than a base metal.*

*It is an early piece, made during the 1930s and is quite rare, especially in this fine condition.*

*The design is well conceived and well-executed, with suitably well-set colourful rhinestones and glass faux jewels.*

An early and relatively rare 1930s Trifari duette pin, of vermeil sterling silver with large emerald pastes, small red and emerald baguettes and small clear rhinestones.

*3.25in (8.5cm) long*

**£200-300** **ROX**

A 1940s Trifari sterling silver American eagle pin, with red and white enamelling, inset rhinestones and blue Lucite 'Jelly Belly' style body.

*These pins were made after the US entry to WWII to demonstrate patriotism. With their strong designs and colours, they are collected and worn for much the same reason today. This piece is particularly dramatic.*

*1.75in (4.5cm) long*

**£150-200** **ROX**

A 1940s Trifari gold-plated sterling silver patriotic American eagle pin, with red, white and blue enamelling.

*2in (5cm) high*

**£80-120** **TR**

A 1940s Trifari Stars and Stripes flag pin, with gold-plated staff and blue and red enamel and clear inset rhinestone flag.

*2.25in (6cm) long*

**£100-150** **ROX**

A Trifari floral bracelet, with clear navette-cut rhinestone petals and faux pearl centres.

*c1950* *6in (15cm) long*

**£150-250** **LB**

A 1930s Trifari Rhodium-plated 'Fruit Salad' wheelbarrow pin, with blue and milky carved glass and clear crystal rhinestones.

*3in (8cm) wide*

**£400-500** **CRIS**

A 1950s Trifari gilt metal balloon brooch, with a satin finish.

*2.25in (5.5cm) high*

**£30-50** **CRIS**

A 1950s Trifari necklace and bracelet, in gold-tone metal with pave-set and baguette-cut rhinestones.

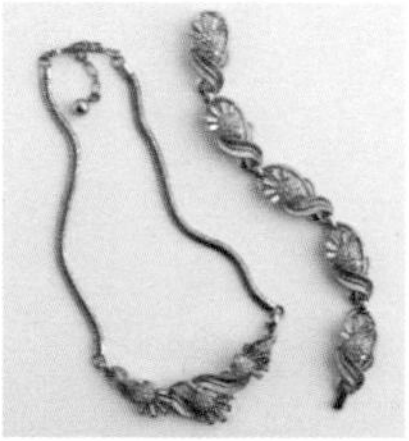

*Necklace 15in (38cm) long*

**£40-60** **ABIJ**

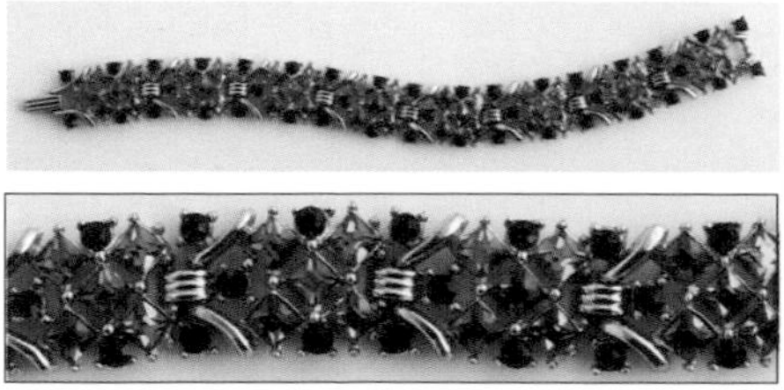

A 1970s Trifari bracelet in gold-tone metal with pale and dark citrine-coloured rhinestones.

*7.5cm (7in) long*

**£40-50** **ABIJ**

A pair of 1940s Miriam Haskell antiqued gilt metal floral earrings, with pink poured glass centres, pink rose montées and emerald and sapphire rhinestones.

*1.25in (3cm) long*

**£60-100** **ROX**

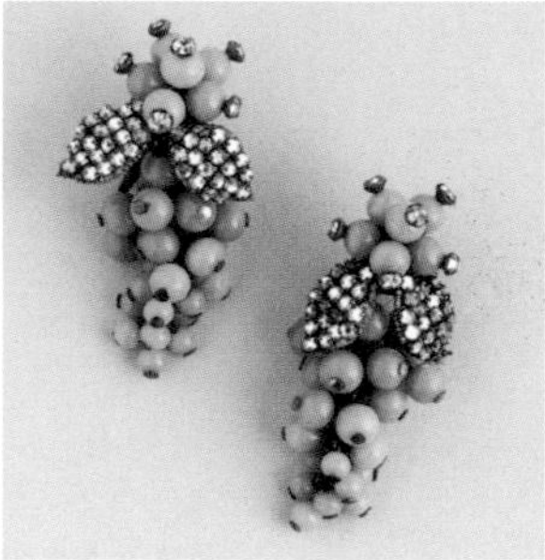

A pair of 1930s Miriam Haskell pink and diamanté drop earrings, unmarked.

*2.25in (6cm) long*

**£60-100** **ROX**

A pair of 1940s Miriam Haskell antiqued gilt metal earrings, with marbled emerald-green poured glass centres encircled by clear rose montées.

*1in (2.5cm) diam*

**£60-90** **ROX**

A 1960s Miriam Haskell pin and pendant earrings, with clusters of seed pearls and metallic coloured beads, the pin with faux baroque pearls, all with pewter coloured poured glass drops.

*Miriam Haskell (1899-1981) established her costume jewellery company with Frank Hess as designer in 1926. During the 1930s her fame spread and she opened retail outlets in major department stores. She began marking her jewellery in the 1940s. Larry Vrba was the designer during the 1970s, with Millie Petronzio taking over from the 1980s onwards.*

*Pin: 3.5in (9cm) wide*

**£80-120** **ROX**

A pair of 1940s Miriam Haskell antiqued gilt metal floral earrings, with clusters of clear rose montées and prong-set clear rhinestone centres.

*1.5in (3.75cm) diam*

**£80-120** **ROX**

A 1940s Miriam Haskell floral pin, with pressed glass, glass beads and rhinestones in shades of pink.

*2.5in (6.25cm) long*

**£150-200** **ROX**

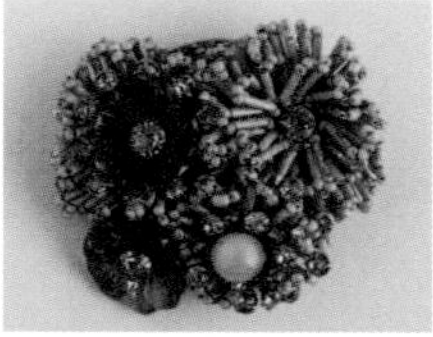

A 1940s Miriam Haskell red and colourless pressed clear glass bead pin.

*2in (5cm) long*

**£100-150** **ROX**

A 1940s Miriam Haskell multiple-pendant necklace and earrings, comprised of rings of small amber glass beads, large faceted citrine glass stones, all linked with silver-tone metal chains incorporating faceted citrine glass beads.

*Necklace 17.5in (45cm) long*

**£400-500** RITZ

A 1940s Miriam Haskell necklace, with two strands of baroque faux pearls, ruby and emerald glass beads, gilt balls and rose montées.

*20in (51cm) long*

**£100-150** ROX

A 1960s Miriam Haskell necklace, with multiple strands of pink and white poured glass beads and a gilt metal clasp with gilt balls.

*15.75in (40cm) long*

**£80-120** ROX

A 1940s Miriam Haskell bracelet, with multiple strands of pink and pearl poured glass beads.

*Clasp: 1.5in (3.75cm) wide*

**£80-120** ROX

## A CLOSER LOOK AT A MIRIAM HASKELL NECKLACE

*The back shows how each element is painstakingly hand-wired onto a complex cast filigree mount.*

*Many of Haskell's necklaces have beaded strands, this has strands decorated with what could be individual pins, adding to the time and skill spent creating it.*

*It is embellished with a profusion of Haskell's signature faux seed pearls, made to a secret recipe in Japan.*

*It also has her lustrous and extra-large 'baroque' pearls, which were supplied exclusively to her.*

A 1940s Miriam Haskell necklace, with pendants.

*Of Haskell's production, her necklaces are often the most loved and desired due to their intricate design, fine workmanship and immense visual impact.*

*6.25in (16cm) wide*

**£800-1,200** MG

COSTUME JEWELLERY

A Dior rhodium-plated pendant cross pin, with prong set, pear-cut and oval royal blue glass stones and aurora borealis rhinestones.

*Christian Dior (1905-57) designed twice yearly costume jewellery collections from 1947-57. After his death, collections continued designed by Mark Bohan, Gianfranco Ferre and John Galliano. Most Dior pieces are stamped with the company name and dated.*

*1958* *3.in (7.5cm) long*

**£100-150** **RG**

A Dior rhodium-plated floral motif pendant pin, with clear rhinestones and faux baroque pearls.

*1963* *4in (10cm) long*

**£100-150** **ROX**

A Dior stylized fruit pin, with faux sapphires, rubies, diamonds and pearls.

*1962* *2.5in (6.25cm) long*

**£250-300** **RG**

A 1960s Dior heart-shaped pin, with oval, round and navette, aquamarine, chalcedony, pale-green and fuchsia-pink prong-set pastes.

*2.75in (7cm) wide.*

**£100-150** **RG**

A Dior rhodium-plated floral necklace and earrings, with round- and navette-cut faux rubies and clear rhinestones.

*1959 Necklace 16in (40cm) long*

**£250-350** **ROX**

A Christian Dior necklace and earrings, signed by Christian Dior, with iridescent glass and aurora borealis stones.

*Dior used many ribbon design stones, but the stones on this piece are of an unusual form. This was because stone forms were often designed for a specific piece, which accounts for their high cost.*

*c1958*

**£300-350** **RG**

## A CLOSER LOOK AT A DIOR NECKLACE

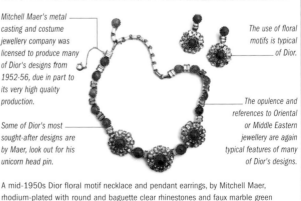

*Mitchell Maer's metal casting and costume jewellery company was licensed to produce many of Dior's designs from 1952-56, due in part to its very high quality production.*

*Some of Dior's most sought-after designs are by Maer, look out for his unicorn head pin.*

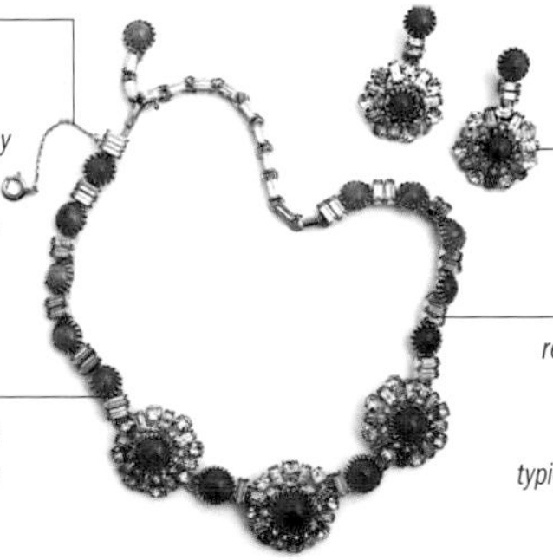

*The use of floral motifs is typical of Dior.*

*The opulence and references to Oriental or Middle Eastern jewellery are again typical features of many of Dior's designs.*

A mid-1950s Dior floral motif necklace and pendant earrings, by Mitchell Maer, rhodium-plated with round and baguette clear rhinestones and faux marble green cabochons.

*Neck: 15in (38cm) long*

**£400-500** **RG**

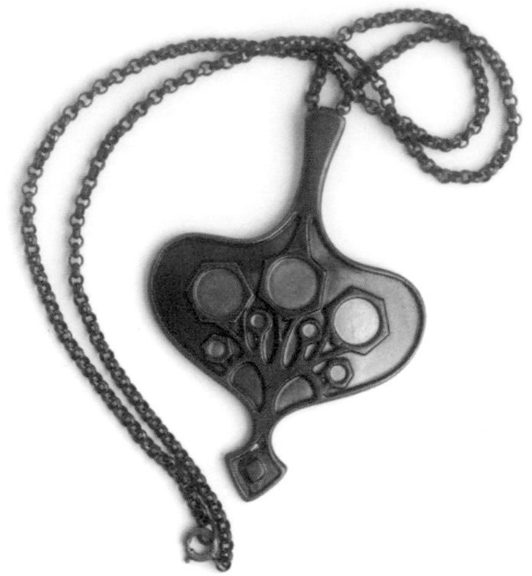

A Norwegian David-Andersen enamelled copper pendant, designed by Unn Tangerud, the back stamped "Design U.Tangerud".

*David-Andersen was founded in Christiana (now Oslo) in 1876, and still produces jewellery today. Tangerud (b.1933) is known for her use of primitive and historical motifs. Here she harks back to the Art Nouveau and Arts & Crafts movements.*

*3.5in (9cm) high*

**£20-30** **NOR**

An Avon necklace and earrings, designed by José Marie Barrera, from the 'Adriatic' collection.

**£15-20** **JJ**

A 1970s B.S.K gold-tone metal pin of an Oriental lady's head and shoulder, with faux pearl earrings.

*1.25in (3cm) high*

**£15-20** **JJ**

A 1930s Marcel Boucher rhodium-plated sterling silver sweet pea brooch, with pearlised enamel, the back with stamped Marcel Boucher logo.

*3.25in (8cm) long*

**£300-350** **RG**

A 1950s Hattie Carnegie fish pin, of black, green and yellow Lucite on a gilt metal mount, with inset clear rhinestone highlights.

*2in (5.cm) long*

**£120-180** **CRIS**

A 1960s Hattie Carnegie electric-blue glass beaded necklace and earrings.

*Earrings 1in (3cm) long*

**£50-60** **ROX**

## A CLOSER LOOK AT A BUTLER & WILSON PIN

*The all-over sparkling rhinestone encrustation contrasting against black elements is typical of Butler & Wilson's designs.*

*Stylized face motifs have been used by many costume jewellery makers, and are popular with collectors.*

*This design harks back to the Art Deco style, which is another feature of many of Butler & Wilson's designs.*

*The proven, demonstrable connection to Bette Davis adds enormously to the value.*

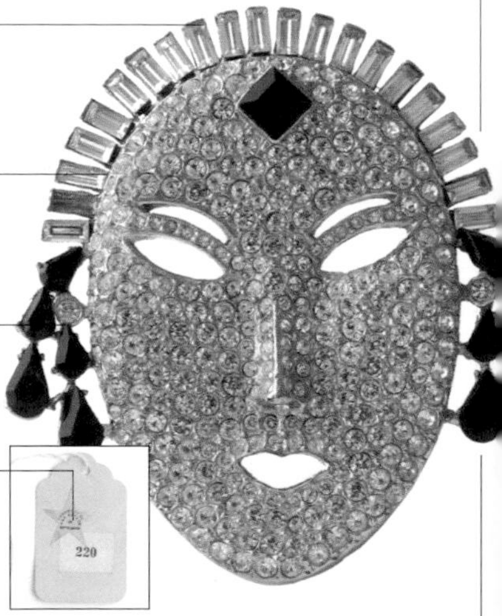


A 1980s Butler & Wilson face pin, the back impressed "20611", given to Bette Davis by a fan and sold in the Doyle's Bette Davis auction as Lot 220, together with the original lot ticket and invoice from Doyle's.

*2.5in (6.5cm) high*

**£800-1,200** **NOR**

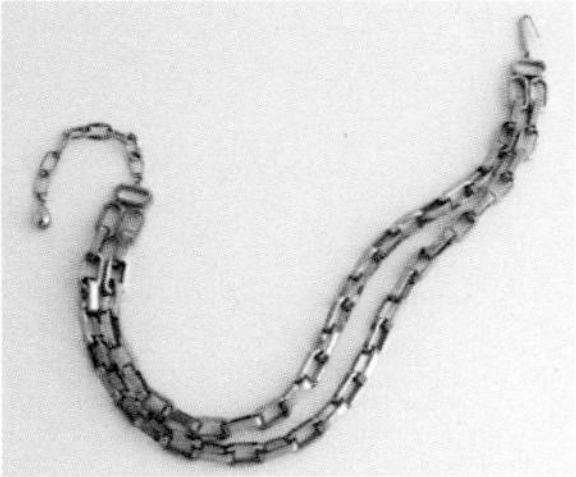

A Hattie Carnegie gold-washed chain-link necklace.

*c1955* *17.5in (44.5cm) long*

**£50-60** **MILLB**

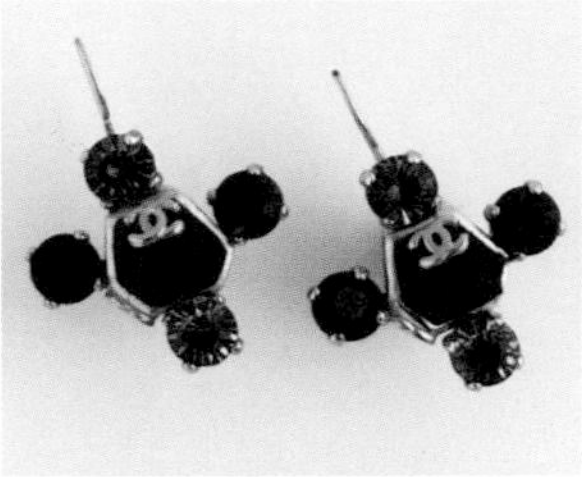

A pair of Chanel 'Maltese Cross' earrings, with poured glass cabochons set in gilt metal, with applied Chanel 'CC' logo.

*2000-01*

**£80-100** **PC**

A Corocraft sterling silver 'Hanging Gardens of Babylon' pin, the reverse with stamped name.

*2.25in (6cm) long*

**£60-90** **BB**

A 1940s Coro 'Jelly Belly' fish Duette pin, inset with crystals.

*Corocraft is famous for its 'Duette' pins, which comprise two separate pins that can be mounted together on a single frame. Here, each fish can also be used as a separate pin. The mechanism was patented in 1931 by Adolphe Katz, Coro's Design Director from 1924.*

*1.75in (4.5cm) long*

**£350-450** **CRIS**

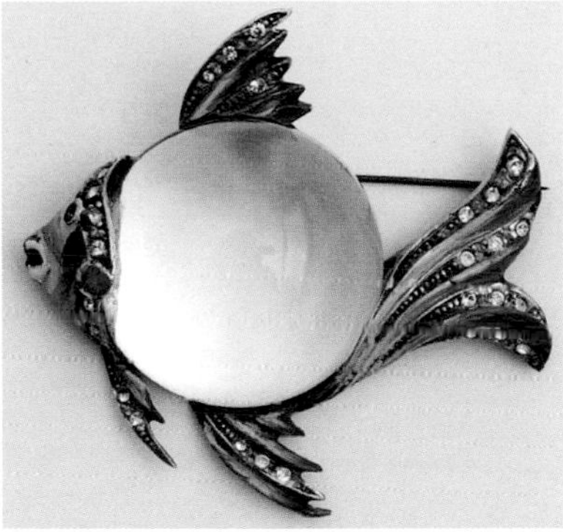

A Corocraft sterling silver fish brooch, designed by Adolph Katz, with enamel decoration and inset and Lucite, signed "Corocraft Sterling America".

*During the war, restrictions on the use of metals meant that many designers had to use alternative materials. Adolph Katz was a friend of Alfred Philippe, Chief Designer at Trifari, who used Lucite in his 'Jelly Belly' pins, hence the similarity of this design to Trifari's 'Jelly Belly' range. 'Corocraft' was the name Coro used for their high-end designs from 1937.*

*1942-45* *2.5in (6.5cm) long*

**£150-250** **RG**

A 1920s Fischel and Nessler sterling silver necklace and pendant earrings, with round- and baguette-cut clear crystal rhinestones, and prong-set, round-, pear- and lozenge-cut cranberry glass beads.

*Necklace 18in (45.75cm) long*

**£350-400** **RG**

A late 1970s Florenza antiqued gold-tone metal Renaissance-style shield-shaped pin, with pendant chains, green enamelling, clear and emerald-coloured rhinestones, a ring of faux pearls, and a faux pearl drop.

*3.5in (9cm) long*

**£60-70** **JJ**

A 1980s Stanley Hagler floral and foliate pin, with yellow and green pressed glass and yellow, red and green faux seed pearls.

*5in (12.5cm) high*

**£250-300** **CRIS**

A 1960s Stanley Hagler fruit pin, with Murano glass beads.

*Hagler was known for the quality of his glass beads. These examples are from the historic glassmaking island of Murano.*

*2.25in (6cm) long*

**£60-80** **CRIS**

A 1980s Stanley Hagler floral pin, with grey faux seed pearls, green poured glass and jade glass beads.

*3.75in (9.5cm) diam*

**£250-300** **CRIS**

## A CLOSER LOOK AT STANLEY HAGLER BANGLE

*Hagler worked for Miriam Haskell during the late 1940s, and her influence shows in his intricate, hand-wired designs.*

*This piece is made more visually stunning by its three dimensional effect, with elements literally 'piled' on top of each other.*

*The use of vibrant, brightly coloured miniature glass beads is a hallmark of Hagler's best designs.*

*The original version of this bangle was made with seed pearls in the 1950s for Wallace Simpson, adding greatly to its desirability.*

A 1970s Stanley Hagler gold-plated bangle, with polychrome moulded glass and glass bead floral motifs, and clear crystal rhinestones.

*7.5in (19cm) circ.*

**£600-800** **CRIS**

A 1950s Har gold-tone and silvered metal key pin, with green and clear crystal rhinestones.

*3.5in (9cm) long*

**£30-40** **JJ**

A 1990s Histoire de Verre pin, with poured glass in metal frames.

*3.25in (8.5cm) long*

**£150-200** **CRIS**

A 1940s Hobé sterling silver bow-shaped pin, with peridot, rose quartz, jonquil and amethyst stones.

*4in (10cm) long*

**£150-200** **CRIS**

A Hollycraft gilt and silver-gilt frame butterfly pin, set with black and white enamel.

*c1970* *2.25in (5.5cm) wide*

**£30-40** **JJ**

A 1940s pair of Joseff of Hollywood 'Russian gold' multiple fish pendant-hoop earrings, each set with a topaz-coloured crystal cabochon.

*3.5in (9cm) long*

**£120-180** **CRIS**

A 1940s pair of Joseff of Hollywood Russian 'Russian gold' pendant owl's head earrings, each suspended from a gold-tone faux pearl.

*2in (5cm) long*

**£120-180** **CRIS**

A 1930s Joseff of Hollywood heart-shaped floral pendant, with graduated teardrop and round faux amethysts and clear rhinestones.

*2.5in (6.25cm) long*

**£100-150** **ROX**

## A CLOSER LOOK AT A JOSEFF OF HOLLYWOOD PIN

*As the company's name suggests, Joseff of Hollywood was best known for its jewellery used by Hollywood film stars on screen.*

*Eugene Joseff was famed for his imitation gold metal, known as 'Russian Gold', which minimised reflection from studio lights due to its semi-matte surface.*

*Stars were used on jewellery designed for Norma Shearer in the 1938 film 'Marie Antoinette' and when Joseff included them in his retail line, they proved immensely popular.*

*Joseff's jewellery is always visually bold and strong - look out for other sky-themed pieces such as his iconic sun and moon pins.*

A 1940s Joseff of Hollywood pendant stars bar pin, each star inset with a clear rhinestone.

*4.5in (11cm) wide*

**£300-400** **CRIS**

A 1950s Lisner brushed gold-tone metal exotic flower pin, with faux pearls.

*3in (7.5cm) long*

**£15-25** **MILLB**

A 1990s pair of Andrew Logan hoop earrings, with segments of orange glass set in gold glittered metal castings.

*2.75in (7cm) diam*

**£120-180** **LB**

A 1940s pair of Mazer Brothers sterling silver floral motif dress clips, with red and purple glass stones and pave-set clear crystal rhinestones.

*11in (3.75cm) wide*

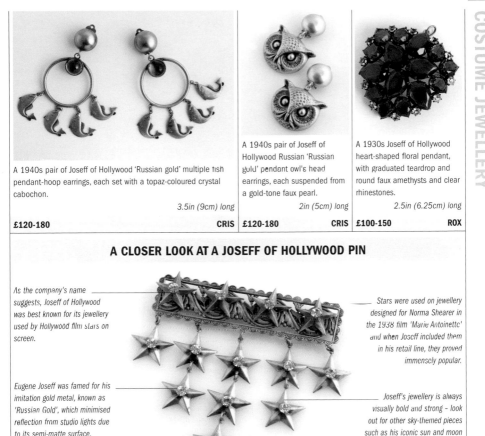

**£140-180** **JJ**

A 1960s-70s Mosell gold-plated necklace, with cast bark effect textured surface, and inset with rhinestones.

**£80-100** **MTS**

A 1940s Napier vermeil sterling silver man-and-wheelbarrow pin, with faux pearls and coral-coloured glass stones.

*1.5in (4cm) high*

**£40-60** **ABIJ**

A 1970s-80s Napier gilt metal Oriental man's head pendant, with facial details in polychrome plastic, lacks chain.

*1.75in (4.5cm) long*

**£25-30** **JJ**

A 1960s-70s Panetta gold-tone metal bracelet, set with faux pearls and clear crystal rhinestones.

*8in (20cm) long*

**£50-60** **ABIJ**

A late 1930s Parco vermeil sterling silver umbrella pin, of three drinkers at a bar, with polychrome enamelling and clear crystal rhinestone highlights.

*1.25in (3cm) high*

**£120-150** **JJ**

A 1970s-80s Pauline gold-tone metal turtle pin, set with a large, marble glass cabochon.

*1.75in (4.5cm) long*

**£40-50** **JJ**

A 1950s Robert gilt metal 'Birdman with Umbrella' pin, with polychrome enamelling.

*Robert was the tradename used by the Fashioncraft Jewelry Company, founded in New York in 1942. In 1960, it changed its name to 'Robert Originals Inc', and used the tradename 'Original by Robert' from 1942 until its closure in 1979.*

*2.5in (6.5cm) long*

**£30-50** **JJ**

A mid-1940s Pennino Bros. vermeil sterling silver bow pin, with aquamarine and rose-pink crystal rhinestones.

*3.75in (9.5cm) long*

**£180-220** **CRIS**

A Rebajes dancer copper pendant, with chain.

*The form of the dancers, as well as the theme, is very similar to paintings and collages by Modern painter Henri Matisse.*

*c1950* *2.25in (6cm) diam*

**£80-120** **MG**

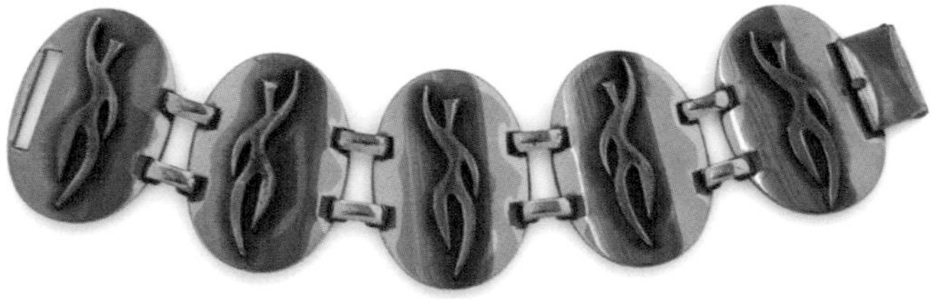

A Rebajes articulated 'Dancer' copper bracelet.

*c1950* *7.5in (19cm) long*

**£120-180** **MG**

## A CLOSER LOOK AT A REBAJES HEAD PIN

*Francisco Rebajes (1906-90) ran a jewellery and objets d'art shop in New York from 1934-67, before returning to his Spanish homeland to make jewellery.*

*This African inspired pin is one of his most iconic and celebrated designs - he also produced other pieces such as plates with similar African designs.*

*He is celebrated for his highly stylized, dramatic Modern designs in copper.*

*Condition and the presence of a good, original patina is vital to value.*

A late 1940s Rebajes 'Ubangi' copper pin, with copper wire necklace and earrings.

*3in (8cm) high*

**£200-250** **CRIS**

A Rebajes hand-wrought metal bull pin.

*c1950* *3in (7.5cm) high*

**£150-250** **MG**

A Nettie Rosenstein vermeil sterling piper fur clip, with coloured enamelling and inset rhinestones.

*2.75in (7cm) high*

**£100-150** **BB**

A 1940s Nettie Rosenstein vermeil sterling silver crab fur clip, with enamelled decoration, the backstamped "Nettie Rosenstein" and "Sterling".

*2in (5cm) long*

**£80-120** **RG**

A rare 1940s Nettie Rosenstein vermeil sterling silver butterfly fur clip, with enamelled detailing, the back signed.

*Nettie Rosenstein was primarily a couturier who also made jewellery, making her pieces quite rare.*

*4in (10cm) long*

**£250-300** **RG**

A 1940s Sandor sprung choker, with two black and blue enamelled panels.

*Sandor was founded in 1938 and closed in 1972. The company is known for its enamelling and the high quality of its manufacture.*

*11.25in (28.5cm) long*

**£150-250** **BB**

A 1950s Elsa Schiaparelli pin and earrings, with prong-set blue cabochons and blue and green crystal rhinestones.

*Pin: 2.5in (6cm) wide*

**£200-250** **CRIS**

A late 1950s Sherman gold-tone metal bracelet and earring, set with large, black-flecked coral glass cabochons surrounded by amber and citrine coloured rhinestones of various cuts, including navette.

*Bracelet: 6.75in (17.5cm) long*

**£120-180** **CRIS**

A Tortolani hand-cast, antiqued gold-plated pewter Devil pin, with ruby red crystal rhinestone eyes.

*c1960* *1.5in (3.5cm) long*

**£50-70** **JJ**

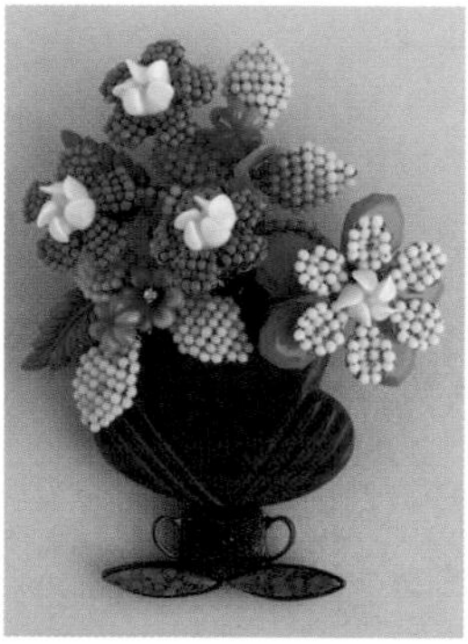

A late 1990s Larry Vrba footed basket-of-flowers pin with carved orange and yellow glass, and jade, coral and yellow glass beads, on a gun-metal frame.

*Larry Vrba was Chief Designer at Miriam Haskell during the 1970s. The use of beads and the general style of this piece show the influence of this position.*

*4.5in (11.5cm) high*

**£100-150** **CRIS**

A Warner gold-tone metal 'Night and Day' flower pin, with opening mechanism.

*This flower has a mechanism that allows the inside petals to be opened up. They are shown closed here. Desirability and prices for these have been rising in recent years, against a limited supply.*

*c1960* *2in (5cm) long*

**£80-120** **LB**

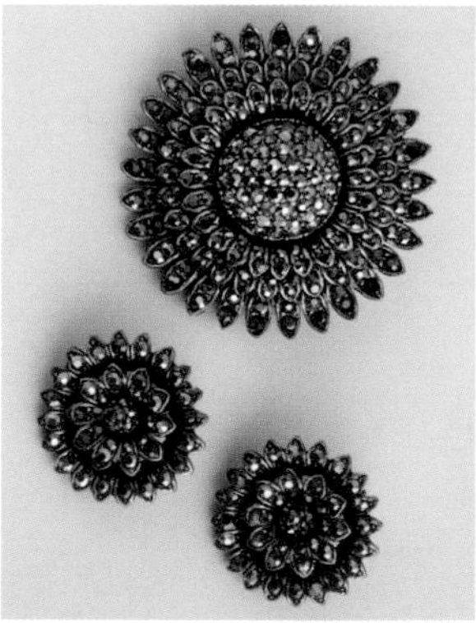

A 1950s Weiss sunflower motif pin and earrings, with inset gold-tone marcasite.

*Pin: 2in (5cm) diam*

**£50-70** **ABIJ**

A 1950s pair of Weiss cream plastic earrings, set with polychrome and clear crystal rhinestones.

*1in (2.5cm) diam*

**£20-30** **JJ**

A 1940s American vermeil sterling silver 'jelly-belly' penguin brooch, with inset rhinestones and Lucite body.

*Unsurprisingly, given their popularity at the time, 'Jelly Belly' designs by Trifari and Corocraft were widely copied by other makers.*

*2in (5cm) long*

**£60-80** **RG**

A 1950s unsigned gold-tone metal heron pin, set with ruby red, sapphire blue and emerald green glass cabochons.

*3in (7.5cm) long*

**£20-25** **CRIS**

A 1960s unsigned gold-tone metal peacock with aqua and turquoise enamelling.

*2.75in (7cm) long*

**£25-35** **CRIS**

A 1950s French unsigned gold-tone metal bird-on-a-branch pin, with pave set turquoise glass stones, and a turquoise cabochon egg.

*1.5in (4cm) high*

**£20-30** **CRIS**

A 1950s unsigned gold-tone metal bird-on-a-branch pin, with red enamelling and pave set clear crystal rhinestones.

*2.25in (5.5cm) high*

**£20-25** **CRIS**

A 1950s unsigned gold-tone metal 'Penguin Family' pin, with brown enamelling, pave-set clear crystal rhinestones and green glass cabochon eyes.

*1.25in (3cm) wide*

**£20 30** **CRIS**

Three 1950s unsigned gold-tone metal chick scatter pins, with inset moonstone, angel skin or lapis blue glass bodies.

*1in (2.5cm) high*

**£10-12 (EACH)** **CRIS**

A 1950s unsigned gold-tone metal butterfly pin, with 'trembler' wings, set with French jet and clear rhinestones.

*2.75in (7cm) wide*

**£40-60** **CRIS**

A 1950s unsigned gold-tone metal butterfly pin, with blue, red and green enamelled wings.

*3in (7.5cm) wide*

**£30-40** **CRIS**

A 1950s unsigned gold-tone metal tortoise pin, with brown enamelled shell and feet, and inset French jet eyes.

*1.75in (4.5cm) wide*

**£10-20** **CRIS**

An 1950s turtle pin, with bakelite cabochons and coral moonstones with lapis.

*2.25in (5.5cm) wide*

**£35-45** **CRIS**

A 1950s unsigned gold-tone metal snail pin, with a blue Lucite shell.

*2in (5cm) long*

**£20-30** **CRIS**

An 1930s unsigned female African head fur clip of cold-enamelled base metal with clear and ruby red crystal rhinestones.

*Butler & Wilson made a near identical pin during the 1980s, but with a silvery instead of a coppery finish. Given the earlier date of this pin, it is likely that they used another example of this pin as inspiration. Founders Nicky Butler and Simon Wilson both sold antique jewellery before turning to costume jewellery design.*

*1.75in (4.5cm) high*

**£50-60** **PC**

An unsigned and unmarked cast metal 'Fu Manchu' fur clip.

*Despite being unmarked, the modelling of his facial expression in particular is of a very good quality.*

*3in (7.5cm) high*

**£25-35** **BB**

A 1960s unsigned gold-washed metal 'My Fair Lady' umbrella pin, with open-and-shut mechanism, here shown shut, with black and white enamelling and clear crystal rhinestone highlights.

*2.5in (6.5cm) long*

**£20-30** **JJ**

An enamelled shoe pin, from the Metropolitan Museum. *2001*

*2in (5cm) long*

**£20-30** **PC**

A 1930s French unsigned rhodium-plated silver 'Fruit Salad' brooch, with prong-set multicoloured glass stones.

*1.75in (4.5cm) long*

**£200-300** **CRIS**

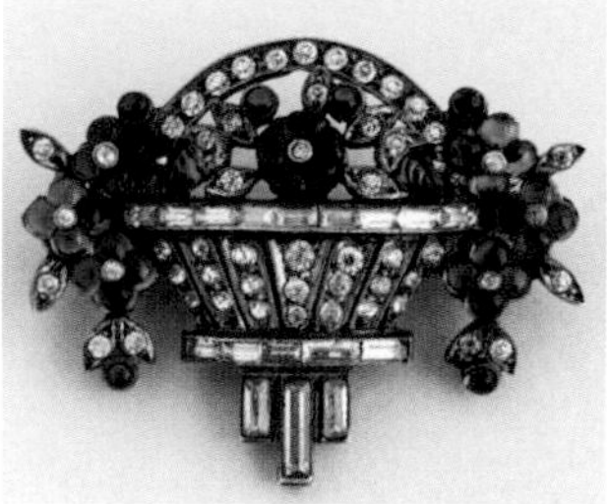

An early 1900s French unsigned sterling silver 'Fruit Salad' hanging-basket-of-flowers pin, with primary coloured cabochons and crystal rhinestones.

*These designs were initially based on Mughal 'Tree of Life' jewellery of India, with Cartier being one of the first companies to produce them. Their multicoloured faux or real jewels soon gained them the nickname 'tutti frutti' or 'fruit salads'. The design of this example is appealing.*

*1.5in (4cm) wide*

**£100-150** **CRIS**

An 1940s American unsigned vermeil sterling silver pin, set with coloured faux pearls and glass stones.

*3in (7.5cm) long*

**£80-120** **RG**

A 1950s unsigned brooch, with pink faceted glass stones.

**£50-60** **PC**

A late 20thC unsigned pin, set all over with aurora borealis rhinestones.

*2.25in (6cm) diam*

**£20-30** **BB**

A 1930s carved amber and gold-tone metal necklace and matching earrings.

*3.5in (9cm) high*

**£120-180** **NOR**

## A CLOSER LOOK AT A CRYSTAL BEAD NECKLACE

*The beads are not made from glass, but from cut and polished rock crystal, which is carefully selected to be as transparent and flawless as possible.*

*In Chinese, they are known as 'Pools of Light', for the amazing refractive and reflective qualities of the rock crystal.*

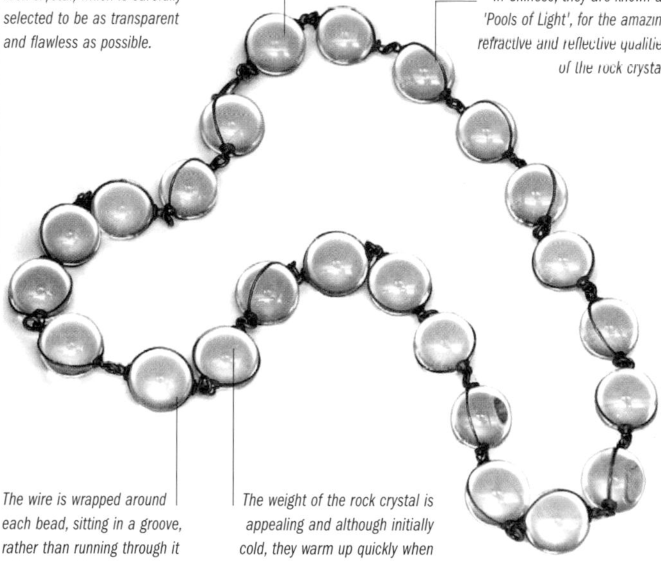

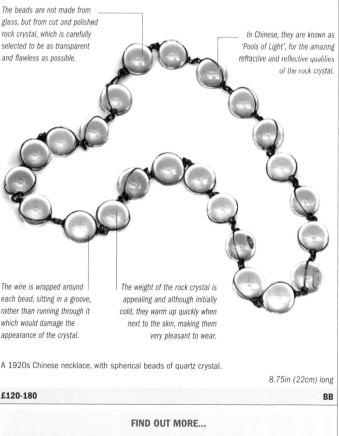

*The wire is wrapped around each bead, sitting in a groove, rather than running through it which would damage the appearance of the crystal.*

*The weight of the rock crystal is appealing and although initially cold, they warm up quickly when next to the skin, making them very pleasant to wear.*

A 1920s Chinese necklace, with spherical beads of quartz crystal.

*8.75in (22cm) long*

**£120-180** **BB**

**FIND OUT MORE...**

**Costume Jewellery**, *by Judith Miller, published by Dorling Kindersley, 2004.*

## COLLECTORS' NOTES

- Although Victorian taste, particularly the fascination for mourning, had downplayed the fun side of jewellery, the Jazz Age of the 1920s and '30s saw a return to glamorous and glitzy pieces. Faux 'diamond' encrusted 'cocktail jewellery' was highly fashionable and Bakelite jewellery also became popular as it allowed ladies of all incomes to afford to buy the latest fashions. This became more important during the hardships of the Great Depression caused by the 1929 Wall Street Crash.

- Plastics could also be carved into myriad shapes and designs, in a rainbow of bright, cheerful colours. Bakelite itself, patented by Dr Leo Baekeland in 1907, is usually found in cream, brown, black and darker colours, although mottled brighter colours are known. Its invention also led to the development of many other plastics, such as cast phenolic, which are grouped under the term 'bakelite' by collectors today.

- In general, consider the colour, form, size, type and level of decoration. Vibrant and bright colours, such as cherry red and strong greens, tend to be the most valuable. However, clear plastics, known collectively under the brand name 'Lucite', have also become popular today. Found in many colours and tones, they are particularly desirable when carved and painted.

- Bangles and bracelets are a popular form, and are often worn by collectors. Chunky examples, made from large pieces of bakelite are more sought-after than thin pieces, partly as they make more of a visual statement. Novelty shapes such as animal pins, which became more widespread during the 1930s, are also sought-after.

- Geometric and highly stylized Art Deco motifs and patterns are among the most desirable. Many are based on flowers, leaves or other natural forms. The most desirable pieces tend to be either deeply and dramatically carved, or intricate and detailed. Examine a piece close-up for signs of repair through polishing away damage or filling holes, and look out for cracks and chips.

A 1930s clear Lucite Scottie dog pin, with gilt metal bow.

*Scottie dogs were highly fashionable during the 1930s, and again during the 1950s. Today, they are a collecting area of their own, which often means prices are higher than for other breeds.*

*3in (8cm) long*

**£150-200** **ROX**

A 1930s black Lucite Scottie dog pin, with inset eye and painted tongue.

*3in (7.5cm) long*

**£60-80** **ROX**

A 1930s carved bakelite Scottie dog pin, with two heads, with inset bead eyes.

**£120-180** **ROX**

A 1930s reverse painted, carved Lucite parrot pin.

*3.5in (9cm) long*

**£60-80** **TR**

A 1930s carved and reverse painted Lucite owl pin.

*3.5in (9cm) long*

**£80-120** **TR**

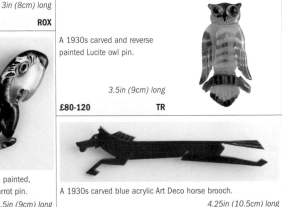

A 1930s carved blue acrylic Art Deco horse brooch.

*4.25in (10.5cm) long*

**£20-30** **JBC**

A 1930s unsigned novelty porter-and-suitcase pin in black, red and blue bakelite with plaited bow, chain and highlights in gilt metal.

*As well as being amusing, this pin is rare and very well designed and made. It has numerous different brightly coloured components. It still retains its 'luggage sticker' transfers and hints at the exclusivity and exoticism of foreign travel by plane or cruise liner, at a time when it was only really affordable by the wealthy.*

*3.25in (8.25cm) long.*

**£150-250** **TM**

## A CLOSER LOOK AT A BAKELITE PIN

*The gently curving, stylized form is very elegant, and the exotic air is popular - all are desirable features of Art Deco design.*

*The head, face and headdress were hand-carved and hand-polished from a single piece of Lucite, requiring skilled work, and were not cast in a mould.*

*The intricate and detailed headdress is finely hand-painted using a number of different colours.*

*It is very rare, comparatively large and still in excellent condition, with no damage to the enamel colours.*

A 1930s Art Deco 'Apple Juice' bakelite pin of a lady's head.

*4in (10cm) high*

**£1,000-1,500** **ROX**

A 1930s cherry red and green bakelite 'Cherries' bar pin, with carved and curved leaves.

*The complexity and condition of these pins is paramount. However, as most are collected and worn, the replaced green 'gimp' stringing on this example does not detract from the overall value.*

*3.25in (8.5cm) high*

**£220-280** **BB**

A late 1930s-40s hand-carved cameo-style black and 'creamed corn' bakelite head oval pin, with metal chain.

*2.25in (6cm) high*

**£120-180** **MG**

An Art Deco red veined and red Catalin 'Bird In Flight' two-piece bar pin, the bird with carved feathers.

*2.75in (7cm) high*

**£50-80** **TSIS**

An Art Deco hand-carved and polished black bakelite life-saving ring pin, with original two-colour gimp stringing.

*1.75in (4.5cm) diam*

**£100-150** **BB**

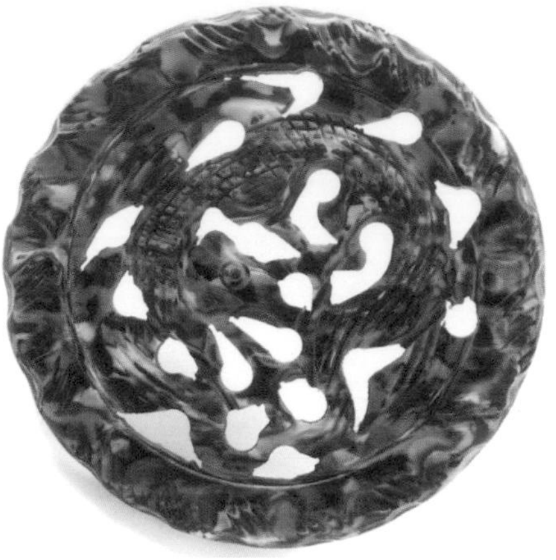

An 'End of the Day' hand-carved bakelite Chinese-style pin.

*Much like glassmaking, this pin takes its name from the fact that at the end of the working day, the remainders of the different coloured plastics were combined together in vats and then cast and carved.*

*3in (7.5cm) diam*

**£350-550** **MG**

A 1930s green bakelite pin, with applied Art Deco 'HC' brass initials.

*2in (5cm) diam*

**£20-30** **BB**

A 1950s multicoloured hand-painted Lucite flower pin.

*1.75in (4.5cm) diam.*

**£12-15** **ECLEC**

A 1920s hand-carved bakelite rose pin, with celluloid bale.

*Although these pins are not too hard to find, the presence of the original, easily broken celluloid 'bale' or ring is rare.*

*2in (5cm) high*

**£20-40** **BB**

A 1950s reverse-carved and filled Lucite rose pin, with black back panel.

*For more information on how this technique is achieved, see the Closer Look on the Apple Juice bakelite bangle with goldfish later in this section.*

*1.75in (4.5cm) long*

**£12-18** **BB**

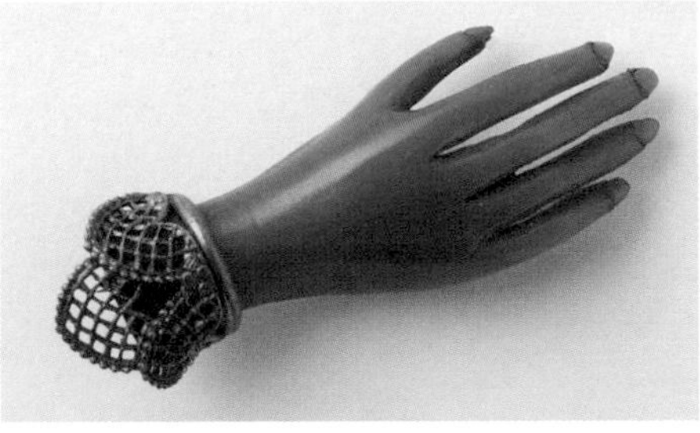

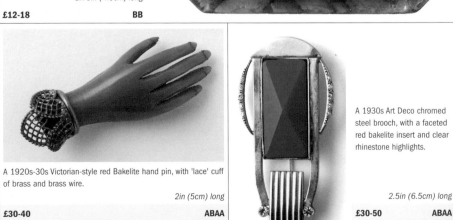

A 1920s-30s Victorian-style red Bakelite hand pin, with 'lace' cuff of brass and brass wire.

*2in (5cm) long*

**£30-40** **ABAA**

A 1930s Art Deco chromed steel brooch, with a faceted red bakelite insert and clear rhinestone highlights.

*2.5in (6.5cm) long*

**£30-50** **ABAA**

An Art Deco bakelite stylized flower pin, with black stem and translucent white petals with incised linear decoration.

*10cm (4in) long*

**£30-40** **ABAA**

A late 1920-30s Art Deco black bakelite stylized torchère-and-buckle pin, with gilt incisions and stylised leaf design.

*The dramatic contrast of black and silver, or black and white, was an enduring combination in Art Deco design. Geometric, clean-lined and often arrow-like forms represented the style's and period's fascination with speed and the machine. Black jewellery moved away from being indicative of mourning, as it had done during the Victorian period, allowing it to make a new style statement. Twinned with inset rhinestones to add sparkle, these pieces made a perfect, glamorous choice for evening wear.*

*11cm (4.25in) long*

**£30-40** **ABAA**

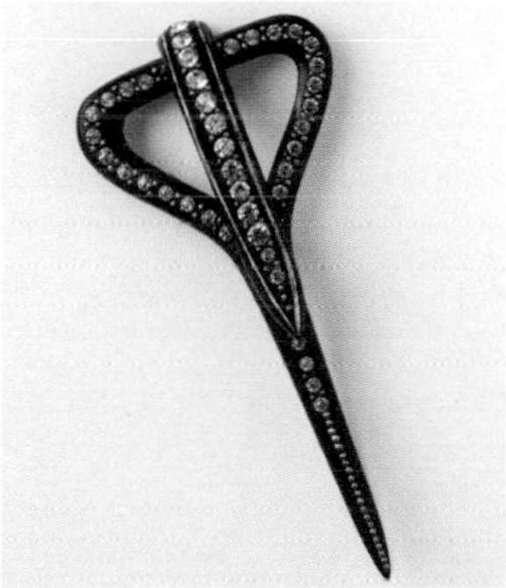

An early 1930s Art Deco black bakelite stylized heart pin, set with clear rhinestones and tiny brass balls.

*9cm (3.25in) long*

**£20-30** **ABAA**

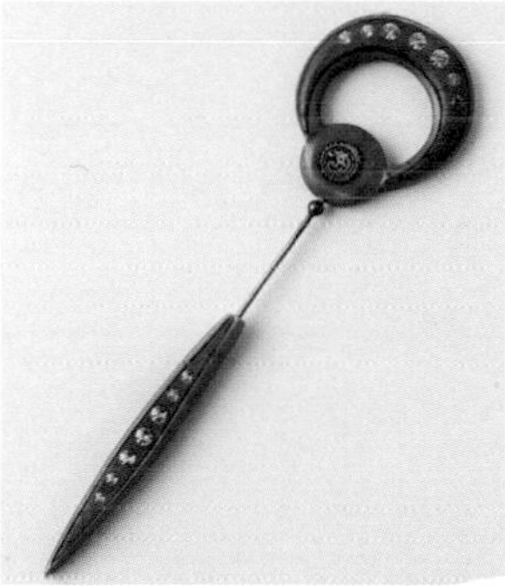

An Art Deco green and gold Bakelite lapel and/or hat pin, set with tiny brass beads and clear and amber coloured rhinestones.

*13.5cm (5.25in) long*

**£30-50** **ABAA**

A late 1920s-30s Art Deco black bakelite twin leaf and bud pin, set with clear rhinestones and tiny brass balls.

*11cm (4.25in) long*

**£20-30** **ABAA**

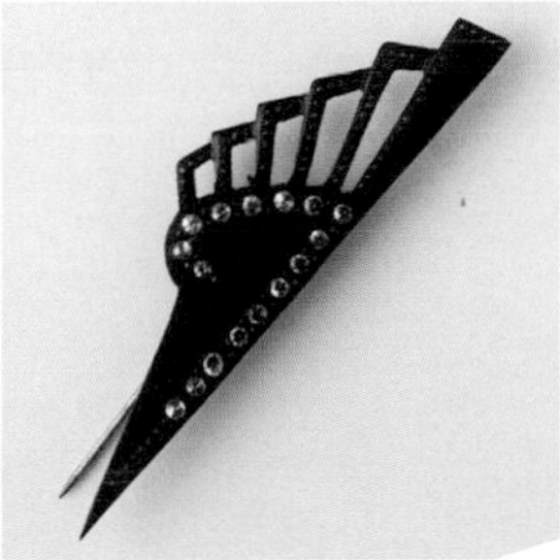

A late 1920s-30s Art Deco fan-shaped black bakelite pin, set with tiny brass balls and clear rhinestones.

*7cm (2.75in) long*

**£20-30** **ABAA**

An early 1930s Art Deco folded scarf pin, in black Bakelite set with clear rhinestones.

*5cm (2in) wide*

**£20-30** **ABAA**

An early 1930s Art Deco black bakelite shield-shaped pin, set with rows of clear rhinestones.

*4.5cm (1.75in) long*

**£25-30** **ABAA**

An Art Deco black bakelite pin, with a diagonal black and white diaper pattern highlighted with clear rhinestones.

*6.5cm (2.5in) wide*

**£25-35** **ABAA**

A late 1920s-30s Art Deco black bakelite 'choker' pin, set with clear rhinestones.

*6.5cm (2.5in) wide*

**£25-35** **ABAA**

A late 1920s-30s dark brown bakelite bowtie pin, set with clear rhinestones.

*6cm (2.25in) wide*

**£25-35** **ABAA**

A late 1920s-30s black bakelite double-knot pin, set with amber rhinestones.

*The rhinestones on this pin were originally clear but have taken on an amber tinge as they have aged.*

*8cm (3in) long*

**£20-30** **ABAA**

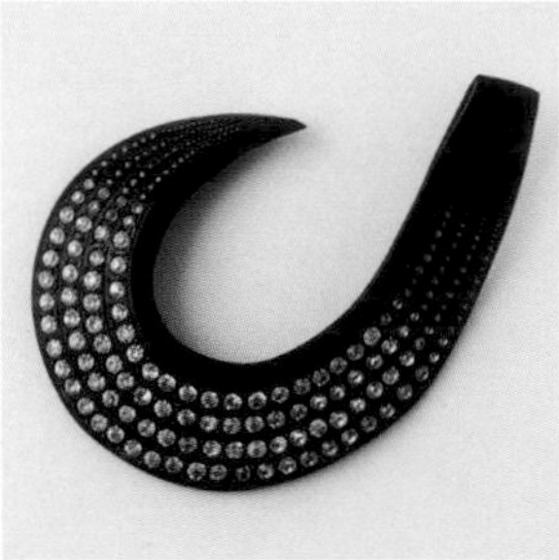

A 1930s curving black bakelite Art Deco hairpin, with four rows of inset brass balls and clear crystal rhinestones.

*8cm (3.25in) long*

**£20-30** **ABAA**

A black bakelite hand pin.

*Hand-shaped pins also appeared in the Victorian era. The material and design helps to date a piece.*

*c1940* *9.5cm (3.75in) long*

**£70-90** **CRIS**

A 1930s laminated, cut and polished bakelite angular pin.

*Different complimentary colours of bakelite panels have been laminated together. The pin has then been cut at an angle and polished to display the different layers.*

*2.25in (6cm) high*

**£35-45** **BB**

A 1930s Art Deco green and black-banded carved bakelite bow brooch, with brass ribbed centre.

*3.75in (9.5cm) long*

**£70-100** **ELI**

## A CLOSER LOOK AT A BAKELITE BANGLE

*This amber coloured type of Lucite is known as 'apple juice' bakelite to collectors and can be found in many different tones.*

*The fish are cleverly carved to add a feeling of depth as they 'swim' around the wrist, showing the care and attention paid to such pieces.*

*The back of the bangle was carved by hand with the small fish, with the recesses then being filled with opaque coloured paint.*

*The bangle is extremely thick, amusing and eminently wearable today - all are desirable features to collectors and lovers of vintage fashion.*

A 1940s 'apple juice' bakelite bangle, reversed carved with goldfish.

*2.5in (7cm) wide*

**£800-1,200** **ROX**

A 1930s 'apple juice' Lucite hinged bracelet, with reverse carved and injected colour flowers and foliage.

*2.75in (7cm) wide*

**£250-300** **BY**

A 1930s Prystal or 'apple juice' bakelite bangle.

*Although the yellow colour is appealing, it is possible that this bangle started off life being clear and colourless, and has changed in colour as it has aged. The thick size and deeply carved geometric pattern is desirable.*

*3.25in (8.5cm) diam*

**£180-220** **BB**

An Art Deco bangle, with elasticated, raised and chamfered squares of onyx- and amber-coloured Bakelite.

*c1940* *Squares: 3cm (1.25in) wide*

**£20-40** **ECLEC**

A 1930s laminated and carved 'apple juice' Lucite and burgundy bakelite bangle.

*3.25in (8.5cm) diam*

**£150-200** **BB**

A 1930s carved faux-tortoiseshell bakelite bangle.

*Early plastics simulating tortoiseshell had been used since the first decades of the 20thC. Tortoiseshell was an expensive and desirable material, particularly with good colouring and in large sizes. Plastics allowed the look to be applied to different, chunkier forms.*

*3.25in (8cm) diam*

**£50-70** **BB**

A 1930s carved and painted 'apple juice' Lucite bangle, the rounded outside decorated with inscribed lines painted in green.

*0.25in (0.5cm) wide*

**£100-150** **DAW**

A 1940s 'apple juice' Lucite and black bakelite articulated bangle, with bands of inset diamanté and elastic stringing.

*3in (8cm) diam*

**£150-200** **MG**

A 1950s plastic bangle, with moulded and painted floral and foliate motifs.

*9in (23cm) circ*

**£15-25** **ECLEC**

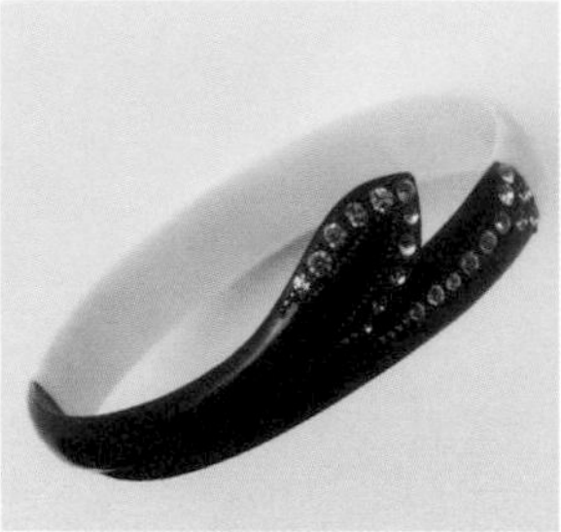

A 1930s black and ivory-coloured bakelite snake bangle set with clear rhinestones and tiny brass beads.

*9in (23cm) circ*

**£25-35** **ABAA**

A heavy cherry red and butterscotch hinged bracelet, domed with crescent clasp.

*Cherry red is one of the most desirable colours for bakelite jewellery, and is often a form of Catalin or 'cast phenolic'.*

*1in (2.5cm) wide*

**£60-80** **DAW**

A 1930s multicoloured striped laminated cast phenolic bangle.

*Combinations of differently coloured plastics are very popular, and would have been more expensive at the time due to the increased work needed to make them.*

*3in (7.5cm) wide*

**£120-180** **BY**

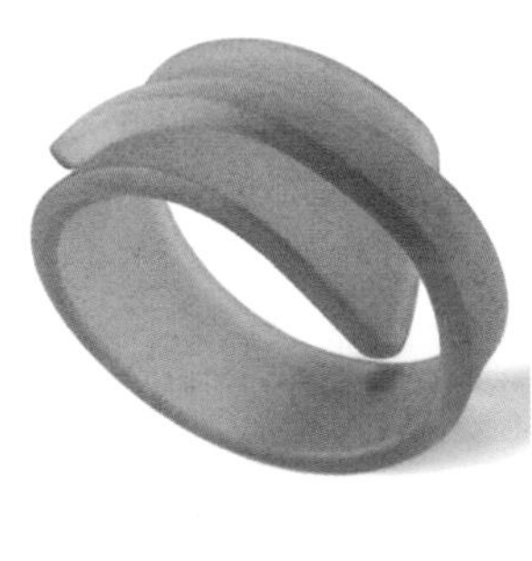

A modern matte yellow plastic curling bangle, formed of a single band of plastic.

*3.25in (8.5cm) diam*

**£10-15** **BB**

A pair of late 1920s-30s black bakelite pendant hoop earrings, set with clear rhinestones of graduated size.

*3.5cm (1.25in) long*

**£20-30** **ABAA**

A pair of 1940s brown bakelite rivetted clip earrings, with engraved circles.

*1.5in (4.5cm) diam*

**£30-40** **BB**

A pair of 1930s green bakelite cube pendant earrings.

*2.5in (6.5cm) high*

**£100-150** **MG**

A pair of 1960s coloured Lucite tapering ring earrings.

*1.5in (4cm) diam*

**£8-12** **BB**

A deep red and yellow mottled bakelite necklace, formed of polished graduated beads.

*The yellow mottling is very subtle and comes through as a lighter red in many places.*

*14.25in (36cm) high*

**£50-80** **BB**

A 1970s 'Yin & Yang' mottled red plastic necklace, the back stamped "Celebrity".

*Oriental, mystical symbols and themes such as the eternal 'Yin Yang' were popular during the 1960s and '70s.*

*Pendant 2.25in (6cm) high*

**£30-40** **TSIS**

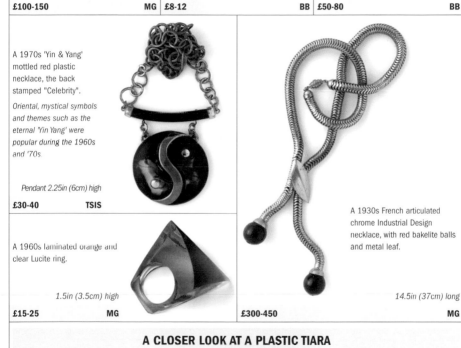

A 1960s laminated orange and clear Lucite ring.

*1.5in (3.5cm) high*

**£15-25** **MG**

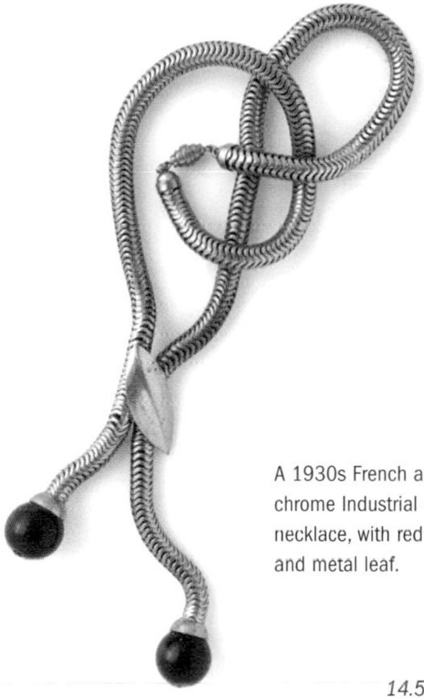

A 1930s French articulated chrome Industrial Design necklace, with red bakelite balls and metal leaf.

*14.5in (37cm) long*

**£300-450** **MG**

## A CLOSER LOOK AT A PLASTIC TIARA

*Auguste Bonaz is a celebrated French Art Deco jewellery designer - simple lines and forms are typical of his work made from the 1900s-40s.*

*Like many of his pieces, this is made from a plastic known as casein, which is formed from milk and also known as 'galalith' - Greek for 'milk stone'.*

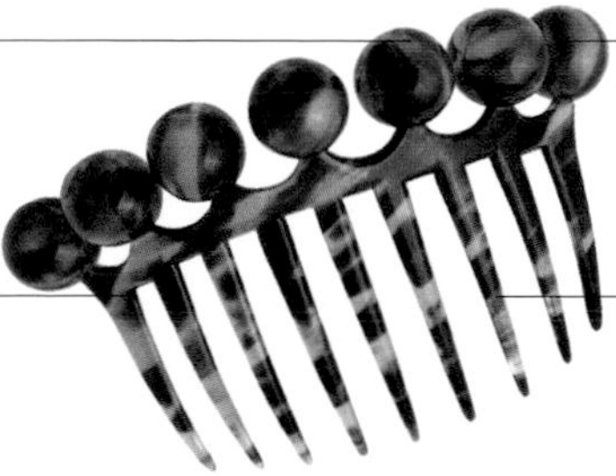

*Galalith is known for its suitability to adopt a wide range of colours, although it can warp and degrade over time. This signed piece is in excellent condition.*

*Bonaz is known for these fashionable hair decorations which can be found in different designs - interestingly Auguste's father made combs.*

An Auguste Bonaz faux-tortoiseshell galalith crown tiara, signed 'Auguste Bonaz'.

*c1900-20* *5.5in (14cm) wide*

**£150-250** **LB**

## COLLECTORS' NOTES

- The ornithologist's worst nightmare, duck decoys are placed in the water by hunters to attract ducks by making them believe the area is safe. Typically, a group of ducks, known as a rig, are placed in various positions to accentuate the illusion of safety.
- The earliest decoys known were made by Native Americans, before the arrival of settlers, from bound bunches of twigs and reeds. They were produced on a larger, commercial scale during the 1800s until the 1920s when commercial bird hunting was outlawed. Most decoys found today date from the latter part of this period, with earlier examples being rarer as they were often lost or damaged through exposure to water and gunfire.
- The industry declined severely after the 1930s, but decoys were still made by craftsmen as a form of folk art, and were typically bought as decorative pieces. Regions have their own styles and body forms, particularly in the US, where decoy collecting is popular. For example, New Jersey and Delaware decoys are nearly always hollow, while Maryland examples are typically solid.
- The form, presence of original paint, detail of the paint and the condition are the major factors that count towards value. Look on the base, as some are marked with a maker's name. Prestigious names include A.E. Crowell, William Bowman and Obadiah Verity. Consult reference books to check that the name is not that of the original owner.
- Today's buyers collect them primarily as a form of previously functional folk art, with interior decorators and those looking for individual statement for a room also adding to the growing community. Look out for the work of some of today's folk artists, which can be highly prized and valuable.

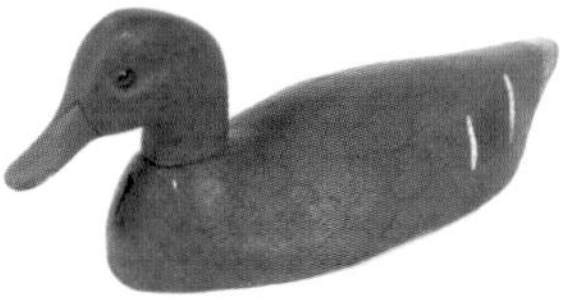

An early 20thC English decoy, painted with black lines to represent feathers, and with inset glass eyes.

**£80-120** **MUR**

An early 20thC decoy, painted with a white wing feather edge detail, and with inset glass eyes.

**£100-150** **MUR**

An early 20thC English decoy, with inset glass eyes.

**£80-120** **MUR**

An early 20thC decoy, painted in brown and greys, with painted yellow and black eyes.

**£70-100** **MUR**

A rare early English painted decoy, with fixed head in sleep position.

*This form is not common.*

**£70-100** **MUR**

An early English mallard decoy, painted in typical colours, with inset glass eyes.

**£100-150** **MUR**

## A CLOSER LOOK AT A DECOY

*Elmer Crowell (1862-1952) is regarded as one of the finest makers of duck decoys, and made both decorative and functional examples.*

*The form is realistic, being well proportioned and modelled, and the pose is natural, which is typical of Crowell's decoys.*

*His decorative shorebirds are among his most sought-after and are finely executed works.*

*The feathers are beautifully painted and very well-detailed, another hallmark of Crowell's work.*

An A. E. Crowell dowitcher decoy, with part-open beak and inset glass eyes, stamped on underside in oval cartouche with maker's name and "High Class Decoys of Every Description, East Harwich, Mass".

*11in (27.5cm) long*

**£7,500-8,500** **NA**

An early English painted decoy, painted in russet red, grey and cream, with two-tone bill and painted eyes.

**£70-100** **MUR**

A Canadian Bluebill Hen decoy, by Ray Pomeroy from Gore Landing, Ontario, the base with unfinished area, signed into the wood with a hot torch.

*1978* *13.75in (35cm) long*

**£80-120** **RAON**

A pair of Canadian Canvas Back working decoys, by W. Simmons of Beamsville, Ontario, signed "W. Simmons Beamsville" on the base.

*1980* *17.25in (44cm) long*

**£200-250 (pair)** **RAON**

A contemporary Canadian 'Ester The Nester' decorative decoy-style folk art bird, by Howard Jasper of Ontario, on a mud and straw nest, mounted on a base.

*14.5in (37cm) long*

**£100-150** **RAON**

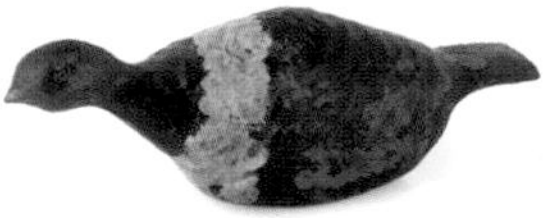

A contemporary 'Dan Quail' decorative decoy-style folk art duck, by Howard Jasper of Ontario, signed on base "HJ".

*12.5in (32cm) long*

**£120-180** **RAON**

A 1950s-60s Canadian carved and painted wood and tin fish decoy, by Basil Secord of Pentanguishene, Ontario.

*9.75in (24.5cm) long*

**£60-80** **TFR**

## COLLECTORS' NOTES

- Walter Elias Disney (1901-66) founded his animation studio with his brother Roy in Hollywood in the early 1920s. Mickey Mouse was developed in 1928, and a vast range of memorabilia followed during the 1930s and '40s. Products from this era tend to be the most sought-after.
- The character, type and rarity of the piece are important factors to value. Marks are also worth considering and can help with dating. For example, finding George Borgfeldt's name included in a mark will usually date it to the early 1930s, as he was the first to receive a license to produce Disney's products. Kay Kamen, legendary salesman and marketeer, is another name to look out for.
- Pieces from the 1930s-40s were usually marked 'Walt Disney Enterprises', and those dating from the late 1940s onwards generally marked 'Walt Disney Productions'. Marks including the copyright symbol are more modern. Other pre-war marks include 'Walter E. Disney' and 'Walt Disney Mickey Mouse Ltd', the latter being used in the UK in the 1930s.
- Another clue to dating can be seen in the characters themselves, particularly Mickey Mouse, who changed his appearance over time. For example, Mickey's 'scary' teeth were removed around 1930, and over time he also lost his tail and rodent-like appearance, becoming rounder and more 'friendly' in form from the 1950s onwards.
- Licensed products tend to be more popular and valuable, however unlicensed examples can be desirable, especially if they are early in date. Major characters generally hold more appeal with collectors, but do not ignore those that are lesser known. The small group of collectors that do collect these rarer examples often pay considerable sums for them to complete their collections.
- Condition is very important. Most Disney products were intended to be played with and have suffered through use. Therefore, mint condition examples, particularly if still in their unopened packaging, can command a premium. Traditional Disney characters are currently attracting less interest from some collectors, so now may be a good time to buy as Mickey's, and his friends' places in history are firmly set.

A 1930s French Depeche 'Mickey Mouse' hand-painted aluminium money bank.

*6in (15cm) high*

**£200-300** **ATK**

An American Crown Toy Co. Mickey Mouse painted composition money bank.

*c1938* *6in (15cm) high*

**£120-180** **BER**

A Pelham Type SL Mickey Mouse' puppet, with original control bar, instruction and box.

*10.25in (26cm) high*

**£80-120** **DN**

A Marx Toys plastic and soft vinyl Minnie Mouse 'Pip Squeek' figure, mint in box.

*1970* *5in (12.5cm) high*

**£4-6** **MEM**

A pair of Mickey and Minnie Mouse hand-painted ceramic toothbrush holders, marked "© Walt Disney".

*These licensed items were probably made in Germany due to the quality of their manufacture and their accurate modelling.*

*4in (10cm) high*

**£200-300** **RH**

A 1970s Severn China Mickey Mouse hand-painted ceramic figure, and two smaller mice.

*3.25in (8cm) high*

**£25-35** **WHP**

A Japanese Mickey Mouse hand-painted ceramic figural pitcher.

*This jug shows how far many of the Japanese makers, who were often only using pictures as examples, departed from Mickey Mouse's true form and colouring.*

*7in (18cm) high*

**£30-40** **BER**

A Pinocchio jointed wood-bodied figurine, with painted composition head and fabric collar and bow.

*7.5in (19cm) high*

**£60-80** **BER**

An Ideal Novelty Co. painted composition and wood 'Flex' Pinocchio, with flex-jointed arms and legs, marked "©Walt Disney".

*c1940* *10in (25.5cm) high*

**£30-40** **BER**

A 1950s Japanese Linemar lithographed tinplate 'Pluto the Drum Major', marked "Walt Disney Productions", with original card box.

*6.25in (16cm) high*

**£200-300** **BER**

A Ferdinand the Bull painted composition figurine, with jointed legs, together with a copy of the original Walt Disney storybook.

*Ferdinand was a bull who would rather smell flowers than fight in bullfights. Accused of being a pacifist allegory at a time of impending world war, the 1935 story by Munro Leaf was adapted into a short film by Walt Disney in 1938.*

*9in (23cm) high*

**£30-40** **BER**

A Marx Toys lithographed tinplate clockwork 'flip-over' Pluto, marked "©1939 Walt Disney Productions".

*c1939* *8in (20cm) long*

**£70-100** **BER**

A 1950s Walt Disney Productions Gus hand-painted ceramic figurine.

*3.5in (9cm) high*

**£10-15** **BB**

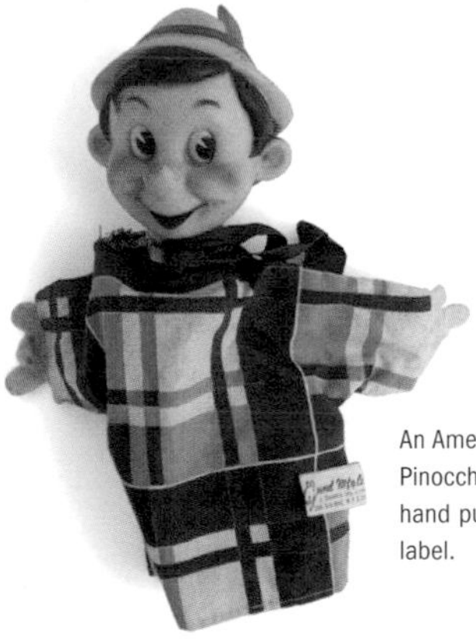

An American Gund Pinocchio vinyl and fabric hand puppet, with original label.

*9in (23cm) high*

**£35-45** **NOR**

A 1950s Brimtoys Cinderella and Prince Charming plastic and metal clockwork toy, marked "With kind permission of Walt Disney Mickey Mouse Ltd" on the box.

*This licensing was used in the UK only. The box is extremely rare.*

*5in (12.5cm) high*

**£20-30** **DSC**

A Marx 'Mickey Mouse Express' lithographed tinplate clockwork toy, marked "Walt Disney Productions", with original box.

*9in (23cm) high*

**£600-700** **BER**

Three rare Britains Disney figures, from Set 1645, comprising Minnie Mouse, Goofy and Pluto, together with a small tinplate flat figure of Mickey Mouse playing the concertina.

**£220-280** **DN**

A 1970s 'Mickey Mouse' Disneyland promotional badge.

*3.5cm (9cm) diam*

**£15-20** **CVS**

A 'Snow White Jingle Club' badge, marked "Walt Disney Enterprises".

*1938* *3.5in (9cm) diam*

**£150-200** **LDE**

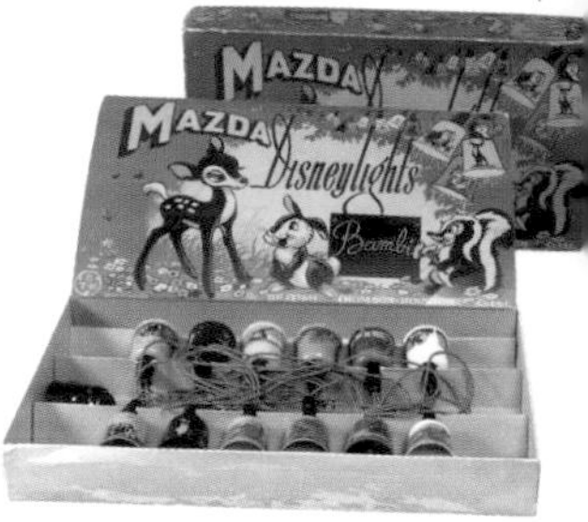


A boxed set of Thomson-Houston Co. 'Bambi' Mazda Disneylights, with 12 lights on a cable and original box and display card.

*Box 16in (40.5cm) long*

**£120-180** **BER**

A boxed set of Nome 'Pinocchio' lights, with eight miniature lights on a cable, each with transfer-printed plastic cover.

*16in (40.5cm) long*

**£120-180** **BER**

A set of 25 paper-covered wooden bricks, each decorated with a Disney character, unmarked.

*1.25in (3cm) wide*

**£10-15** **BH**

'Mickey Mouse Story Book', published by David McKay.

*1931* *8.5in (21.5cm) high*

**£60-80** **BER**

A rare 1930s Italian Saiwa 'Biscotti Topolino' biscuit tin, with licensed lithographs of Mickey Mouse, marked "By Special Permission Walt Disney".

**£1,000-1,500** **BER**

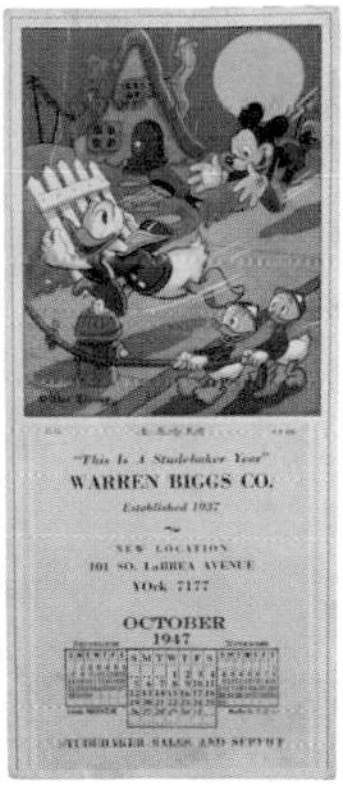


A Warren Biggs Co. calendar card for October 1947, with Donald Duck and Mickey Mouse.

*9in (23cm) high*

**£15-25** **LDE**

A 1980s Mickey Mouse printed silk tie.

**£10-20** **S&T**

A Walt Disney animation cel from 'The Aristocats', showing Duchess and her daughter Marie, stamped with studio authenticity stamp.

*1970* *14in (35.5cm) wide*

**£250-350** **POOK**

## A CLOSER LOOK AT DISNEY SHEET MUSIC

*The film was released as an eight minute short film in 1943 and starred Donald Duck, It was used as anti-Nazi war propaganda to promote the US war effort.*

*The music was written by Oliver Wallace in the 1942 and commented on Germany's re-armament, the strict Nazi regime and wartime shortages.*

*In 1942, Spike Jones released a successful version of the song, prompting Disney to change the title of the film to match the song.*

*Before the film was released it had the title of 'Donald Duck in Nutzi Land'.*

A 'Der Fuehrer's Face' un-released Walt Disney film sheet music.

*1942* *12in (30.5cm) high*

**£25-35** **NOR**

## COLLECTORS' NOTES

- Barbie made her debut at the 1959 American Toy Fair in New York City. She was designed by Ruth and Elliot Handler, founders of Mattel, who were inspired by a 'Lilli' doll bought by Ruth for her daughter. Ruth thought that as her daughter grew, she would need a more interesting three-dimensional doll to replace the paper fashion dolls popular at the time.
- Barbie received mixed reviews at first, as she was so unlike any other doll produced before. However, the public grew to love her and, from 1960, her popularity became assured. Two of her most popular attractions were the range of hair colours and styles, and the ever-increasing array of modern outfits that could be bought for her.
- Collectors tend to focus on dolls made before 1972, as these are considered true 'vintage' dolls. Learn the different faces and hairstyles used over the years, as these will help to date a Barbie. For example, if she has 'bubble cut' hair, she dates from between 1961 and 1967.
- Barbies with 'pony tail' hairstyles were produced between 1959 and 1964 and are highly sought-after, with around six different types available. Beware, as this hairstyle was reproduced by Mattel during the 1990s, so look at other features including eyes, skin tone and style of head.
- Barbie's earliest eye colour was white, then blue. Barbie is marked on her bottom, with the marks helping to date and identify her. The date shown is not the date she was made, but the patent date, meaning she was made sometime after that.
- As many Barbies were sold, condition and completeness are vitally important. Dolls that have not been played with and complete examples with boxes and accessories will be worth more. Most collectors look for examples that show very light signs of wear from play, but are complete – if the condition is better, the value usually rises. Examine ears for green stains caused by early metal earrings.

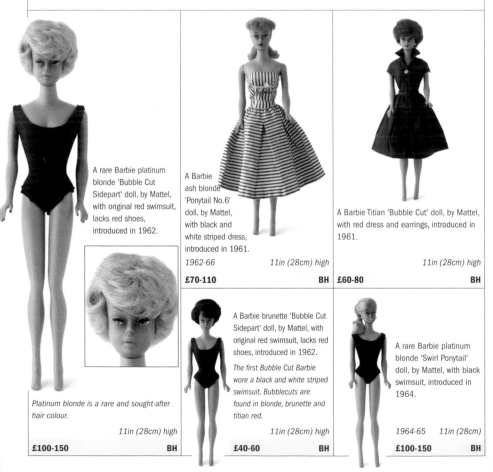

A rare Barbie platinum blonde 'Bubble Cut Sidepart' doll, by Mattel, with original red swimsuit, lacks red shoes, introduced in 1962.

*Platinum blonde is a rare and sought-after hair colour.*

*11in (28cm) high*

**£100-150** **BH**

A Barbie ash blonde 'Ponytail No.6' doll, by Mattel, with black and white striped dress, introduced in 1961.

*1962-66* *11in (28cm) high*

**£70-110** **BH**

A Barbie Titian 'Bubble Cut' doll, by Mattel, with red dress and earrings, introduced in 1961.

*11in (28cm) high*

**£60-80** **BH**

A Barbie brunette 'Bubble Cut Sidepart' doll, by Mattel, with original red swimsuit, lacks red shoes, introduced in 1962.

*The first Bubble Cut Barbie wore a black and white striped swimsuit. Bubblecuts are found in blonde, brunette and titian red.*

*11in (28cm) high*

**£40-60** **BH**

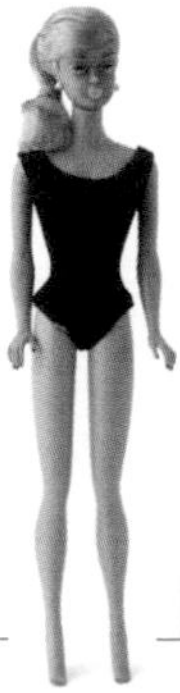

A rare Barbie platinum blonde 'Swirl Ponytail' doll, by Mattel, with black swimsuit, introduced in 1964.

*1964-65* *11in (28cm)*

**£100-150** **BH**

A Barbie titian 'Swirl Ponytail' doll, by Mattel, with red swimsuit.

*1964-65* *11in (28cm) high*

**£70-90** **BH**

A Barbie 'Miss America' doll, by Mattel, with dress, cape, shoes and crown, lacks red rose garland.

*1974* *11in (28cm) high*

**£20-30** **BH**

## A CLOSER LOOK AT A BARBIE

*Twist 'N' Turn Barbie, with her pivoting waist, was released in 1967 and went on to become the most popular version produced.*

*Her eyelashes are rooted rather than molded and painted on.*

*She came with many different hair colours with exotic names such as 'Go Go Co Co' and 'Summer Sand' - titian red and platinum blonde are perhaps the rarest.*

*She had a more youthful looking face, made using a new mold.*

A rare Barbie 'Twist 'N' Turn' red-haired doll, by Mattel, with green skirt and silver top and boots.

*1967* *11in (28cm) high*

**£100-150** **BH**

A 'Skipper' red-haired doll, by Mattel, with replaced white skirt, red top and hairband, introduced in 1964.

*Barbie's little sister originally had a brass hairband, which can be worth around £10 when found. She was originally dressed in a red swimsuit with white stripes.*

*9.25in (23.5cm) high*

**£35-45** **BH**

A Skipper blonde 'Quick Curl' doll, by Mattel, in a red minidress, with metal fibres in her curly hair.

*The metal fibres allowed her hair to stay curled after it had been styled.*

*1973-75* *9in (23cm) high*

**£10-15** **BH**

A 'Casey' red-haired doll, by Mattel, wearing a green and yellow stripy skirt and blue top with collar, introduced in 1966.

*Casey was the friend of Barbie's 'modern' cousin, Francie. She was re-released in 1974.*

*10.75in (27.5cm) high*

**£30-40** **BH**

A 'Midge' titian doll, by Mattel, in a Hawaiian outfit with green grass skirt.

*Midge was introduced in 1963. Look out for examples without freckles, which can be more desirable and valuable.*

*1963-66* *11in (28cm) high*

**£25-35** **BH**

## COLLECTORS' NOTES

- Most early dolls were homemade, being formed from fabric or carved wood. The industry's first boom was centred on Germany and France from the mid-late 19th century to the 1930s, when makers such as Armand Marseille, Kammer & Reinhardt, Jumeau and others created dolls with heads made from moulded bisque. The incised numbers and letters on the back of the head can help identify a doll, as can the facial characteristics.
- Look for well-known makers, and clean, undamaged bisque that has been well-painted. Replaced bodies devalue a doll, but original clothes add to it considerably. Dolls continued to be made in fabric, and were also made in wax and composition. Composition is a mixture of plaster, wood pulp, glue and other ingredients, that produced a resilient, inexpensive material that could be easily moulded and painted. It was used from c1900s to the 1950s when it was superseded by the more economical and versatile plastic.
- As generations of collectors change, interest also changes, and new markets emerge. Hard and soft plastic dolls have seen a rise in interest and values as the people who loved them as children decide to collect them today. Look for major names such as Madame Alexander, Terri Lee, Vogue, Ideal and Pedigree.
- The highest prices are reserved for those in truly mint condition, including their complete original clothes. Hairstyles should also be original with restyled, and in particular cut hair, reducing value considerably. Look for detailed clothing and original boxes. Character dolls can also be sought-after, be they based on real-life people or fictional characters.

An American Fulper bisque doll, with sleeping eyes and fully jointed body, one finger repaired.

*19in (48.5cm) high*

**£80-120** **BER**

A German Max Handwerck '283' bisque doll, with brown glass sleeping eyes, original body, waist length ringlet wig, with dress embellished with ribbon, and a hat.

*20in (51cm) high*

**£100-150** **BER**

A German Kammer & Reinhardt '43' bisque doll, with blue glass eyes on rocker, open mouth with teeth, worn and repainted hands, and burgundy coloured dress, minor colour loss on nose and cheeks.

*18in (45.5cm) high*

**£60-80** **BER**

A German bisque shoulder-head doll, with fixed brown eyes, painted eyebrows and lashes, open mouth with four teeth, blonde platted wig, and kid body, with fracture above right eye, hands incomplete.

*16in (41cm) high*

**£60-80** **SAS**

A bisque closed mouth shoulder head doll, incised "I/8", with brown glass eyes, gusseted leather body, bisque forearms, patched at knee, one thumb chipped, minor colour loss of cheeks and nose.

*21in (53.5cm) high*

**£100-150** **BER**

A 1920s Japanese bisque baby head doll, incised "3-11", with blue glass eyes, original bent limb body, moulded and painted hair, hands repaired and repainted.

*18in (45.5cm) high*

**£50-80** **BER**

An unclothed German porcelain doll, with painted facial features.

*15.25in (38.5cm) high*

**£70-100** **SAS**

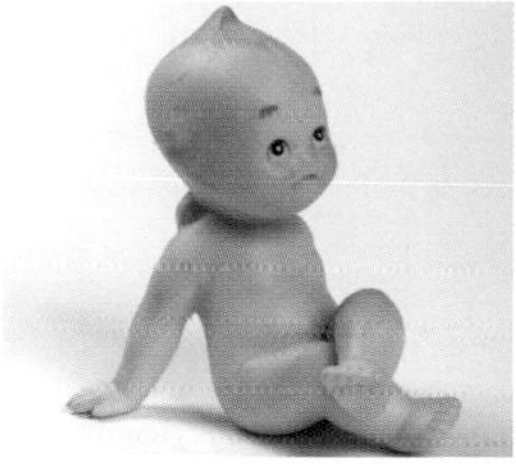

A Kewpie seated 'Action' bisque doll, with upcast eyes.

*c1910* *5in (12.5cm) high*

**£300-350** **BEJ**

## A CLOSER LOOK AT A HEUBACH DOLL

*Gebruder Heubach are known for their extremely fine quality, well-moulded doll faces, which are also well-painted.*

*The company is also renowned for its expressive character dolls. Googly eye dolls were popular during the 1910-20s.*

*A lever on the back of the head moves the eyes – this is a desirable feature.*

*It was made for import company Eisenmann & Co. (Einco), which was one of the companies that became the important British toy maker Chiltern Toys.*

A rare German Gebruder Heubach for Einco 'Googly' eye doll, with lever to move eyes, on a composition body, dressed as a Scotsman.

*The unusual and well-made Scottish costume also makes this doll desirable, and counts towards its value.*

*c1915* *12in (30.5cm) high*

**£2,800-3,000** **BEJ**

A German glazed white porcelain shoulder head 'Berta' type doll, with painted blue eyes, red cheeks and blonde moulded hair, impressed 'Germany'.

*6in (15cm) high*

**£120-180** **WDL**

An Italian Lenci pressed felt 'Lucia' girl doll, with ivory floral print dress, yellow felt hat, and rectangular paper tag.

*14in (35.5cm) high*

**£220-280** **BER**

An Italian Lenci pressed felt 300 series boy doll, with painted features, side glancing eyes, original clothing and replaced shoes.

*Lenci was founded in 1918 in Turin, Italy, and were the first company to produce dolls from painted, pressed felt. By the 1920s, the company was renowned for its designs, The popular 300 series dolls have felt torsos, and their pouty and character dolls are especially sought-after.*

*c1930* *17in (43cm) high*

**£800-1,200** **BER**

A Raynal cloth doll, with painted, pressed felt face, brown mohair wig, jointed cloth body, celluloid hands, and original costume.

*These was made to imitate the popular Lenci dolls of the 1920s and '30s.*

*20.5in (52cm) high*

**£100-150** **SAS**

## A CLOSER LOOK AT A LENCI DOLL

*During the late 1920s and '30s there was an increased interest in travel and foreign countries - Lenci reflected this with their range of 300 series dolls in national costume.*

*Each country was represented by a boy and a girl doll, Spain's Matador is paired with a similarly dressed Senorita.*

*Although customers tended to buy pairs as this is how they were displayed, the Matador is harder to find than the Senorita.*

*He still retains his original clothing, which is rare and his face is in bright, clean condition, with good detailing.*

An Italian Lenci pressed felt 'Matador' 300 series boy doll, with original clothing, side glancing eyes, pierced ears with brass earrings, black mohair wig and high leather boots.

*c1930* *17in (43cm) high*

**£1,800-2,200** **BER**

A 1920s Merrythought 'Negro Girl' felt pyjama case doll, with early label to back, some fading to dress.

*19.5in (49.5cm) high*

**£22-28** **GAZE**

An S.F.B.J. composition doll, with fixed brown eyes, painted eye brows and lashes, open mouth, jointed wood body wearing a cream dress, with green hat and blazer, one tooth missing.

*19.5in (49.5cm) high*

**£100-150** **SAS**

A German wax-over composition doll, with blue pierced ears, blonde mohair wig, cloth body, composition limbs, moulded and painted boots, original blue frock and net over-dress, with a glass dome (not shown).

*17.5in (57cm) high*

**£150-200** **SAS**

An American Horsman 'He-Bee' composition swivel-neck doll, with painted features, light green romper suit with pink booties, some peeling paint to arms.

*This doll is in the style of the illustrations of children produced by American illustrator Charles Twelvetrees for the Pictorial Review. The bases of the feet are usually marked. Beware of modern reproductions produced by Horsman in the 1990s, which are made from bisque and do not show signs of age.*

*c1926* *10.5in (26.5cm) high*

**£200-300** **BER**

A Canadian Noma Toys Ltd composition Kewpie doll, licensed by Rose O'Neill, with original transfer to chest and rare original box.

*11in (28cm) high*

**£200-300** **BER**

A Madame Alexander 'Alexander-kins' hard plastic straight-leg walker doll, with brunette hair and original pink dress, hat, shoes and socks.

*1956-64* *8in (20cm) high*

**£70-90** **BH**

A Vogue Ginny hard plastic bent knee-walker doll, with platinum blond hair, green dress and hat, shoes and socks.

*7.5in (19cm) high*

**£80-120** **BH**

A Madame Alexander 'Alexander-kins' hard plastic bent-knee walker doll, with 'Tosca' hair, original blue dress with tag, shoes and socks.

*1956-64* *8in (20cm) high*

**£40-60** **BH**

A 1960s Madame Alexander vinyl 'Wendy Baby' doll, with romper suit and hat.

*7.5in (19cm) high*

**£60-80** **BH**

A 1950s Ideal 'Saucy Walker' hard plastic doll, with original clothes and short hair, the back of the head moulded "Ideal Doll".

*Although the hair was meant to be short, a previous owner has cut off her plaits. This is a recognisable and important characteristic of Saucy Walker dolls.*

*22in (56cm) high*

**£40-60** **MEM**

A Madame Alexander 'Alexander-kins' hard plastic bent-knee walker doll, with blond hair, original blue dress with red trim and tag, hat, shoes and socks.

*1956-64* *8in (20cm) high*

**£40-60** **BH**

A Vogue 'Ginny' hard plastic bent knee-walker doll, with 'Funtime Beach' outfit.

*1957-62* *8in (20cm) high*

**£40-60** **BH**

A 1960s clockwork Japanese girl doll, made of vinyl, metal and composition.

*8.5in (21.5cm) high*

**£15-20** **DSC**

## COLLECTORS' NOTES

- In the 19th century, doorstops were used to keep doors open to aid ventilation. Most were produced between the late 19th century and the 1940s.
- Although mass-produced in cast iron, doorstops were usually painted by hand, lending them a uniqueness and folk art appeal. Consequently, they appeal to folk art collectors as well as those collecting by foundry or subject matter. Animals, people, plants and flowers are all popular subjects. The shape and theme are the most important indicators of value, with flowers being the most common form.
- In the late 1930s and 40s, companies reduced the amount of iron used in manufacturing doorstops in response to the war effort, with the result that pieces from this period weigh less than earlier examples. Production dwindled with the introduction of air conditioning in the 1950s.
- Key makers include Hubley, (est. 1894), Bradley & Hubbard (founded 1854), The Albany Foundry Co. (1897-1932) and Littco Products (est. 1916).
- Modern reproductions are common. These usually have rough, sandy-feeling surfaces and, if cast in two pieces, the joins will not fit snugly. If the paint is bright, it may be repainted or a reproduction. Examine the moulding as the detail will not be as fine as that found on older, original versions.
- Condition is important. Badly damaged paint, rust and repainting reduces the value considerably.

A Hubley 'Apple Blossoms' cast iron doorstop, painted in colours, and marked "329 Hubley" to reverse.

*7.5in (19cm) high*

**£140-160** **BER**

A Hubley 'Lilies of the Valley' cast iron doorstop, painted in colours, marked "189".

*10.5in (26.5cm) high*

**£180-220** **BER**

A Hubley 'Marigolds' cast iron doorstop, painted in colours and marked "#315 Made in USA".

*By examining the flowers, one can see that this is an ornate and very well cast example. It is also in near mint condition.*

*8in (20cm) high*

**£180-220** **BER**

A Judd Co. cast iron doorstop, no. 1252, painted in colours.

*9.5in (24cm) high*

**£80-120** **BER**

A Judd Co. 'Poinsettia' cast iron doorstop, no.1232, painted in colours.

*This is a desirable doorstop.*

*10in (25.5cm) high*

**£200-300** **BER**

A Hubley 'Jonquils' cast iron doorstop, painted in colours.

*8in (20cm) high*

**£180-220** **BER**

A Hublcy 'Scottie Dog' cast iron doorstop, painted black.

*8.25in (21cm) high*

**£180-220** **BER**

A Hubley 'Cocker Spaniel' cast iron doorstop, painted in black and white.

*11in (28cm) long*

**£200-300** **BER**

A Spencer of Connecticut 'Art Deco Terrier' cast iron doorstop, painted in black and white, with wedge back.

*6in (15cm) high*

**£150-200** **BER**

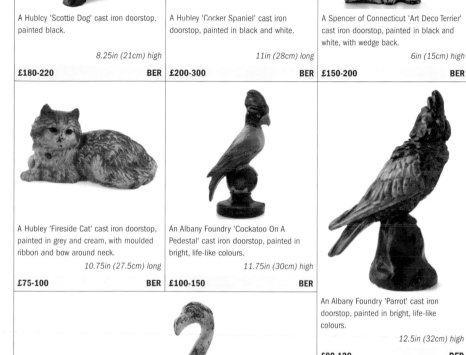

A Hubley 'Fireside Cat' cast iron doorstop, painted in grey and cream, with moulded ribbon and bow around neck.

*10.75in (27.5cm) long*

**£75-100** **BER**

An Albany Foundry 'Cockatoo On A Pedestal' cast iron doorstop, painted in bright, life-like colours.

*11.75in (30cm) high*

**£100-150** **BER**

An Albany Foundry 'Parrot' cast iron doorstop, painted in bright, life-like colours.

*12.5in (32cm) high*

**£80-120** **BER**

A Hubley 'Flamingo' cast iron doorstop, old repaint in in green, brown and pink.

*Flamingos, like Scottie dogs, have quite a collectors' following, particularly around Miami and Florida. 'Exotic' animals tend to be more valuable – cats and dogs are more common.*

*10.25in (26cm) high*

**£250-300** **BER**

A cast iron doorstop of an elephant, with his truck raised, finished in cream.

*Hubley produced an elephant in a very similar pose.*

*8in (20cm) high*

**£40-60** **BB**

A cast iron doorstop as a monkey, cast in three parts and finished in brown with textured 'fur'.

*8.75in (22cm) high*

**£150-200** **BER**

A 'Rabbit Eating Carrot' cast iron doorstop, painted in colours.

*This chubby chappy was designed by Harrison Cody.*

*8.5in (21.5cm) high*

**£180-220** **BER**

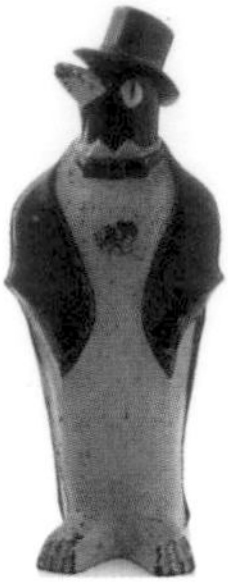

A Hubley 'Penguin In Top Hat' cast iron hollow cast doorstop, painted in black, white and yellow.

*10.5in (26.5cm) high*

**£180-220** **BER**

A National Foundry 'Southern Belle' cast iron doorstop, painted in colours.

*Orange and black is a very unusual colour combination.*

*11.75in (30cm) high*

**£80-120** **BER**

A Littco Products 'Woman Skier' cast iron doorstop, painted in typical colours.

*This is both a rare and a desirable doorstop.*

*12.5in (32cm) high*

**£750-1,000** **BER**

A National Foundry 'Dancing Girl' cast iron doorstop, with a light blue dress, with an old repaint.

*This is the rarer of two similar dancing girl doorstops – the more common example has her hands held together above her head.*

*8.5in (21.5cm) high*

**£75-100** **BER**

An 'Oriental Girl' cast iron doorstop, painted in colours in the Art Deco style.

*8in (20cm) high*

**£140-160** **BER**

A Hubley 'Small Mammy' cast iron doorstop, painted in typical red and white.

*8.5in (21.5cm) high*

**£200-250** **BER**

## A CLOSER LOOK AT A LITTCO DOORSTOP

*This piece is in excellent overall condition, with its original paint, and even retains its extremely rare original label.*

*This is one of only four known examples of this extremely rare doorstop.*

*Of the four, this is the one in the best condition.*

*With the girl dressed up as a 'ghost' holding a pumpkin, this falls into the popular Halloween memorabilia field too, appealing to collectors of that area as well.*

A 1930s Littco Products cast iron doorstop, in the form of a girl in a white cloak holding a pumpkin, with original label to reverse.

*Littco Products was a brand name of the Littlestown Hardware & Foundry Co Inc, of Littlestown, Pennsylvania. Founded in 1916, it made doorstops from around 1930, ceasing production of civilian castings after the war. Most of its production was sold in gift or flower shops on the East Coast of the US, and it is particularly known for its Aunt Jemima, Mary Quite Contrary and Huckleberry Finn doorstops.*

*14in (35.5cm) high*

**£35,000-40,000** **BER**

A Judd Co. 'Major Domo' cast iron doorstop, with strong painted colours and showing the Major at attention.

*5in (12.5cm) high*

**£80-120** **BER**

A 'Drum Major' cast iron doorstop, heavily cast in marching pose and painted in colours.

*13.5in (34.25cm) high*

**£180-220** **BER**

A 'Sailor' cast iron doorstop, with old but sympathetic re-paint.

*11.75in (30cm) high*

**£400-500** **BER**

A Bradley & Hubbard 'Gnome Warrior' cast iron doorstop, no.7785.

*It's likely that this hard-to-find doorstop's similarity to Gimli in 'Lord of the Rings' adds to its popularity and value!*

*13.5in (34.5cm) high*

**£1,000-1,500** **BER**

An English 'Judy' cast iron doorstop, holding a miniature baby 'Punch', with a wooden base and painted in colours.

*This is also found in an unpainted version.*

*12in (30.5cm) high*

**£280-320** **BER**

An English 'Mr Punch' cast iron doorstop, dressed as Julius Caesar with a dog by his side, with a wooden base and painted in colours.

*12in (30.5cm) high*

**£280-320** **BER**

A rare 'Dancing Girls' cast iron doorstop, with wedge back.

*10.5in (26.5cm) high*

**£350-400** **BER**

A Hubley 'Cape Cod' cast iron doorstop, showing an ocean-side home.

*7.25in (18.5cm) high*

**£150-200** **BER**

## COLLECTORS' NOTES

- Erotic collectables are highly sought after, particularly early examples from the 18th and 19th centuries. Pieces from the 20th century are more plentiful, accessible and affordable. Much of the value depends on the subject matter. Popular girls will usually have a large following, meaning prices can be high. Look out for well-known and influential photographers, as this can affect value too.
- The 1950s and '60s are particularly 'hot' areas, with the glamour girl being a popular motif. Key magazines, such as Playboy, and shoots early on in a model's career are often highly desirable. Although a great many later editions of Playboy sold out, the first edition is extremely valuable. Also look for appealing artwork from a design perspective, and consider the design the ethics of the period it was produced in. Condition is important, with many of the 1950s and '60s pieces in particular not being made to last.

"Silk Stocking Stories", May 1937.

*11in (28cm) high*

**£25-35** **NOR**

"Celebrity", December 1955, with Norma Dean cover, and including stories on Marilyn Monroe and James Dean.

*5.75in (14.5cm) high*

**£8-12** **NOR**

"Tops", February 1955, the cover with Barbara Darrow, including stories on Dirk Bogart and Vivienne Leigh.

*5.75in (14.5cm) high*

**£8-12** **NOR**

"TV Girls & Gags", March 1957, the cover with a Bunny Yaeger shot of Marley Sanderson on cover.

*Yaeger was a glamour model who moved behind the camera, winning 'Photographer of the Year' in 1959.*

*5.75in (14.5cm) high*

**£10-15** **NOR**

"Caper", May 1959, with cover shot of June Wilkinson by Russ Meyer, in near-fine condition.

*Wilkinson was a natural brunette but had dyed her hair blond by 1960. Her first appearance in Playboy was in September 1958, and she was so popular that she appeared again in August 1959 and once again in 1960, with Heffner nicknaming her 'The Bosom'.*

*11in (28cm) high*

**£15-25** **NOR**

"Glance", June 1959, with June Wilkinson centrefold, also including a Rita Moreno story.

*11in (28cm) high*

**£10-15** **NOR**

A Folies Bergere brochure, with red felt cover and gilt embossed glamour girl artwork.

*Here the cover artwork, that harks back to the Art Deco period, lifts the value of this magazine.*

*c1965 12.5in (31.5cm) high*

**£10-15** **NOR**

Timothy Greenfield-Sanders and Gore Vidal, "XXX 30 Porn Star Portraits", published by Bullfinch Press.

*This book shows portraits of each star clothed and unclothed, drawing attention to their faces. Celebrity contributors included John Malkovich, Gore Vidal and Salman Rushdie. The cover shows Jenna Jameson, and other stars include Lukas Ridgeston and Belladonna.*

*2004* *12.25in (31cm) high*

**£12-18** **NOR**

Hajime Sorayama, "Hyper Illustrations", published by Bijutsu Shuppan-Sha, Japan.

*Here Japanese illustrator Sorayama (b.1947) presents typically 1980s airbrushed images of androids as erotic fantasies.*

*1989*

**£18-22** **NOR**

Hajime Sorayama, 'Hyper Illustrations Part 2', published by Bijutsu Shuppan-Sha.

*1989* *12in (30.5cm) high*

**£18-22** **NOR**

A salesman's sample calendar, featuring Jayne Mansfield.

*1968* *16in (40.5cm) high*

**£7-10** **BH**

A 1960s glamour girl tin, with a girl posing with a cocktail in a gold mini-dress.

*8.5in (21.5cm) high*

**£20-30** **MTS**

A 1959 Playboy Playmate' calendar, including Jayne Mansfield as 'Miss July', retaining original sleeve.

*The original sleeve is rare, and Jayne Mansfield is a desirable subject.*

*1959* *12.5in (32cm) high*

**£80-120** **CVS**

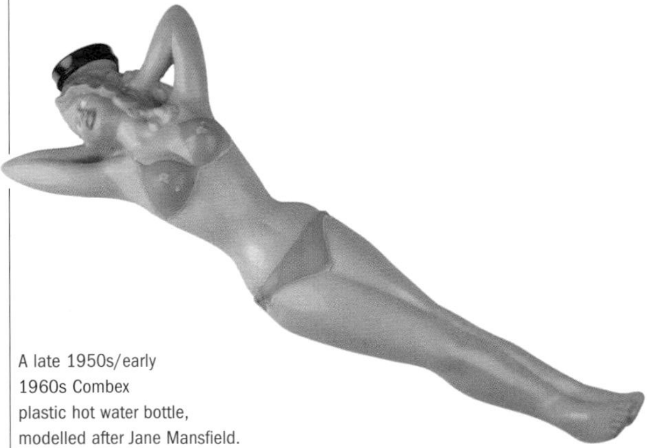

A late 1950s/early 1960s Combex plastic hot water bottle, modelled after Jane Mansfield.

*20in (51cm) high*

**£80-120** **MA**

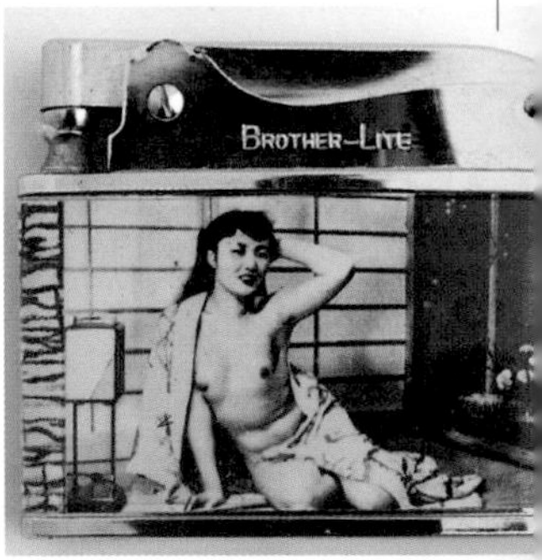


A 1950s Japanese Brother-Lite pin-up girl lighter, with photographic image of a an oriental glamour girl.

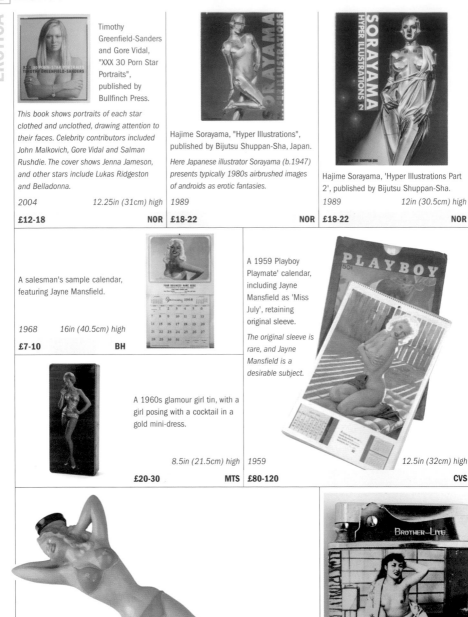

**£10-15** **CVS**

## COLLECTORS' NOTES

- Today it is easier than ever to own a piece of memorabilia or merchandise connected to your favourite film or movie star. While items personally owned by an actor or props used and seen on screen occupy the top bracket, more mass-produced items, such as magazines, production crew kit, and promotional material, can be much more affordable.
- Always buy from a reputable source, as provenance is very important. Today, studios release props and other memorabilia after production and this should always come with a certificate of authenticity. Wile this means you may not get a 'bargain', you can be assured it is the genuine article.
- Stars like Marilyn Monroe and James Dean are perennial favourites. As they were popular during their own lifetime there is a vast amount of memorabilia on the market to suit all budgets.

'Dangerous Years' & 'Invisible Wall', US double bill half-sheet poster.

*This was one of Marilyn Monroe's first movies.*

*1947* *28in (71cm) high*

**£80-120** **ATK**

"Picture Post", April 24th, 1954, with Marilyn Monroe cover.

*13in (33cm) high*

**£80-120** **VM**

"Movie Stars", March 1954, with Marilyn Monroe cover.

**£32-38** **NOR**

"Le Film Complet", no.613, 18th April, 1957, French magazine with nine pages on Marilyn Monroe in "Bus Stop".

*1957*

**£15-20** **GAZE**

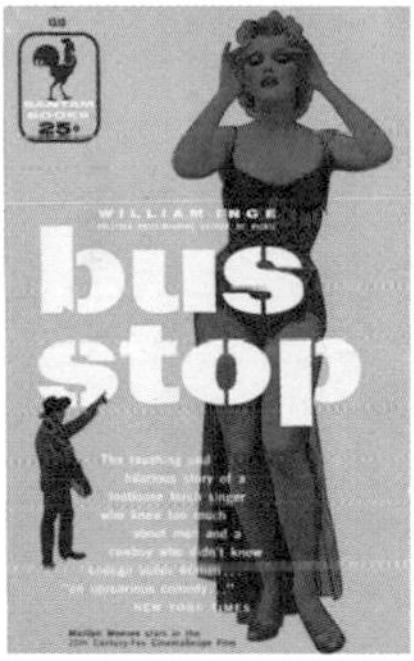


"Bus Stop", William Inge, first paperback edition published by Bantam Books, New York, novelization of the original play by the author with star Marilyn Monroe on the cover.

*1956*

**£10-15** **MBO**

"Life", May 25th, 1959, International edition with Marilyn Monroe in "Some Like It Hot" cover and feature.

*14in (35.5cm) high*

**£80-120** **VM**

A Tate Gallery 'Warhol' exhibition poster, featuring Warhol's 1964 portrait of Marilyn Monroe.

*1971* *30in (58cm) high*

**£50-70** **PC**

"Photoplay", March 1957, with Jayne Mansfield cover.

*With her platinum blonde hair and hourglass figure, actress and centrefold model Jayne Mansfield was a contemporary and rival of Marilyn Monroe, although she failed to land the high profile roles of Monroe. She also died young in a tragic road accident at the age of 34.*

*10.75in (27.5cm) high*

**£25-35** **NOR**

A Palitoy 'Talking Dalek' silver and blue battery-operated toy, in excellent condition, in fair condition original box.

*1975*

**£70-100** **SAS**

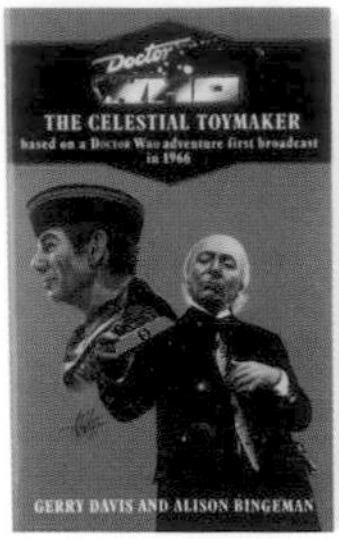


Gerry Davis & Alison Bingeman, "Doctor Who: The Celestial Toymaker", published by Target.

*1986*

**£3-5** **ZDB**

Andy Lane & Jim Mortimer, "The New Doctor Who Adventures: Lucifer Rising", published by Dr Who Books an imprint of Virgin Publishing Ltd.

*1993*

**£3-5** **ZDB**

A "Doctor Who – The Eighties" annual, published by Virgin Publishing.

*As the collecting market matures, interest in the later incarnations of the Doctor has risen.*

*1996* *12in (30.5cm) high*

**£20-30** **TP**

An E.T. The Extra Terrestrial 'E.T. & Elliot Powered Bicycle' toy, by Ljn, mounted on card.

*c1982* *9.25in (23.5cm) high*

**£10-15** **NOR**

A Buck Rogers night light, by G.E.C., with image of Buck and Twiki, mounted on card.

*5.5in (14cm) high*

**£7-10** **NOR**

A pair of "Fifth Element" promotional gold-plated cufflinks and matching tie pin, boxed.

*c1997*

**£40-50** **NOR**

A "Fifth Element" promotional Swatch watch, GK260, mint and boxed.

*This appeals to both film memorabilia collectors and Swatch collectors. Fifth Element memorabilia is quite scarce and the film has a cult following.*

*c1997*

**£100-150** **NOR**

A Walt Disney Studios original production cel from "Mother Goose goes to Hollywood", depicting 'Three Men in a Tub.

*11in (28cm) wide*

**£450-550** **AAC**

A Walt Disney Studios original production cel, possibly from "Winnie the Pooh and Tigger Too!", featuring Tigger and Rabbit, framed.

*Although Tigger is a popular character, the value would have been higher is Winnie the Pooh was included.*

*c1974* *20in (51cm) wide*

**£70-100** **PC**

A Walt Disney Studios original production cel from "The Mickey Mouse Club" show, featuring Mickey Mouse in the opening sequence, framed.

*This appeals to collectors of Disney memorabilia as well as collectors of animation art.*

*19in (48.5cm) high*

**£800-1,200** **PC**

A Turner Entertainment Company original production cel no. CJ75-332-013 from "How the Grinch Stole Christmas", featuring the Grinch holding onto Max's foot, signed by artist Chuck Jones, together with a certificate of authenticity, framed.

*1966* *21in (53.5cm) wide*

**£800-1,200** **PC**

A limited edition Warner Brothers animation art cel from "Pepé in Tulips", from an edition of 500, featuring Pepé le Pew, signed by artist Chuck Jones and with a certificate of authenticity, framed.

*The popularity of animation cels has lead studios to release limited edition copies from popular films and shorts. Look for examples with a small edition run, ideally under 1,000.*

*1989* *21in (53.5cm) wide*

**£250-350** **PC**

A Warner Brothers animation art cel no. CJS26-084-022 from "From Here to Eternity", featuring Bugs Bunny and Yosemite Sam, signed by artist Chuck Jones, and with a certificate of authenticity.

*1996* *20in (51cm) wide*

**£200-300** **PC**

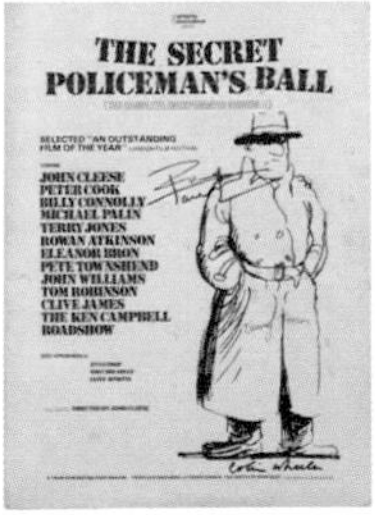


A 'The Secret Policeman's Ball' programme, bearing signatures of Michael Palin, Terry Jones, Rowan Atkinson and Pete Townshend.

*1979*

**£25-35** **GAZE**

A black MA2 flying crew jacket from 'Event Horizon', with fur collar and "Event Horizon Crew '97" embroidered on the left breast in silver with the Event Horizon logo on the back.

*1997* Size XL

**£150-200** **PC**

David O. Selznick's leather-bound script and a mounted Venice Film Festival trophy for "Viva Villa!", the base with plaque reading "To David O. Selznick, Producer of the Film "Viva Villa!", for the Best Picture of the Year International Motion Picture Exhibit, Rome 1936.

*Actor Wallace Beery won the best actor gold medal at the 1934 Venice Film Festival and director Jack Conway also won a Special Recommendation at same year.*

*c1934-36*

**£450-550** **ROS**

## COLLECTORS' NOTES

- Spurred on by the renewed interest in classic 1930s and '40s horror movies, publisher James Warren, and horror fan and collector Forrest J Ackerman initially conceived 'Famous Monsters of Filmland' as being a one-shot publication in October 1958.
- The magazine was such a hit with horror fans that it managed a 191 issue run, plus 10 yearbooks until the publication closed in 1983. It counts Stephen King, Gene Simmons and Steven Spielberg among its readers. Warren also produced a number of other similarly themed magazines featuring illustrated horror stories, thereby circumventing the Comics Code Authority ruling, which it did not apply to magazines. This success also lead to number of rival publications, such as "Vault of Horror", "Monsters and Things" and "World Famous Creatures".
- With the popularity of movies like "Star Wars" and "Closer Encounters of the Third Kind", covers and content became more influenced by science fiction movies and readership levels dropped. The title eventually closed in 1983 but was resurrected by Ray Ferry in 1993, initially with Ackerman participating, however Ackerman left after 10 issues and sued Ferry in 1997. Ferry continues to publish the magazine today.
- Given the nature of the material, look for complete examples in good, undamaged condition, while examples in very fine to mint condition will fetch a premium. Issues with classic cover art featuring popular horror characters like Dracula and Frankenstein's Monster and by artists such as Basil Gogos and Albert Nuetzell are desirable. Certified Guaranty Company grading can increase the value.

"Famous Monsters of Filmland", no.1, published by Central Publications Inc., with Frankenstein cover, marked 'Collector's Edition', in fine condition.

*The magazine was initially only going to be a one-shot publication, explaining the 'Collector's Edition' tag on the cover.*

*1958* *10.5in (26.5cm) high*

**£1,000-1,500** **NOR**

"Famous Monsters of Filmland", no.2, 1959, published by Central Publications Inc., in near fine condition.

*1959* *10.5in (26.5cm) high*

**£80-120** **NOR**

"Famous Monsters of Filmland", no.3, April 1959, published by Central Pub. Inc., with Jim Warren cover, in near fine condition.

*1959* *10.5in (26.5cm) high*

**£250-300** **NOR**

"Famous Monsters of Filmland", no.4, August 1959, published by Central Publications Inc, with Albert Nuetzell cover artwork and rare 'Ghoul's Eye' amusement park ride sticker, in fine condition.

*1959* *10.5in (26.5cm) high*

**£400-500** **NOR**

"Famous Monsters of Filmland", no.5, November 1959, published by Central Publications Inc, with Albert Nuetzell cover artwork of Béla Lugosi, in fine condition.

*1959* *10.5in (26.5cm) high*

**£70-100** **NOR**

"Famous Monsters of Filmland" no.6, February 1960, published by Central Publications Inc, with Albert Nuetzell cover artwork of King Kong, in fine condition.

*1960*

**£100-150** **NOR**

"Famous Monsters of Filmland", no. 7, June 1960, published by Central Publications Inc, with Albert Nuetzell cover artwork of John Zacherley, in fine condition.

*1960* *10.5in (26.5cm) high*

**£250-300** **NOR**

"Famous Monsters of Filmland", no.8, September 1960, published by Central Publications Inc, with Albert Nuetzell cover artwork, in near mint condition.

*1960* *10.5in (26.5cm) high*

**£80-120** **NOR**

"Famous Monsters of Filmland", no.9, November 1960, published by Central Publications Inc, with Basil Gogos cover artwork of Vincent Price in "The House of Usher", in very good-plus condition.

*This was the first cover done by Gogos for Famous Monsters. He went on to create 50 other covers, many of which have become iconic images of the period.*

*1960* *10.5in (26.5cm) high*

**£60-90** **NOR**

"Famous Monsters of Filmland", no.10, January 1961, published by Central Publications Inc, with Basil Gogos cover artwork of Claud Rains as the Phantom of the Opera, in very good condition.

*1961* *10.5in (26.5cm) high*

**£35-45** **NOR**

"Famous Monsters of Filmland", no.11, April 1961, published by Central Publications Inc, with Basil Gogos cover artwork of 'Gorgo', a British variation on Godzilla, in fine condition.

*1961* *10.5in (26.5cm) high*

**£70-100** **NOR**

"Famous Monsters of Filmland", no.12, June 1961, published by Central Publications Inc, with Basil Gogos cover artwork of the Werewolf from "Curse of the Werewolf", in very good-plus condition.

*1961* *10.5in (26.5cm) high*

**£20-30** **NOR**

"Famous Monsters of Filmland", no.13, August 1961, published by Central Publications Inc, with cover artwork by Basil Gogos, in very good-plus condition.

*1961* *10.5in (26.5cm) high*

**£60-90** **NOR**

"Famous Monsters of Filmland", no.14, October 1961, published by Central Publications Inc, with Basil Gogos cover artwork of Vincent Price in "The Pit & the Pendulum".

*1961* *10.5in (26.5cm) high*

**£20-30** **NOR**

"Famous Monsters of Filmland", no.15, January 1961, published by Central Publications Inc, with Basil Gogos cover artwork of John Zacherley, in fine condition.

*1961* *10.5in (26.5cm) high*

**£70-100** **NOR**

### FIND OUT MORE...

**Gathering Darkness**, *www.gdarkness.com/monstermags/*

**Famous Monsters Chronicles**, *edited by Dennis Daniel, published by Fantaco, 1991.*

## COLLECTORS' NOTES

- Although machine-made pressed glass had been produced since the early 19th century, inspired by more expensive cut glass, the examples in this section were largely inspired by the work of Rene Lalique. As this glass was only fashionable during the 1920s and '30s, it can be hard to find today, particularly the rarer examples.
- Jobling and Bagley in Britain and Walther & Sohn in Germany were notable manufacturers, although many Czechoslovakian factories also produced similar pressed glass, often in strongly Art Deco styles. Numerous different shapes were made, with most being both decorative and functional. Centrepieces are a mainstay and were highly popular at the time, particularly as wedding gifts among the middle classes. Vases were the next most popular object.
- Colours affect value, with opalescent glass being the most desirable. The stronger the opalescence, the more valuable it will be. British companies generally used green, pink, blue, amber and clear 'flint', while Czechoslovakian companies had a wider range of colours and tones, including turquoise. German examples, such as those by Walther, are usually stronger in tone.
- Scratches, scuffs, chips and cracks will reduce value considerably. All values given here reflect undamaged examples in mint condition. Surprisingly, mould lines, internal bubbles and even internal ash (workers were allowed to smoke while working) do not affect value. However, a collector will always prefer a perfect piece.
- Modern reproductions exist and are of little interest to collectors. These are generally lighter in weight than originals and sometimes in different tones of colour, or slightly smaller sizes. Frosted areas can also be rougher, as they are sandblasted rather than gently etched with acidic fumes.

A 1930s German Walther pink pressed glass four-piece centre piece, with figure of a woman feeding geese.

*This is the rarest of the smaller centrepieces that feature ladies in bowls.*

*8.25in (21cm) high*

**£120-180** **AAB**

A 1930s German Walther 'Seagulls' amber pressed glass four-piece centrepiece, with black glass base.

*10.75in (27cm) high*

**£70-100** **AAB**

A 1930s Sowerby 'Squirrel Bowl' amber pressed glass three-piece centrepiece, with "Registered Number Applied For" acid stamp.

*8.25in (20.5cm) high*

**£70-100** **AAB**

A 1930s Czechoslovakian green pressed glass 'September Morn' four-piece centrepiece.

*Like the bowl shown in last year's edition of this book, this figurine was inspired by Paul Chabas' 1912 'September Morn' painting, which became famous after US critic Anthony Comstock demanded the 'dirty picture' be withdrawn from exhibition. This particular piece is found in a number of green tones. The nose is often damaged as the figurine is prone to falling over. The bowl is similar to many pieces by Guggenheim, but is a different shape upon closer inspection.*

*Bowl 10.25in (26cm) diam*

**£70-100** **AAB**

A 1930s Bagley & Co. green pressed glass three-piece 'Andromeda' centrepiece, the base moulded "Made in England".

*The bowl is an Equinox vase pattern but the rim has been turned out and down with wooden tools. The shape is meant to represent crashing waves.*

*12in (30.5cm) diam*

**£120-180** **AAB**

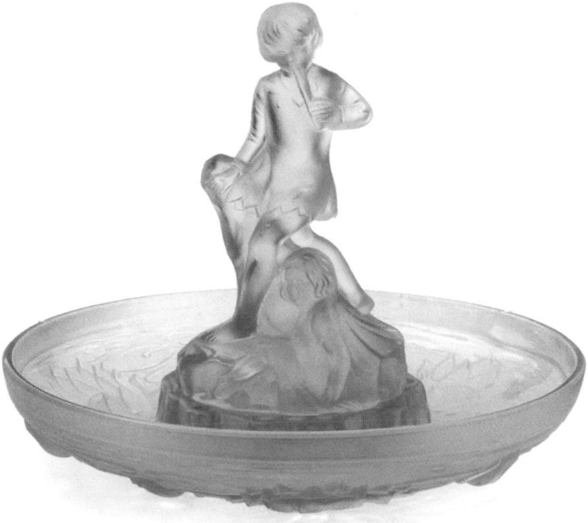

A 1930s German Walther green pressed glass Peter Pan 'Flotenspieler' three-piece centrepiece, with 'float bowl'.

*This design was available with either a striped or a plain coat. The striped coat is rarer, but there is no real difference to the value. 'Flotenspieler' is German for 'flute player'.*

*9.75in (25cm) high*

**£200-250** **AAB**

A 1930s Czechoslovakian pink pressed glass three-piece centrepiece and lamp.

*A lamp can be fitted beneath the figure, lighting the whole piece, and flowers can be inserted into the holes.*

*Bowl 11.75in (30cm) diam*

**£150-200** **AAB**

A late 1930s German Walther blue pressed glass two-piece Muschel dish, possibly designed as a soap dish.

*This can be seen in Walther's 1936 catalogue, but it may have been in production before then.*

*9.5in (24cm) high*

**£150-250** **AAB**

A 1930s Czechoslovakian green pressed glass kneeling lady and bowl on a stand, unmarked.

*The curving base of this bowl is often found damaged. They were reputedly used to promote perfume in shops, the bowl being filled with a particular scent.*

*9.25in (23.5cm) high*

**£200-300** **AAB**

A 1930s Jobling 'Three Graces' pink pressed glass comport, cat. no.2593, with registered design number 799881 for 2nd February 1935.

*7.5in (19cm) high*

**£150-200** **AAB**

A 1930s Bagley colourless, clear pressed glass 'Wyndham' Art Deco vase, from the 'Wyndham' series.

*9.5in (24cm) high*

**£35-45** **AAB**

A 1930s Czechoslovakian pressed glass vase, with two acid-frosted ladies holding up a octagonal faceted trumpet vase.

**£100-150** **AAB**

A 1930s Schlevogt 'malachite' pressed glass vase, Hoffman design, shape no.1006, marked "JH No.27" in gilt.

*8.75in (22cm) high*

**£300-400** **AAB**

## COLLECTORS' NOTES

- Carnival glass is the term given to pressed glass that has been sprayed with chemicals to give an iridescent surface effect. It gained this name during the 1960s possibly because it had been given away at fairs. It is also known as 'Poor Man's Tiffany', as it was inexpensive and allowed people to aspire to the Tiffany look without paying high prices.
- It was primarily made from the 1900s to the 1930s and US factories were the most important producers. By the 1920s, other factories in Sweden, Germany, England and Australia took over, and the US dominance began to wane. Notable names in the US include Northwood (1888-1925) who became Dugan Diamond after 1913, Imperial Glass Co. (est. 1902) and Fenton Art Glass (est. 1904).
- A number of factors are used to identify and value carnival glass, including the pattern, colour, size, shape and level of iridescence. To identify the colour properly, hold a piece up so that light shines through it. The most common colour is the orange 'marigold', with red and sky blue being very rare. Examples with a creamy white opalescence are rarer.
- Examine patterns carefully, as they have a major impact on value and can help to identify a maker. Patterns that were popular in their day are likely to fetch a lower value today as more were made so more will have survived. The shape also counts: ruffled bowls are commonly found, but flatter plates are rare. Sometimes a combination of pattern and form makes a piece very rare.
- The level of iridescence is important: those with strong, deep iridescence with a wide range of shimmering colours are the most desirable. Examine the edges for damage, which will look 'polished' and will not have an iridescent surface. Shining light through a piece will also show repairs and damage.

A Northwood 'Good Luck' pattern amethyst Carnival glass ruffled piecrust bowl.

*This can be found in many colours with a basketweave or chequerboard design on the exterior.*

*8.5in (21.5cm) diam*

**£150-200** **BA**

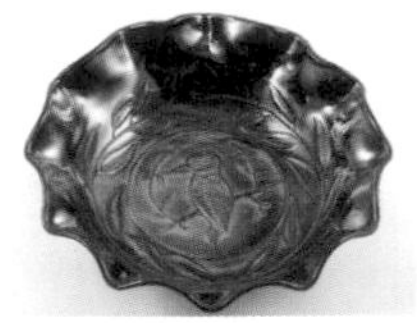

An Australian Crystal Glass Co. 'Kingfisher' pattern amethyst Carnival glass ruffled bowl.

*This pattern was first made in 1923.*

*9.5in (24cm) wide*

**£100-150** **BA**

A 'Windmill' pattern amethyst Carnival glass ruffled footed bowl.

*8in (20cm) diam*

**£60-80** **BA**

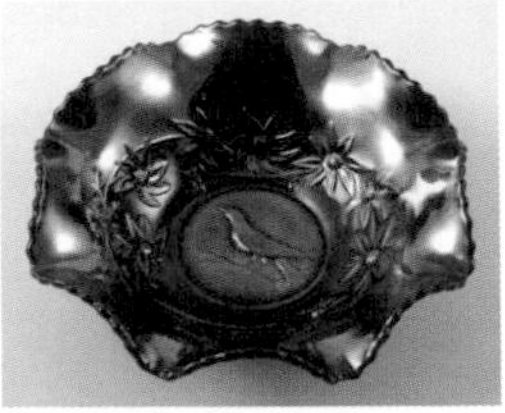

An Australian Crystal Glass Co. 'Magpie' pattern amethyst Carnival ruffled glass bowl.

*The bird is probably a New Zealand Parson bird, not a magpie.*

*5.5in (14cm) diam*

**£50-70** **BA**

A Fenton 'Peacock and Grape' pattern amethyst Carnival glass ruffled bowl.

*8.75in (22cm) diam*

**£40-60** **BA**

A Fenton 'Dragon and Lotus' pattern amethyst Carnival glass bowl.

*Plates in this well-known pattern are rare.*

*8.5in (21.5cm) wide*

**£50-70** **BA**

A Northwood 'Three Fruits' pattern amethyst Carnival glass bowl.

*8.75in (22cm) diam*

**£50-70** **BA**

A Millersburg 'Peacock' pattern amethyst Carnival glass sauce dish.

*The level of iridescence on this example is very good.*

*5.75in (14.5cm) diam*

**£40-60** **BH**

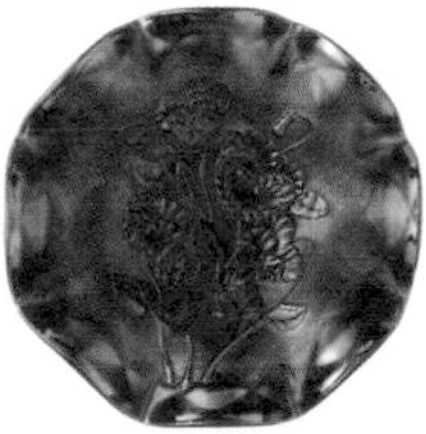

An Imperial 'Pansy' pattern amethyst Carnival glass ruffled bowl.

*8.25in (21cm) diam*

**£70-90** **BH**

An Imperial 'Windmill' pattern amethyst Carnival glass bowl.

*7.25in (18.5cm) diam*

**£80-120** **BA**

A Northwood 'Acorn Burrs' amethyst Carnival glass bowl.

*This deeply moulded pattern is one of Northwood's best and was introduced around 1911.*

*4.75in (12cm) high*

**£30-40** **BA**

A Fenton 'Wild Blackberry' pattern amethyst Carnival glass ruffled bowl.

*6.5in (16.5cm) diam*

**£50-70** **BA**

A Dugan Diamond 'Question Marks' pattern amethyst Carnival glass two-handled compote.

*1910-20* *6.5in (16.5cm) wide*

**£40-60** **BA**

A Northwood 'Fine Cut and Roses' pattern amethyst Carnival glass three-footed bowl.

*4in (10cm) high*

**£25-35** **BH**

An Imperial 'Hobstar Flower' pattern amethyst Carnival glass goblet, with a flared scalloped rim.

*This is most commonly found in the purple amethyst colour and is surprisingly scarce in marigold.*

*4.75in (12cm) high*

**£40-50** **BH**

A Diamond 'Stork and Rushes' pattern amethyst Carnival glass punch cup.

*Tumblers can be found with beaded rims, as here, or lattice rims. Blue is a rare colour.*

*2.75in (7cm) high*

**£20-30** **BA**

An Imperial 'Pansy' pattern amethyst Carnival glass nappy.

*A nappy is a shallow cup or dish.*

*6.5in (16.5cm) diam*

**£50-70** **BA**

## A CLOSER LOOK AT A WATER SET

*The pattern is detailed and deeply moulded, with strong visual appeal.*

*This pattern has only been found in Carnival glass on this water set, a berry set, an ice cream set and a rose bowl.*

*It was first shown in Imperial's 1909 catalogue in clear, colourless 'crystal' glass.*

*This water set is only known in purple amethyst, although individual tumblers are known in marigold.*

An Imperial 'Diamond Lace' pattern amethyst Carnival Glass pattern pitcher and six tumblers.

*Pitcher 8.75in (22cm) high*

**£200-300** **MAC**

A Northwood 'Grape & Cable' pattern amethyst Carnival Glass hatpin holder.

*Fenton and Northwood both produced very similar Grape & Cable patterns. The cable is replaced by a plain band on this example, showing it is a variant of Northwood's pattern. Note the excellent 'electric' iridescence.*

*6.75in (17cm) high*

**£120-180** **BH**

An Imperial 'Heavy Grape' pattern amethyst Carnival glass nappy.

*5.25in (13.5cm) diam*

**£50-70** **BA**

A Fenton 'Butterfly and Fern' pattern amethyst Carnival glass tumbler, from a water set.

*4in (10cm) high*

**£40-60** **BA**

## A CLOSER LOOK AT A FENTON BOWL

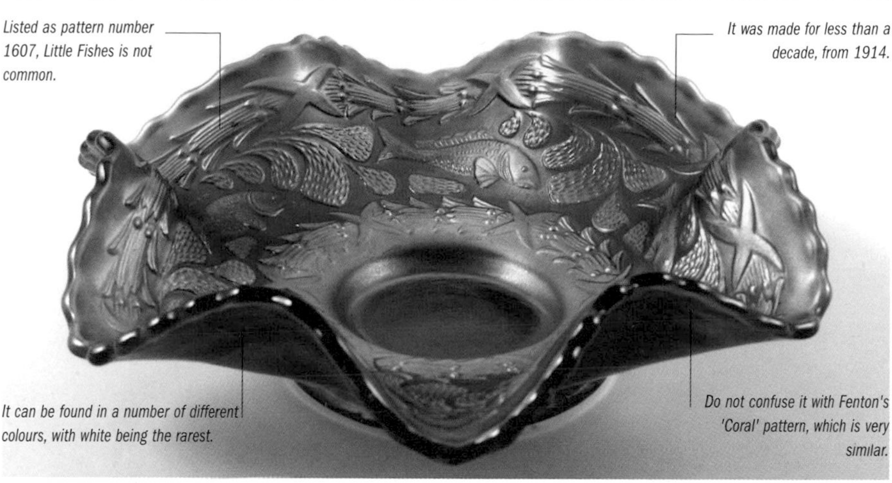
Listed as pattern number 1607, Little Fishes is not common.
It was made for less than a decade, from 1914.
It can be found in a number of different colours, with white being the rarest.
Do not confuse it with Fenton's 'Coral' pattern, which is very similar.

A Fenton 'Little Fishes' pattern marigold Carnival glass ruffled bowl.

*1914-c1922*

*6in (15cm) diam*

**£70-90** BA

A Diamond Glass 'Pony' pattern marigold Carnival glass bowl.

*Pony is usually found in bowl forms. Plates and Aqua colour items in this pattern are very rare.*

*8.25in (21cm) diam*

**£40-60** BA

A Northwood 'Good Luck' pattern marigold Carnival glass ruffled dish, with excellent 'electric' iridescence.

*Scarcer variations have less flowers, may also have a stippled pattern, and are more desirable.*

*8.75in (22.5cm) diam*

**£80-120** BH

An Australian Crystal Glass Co. 'Kangaroo' pattern marigold Carnival glass bowl.

*This pattern was patented in 1924.*

*5in (12.5cm) diam*

**£60-80** BA

A Northwood 'Wishbone' pattern marigold Carnival glass footed bowl.

*The exterior of this bowl can be plain or decorated with a basketweave pattern.*

*7.5in (19cm) diam*

**£40-60** BA

An Australian Crystal Glass Co. 'Swan' pattern marigold Carnival glass bowl.

*9in (23cm) diam*

**£80-120** BA

A 'Hobnail and Button' pattern marigold Carnival glass bowl.

*6.5in (16.5cm) diam*

**£30-50** BA

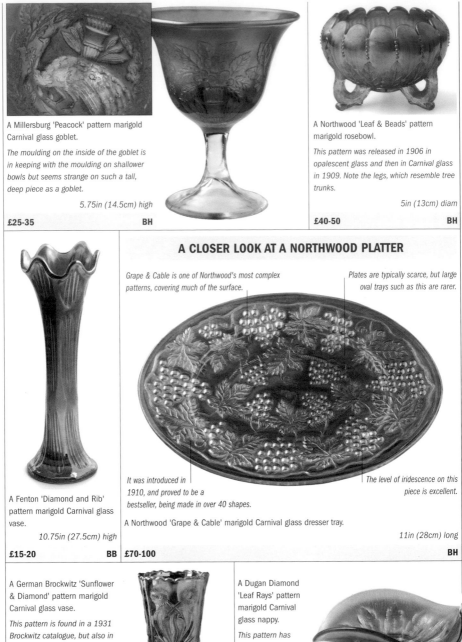

A Millersburg 'Peacock' pattern marigold Carnival glass goblet.

*The moulding on the inside of the goblet is in keeping with the moulding on shallower bowls but seems strange on such a tall, deep piece as a goblet.*

*5.75in (14.5cm) high*

**£25-35** **BH**

A Northwood 'Leaf & Beads' pattern marigold rosebowl.

*This pattern was released in 1906 in opalescent glass and then in Carnival glass in 1909. Note the legs, which resemble tree trunks.*

*5in (13cm) diam*

**£40-50** **BH**

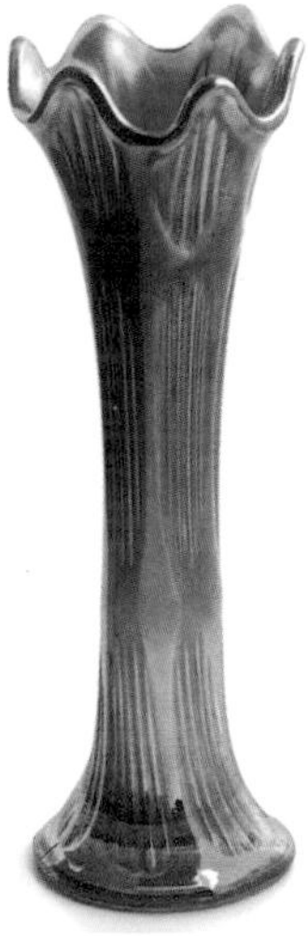

A Fenton 'Diamond and Rib' pattern marigold Carnival glass vase.

*10.75in (27.5cm) high*

**£15-20** **BB**

## A CLOSER LOOK AT A NORTHWOOD PLATTER

*Grape & Cable is one of Northwood's most complex patterns, covering much of the surface.*

*Plates are typically scarce, but large oval trays such as this are rarer.*

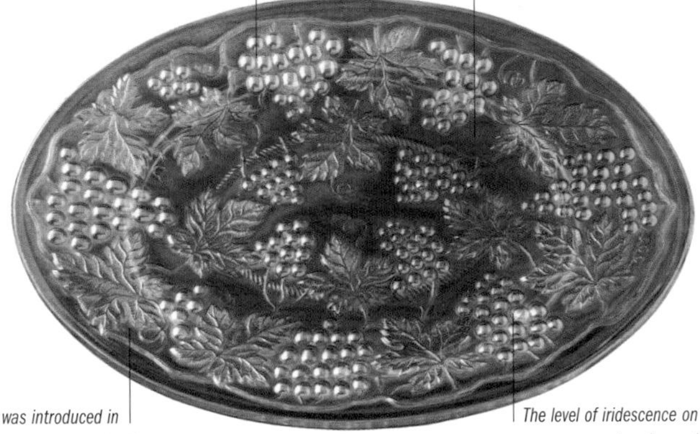

*It was introduced in 1910, and proved to be a bestseller, being made in over 40 shapes.*

*The level of iridescence on this piece is excellent.*

A Northwood 'Grape & Cable' marigold Carnival glass dresser tray.

*11in (28cm) long*

**£70-100** **BH**

A German Brockwitz 'Sunflower & Diamond' pattern marigold Carnival glass vase.

*This pattern is found in a 1931 Brockwitz catalogue, but also in catalogues from Swedish factory Eda, and is thus indicative of the exchange of patterns between European factories.*

*9.25in (23.5cm) high*

**£40-50** **BH**

A Dugan Diamond 'Leaf Rays' pattern marigold Carnival glass nappy.

*This pattern has only been found on this shape, typically with low iridescence.*

*6.75in (17cm) long*

**£25-35** **BA**

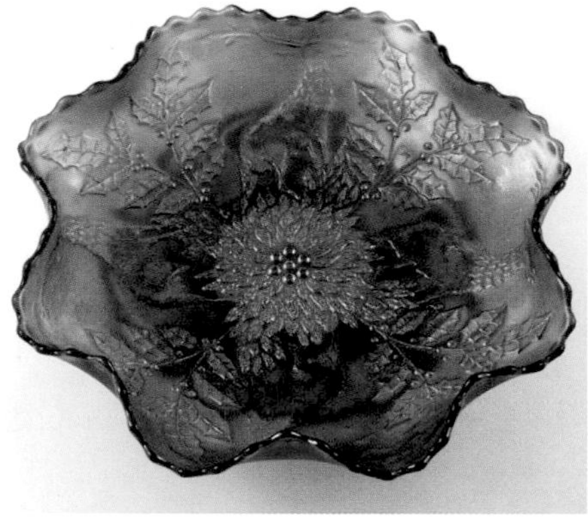

A Fenton 'Stag and Holly' pattern green Carnival glass bowl.

*Released in 1912, this pattern is only found on bowls and plates. Look out for amber glass examples, which are rare.*

*8.5in (21.5cm) diam*

**£70-90** **BA**

A Northwood 'Good Luck' pattern green Carnival glass bowl.

*Green is a comparatively rare colour for Carnival glass.*

*8.25in (21cm) diam*

**£100-150** **BA**

A Fenton 'Butterflies' pattern green Carnival glass two-handled compote.

*Look closely at patterns! As this has a band of butterflies near the rim as well as one in the centre, it is a different pattern to the one on the right. In this case it is also by a different maker.*

*7in (18cm) diam*

**£40-60** **BA**

A Northwood 'Butterfly' pattern green Carnival glass two-handled compote.

*This pattern is usually found with a plain exterior. The 'threaded' exterior shown here is less common.*

*7.5in (19cm) wide*

**£50-70** **BA**

A Northwood 'Grape & Cable' pattern green Carnival glass milk jug.

*3in (7.5cm) high*

**£40-60** **BA**

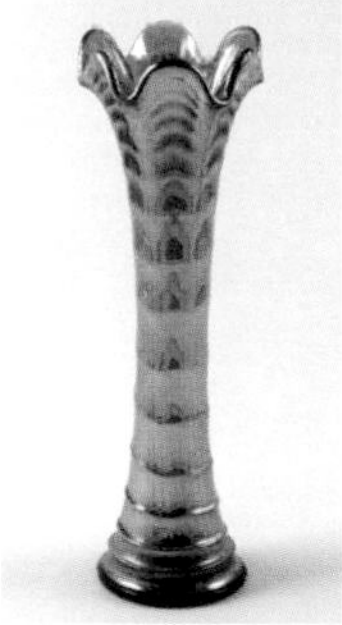

An Imperial 'Ripple' pattern green Carnival glass vase.

*9in (23cm) high*

**£30-40** **BA**

A Northwood 'Singing Bird' pattern green Carnival glass tumbler.

*Look out for the very rare jug in this pattern, which is effectively similar in form to the tumbler shown here, but with a handle and 'pulled' rim forming a spout.*

*4in (10cm) high*

**£60-80** **BA**

A Northwood 'Bushel Basket' electric blue bowl with two handles, with excellent iridescence.

*4.75in (12cm) high*

**£100-150** **BH**

A Fenton 'Open Edge Basketweave' cobalt blue Carnival glass cabinet basket.

*This pattern is rare in pastel colours and plate shapes.*

*2.75in (7cm) high*

**£20-30** **BH**

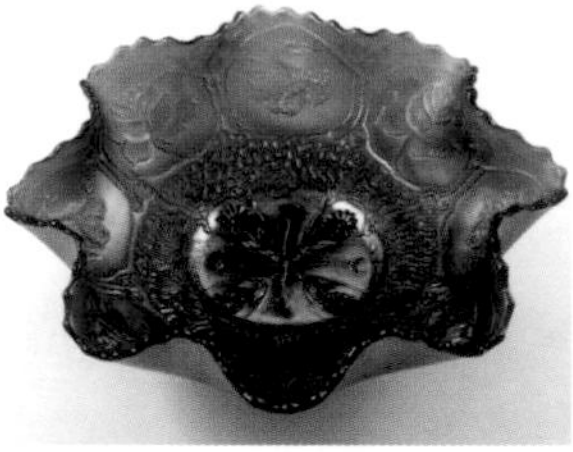

A Fenton 'Dragon and Lotus' pattern blue Carnival glass ruffled bowl.

*8.5in (21.5cm) diam*

**£80-120** **BA**

A Dugan Diamond peach opalescent 'Question Marks' Carnival glass bonbon dish, with two handles.

*This pattern is also found on compotes and a plate. Exteriors are usually plain, but those with additional patterns are more valuable.*

*4in (10cm) high*

**£40-60** **TSIS**

A Northwood 'Poppy' pattern ice blue Carnival glass oval pickle dish.

*This is a rare colour and non-Carnival opalescent blue is even rarer.*

*8.5in (21.5cm) wide*

**£200-300** **GL**

A Dugan 'Raindrops' pattern peach opalescent Carnival glass ruffled bowl.

*This is a comparatively scarce pattern, which is usually found in this colour. Purple is the most desirable colour, particularly if the iridescence is striking.*

*8.5in (21.5cm) diam*

**£40-60** **BH**

A Fenton 'Dragon and Lotus' pattern peach Carnival glass ruffled bowl.

*8in (20.5cm) diam*

**£10-20** **AS&S**

A Dugan 'Heavy Grape' pattern yellow Carnival glass tazza table centrepiece.

*Although this looks like marigold, the colour is in fact yellow.*

*8.25in (21cm) high*

**£15-25** **MAC**

A Fenton 'Sailboats' yellow Carnival glass plate.

*Not only is this a rare plate and in a scarce colour, it is also a variant of the Sailboats pattern, having fewer trees on the lakeside and a windmill on the left of the boat.*

*6.25in (16cm) diam*

**£70-100** **BH**

A Dugan 'Roundup' pattern white ruffled dish.

*This pattern was introduced in around 1910 and is only found on plates and bowls. It is rare on plates and in white.*

*9.25in (23.5cm) diam*

**£70-100** **BH**

A Northwood 'Bushel Basket' Lavender Carnival glass bowl, with two handles.

*Lavender is a scarce colour.*

*4.75in (12cm) high*

**£100-150** **BH**

**FIND OUT MORE...**

**The Standard Encyclopedia of Carnival Glass**, *by Bill Edwards and Mike Carwile, published by Collector Books, 2002.*

**The Pocket Guide to Carnival Glass**, *by Monica Lynn Clements and Patricia Rosser Clements, published by Schiffer Publishing, 2001.*

## COLLECTORS' NOTES

- Chance Glass, founded in 1824 outside Birmingham, began by producing glass for industrial, scientific and commercial uses. In 1934, it produced its first domestic tablewares, made from pressed glass. In 1951, pressed glass was abandoned due to a rise in related taxes, and the 'Fiesta' range was introduced.
- Fiesta was made from 'slumped glass'. A thin, flat glass panel was placed above a mould, or solid object. The glass was then heated, causing it to become pliable. Gravity would then cause it to fall into or onto the mould and take its form. Tools were sometimes used to manipulate the glass, notably with handkerchief vases. The panels were also decorated with lithographic designs, which were later screen-printed.
- Although a number of notable designers worked for Chance, such as Robert Goodden, Margaret Casson and Michael Harris, many designs were produced by a team of in-house designers who have remained unidentified. One of the most famous and popular forms was the Handkerchief vase, released in 1958 and based on Paolo Venini and Fulvio Bianconi's design for Venini, in 1949.
- Also known as 'Posy Vases', they were produced in four different sizes: 4in high; 5in high; 7in high; and 8in high. The medium and largest sizes tend to be the scarcest. Some patterns are also rare, as are some patterns in certain colours. In 1981, Chance Glass' management bought out the Fiesta range, which they continued to produce under the name 'Fiesta Glass' into the 1990s.
- Always examine the pattern carefully, particularly around the rounded base of handkerchief vases. As the pattern was usually printed on the outside, it is prone to scratching and wear, which reduce value. The same applies to the gold rim found on many shapes – the brighter and more intact, the better. Look closely at the corners of handkerchief vases, to ensure they are not chipped.

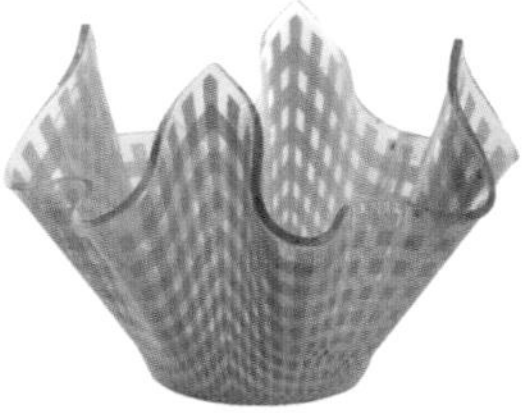

A 1960s Chance Glass white 'Gingham' pattern small handkerchief vase.

*4in (10cm) high*

**£30-40** **MHT**

A Chance Glass red 'Gingham' pattern small handkerchief vase.

*Gingham was designed in 1977 and produced into the early 1980s, under Fiesta Glass.*

*4in (10cm) high*

**£30-50** **MHT**

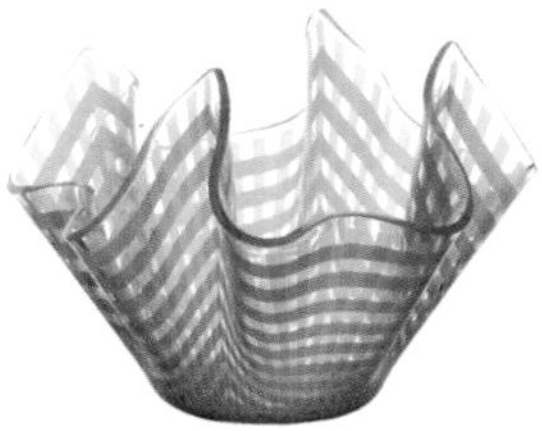

A Chance Glass green 'Gingham' pattern small handkerchief vase.

*4in (10cm) high*

**£30-50** **GC**

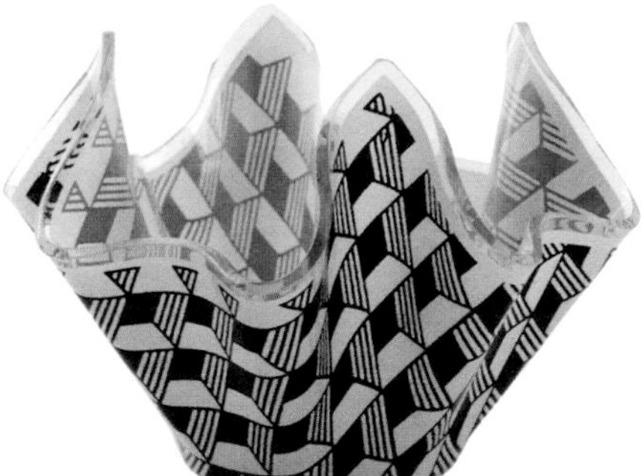

A 1960s Chance Glass red 'Carre' pattern handkerchief vase.

*Some collectors call these 'Escher', due to the pattern's similarity to graphics by artist M.C. Escher. The pattern is one of the hardest ones to find.*

*4in (10cm) high*

**£40-60** **MHT**

A Chance Glass purple 'Cordon' pattern handkerchief vase.

*Designed around 1960, Cordon is perhaps the most commonly found pattern produced and can be found in a number of different colours – the purple colourway is the only one that is transparent.*

*4in (10cm) high*

**£30-40** **MHT**

A Chance Glass orange 'Cordon' pattern large handkerchief vase.

*7in (18cm) high*

**£70-90** **MHT**

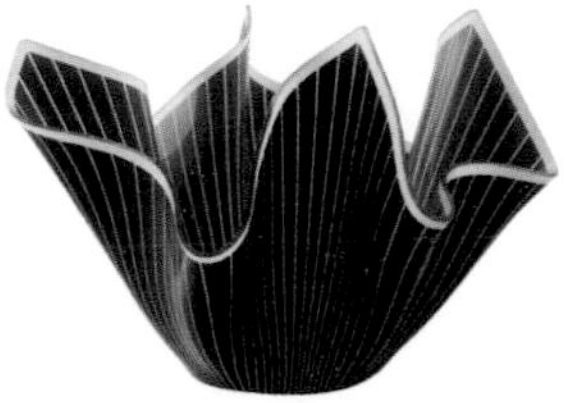

A Chance Glass black 'Cordon' pattern large handkerchief vase.

*7in (18cm) high*

**£70-90** **MHT**

A rare Chance Glass ruby cased, intaglio-cut large handkerchief vase.

*Few examples of this design are known – the ruby casing is cut back in horizontal lines to show the clear, colourless layer.*

*7in (18cm) high*

**£100-150** **MHT**

A Chance Glass red 'Polka Dot' pattern large handkerchief vase.

*Red is one of the more commonly seen colours in this pattern. However, look out for the reverse – red dots on a white background – as this is very rare.*

*7in (18cm) high*

**£60-80** **GC**

A Chance Glass black 'Psychedelic (Pop Art)' pattern small handkerchief vase.

*This hard-to-find pattern is very desirable. Red and white is scarcer than black and white.*

*4in (10cm) high*

**£50-70** **MHT**

A Chance Glass black 'Polka Dot' pattern small handkerchief vase.

*4in (10cm) high*

**£35-45** **MHT**

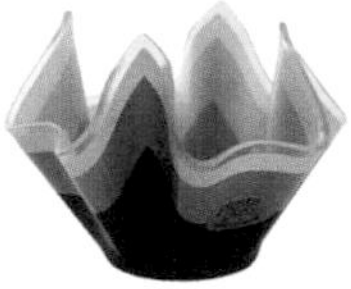

A 1980s Fiesta Glass 'Wide Bands' small handkerchief vase, with Fiesta Glass oval gold foil label.

*4in (10cm) high*

**£30-50** **MHT**

## A CLOSER LOOK AT A HANDKERCHIEF VASE

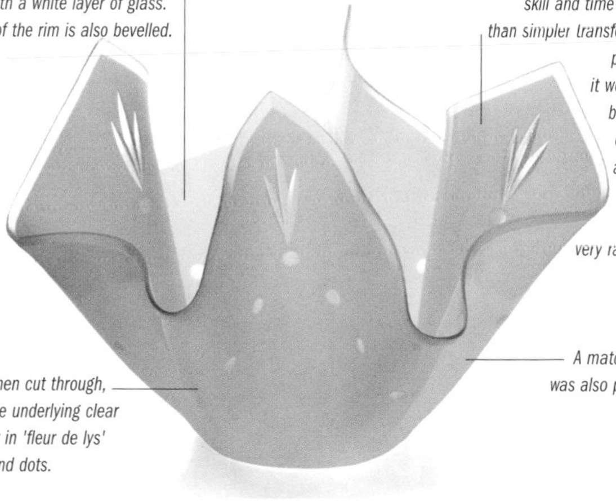

*The clear, colourless glass panel was covered with a white layer of glass. The edge of the rim is also bevelled.*

*This requires more skill and time to create than simpler transfer-printed patterns – it would have been more expensive and fewer sold, making it very rare today.*

*This was then cut through, down to the underlying clear glass layer in 'fleur de lys' patterns and dots.*

*A matching tray was also produced.*

A very rare Chance Glass 'Pearl' intaglio-cut large handkerchief vase.

*7in (18cm) high*

**£150-200** **GC**

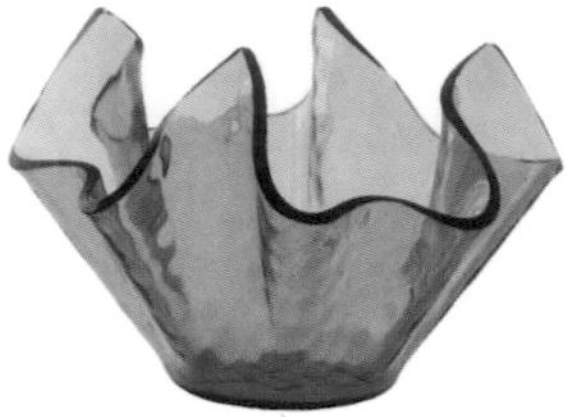

A 1970s Chance Glass double-rolled blue 'Flemish' textured pattern small handkerchief vase.

*4in (10cm) high*

**£30-40** **MHT**

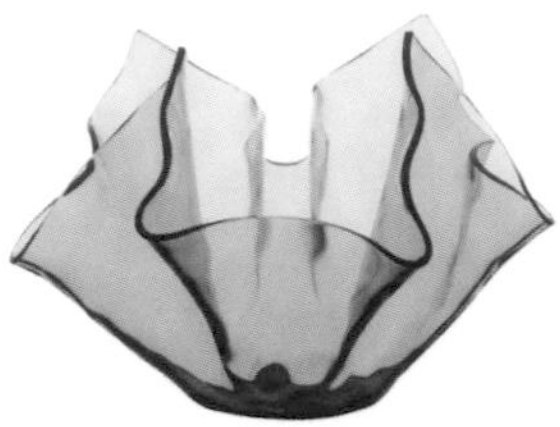

A 1970s Chance Glass blue 'Flemish' textured pattern large handkerchief vase.

*Textured glass was used in the Handkerchief vase range from 1970.*

*7in (17cm) high*

**£70-90** **GC**

A 1970s Chance Glass amber 'Hammered' textured pattern small handkerchief vase.

*4in (10cm) high*

**£30-40** **MHT**

A 1970s Chance Glass green 'Cotswold' textured pattern small Handkerchief vase.

*4in (10cm) high*

**£30-40** **MHT**

A 1970s Chance Glass silk screen printed 'Honeysuckle' pattern large dish, designed in 1970.

*8.75in (22cm) diam*

**£15-20** **GC**

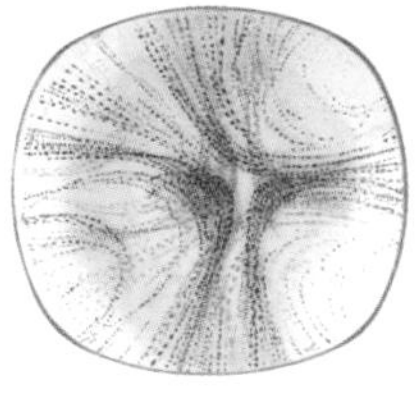

A 1970s Chance Glass 'Gold Spray' pattern small dish, with gilt rim, designed in 1970.

*Unusually, each of the two colours is printed on a different side, rather than on one side only.*

*4.25in (11cm) diam*

**£15-20** **GC**

A 1970s Chance Glass silk screen-printed 'Honeysuckle' pattern small dish, designed in 1970.

*Even though the pattern is different between the large and smaller sizes the honeysuckle flower element is the same size, showing they used the same template.*

*5.25in (13.5cm) diam*

**£10-15** **GC**

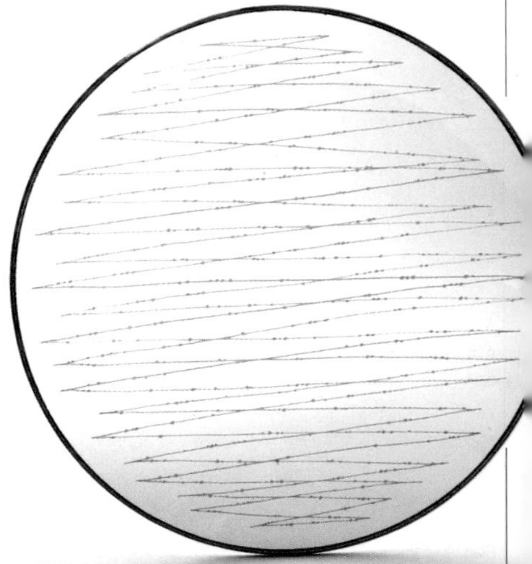

A Chance 'Night Sky' pattern Fiestaware dish, designed by Margaret Casson in 1958.

*8.25in (21cm) diam*

**£30-40** **MHT**

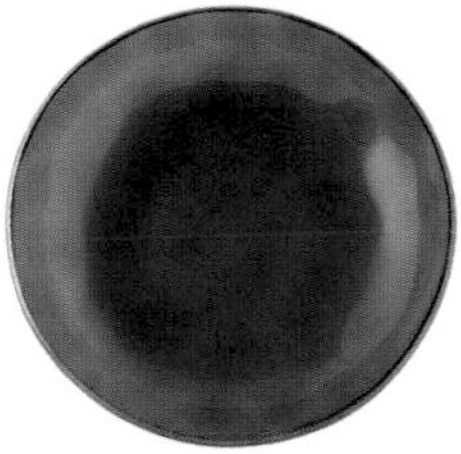

A Chance Glass cobalt blue 'Flemish' textured pattern dish.

*Chance also made glass window panels for domestic, commercial and industrial uses – it often used the same panels to make its tableware. The term 'Aqualux' should only be applied to pre-WWII textured glass items.*

*6.75in (17cm) diam*

**£15-20** **GC**

A Chance Glass 'Lotus' pattern plate, with shaped rim.

*Lotus was designed around 1974, at the same time as Canterbury. Like all patterns applied after 1971, it was screenprinted, and not applied using lithography.*

*9.5in (24cm) diam*

**£35-45** **MHT**

A late 1970s Chance 'Canterbury' pattern teardrop-shaped dish, with original Chance Glass oval gold foil label.

*This pattern can also be found in a vibrant red-orange.*

*11.5in (29cm) long*

**£35-40** **MHT**

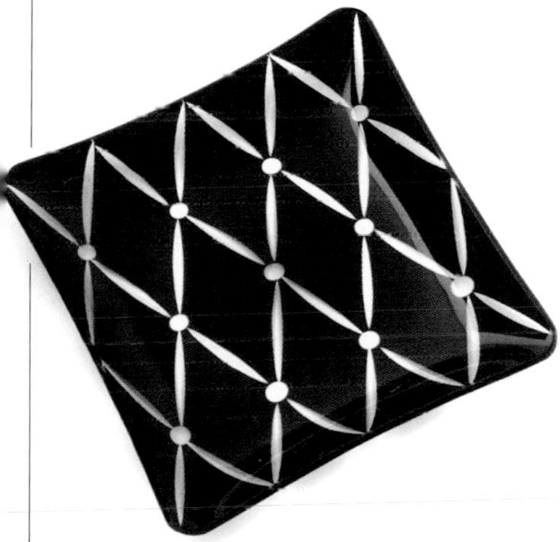

A Chance Glass rare ruby red intaglio cut ashtray or square dish.

*Here, a clear, colourless glass panel is flashed (or covered) with a red panel of glass. This outer layer is then cut away to reveal the colourless glass underneath.*

*5.5in (14cm) wide*

**£40-60** **GC**

An extremely rare Chance Glass 'Green Leaves' beaker, with screen-printed stylized leaf, line and dash pattern and gilt rim, designed in 1958.

*This is a variation of the more commonly seen tri-partite leaf pattern. Chance often re-designed patterns to match different forms and tasks.*

*4in (10cm) high*

**£15-20** **GC**

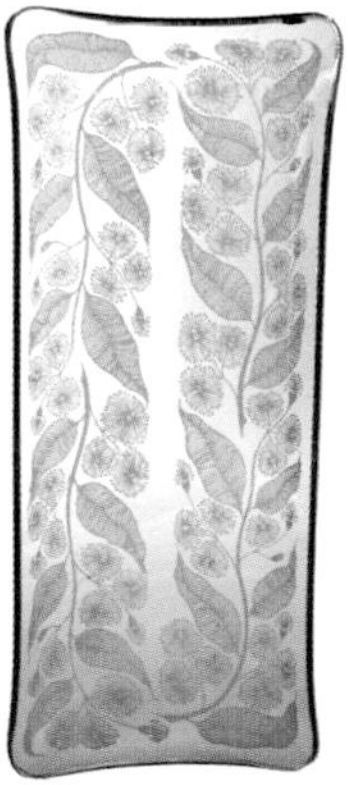

A Chance Glass 'Calypto' pattern Fiestaware rectangular dish.

*This pattern was designed by Michael Harris in 1959, when studying Industrial Glass at the Royal College of Art in London. He later went on to found Mdina Glass and Isle of Wight Studio Glass.*

*8.5in (21.5cm) wide*

**£20-30** **MHT**

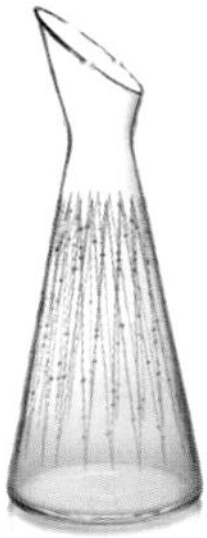

A 1960s Chance Glass 'Night Sky' Giraffe carafe, designed by Margaret Casson in 1958.

*Casson based her design on astronomical charts. The bizarrely named 'Giraffe' carafe was made elsewhere as Chance did not make hollow ware.*

*12in (30.5cm) high*

**£150-200** **GC**

**FIND OUT MORE...**

**Chance Expressions**, *by David Encill, ISBN: 978-0-9549196-1-0, www.chanceglass.net.*

A 1930s Stuart cut glass vase, with chevron and circle pattern.

*Despite being by a new wave of designers during the 1930s and '50s, comparatively few of these modern cut designs were produced by Britain's long-established cut glass factories, based in Stourbridge. Demand was still primarily for traditional cut designs, with these simpler, often more dramatic, designs being largely overlooked. The same was true of today's collectors until an exhibition in London in 2003 allowed people to reappraise the ranges produced.*

*7.75in (19.5cm) high*

**£60-90** **GC**

A Webb Corbett cut glass vase, cut with a stylized design of ears of wheat, the base etched "Webb Corbett Made in England".

*9.25in (23.5cm) high*

**£100-150** **GC**

A Stevens & Williams 'Cactus' cut vase, designed by Keith Murray, with acid mark to base.

*Murray produced over 20 designs incorporating cacti from 1935-39.*

*c1937* *7in (17.5cm) high*

**£350-450** **GAZE**

## A CLOSER LOOK AT A CUT GLASS PLAQUE

*This is typical of Webster's work after 1969, which often incorporated optical or plate glass combined with other materials such as wood or stone.*

*The Pye Television awards were given to prestigious people in the industry whose names are usually on a plaque on the base. Eight were made each year over 13 years and very few have come to the market.*

*Here the curved form cleverly mimics a television screen.*

*Webster created a number of engraved glass awards for different organisations.*

*Webster was extremely skilled at copper wheel engraving, as this piece demonstrates, but her work is hard to find.*

A Jane Webster copper wheel-engraved Pye Television Award, with maiden playing a lute and gilt filled laurel wreath, sandblasted abstract border and asymmetric, organic carved wood plinth, together with original fitted presentation box.

*According to Geoffrey Beard's 'International Modern Glass' (1976), Webster was born in the mid-1930s in Tanganyika. She trained as a sculptor at the Southern College of Art, Portsmouth, before moving to Stourbridge College of Art where she gained a National Diploma in Design, with first class honours. She was then awarded a Scholarship to the Royal College of Art to study glass further and went on to have a successful studio in London until the late 1980s.*

*Plaque 9in (23cm) high*

**£400-600** **PC**

A Walsh Walsh intaglio cut and engraved 'Water Lily' bowl, marked "Walsh England".

*c1935* *9.75in (25cm) wide*

**£100-150** **JH**

## COLLECTORS' NOTES

- Over the past decade, the modern glass designs produced in the former Communist country of Czechoslovakia since the end of WWII have become increasingly popular. Many were highly revolutionary at the time, but were largely hidden from the West by the 'Iron Curtain' except at exhibitions. Only in the years following the Velvet Revolution in 1989, have glass collectors and researchers been able to find out more.
- The complexity of the piece, the designer and the size are major considerations towards value. Hot-worked, enamelled, engraved and cut pieces that are unique and were influential tend to fetch the highest sums. Some designs were copied or reproduced on a mass scale, much like designs in Murano, and these can offer a more affordable route into the market.
- The same price point can be applied to the great number of high quality pressed glass designs produced by companies working as part of the Sklo Union. Leading and influential designers whose work is sought-after today include Stanislav Libensky, Frantisek Vízner, Pavel Hlava, Rene Roubícek and Jirí Harcuba. Some had their own specialisms, such as cutting or engraving, but many worked across the full spectrum of working methods.
- It is worth studying reference books and contemporary sources in order to build up a working knowledge of who was responsible for what design, and when it was produced. Much work is not signed, with labels having been removed over time, and a considerable amount of research is yet to be completed. Nevertheless, the area looks set to grow in terms of interest and value over the next few years.

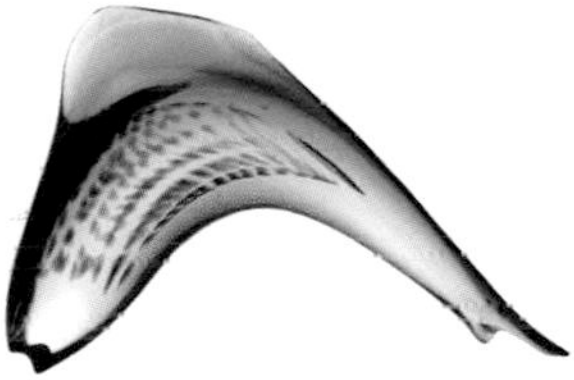

An Exbor coloured glass leaping fish, designed by Stanislav Klemes or Stanislav Honzik, with cut decoration to the fin.

*12.5in (32cm) long*

**£100-150** **PC**

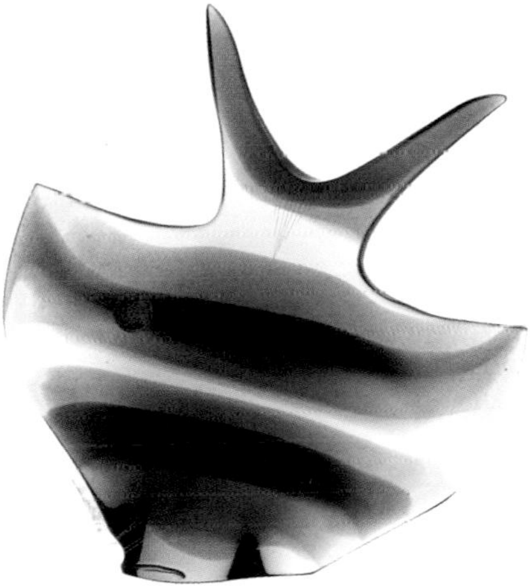

An Exbor coloured glass fish, designed by Stanislav Klemes or Stanislav Honzik, with decoration to the fin and tail and foil sticker.

*Klemes and Honzik both designed a number of colourful, abstract fish designs, with cut and polished detailing.*

*8.75in (22cm) high*

**£100-150** **PC**

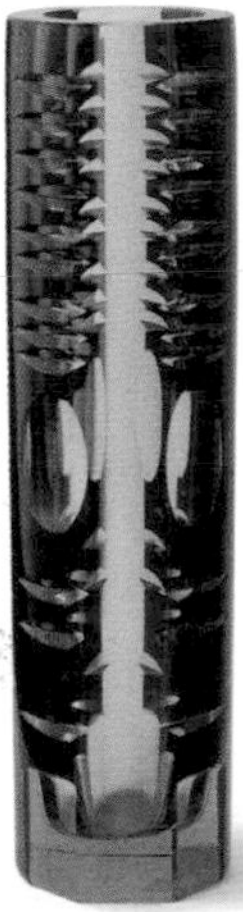

A Borske Sklo faceted glass vase, designed by Karel Wunsch, pattern no.46301, from the Dual series, the amber body cased with blue cut with a geometric pattern.

*12in (30.5cm) high*

**£100-150** **DN**

A Moser octagonal glass vase of clear, colourless glass cased in blue and cut through with facets.

*5.5in (14cm) high*

**£80-120** **TCM**

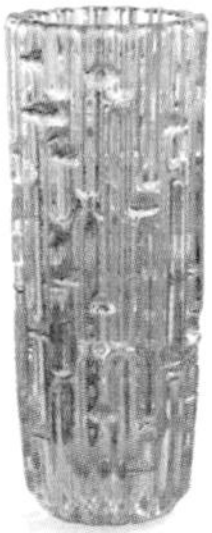

A 1970s Sklo Union pressed glass vase, pattern no.20082, designed by Frantisek Vízner in 1965 and made at the Hermanova Hut.

*9.75in (25cm) high*

**£28-32** **FD**

A Borske Sklo, Novy Bor green and red vase, designed by Pavel Hlava, with cut and polished exterior.

*These stunning vases, with an almost veiled, optical effect to the colour, and polished and curving surfaces, were first exhibited in 1957. They were made in a number of different tall shapes and colours, and were inspired by Hlava's experience of working with glassmakers at the furnace at the Chribska Glassworks in 1955.*

*c1958* *8.25in (21cm) high*

**£700-900** **JH**

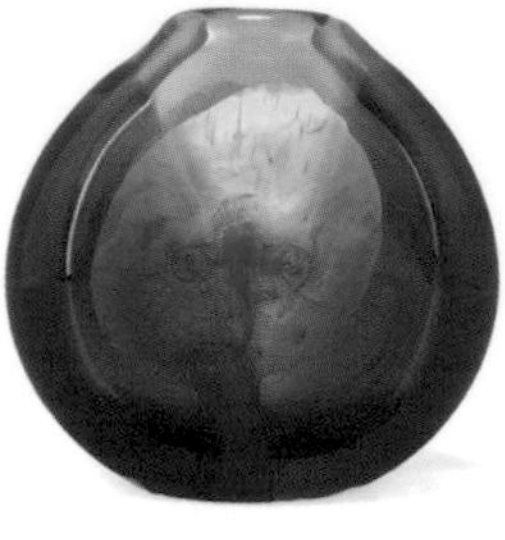

A Moser vase, designed by Jiří Suhajek, the clear glass body with yellow and green inclusions, and amber coloured partial casing.

*Suhajek was the third designer at Moser, working there from 1972-79, and continues to collaborate with the factory to this day.*

*c1974* *7.5in (19cm) high*

**£700-1,000** **QU**

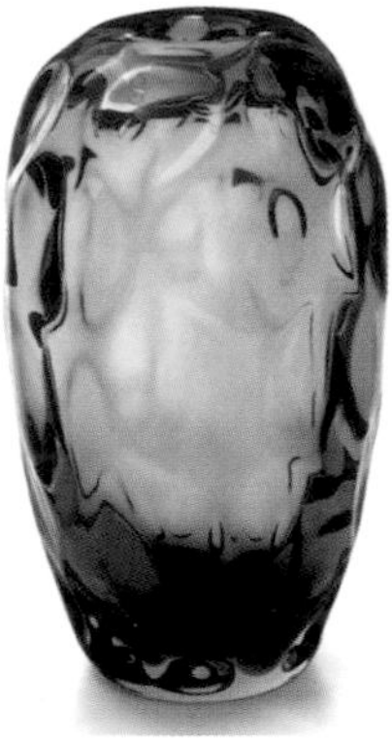

A Chribska blue and colourless cased amber hot-worked glass vase, designed by Josef Hospodka, with optical effect.

*Hospodka is known for his hot-worked, almost studio glass, designs produced for Chribska in the early 1960s. His designs have both been copied and adapted widely, making attributions difficult.*

*7.5in (19cm) high*

**£40-60** **GC**

A 1960s-70s Czechoslovakian hand-blown art glass bowl, possibly designed by Josef Hospodka or Maria Stahlikova.

*These cased, brightly coloured bowls and dishes are often mistaken for Murano glass of the same period, if unlabelled.*

*6in (15cm) high*

**£28-32** **GAZE**

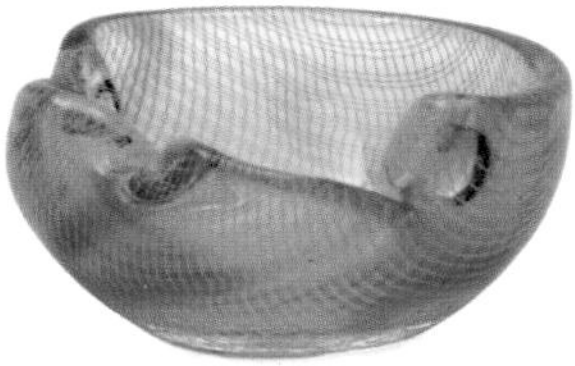

A 1950s Harrrachov Glassworks (Borske Sklo) 'Harrtil' bowl, with internal woven glass fibres and green trail, designed by Milos Pulpitel and Milan Metalek.

*4.75in (12cm) wide*

**£40-60** **JH**

A Czech mould blown 'end of day' bowl, the base acid-stamped "Czechoslovakia".

*8in (20cm) diam*

**£50-60** **BB**

A 1960s Bohemia Glassworks cut ashtray, designed by Vladimir Zahour and made at the Podebrady factory, the square footed body cut with facets at different angles, with a polished pontil mark.

*3in (7.5cm) high*

**£150-200** **GC**

## FIND OUT MORE...

**Czech Glass 1945-80: Design in an Age of Adversity**, *editor Helmut Ricke, published by Arnoldsche, 2006.*

## COLLECTORS' NOTES

- Dartington Glass was founded in June 1967, by the charitable Dartington Hall Trust, with the aim of revitalising the surrounding rural community in Devon by introducing a new industry. Frank Thrower, who had worked as Wuidart & Co. and Portmeirion was appointed Designer. His experience selling Scandinavian glass at both companies, and designing glass for Portmeirion, allowed him to create successful designs.

- Master glassmaker and glass factory manager, Eskil Vilhelmsson, was employed from Sweden's Björkshult factory, along with other Scandinavian glassmakers, who made glass and taught their skills. The range was successful, with decorative wares being particularly popular with collectors today. The 'textured' range is especially popular, with collectors aiming to own an example of every shape in every colour.

- Shape, colour and size are important considerations. Some shapes are rarer than others, particularly early or large designs. Flame and Kingfisher tend to be more desirable colours than Midnight and the common Clear. Tablewares and stemwares are generally less popular with collectors, although decanters attract interest from a dedicated group.

- After a few years of being largely ignored by collectors, Throwers' designs are becoming increasingly sought-after, particularly his hallmark designs. From 1982-87, the company was in partnership with Wedgwood Glass, and Thrower produced many more designs for them. These later designs are currently less popular than earlier ranges, so now may be the time to buy. Always examine a piece closely for damage and liming from water as this detracts from the colour of the glass and interrupts the design.

A Dartington Glass FT60 Kingfisher blue mould-blown textured vase, designed by Frank Thrower in 1968, with moulded stylised flower pattern.

*4.75in (12cm) high*

**£20-30** **GC**

A rare Dartington Glass FT65 Kingfisher blue mould-blown textured vase, designed by Frank Thrower in 1968.

*6in (15.5cm) high*

**£60-80** **GC**

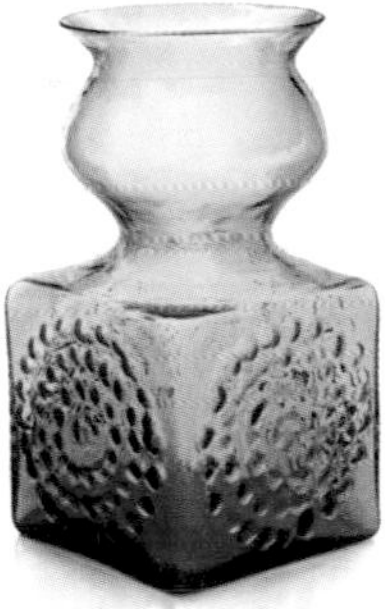

A Dartington Glass FT62 Kingfisher blue mould-blown textured vase, designed by Frank Thrower in 1968, with moulded dots pattern and shaped top with flared rim.

*6in (15cm) high*

**£50-80** **GC**

A Dartington Glass FT2 Kingfisher blue mould-blown textured vase, designed by Frank Thrower in 1967, with moulded stars and dot design.

*3.5in (9cm) high*

**£30-40** **GC**

A Dartington Glass FT58 Kingfisher blue mould-blown textured vase, designed by Frank Thrower in 1967, with moulded Greek Key pattern.

*This large size is rare, smaller sizes are much more common.*

*9.5in (24cm) high*

**£70-100** **GC**

A Dartington Glass FT72 Kingfisher blue mould-blown textured vase, designed by Frank Thrower in 1968, with moulded Greek Key pattern and hammered effect flared rim.

*3.5in (9cm) high*

**£30-40** **GC**

A Dartington Glass FT66 Midnight grey mould-blown textured vase, designed by Frank Thrower in 1968, with geometric patterns and a hammered effect flared rim.

*5in (13cm) high*

**£30-40** **GC**

A Dartington Glass FT98 Midnight grey mould-blown bark textured small vase, designed by Frank Thrower in 1968.

*2.5in (6.5cm) high*

**£15-20** **GC**

A scarce Dartington Glass FT108 Flame red 'X-Certificate' hexagonal vase, designed by Frank Thrower in 1969.

*Making waves at the time, even after the free-living '60s, the design is based on the form of the human nipple. 'Flame' red is the rarest colourway.*

*4.25in (11cm) high*

**£150-200** **GC**

Two Dartington Glass FT72 Flame red mould-blown textured vase, designed by Frank Thrower in 1968s, with moulded Greek Key patterns.

*Flame can often appear orange, particularly when light is passed through it, as here.*

*3.5in (9cm) high*

**£80-120 (each)** **MHT**

A Dartington Glass FT23 Kingfisher blue mould-blown rectangular vase, designed by Frank Thrower in 1967, with stylized flower designs.

*9.75in (24.5cm) high*

**£300-400** **GC**

A Dartington Glass FT35 cased blue 'Sunflower' floor vase, designed by Frank Thrower in 1967.

*This enormous mould blown vase was produced from 1967-70 in un-cased colourless, Midnight grey and Kingfisher blue. It was then re-introduced in 1994 in cased dark blue and cased green. The bases on the later re-issues were also acid-etched with a "D" and "VA No.1033" markings.*

*15.25in (39cm) high*

**£400-500** **GC**

Two Dartington Glass FT228 Clear mould-blown 'Daisy' vases, designed by Frank Thrower in 1979.

*Largest 7in (18cm) high*

**£30-50 (each)** **MHT**

A Dartington Glass FT74 Flame red 'Top Hat' vase, designed by Frank Thrower in 1968, with polished pontil mark.

*Flame is the rarest colour produced by Dartington, and is produced using the chemical element Selenium. Somewhat like Amberina, reheating the orange glass mix after the vase was formed turned it into a rich and varied red.*

*8in (20.5cm) high*

**£150-200** **GC**

## A CLOSER LOOK AT A DARTINGTON GLASS VASE

*The shape is mould blown and is one of two vase designs by Thrown that incorporating faces. The other, head-shaped vase, is rarer still.*

*It was probably inspired by the figural and face designs being produced in Scandinavia by designers such as Eric Hoglund.*

*It was deemed comparatively ugly at the time, and was also expensive, so few examples sold compared to Dartington's other vases.*

*It was made in Clear, Midnight grey and Kingfisher blue and was only produced until around 1970.*

A very rare Dartington Glass FT16 Kingfisher blue 'Face' vase, designed by Frank Thrower in 1967.

*5.75in (14.5cm) high*

**£300-400** **GC**

A Dartington Glass FT27 Clear 'Inga' decanter, designed by Frank Thrower in 1967.

*14.5in (37cm) high*

**£30-50** **GC**

A Dartington Glass FT44 Clear decanter, designed by Frank Thrower in 1967, with cylindrical stopper.

*10.5in (26.5cm) high*

**£15-20** **GC**

A Dartington Glass FT85 Clear decanter, designed by Frank Thrower in 1968.

*10.75in (27cm) high*

**£30-40** **GC**

A Dartington Glass FT156 Clear 'Ripple' sherry decanter, designed by Frank Thrower.

*12in (30.5cm) high*

**£20-30** **GC**

### FIND OUT MORE...

**Frank Thrower & Dartington Glass**, *by Eve Thrower & Mark Hill, published by www.markhillpublishing.com, 2007, ISBN: 978-0-9552865-2-0.*

## COLLECTORS' NOTES

- Depression glass is inexpensive, mass-produced, coloured or clear tableware, produced during the 1920s and Great Depression of the 1920s and '30s, hence its name. It was made using a tank-moulding process, where glass ingredients were melted in a tank and forced through pipes into moulds.
- Six companies were responsible for most of the glass available today, the most popular among collectors include: Anchor Hocking Glass Co, Jeanette, Indiana Glass Co. and Hazel Atlas. Depression glass pieces were usually used as promotional giveaways in petrol stations, cereal boxes or cinemas, and were inexpensive to buy.
- Colours are typically bright, to counteract the drabness of the Great Depression era. Green is one of the most typical, with the majority produced by Anchor Hocking. Pink is as popular today as it was during the 1920s. During the mid-1930s, tastes began to revert to clear glass, and colourless 'Crystal' was often used. These pieces are heavier in weight.
- Most collectors collect by pattern, which were often named after festive, historical, geographic or natural themes. Examine patterns carefully and learn how to recognize them, as patterns usually identify the manufacturer. 'Jubilee' is a highly sought-after pattern, but other patterns are very similar and are often mistaken for it.
- Examine glass closely for damage – try to examine it clean. Some wear through use, shown by light criss-crossing lines, is acceptable, but chips and cracks are not. Bubbles and ripples give pieces character and are also acceptable. Be aware – reproductions do exist, so get to know the feel and appearance of originals. Reproduction colours are usually paler or different in tone – reproduced pink contains more orange than the original. Certain patterns were also not produced in some colours. The pattern on reproductions is not usually as fine as the original or it is unusually sharp, with no signs of age.

A Hazel Atlas Glass Co. green 'Royal Lace' pattern Depression glass cookie jar.

*These also appeal to cookie jar collectors. Beware of Cobalt blue examples, which are later reproductions.*

*1934-41* *7.5in (19cm) high*

**£30-50** **BH**

A Hazel Atlas Glass Co. green 'Royal Lace' Depression glass salt shaker, with metal top.

*1934-41* *4.25in (10.5cm)*

**£20-30** **BH**

A Hazel Atlas Glass Co. green 'Royal Lace' pattern Depression glass dinner plate.

*1934-41* *9.75in (25cm)*

**£12-18** **BH**

A Hazel Atlas Glass Co. pink 'Royal Lace' pattern Depression glass oval platter.

*1934-41* *12.5in (32cm) diam*

**£18-25** **BH**

A Hazel Atlas Glass Co. 'Royal Lace' pink Depression glass tumbler.

*1934-41* *4.25in (11cm) high*

**£10-15** **BH**

A Hazel Atlas Glass Co. cobalt blue 'Royal Lace' pattern Depression glass cup and saucer.

*Blue is a desirable colour. Very deep blue tones generally indicate a reproduction.*

*1934-42* *5.5in (14cm) diam*

**£20-25** **BH**

A Jeanette Glass Co. pink 'Adam' pattern Depression glass square dinner plate.

*Beware of butter dishes in this pattern, in pink and green, as these are reproductions.*

*1932-34* *9in (23cm) wide*

**£10-15** **BH**

A Fostoria Crystal 'American' pattern Depression glass beer mug.

*1915-86* *4.75in (12cm) high*

**£25-35** **BH**

A Fostoria Crystal 'American' pattern Depression Glass oil cruet.

*1915-86* *6.5in (16.5cm) high*

**£15-20** **BH**

A Hocking Glass Co. green 'Block Optic' pattern Depression glass juicer.

*1929-33* *5.75in (14.5cm) diam*

**£15-25** **TM**

A Hocking Glass Co. green 'Block Optic' pattern Depression glass juicer.

*The placing of the handle, as here, is scarcer than when it is opposite the spout.*

*1929-33* *6in (15.5cm) diam*

**£20-25** **TM**

An Anchor Hocking Crystal 'Bubble' pattern Depression glass plate.

*1937-65* *6.5in (16.5cm) diam*

**£5-10** **GROB**

A Jeanette Glass Co. green 'Cherry Blossom' pattern Depression glass footed bowl.

*Crystal, Jadeite and red are the rarest colours, but watch out for reproductions and fakes, such as a children's butter dish.*

*1930-39* *10.5in (26.5cm) diam*

**£40-50** **BB**

A 1930s Paden City Glass Co. red 'Crow's Foot' pattern Depression glass cup and saucer.

*6in (15.5cm) diam*

**£5-10** **BH**

A 1930s Paden City Glass Co. red 'Crow's Foot' pattern Depression glass soup bowl.

*4.5in (11.5cm) diam*

**£8-12** **BH**

A Macbeth-Evans Glass Co. pink 'Dogwood' pattern Depression glass dinner plate.

*The 'Dogwood' pattern in yellow is rare, particularly in the cereal bowl form. Crystal pieces are less desirable, usually worth around half the value of coloured pieces.*

*1929-32* *9.25in (23.5cm) diam*

**£10-15** **BH**

A Jeanette teal 'Doric & Pansy' pattern Depression glass bowl.

*Pink and colourless 'Crystal' are the two rarest colours in this pattern.*

*1937-38* *4.5in (11.5cm) diam*

**£7-10** **GROB**

A Jeanette pink 'Floral' pattern Depression glass footed conical tumbler.

*1931-35* *4.75in (12cm) high*

**£10-15** **TM**

## A CLOSER LOOK AT A DEPRESSION GLASS TUMBLER

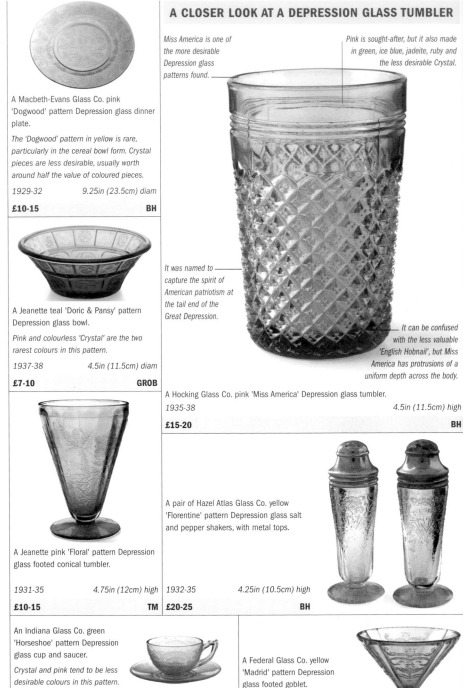

*Miss America is one of the more desirable Depression glass patterns found.*

*Pink is sought-after, but it also made in green, ice blue, jadeite, ruby and the less desirable Crystal.*

*It was named to capture the spirit of American patriotism at the tail end of the Great Depression.*

*It can be confused with the less valuable 'English Hobnail', but Miss America has protrusions of a uniform depth across the body.*

A Hocking Glass Co. pink 'Miss America' Depression glass tumbler.

*1935-38* *4.5in (11.5cm) high*

**£15-20** **BH**

A pair of Hazel Atlas Glass Co. yellow 'Florentine' pattern Depression glass salt and pepper shakers, with metal tops.

*1932-35* *4.25in (10.5cm) high*

**£20-25** **BH**

An Indiana Glass Co. green 'Horseshoe' pattern Depression glass cup and saucer.

*Crystal and pink tend to be less desirable colours in this pattern.*

*1930-33* *6in (15cm) diam*

**£6-9** **BH**

A Federal Glass Co. yellow 'Madrid' pattern Depression glass footed goblet.

*1932-39* *3in (7.5cm) high*

**£5-8** **BB**

A Hocking Glass Co. pink 'Miss America' Depression glass creamer.

*The butter dish can fetch up to £100, but beware of reproductions. Always compare to a genuine piece in terms of colour and feel.*

*1935-38* *4in 4in (10cm) high*

**£8-12** **BH**

A New Martinsville Glass Co. ruby red 'Moondrops' pattern Depression glass goblet.

*1932-40* *4.75in (12cm) high*

**£10-15** **CA**

A Hocking Glass Co. pink 'Old Colony' pattern Depression glass cereal bowl.

*Crystal pieces are worth roughly half the value of pink, the other only colour produced. Check the pattern carefully, as it is similar to designs by other companies.*

*1935-38* *6.5in (16.5cm) diam*

**£10-15** **BH**

A Federal Glass Co. yellow 'Patrician' pattern Depression glass dinner plate.

*1933-37* *9in (23cm) diam*

**£4-6** **BH**

A Federal Glass Co. pink 'Sharon' pattern Depression glass dinner plate.

*1935-39* *9in (23cm) diam*

**£7-10** **BH**

A Federal Glass Co. pink 'Sharon' pattern Depression glass sugar bowl.

*1935-39* *3.25in (8cm) high*

**£5-8** **BH**

A Federal Glass Co. pink 'Sharon' pattern Depression glass berry bowl.

*1935-39* *5in (13cm) diam*

**£5-8** **BH**

A Cambridge Glass Co. pink depression glass swan bonbon dish, the base marked with a "C" in a triangle, mould no.1043.

*The Cambridge Glass Co. (1902-58) produced swans in six different sizes from 1928-58. The feather detail shows that this dates from between 1928 and 1939, when the detail was reduced, leaving just outlines.*

*1928-39* *21cm (8.5in) long*

**£100-125** **BH**

## COLLECTORS' NOTES

- Ronald Stennett-Willson (b.1915) is one of late 20th century Britain's most important glass designers. He began his career in 1946 at glass importers Rydbeck & Norstrom in London. In 1951, he left to become sales director at J. Wuidart & Co. Ltd., who imported Scandinavian ceramics and glass from companies such as Rorstrand, Orrefors and Kosta. Within a few years, Stennett-Willson became Managing Director.
- During the 1950s, he designed glass for Wuidart, which was manufactured by Björkshult, Stromberg and Johansfors, among others. He also produced designs for Lemington Glass in Scotland from 1960-62. In 1961 he left Wuidart and became Reader and part-time tutor in Industrial Glass at the Royal College of Art, London. In 1964, he opened his own shop, 'Choses', in London, which was followed by a glass import company called Wilmart in 1964.
- In 1967, Stennett-Willson founded King's Lynn Glass in Norfolk, and was responsible for all of its designs. Among his most popular designs are the 'Sheringham' candlestick and the 'Top Hat' vases. The company was a great success and was acquired by Wedgwood in 1969, as it felt the company would benefit its US sales and add modern glass to its portfolio of products.
- Many King's Lynn designs were continued under Wedgwood, and more were introduced. Stennett-Willson retired in 1979 and the company entered a decline in business, resulting in it merging with Dartington Glass in 1982. Dartington's designer, Frank Thrower, then became the designer for the merged 'Wedgwood Crystal' group, and produced new designs.
- In 1987, Waterford merged with Wedgwood Crystal and Dartington left the group. 1992 saw the final closure of the King's Lynn glass factory. Since then, Stennett-Willson's landmark modern designs, some only produced for a few years, have been rising in value as collectors and glass historians reappraise their importance.

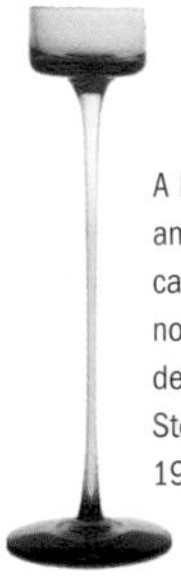

A King's Lynn large amber 'Brancaster' candleholder, shape no.RSW15, designed by Ronald Stennett-Willson in 1967.

*Supremely elegant, the Brancaster has a delicate hollow stem. The shape was produced by Wedgwood after the take-over in 1969.*

*11.5in (29cm) high*

**£50-70** **GC**

Two King's Lynn purple 'Brancaster' candleholders, shape no.RSW15, in small and medium size, designed by Ronald Stennett-Willson in 1967.

*Smallest 5.5in (14cm) high*

**L: £20-30 R: £30-40** **GC**

A King's Lynn small amber 'Brancaster' candlestick, shape no.RSW15, designed by Ronald Stennett-Willson in 1967.

*5.5in (14cm) high*

**£20-30** **GC**

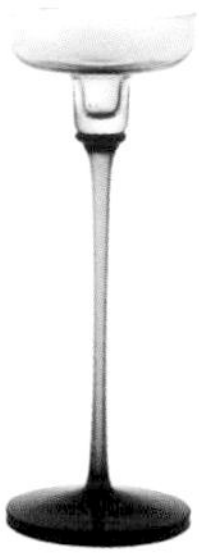

A King's Lynn light blue and colourless 'Wide Bowl' candleholder, designed by Ronald Stennett-Willson in 1967.

*7.75in (20cm) high*

**£100-150** **GC**

A King's Lynn light blue and colourless 'Wide Bowl' candleholder, designed by Ronald Stennett-Willson in 1967.

*10.25in (26cm) high*

**£80-120** **GC**

Two King's Lynn blue 'Sandringham' candlesticks, shape no.RSW22, in small and medium size, designed by Ronald Stennett-Willson in 1967.

*Tallest 6.5in (16.5cm) high*

**L: £30-40 R: £40-60** **GC**

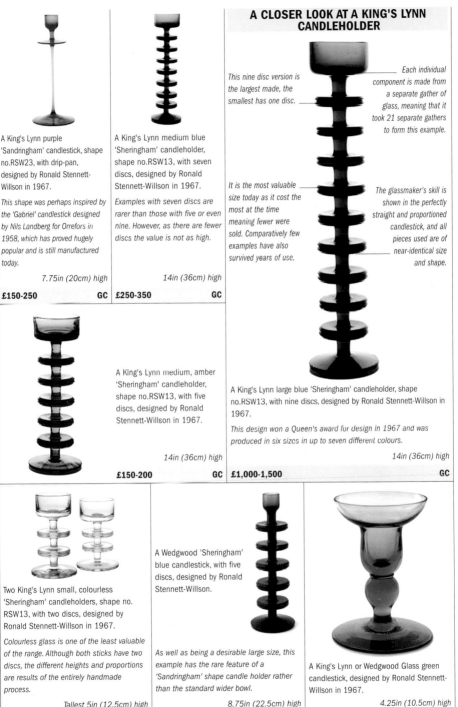

A King's Lynn purple 'Sandringham' candlestick, shape no.RSW23, with drip-pan, designed by Ronald Stennett-Willson in 1967.

*This shape was perhaps inspired by the 'Gabriel' candlestick designed by Nils Landberg for Orrefors in 1958, which has proved hugely popular and is still manufactured today.*

*7.75in (20cm) high*

**£150-250** **GC**

A King's Lynn medium blue 'Sheringham' candleholder, shape no.RSW13, with seven discs, designed by Ronald Stennett-Willson in 1967.

*Examples with seven discs are rarer than those with five or even nine. However, as there are fewer discs the value is not as high.*

*14in (36cm) high*

**£250-350** **GC**

## A CLOSER LOOK AT A KING'S LYNN CANDLEHOLDER

*This nine disc version is the largest made, the smallest has one disc.*

*Each individual component is made from a separate gather of glass, meaning that it took 21 separate gathers to form this example.*

*It is the most valuable size today as it cost the most at the time meaning fewer were sold. Comparatively few examples have also survived years of use.*

*The glassmaker's skill is shown in the perfectly straight and proportioned candlestick, and all pieces used are of near-identical size and shape.*

A King's Lynn large blue 'Sheringham' candleholder, shape no.RSW13, with nine discs, designed by Ronald Stennett-Willson in 1967.

*This design won a Queen's award for design in 1967 and was produced in six sizes in up to seven different colours.*

*14in (36cm) high*

**£1,000-1,500** **GC**

A King's Lynn medium, amber 'Sheringham' candleholder, shape no.RSW13, with five discs, designed by Ronald Stennett-Willson in 1967.

*14in (36cm) high*

**£150-200** **GC**

Two King's Lynn small, colourless 'Sheringham' candleholders, shape no. RSW13, with two discs, designed by Ronald Stennett-Willson in 1967.

*Colourless glass is one of the least valuable of the range. Although both sticks have two discs, the different heights and proportions are results of the entirely handmade process.*

*Tallest 5in (12.5cm) high*

**£20-30 (each)** **GC**

A Wedgwood 'Sheringham' blue candlestick, with five discs, designed by Ronald Stennett-Willson.

*As well as being a desirable large size, this example has the rare feature of a 'Sandringham' shape candle holder rather than the standard wider bowl.*

*8.75in (22.5cm) high*

**£100-150** **GC**

A King's Lynn or Wedgwood Glass green candlestick, designed by Ronald Stennett-Willson in 1967.

*4.25in (10.5cm) high*

**£30-40** **GC**

A King's Lynn or Wedgwood Glass purple cylindrical candlestick, designed by Ronald Stennett-Willson in 1967.

*3.25in (8.5cm) high*

**£30-40** **GC**

A King's Lynn blue cylindrical glass vase, shape no.RSW20, from the Rustic range, designed by Ronald Stennett-Willson in 1967.

**£40-60** **GC**

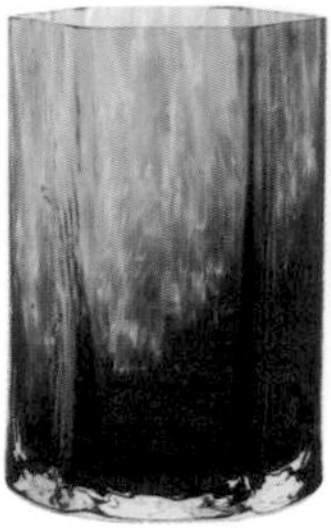

A Wedgwood Glass hexagonal vase, shape no.RSW252, with mottled blue pattern and clear, colourless casing, designed by Ronald Stennett-Willson in 1970.

*These vases were blown into moulds and rolled in chips of a darker colour to give the mottled appearance. They were produced from 1970-74.*

*8.5in (21.5cm) high*

**£60-80** **GC**

A Wedgwood Glass rectangular vase, possibly shape no.RSW251, with mottled green pattern and clear, colourless casing, designed by Ronald Stennett-Willson in 1970.

*1970* *8.5in (21.5cm) high*

**£80-100** **GC**

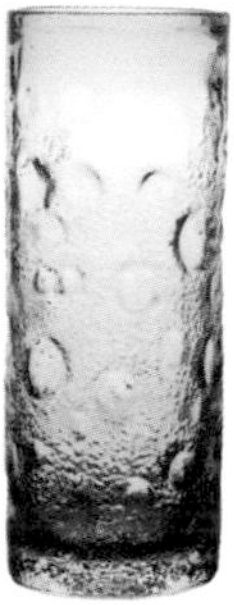

A King's Lynn amber mould-blown textured cylindrical vase, shape no. RSW25, designed by Ronald Stennett-Willson in 1968.

*This vase was produced to commemorate the moon landing in 1967. Another variation is known with moulded square and diamond shapes. Both were produced from 1968-c1970.*

*c1969*

**£70-90** **GC**

A Wedgwood Glass mould-blown textured green cylindrical vase, designed by Ronald Stennett-Willson in 1975.

*1975-78* *8.5in (21cm) high*

**£70-100** **GC**

A Wedgwood Glass mould-blown textured green cylindrical bowl, shape no.RSW267, designed by Ronald Stennett-Willson in 1975.

*1975-78* *8.25in (21cm) high*

**£30-50** **GC**

## A CLOSER LOOK AT A WEDGWOOD VASE

*The Studio range was made under Stennett-Willson's direct supervision.*

*Each piece was handmade and is unique - even those produced in small quantities are unique in their exact patterning.*

*It was produced partly in response to the growing Studio glass movement, which focused on producing unique pieces of handmade glass. They also acted as exhibition pieces showcasing the company's skills.*

*Other vases in the range were made using the Aerial process (see pp.301-310) pioneered at Orrefors in Sweden in 1937 and tend to be more valuable, often fetching from £500 upwards.*

A Wedgwood Glass yellow bowl, shape no. RSW103/5, from the 'Studio' range, with an applied orange trail, designed by Ronald Stennett-Willson.

*c1975* *7in (18cm) high*

**£300-400** **GC**

A Wedgwood Glass pink vase, shape no.RSW103/?, from the 'Studio' range, with flared rim, designed by Ronald Stennett-Willson.

*c1975*

**£300-500** **GC**

A King's Lynn purple footed fruit bowl, shape no.RSW6, designed by Ronald Stennett-Willson in 1967.

*c1968* *5in (13cm) high*

**£180-220** **GC**

A King's Lynn blue footed fruit bowl, with shaped stem, shape no.RSW52, designed by Ronald Stennett-Willson in 1967.

*c1968* *9in (23cm) high*

**£100-150** **GC**

A Wedgwood Glass footed hurricane lantern, with ball knopped stem and mottled tortoiseshell bowl, designed by Ronald Stennett-Willson.

*c1970* *11.25in (28.5cm) high*

**£100-150** **GC**

A Wedgwood Glass cased squat vase, with mottled tortoiseshell pattern, designed by Ronald Stennett-Willson.

*c1970* *5in (13cm) high*

**£80-120** **GC**

A Wedgwood Glass cased squat vase, with striated pink pattern, designed by Ronald Stennett-Willson.

*c1970* *5in (13cm) high*

**£80-120** **GC**

A King's Lynn large orange mould blown 'Rustic' range vase, shape no. RSW20, and a small 'Top Hat' vase, shape no. RSW21, both designed by Ronald Stennett-Willson in 1967.

*This form was not produced after the take-over by Wedgwood in 1969. Orange is a rare colour.*

*1967-69* *Tallest 7.5in (19cm) high*

**Left: £100-150 Right: £80-120** **GC**

## A CLOSER LOOK AT A SET OF GLASSES

*These are slightly taller than the LSW611 tumbler, which had such a low centre of gravity that it was almost impossible to over-turn.*

*Lemington Glass was a subsidiary of G.E.C. Osram who, from 1959, produced around 40 designs by Stennett-Willson.*

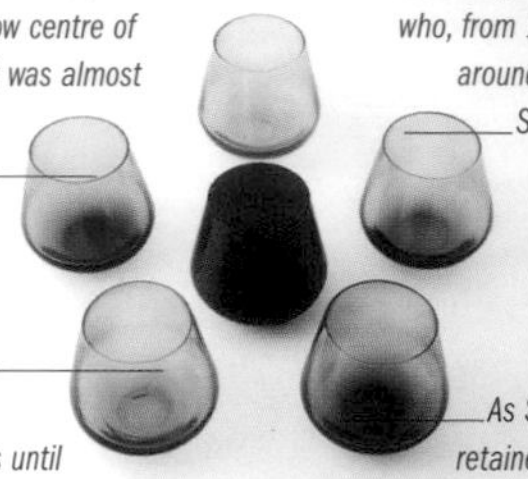

*The different colours were intentional as until then most table glass was colourless or produced in single colours, with different colours only coming from abroad.*

*As Stennett-Willson retained the copyright for his designs, they could be produced by any of the companies he worked for.*

A set of six Lemington Glass 'Harlequin' tumblers, shape no. LSW17, designed by Ronald Stennett-Willson in 1959.

*1960-62* *3.5in (9cm) high*

**£100-150** **MHT**

A King's Lynn amber decanter shape no. RSW43, with a clear, colourless stopper with internal bubbles, designed by Ronald Stennett-Willson in 1968.

*Produced from 1968-74, this decanter was produced in three colours, being colourless, blue or amber.*

*1968-74* *12.5in (32cm) high*

**£60-90** **GC**

A King's Lynn or Wedgwood Glass whisky decanter, shape no. RSW60, with heavy dimple moulded base, designed by Ronald Stennett-Willson in 1969.

*1969-72* *9.5in (25cm) high*

**£40-60** **GC**

A set of six J. Wuidart & Co. 'Harlequin' multicoloured 'Vortex' tumblers, designed by Ronald Stennett-Wilson.

*Previously thought to have been manufactured by Stromberg, these were in fact made by Stevens & Williams and appeared in Wuidart's 1953-54 catalogue listed as a 'Vortex Table Service in English Lead Crystal'.*

*Each 3.5in (9cm) high*

**£50-70** **MHT**

A King's Lynn green 'Topiary' paperweight, shape no. RSW11, designed by Ronald Stennett-Willson in 1967.

*4in (10cm) high*

**£20-30** **GC**

A King's Lynn orange 'Topiary' paperweight, shape no. RSW11, designed by Ronald Stennett-Willson in 1967.

*This combines the air bubbles found in the Saturn range with the randomly formed blobs of coloured glass found in the 'Topiary' range.*

*3.75in (9cm) high*

**£20-30** **GC**

## COLLECTORS' NOTES

- Liskeard Glass was founded by John Randle in Liskeard, Cornwall in 1970. Acting as a small, independent glassworks with only a few glassmakers, it produced tableware in colourless glass, and decorative wares in coloured and colourless glass. Tableware comprised of two candleholders, a range of wine glasses and jugs and tankards.
- However the company is best known for its art glass, most particularly the 'Knobbly' range designed by Jim Dyer in 1970. Very similar at first glance to Whitefriars' 'Knobbly' range, designed by William Wilson and Jim's relation Harry Dyer in 1963, it is different on closer inspection. Whereas Whitefriars' 'knobbles' are rounded, Liskeard's have a flat circle around a small raised, rounded lump. Colourless glass also heavily cases a single coloured core.
- The company was acquired in 1979 by Timothy Bristow, who had trained under Michael Harris at Isle of Wight Studio Glass. It is now run as Merlin Glass by Liam Carey, who acquired the company in 1983, having worked there since 1976. Production ranges changed during the 1980s, and the company now primarily produces art glass door handles.

A Liskeard Glass large colourless Knobbly vase.

*Liskeard Knobbly vases are typically stamped with a prunt of the company's monogram, as seen in the detail.*

*6in (15.5cm) high*

**£30-40** **GC**

A Liskeard Glass medium Knobbly vase.

*4.75in (13cm) high*

**£30-35** **GC**

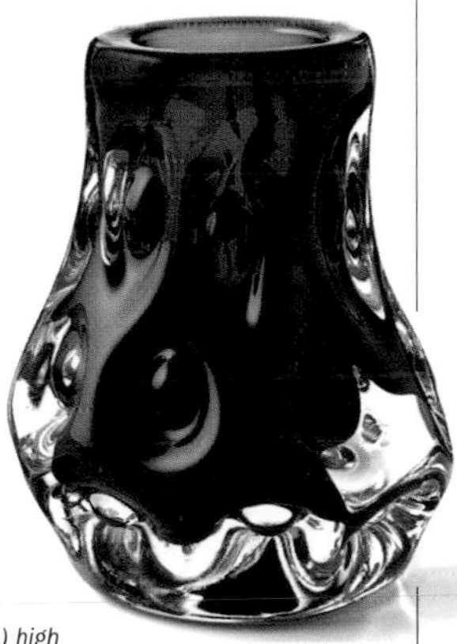

A Liskeard Glass large amethyst Knobbly vase.

*This strong, deep amethyst colour tends to be the more popular colourway.*

*5.75in (14.5cm) high*

**£30-40** **GC**

A Liskeard greyish blue Knobbly cylinder vase.

*4.25in (10.5cm) high*

**£25-35** **GC**

A Liskeard Glass colourless cylindrical Knobbly vase or candleholder.

*6.75in (10.5cm) high*

**£20-30** **GC**

A Liskeard Glass green Knobbly ashtray.

*4.5in (11.5cm) diam*

**£15-20** **GC**

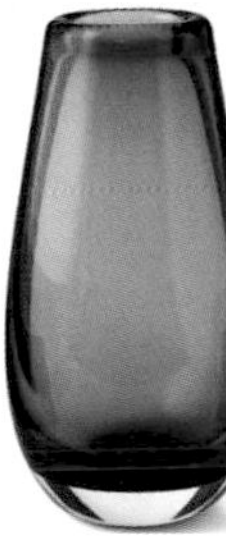

A Liskeard green teardrop-shaped vase, the base with impressed pontil mark.

*4.25in (10.5cm) high*

**£25-35** **GC**

## COLLECTORS' NOTES

- Michael Harris (1933-94) founded Mdina Glass on Malta in 1968. Harris had learnt studio glass techniques with Sam Herman at the RCA, and adapted them so that they could function on a commercial basis. Typical colours comprise the greens, blues and sandy ochres of the Mediterranean landscape. Forms are generally chunky, curving and are rendered in thick glass.
- Harris' most characteristic form, the 'Fish' vase, is the most desirable, but any piece that can be dated to the period he ran the studio (1968-72) is sought-after. Large pieces are rarer, as production was aimed at the export and tourist market, which favoured smaller sizes. Examples signed with Harris' name are exceptionally rare, as he did not like to sign his work. Pieces made after he left in 1972 tend to be less desirable, but all Mdina glass has risen in value over recent years and this looks set to continue.
- After leaving Malta, Harris founded his second factory on the Isle of Wight in the same year. Ranges from the 1970s tend to be executed with broad swirls of mottled, cloud-like colour, such as deep blues, pinks, golds and browns. The turning point in the factory's history came in 1978, when Harris and RCA student William Walker devised the 'Azurene' range, where surfaces are decorated with silver and 22ct gold leaf.
- As the market is still growing, look out for rarities produced for short periods of time, as these can be valuable. The experimentation begun by Harris has been continued by his son Timothy and widow Elizabeth, and many innovative and colourful ranges have been produced. As with Mdina, both values and the number of collectors are increasing rapidly, making this a vibrant and exciting collecting area.

A Mdina Glass globe vase, with bubbly dark green exterior and bubbly yellow interior, designed by Michael Harris.

c1969 5in (13cm) high

**£30-50 GC**

A Mdina Glass tapered vase, designed by Michael Harris, with bubbly dark green exterior and bubbly yellow interior.

*This is a very unusual shape. The thick 'button' rim and colour show this to be an early piece.*

c1969 6in (15.5cm) high

**£30-40 GC**

A rare Mdina Glass 'Chinese Bowl', designed by Michael Harris, with mottled green body and applied trailed colourless glass symbols.

c1971 4.25in (11cm) high

**£120-180 GC**

A large Mdina Glass doorstop, with internal colouring and heavy colourless casing.

*Large stops such as this are scarce as they often cracked apart when cooling in the annealing oven due to internal stresses.*

4.75in (12cm) high

**£50-60 GC**

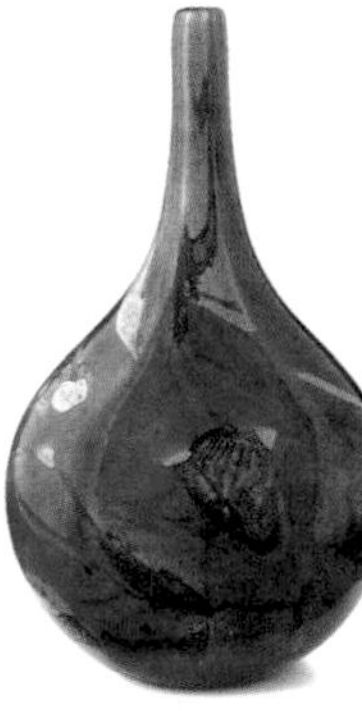

A 1970s-80s Mdina Glass 'Tiger' Lollipop bottle.

*'Tiger' and 'Earthtones' were introduced after Harris left Mdina Glass.*

8.75in (22.5cm) high

**£30-40 GC**

A scarce Mdina Glass vase, designed by Michael Harris and possibly made by Ettore or Vicente Boffo, with strapped patterns on an amber yellow ground and with polished concave pontil mark.

*Note the similarity to Peter Wheeler's Studio range for Whitefriars, the company the Boffos left to work for Harris on Malta. It is perhaps understandable that they bought some of their experience with them.*

c1971 7in (18cm) high

**£40-60 ART**

A late 1970s-80s Mdina Glass bottle, with blue-green trails over an orange body.

*12.75in (32.5cm) high*

**£20-30** **GC**

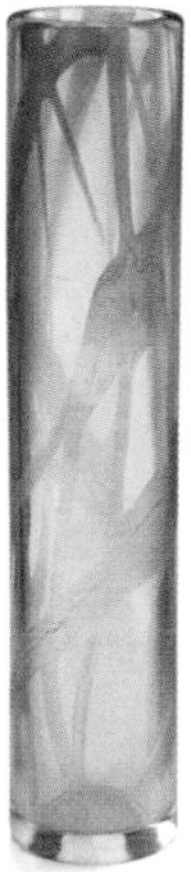

An Isle of Wight Studio Glass 'Ribbons White' cylinder vase.

*1988-90 9.75in (24.5cm) high*

**£50-80** **GC**

A late 1970s-80s Mdina Glass 'Earthtones' angular vase.

*4.25in (11cm) high*

**£30-40** **GC**

## A CLOSER LOOK AT AN ISLE OF WIGHT STUDIO GLASS VASE

*The impetus for this range was provided by Jonathan Harris, Michael's other son, although Michael and Timothy worked closely with him to create the production procedure and final result.*

*The process used to make this design is complex, using pre-designed screen-printed decals to create a 'reverse transfer' in 22ct gold leaf.*

*This shape is a unique prototype trial piece utilising decals from both the 'Elizabethan Tapestry' and 'Mosaic' ranges. It was not offered as part of the range.*

*The range was expensive due to the time involved in making it and comparatively few pieces sold, making examples hard to find today.*

An Isle of Wight Studio Glass 'Elizabethan Tapestry', 'Renaissance II' and 'Mosaic' vase.

*c1989 5in (13cm) high*

**£120-180** **PC**

An Isle of Wight Studio Glass violet swirl squat vase, with concave 'coachbolt' prunt.

*This piece is from an early experimental range. The 'coachbolt' prunt indicates that it was made in early 1973.*

*1973 3.25in (8cm) high*

**£70-100** **GC**

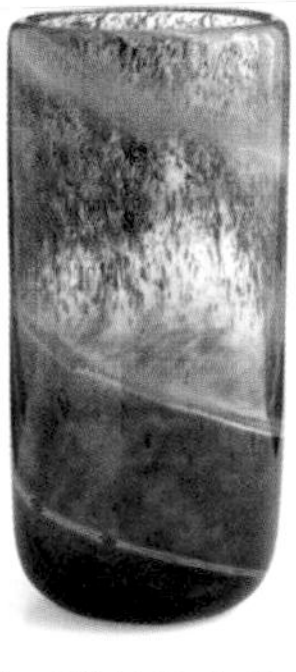

An Isle of Wight Studio Glass 'Aurene' vase, with streaks of silver chloride and impressed 'flame' pontil mark to base.

*1974-c1980 8.25in (21cm)*

**£80-120** **ART**

An Isle of Wight Studio Glass 'Aurene' double-cased bottle, with wide silver chloride streaks and impressed 'flame' pontil mark to base.

*This was originally intended to have a stopper. The double casing and deep colours suggest this to be an earlier example.*

*1974-c1978 5.25in (13.5cm)*

**£50-70** **GC**

### FIND OUT MORE...

**Michael Harris: Mdina Glass & Isle of Wight Studio Glass**, *by Mark Hill, published by Mark Hill Publishing, www.markhillpublishing.com, ISBN 978-0-9552865-1-3.*

**http://www.isleofwightstudioglass.co.uk**

## COLLECTORS' NOTES

- The 20th century has seen some remarkable changes and designs being produced on the historic island of Murano, in Venice. Glass has been made on the island since the 13th century, with glassmakers moving there from Venice to protect the mercantile capital city from the threat of fire spreading from the furnaces. As demand for their glass declined, factories and designers broke away from the centuries' old traditions, producing new, innovative and often exuberant designs.
- Many historic techniques, such as 'zanfirico', were updated from the 1930s onwards into a range of simple, modern forms with typically bright colours. By the 1950s, the revolution in design had really taken hold and, today, it is pieces from the middle decades of the century that are most keenly collected. 'Sommerso' glass is one of the most popular techniques. Always look for well-balanced and proportioned shapes with very clearly demarcated differently coloured layers.
- Value is largely based around the name of the glass factory, and particularly the designer. Notable names such as Seguso, Barovier & Toso and Venini occupy the top of the market, together with designers such as Fulvio Bianconi, Paolo Venini, Flavio Poli and Alfredo Barbini. Much work is not signed or marked, with identification being based on the form, techniques and colours. Original labels will also help to narrow down identification of a piece.
- However, many of their successful designs were copied by the numerous glass factories on the island, so it is best to research shapes, colours and forms in reference books and to handle and see as much identified glass as possible in museum collection in order to build up a good working knowledge. Animals are one area where this is important, as so many novelty forms are still being produced, and it is often easy to over look an important early design.
- Nevertheless, for those working on a smaller budget, this area of the market allows enormous scope to build a collection. Always consider technique and size, the more complicated and large the better, but don't forget the instant 'eye appeal' that a brightly coloured, modern design may have.
- For those with larger budgets, the new work of today's designers is certainly worth considering. Many, such as Vittorio Ferro, still use traditional techniques, but have updated them into a modern style. Others follow recent design trends such as Postmodernism, or develop artistic styles of their own, such as Bruno Pedrosa.

A Seguso Vetri d'Arte sommerso vase, model no.13886, designed by Flavio Poli, with original factory label.

*c1951* *14.75in (37cm) high*

**£1,000-1,500** **FIS**

An Archimede Seguso 'Polveri' vase, the clear glass body with applied gold foil and blue powdered enamel inclusions, with paper label reading "Made in Murano Italy".

*1953-54* *4.25in (11cm) high*

**£550-650** **QU**

An Archimede Seguso sommerso vase, the blue internal body cased in milky blue/white clear glass, with maker's label.

*c1965* *7.5in (19cm) high*

**£180-220** **QU**

A Seguso Vetri d'Arte cherry red and violet blue sommerso bowl with handle, designed by Flavio Poli.

*c1955*

**£300-400** **QU**

A Seguso Vetri D'Arte green and yellow sommerso tapering cylindrical vase, designed by Flavio Poli.

*c1960* *11.25in (28.5cm) high*

**£200-300** **GC**

## A CLOSER LOOK AT A SEGUSO VASE

*Sommerso is the Italian for 'submerged' and is used to describe this type of Murano cased glass.*

*Casing describes a molten coloured body that is seamlessly covered in another layer or an number of layers of differently coloured, or colourless, glass.*

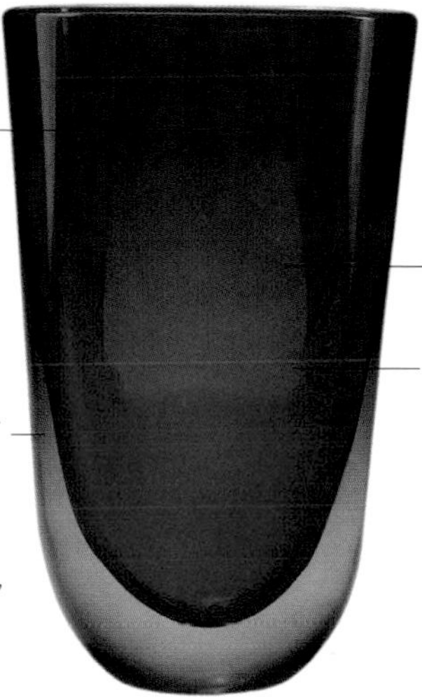

*Flavio Poli (1900-84) is considered the best and most famous sommerso designer and he won many awards for his designs from the 1940s-50s.*

*This is typical of his emphasis on simple, curving forms and vibrant colours. Look out for his large teardrop-shaped 'Valva' vases that can be worth over £2,000.*

A Seguso Vetri d'Arte sommerso vase, designed by Flavio Poli, the fuchsia coloured body cased in purple and pale blue glass.

*1954* *9.5in (24cm) high*

**£450-550** **QU**

A 1960s Seguso Vetri D'Arte large yellow cased over red sommerso bowl, probably designed by Flavio Poli, with polished rim, acid-etched "Seguso" to base.

*10.75in (27cm) diam*

**£250-350** **GC**

An Archimede Seguso pink glass vase, blown into a ribbed mould and twisted, cased in colourless glass, with remnants of paper label.

*Archimede Seguso joined a Murano-based glass company in 1933, which became Seguso Vetri D'Arte in 1937 with Seguso himself as master glass blower. Flavio Poli joined in 1934, and in 1942 Seguso left to found his own glassworks.*

*c1955* *10.75in (27cm) high*

**£400-600** **QU**

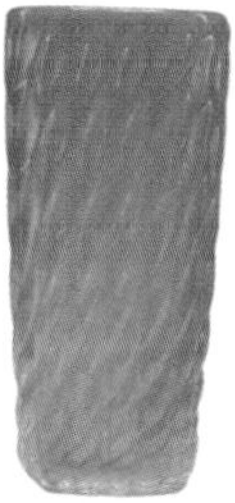

A Murano pink glass vase, attributed to Archimede Seguso, blown into a ribbed mould and twisted to give an optic pattern, and cased in colourless glass.

*c1955* *12in (30.5cm) high*

**£180-220** **QU**

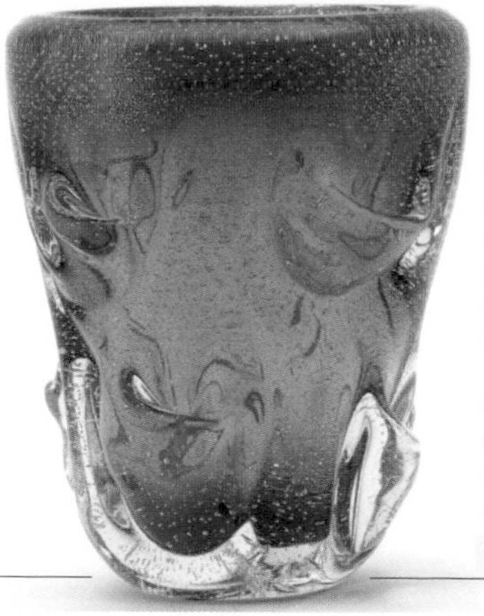

A Seguso Vetri D'Arte green cased bullicante vase, designed by Flavio Poli, with gold foil and bubble inclusions and exterior with pulled decoration.

*Bullicante is formed by rolling the molten body over a table set with pins, which indent the glass. The body is then covered with a layer of clear glass, trapping air bubbles in the indentations. Moulds containing protrusions can also be used. The process is typically repeated a number of times.*

*c1960* *8.5in (21.5cm) high*

**£250-350** **SDR**

A Venini fasce orrizontali decanter, designed by Fulvio Bianconi, with applied yellow ribbons on a blue ground, and a colourless stopper with a matching yellow ball.

*c1957* *16in (40.5cm) high*

**£750-850** **JH**

A Venini fasce orrizontali decanter, designed by Fulvio Bianconi, with applied red ribbons on a green ground and a matching spherical ball stopper, with three line "venini murano ITALIA" acid stamp.

*c1957* *19in (48.5cm) high*

**£1,000-1,500** **SDR**

A 1950s Venini fasce orrizontali decanter and two (of six) glasses, designed by Fulvio Bianconi, with red ribbons around smoky amber bodies and matching stopper, with pre-1960 acid stamp to base.

*Tumbler 4.5in (11.5cm) high*

**£1,200-1,800 (set)** **JH**

A Venini blue cased velato vase, designed by Paolo Venini, with ground surface, "venini murano ITALIA" acid stamp to base.

*With velato, the near-matte 'satin' surface effect is not created with acid, but is made through careful use of a grinding wheel.*

*c1955* *15in (38cm) high*

**£1,200-1,800** **QU**

A Venini a canne pitcher, the clear glass body overlaid with red, green and blue canes, with clear glass applied handle, with "venini murano ITALIA" acid stamp.

*c1955* *10in (25.5cm) high*

**£450-550** **SDR**

A Venini a bolle tapering cylindrical vase, with factory paper label.

*The 'a bolle' technique is essentially the same as that used for the 'bullicante' vase also in this section.*

*c1950* *13.5in (34.5cm) high*

**£450-550** **QU**

A Venini 'Opalino' vase, designed by Paolo Venini, the clear and opaque white body cased in chocolate brown glass, with "venini murano ITALIA" acid stamp.

*c1950* *15in (38cm) high*

**£220-280** **QU**

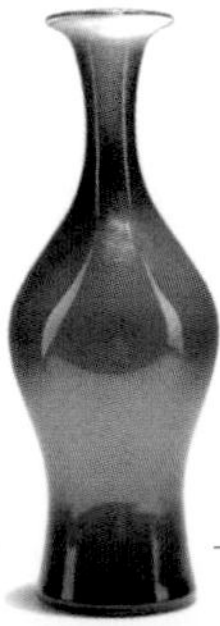

A Venini a fasce vase, designed by Fulvio Bianconi, the clear glass body with applied bands of black, green, red and blue glass.

*1953* *14in (35.5cm) high*

**£3,500-4,500** **QU**

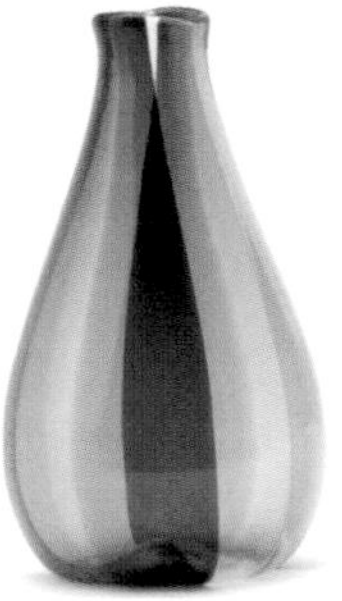

A Venini spicchi glass vase, designed by Fulvio Bianconi, with applied vertical panels in aubergine, yellow and charcoal glass over a clear, colourless glass body, with three line "venini murano ITALIA" acid stamp.

*This technique has been copied by many factories. This subtle combination of colours is very unusual.*

*8.25in (21cm) high*

**£1,500-2,000** **SDR**

A Venini occhi vase, designed by Tobia Scarpa in 1960, the clear, colourless glass body covered with red bordered murrines, with acid stamp to base.

*These bottles, and vases in the same pattern, are still being produced today. 'Occhi' is Italian for 'eyes'.*

*8.75in (22cm) high*

**£700-1,000** **FIS**

A Venini sommerso vase, designed by Paolo Venini, the orange body cased in olive green glass at the base and clear glass all over, with "venini murano ITALIA" acid stamp to base and factory paper label.

*This shape was designed for the finely cut Inciso range, and is very rarely found without the surface cutting.*

*c1954* *10.75in (27.5cm) high*

**£1,500-2,000** **QU**

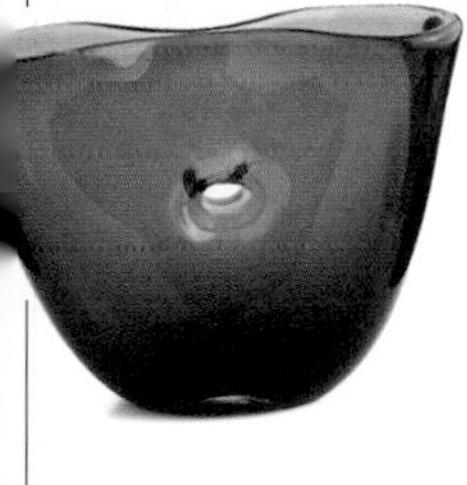

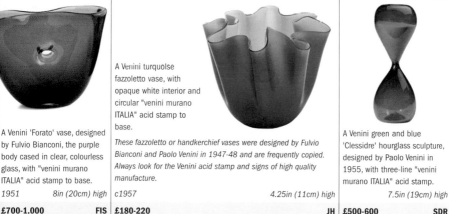

A Venini 'Forato' vase, designed by Fulvio Bianconi, the purple body cased in clear, colourless glass, with "venini murano ITALIA" acid stamp to base.

*1951* *8in (20cm) high*

**£700-1,000** **FIS**

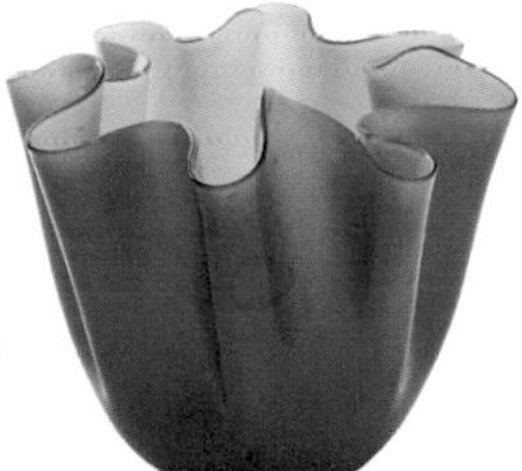

A Venini turquoise fazzoletto vase, with opaque white interior and circular "venini murano ITALIA" acid stamp to base.

*These fazzoletto or handkerchief vases were designed by Fulvio Bianconi and Paolo Venini in 1947-48 and are frequently copied. Always look for the Venini acid stamp and signs of high quality manufacture.*

*c1957* *4.25in (11cm) high*

**£180-220** **JH**

A Venini green and blue 'Clessidre' hourglass sculpture, designed by Paolo Venini in 1955, with three-line "venini murano ITALIA" acid stamp.

*7.5in (19cm) high*

**£500-600** **SDR**

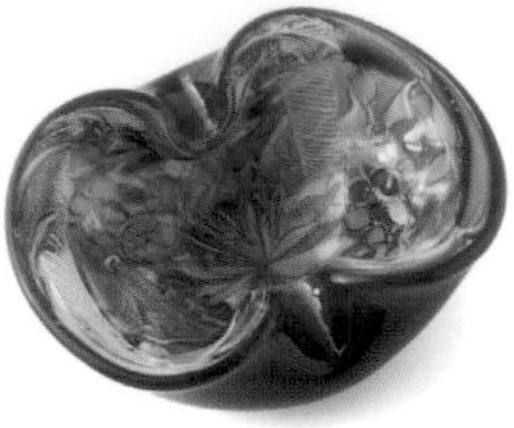

A 1950s Murano glass emerald green ashtray, probably from the A.V.e.M Bizzantina range, with murrine and aventurine inclusions, and cigarette rests.

*5.5in (14cm) diam*

**£30-40** **AG**

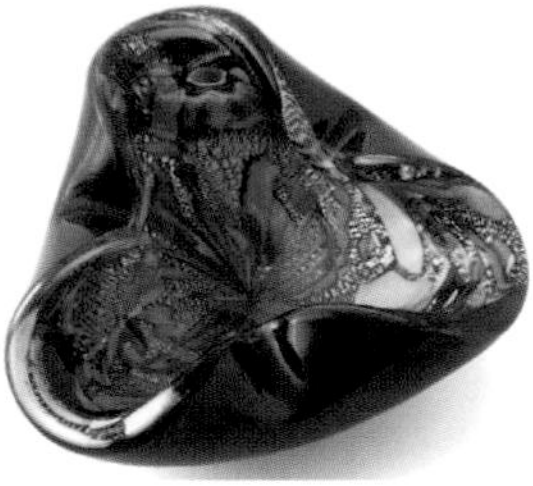

A 1950s A.V.e.M Murano glass dish, probably from the 'Bizzantina' range, with silver foil, coloured and murrine inclusions.

*6.25in (16cm) diam*

**£40-60** **AG**

## A CLOSER LOOK AT A MURANO GLASS DISH

*A.V.e.M. stands for 'Arte Vetreria Muranese', which was founded c1932. It flourished during the 1950s under the guidance of Giorgio Ferro and then designer Ansolo Fuga from 1955-68.*

*Small bowls, dishes and toothpick holders are more commonly found, and the colours of base glass include red, cobalt blue and green.*

*This range is known as 'Tutti Frutti' or 'Bizzantina' and is popular with collectors, even though a designer's name has not yet been firmly attributed.*

*Short sections of coloured canes, murrines and gold foil are added to the surface in a random pattern, making each piece unique.*

A 1950s A.V.e.M. Murano glass oval dish, with shaped edge and murrine, gold foil and cut cane inclusions on a red base.

*It is rumoured that a forgotten storeroom containing a large number of pieces from this range was discovered on Murano some years ago.*

*12.75in (32.5cm) wide*

**£120-150** **TGM**

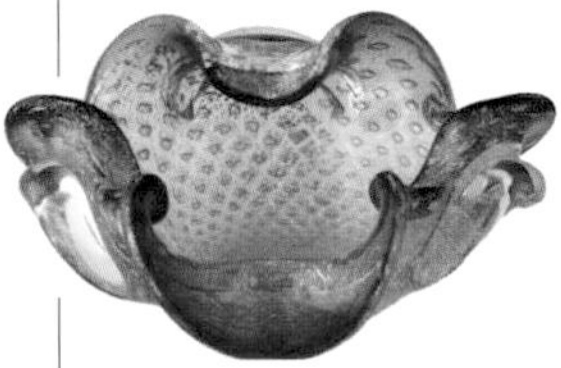

A 1960s green Murano glass bowl or ashtray with silver foil inclusions, internal controlled bubbles and a pulled rim.

*5in (13cm) long*

**£20-30** **BB**

A Murano glass tear-drop shaped sommerso vase, of green cased in yellow.

*This recalls the work of Flavio Poli for Seguso, although the quality and design indicates it is not by him.*

*c1960* *8in (20cm) high*

**£70-100** **QU**

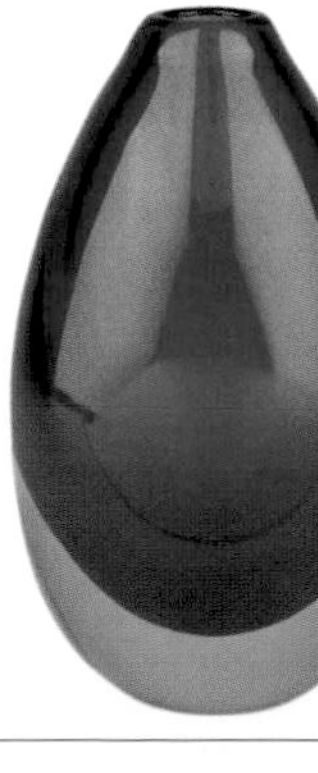

A Murano glass sommerso vase, with pulled side 'horn', the aqua green vase cased in darker green and heavily cased again in lemon yellow.

*8in (20cm) high*

**£150-250** **HLM**

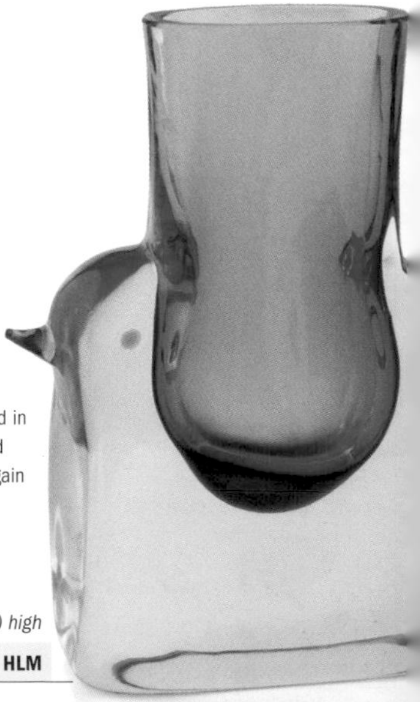

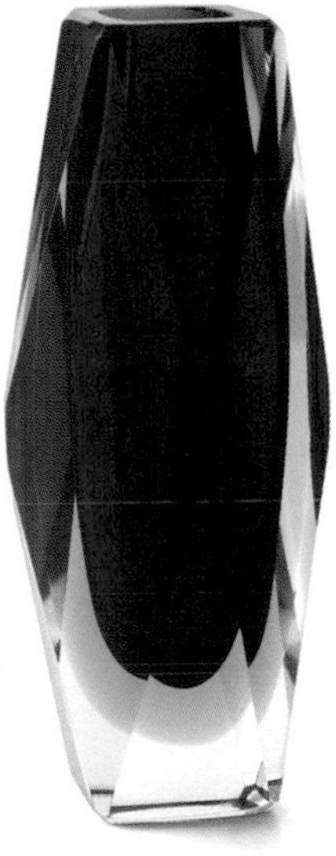

A Murano glass faceted red and yellow sommerso vase.

*6.75in (17cm) high*

**£50-80** **GAZE**

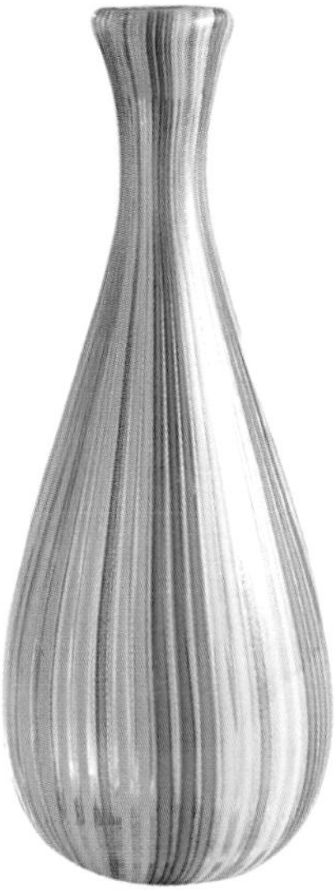

A Barovier & Toso 'Canne Policrome' tear-shaped glass bottle, lacks stopper, unmarked.

*10.75in (27.5cm) high*

**£300-400** **SDR**

A Barovier & Toso 'Pezzo Unico di Prova' vase, designed by Ercole Barovier, the clear glass body covered with a fused and flattened green trail in a lattice design.

*Barovier was founded in 1878, with Ercole Barovier (1889-1974) joining in 1919. He went on to bring great renown to the factory, using many different complex techniques. Perhaps his most famous are the swirling 'Oriente', the patchwork 'Intarsio' and the 'Parabolico' woven effect technique.*

*1955-60* *10in (25.5cm) high*

**£1,000-1,500** **QU**

A Barovier & Toso 'Euganeo' vase, designed by Ercole Barovier, in clear glass with green and white powdered enamel colouring and iridescent finish, with paper label.

*1951* *10.25in (26cm) high*

**£400-600** **QU**

A Barovier & Toso 'Efeso' jug, designed by Ercole Barovier, with bubbly cobalt blue metallic oxide inclusions on the surface.

*1964* *11.5in (29cm) high*

**£300-400** **QU**

A Barovier & Toso 'Neomurrino' vase, designed by Ercole Barovier, with white murrines with black edges on a clear glass core, the base engraved "Barovier & Toso Murano".

*1972* *8.75in (22cm) high*

**£600-700** **QU**

A Bruno Pedrosa 'Rainbow' sommerso and blown glass vase, with applied features, signed "Pedrosa 2003" to the base and with his official cruciform monogram mark.

*Brazilian Bruno Pedrosa designs his pieces and then guides the glassmaster's hand, using it as a brush to execute his designs. All his pieces including his paintings, tapestries, jewellery and sculpture are named and signed, as well as bearing his cruciform mark. He keeps a record of every piece he has made, when it was made, what it was called and to where or to whom it was sold.*

*2003* *12.5in (32cm) high*

**£2,000-3,000** **VET**

A Vittorio Ferro multicoloured terrazzo murrine carafe-style vase, designed, made by Vittorio Ferro and signed "Vittorio Ferro 1990" on the base.

*These murrines are known as 'terrazzo' from their appearance, which is similar to traditional Venetian floors, made from compressed stone granules. Vittorio Ferro (b.1932) is renowned for his complex murrine work, which he learnt and perfected at Fratelli Toso. He then worked at the De Majo factory in the 1980s and has since been producing his own designs, of which this is an excellent example.*

*1990* *14in (35.5cm) high*

**£2,800-3,200** **PC**

## A CLOSER LOOK AT A MURANO GLASS SCULPTURE

*Berengo Fine Arts was founded on Murano in 1990, and has its own furnace.*

*Riccardo Licata (b1929) is a notable glass artist as well as being a sculptor, stage designer, printmaker and mosaicist. His work is highly sought-after by collectors.*

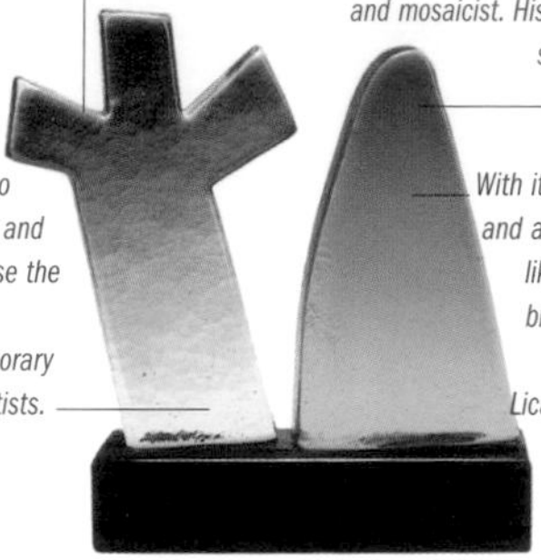

*It aims to promote and popularise the work of contemporary glass artists.*

*With its strong linear and almost 'cartoon like' elements in bright colours, it is typical of Licata's work and has a strong Postmodern aesthetic.*

A limited edition Berengo Fine Arts cast sculpture of a cross and horn or fin, designed by Riccardo Licata, from an edition of 99, engraved "Licata '90, 34/99".

*1990* *10.5in (26.5cm) high*

**£450-550** **QU**

A Bruno Pedrosa 'Bozios Sea Colour' blown and sommerso vase, signed on the base by Pedrosa and bearing his cruciform monogram.

*2003* *15.75in (40cm) high*

**£2,000-3,000** **VET**

A Memphis Extra three-piece yellow, blue and orange Murano glass sculpture, designed by Andrea Anastasio, the base engraved "A. Anastasio per Memphis.

*Memphis is the name of the influential group of Postmodern designers founded in 1980 and led by Ettore Sottsass. Many of their designs are still made today.*

*18.5in (47cm) long*

**£200-300** **QU**

A black and white 'incalmo' vase, designed and made by Andrea Zilio, the base signed "Andrea Zilio '99".

*Incalmo describes the process of joining two bodies of differently coloured glass together. It is a difficult process, as it is hard to make each piece the same size, and there is a risk of the piece splitting apart as the different colours of glass cool at different temperatures.*

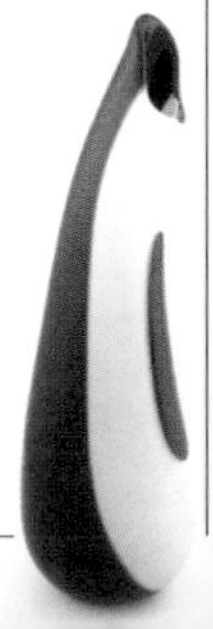

*1999* *19.75in (50cm) high*

**£2,000-2,500** **ANF**

An Alfredo Barbini flying duck, of hot-worked black glass with gold foil inclusions cased in clear, colourless glass, mounted on a hemispherical stand with gold foil inclusions.

*c1960* *7.5in (19cm) high*

**£150-200** **QU**

A 1950s-60s Vetro Artistico Vetreria hot-worked cockerel, with "Made in Murano" gold and red foil label.

*11.75in (30cm) high*

**£30-40** **BB**

A pair of Seguso Vetri d'Arte sommerso ducks, designed by Flavio Poli, of hot-worked cherry red and cobalt blue glass, cased in clear, colourless glass.

*Although bird figurines were produced by many glass factories on Murano, these examples are very large, well-made and were designed by a famous artist, known for his sommerso pieces.*

*c1960* *Tallest 18.25in (46.5cm) high*

**£600-700** **QU**

An Aureliano Toso duck, designed by Dino Martens, of clear, colourless glass with internal orange and white threads, the applied beak, claws and eyes with gold foil inclusions.

*Although this threaded pattern had been used for many decades, this format is recognisable as being by Martens, or those that copied him.*

*c1960* *10in (25.5cm) high*

**£350-450** **QU**

A Murano glass black and white striped bird, with an orange beak, unmarked.

*5.25in (13.5cm) high*

**£10-15** **BB**

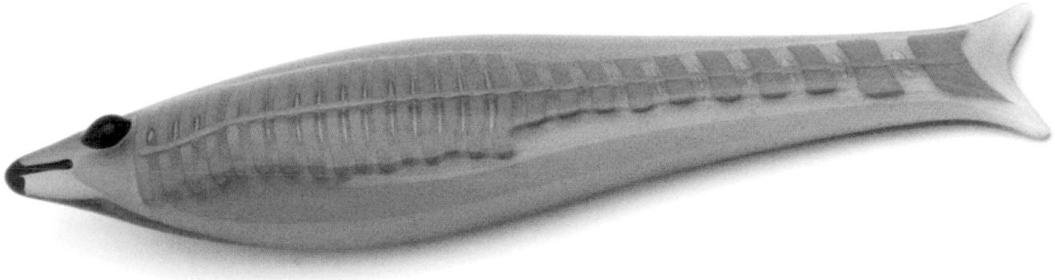

An early 1950s Venini & Cie. blown glass fish, designed by Kenneth George Scott, in ochre, orange and black with applied details.

*13.5in 34.5cm) long*

**£650-750** **SDR**

A Venini & Cie. 'Corroso' fish, designed by Tyra Lundgren, of wine-red glass with applied fins and tail and a matte iridescence.

*This also appears in Venini's catalogue raisonée in blue. Freelance designer Lundgren designed tableware for Finland's Arabia and Czechoslovakia's Moser, before working at Venini from 1937. Her 1937-38 pieces include a leaf-shaped bowl, birds and fish, all of which won awards at the famed Biennale exhibitions. Due to the onset of WWII, examples are scarce today.*

*c1937-38* *23.5in (60cm) long*

**£3,000-4,000** **QU**

A Vetreria Gino Cenedese cased fish, designed by Antonio da Ros, with yellow, blue and pink glass inclusions.

*c1950* *13.75in (34.5cm) long*

**£800-1,200** **VZ**

A Murano glass 'aquarium', designed by or after Riccardo Licata for Gino Cenedese, the clear glass block with two multicoloured fish and pond weed.

*c1960* *3.5in (9cm) high*

**£100-150** **QU**

A Vetreria Artistica Barovier & Cie hot-worked glass monkey, designed by Ercole Barovier, in iridised clear and dark violet glass.

*This is an exceptionally early date for such a whimsical design. Barovier made a small number of animal forms during this period, all of which are very rare and highly desirable, particularly the crackled 'Primavera' series which could never be repeated.*

*1930* *7.25in (18.5cm) high*

**£2,500-3,500** **QU**

A colourless, hot-worked glass horse's head, unmarked but probably by Seguso.

*These heads are actually quite complex to make as they are not moulded, but made freehand by trailing and manipulating the molten glass. This is a well-proportioned example.*

*8.75in (22cm) high*

**£150-200** **GC**

An Alfredo Barbini squirrel candlestick, of hot-worked clear glass cased in black, the branch, fruit and nuts in clear glass with coloured, gold foil and gold powder inclusions.

*c1960* *7.25in (18.5cm) high*

**£700-1,000** **QU**

**FIND OUT MORE...**

**DK Collectors' Guide: 20th-Century Glass**, *by Judith Miller, published by DK, 2005, www.dk.com/judithmiller*

## COLLECTORS' NOTES

- In 1819, the Moor Lane Glasshouse on Brierley Hill, near Stourbridge, was renamed Stevens & Williams. In 1931, it gained the name Royal Brierley after a visit from King George V. Although it is best know for its cut and engraved glass designs, it also produced a small number of other art glass ranges.
- As the studio glass movement took hold and handmade 'studio glass' became more desirable and popular, Royal Brierley decided to take advantage of the trend. In 1986, they asked Michael Harris at Isle of Wight Studio Glass to design a range that gave the effect of studio glass but could be easily produced on their factory production line.
- Harris and his family adapted one of their existing ranges, which had a lightly textured surface that was strongly iridised, by fuming it with metallic oxides. Brierley took the range on and applied it to vase and bowl forms, perfume atomisers and to existing light fitment forms. It became known as the 'Studio' range and was produced with different surface effects in pink and white and a deep blue/black.
- Most pieces bear a 'Royal Brierley Studio' acid stamp on the base, but gold foil labels were also used. Examine the edges of rims carefully for signs of damage such as chips and smaller 'fleabites' as these can be hard to satisfactorily polish away without compromising the surface design.

A Royal Brierley 'Studio' range bowl, with acid stamp to base.

*Even though the form is the same, note the slightly different finish to the example below.*

*8in (20cm) diam*

**£50-70** **GC**

A Royal Brierley 'Studio' range bowl.

*Turning this bowl over shows clearly that the form is an inverted lampshade.*

*8in (20cm) diam*

**£50-70** **GC**

A Royal Brierley 'Studio' range low baluster vase.

*4in (10cm) high*

**£20-30** **GC**

A Royal Brierley 'Studio' range small globe vase.

*4.25in (11cm) high*

**£30-40** **MHC**

A Royal Brierley 'Studio' range pink vase.

*9.25in (23.5cm) high*

**£50-80** **GC**

A Royal Brierley 'Studio' range white mottled vase.

*9in (23cm) high*

**£70-100** **GC**

The trial piece for the Royal Brierley 'Studio' range, designed and made by Michael and Timothy Harris at Isle of Wight Studio Glass, signed "TMH Nov 86 C".

*1986* *7in (18cm) high*

**£500-700** **PC**

## COLLECTORS' NOTES

- Scandinavian glass from the post war period has boomed in popularity, and value, recently. Not only have collectors re-appraised its importance to 20th century design over the past decade, but the area has received increasing amounts of coverage outside specialist publications, drawing popular attention. As more research is published, and designs are attributed to factories and designers, the area continues to grow.
- There are three main styles to consider; an asymmetric style with curving forms and cool colours inspired by natural forms such as buds and leaves; a clean-lined, geometric Modern style that is typically found in bright colours, and styles with textured surfaces. Generally speaking, the asymmetric style dates from the 1950s, while glass with textured surfaces and the geometric look, date from the mid-1960s to '70s.
- The factory and the designer count considerably towards value, and an engraved mark on the base will help identify both. However, the overall style of a piece, the colour, and the way it is made will also help to identify the maker and the designer. Factories to look out for include Orrefors, Kosta Boda, Iittala, Riihimäen Lasi Oy and Holmegaard.
- Leading designers whose work was influential include Vicke Lindstrand, Simon Gate, Tapio Wirrkala, Sven Palmqvist, Per Lütken, Tamara Aladin and Nanny Still. Some designers, such as Lindstrand, moved between factories, and factories themselves were frequently merged with others. However, it is also often the 'eye appeal' or technical skill of a piece that draws attention.
- Pieces by Riihimäen Lasi Oy and Holmegaard are currently popular, and look to remain so, for their modern 'Pop' forms and bright colours. Keep an eye out for secondary factories and designers whose work is still being researched, as now may be the time to buy. These include Strömbergshyttan, John Orwar Lake for Ekenas, and Eric Höglund for Boda.
- Always consider how a piece was made, and its colour, as some techniques and colours can be rare. A unique 'graal' vase will always be worth more than a mould blown production line piece, although both have their fans. Examine pieces closely, avoiding those with chips, cracks, scratches or lime marks from water. These detract from the purity of colour and form so typical of this type of glass.

An Afors glass vase, designed by Ernest Gordon, with pulled rim and engraved tri-partite stylized face design, the base engraved "Ernest Gordon afors GS 1071".

*Ernest Gordon (b.1926) worked for Afors from 1954-61. He produced designs that were highly modern in terms of the engraved design or colour, yet also followed the organic, asymmetric trend of Scandinavian glass design of the time. Attributed designs are not as commonly found today as those by other designers.*

*c1956* *8.25in (21cm) high*

**£300-400** **GM**

A late 1960s Boda Afors footed bowl, designed by Bertil Vallien, the foot inscribed "Boda Afors B.Vallien".

*Afors and Boda merged in 1964, and would have probably used both brand names for a period of time.*

*7in (18cm) high*

**£70-100** **NPC**

A Kosta bud vase, designed by Vicke Lindstrand, with interior acid-etched surface, signed on the base "Kosta LH1834".

*The 'L' prefix indicates this was designed by Lindstrand. c1963*

*6in (15cm) high*

**£60-90** **MHT**

A Kosta facet-cut waisted vase, by an unknown designer, the base engraved "Kosta XXX 5768".

*7.5in (19cm) high*

**£40-60** **MHT**

A Kosta cylindrical vase, designed by Vicke Lindstrand, with graduated colours and internal air bubble and original label, the base signed "Kosta LH 1889".

*c1965* *9in (23cm) high*

**£180-220** **MHT**

A Kosta 'Oktober Nr.4661' glass vase, designed by Vicke Lindstrand, engraved all over with a scene of stylized trees, the base engraved "Kosta 46661 Lindstrand".

*1951* *9.5in (24cm) high*

**£700-1,000** **GM**

A large Kosta Boda 'Network' bottle, designed by Bertil Vallien, from the Artist Collection, signed to base.

*The blue prunt shows that this was a studio, or 'atelier', piece. This large size is hard to find.*

*10.75in (37.5cm) high*

**£150-200** **MHT**

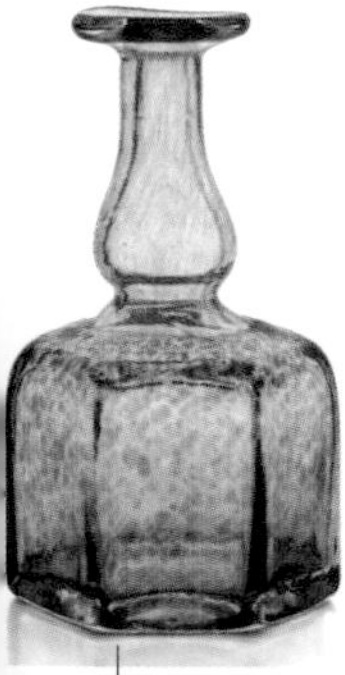

A Kosta Boda miniature bottle, designed by Bertil Vallien, from the 'Artist Collection'.

*This bottle is from a small range of handmade glass that was also given away to first class passengers on SAS, Scandinavia's airline. The range has risen enormously in popularity, and value, over the past year.*

*4in (10cm) high*

**£25-35** **NPC**

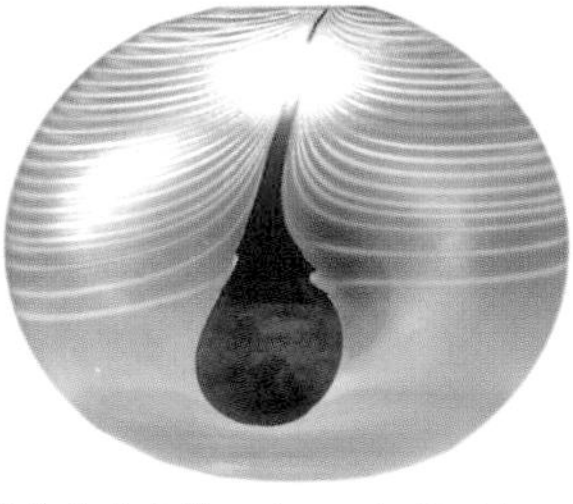

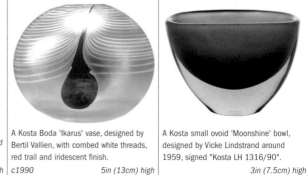

A Kosta Boda 'Ikarus' vase, designed by Bertil Vallien, with combed white threads, red trail and iridescent finish.

*c1990* *5in (13cm) high*

**£100-150** **QU**

A Kosta small ovoid 'Moonshine' bowl, designed by Vicke Lindstrand around 1959, signed "Kosta LH 1316/90".

*3in (7.5cm) high*

**£70-100** **MHT**

An Orrefors octagonal vase, designed by Simon Gate, finely engraved with a figure of an exotic dancer, with machine-cut rim.

*c1935* *9.5in (24cm) high*

**£180-220** **JN**

An Orrefors vase, designed by Vicke Lindstrand, with optic ribbing and engraved pattern of a lady amidst bubbles, the base engraved "of.L.1191.33.E.9".

*1982* *8.25in (21cm) high*

**£800-1,200** **GM**

An Orrefors 'Fiskegraal' vase, designed by Edward Hald in 1937, the base signed "Hald Orrefors 1938".

*1938* *5in (13cm) high*

**£2,000-3,000** **VSP**

## A CLOSER LOOK AT A ORREFORS VASE

*The graal technique was developed at Orrefors by glass master Knut Bergqvist and designer Simon Gate in 1917.*

*Surprisingly for such a complex and time-consuming process, this design was part of Orrefors' standard production range and thousands were produced from 1937-88.*

*A coloured 'blank' is built up and engraved or cut with the design before it is cased in clear glass and blown outwards and shaped to create its final form.*

*The '1596D' engraving allows this piece to be dated to 1952 - early examples tend to be more complex and desirable.*

An Orrefors 'Fiskegraal' (Fish Graal) vase, designed by Edward Hald in 1937, the base engraved "Graal 1596D" and "Edward Hald".

*1952* *4.75in (12cm) high*

**£450-550** **JN**

An Orrefors Art Deco cut glass footed bowl, designed by Vicke Lindstrand, the base signed "Orrefors LA355" and dated.

*1931*

**£100-150** **JH**

An Orrefors 'Ariel' vase, designed by Ingeborg Lundin, the base engraved "Orrefors Ariel Nr. 760 N Ingeborg Lundin".

*Ariel was developed by Vicke Lindstrand, Gustav Bergqvist and Edvin Ohrstrom in 1937, and is similar to the graal process. The difference is that the sandblasted design is deeper, producing cavities that are filled with air, which is trapped under the final, colourless clear layer of glass. As a result, the designs tend to be simpler and more 'fluid'.*

*1964* *6in (15.5cm) high*

**£700-1,000** **QU**

An Orrefors 'Ravenna' bowl, designed by Sven Palmqvist in 1948, the base engraved "Orrefors Ravenna Pu 230 Sven Palmqvist".

*Ravenna is made by fusing flat glass masses on to a body to form a 'blank' and sandblasting a design into it, here with squares. These concave areas are then filled with coloured glass powder. The piece is then reheated, cased and blown into a mould to give the final form. The effect is like stained glass windows or a Byzantine mosaic, the latter of which Palmqvist said was his inspiration.*

*1952* *10in (25.5cm) wide*

**£700-1,000** **QU**

An Orrefors 'Expo' large charger, designed by Sven Palmqvist, the base engraved "Orrefors Expo PM 243-62 Sven Palmqvist".

*1962* *20.5in (52cm) diam*

**£350-450** **FRE**

An Orrefors freeblown blue vase, designed by Nils Landberg, the base engraved "Expo N.IL 925-68".

*1968* *6in (15cm) high*

**£100-150** **GAZE**

An Orrefors opalescent bowl, designed by Sven Palmqvist from 1948, from the Selina range, with wavy rim, signed on the base "Orrefors Tal 3090/1".

*Orrefors' opalescent glass is rare. The Selina range is typified by its free-formed, wavy rims.*

*2.25in (6cm) high*

**£30-50** **TGM**

A Swedish Orrefors red 'Fuga' centrifuge moulded bowl, designed by Sven Palmqvist, the base moulded "Orrefors Fuga".

*This bowl is 'cast' by spinning the mould at speed in a centrifuge, with the molten glass being forced around the mould evenly by the forces. Palmqvist first considered the idea in 1934, but it was not until 1954 that he formulated a method, won a patent for it, and production began. Prestigious Stockholm department store NK was the first to sell the range.*

*5in (12.5cm) diam*

**£10-15** **GAZE**

An Orrefors 'Dusk' vase, designed by Nils Landberg in 1956, the base engraved "Orrefors 3595/1".

*7in (17.5cm) high*

**£70-100** **BMN**

A late 1970s-80s Iittala 'Stellaria' vase, designed by Tapio Wirkkala in 1978, the base engraved "Tapio Wirkkala 3450".

*9.5in (24cm) diam*

**£150-250** **QU**

An Iittala vase, designed by Tapio Wirkkala in 1959, with acid-etched and polished finish, the base signed "Tapio Wirkkala 3502".

*This vase is often called the 'Cog' due to the shape's resemblance when viewed from above. It was also available in different colours.*

*1959-69* *6.5in (16.5cm) high*

**£250-300** **MHT**

## A CLOSER LOOK AT AN IITTALA VASE

*The natural inspiration behind the bark-like surface of this range is typical of much Scandinavian glass. This range also set a trend for textured glass in the 1960s and '70s.*

*Initially the glass was blown into a wooden mould that had a bark-like texture. Later textured metal moulds were used to ensure consistency.*

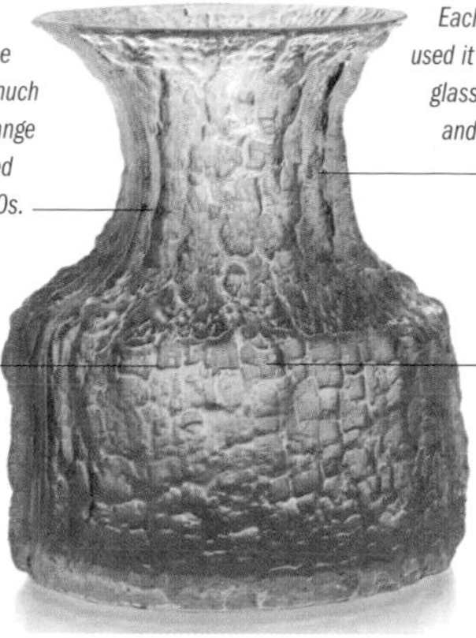

*Each time the mould was used it was burnt by the hot glass, altering the surface and reducing the level of detail.*

*This example is large and has an excellent level of all over texture, making it highly desirable.*

An Iittala 'Finlandia' mould-blown vase, designed by Timo Sarpaneva in 1964, the base engraved "Timo Sarpaneva 7751".

*The range consisted of a number of shapes, and was produced from 1964-71.*

*c1965* *7in (17.5cm) high*

**£500-600** **GM**

An Iittala 'Avena' vase, designed by Tapio Wirkkala in 1968, model no. 3429, the base engraved "Tapio Wirkkala".

*This is also available in clear, colourless glass.*

*c1970* *9.5in (24cm) high*

**£250-300** **QU**

An Iittala glass cased vase, designed by Tapio Wirkkala in 1960, with sandblasted and polished finish, the base engraved "Tapio Wirkkala 3306".

*1960-65* *7in (18cm) high*

**£250-350** **BONBAY**

A pair of Iittala 'Ultima Thule' tankards, designed by Tapio Wirkkala in 1968, with original labels.

*This is one of Wirrkala's most celebrated and commercially successful designs, and is still available today in certain shapes. The design was a commission for Finnair, for use in its cabin meal service, with the first piece being a tumbler. A year later, the range was widened to include other shapes, and was also available on general release.*

*4.75 in (12cm) high*

**£50-70** **MHT**

A Holmegaard smoke grey asymmetric dish, designed by Per Lütken, the base engraved "Holmegaard 19 PL 57".

*1957* *12.75in (32.5cm) long*

**£60-80** **GAZE**

A Holmegaard pale green 'Naebvase' (Beak vase), designed by Per Lütken in 1951 and produced from 1952-76, the base engraved "Holmegaard 19 PL 57".

*1957* *10.25in (26cm) high*

**£30-50** **GAZE**

A Holmegaard/Odense large amber 'Gul' vase, designed by Otto Brauer in 1962.

*Look out for versions with a white interior cased in a bright colour such as red, as these can be worth up to three times more, depending on size and colour.*

*1962-80* *20in (51cm) high*

**£80-120** **FD**

A Holmegaard blue and white cased glass vase, designed by Per Lütken in 1968, from the 'Carnaby' range.

*Note where the transparent blue casing is thinner, resulting in a lighter tone.*

*1969-76* *9in (23cm) high*

**£100-150** **FD**

A pair of Kastrup graduated opaque white Opaline-type small shot glasses, designed by Jacob Bang, each with tapered foot and wider tapered bowl.

*These accompanied Bang's angular opaque white decanter with a raffia bound neck.*

*4.25in (11cm) high*

**£30-50** **HLM**

A 1970s Holmegaard/Odense yellow 'Hivert' schnapps decanter, designed by Hjordis Olsson and Charlotte Rude in 1970, with white metal topped cork stopper.

*Without the stopper, the decanter is generally worth only half this value.*

*5in (13cm) high*

**£30-50** **MHT**

A Holmegaard 'Perlemer' studio goblet, designed by Per Lütken, the foot engraved "Holmegaard PL 2380".

*c1970* *7in (18cm) high*

**£80-100** **GC**

A Riihimäen Lasi Oy large red 'Kasperi' vase, designed by Erkki Tapio Siiroinen, with original label and fully signed to base.

*c1974* *12in (30.5cm) high*

**£120-180** **MHT**

A Riihimaen Lasi Oy small green 'Kasperi' vase, designed by Erkki Tapio Siiroinen, with original label and fully signed to base.

*c1974* *8.25in (21cm) high*

**£70-90** **MHT**

A Riihimäen Lasi Oy blue 'Pompadour' vase or candlestick, designed by Nanny Still in 1967, with original label.

*1967-73* *7.5in (19cm) high*

**£40-60** **MHT**

A Riihimäen Lasi Oy 'Aitan Lukko' (Grain Barn) clear mould blown vase, designed by Helena Tynell in 1968, from the Vanha Kartano (Country House) series.

*1968-74* *8.25in (21cm) high*

**£100-150** **GAZE**

A Riihimäen Lasi Oy smoke 'Aitan Lukko' (Grain Barn) vase, designed by Helena Tynell in 1974, from the 'Country House' range.

*1968-74* *7.75in (21.5cm) high*

**£120-180** **MHT**

A Riihimäen Lasi Oy red 'Emma' vase, designed by Helena Tynell in 1968, from the Vanha Kartano (Country House) series.

*Red is one of the most desirable colours, perhaps due to its vibrancy and the fact that it is so typical of this type of Scandinavian glass from this period.*

*1968-74* *8.25in (21cm) high*

**£100-150** **MHT**

A Riihimäen Lasi Oy yellow 'Piironki' vase, designed by Helena Tynell in 1968, from the Vanha Kartano (Country House) series.

*1968-74* *8.25in (21cm) high*

**£120-140** **MHT**

A Riihimäen Lasi Oy mould blown cased vase, designed by Tamara Aladin in 1967, shape no.1472.

*This vase was included in Riihimäki's 'Export Collection' sold by retailers such as Boots the Chemists in the UK during the 1970s. Although many of the designs in this collection have not yet been fully attributed, this is one of the few designs that is listed in Riihimäki catalogues as being by Aladin.*

*9.75in (25cm) high*

**£50-80** **MHT**

A Riihimäen Lasi Oy 'Ruusu' (Rose) mould blown vase, designed by Tamara Aladin in 1970, shape no. 1477.

*This form is also available in a shorter size.*

*1970-76* *12in (30cm) high*

**£50-80** **GAZE**

A late 1970s Riihimäen Lasi Oy tobacco brown vase, probably designed by Tamara Aladin.

*7in (18cm) high*

**£25-35** **NPC**

A Riihimäen Lasi Oy 'Aurinko' (Sun) mould blown vase, designed by Helena Tynell in 1964, with original 'Finncristall' foil label.

*These were produced in a number of different colours, and with wide or narrow neck rims. Beware of later Italian copies, which tend to be lighter in weight and often have a slightly rougher surface. The Finncristall label indicates an exported piece.*

*1964-74* *5in (12.5cm) high*

**£30-40** **GAZE**

## A CLOSER LOOK AT A CARAFE

*This form was inspired by the onion shaped domes of the Kremlin in Moscow, hence its name.*

*It is made up of two pieces; a carafe (below) and a stoppered decanter (above), with each piece being in a different colour.*

*Kaj Franck (1911-89) was a renowned modern glass designer who revolutionised the company's designs as its art director from 1950-76, bringing them into the modern age.*

*The design inspired Frank Thrower to produce his FT4 decanter design for Dartington Glass in 1967 - neither were commercially successful and are rare today.*

A Finnish Nuutajärvi Nöstjo glass 'Kremlin Kellot' (Kremlin Bells) carafe, designed by Kaj Franck in 1957.

*c1959*

*13.5in (34cm) high*

**£800-1,200** **GM**

A Björkshult amber mould blown beaker, with two ribs and original label.

*Björkshult glass was imported into the UK by Wuidart, run by Ronald Stennett-Willson, and also produced some of Stennett-Willson's own designs.*

*3.25in (8cm) high*

**£7-10** **GC**

An Ekenas bowl, designed by John Orwar-Lake, with internal, cloudy bubbles, signed "Ekenas Sweden Jo Lake L.1456/17".

*Little is known about Orwar-Lake, but vases and bowls in this colourway tend to be the most commonly found of his designs. Less common is a reddy-orange colourway, but this tends to be less desirable. The rarest and most valuable shape in either colourway is a large charger, which can be worth £200.*

*8.25in (21cm) wide*

**£80-120** **MHT**

A 1960s Magnor large green cased dish, designed by Eystein Sandnes, with white internal spirals to the underside, the base engraved "Magnor".

*Sandnes (b.1924) also designed for ceramics manufacturer Porsgrund.*

*15.75in (40cm) wide*

**£70-90** **MHT**

A Nuutajärvi Nötsjo controlled air bubble small bowl, designed by Kaj Franck, the base engraved "Nuutajärvi'.

*2.75in (7cm) high*

**£80-120** **BB**

A Ruda green mould blown vase, with abstract high relief design.

*This design is often mistakenly attributed to one the Sklo Union factories in Czechoslovakia.*

*c1965* *7in (18cm) high*

**£50-70** **MHT**

A tall goblet, attributed to Bengt Orup at Johanfors.

*15.75in (40cm) high*

**£50-70** **MHT**

A Swedish tall red waisted cased vase, possibly by Gullaskruf.

*11in (28cm) high*

**£18-22** **NPC**

A cylindrical waisted brown, cased vase, with an internal bubble to base, by an as yet unidentified maker.

*9in (23cm) high*

**£25-35** **NPC**

A Swedish large tiered blue mould blown vase, by an as yet unidentified maker.

*11.5in (29cm) high*

**£30-40** **NPC**

A Strömbergshyttan lead crystal decanter, probably designed by Gerda Strömberg, with original label.

*12in (30cm) high*

**£60-80** **NPC**

A Scandinavian clear pillow-shaped bowl, engraved with "Norwegian Motorists' Visit September 1955", and with a monogram, but otherwise unsigned.

*c1955* *6.75in (17cm) high*

**£25-35** **GAZE**

## FIND OUT MORE...

**20th-Century Glass,** *by Judith Miller, published by DK, 2005.*

**Scandinavian Ceramics & Glass In The Twentieth Century,** *by Jennifer Opie, published by V&A Publications, 1989.*

**20th Century Factory Glass,** *by Leslie Jackson, published by Mitchell Beazley, 2000.*

## COLLECTORS' NOTES

- The creation of art glass spheres and orbs derived from the creation of contemporary glass marbles. As glass artists learned new skills, they pushed the boundaries by making progressively larger examples. The designs are not painted on the outside, but are made from glass and contained within, and make up, the sphere.
- Examples need to be handled to experience the design and artistry properly. It takes great skill to make most examples. The best are highly intricate, with many components formed in hot glass, and often take advantage of the optical properties of glass and use the borosilicate, 'crystal' glass domes to magnify the design.
- Names to look out for include David Salazar, Rolf & Genie Wald, Paul Standkard, Christopher Rice and Chris Juedemann. However, also look out for the work of new, younger artists. Many incorporate references to pop culture, making this a young and vibrant market. The use of murrines (glass tiles containing a pattern), the 'rake pull' technique and underwater scenes are currently particularly popular.

A Drew Fritts 'Luna Moth' rake pull sphere, from the Butterfly Series.

*Rake pull involves pulling and dragging the molten glass into a pattern.*

*2in (5cm) diam*

**£50-80** BGL

An F. Eddie Seese furnace worked six-panel lobe core swirl sphere, with rows of small controlled bubbles, signed "F.E.S. 05".

*1.75in (4.5cm) diam*

**£30-40** BGL

A Fritz Lauenstein multi-coloured onionskin furnace sphere.

*1.5in (4cm) diam*

**£12-18** BGL

A James Hart abstract dichroic core reverse twist onionskin sphere.

*1.75in (4.5cm) diam*

**£18-22** BGL

A Scott Young undersea bouquet torchwork sphere, with murrine fish to the sides.

*1.25in (3cm) diam*

**£10-15** BGL

An Andrew Gregorich WigWam Rake Pull sphere, with torchworked surface decoration.

*These 'WigWam' designs are becoming increasingly popular.*

*2in (5cm) diam*

**£80-120** BGL

A Jerry Kelly torchwork murrine sphere.

*The coloured elements are 'pulled' into the sphere under the pressure of a vacuum.*

*1.75in (4.5cm) diam*

**£35-45** BGL

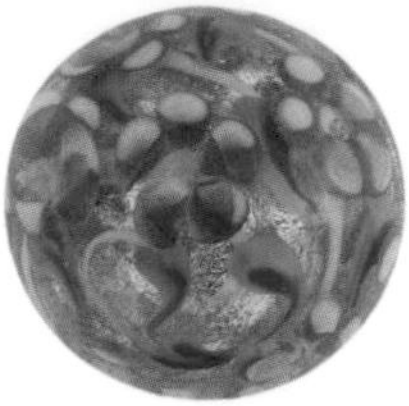

A Cathy Richardson dichroic base torchwork sphere, with torchworked floral design on the surface.

*Richardson is best known for her celebrated spheres of seabeds and marine life.*

*1.5in (4cm) diam*

**£40-50** **BGL**

A John Kubuki encased flora torchwork sphere, signed in kanji.

*1.25in (3cm) diam*

**£35-45** **BGL**

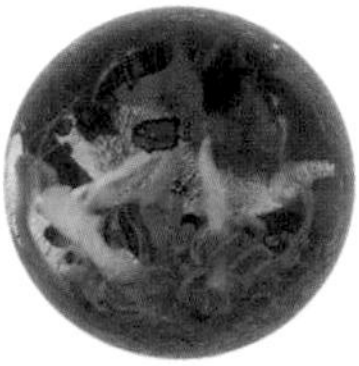

A Cindy Hyer Morgan aquarium scene sphere, with torchworked details, dichroic background and murrine fish.

*2in (5cm) diam*

**£30-40** **BGL**

A Jesse Taj 'Cat In The Hat' glass sphere, using torchworked murrine canes, signed "Taj 03".

*Taj is renowned for his detailed, well-formed murrines, which often focus on icons in popular culture or natural subjects.*

*2003* *1.5in (4cm) diam*

**£120-180** **BGL**

## A CLOSER LOOK AT A SPHERE

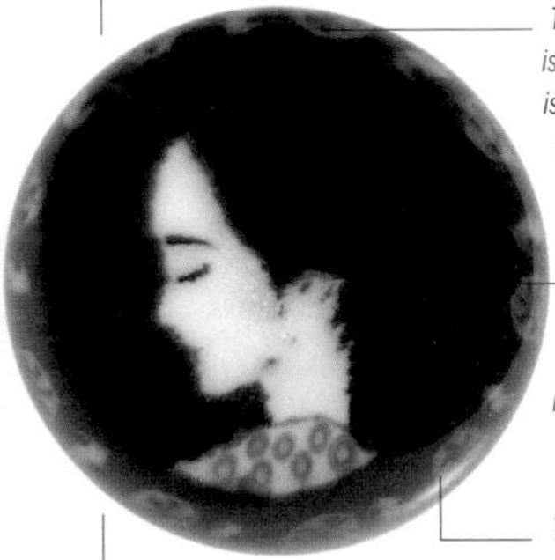

*The lady's face and background is one large, solid murrine, which is sliced from a larger rod with a design through it, like a stick of rock.*

*The design in the rod is comprised of many thousands of thin rods, each making up the design like pixels on a computer screen.*

*This time-consuming and labour intensive process was first practiced by the the Ancient Egyptians and Romans, and was revived on Murano.*

*Around the main murrine, they have added other, smaller and less complicated murrines including their signature murrine.*

A Chris & Lissa Juedemann 'Silhouette' sphere, with self-made murrines, blue and white signature cane, and signed "CEJ2004".

*The Juedemanns often depict personalities and iconic images from today's political and cultural scenes.*

*1.5in (4cm) diam*

**£120-180** **BGL**

A David Salazar dichroic Parrot with Harvest Moon' furnace and torchworked sphere.

*David Salazar is a noted glass artist working in the 'California Technique' of painting with molten glass. A nature lover, he has worked with hot glass for over 25 years and worked at the famous Lundberg Studios.*

*1.5in (4cm) diam*

**£30-40** **BGL**

### FIND OUT MORE...

**The Encyclopedia of Modern Marbles, Spheres & Orbs**, *by Mark Block, published by Schiffer Books, 2005.*

## COLLECTORS' NOTES

- In 1881, Frederick Stuart acquired the Red House Glass Works at Wordsley, near Stourbridge, and renamed it Stuart & Sons in 1885. From then on, the company was renowned primarily for its high quality cut, etched and engraved crystal, employing modern designers and cutters such as Ludwig Kny and John Luxton over the coming decades.
- In 1980, they acquired Strathearn Glass, based in Crieff, Scotland, previously known as Vasart. The company had been founded by the Ysarts who had been partly responsible for the Monart range of art glass. During the mid-1980s, the company was called Stuart Strathearn and new designs were introduced, with a major designer at this time being Iestyn Davies.
- Davies produced two major ranges in 1986, 'Ebony & Gold' and 'Dark Crystal'. Both were mould-blown and used the same opaque black glass bodies. 'Dark Crystal' had a mottled, almost volcanic textured, red coating created with powdered enamels. 'Ebony & Gold' was decorated with sections of gold leaf that was fragmented as the piece was blown outward.
- These pieces are frequently mistaken for the 'Azurene' range developed by Michael Harris and William Walker at the Isle of Wight Studio Glass in 1978. It is likely Davies was inspired by Harris' designs when he worked with, and produced designs for, Harris between 1984 and 1985. However, Stuart's designs are different, – more of the black body is shown, the shapes are different, and Stuart's range does not use gold and silver leaf together. Each piece is also entirely mould-blown, resulting in a body of roughly the same thickness all over. The rims are also flat and machine-finished.
- Most examples are marked on the base with the 'Stuart England' acid mark. Although the leaf is bonded to the glass surface in the heat of the furnace, it is prone to wear, particularly during the production process. Examine pieces for such damage, as this reduces the value. Large pieces are much harder to find than smaller pieces, and command higher values today. The range was expensive at the time and was not successful, so was withdrawn after a few years.

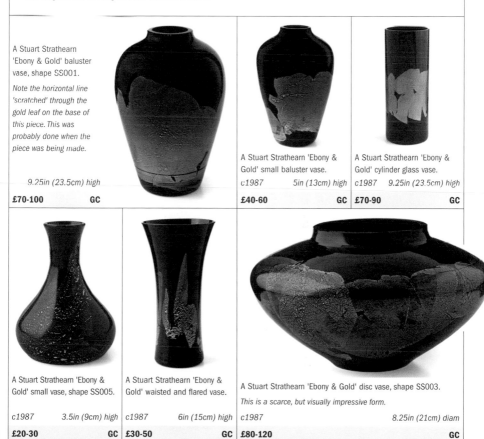

A Stuart Strathearn 'Ebony & Gold' baluster vase, shape SS001.

*Note the horizontal line 'scratched' through the gold leaf on the base of this piece. This was probably done when the piece was being made.*

*9.25in (23.5cm) high*

**£70-100** **GC**

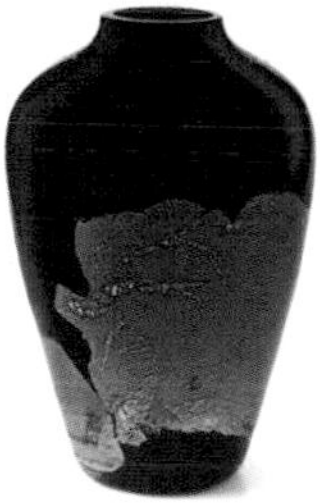

A Stuart Strathearn 'Ebony & Gold' small baluster vase.

*c1987* *5in (13cm) high*

**£40-60** **GC**

A Stuart Strathearn 'Ebony & Gold' cylinder glass vase.

*c1987* *9.25in (23.5cm) high*

**£70-90** **GC**

A Stuart Strathearn 'Ebony & Gold' small vase, shape SS005.

*c1987* *3.5in (9cm) high*

**£20-30** **GC**

A Stuart Strathearn 'Ebony & Gold' waisted and flared vase.

*c1987* *6in (15cm) high*

**£30-50** **GC**

A Stuart Strathearn 'Ebony & Gold' disc vase, shape SS003.

*This is a scarce, but visually impressive form.*

*c1987* *8.25in (21cm) diam*

**£80-120** **GC**

A Val St Lambert 'Eldorado' glass vase, designed and made by Samuel Herman, the base engraved "Val. S. Lambert/ L. L. S. J. H."

*Glassmaker Louis LeLoup collaborated with Herman on these works, before leaving Val St Lambert to found his own studio in the same town in 1971.*

*c1970 19.25in (49cm) high*

**£100-150 QU**

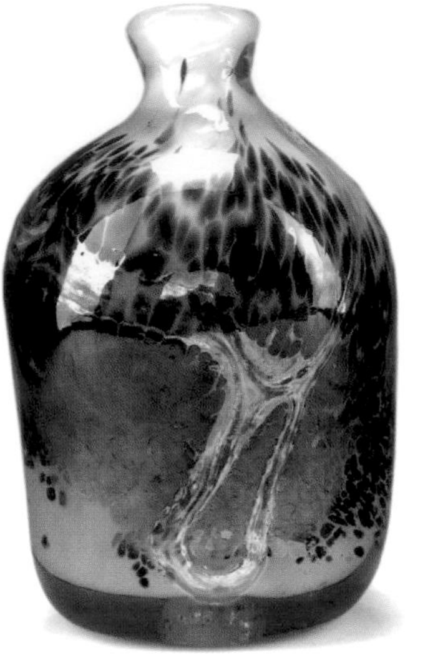

A Val St Lambert vase, designed by Samuel Herman, the opaque white body with applied flattened trail, the base engraved "Val St Lambert sjh".

*c1980 9.25in (23.5cm) high*

**£100-150 QU**

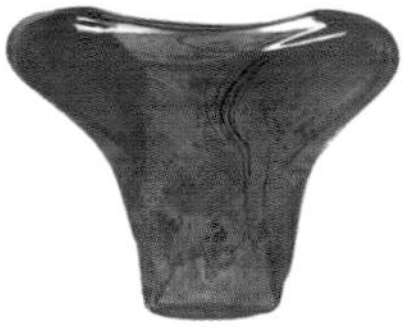

A Samuel Herman studio glass vase, of clear glass decorated with metallic oxides and silver chloride, the base engraved "Samuel J. Herman 1981".

*1981 7in (17.5cm) high*

**£200-250 QU**

A Samuel Herman studio glass vase, the cased opaque white body with violet spots and iridescent silver chloride trail, the base engraved "Samuel J Herman 1974".

*Samuel Herman (b.1936) learnt studio glass techniques under Dominick Labino and Harvey Littleton at the University of Wisconsin. In 1966, he came to London where he succeeded Michael Harris as head of the Glass department at the Royal College of Art. He went on to found the influential Glasshouse in London in 1969 as well as his own studio. He remains one of the most influential studio glassmakers alive today and wise collectors have already identified his work as a hot tip for the future.*

*1974 10.75in (27cm) high*

**£250-350 QU**

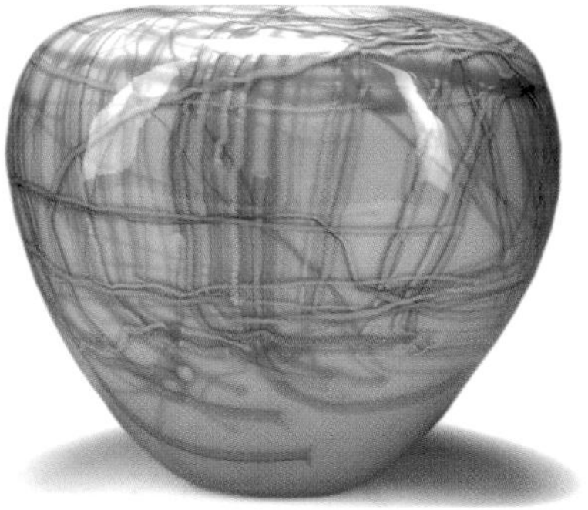

A Venini & Cie vase, designed by Mary Ann 'Toots' Zynsky, the translucent white body with applied green, pink and blue canes, the base engraved "Zynsky venini 88".

*Although not necessarily an example of studio glass in its strictest sense, 'Toots' Zynsky is a notable and popular studio glass artist.*

*1988 6.75in (17cm) high*

**£450-550 QU**

A Peter Layton studio glass 'Paradiso' dropper bottle.

*This shape, was inspired by a play of Dr Faustus and is derived from the traditional poison bottle used by villains.*

*2004 8in (20cm) high*

**£400-500 PL**

A Grant Ede green and black swirled art glass vase, signed to base, with ground and broken pontil.

*This vase is very similar to those produced by Monart.*

*8.25in (21cm) high*

**£80-120 GAZE**

## COLLECTORS' NOTES

- Whitefriars was founded in London in the 1600s and was acquired by James Powell in 1834, when it became known as 'Powell & Sons'. In 1926, the factory moved to Wealdstone, Middlesex, and became known as Whitefriars once again in 1962. For simplicity, most collectors refer to much of the glass produced by the company during the 20th century as 'Whitefriars'.
- In 1954, Geoffrey Baxter was employed as designer, and went on to produce many of the most popular and valuable designs in today's market. His innovative and modern designs were inspired by the modernity, clean lines and strength of colour of Scandinavian glass of the same period. However, he pursured his own idiosyncratic direction.
- 1967 saw the unveiling of Baxter's 'Textured' range that was to become the pinnacle of his achievements and is the most sought-after today. Moulds with internal textures were used to create glass with strong surface decoration, and in bright colours that matched the interiors of the time. The 'Studio' range, designed by Peter Wheeler and Baxter, is also highly collectable, with each piece being unique.
- Always consider the form, size and colour of a piece as these factors affect value considerably. New colours were introduced in 1969. Key designs such as the 'Banjo' and 'Drunken Bricklayer' have become icons of modern design, although prices have reached a plateau over the past year. Rarities, where fewer examples were known to have been made, continue to rise in value.
- Smaller pieces from the 'Late Textured' range of the 1970s are not currently as desirable as they arguably lack the visual impact, large sizes and 'freshness' of the original late 1960s designs. As such, they may make wise investments while prices are low.

A Whitefriars sapphire blue glass bowl, the shape and pattern designed by Barnaby Powell, unsigned, small chips to top rim.

*Some of the abstract patterns on these bowls were designed by Albert Tubby, a glass cutter at the time. Many combine areas of polished and unpolished cutting.*

*c1932* *9in (22.5cm) diam*

**£180-220** **WW**

A 1950s Whitefriars ruby red lobed and cased vase, designed by William Wilson, pattern no.9286, with internal bubbles.

*7.25in (18.5cm) high*

**£15-20** **GAZE**

A Whitefriars tricorn red bowl, designed by Geoffrey Baxter in 1963, shape no.9588.

*1964-70* *11.75in (30cm) diam*

**£120-180** **MHT**

A Whitefriars indigo blue 'Banjo' vase, designed by Geoffrey Baxter in 1966, shape no.9681, with tiny fleabites to the rim.

*Only 228 Banjo vases were produced in indigo, making them rarer than the 683 that were produced in tangerine. Aubergine and colourless flint are rarer still. The rarest is ruby red, of which only one has ever been found.*

*12.25in (31cm) high*

**£1,000-1,500** **WW**

A Whitefriars tangerine 'Banjo' vase, designed by Geoffrey Baxter in 1966, shape no.9681.

*Tangerine was not one of the original three colours used for the Banjo vase, but was added in 1969, together with kingfisher blue.*

*c1969-73* *12.5in (32cm) high*

**£700-900** **GC**

A Whitefriars tangerine 'Hoop' vase, designed by Geoffrey Baxter in 1966, pattern no.9680.

*1969-72* *11.5in (29cm) high*

**£250-350** **WW**

A large Whitefriars meadow green bark vase, designed by Geoffrey Baxter in 1966, pattern no.9691.

*c1970-72* *9in (23cm) high*

**£70-90** **TCS**

A Whitefriars ruby red 'Chess Board' textured glass vase, by Geoffrey Baxter, shape no.9817, from the Late Textured range.

*c1974* *6in (15cm) high*

**£60-80** **GC**

A very rare Whitefriars Streaky Amber full lead crystal lampbase or large vase, designed by Geoffrey Baxter, pattern no.9856, from the Cirrus range.

*c1980* *9.25in (23.5cm) high*

**£150-200** **GC**

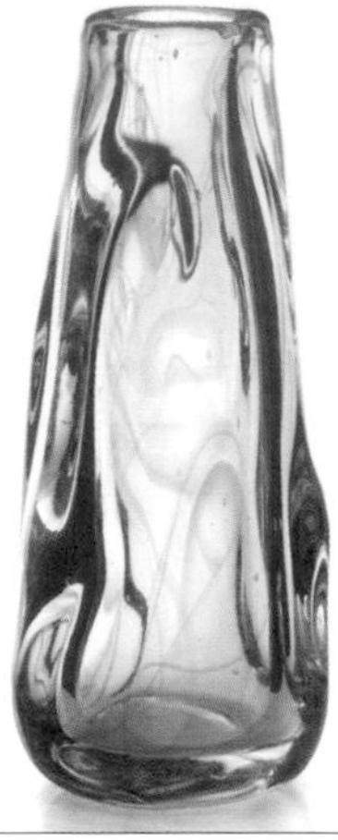

A Whitefriars aqua green full lead crystal Knobbly vase, pat no.9856, with flared rim.

*Although very close to Harry Dyer's 1964 designs, these later versions have slightly flared rims. Being made from full lead crystal, they are also heavier in weight.*

*c1980* *11in (24.5cm) high*

**£80-120** **GC**

A Whitefriars Studio range 'Peacock' vase, designed by Peter Wheeler in 1969, pattern no.S13, with peacock-coloured base and random silver chloride trailing.

*Wheeler was Baxter's assistant and was responsible for much of the Studio range. The striking colours and rarity, particularly in this form, make these prized and valuable designs.*

*1969-70* *11.5in (29cm) high*

**£700-1,000** **TCS**

## A CLOSER LOOK AT A WHITEFRIARS VASE

*The Studio range was released in 1969 in answer to the growing studio glass movement that was making an impact both on sales and within the glass industry.*

*Silver chloride has been included in the hand-applied trails, resulting in the deeper colours that compliment the amber body.*

*The 'New Studio' range was introduced in 1970 and used different colours to the original range.*

*Whitefriars was suffering from a major decline in sales at that time, leading to its closure in 1980, so few of these expensive pieces sold making them rare today.*

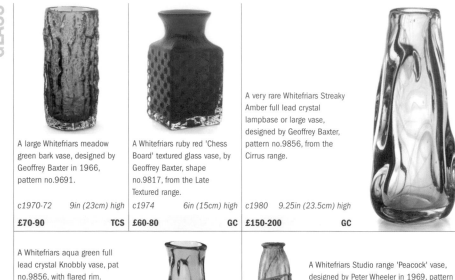

A Whitefriars gold amber cylinder vase, designed by Geoffrey Baxter, pattern no.9882, from the New Studio range, with silver chloride strapping to centre.

*1978-80* *10in (25.5cm) high*

**£500-600** **TCS**

A Whitefriars gold-coloured full lead crystal small Knobbly vase, designed by Geoffrey Baxter, pattern no.9608.

*9.25in (23.5cm) high*

**£50-80** **GC**

### FIND OUT MORE...

**Whitefriars Glass**, *by Lesley Jackson, published by Richard Dennis, 1996.*

## COLLECTORS' NOTES

- As the consumption of wine in the home has risen over the past few decades, wine glasses have become as common in many households as cups and saucers, and mugs. Over the 20th century, many designers have produced wine glass designs to complete a tableware service or to accompany their more decorative vases and bowls. Decanters have already been the subject of a major book, and form many collections, but wine glasses have yet to receive the attention they surely deserve.

- Prices are currently low, partly as they were typically produced and sold in sets and in large quantities, and they can make an affordable way to buy into the work and 'look' of certain designers. Many designs were highly successful, with some still being produced today. Consult original company catalogues and look in reference books to learn the shapes and colours used, as examples are very rarely signed and labels have usually been removed for use.

- Much like antique chairs, some have built 'harlequin' collections made up of many different individual examples. Eminently usable, they can add fun and variety to a formal dining table, or be used individually, with some glasses suiting certain wines. Some 20th century designs were based on historic examples, and many of today's designers continue to use them, and the glass designs derived from them, as inspiration. Many 20thC designers also copied or were inspired by the work of their contemporaries.

- Although prices for earlier, 18th and 19th century examples have generally fallen over the past few years, now is the time to buy as current values make them excellent value for money and it is likely that values will rise again. Also consider more mass-produced designs made during the early to mid-19th century, shown at the end of this section. These handmade, hand-cut glasses can usually be found for around £20-50 and act as robust, highly functional historic talking points.

A Boda amber bubbled glass wine goblet, designed by Eric Hogland.

*Both the colour and thick, almost artisan-made, type of bubbly glass are typical of Hogland's designs for Boda.*

*6.75in (17cm) high*

**£35-40** **GC**

A pair of M.V.M. Cappellin Murano glass dessert wine glasses, with wide feet and hollow ovoid stems.

*c1928* *5in (12.5cm) high*

**£200-250** **VZ**

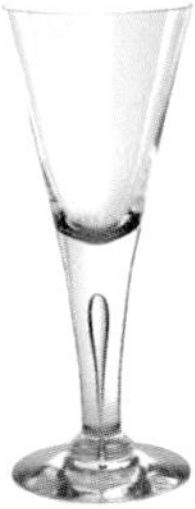

A Dartington 'Sharon' colourless wine glass, FT115, with internal bubble, designed by Frank Thrower in 1970.

*7.5in (19cm) high*

**£10-15** **GC**

A Dartington Glass Midnight grey 'Dartington' wine goblet, FT553, designed by Frank Thrower in 1968.

*This was an early and short-lived design, similar to Ronald Stennett-Willson's 'Tower' design.*

*6.5in (16.5cm) high*

**£20-25** **GC**

A Dartington Glass 'Regency' wine goblet, FT118, designed by Frank Thrower in 1971.

*1971-85* *5.5in (14cm) high*

**£20-30** **GC**

A Dartington 'Rummer' wine goblet, FT104, designed by Frank Thrower in 1967-68.

*5.75in (14.5cm) high*

**£10-20** **GC**

A King's Lynn/Wedgwood Glass wine glass, designed by Ronald Stennett-Willson.

*c1967* *7.5in (19cm) high*

**£40-60** **GC**

An Orrefors amber wine glass, designed by Simon Gate in 1918, with ribbed stem and flared rim.

*This glass was designed for Sandvik and retailed by Heal's under the name 'Astrid' until 1966. It is accompanied by an elegant decanter with a leaf-shaped stopper.*

*7.25in (18.5cm) high*

**£10-20** **GC**

## A CLOSER LOOK AT A WINE GLASS

*This is a hard to find version of one of Ronald Stennett-Willson's most celebrated designs. His Sheringham candlesticks are far easier to find, see pages 282-286 for examples.*

*Each piece was made from a separate gather of glass, meaning five separate gathers had to be formed for this glass.*

*The time-consuming process of forming and blowing this glass, combined with the skill required to join all the pieces together properly, led to, what was then, a high retail price of 47/6d (£2.35).*

*Its high price meant that it did not sell well, and when Wedgwood acquired King's Lynn in 1969, they discontinued the design, making it scarce today.*

A King's Lynn 'Sheringham' wine glass, no.RSW16, designed by Ronald Stennett-Willson in 1967.

*1967-69* *6.25in (16cm) high*

**£70-100** **GC**

A Pukeberg wine goblet, probably designed by Goran Warff, with grey glass stem and bowl with martelé (hammered) effect, and colourless foot.

*7.5in (19cm) high*

**£20-30** **GC**

A Stromberg light blue wine goblet, with one piece conical bowl and twisted stem, with stepped foot.

*5in (13cm) high*

**£20-25** **GC**

A Stromberg bud-like wine goblet, probably designed by Gerda Stromberg, with optical effect.

*5in (13cm) high*

**£15-20** **GC**

A Stromberg two-colour wine glass, of organic form with one-piece stem and foot.

*4.25in (11cm) high*

**£15-20** **GC**

A late 1930s Stuart 'Woodchester' wine glass, the bowl cut with a stylized ferm leaf pattern, the base with "Stuart" acid stamp.

*This elegant and long-lived design was released in 1935, and applied to over 30 different shapes.*

*6.75in (17cm) high*

**£20-30** **GC**

A J. Wuidart & Co. wine glass, designed by Ronald Stennett-Willson in 1955, with banded knop, with original company label.

*Stennett-Willson designed for the distributor and wholesaler Wuidart from 1952-56. This glass was made by Björkshult of Sweden, which is where Dartington Glass' factory manager and many of their blowers came from 12 years later.*

*1955-57* *5.5in (14cm) high*

**£30-40** **GC**

A Wedgwood Glass wine goblet, designed by Ronald Stennett-Willson, with original label.

*5.75in (14.5cm) high*

**£40-60** **GC**

A J. Wuidart & Co. 'Whirl' wine glass, designed by Ronald Stennett-Willson, with bulbous four-part knop.

*4.75in (12cm) high*

**£15-20** **GC**

A Georgian champagne flute, with high panel cutting, on collar and blade knop stem.

*c1820* *7in (18cm) high*

**£30-50** **AG**

A Victorian panel-cut tavern rummer.

*5.25in (8cm) high*

**£15-20** **AG**

A Victorian U-bowl tavern rummer, with gadget mark.

*A gadget was a 19thC metal device used in glass production to hold a wine glass at the base so that the bowl could be formed and finished. It had metal jaws that clamped down on the foot to hold the glass. These jaws were of different shapes and sizes and left impressions on the foot known as 'gadget marks'.*

*c1870* *5.5in (14cm) high*

**£25-35** **AG**

A Dutch Leerdam 'Unica' vase, designed by Floris Meydam, the clear glass body with horizontal ribbons of yellow and green, the base inscribed "Leerdam Unica MF 36 H FMeydam".

*Although most of Leerdam's glass was designed by Andreas Dirk Copier, many postwar designs were by Floris Meydam (b.1919), who trained under Copier and worked for Leerdam from 1949-86. Curving organic cylinders, ovals and circles are typical of his designs.*

*6.5in (16.5cm) high*

**£500-600** **QU**

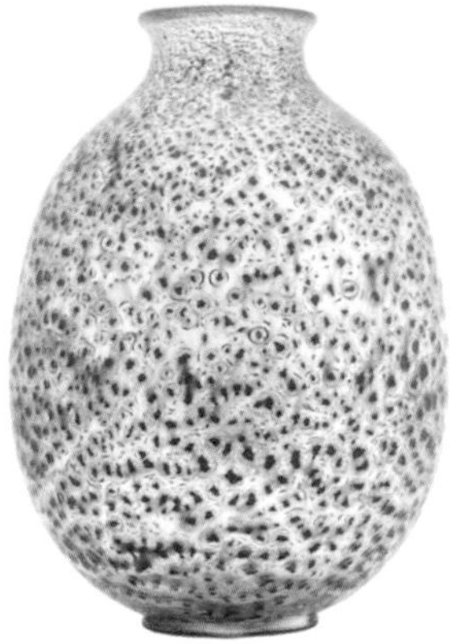

A Dutch Leerdam 'Unica' large bulbous glass vase, with metallic inclusions, the base engraved "Leerdam Unica/E234/AD Copier".

*Andreas Dirk Copier (1901-91) joined Leerdam in 1914, and worked as artistic director from 1927-71. His hand-blown art glass 'Unica' range was introduced c1923, and early examples have mottled bubbled or crackled coloured patterning.*

*16.25in (41.5cm) high*

**£2,000-3,000** **SDR**

A Dutch Leerdam cobalt blue jug, possibly designed by Andreas Dirk Copier, with "LG" acid stamp.

*7in (18cm) high*

**£70-100** **GC**

A Dutch Leerdam ribbed spherical vase, with slight iridescence, with "LG" acid stamp to base.

*3.25in (8.5cm) high*

**£30-40** **GC**

A 1930s Loetz 'Tango' orange glass vase, designed by Michael Powolny, with applied cobalt blue handles and rim.

*5in (12.5cm) high*

**£100-150** **SDR**

A Monart tapering cylindrical vase, the mottled turquoise body with blue and aventurine inclusions to the rim.

*7.75in (20cm) high*

**£80-100** **PC**

A Muller Frères vase, with low relief stylized bird moulded design and matte, acid-etched finish.

*Muller Frères' most prolific period was from c1900-30. The Great Depression hit business seriously, and it closed in 1936.*

*9.75in (25cm) high*

**£180-220** **NPC**

A 1930s Muller Frères Art Deco vase, with low relief moulded geometric pattern and matte acid-etched finish.

*9.75in (25cm) high*

**£120-180** **NPC**

A Peill & Putzler mould-blown vase, designed by Horst Tuselmann, with shaded grey colouring, polished clear protrusions, and overall matte, acid etched finish, the base with etched "P".

*c1970* *4in (10cm) high*

**£120-180** **QU**

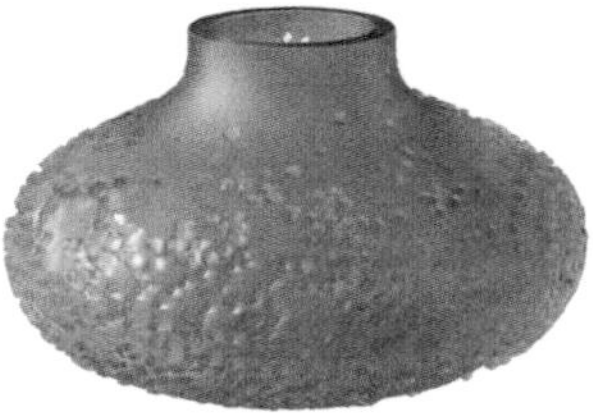

A Peill & Putzler mould blown vase, designed by Horst Tuselmann, with polished clear prunts, and overall matte, acid-etched finish.

*Peill & Putzler was created in 1946 when Gebruder Putzler (founded 1869) merged with Peill & Sohn (founded 1903) and the merged company moved to Duren, Germany. The company employed a number of designers including Wilhelm Wagenfeld and Horst Tuselmann, who was their leading designer from the 1960s until the factory closed in 1997.*

*8.5in (21.5cm) diam*

**£150-200** **GC**

A 1970s Schott Zweisel heavily cased 'bullet' shaped vase, designed by Heinrich Loffelhardt.

*9.5in (24cm) high*

**£25-35** **GC**

A 1930s Sabino dark blue glass vase, decorated with moulded overlapping rays around the body with gilt highlights, the base with etched mark.

*Although dramatic and indicative of the Art Deco period, examples of Sabino's opalescent glass that resembles Lalique tends to be more popular.*

*8.5in (21.5cm) high*

**£70-100** **CHEF**

An Italian SI.AN. Cristallerie red and opaque yellow glass vase, with original foil label.

*Probably dating from the 1970s, this bold design crosses both Scandinavian modern and Italian Postmodern design. SI.AN. Cristallerie of Empoli produces domestic table and decorative glass wares.*

*9.75in (25cm) high*

**£50-80** **GC**

## A CLOSER LOOK AT A STEVENS & WILLIAMS RAINBOW VASE

*Stevens & Williams Rainbow glass is comparatively uncommon and highly desirable. This piece is large and has delicate tonal variations.*

*The top is cut with circular 'lenses', which are typical of the period, and add an interesting optical effect.*

*This design was introduced in 1938 and was only in production for a year or two, due to the onset of WWII.*

*It is described in company record books as being 'light blue and green rainbow cased inside'.*

A rare Stevens & Williams (Royal Brierley Crystal) two colour, lens-cut 'Rainbow' vase, pattern no.68307.

*c1939* *10in (25.5cm) high*

**£300-500** **GC**

## A CLOSER LOOK AT A PAIRPOINT ART DECO TAZZA

*The silver overlay was probably made by Rockwell, and is typically Art Deco in style. It also incorporates a leaping gazelle, a motif frequently found in Art Deco designs.*

*The tazza form and black amethyst glass display the silver pattern well. It is decorated on both the foot and the rim of the bowl.*

*This piece would have been expensive in its day as fewer would have been made and sold. It is very rare and sought-after today.*

*Bowls and candlesticks were also made, and the type of pattern and colour of the glass can vary. Black is a popular colour however.*

A Pairpoint Art Deco black amethyst glass tazza, with silver overlay, and controlled air bubble knop on stem.

*c1925* *7.5in (19cm) high*

**£80-120** **TSIS**

A Stevens & Williams pink and green candy striped 'Rainbow' glass type bowl.

*7in (18cm) diam*

**£70-90** **MHT**

A Waterford Society keepsake box and lid, marked "Waterford WS 2001", with box.

*2001* *2.75in (7cm) wide*

**£8-12** **BEL**

A WMF bell-shaped bowl with flared rim, the honey-coloured glass with strong golden iridescence, with delicate craquelure work on rim.

*c1930* *6in (15cm) diam*

**£45-55** **VZ**

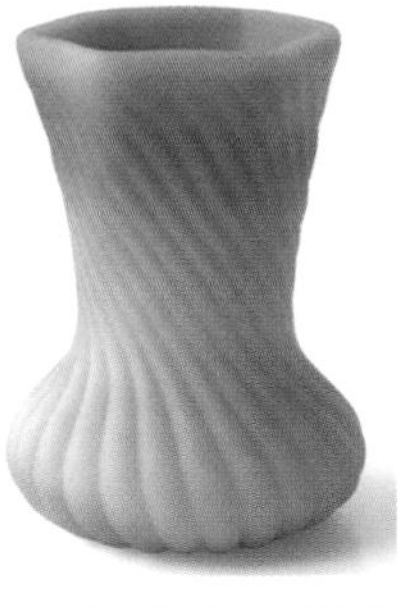

A 'Burmese' barley twist vase, possibly by Thomas Webb & Sons, with hexagonal rim and matte finish.

*The graduated yellow to pink 'Burmese' glass was developed in 1881 by Frederick Shirley at the Mouth Washington Glass Co. in the US. In 1886, Thomas Webb gained the license to make it in the UK, and it was marketed under the name of 'Queen's Burmese'. Reproductions are known to have been made as late as 1960.*

*4.25in (10.5cm) high*

**£40-60** **PC**

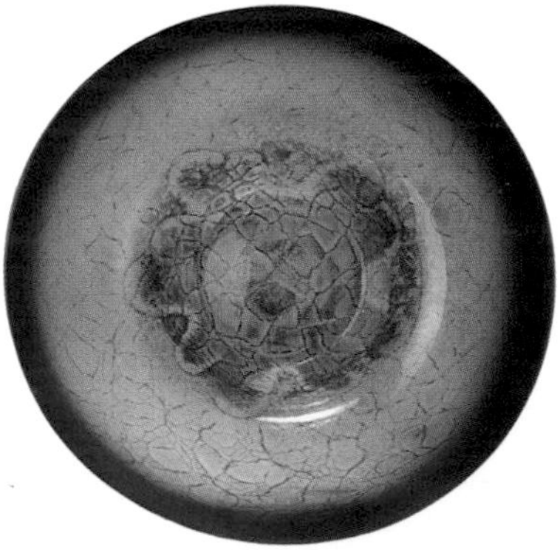

A WMF 'Ikora' bowl, with fine bubbly orange-red oxide inclusions around a bright green centre, small crack on inner wall of base.

*c1930* *15.5in (38.5 cm) diam*

**£100-150** **VZ**

## COLLECTORS' NOTES

- The customs and iconography relating to celebrating holidays have a rich and lengthy history resulting in images that we may no longer associate with that particular event.
- The rosy-cheeked Santa Claus in his white-trimmed red suit was popularized (but not created) by Haddon Sundblom working for Coca-Cola in the 1930s and many today consider this the traditional depiction of Santa. However, early illustrations from the turn of the century depict him in a variety of outfits, examples of which are sought-after today. Early pieces in general are desirable and were usually produced in Germany from papier-mâché until the beginning of WWII. Later examples were produced in Japan and the US, often in plastic. From the 1960s onwards, memorabilia was more likely to be mass-produced and lower quality, making examples from this period less desirable.
- Much Hallowe'en memorabilia reflects its rural roots in Scotland – the custom was brought to the US by Scottish immigrants in the 1880s. Vegetable-shaped candy containers, figurines and centrepieces are common. The more frightening objects, ghouls and the like, are always popular. Hallowe'en postcards are a popular collecting area and appeared in the late 1880s in the US and Germany. Embossed and ornate examples in mint condition are the most desirable, as are those by Brundage, Clapsaddle and Schmucker. However unsigned examples are a great way to amass an affordable collection that is easy to store and display.

A 'Jolly Hallowe'en' vegetable man falling in tub postcard.

*5.5in (14cm) wide*

**£10-15** **SOTT**

A Hallowe'en embossed postcard, of a boy and girl carrying a pumpkin. *1908* *5.5in (14cm) wide*

**£12-18** **SOTT**

A 'Happy Hallowe'en' embossed postcard, printed by International Art Publishing Co, with 1908 copyright.

*5.5in (14cm) wide*

**£12-18** **SOTT**

A Hallowe'en Greetings' card, with red border, pumpkins, lady and hand mirror, "Made in Saxony".

*5.5in (14cm) wide*

**£10-15** **SOTT**

A Hallowe'en embossed postcard, with vegetable head figures, and gilt highlights.

*5.5in (14cm) wide*

**£8-12** **SOTT**

A 'Jolly Hallowe'en May Fortune Smile on You' silver painted embossed postcard, with witch.

*5.5in (14cm) wide*

**£18-22** **SOTT**

A 'Joyous Hallowe'en' gate postcard.

*5.5in (14cm) wide*

**£10-15** **SOTT**

A 'Best Hallowe'en wishes' embossed postcard, decorated with pumpkin and girls and gold foil highlights.

*5.5in (14cm) wide*

**£10-15** **SOTT**

A 'Jolly Hallowe'en' lady in mirror postcard, by Fred C. Lounsbury, with 1907 postmarks.

*5.5in (14cm) wide*

**£8-12** **SOTT**

A 'Hallowe'en Greetings', embossed gold postcard.

*1912* *5.5in (14cm) wide*

**£12-18** **SOTT**

A German 'With All Hallowe'en Greetings' postcard, dated October 31st, 1909.

*5.5in (14cm) wide*

**£10-15** **SOTT**

A 'Happy Hallowe'en' postcard, with boy and pumpkin.

*1911* *5.5in (14cm) wide*

**£8-12** **SOTT**

A Hallowe'en embossed postcard, with gilt detailing and Vegetable heads in car.

*5.5in (14cm) wide*

**£10-15** **SOTT**

An 'All Hallowe'en' embossed postcard, by TR Co., with large pumpkin, and witch flying above.

*5.5in (14cm) wide*

**£10-15** **SOTT**

A Hallowe'en moon embossed postcard.

*5.5in (14cm) wide*

**£12-18** **SOTT**

A 1920s German small vegetable man composition 'roly poly', weighted base.

*2.25in (5.5cm) high*

**£100-120** **SOTT**

A pressed pulp card roly-poly jack-o'-lantern vegetable man lantern.

*9in (22.5cm) high*

**£250-350** **SOTT**

## A CLOSER LOOK AT A JACK-O'-LANTERN MAN

*This delicate automated figure has survived in relatively good condition given his age.*

*His head is made from clay-sprayed papier-mâché and has its original painted features. It also display bright colours.*

*Wind-up Hallowe'en figures are unusual and this would have been more expensive than static examples at the time of manufacture.*

*His original clothes are in complete and unfaded condition.*

A 1920s German wind-up walking jack-o'-lantern man, with fabric clothes.

*7in (18cm) high*

**£400-600** **SOTT**

A German large composition vegetable man, with black fabric-covered squeaker hat.

*The hat would be pushed down to make a noise and would eventually stay compressed. This example is in original condition although the squeaker isn't working any longer.*

**£220-280** **SOTT**

A German clay-sprayed card egg-shaped vegetable man, on springy legs on a sweets box.

*9.5in (24cm) high*

**£300-400** **SOTT**

A German wooden and papier-mâché cat rackett clacker.

*10.25in (26cm) high*

**£80-120** **SOTT**

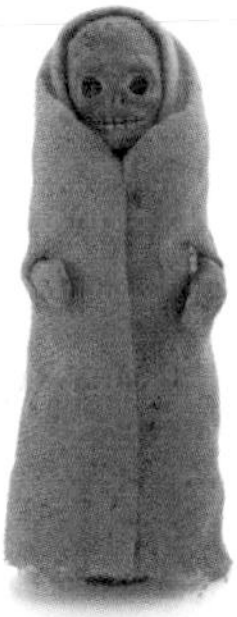

A very rare 1920s German gauze-covered card sweets holder, with painted plaster/chalk skeleton.

*4.25in (11cm) high*

**£200-250** **SOTT**

A 1920s German ceramic dressed Santa Claus sweets container, with early tree, good luck mushroom, and sack.

*7.5in (19cm) high*

**£350-450** **SOTT**

## A CLOSER LOOK AT A SANTA CLAUS FIGURE

*The term belsnickle comes from the Pennsylvania Dutch and is a corruption of Pelz-Nickel or Pelts Nicholas meaning 'St. Nicholas in fur.'*

*These early figures were made from papier-mâché, a fragile material meaning few examples survive.*

*He retains his wooden backpack, which is unusual.*

*The red-suited figure we are used to seeing today was popularized through Haddon Sunblom's depictions of the character for Coca-Cola. Other coloured figures were produced, such as the brown examples on this page, but the blue mohair coat is unusual.*

A rare and early German blue mohair coat Santa Claus belsnickle figurine, with wooden backpack.

*c1918* *8.5in (21.5cm) high*

**£600-800** **SOTT**

An early Belsnickle Santa Claus, on wooden base, with long coat and feather tree.

*A number of things point to this being an early example. His stuffed hat, lined coat and the tree made from a feather.*

*7.5in (19cm) high*

**£300-400** **SOTT**

A 'Merry Christmas' advertising clicker, with Santa Claus, marked "Kirchhof USA".

*1.75in (4.5cm) high*

**£30-40** **LDE**

A 'Grants Toy Dept.' Christmas advertising clicker.

*1.75in (4.5cm) high*

**£30-40** **LDE**

A very early hand-painted pressed card and plaster-dipped sweets container, of a bunny in clown suit, base printed "Made in Germany".

*c1915* *7.5in (19cm) high*

**£250-300** **SOTT**

A red, white and green roly-poly rabbit sweets container, base printed "Germany".

*Look at the font on the marked base as well as the material as these help to date a piece. This can also be dated to pre-WWII as it is marked simply "Germany" rather than "West Germany".*

*5.5in (14cm) high*

**£100-150** **SOTT**

A hand-painted composition girl bunny sweets container, printed "Germany".

*6.25in (16cm) high*

**£60-80** **SOTT**

A 1920s German composition nodding head rabbit, with glass eyes, dressed in suit, the card base printed "Germany".

*6.75in (17cm) high*

**£100-150** **SOTT**

A German pink and blue plaster Easter rabbit sweets container, marked "MADE IN GERMANY US Zone".

*Unusual colour combinations for an Easter bunny are rare and make them more desirable. This mark was only used between 1945-53.*

*6.75in (17cm) high*

**£60-80** **SOTT**

A green and white plaster sweets container rabbit, base printed "Germany".

*This green and white colour combination is unusual and is worth more than the pastel version also on this page.*

*6.75in (17cm) high*

**£80-120** **SOTT**

A 1930s Japanese rabbit in a basket sweets container, with cotton bunting rabbit.

*2.75in (7cm) high*

**£60-90** **SOTT**

A 1920s German squeaky body sweets container, with sprung gauze-covered body and plaster-dipped card head.

*6in (15cm) high*

**£120-180** **SOTT**

A very rare 1930s Japanese cotton ball chick, with crêpe hat, with "MADE IN JAPAN" label.

*7.75in (19.5cm) high*

**£25-30** **SOTT**

## COLLECTORS' NOTES

- Although enjoying a heritage of many centuries, most of what is known and collected as 'Inuit art' today was made from the mid-20thC onwards. In 1949, a young Canadian artist called James Houston visited the Canadian Arctic to find out if the native art was appealing and could be commercial. His initial purchases sold out rapidly and both the government and Hudson Bay company became involved. During the 1960s, organised trading and collecting began in earnest and popularity swiftly grew.
- The majority of works are sculptures carved from green or grey hardstone or whalebone. Prints and fabrics are also produced and collected. Subject matter focuses on traditional Inuit life and surroundings including the Inuit themselves, Arctic animals, Inuit myths and more abstracted forms. The artist counts greatly towards value, with works by leaders such as Osuitok Ipeelee, John Tiktak, John Pangnark, Jessie Oonark and Karoo Ashevak being hotly sought-after.
- Due to the growing popularity of the area and increased trade, there are also a great many mediocre and even poor quality artworks available. By comparison, these have little chance of becoming desirable or collectable in future, so learn about forms, artists and market trends by reading books and visiting dealers and auctions to view examples. Look for well-executed, stylized and even abstracted designs, often with an inherent wit or humour.
- Many pieces are signed on the bottom with 'syllabics', the Inuit form of 'verbal' lettering, or with a 'disc number' beginning with an 'E' or 'W' that also identifies the artist. Numbers in brackets in the caption indicate the disc number, and also birth and death dates, if known. The market for Inuit art has seen rapid development over the last 25 years, with interest from across the world, and this looks sets to continue.

A green soapstone bird, by Abraham Etungat (E7-809) from Cape Dorset, with outstretched wings.

*c1980* *9.75in (25cm) high*

**£800-1,200** **WAD**

A soapstone 'Bird' figure, by Abraham Etungat (E7-809) from Cape Dorset, signed in syllabics.

*6.25in (16cm) wide*

**£600-700** **WAD**

A green soapstone bird, by Aqjangajuk Shaa (E7-1065), with upswept wings.

*This is an extremely large and visually impressive example in a pose full of action and movement. Shaa (b.1937) began carving at the age of 17 and participated in the notable 1971 travelling exhibition of Inuit art. In 2003 he was elected as a member of the Royal Canadian Academy.*

*32in (81cm) high*

**£2,500-3,000** **WAD**

A soapstone owl sculpture, by Joe Talirunli (E9-818) from Povungnituk, signed in Roman script.

*3.5in (9cm) high*

**£1,200-1,800** **WAD**

A pink stone owl, by Manasie Akpaliapik (E5-1155), with inset eyes, beak and claws, signed in syllabics.

*8in (20cm) high*

**£800-1,200** **WAD**

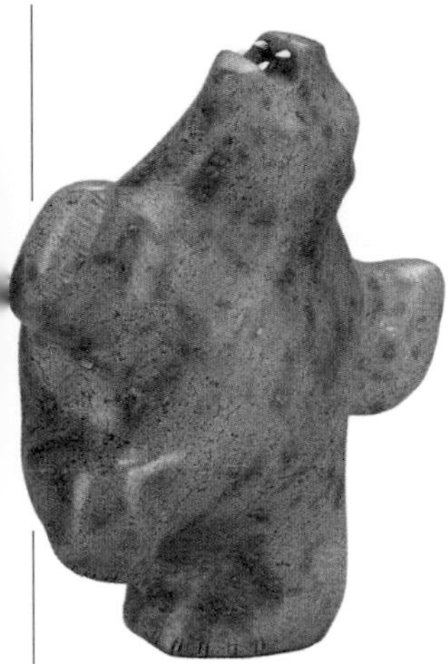

A mottled green soapstone dancing polar bear, by Pauta Saila (E7-990) from Cape Dorset,with inset teeth.

*10.5in (27cm) wide*

**£3,500-4,000** **WAD**

## A CLOSER LOOK AT AN INUIT SCULPTURE

*Pauta Saila (b.1916) is particularly known for his monumental, stylized dancing polar bears which vary in their sense of movement - this one is a superb example.*

*The pose of a bear dancing on one foot is a hallmark of his. The solid form of the sculpture suggests a bear's immense strength – a factor which is balanced by the whimsical, almost delicate pose.*

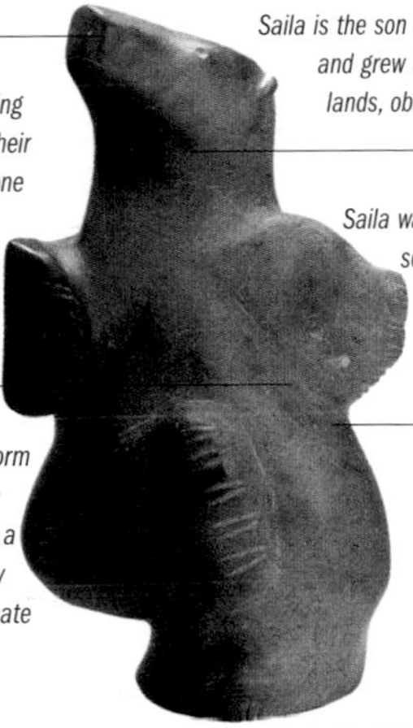

*Saila is the son of an important Inuit leader and grew up on the family's extensive lands, observing polar bears at close quarters.*

*Saila was chosen to represent Inuit sculpture at the International Sculpture Symposium in 1967, and his work is in many important public and private collections.*

A soapstone 'Dancing Polar Bear' figure, by Pauta Saila (E7-990) from Cape Dorset, signed in syllabics.

*Saila is also known for his works on paper, and is married to Pitaloosie Saila, best known for her works on paper.*

*13in (33cm) high*

**£6,500-7,500** **WAD**

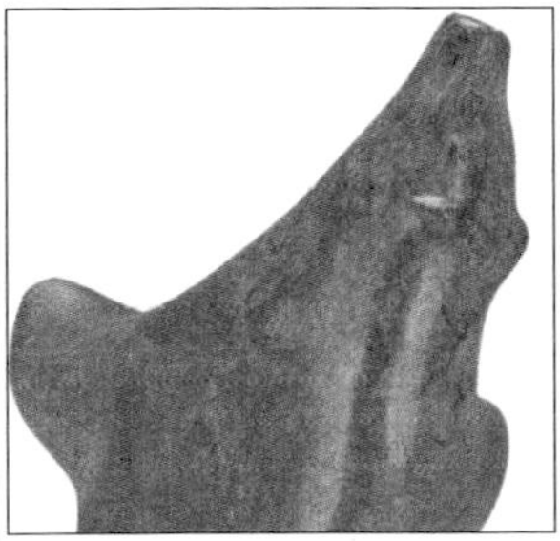

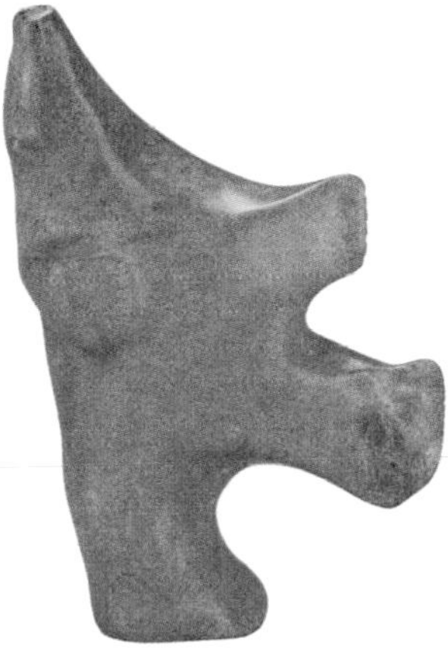

A grey-green soapstone dancing polar bear, by Pauta Saila (E7-990) from Cape Dorset, signed in syllabic and dated "1998" and inscribed "my last bear".

*1998* *12.5in (32cm) high*

**£3,200-3,800** **WAD**

A soapstone 'Dancing Polar Bear' figure, by Davie Atchealak (E7-1182) from Iqaluit.

*15in (38cm) high*

**£1,500-2,000** **WAD**

A dark soapstone polar bear, by Josiah Nuilaalik (E2-385) from Baker Lake, with inset teeth, signed in syllabics.

*11in (28cm) high*

**£450-550** **WAD**

A dark soapstone polar bear, by Peter Pitseolak (E7-970) from Cape Dorset, signed in syllabics.

*5in (11cm) wide*

**£200-300** **WAD**

A green soapstone musk ox, by Seepee Ipellie (E7-511) from Iqaluit, with inset horns, signed in syllabics.

*9.75in (25cm) high*

**£400-500** **WAD**

A soapstone 'Musk Ox' figure, by William Angivgalokak (W2-168) from Coppermine.

*c1974* *4in (10cm) long*

**£150-200** **WAD**

A soapstone and carved antler 'Musk Ox' figure, by Mark Tungilik (E3-320), signed in syllabics.

*5.25in (13.5cm) long*

**£800-1,200** **WAD**

A soapstone and carved antler inset 'Musk Ox' figure, by Judas Ullulaq (E4-342) from Gjoa Haven.

*Many of Ullulaq's (1937-99) sculptures are both unusual and dramatic, often making use of inset horn and having bizarre (sometimes amusing) expressive faces. He was a founder of the Netsilik school, known for its extravagant style closely associated with shamanism and asymmetry.*

*7in (18cm) high*

**£2,500-3,500** **WAD**

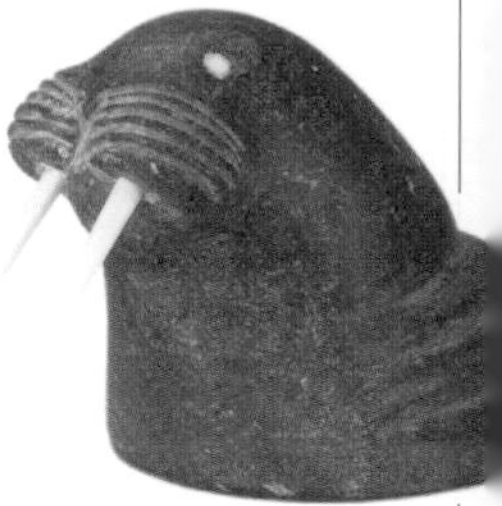

A grey soapstone walrus, by an unidentified artist, with inset eyes and teeth.

*c1955* *4in (10cm) high*

**£150-200** **WAD**

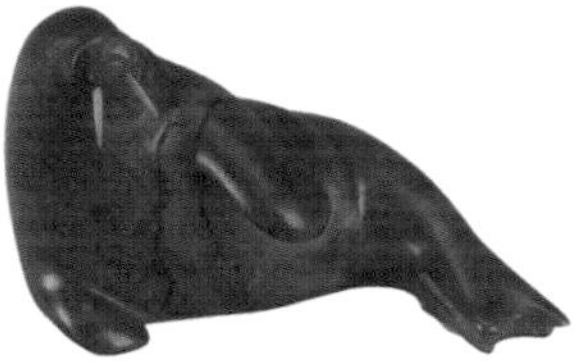

A green soapstone walrus, by Zebedee Enoogoo (E5-243) from Arctic Bay, with inset ivory tusks, signed in Roman with disc number.

*c1960* *5in (13cm) wide*

**£400-500** **WAD**

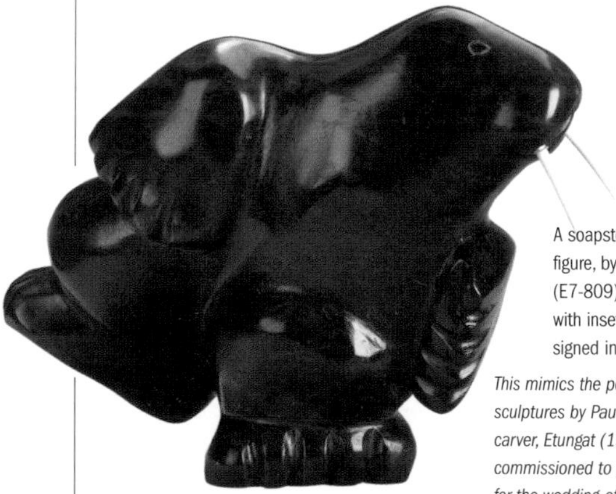

A soapstone 'Dancing Walrus' figure, by Abraham Etungat (E7-809) from Cape Dorset, with inset carved ivory tusks, signed in syllabics.

*This mimics the popular dancing bear sculptures by Pauta Saila. A notable carver, Etungat (1911-99) was commissioned to produce a sculpture for the wedding of Diana, Princess of Wales and Prince Charles.*

*20in (51cm) high*

**£2,800-3,200** **WAD**

A soapstone 'Transformation' figure, by Naleniktemela (E7-71) from Lake Harbour, signed in syllabics.

*Figurines showing a human transforming into an animal, or animals transforming into other animals are commonly found and represent the mysterious, Shamanistic side of Inuit legends.*

*13in (33cm) high*

**£450-550** **WAD**

## A CLOSER LOOK AT AN INUIT SCULPTURE

*The form and whimsical, almost humourous, design is appealing to today's collectors.*

*The modern, abstracted face, which is set with carved antler is striking.*

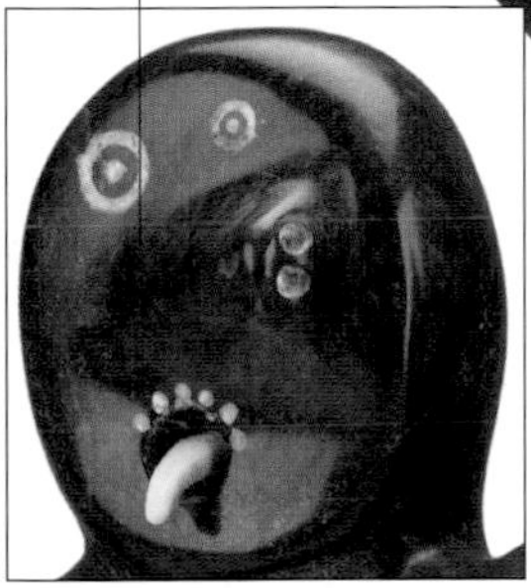

*A similar piece was exhibited in an exhibition held at Winnipeg Art Gallery in 2000 and featured in the catalogue by Darlene Wight.*

*The feature of the hole is very unusual, particularly with an inset, swinging heart.*

A soapstone 'Man with Heart' figure, by Samuel Ullikatalik, with carved inset antler.

*11in (28cm) high*

**£2,500-3,000** **WAD**

A dark soapstone mother and child figure, by Mathew Aqigaaq (E2-350) from Baker Lake, signed in syllabics.

*9.75in (25cm) high*

**£1,500-2,000** **WAD**

A soapstone and antler 'Woman With Seal' figure, by Samuel Nahaulaituq (E4-288), signed in syllabics.

*13in (33cm) high*

**£800-1,200** **WAD**

A soapstone and antler 'Hunter' figure, by Barnabus Arnasungaaq (E2-213) from Baker Lake, signed in syllabics.

*5in (12.5cm) high*

**£500-600** **WAD**

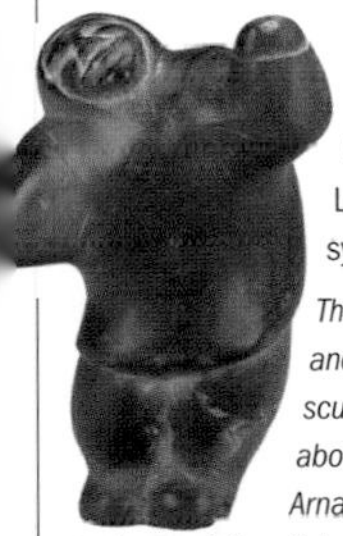

A soapstone figure, by Barnabus Arnasungaaq (E2-213) from Baker Lake, signed in syllabics.

*The sense of movement and the fame of the sculptor raises this piece above the ordinary. Arnasungaaq is a well-known, influential sculptor from the Baker Lake area and contributed to the first Keewatin art exhibition held at the Winnipeg Art Gallery in 1964.*

*6.5in (16.5cm) high*

**£1,200-1,800** **WAD**

A soapstone figure, by an unidentified artist, with inscribed disc number.

*c1960* *4in (10cm) high*

**£280-320** **WAD**

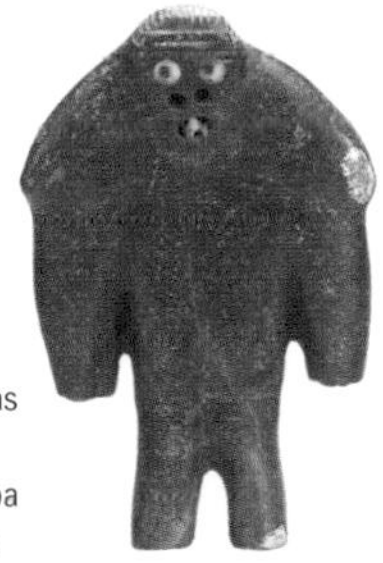

A soapstone and antler figure, by Judas Ullulaq (E4-342) from Gjoa Haven, signed in syllabics.

*Ullulaq's idiosyncratic style with inlays and heavily carved parallel lines is apparent.*

*5.75in (14.5cm) high*

**£800-1,200** **WAD**

A soapstone 'Figure' sculpture, by John Pangnark (E1-104) from Arviat, signed in syllabics.

*5in (12.5cm) high*

**£500-700** **WAD**

A grey soapstone hooded Inuk, by John Pangnark (E1-104) from Arviat.

*6in (15cm) high*

**£1,000-1,500** **WAD**

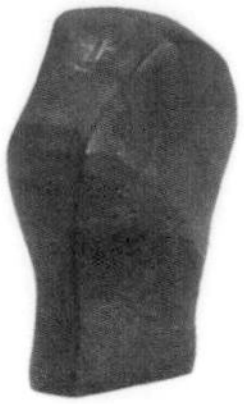

A soapstone 'Figure' sculpture, by John Pangnark (E1-104) from Arviat.

*4.5in (11.5cm) high*

**£1,800-2,200** **WAD**

A 'Figure' soapstone Inuk sculpture, by John Pangnark (E1-104) from Arviat, signed in syllabics.

*Inuk is the singular form of Inuit, roughly translating as 'human being'.*

*4.5in (11.5cm) high*

**£1,500-2,000** **WAD**

A soapstone 'Opposing Figures' sculpture, by John Pangnark (E1-104) from Arviat, signed in syllabics.

*Pangnark (1920-1980) is renowned for his, typically small scale, abstract sculptures that are lightly engraved with a stylized face. Most forms are highly abstracted and are reminiscent of mountains, hills or Inuit huddled on the ground against the cold wind, with the face only occupying a tiny area of the surface. Values vary, often depending on the size, sense of weight and form, and visual appeal of the piece. Double figures, such as this example, are comparatively scarce.*

*4in (10cm) long*

**£3,200-3,800** **WAD**

A grey soapstone bust of an Inuk, by John Pangnark (E1-104) from Arviat.

*2.25in (6cm) high*

**£500-600** **WAD**

A soapstone 'Bust' figure, by John Kavik (E2-290) from Rankin Inlet.

*3in (7.5cm) high*

**£280-320** **WAD**

A soapstone 'Bust' figure, by John Tiktak (E1-266) from the Rankin Inlet, signed in syllabics.

*Tiktak (1916-81) devoted himself to art from 1962. In 1970, he was well-known enough to be given the first retrospective devoted to an Inuit artist. He is known for his abstracted sculptures of heads and the mother and child theme, and his work is in many private and public collections.*

*6in (15cm) high*

**£2,200-2,800** **WAD**

A limited edition 'Shaman Entering The Drum Dance' serigraph, by Luke Anguhadluq (1895-1982), from an edition of 59.

*1976* *30in (76cm) high*

**£1,000-1,500** **WAD**

A 'Challenging Wrestle' silkscreen print, by Jessie Oonark (1906-1985).

*1976* *30in (76cm) wide*

**£500-600** **WAD**

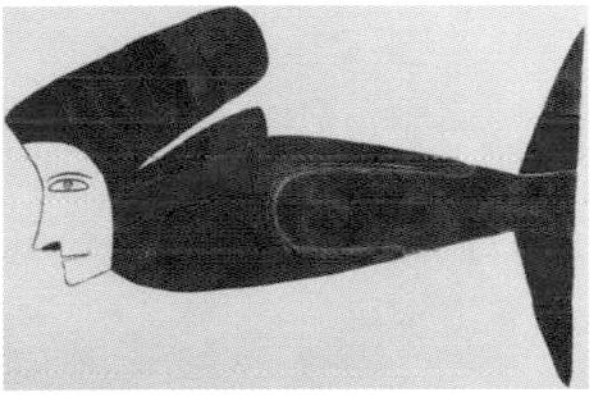

A limited edition 'Fish Woman' stencil print, by Jessie Oonark (1906-85), from an edition of 55.

*1979* *36.5in (92.5cm) wide*

**£1,200-1,800** **WAD**

A limited edition 'All Different Thoughts' stencil print, by Irene Avaalaaqiaq Tiktaalaaq (b.1941), from an edition of 50.

*1978* *30in (76cm) wide*

**£450-550** **WAD**

## A CLOSER LOOK AT AN INUIT PRINT

*Oonark (1906-85) had her first works published in 1960, at the age of 54, and became a prolific and influential artist over the next 19 years.*

*The bold areas of flat colour are a hallmark of Oonark's style and are derived from Inuit sewing designs - Oonark is also known for her wall hangings and textiles.*

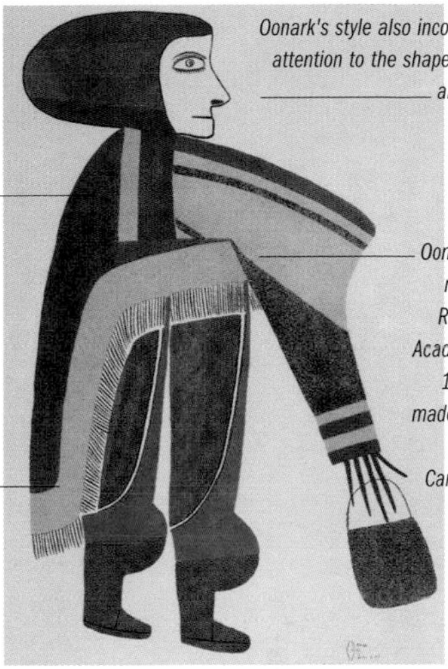

*Oonark's style also incorporates close attention to the shapes of these flat areas of colour.*

*Oonark became a member of the Royal Canadian Academy of Arts in 1975, and was made an Officer of the Order of Canada in 1984.*

A limited edition 'Big Woman' stencil print, by Jessie Oonark, from an edition of 46.

*1976* *34.56in (87.5cm) high*

**£1,500-2,000** **WAD**

A limited edition 'The Shaman Calls His Friends' stencil print, by Irene Avaalaaqiaq Tiktaalaaq (b.1941), from an edition of 50.

*1980* *29.5in (75cm) wide*

**£150-200** **WAD**

A limited edition 'A Wild Life' stonecut and stencil print, by Marion Tuu'Luuq (1910-2002), from an edition of 50.

*1976* *37in (94cm) wide*

**£250-300** **WAD**

### FIND OUT MORE...

**The Inuit Art Center** - *www.ainc-inac.gc.ca*

**'Inuit Art: An Introduction'**, *by Ingo Hessel, Dieter Hessel and George Swinton, published by Douglas & McIntyre, 2003.*

**'Sculpture of the Inuit'**, *by George Swinton, published by McLelland & Stewart, 1999.*

## COLLECTORS' NOTES

- Keys have been made for over four thousand years – for as long as mankind has had precious possessions to protect. The value of keys is not always dependant on their age. Some ancient keys, found at archeological digs, can be acquired for comparatively small sums of money considering their age. Bronze was the primary material from AD650-1050, with iron taking over afterwards.
- Consider the form and decorative appeal of a key. Those with complex wards and decorative bows, or in novelty forms, tend to be the most valuable. The Renaissance saw the first highly decorative keys being made. The 17th and 18th centuries saw an enormous growth in key manufacture. Highly decorative, ornate European examples can command values of a few hundred pounds of more. Look out for large examples, as size can count towards value.
- Keys produced after the late 19th century tend to be of considerably less interest. However, solid gold watch keys, watch keys with makers names or attached pencils, and keys with novelty functions or forms can generate some interest. Although not of enormous value, Joseph Bramah's 'unpickable' locks and keys are interesting. Condition is also worth considering, with missing parts and serious rust reducing value.

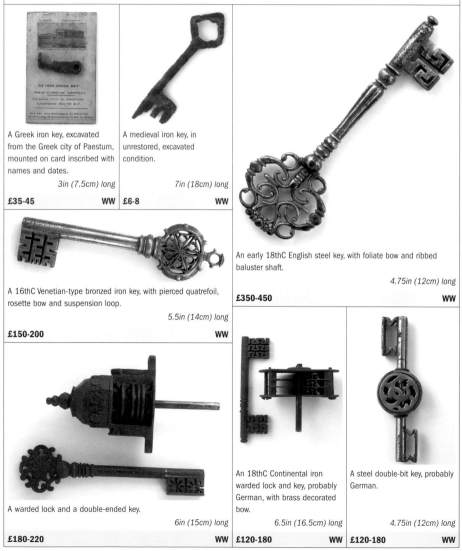

A Greek iron key, excavated from the Greek city of Paestum, mounted on card inscribed with names and dates.

*3in (7.5cm) long*

**£35-45** **WW**

A medieval iron key, in unrestored, excavated condition.

*7in (18cm) long*

**£6-8** **WW**

An early 18thC English steel key, with foliate bow and ribbed baluster shaft.

*4.75in (12cm) long*

**£350-450** **WW**

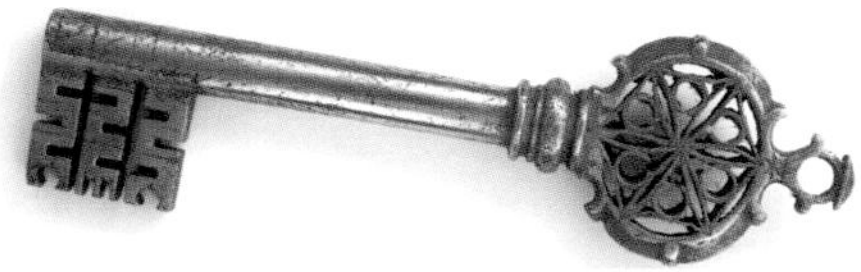

A 16thC Venetian-type bronzed iron key, with pierced quatrefoil, rosette bow and suspension loop.

*5.5in (14cm) long*

**£150-200** **WW**

A warded lock and a double-ended key.

*6in (15cm) long*

**£180-220** **WW**

An 18thC Continental iron warded lock and key, probably German, with brass decorated bow.

*6.5in (16.5cm) long*

**£120-180** **WW**

A steel double-bit key, probably German.

*4.75in (12cm) long*

**£120-180** **WW**

A rare and early herb chopper, by James Cam, with original boxwood handle and maker's stamp to the semi-circular blade, in very good condition.

*James Cam was a noted late 18thC and early 19thC toolmaker, based in Sheffield.*

**£40-60** **MUR**

A 19thC kitchen chopper, with later handle, in very good condition.

**£60-80** **MUR**

An early 19thC decorative herb chopper, with original yew handle, in very good condition.

*The semi circular shape and moving handle allowed the blade to be rocked, easily chopping the herbs finely.*

**£100-150** **MUR**

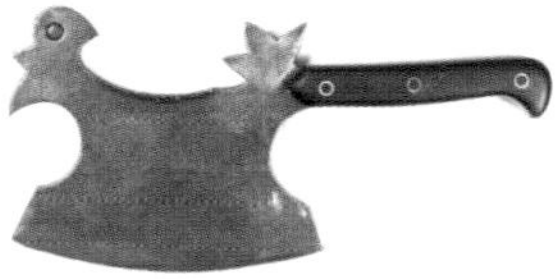

A 19thC decorative kitchen chopper, in the shape of a cockerel, in very good condition.

**£180-220** **MUR**

A rare early 19thC asparagus knife, with horn handle, in very good condition.

**£80-120** **MUR**

A rare three-legged cherry stoner, by Scott Bastinone, in very good condition.

**£60-70** **MUR**

A 19thC European 'fox' chopper, with ebony handle, in very good condition.

*Figural choppers are rare and desirable. The more obviously figural, the better. The fox also plays on stories of foxes in the chicken house.*

**£550-650** **MUR**

An American Reading Hardware Co. mechanical apple peeler, in very good condition.

**£100-150** **MUR**

An unusual 19thC bronze scale weight, in very good condition.

*5in (12.5cm) long*

**£60-80** **MUR**

A Robert Welch candlestick, made from vitreous cast iron at Chipping Campden.

*Note the similarity to Ronald Stennett-Willson's complex 'Sheringham' candleholder designed for King's Lynn Glass in 1967.*

*c1964 5.75in (14.5cm) high*

**£45-50** **MHT**

A pair of 1930s Danish Meka sterling salt and pepper pots, in the form of fish with enamelled eyes and fin decoration, the base moulded "Meka Denmark Sterling".

*2.25in (5.5cm) high*

**£30-50** **GAZE**

A green 'Chicken of the Sea' tuna mayonnaise serving dish, the base moulded "Made in California Chicken of the Sea Tuna Baker-Salad Server. Pat Applied For", with metal base.

*These are also found in burgundy and yellow, and were a free promotion redeemed by sending labels from tins of tuna.*

*8.5in (22cm) high*

**£40-60** **HLM**

## A CLOSER LOOK AT A SET OF KRENIT WARE BOWLS

*Krenit Ware bowls were designed in in 1953, by Herbert Krenchel, a Danish professor of mechanical engineering.*

*They won a gold medal when exhibited at the prestigious Milan Triennale in 1954.*

*They are acid resistant and fire-proof.*

*They were produced by Danish manufacturer Torben Orskov in a number of different sizes - the larger the more valuable.*

*Produced from cold-pressed steel, they are enamelled in glossy colours inside and matte black on the outside. Chips to the enamel devalue examples considerably.*

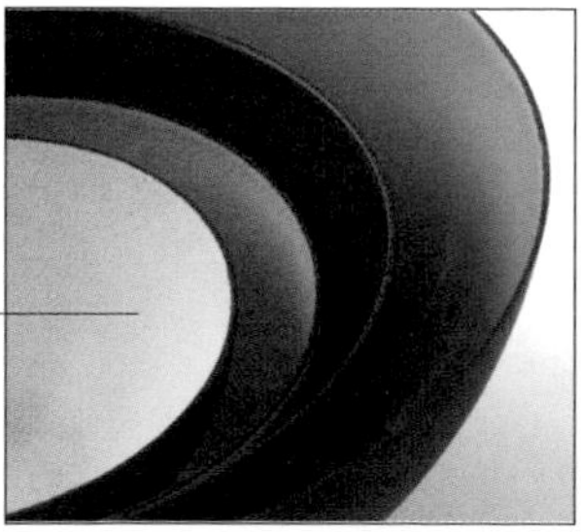

Four different Danish Krenit Ware enamelled metal bowls, designed by Herbert Krenchel in 1953, with coloured interiors and black exteriors.

*Krenchel also designed a pair of melamine salad servers as part of the range.*

*Largest 6.25in (16cm) diam*

**£50-120 (each)** **HLM**

A 1960s Braun orange plastic-cased coffee grinder, designed by Dieter Rams.

*10.75in (27.5cm) high*

**£8-12** **GAZE**

## COLLECTORS' NOTES

- Lighting can be a simple and highly effective way to add a period touch to a home that proves functional as well as decorative. With the current vogue for retro styles and individualism looking set to remain popular, lamps should continue to be desirable.
- Currently, the 1930s and the 1950s-60s provide the two main periods for collectors to focus on. The modernity of clean lines, simple geometric forms and, cool and classic, or strong and contrasting, colours of the Art Deco style are sought-after as they fit in many of today's modern interiors. This period also saw many whimsical lamps being made, particularly in animal forms.
- Look for quality of manufacture and any notable manufacturer's names. However, it is adherence to a particular style and instant 'eye appeal' that are usually the most important factors. Examine a lamp closely for signs of wear or damage, and always have a vintage lamp inspected by a qualified electrician before plugging it in.

A hand-carved alabaster night light, probably modelled on an US lighthouse.

*Lit from within, alabaster gives a gentle, warm glow.*

*c1935* *7.5in (19cm) high*

**£120-180** **DETC**

A Hirsch figural alabaster lighthouse lamp, with a spelter keeper holding a lantern and a large anchor, on a slate base with cracks.

*c1930* *10in (25.5cm) high*

**£300-400** **DETC**

A German 'iron forge' spelter and alabaster lamp, with ironworker and illuminated 'flame'.

*8in (20.5cm) high*

**£200-300** **DETC**

A finely detailed cast spelter lamp, in the form of a cobbler's house and workshop, with customer outside and cobbler inside.

*This is a finely detailed American copy of a bronze and ivory Austrian original. US companies bought the rights to reproduce the work of many Austrian artists in this way, including Bergman.*

*11.5in (29cm) high*

**£250-350** **DETC**

A white onyx figural lamp, depicting a polar bear group on an iceberg.

*The polar bear was a popular motif during the Art Deco period, with a famous stylized sculpture by Francois Pompon being displayed in the original Paris Exhibition in 1925.*

*10in (25.5cm) high*

**£400-500** **DETC**

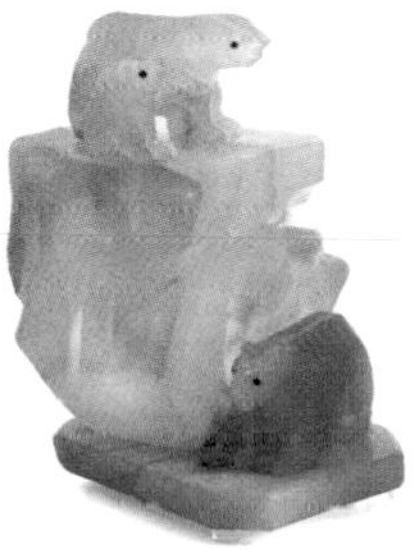

An American Gibson of New York playing cat night light, with original neon bulb and maker's sticker.

*c1935* *7in (18cm) long*

**£180-220** **DETC**

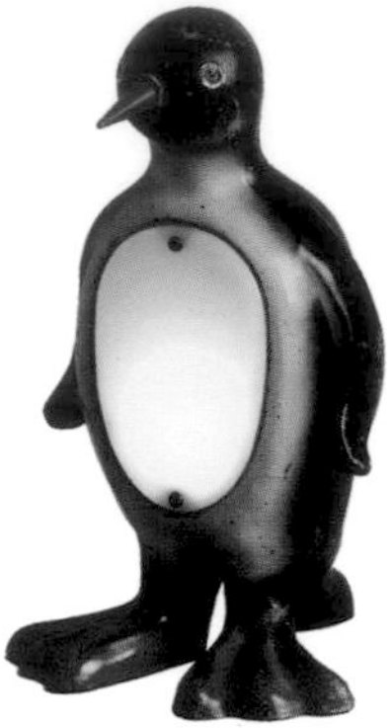

A rare 1930s enamelled metal penguin night light, the Catalin beak as the switch.

*10.25in (26cm) high*

**£200-250** **DETC**

A figural lamp in the form of a parrot, of painted cast iron, holding the bulb in a cage from its beak.

*c1935* *15in (38cm) high*

**£300-400** **DETC**

A French hand-painted earthenware figural lamp, with polychrome glaze, inscribed "Mary E" to the bottom.

*c1935* *13.5in (34.5cm) high*

**£120-180** **DETC**

A frosted green and uncoloured glass 'Saturn' lamp, with internally painted stars and planets.

*These lamps were produced to commemorate the 1939 New York World's Fair, which celebrated technology and the future. This theme is shown in the planet-shaped shade and the stars and planets depicted on it.*

*c1939* *12.25in (31cm) high*

**£120-180** **DETC**

## A CLOSER LOOK AT A LAMP

*The base is made from hand-painted moulded plaster, which is fragile and prone to damage, this example is in excellent condition.*

*This lamp retains its original shade, which has boosted the value by at least a third.*

*Cast plaster lamps such as these were often sold in pairs.*

*The fairground subject matter, form and colourful finish makes this extremely appealing.*

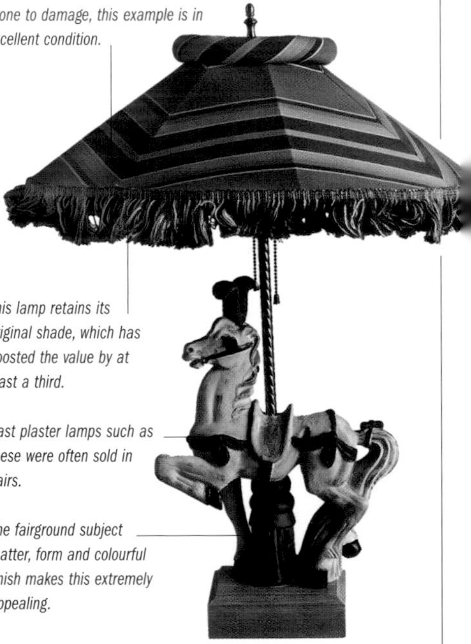

A 1940s painted plaster, wood and brass 'carousel horse' table lamp, with original fabric shade.

*27.5in (70cm) high*

**£100-150** **DETC**

## COLLECTORS' NOTES

- The market for magic memorabilia has seen a recent boom in interest thanks to books and films, such as the Harry Potter series, that have revealed the activity to younger people. Celebrity illusionists and magicians such as David Blaine, Derren Brown and Criss Angel have also drawn attention to the area. Memorabilia focuses primarily on instructional literature and the promotional material produced for magicians and their acts. This comprises books, advertising posters and cards, and other ephemera.
- The focus of most of today's collectors is on pieces produced from the mid-late 19th century to the 1940s. Look out for 'scaling' or throw cards, which were small promotional cards thrown by the magician with incredible accuracy at individuals in the audience. Rarer still are props and apparatus used in acts, which are not to be confused with mass-produced games for children. Nevertheless, these are also highly collectable when complete and bearing charming graphics.
- Value is decided by a number of factors including the fame of the magician, the visual appeal of the piece, its age and its rarity. Pieces related to leading illusionists and magicians such as Harry Houdini, Charles Carter and Howard Thurston tend to fetch the highest prices, particularly if they were known for producing well-designed pieces. Always aim to buy pieces that represent the magic and mystery of illusionism, and also the character of the performer.

"The Boy's Own Magic & Trick Books Tricks & Deceptions With Cards", published by Aldine Publishing Co., with pictorial title page, illustrations and original pictorial wrappers.

*c1895*

**£20-25** **BLO**

'DeLaMano's Great Magic Book', with illustrations and original pictorial wrapper, published by NY Popular Publishing Co., New York.

*DeLaMano was a French travelling magician and these books would have been sold at his shows.*

*c1880*

**£45-55** **BLO**

Dryasdust, 'The Wizard's Mantle', the preface inscribed "with the author's compliments", with printed illustrations designed by the author and original pictorial cloth.

*An edition was published in 1903 with M.Y. Halidom named as the author.*

*c1900*

**£120-180** **BLO**

The Magical Monthly, edited by Edward Bagshaw, a complete set of volumes 1-3, with insides, with rexine backed boards, and a duplicate of the first volume.

*1923-1926*

**£40-60** **BLO**

A 'Le Livre Magique' flickbook, with eight paired stencil-coloured woodcut illustrations repeated six times, loose in original pictorial wrappers, printed in Paris.

*Subjects illustrated include performing monkeys and bears, Punch and Harlequin, acrobats, and others. Flick or flipbooks were introduced in the mid-19thC and are effectively a form of pre-cinema animation. Each page has a slightly different image that gives the illusion of movement when it is flipped through.*

*1863*

**£400-500** **BLO**

An American Crest Trading Co.'Standard and Up-to-Date Magic' illustrated catalogue, with illustrations and original pictorial wrappers.

*c1907*

**£40-80** **BLO**

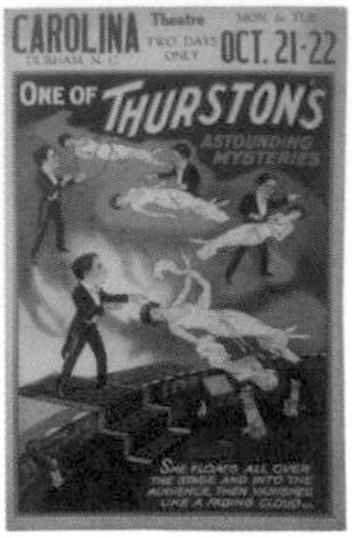


A window card advertising 'Thurston's Astounding Mysteries in Carolina, Durham NC' on Oct 21 and 22nd, showing the magician levitating people, printed by The Otis Litho Co. of Cleveland Ohio.

*American Howard Thurston (1869-1936) became one of the most famous magicians of the early 20thC. Like Newmann and Carter, he is known for his lavish and high quality promotional materials, which were produced throughout his career and included posters, books, cards, coins and more.*

*22.25in (56.5cm) high*

**£250-350** **PWE**

A 'Thurston – World's Famous Magician' colour lithographed advertising window card, showing the magician with two devils on his shoulders.

*22.25in (56.5cm) high*

**£250-350** **PWE**

A Newmann The Great advertising card, showing the magician surrounded by a question mark in smoke emitting from a censor, on a red ground.

*c1913 14.5in (35.5cm) high*

**£150-200** **PWE**

A 'Davis The Man Who Mystifies' colour lithographed advertising window card, showing the magician pulling a rabbit out of a hat.

*22in (56cm) high*

**£60-80** **PWE**

A 'Reno Master of Magic' colour lithographed advertising card, showing the magician performing several tricks.

*16.25in (41cm) wide*

**£50-80** **PWE**

A 'Carter the Great Magician' large colour lithographed poster, printed by Otis Litho, Cinn., OH, captioned 'Shooting a marked bullet', linen mounted in two sections.

*American born illusionist Charles Carter (1874-1936) left the US due to strong competition, seeing more success overseas. He is known to collectors today for his high quality promotional material, such as this poster, which is highly collectable. Interest has mushroomed due to the publication of the best-selling 'Carter Beats the Devil' book in 2002.*

*106in (269cm) high*

**£500-700** **JDJ**

A large Gogia Pasha colour printed poster, with central portrait and line illustrations of various tricks and illusions.

*40in (101.5cm) high*

**£10-15** **BLO**

An International Brotherhood of Magicians (British Ring) handbill for the 'Grand International Gala of Magic' to be held at the Winter Garden, Eastbourne, England on October 4th, featuring a number of prominent magicians.

*14.75in (37.5cm) high*

**£20-25** **BLO**

A large 'The Magic Mirror' hand-coloured lithographed pictorial label for a fortune-telling game, depicting a magician showing a young woman a future view of her and her groom at the altar.

*11.5in (29.5cm) wide*

**£60-80** **BLO**

A coloured lithograph of Servais LeRoy performing 'The Flesh and the Devil' illusion, published by Charles Lane, Brighton, framed and glazed.

*Jean-Henri Servais LeRoy (1865-1953) was a notable illusionist who was admired by both Houdini and Thurston and is best known for his trio act 'LeRoy, Talma & Bosco'.*

*c1900* *10in (25.5cm) wide*

**£220-280** **BLO**

## A CLOSER LOOK AT A MYSTERY CLOCK

*Jean-Eugène Robert-Houdin (1805-71) was a French clock and watch maker, and also a skilled illusionist who used his technical knowledge in many of his tricks.*

*He is seen by many as the father of modern conjuring and illusions, with Erich Weiss adopting the name 'Houdini' in his honour.*

*Mystery clocks are so-called as they have no visible mechanism to enable the hands to turn to tell the time.*

*He introduced mystery clocks in the late 1830s, and this is an excellent example with fine quality materials and construction.*

A French fine Jean-Eugène Robert-Houdin mystery clock, the thin glass dial with single hour hand and metal rim above the tiered bronze casing with gilt decoration, on gilt wooden plinth, the dial lettered 'Robert-Houdin Paris'.

*c1840* *16.5in (42cm) high*

**£10,000-15,000** **BLO**

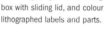

An American McLoughlin Brothers 'Chiromagica' game, in mahogany box with sliding lid, and colour lithographed labels and parts.

*c1870* *11in (28cm) wide*

**£550-650** **BLO**

A 'Flower and Fishbowl Production' magic illusion apparatus, comprising a velvet covered platform on a chromed metal stand, a large circular cover decorated with painted flowers, and a large glass bowl, the latter in original case.

*This was commissioned from renowned New York illusion equipment maker Rudy Schlosser by the legendary magician and escapologist Harry Houdini (Erich Weiss). It later passed into the care of Bill Vagel who performed as 'Mystic Craig', from whose estate it passed to the present owner and sale.*

*17.75in (45cm) high*

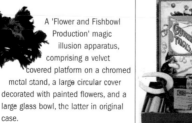

**£3,000-4,000** **BLO**

An English Glevum 'Conjuring Tricks' child's magic set, containing a magic wand, magic coral beads, the magic cube, an ever-changing card trick, a horse-shoe puzzle trick, a heart puzzle, magic book, and nail trick, together with 12-page Instruction pamphlet.

*Always check that all the contents are present and intact, as many tricks were broken or lost.*

*c1920*

**£70-90** **BLO**

A Merv Taylor aluminium and metal 'Wrist Chopper', with engine-turned decoration on upright surfaces, and photocopied instructions.

*14.25in (36.5cm) high*

**£180-220** **BLO**

A transitional 'Leighton Ground Pontil' handmade marble.

*These are so-called as they were apparently made by James Leighton & Co. of Ohio in the late 1890s, although they may in fact originate from Germany. Look out for oxblood swirls as these can double or triple this value.*

*c1880s-1920s* *0.75in (2cm) diam*

**£40-50** **AB**

A transitional 'Oxblood' handmade marble.

*This is a rare marble in a rare and desirable colour.*

*0.75in (2cm) diam*

**£650-750** **AB**

A 1920s-30s Christensen Agate Company machine-made 'Electric Yellow Slag' marble.

*0.5in (1.5cm) diam*

**£30-40** **AB**

A Christensen Agate Company 'Guinea' machine-made marble.

*0.5in (1.5cm) diam*

**£150-250** **AB**

A 'Pinwheel' hand-painted china marble, with pink band and green flower motif.

*c1890* *0.75in (4.5cm) diam*

**£40-60** **AB**

A 'The News Bee Marble Competition' badge.

*1in (3cm) diam*

**£60-80** **LDE**

A 1928 'Bulletin Marble Shooter' pin.

*Vintage badges such as this are rare as few were produced for these comparatively small events, and many were damaged or lost over the years.*

*1928* *1in (2.5cm) diam*

**£60-80** **LDE**

A very rare spelter alloy 'The Marble Shooter' figural trophy, impressed "C.L' Chilon" and with inscribed brass plaque reading 'Seventh National Marble Tournament, Ocean City, NJ, 1929, won by Marion Aiello, Champion Northern League, sponsored by The Akro Agate Co. Clarksburg W.VA', in undamaged condition.

*This is one of only 48 examples ever made. Most have been lost or damaged, as the piece is large, cumbersome and relatively unwieldy. Most damaged examples have detached heads.*

*c1928* *13.25in (33.5cm) high*

**£2,500-4,000** **AB**

An American by Oro-Tone 'Orola' record player, with electric folding pick-up arm over needle bowl, speed control, knob and twin lead sockets, in circular nickelled hinged case.

*c1930* *12in (30.5cm) diam*

**£180-220** **EG**

An Edison Model D Standard 'Home' phonograph, No.360887D, with Combination gearing, C reproducer and oak case, restored.

*Combination gearing allowed it to play both two- and four-minute cylinders.*

*c1910*

**£120-180** **EG**

A German Symphonion Musikwerke 4.5in disc player, with a 20-teeth comb and ten metal discs.

*Look out for large examples and fancy cases, as these can be worth over twice the value of this simple example.*

*c1890*

**£220-280** **ATK**

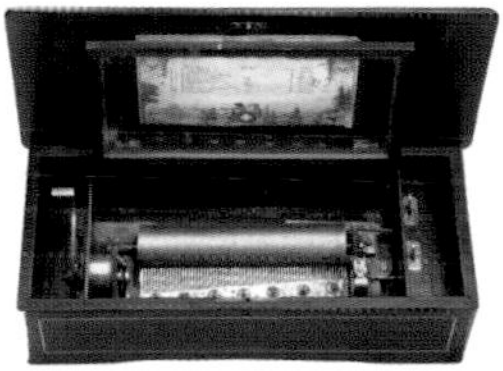

A Swiss brass cylinder walnut musical box, with eight melodies, comb with 66 teeth, with original tune sheet, unmarked.

*c1880* *20.5in (51cm) wide*

**£350-450** **ATK**

An Italian silk-lined wooden musical box, with wax putto doll automaton, the putto raising its head and opening its eyes when the music plays.

*A label indicates that this was made by Giovanni Pusso of Naples, who also made religious articles. Automaton music boxes are rare and desirable.*

*c1930* *10.5in (26cm) wide*

**£450-550** **ATK**

A 1970s Wurlitzer Duet jukebox, with chrome mounts and an illuminated front panel.

**£200-300** **SWO**

A rare 1920s American National Co. 'Microphone Dancer', the articulated wood and card figure jiggling around to music by a vibrating mechanism in the base.

*12in (30cm) high*

**£250-350** **SWO**

A Searchlight gramophone horn, with ribbed bell and remnants of blue paint.

*31in (78.5cm) long*

**£45-55** **EG**

## COLLECTORS' NOTES

- Cast iron money banks are divided into two categories: mechanical banks with movements started by inserting a coin or pulling a lever, and static 'still banks'. Mechanical banks are generally the more desirable and valuable type, as well as the most interesting and varied.
- The first cast iron money bank of this type was patented in 1869, although money banks had existed previously. It was made by J.&E. Stevens & Co of Cromwell, Connecticut, who went on to become a prolific maker. Other known makers include the Hubley Manufacturing Co who also made doorstops and other metal toys, Kyser & Rex (1879-1898) and the Shepard Hardware Manufacturing Company (1882-1892).
- Collectors focus strongly on condition, which is most applicable to the paint. A bank in excellent condition can be worth over ten times more than one in average condition. The level of rarity will also increase prices.
- Mechanisms should work, all parts should be intact, and the coin trap should be original. Repainting devalues a bank, so look closely at the paint, which should have depth, a patina built up over roughly a century, and perhaps show signs of crazing from age.
- There are many fakes and reproductions, especially of mechanical and 'Jolly Bust' banks. Typical hallmarks of fakes include joints that do not 'fit' together well, rough surfaces and less fine detailing. The form may also be slightly different and internal components are often clearly modern. Some are aged to look 'rusty' and old.

A National Products Inc. die-cast metal beige 1949 Dodge Coronet promotional money bank, with silver detailing, trunk and hood embossed "Dodge", side front panels embossed "Coronet", bottom reads "Authentic Scale Model Dodge", white rubber tyres with tin hubs, in near mint condition.

*8in (20cm) long*

**£150-200** **BER**

A National Products Inc. die-cast metal maroon 1947 Chevrolet Fleetline promotional money bank, roof imprint reads 'Chevrolet Grand Rapids, MICH.', painted in maroon overall with silver detailing, minor roof rub, otherwise in very good condition.

*6.5in (16.5cm) long*

**£100-150** **BER**

A rare National Products Inc die-cast metal 1946-8 Chrysler New Yorker promotional automobile, some chipping.

*6.5in (16.5cm) long*

**£120-180** **BER**

A Kenton cast iron three dial 'Radio' money bank, painted in red, with three nickel knobs.

*4.5in (11.5cm) high*

**£100-150** **BER**

A J. & E. Stevens cast iron 'Treasure Safe' still money bank, with nickel finish and key and combination lock.

*This bank is known for its highly detailed moulding.*

*5.25in (13.5cm) high*

**£30-40** **BER**

A C.Hart Mfg Co. cast iron 'Safe Deposit' still money bank, painted in red and gold, with combination lock.

*5.25in (13.5cm) high*

**£120-180** **BER**

A very rare cast iron Kyser & Rex 'Coin Registering Bank' still money bank, painted in red and gold.

*As well as being exceptionally rare and very well moulded with good details, this example is in truly excellent condition, with very little loss to the paintwork. Its rarity is largely due to the fact that it was deemed boring in its day, so very few were sold.*

*7in (18cm) high*

**£4,000-5,000** **BER**

A J. & E. Stevens cast iron 'Home Savings Bank', with japanned exterior and dog's head roof finial.

*c1891 5.75in (14.5cm) high*

**£120-180** **BER**

A 1930s Hubley cast iron 'Duck' still money bank, in excellent condition.

*4.75in (12cm) high*

**£120-180** **BER**

A Hubley cast iron 'Circus Elephant' still bank, painted in colours, in excellent condition.

*4in (10cm) high*

**£150-200** **BER**

A Kenton cast iron 'Round Duck' money bank, painted in blue and red, with large trap cover to base.

*The red detailing has been repainted, which reduces the value.*

*4.5in (11.5cm) high*

**£150-200** **BER**

A painted cast iron 'Bull Dog Bank' money bank, the base stamped "Patd Apr27 1880".

*8in (20cm) high*

**£220-320** **PWE**

A Grey Cast Iron Company cast iron green painted 'Doughboy' money bank, minor chips to face.

*c1919 7in (17.75cm) high*

**£220-280** **BER**

An English Sydenham & McOustra cast iron black finished 'Save And Smile' money bank, with painted eyes and lips.

*4in (10cm) high*

**£100-150** **BER**

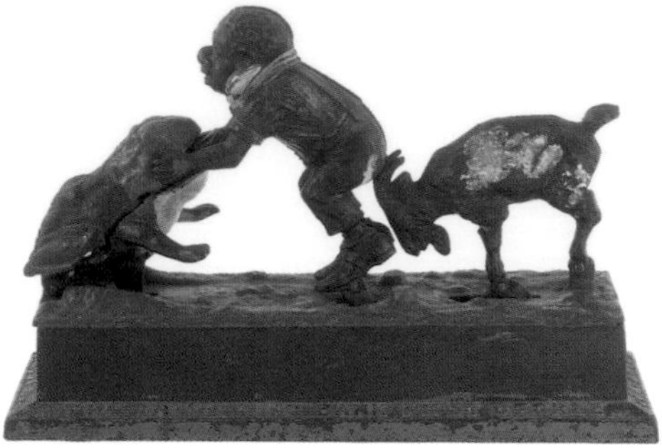

A very rare Mechanical Novelty Works 'The Initiating Bank, First Degree' money bank.

*The goat's head butts the man's bottom and, as he moves forward, he deposits the coin in the frog's mouth. Although there is considerable paint loss, this is a very rare bank.*

*c1880* *10.75in (27cm) long*

**£3,000-4,000** **PWE**

A Hubley cast iron 'Trick Dog' mechanical money bank, with solid base, placing a coin in the dog's mouth and pressing the lever makes the dog jump through the hoop and deposit the coin into the barrel.

*c1906*

**£350-450** **BER**

A J. & E. Stevens Co cast iron 'Bread Winners Bank' mechanical money bank, designed by Charles A. Bailey.

*Place the coin in the end of the club, raise the hammer, press the button and Labour strikes Monopoly, 'sending the rascals up' as the coin falls into the loaf of bread. This sort of political comment can be popular, and even though this example was repainted, it is an early repaint and is a comparatively scarce model.*

*c1886*

**£4,000-5,000** **BER**

A Shepard Hardware Co. cast iron 'Speaking Dog' mechanical money bank, with a maroon base, girl wearing a red coat, replaced trap cover.

*This was designed by Charles Shepard and Peter Adams and patented on 20th October 1885. Place a coin on the plate held by the girl, press the thumbpiece, and the girl's arm moves quickly and deposits the coin through a trap door in the bench. At the same time, the dog opens and closes his mouth as if speaking. The version with a blue coat is usually worth more: this form is generally more common.*

**£420-480** **BER**

## A CLOSER LOOK AT A MECHANICAL MONEY BANK

*This popular, lively and desirable money bank was designed by Charles A. Bailey and patented c1891.*

*Place a coin under the feet of the driver and press the lever. The boy jumps into the road and scares the donkey, which rears up, throwing the driver and cart backwards - the coin falls into the cart and vanishes.*

*This example is worth as much as it is as so much of the original paint still remains.*

*An example in lesser condition with little paint remaining may fetch between £300-500.*

A J.&E. Stevens cast iron 'Bad Accident' mechanical money bank, painted in colours.

*10.25in (26cm) long*

**£1,200-1,800** **BER**

A Shepard Hardware Co cast iron 'Jonah & The Whale' mechanical money bank.

*This bank was designed by Peter Adams and patented on 15th July 1890. Place a coin on Jonah's head and press the lever. The man moves as if to throw Jonah overboard, and the whale opens his mouth. The coin slides off Jonah's head and into the whale. Releasing the lever makes the whale's mouth keep moving afterwards.*

**£1,000-1,500** **BER**

A J. & E. Stevens cast iron yellow painted 'Cabin Bank' mechanical money bank.

*This bank was designed by Edward L. Morris and patented on 2nd June 1885. Place the coin on the roof slot, pull the lever and the man stands on his head and kicks the coin into the back of the bank.*

**£280-320** **BER**

A J.& E. Stevens & Co. cast iron 'Novelty Bank' money bank, painted in colours.

*This bank was designed by C.C. Johnson and patented on the 28th October 1873. When the cashier has received the coin, a light touch closes the door and deposits the coin via the opening in the vault. This example has been 'over cleaned' removing the patina and changing the paint colours.*

**£180-220** **BER**

A J&E Stevens cast iron 'Mule Entering Barn' mechanical money bank, painted in red and white, the base moulded "Patd Aug 3D 1880", in excellent condition.

*This bank was designed by Edward L. Morris and patented on the 6th January 1880. Pressing a knob at the donkey's feet flips the coin into the barn and a dog pops out.*

*8.75in (22cm) long*

**£550-650** **PWE**

A Shepard Hardware Co. cast iron 'Uncle Sam' mechanical money bank.

*This bank was designed by Charles Shepard & Peter Adams and patented on 8th June 1886. Place a coin in Sam's hand, press the button on the stand and the satchel opens, with the arm lowering to drop the coin inside. The pivot-mounted jaw also moves comically throughout.*

**£600-700** **BER**

## A CLOSER LOOK AT A MONEY BANK

*This example is rare as would-be savers, usually children, preferred colourful and fun, complex mechanisms and stories.*

*The movement is comparatively simple – the small dog is tipped over by gravity when the coin is placed on the tray and unbalances him.*

*The rarity of this bank is reinforced as the dog often became detached and was lost, and the rest was discarded.*

*The paintwork is still largely intact, but this simply modelled money bank is rare and desirable in any condition.*

*This money bank was patented by Kyser & Max on 21st September 1880.*

An extremely rare Kyser & Rex cast iron 'Dog Tray Bank' gravity action money bank, designed by Louis Kyser and Albert Rex, dog repainted.

*4.25in (11cm) high*

**£1,000-1,500** **BER**

A Shepard Hardware Co. Santa Claus mechanical money bank, in very good condition.

*Designed by Charles Shepard & Peter Adams and patented on 15th October 1889, placing a coin in Santa's hand and pressing the lever flips the coin down the chimney.*

**£600-700** **BER**

A contemporary cast iron 'Penny Pineapple' mechanical money bank, painted in colours.

*This was made to commemorate Hawaii's induction as the 50th state of the United States, in 1959. It has a similar action to the 'Jolly Bust' money banks.*

*9in (23cm) high*

**£70-90** **BER**

## A CLOSER LOOK AT A MONEY BANK

*Despite its political incorrectness, this is the most commonly faked and reproduced money bank.*

*Look for signs of age - screw holes should not be bright and fresh and the base should have signs of wear consistent with age. Beware of uniformly deep scratches.*

*On originals, the joins are better moulded and fit closer together.*

*Reproductions and fakes often have rougher surfaces and the paint is gloopy and bright, with no signs of patina of ages.*

An original Sydenham & McOustra cast iron 'Jolly Bust' mechanical money bank, painted with a red coat, his eyes and tongue roll back when he swallows the coin.

**£200-300** **BER**

A Hubley cast iron white painted 'Elephant Howdah' pull tail money bank.

*Place the coin in the end of the elephant's trunk and pull his tail to swing the trunk over the howdah, depositing the coin into the front of it.*

*c1930*

**£250-350** **BER**

A lithographed tinplate 'Monkey & Parrot' mechanical money bank, attributed to Selheimer & Strauss, with lever flipping the coin on the monkey's hand into the opening parrot's mouth.

*c1925*

**£120-180** **BER**

A 1950s West German lithographed tinplate 'Shell Service Station' still bank.

*When a coin is inserted in the roof slot, a door swings open and an attendant comes out.*

*5.75in (14.5cm) long*

**£100-150** **BER**

## COLLECTORS' NOTES

- The market for collectable vintage fountain pens began in earnest during the late 1970s and grew throughout the 1980s and early 1990s, arguably reaching its peak in the late 1990s. The most popular brands are household names, and include Parker, Waterman and Montblanc. The production of other, now closed, companies that have now faded from the public consciousness such as Conklin, De La Rue and Mabie Todd, are also collectable. However, the major brands still generally attract the highest prices.
- In the past, collectors tended to focus on pens produced in their own countries. The growth in trade over the internet, the fact that pens can be shipped both easily and cost-effectively, and the rise in price of the best pieces has led collectors to look farther afield. As a result, many smaller brands such as Britain's Conway Stewart have become more collectable across the world. More modern pens, such as the Parker 75,with its many variations have also become the focus of many collectors' attention.
- As well as the brand, the size, rarity and quality of the pen counts. Many pen collectors are men, and larger pens that fit their hands better and have a more immediate visual impact tend to be more desirable. Those with strong decorative qualities such as precious metal or gold-plated overlays, lacquerwork designs or unusual celluloids also tend to be more valuable. Rare pens among these attract the highest prices, particularly if early or unusual.
- Condition is very important as they are often bought to be used, and a pen should be complete and undamaged. Although it is important that a pen has its original nib, there is generally little value in the nib itself, unless the nib is rare or very large and thus typically rare. Most nibs can be changed easily and there is a booming trade in spare parts.

An English Conway Stewart Dinkie no.540 pen, multicoloured marble casein lever-filler with Conway Stewart 14ct gold nib.

*Multicoloured Dinkies such as these, which represent the colours of the Jazz Age, are scarce. The plastic used often bows and warps through age and use, but this example is in excellent condition.*

*1928-32*

**£80-120** **BLO**

A rare English Conway Stewart Dinkie no.540 pen, multicoloured blue, purple, bronze and black marble celluloid with Conway Stewart 14ct gold medium nib, in excellent condition.

*c1937-40*

**£70-100** **BLO**

An English Conway Stewart 100 'cutaway demonstrator', black oversize pen with cut-away barrel to show the working of interconnected O-ring, lever and pressure bar, with Duro 20 medium nib, in very good condition.

*Conway Stewart demonstration pens are extremely rare. A standard no.100 may be worth around £60-90 in excellent condition.*

*1954-58*

**£80-120** **BLO**

A 1930s English Conway Stewart no.380 'Reverse Cracked Ice' pen, ice-blue silver pearl celluloid with black veins, Conway Stewart 14ct gold nib, minor fading, otherwise in excellent condition.

**£120-180** **BLO**

A 1950s English Conway Stewart no.58 'Tiger's Eye' celluloid lever-filling pen, with Conway Stewart medium nib, with light wear on an attractive finish.

**£100-150** **BLO**

A Conway Stewart no.22 'Floral' lever-filling pen, the floral design printed paper encased in clear celluloid, with a Conway Stewart no.5 medium nib, with typical ambering to the paper.

*It was once thought that only around 200 of these pens were made, however, given the number that have appeared for sale over the past decade, this would seem untrue. Examples without the usual amber discolouring to the paper can be worth up to twice this amount. The design was re-released as a limited edition of 50 enamelled pens in 1999.*

*c1955*

**£250-350** **BLO**

A Mabie Todd & Co un-numbered pearl grey snakeskin and red veined celluloid Self-Filler pen, with rolled gold trim and broad cap band and Swan no.1 fine nib, in excellent condition.

**£30-40** **BLO**

A Mabie Todd & Co un-numbered pearl grey snakeskin and green veined celluloid Self-Filler, with chrome trim and narrow cap band and Swan no.1 fine nib, in mint 'new-old stock' condition.

*New-Old stock refers to an item in the same unused condition as it left the factory. These are usually unsold stock from a shop or factory.*

**£30-40** **BLO**

A Mabie Todd & Co Swan L312/88 Leverless pen, with green lizard skin celluloid and later Swan 3G medium nib, in excellent, restored condition.

*This is a particularly sought-after celluloid, but is often found with cracks in the cap, or opening seams, where the plastic was rolled to form a tube. Many examples found are restored. The large no.6 size can be worth over £250.*

**£120-180** **BLO**

A Mabie Todd & Co Swan L312/87 Leverless pen, with blue lizard skin celluloid and later Swan 2 broad nib, in excellent condition noting a small crack in cap lip.

**£80-120** **BLO**

A Mabie Todd & Co 'Le Merle Blanc' pen, with pink, bronze and black marbled celluloid, chrome trim and Warranted 14ct medium nib, in mint condition.

*This pen was produced for export to the French market, as indicated by the partially French barrel imprint. This scarce pen is made even rarer by the unusual and attractive plastic.*

*c1937*

**£400-500** **BLO**

An English Burnham prototype pen, light and royal blue pearl acrylic lever-filler, with gold-plated trim and glass nib, in mint condition.

*Hand-made by John Burnham, but never put into production.*

*c1960*

**£180-220** **BLO**

A rare 1940s-50s English Esterbrook 'Relief' no.12 lever-filling pen, 'Tiger's Eye' (golden-bronze pearl and lined spiral marble) celluloid with 'R' clip and gold Relief Esterbrook 14ct medium-oblique nib, in excellent condition.

**£180-220** **BLO**

A 1920s English National Security 'Rosemary' lever-filling pen, mottled hard rubber full-length slender pen with rolled gold cap band and threaded post with Warranted nib, in green marbled Rosemary hard box with instructions, and similar ringtop pencil, pen lacks iridium, otherwise excellent or better, rare in this condition and with its box.

**£40-60 (set)** **BLO**

A 1920s English Platignum A1 Major, red and black ripple hard rubber lever-filler, shaped metal Platignum A1 Major nib and lever, in excellent condition.

*This is an early hard rubber Platignum with a rare nib. Most Platignums date from the postwar period and are worth under £5.*

**£40-50** **BLO**

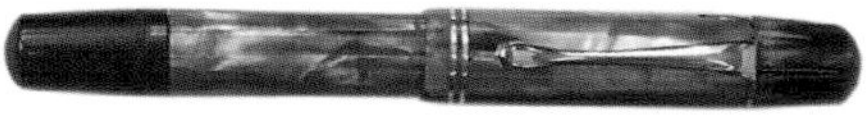

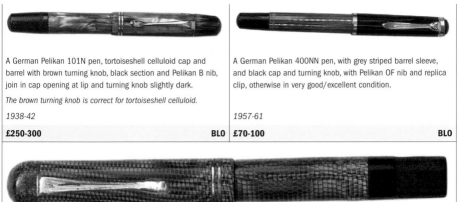

A German Pelikan 101N pen, tortoiseshell celluloid cap and barrel with brown turning knob, black section and Pelikan B nib, join in cap opening at lip and turning knob slightly dark.

*The brown turning knob is correct for tortoiseshell celluloid.*

*1938-42*

**£250-300** **BLO**

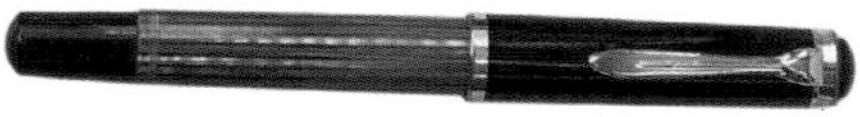

A German Pelikan 400NN pen, with grey striped barrel sleeve, and black cap and turning knob, with Pelikan OF nib and replica clip, otherwise in very good/excellent condition.

*1957-61*

**£70-100** **BLO**

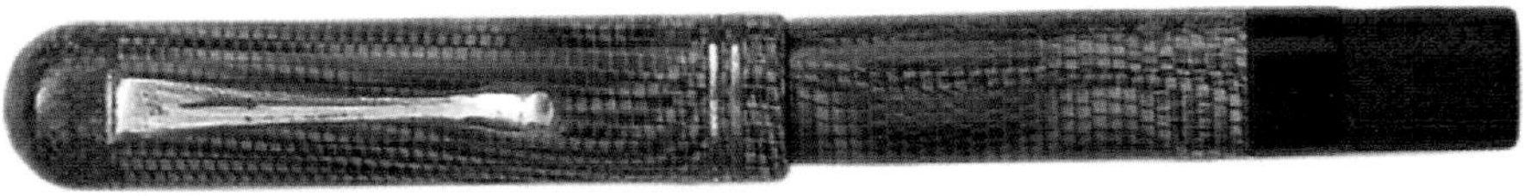

A Pelikan 100 'Cobra' with grey snakeskin effect celluloid cap and barrel and short clip screw, with Pelikan 585 nib, some splits and wear.

*This is a very rare plastic, made for export only. Always examine the body carefully, as they are frequently found with cracks and splits.*

*c1938*

**£450-550** **BLO**

A German Pelikan 400NN transparent piston-filling pen demonstrator pen, with Pelikan 14c 585 OF nib, in excellent condition.

*Genuine Pelikan vintage demonstrators are very rare. They are typically both colourless and transparent.*

*1956-65*

**£300-400** **BLO**

A 1980s German Pelikan black M800 five-piece set, comprising an M800 pen with Pelikan two-colour 14C-585 medium nib, a K800 twist-action ballpoint pen with tag, a D800 capped rollerball with tag, matching pencil, and R800 small-size capped rollerball, in mint condition, with five boxes and booklet.

**£280-320 (set)** **BLO**

A 1990s German Pelikan Souverän M200 pen and ballpen, tortoiseshell and brown piston-filler with gold-plated 'B' nib and matching ballpen, in hard Pelikan box with guarantee, in mint condition.

*This is a rare finish for the 200, which is usually found in plain black.*

**£150-200** **BLO**

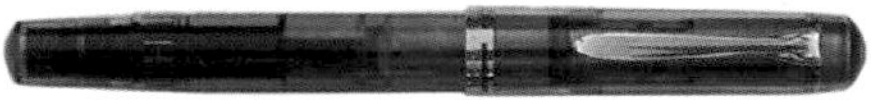

A German Pelikan M250 transparent green pen, with Pelikan metal medium nib, in mint condition with box and guarantee.

*This is almost certainly from the un-numbered special edition of 3,000 pieces made for the American market in 1989.*

*1989*

**£80-120** **BLO**

A 1990s German Pelikan transparent green Souverän M800 piston-filler, with two-colour 14ct 585 OBB nib, in modern Pelikan hard case, in near mint condition.

*The M800 is the largest size of pen made by Pelikan. The scarce double broad oblique nib adds to the value.*

**£280-320** **BLO**

## A CLOSER LOOK AT A MONTBLANC PEN

*Popular with a number of makers during the 1920s, safety pens have a mechanism that allows the nib to be retracted into the body by turning a knob at the end of the barrel.*

*Octagonal Montblanc safety pens are much rarer than cylindrical examples.*

*They are called safety pens as, once the nib has been retracted, the cap fits tightly over the top, and has a cork stopper inside to prevent any ink leakage.*

*This pen is also a large no.6 size. It is in excellent condition.*

A rare German Montblanc 6-F octagonal safety filling pen, octagonal black hard rubber with 18ct 6 fine nib, in excellent condition.

*1924-29*

**£500-600** **BLO**

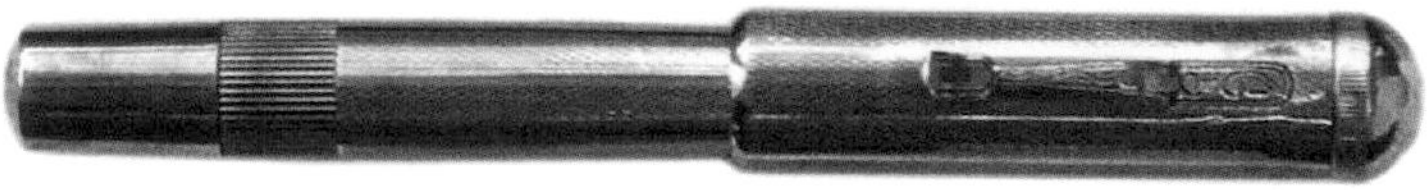

A very rare German Montblanc yellow-metal safety filling pen, marked "585" on the clip and signed "Mont -M Blanc" with alternating engine-turned and plain panels and Montblanc 2 medium nib with heart-shaped vent, barrel threads replaced with black hard rubber, otherwise in excellent condition.

*Montblanc pens with original factory precious metal overlays are rare. Many modern or vintage overlays were applied by jewellers at the request of collectors or original buyers.*

*1925-28*

**£700-900** **BLO**

A rare Danish Montblanc 35 Masterpiece push-knob filling pen, coral red with 4810 medium nib, in later Montblanc hard duo box, in good condition, with engraved name and date.

*Montblanc had a factory in Denmark during the 1930s and '40s and vintage Mont Blanc pens are often found in Scandinavia. As pipe smoking was so popular in these countries during this time, many have burn marks as they were used as pipe tampers.*

*1935-46*

**£200-300** **BLO**

A rare German Montblanc 322 EF button-filling pen, pearl and black marbled celluloid with Warranted a nib, barrel slightly amberised, lightly engraved name.

*1935-38*

**£350-450** **BLO**

A German Montblanc 244-F 'PL' piston-filling pen, platinum pearl striated celluloid with Montblanc fine nib, in large Montblanc mock croc card box, in excellent condition.

*1950-54*

**£300-400** **BLO**

A 1930s German new-old-stock Osmia 62M pen, bronze pearl with black lattice and visible inkwindow, Osmia 3 .585 gold medium nib, an attractive pen.

**£80-120** **BLO**

A German Soennecken Rheingold 616 pen, black, with yellow ink window and Soennecken medium metal nib, in excellent or better condition, recently restored.

*c1938*

**£120-180** **BLO**

## A CLOSER LOOK AT A PARKER VACUMATIC

*This plastic is extremely rare and does not appear on any other pen by Parker or any other manufacturer.*

*Only four or five examples are known, of which this is one.*

*It is a prototype pen, produced for management to decide on plastics to be used for the new Vacumatic range, which had been released in 1933.*

*The cream grid plastic is close to the later 'Golden Web' design plastic introduced c1936, and this pen is likely to have led to its development.*

A Parker prototype Vacumatic, with cream and dark brown celluloid, full barrel imprint, 'lockdown' filler and Parker Vacumatic Arrow nib, some darkening from use.

*1935*

**£1,800-2,200** **BLO**

A Parker 15 eyedropper-filling pen, with corrugated abalone-covered barrel, chased gold-filled bands and gold-filled filigree cap, and Parker Lucky Curve 2 nib with teardrop vent, in very good to excellent condition.

*This is a rare, early pen that is typical of the ornate style of expensive pens produced in the early decades of the 20thC. Examples were also made with flat abalone barrels, and with bulging barrels, often known as 'Pregnant' pens. Always check the abalone carefully as panels are often replaced.*

*1910-18*

**£850-950** **BLO**

An American Parker model 33 eyedropper-filling pen, gold-filled half-overlaid filigree with matching cap crown, and Parker Lucky Curve Pen 2 nib, initialled, minor brassing.

*c1905-18*

**£180-220** **BLO**

An American Parker model 16 eyedropper, gold-filled filigree-overlay signed on cap and barrel overlay, with Parker Lucky Curve medium nib, initialled and dated 1909, otherwise in very good condition.

*c1905-15*

**£180-220** **BLO**

An American Parker 16 Jack-Knife Safety eyedropper-filling pen, gold-filled filigree covered long barrel, 'turban' cap, hourglass section and with Parker Lucky Curve Pen 3 keyhole nib, in excellent condition, a rare early version with the hourglass shaped section.

*1908-12*

**£350-450** **BLO**

An American Parker Junior Vacumatic filling pen, jet celluloid with ink windows running the full length of the barrel, aluminium lock-down plunger-filler, gold Parker USA Arrow nib, a rare and short-lived variation; professionally overhauled.

*1936*

**£60-80** **BLO**

A Canadian Parker Senior Maxima Vacumatic filling pen, Jet black celluloid, with aluminium Speedline-filler and Parker Vacumatic two-colour arrow medium-fine nib, barrel needs cleaning on the inside to remove ink bloom.

*1939*

**£80-120** **BLO**

A 1930s Canadian Parker Televisor Standard button-filling pen, silver and black lined celluloid with Parker Fountain Pen Canada medium nib, in good/very good condition.

**£60-80** **BLO**

An English Parker Maxima Duofold pen, green, with large arrow Parker 50 medium nib, in card Parker box with leaflet, engraved name.

*The large Maxima with the correct nib is worth the most, other 1950s English Duofolds are typically up to £10 in used condition.*

*c1959*

**£40-60** **BLO**

A 1950s American Parker 51 Custom pen, Midnight Blue with gold-filled Insignia (converging line) design cap and fine nib, in very good to excellent condition.

**£50-70** **BLO**

A 1950s English Parker 51 Custom pen, burgundy with rolled gold Insignia (converging line) design cap and fine nib, in Parker 51 'mock croc' box, in 'inked mint' condition, with remains of chalk marks.

**£80-120** **BLO**

A 1960s English Parker 61 Custom Heirloom fountain pen and propelling pencil, Rage red capillary-filler with two-colour rainbow cap (in yellow and brown) and fine nib, matching pencil, in Parker duo polka-dot hard box with instructions, in near mint condition.

*Rage red is a desirable and hard to find colour, and the 'Rainbow' cap is equally scarce. The design did not wear well, and most examples found are heavily scratched and faded.*

**£70-90** **BLO**

An English Parker 61 'Heirloom' pen, Vista Blue capillary action filler with pink and green rolled-gold 'rainbow' cap and medium nib, scratches on Teflon-coating, otherwise in near mint condition with chalk marks.

*c1964-67*

**£80-120** **BLO**

A 1970s French Parker 75 Place Vendôme 'Flammé ' pattern pen, silver-plated, with metal section ring (without '0' reference) and Parker 585 France fine nib, in mint condition, with tag.

**£80-120** **BLO**

A new-old-stock French Parker 75 'Godron' pattern pen, gold-plated with flat tassies, "20µ" mark, broad gold-plated section ring with '0' reference and Parker .750 France medium nib, inked mint, with tag.

*This a rare example of an early Parker 75 made at the Meru factory in France. It retains the flat tassies found only on the first series of pens, and uses the 'µ' symbol to indicate the thickness of gold electroplate. These features were phased out during the early-mid-1970s.*

*c1968-71*

**£300-400** **BLO**

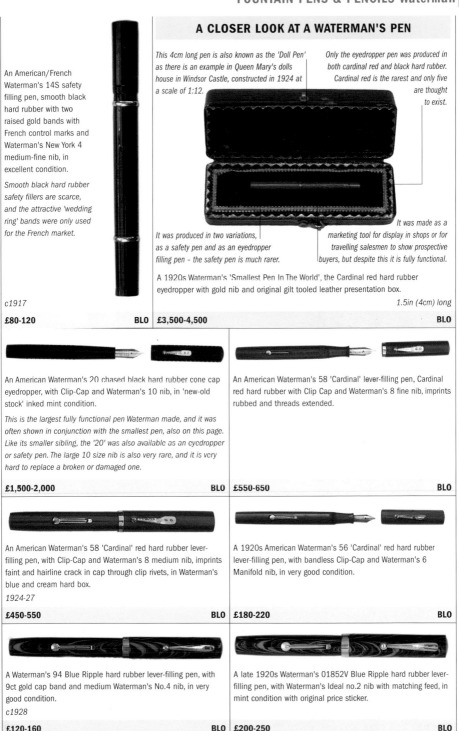

An American/French Waterman's 14S safety filling pen, smooth black hard rubber with two raised gold bands with French control marks and Waterman's New York 4 medium-fine nib, in excellent condition.

*Smooth black hard rubber safety fillers are scarce, and the attractive 'wedding ring' bands were only used for the French market.*

*c1917*

**£80-120** **BLO**

## A CLOSER LOOK AT A WATERMAN'S PEN

*This 4cm long pen is also known as the 'Doll Pen' as there is an example in Queen Mary's dolls house in Windsor Castle, constructed in 1924 at a scale of 1:12.*

*Only the eyedropper pen was produced in both cardinal red and black hard rubber. Cardinal red is the rarest and only five are thought to exist.*

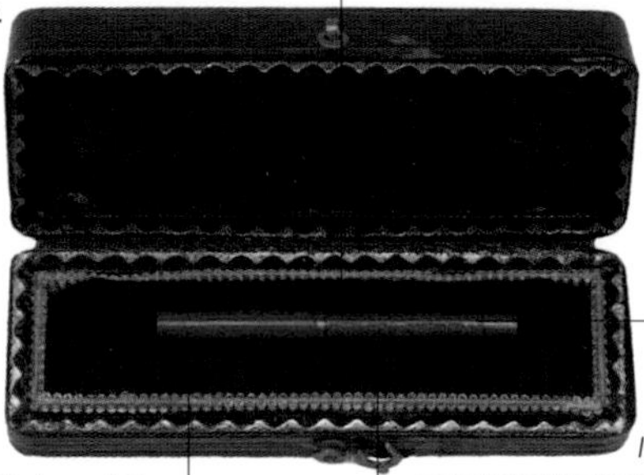

*It was produced in two variations, as a safety pen and as an eyedropper filling pen - the safety pen is much rarer.*

*It was made as a marketing tool for display in shops or for travelling salesmen to show prospective buyers, but despite this it is fully functional.*

A 1920s Waterman's 'Smallest Pen In The World', the Cardinal red hard rubber eyedropper with gold nib and original gilt tooled leather presentation box.

*1.5in (4cm) long*

**£3,500-4,500** **BLO**

An American Waterman's 20 chased black hard rubber cone cap eyedropper, with Clip-Cap and Waterman's 10 nib, in 'new-old stock' inked mint condition.

*This is the largest fully functional pen Waterman made, and it was often shown in conjunction with the smallest pen, also on this page. Like its smaller sibling, the '20' was also available as an eyedropper or safety pen. The large 10 size nib is also very rare, and it is very hard to replace a broken or damaged one.*

**£1,500-2,000** **BLO**

An American Waterman's 58 'Cardinal' lever-filling pen, Cardinal red hard rubber with Clip Cap and Waterman's 8 fine nib, imprints rubbed and threads extended.

**£550-650** **BLO**

An American Waterman's 58 'Cardinal' red hard rubber lever-filling pen, with Clip-Cap and Waterman's 8 medium nib, imprints faint and hairline crack in cap through clip rivets, in Waterman's blue and cream hard box.

*1924-27*

**£450-550** **BLO**

A 1920s American Waterman's 56 'Cardinal' red hard rubber lever-filling pen, with bandless Clip-Cap and Waterman's 6 Manifold nib, in very good condition.

**£180-220** **BLO**

A Waterman's 94 Blue Ripple hard rubber lever-filling pen, with 9ct gold cap band and medium Waterman's No.4 nib, in very good condition.

*c1928*

**£120-160** **BLO**

A late 1920s Waterman's 01852V Blue Ripple hard rubber lever-filling pen, with Waterman's Ideal no.2 nib with matching feed, in mint condition with original price sticker.

**£200-250** **BLO**

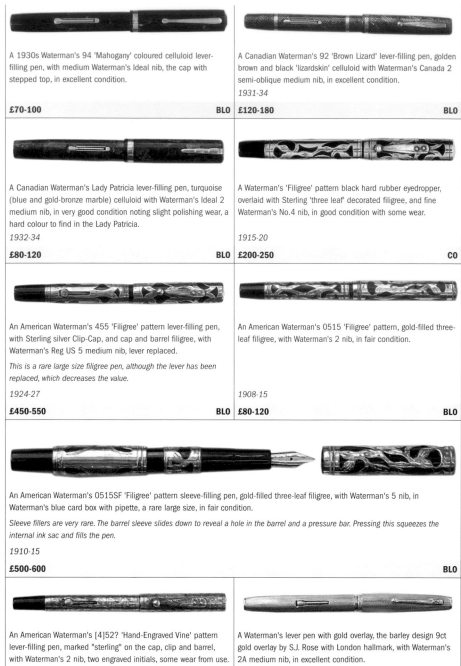

A 1930s Waterman's 94 'Mahogany' coloured celluloid lever-filling pen, with medium Waterman's Ideal nib, the cap with stepped top, in excellent condition.

**£70-100** **BLO**

A Canadian Waterman's 92 'Brown Lizard' lever-filling pen, golden brown and black 'lizardskin' celluloid with Waterman's Canada 2 semi-oblique medium nib, in excellent condition.

*1931-34*

**£120-180** **BLO**

A Canadian Waterman's Lady Patricia lever-filling pen, turquoise (blue and gold-bronze marble) celluloid with Waterman's Ideal 2 medium nib, in very good condition noting slight polishing wear, a hard colour to find in the Lady Patricia.

*1932-34*

**£80-120** **BLO**

A Waterman's 'Filigree' pattern black hard rubber eyedropper, overlaid with Sterling 'three leaf' decorated filigree, and fine Waterman's No.4 nib, in good condition with some wear.

*1915-20*

**£200-250** **CO**

An American Waterman's 455 'Filigree' pattern lever-filling pen, with Sterling silver Clip-Cap, and cap and barrel filigree, with Waterman's Reg US 5 medium nib, lever replaced.

*This is a rare large size filigree pen, although the lever has been replaced, which decreases the value.*

*1924-27*

**£450-550** **BLO**

An American Waterman's 0515 'Filigree' pattern, gold-filled three-leaf filigree, with Waterman's 2 nib, in fair condition.

*1908-15*

**£80-120** **BLO**

An American Waterman's 0515SF 'Filigree' pattern sleeve-filling pen, gold-filled three-leaf filigree, with Waterman's 5 nib, in Waterman's blue card box with pipette, a rare large size, in fair condition.

*Sleeve fillers are very rare. The barrel sleeve slides down to reveal a hole in the barrel and a pressure bar. Pressing this squeezes the internal ink sac and fills the pen.*

*1910-15*

**£500-600** **BLO**

An American Waterman's [4]52? 'Hand-Engraved Vine' pattern lever-filling pen, marked "sterling" on the cap, clip and barrel, with Waterman's 2 nib, two engraved initials, some wear from use.

*c1923*

**£120-180** **BLO**

A Waterman's lever pen with gold overlay, the barley design 9ct gold overlay by S.J. Rose with London hallmark, with Waterman's 2A medium nib, in excellent condition.

*S.J. Rose was an accomplished jeweller who held the Royal Warrant and is known to have created overlays for Waterman and Mont Blanc pens.*

*1959*

**£180-220** **BLO**

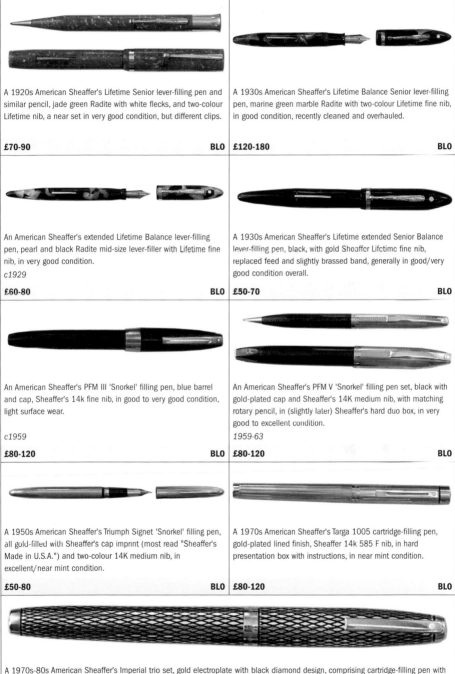

A 1920s American Sheaffer's Lifetime Senior lever-filling pen and similar pencil, jade green Radite with white flecks, and two-colour Lifetime nib, a near set in very good condition, but different clips.

**£70-90** **BLO**

A 1930s American Sheaffer's Lifetime Balance Senior lever-filling pen, marine green marble Radite with two-colour Lifetime fine nib, in good condition, recently cleaned and overhauled.

**£120-180** **BLO**

An American Sheaffer's extended Lifetime Balance lever-filling pen, pearl and black Radite mid-size lever-filler with Lifetime fine nib, in very good condition.

*c1929*

**£60-80** **BLO**

A 1930s American Sheaffer's Lifetime extended Senior Balance lever-filling pen, black, with gold Sheaffer Lifetime fine nib, replaced feed and slightly brassed band, generally in good/very good condition overall.

**£50-70** **BLO**

An American Sheaffer's PFM III 'Snorkel' filling pen, blue barrel and cap, Sheaffer's 14k fine nib, in good to very good condition, light surface wear.

*c1959*

**£80-120** **BLO**

An American Sheaffer's PFM V 'Snorkel' filling pen set, black with gold-plated cap and Sheaffer's 14K medium nib, with matching rotary pencil, in (slightly later) Sheaffer's hard duo box, in very good to excellent condition.

*1959-63*

**£80-120** **BLO**

A 1950s American Sheaffer's Triumph Signet 'Snorkel' filling pen, all gold-filled with Sheaffer's cap imprint (most read "Sheaffer's Made in U.S.A.") and two-colour 14K medium nib, in excellent/near mint condition.

**£50-80** **BLO**

A 1970s American Sheaffer's Targa 1005 cartridge-filling pen, gold-plated lined finish, Sheaffer 14k 585 F nib, in hard presentation box with instructions, in near mint condition.

**£80-120** **BLO**

A 1970s-80s American Sheaffer's Imperial trio set, gold electroplate with black diamond design, comprising cartridge-filling pen with medium nib, capped soft-tip, and clip-action ballpoint pen, pen and softip in near mint/mint condition, ballpoint pen in good to very good condition.

**£70-100 (set)** **BLO**

## A CLOSER LOOK AT A LIMITED EDITION MONT BLANC PEN

*The pattern is based on a 1920s Mont Blanc overlay design, and the form is similar to the safety pens produced at that time, so it reflects the company's heritage.*

*Modern limited editions by notable makers have become sought-after and risen in price in recent years providing they are in mint condition with all their packaging. This pen originally retailed for $1,650 or about £900.*

*The Octavian was the second in the series of annual limited editions produced by Montblanc from 1992.*

*The edition size of 4,810 pieces is taken from the height of the Mont Blanc mountain in metres. Low edition numbers can be even more sought-after.*

A limited edition German Montblanc 'Octavian' pen, from an edition of 4,810, silver spider's web filigree overlay, two-colour 4810 'spider' F nib, with box and paperwork, in 'inked mint' condition.

*1993*

**£2,500-3,500** **BLO**

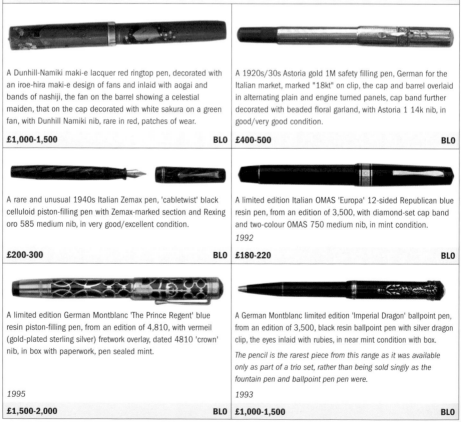

A Namiki maki-e lacquer pen, decorated with plants and butterflies, in red, green and gold iroe-hiramaki-e, with takamaki-e, bands of nashiji and inlaid with aogai and raden, the barrel with a vase with a flowering hydrangea, the cap decorated with five differently sized butterflies, stamped "T331 Made in Japan" on the post and fitted with a Pilot 3 nib, an unusual pattern, some wear.

**£1,500-2,000** **BLO**

A Dunhill-Namiki maki-e lacquer red ringtop pen, decorated with an iroe-hira maki-e design of fans and inlaid with aogai and bands of nashiji, the fan on the barrel showing a celestial maiden, that on the cap decorated with white sakura on a green fan, with Dunhill Namiki nib, rare in red, patches of wear.

**£1,000-1,500** **BLO**

A 1920s/30s Astoria gold 1M safety filling pen, German for the Italian market, marked "18kt" on clip, the cap and barrel overlaid in alternating plain and engine turned panels, cap band further decorated with beaded floral garland, with Astoria 1 14k nib, in good/very good condition.

**£400-500** **BLO**

A rare and unusual 1940s Italian Zemax pen, 'cabletwist' black celluloid piston-filling pen with Zemax-marked section and Rexing oro 585 medium nib, in very good/excellent condition.

**£200-300** **BLO**

A limited edition Italian OMAS 'Europa' 12-sided Republican blue resin pen, from an edition of 3,500, with diamond-set cap band and two-colour OMAS 750 medium nib, in mint condition.

*1992*

**£180-220** **BLO**

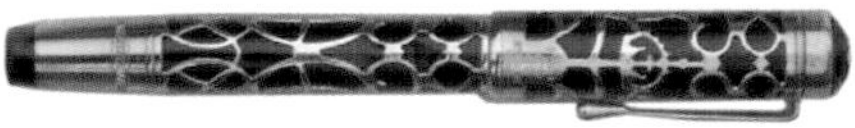

A limited edition German Montblanc 'The Prince Regent' blue resin piston-filling pen, from an edition of 4,810, with vermeil (gold-plated sterling silver) fretwork overlay, dated 4810 'crown' nib, in box with paperwork, pen sealed mint.

*1995*

**£1,500-2,000** **BLO**

A German Montblanc limited edition 'Imperial Dragon' ballpoint pen, from an edition of 3,500, black resin ballpoint pen with silver dragon clip, the eyes inlaid with rubies, in near mint condition with box.

*The pencil is the rarest piece from this range as it was available only as part of a trio set, rather than being sold singly as the fountain pen and ballpoint pen pen were.*

*1993*

**£1,000-1,500** **BLO**

## COLLECTORS' NOTES

- Sampson Mordan and John Isaac Hawkins patented the first mechanical propelling pencil in 1822. A year later, Hawkins left the partnership and stationer Gabriel Riddle acquired a share of the rights until 1837. Their success provided Mordan with the income to become a great success during the late 19th century. Early examples from the 1830s are desirable, and pieces from the 1820s are very rare.
- The quality of manufacture, decorative appeal, materials and quality of work affect value considerably. Look for novelty forms, most of which were made in the 1880s and 1890s, or finely worked and inlaid examples, most of which tend to date from earlier in the decade. Many other makers copied Mordan's pencils once the patent had expired, or developed their own designs, but the same guidelines apply to value.
- Look closely at all parts of a pencil for markings. Not all early silver examples bear hallmarks, and the maker's name or the way it is shown can help to date a piece to a period. 'Combinations' including pen nib holders, knives and other accessories can also help to boost the value.

A Mordan & Riddle silver 'Everpoint' pencil, with barley pattern shaft, cast foliate band and ring slide, and bud terminal over a lead reserve, marked "S. Mordan & Cos. Patent", with London hallmark.

*1829*

**£150-200** BLO

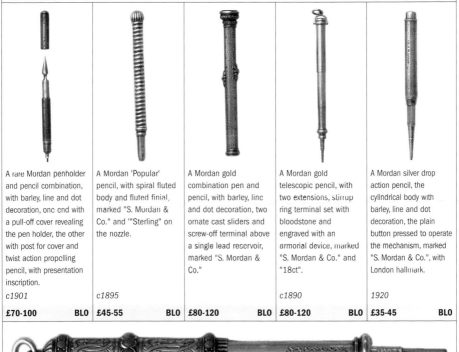

A rare Mordan penholder and pencil combination, with barley, line and dot decoration, one end with a pull-off cover revealing the pen holder, the other with post for cover and twist action propelling pencil, with presentation inscription.

*c1901*

**£70-100** BLO

A Mordan 'Popular' pencil, with spiral fluted body and fluted finial, marked "S. Mordan & Co." and '"Sterling" on the nozzle.

*c1895*

**£45-55** BLO

A Mordan gold combination pen and pencil, with barley, line and dot decoration, two ornate cast sliders and screw-off terminal above a single lead reservoir, marked "S. Mordan & Co."

**£80-120** BLO

A Mordan gold telescopic pencil, with two extensions, stirrup ring terminal set with bloodstone and engraved with an armorial device, marked "S. Mordan & Co." and "18ct".

*c1890*

**£80-120** BLO

A Mordan silver drop action pencil, the cylindrical body with barley, line and dot decoration, the plain button pressed to operate the mechanism, marked "S. Mordan & Co.", with London hallmark.

*1920*

**£35-45** BLO

A Mordan gold pencil, with one extension, the body with engraved Gothic design and set with coral cabochons, the domed godron terminal with swivelling ring, marked "S. Mordan & Co." and "18ct".

*This is an extremely fine pencil, with workmanship and attention to detail that is typical of Mordan's best quality pencils.*

*c1880*

**£500-700** BLO

A Mordan 'Thornhill's Soda Water' white metal advertising pencil, the bulb shaped body embossed "Thornhill's Soda Water", the pencil marked "S. Mordan & Co.", three engraved initials and mechanism needs attention.

*This is a very rare advertising pencil by Mordan. The shape represents the gas bulbs used in soda siphons. When found, these pencils are often dented.*

*c1900*

**£220-280** **BLO**

A John Bettridge silver porte crayon, with plain body, ring design slide and plain polished seal terminal.

*1815-20*

**£60-70** **BLO**

A French or English unmarked gold porte crayon, with plain shaft, cast foliate slider, bands and terminal set with a crest of a hawk on a glove.

*c1820*

**£280-320** **BLO**

A Lund Patent pencil, with an ivory body cut with a spiral, and gold slide and bud terminal with dot decoration.

*The gold additions are rare, particularly in such a decorative form.*

*c1858*

**£80-120** **BLO**

A W.H. Woodward silver pen and pencil combination, the hexagonal shaft with engraved foliate decoration, two ornate slides and screw-off cast terminal over a lead reserve, with Birmingham hallmark.

*1899*

**£40-50** **BLO**

A late 18thC English varnished wood penner, with hinged cover, glass inkbottle, and compartment for quills, rare and unusual, lacks cork, otherwise in very good condition.

*7.25in (8.5cm) long*

**£220-280** **BLO**

A rare late 18thC English silver penner, unmarked, with reversible barrel nib, tapered cylindrical shaft and slip-off well, both with bands of diagonal ribbed decoration, lacks stopper and end of nib holder bruised, otherwise in excellent condition.

**£150-200** **BLO**

## A CLOSER LOOK AT A MORDAN NOVELTY PENCIL

Mordan are well-known for their novelty shaped pencils, which were produced in the late 19thC and are all of high quality.
This example is not complete and does not contain its mechanism. Had it been complete and in working order, its value may have doubled.
The Ally Soper pencil was thought to be 'mythical' until this example was found.
Although this example is not signed by Mordan, it is thought that the company produced them for retailers, whose names may have been marked on them instead.


A late 1880s English 'Ally Soper' silver novelty pencil, the figural case in excellent condition, but lacking mechanism apart from the pencil tube marked "McMichael".

*Ally Soper, of 'Ally Soper's Half Holiday' which ran from 1884-90, was portrayed as a mock-gentrified working class drunk, who would commit social faux-pas while living the good life. This caricatured figure followed traditions set by William Hogarth and George Cruickshank.*

*c1888*

**£900-1,200** **BLO**

## A CLOSER LOOK AT A SHELDON TRAVELLING SET

*John Sheldon (1808?-1863) is renowned for his inventiveness and ingenuity in making multi-functional writing equipment, often aimed at the traveller.*

*This tiny box provided all a traveller would need, including pen, pencil, paper, postal balance, toothpick, coin gauge, stamps, a tape measure and seals.*

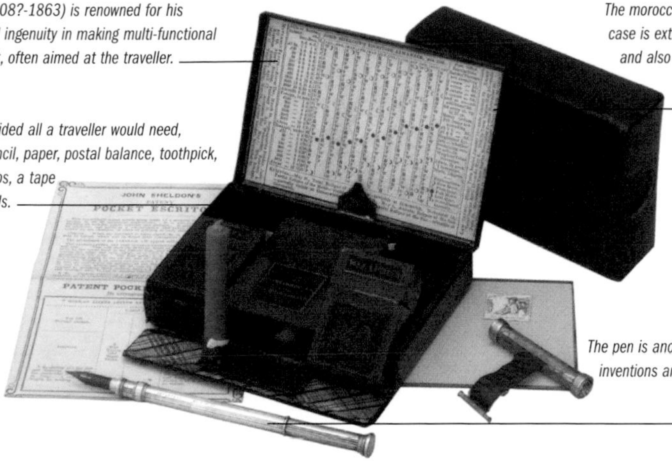

*The morocco leather-covered case is extremely well-made and also has the almanac for 1845 inside the lid.*

*The pen is another of Sheldon's inventions and combines pen, pencil, seal and postal balance.*

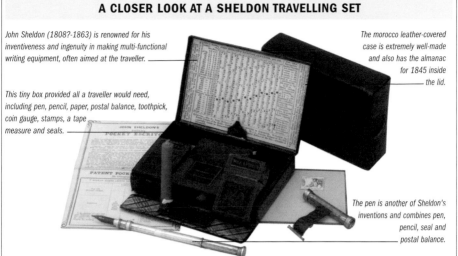

A rare English John Sheldon 'Patent Escritoire', with original contents, only lacking the blotter and India rubber.

*c1845* *4in (10cm) wide*

**£2,200-2,800** **BLO**

A German or Austrian leather-covered copper travelling patent writing set, with stamp box, inkwells, penwipe, a compartment for nibs and a telescopic pen holder.

*c1900* *3in (7.5cm) wide*

**£150-200** **BLO**

A German leather-covered copper travelling writing set with roller blotter, lift-up candle holder, penwipe, inkwell, nib compartment, and clamps inside the lid to hold a pen.

*c1880s* *4.5in (11cm) wide*

**£120-180** **BLO**

A German leather-covered brass travelling writing set, with vesta case, inkwell, fold-down side acting as a candle-holder, concealed drawer for stamps or nibs, and lid clamps holding an earlier gold pen/pencil combination.

*c1900* *3.75in (9.5cm) wide*

**£180-220** **BLO**

A German leather-covered brass pocket writing set, with a pair of inkwells with catch-covers flanking a penwipe, and a grooved pentray/rest.

*c1900* *4in (10cm) wide*

**£70-100** **BLO**

An English small red Morocco leather travelling writing compendium, with compartments to hold quills and a flap covering a glass ink bottle with a silver plated and cork stopper.

*c1810-20* *(closed) 4.5in (11.5cm) long*

**£150-200** **BLO**

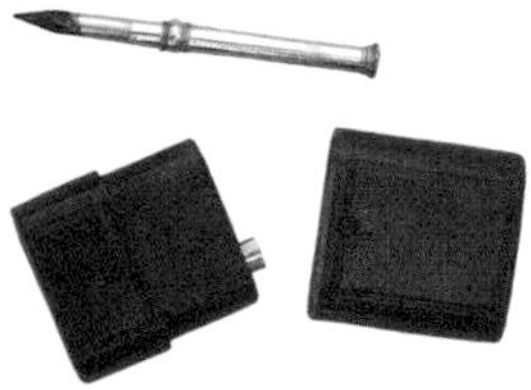

An English red Morocco leather-covered pressed card travelling inkpot and pen, with a silver-plated inkwell, lacks stopper, and silver sliding pen.

*c1815* *2.25in (5.5cm)*

**£70-100** **BLO**

A rare 18thC English turned and polished horn inkhorn, with screw-off cover and screw-off base with pierced wooden plate.

*Inkhorns were portable inkwells, and as well as holding ink, held 'pounce' powder that was used to dry the ink.*

**£180-220** **BLO**

A rare Perry & Co. swivelling ceramic patent 'Perryian Gravitating Inkstand', with moulded brass base and sprung enclosure.

*c1820* *6.25in (16cm) wide*

**£180-220** **BLO**

Two English novelty tin inkwells, in the form of a teapot and a cream pail, each containing a ceramic well.

*c1840-50* *Largest 4.25in (11cm) wide*

**£120-180** **BLO**

An English or French novelty 'fireman's helmet' spelter inkwell, with hinged cover, chinstrap damaged.

*c1870* *4in (10cm) high*

**£35-45** **BLO**

A Japanese brass wire inkwell in the form of a fishing creel, the lid cast with fish, and a cast crab climbing up the side.

*The attention to detail, subject matter and material makes this a desirable piece, as well as helping to identify its country of manufacture.*

*c1910*

**£250-350** **BRI**

An English globe inkwell, covered with colour lithographed gores, with flattened base at the Antarctic and button release, the interior with inkbottle and penwipe.

*c1880s* *2in (5cm) diam*

**£120-180** **BLO**

A German Meissen-style porcelain inkwell, decorated in underglaze blue, crossed sword mark on base and incised "Y38 6" and stamped "29".

*c1880s* *2.75in (7cm) diam*

**£45-55** **BLO**

A Continental carved and polished wood novelty 'Harry' dog inkwell.

*Harry's front paws are attached to the lid and his back paws are sprung, allowing him to be rocked back to access the ink inside the well.*

*c1910* *9in (23cm) high*

**£550-650** **SWO**

A very rare William Mitchell red leather folder, containing six leaves of 91 different styles of nib, arranged in groups of three of each type, with ink titles and prices, and cloth interleaves, with gilt tooling to exterior, lacks ten nibs.

*c1850s*

**£1,500-2,000** **BLO**

A mid-to late 19thC English burgundy morocco case pocket case, illustrating the step-by-step process in making a Joseph Gillot nib, with four panels with sections labelled 'A-R', illustrating each step in the manufacture of steel nibs.

**£1,000-1,500** **BLO**

A late 19thC leather, card and gilt pen nib holder, with chromo-lithographed Baxter print of Prince Napoleon Bonaparte, from the 'Queen & Heroes of India' series.

*2.25in (6cm) high*

**£40-50** **CBE**

An extremely rare Mordan & Co. card box for leads, the cover embossed "Mordan & Cos Best H Cumberland Lead" with a royal coat-of-arms, the remainder decorated with a star-and-dot pattern.

*c1850s* *1in (2.5cm) wide*

**£25-35** **BLO**

A English silver seal and wax-holder, the tube with sprung action jaws to release or clamp a piece of sealing wax, marked "Rd. 441581".

*1904*

**£120-180** **BLO**

A small pen knife sharpening stone, with wooden handle and card slip cover.

*This is an unusually small size. These are usually found in larger sizes and in burgundy card slip cases.*

*c1840* *4in (10cm) long*

**£80-120** **MHC**

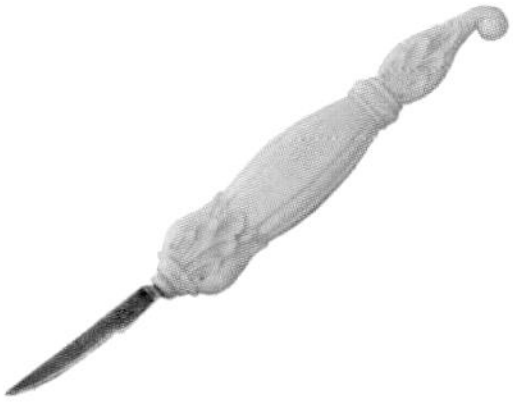

A English or French quill knife, with a ornately carved ivory handle and slightly curved steel blade.

*c1830* *13.5cm (5.25in) long*

**£80-120** **BLO**

A 19thC Scottish four-colour hardstone eight inch octagonal rule, made of alternating sections of four different coloured hardstones.

*8in (20cm) long*

**£150-200** **BLO**

A mid-19thC English 'Appleton's Patent' ruler, with stamped brass endplates and mahogany and ebony roller rules.

*9.25in (23.5cm) long*

**£35-45** **BLO**

A rare mid-19thC boxwood compendium desk stand, carved in the image of a hand resting on a textured surface, with four removable components.

*c1850s*

**£600-700** **BLO**

A 'Merry Phipson & Parker's' gilt brass letter clip, with Royal Arms and black japanned spring, marked "Reg Octr 3 1843 No 24".

*This is an extremely early registered design, only the 24th issued since the Design Act was passed in 1842.*

*5in (12.5cm) long*

**£70-100** **BLO**

A rare English E. Smith gilt brass quill pen file, marked "E. Smith 3 Cheapside" on the turning nut to the metal file-plate, with Registered Design lozenge for June 1882.

*2.75in (7cm) long*

**£100-150** **BLO**

An English Sampson Mordan silver 'Boot Wipe' penwipe, with articulated handles and black bristles, London hallmark.

*1894* *2in (5cm) wide*

**£200-250** **BLO**

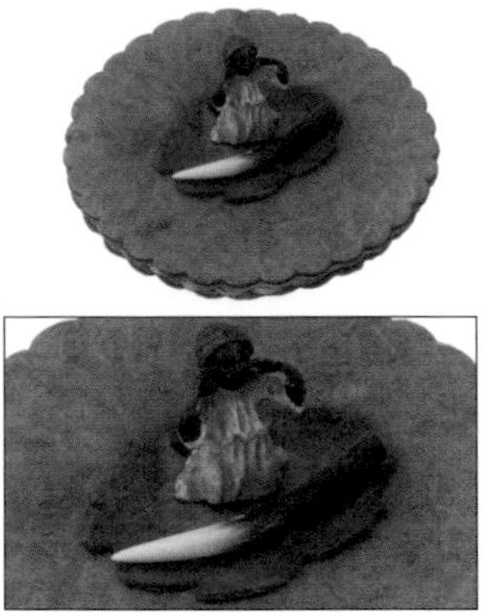

A late 19thC cold-painted figural penwipe, probably German, modelled as a weeping Arab kneeling before an elephant tusk, with leather pads and wipe.

*3.75 in (9.5cm) diam*

**£60-80** **BLO**

A German silver and duck egg blue guilloché enamel stamp damper and desk seal, marked "DRGM 925 Germany".

*c1910* *1.75in (4.5cm) high*

**£280-320** **BLO**

An American Thompson Eng & Mfg Co. aluminium desk postal balance, with "3c per oz 1st class and 6c per oz Airmail" printed card to base.

*Its the use of aluminium, and the appeal of the 'Machine Age', almost architectural, form and design that makes this balance desirable. The conical top unscrews and overturns to reveal the sprung scale and form the tray.*

*3.25in (8cm) high*

**£40-60** **BB**

A mid-to late 19thC English Perry & Co. patent brass postal balance, calibrated from 0-12oz.

*5.5in (14cm) long*

**£45-55** **BLO**

A 1920s American Art Deco Parker desk base, with Elgin clock and green enamel and gold geometric inserts, the tulip marked "Parker Pat Appld For".

**£280-320** **BLO**

A 1920s Wahl-Eversharp onyx desk base, with a spelter English Setter dog, green/bronze tulip and Gold Seal desk pen with Wahl Eversharp nib.

**£150-200** **GORL**

A rare English Waterman's annodised copper desk light and pen stand, with adjustable shade, ornate pillar, and base with bakelite Waterman's desk pen holder.

*c1920* *15in (38cm) high*

**£300-400** **BLO**

## A CLOSER LOOK AT A DUNHILL BRIDGE SET

*This set was made for and retailed by Alfred Dunhill, who are renowned for their luxurious gentlemen's accessories and driving accessories.*

*With its specially fitted case marked 'Alfred Dunhill', this set has not been seen before, so may have been a one-off commission.*

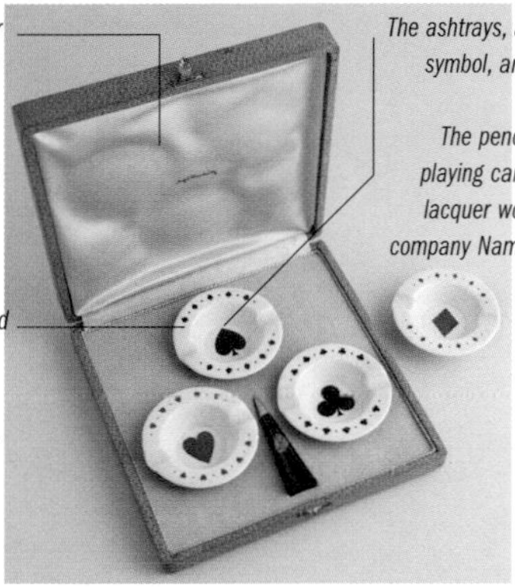

*The ashtrays, arranged like a club symbol, are by Royal Doulton.*

*The pencil is decorated with playing cards motifs in maki-e lacquer work by the Japanese company Namiki, and would have taken many weeks to complete.*

An Alfred Dunhill bridge set, comprising four Royal Doulton ashtrays and a Dunhill Namiki maki-e lacquer bridge pencil signed by Kosai, in a fitted Alfred Dunhill case.

*It is the pencil that holds much of the value of this set.*

*c1932* *pencil 3in (8cm) high*

**£400-600** **PC**

A French Dunhill-Namiki 'Une Fleur, Un Oiseau' advertisement, from 'Punch' magazine.

*Colour advertisements for Dunhill-Namiki pens are extremely rare. Most advertising at the time used monochrome, largely due to the cost of colour printing technology of the period.*

*1930*

**£35-45** **BLO**

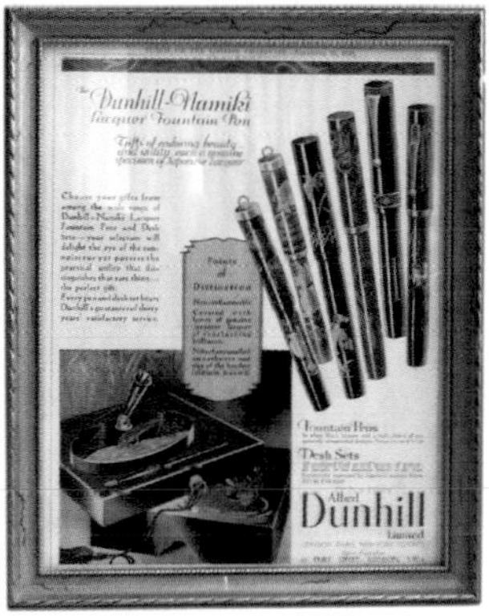


A Dunhill-Namiki colour advertisement, from 'Punch', Dec. 10 1930, showing six different flat-top pens and a desk base and box, in excellent condition, framed and glazed.

*1930* *12in (31cm) high*

**£250-350** **BLO**

A 1950s Waterman advertisement, of a hand holding a 'Waterman' pen, designed by Pierre Lacroix.

**£3-5** **BLO**

A 1920s 'Swan Inks' enamel advertising sign, in extremely good condition.

*16in (40cm) wide*

**£60-80** **GWRA**

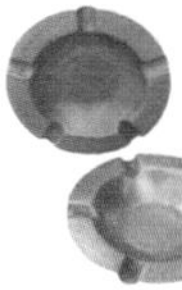

A pair of English Waterman's hand-crafted hammered aluminium ashtrays, stamped "Waterman's Ideal Fountain Pen" on the front and "Aluminium Hand Made By Crippled Boys" and "Hand Made by Cripples" on the reverse.

*c1920*

**£60-80** **BLO**

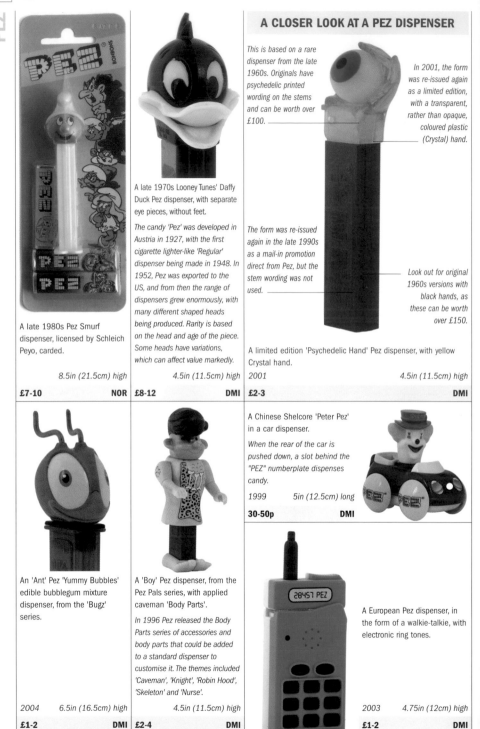


A late 1980s Pez Smurf dispenser, licensed by Schleich Peyo, carded.

*8.5in (21.5cm) high*

**£7-10** **NOR**

A late 1970s Looney Tunes' Daffy Duck Pez dispenser, with separate eye pieces, without feet.

*The candy 'Pez' was developed in Austria in 1927, with the first cigarette lighter-like 'Regular' dispenser being made in 1948. In 1952, Pez was exported to the US, and from then the range of dispensers grew enormously, with many different shaped heads being produced. Rarity is based on the head and age of the piece. Some heads have variations, which can affect value markedly.*

*4.5in (11.5cm) high*

**£8-12** **DMI**

## A CLOSER LOOK AT A PEZ DISPENSER

*This is based on a rare dispenser from the late 1960s. Originals have psychedelic printed wording on the stems and can be worth over £100.*

*In 2001, the form was re-issued again as a limited edition, with a transparent, rather than opaque, coloured plastic (Crystal) hand.*

*The form was re-issued again in the late 1990s as a mail-in promotion direct from Pez, but the stem wording was not used.*

*Look out for original 1960s versions with black hands, as these can be worth over £150.*

A limited edition 'Psychedelic Hand' Pez dispenser, with yellow Crystal hand.

*2001* *4.5in (11.5cm) high*

**£2-3** **DMI**

An 'Ant' Pez 'Yummy Bubbles' edible bubblegum mixture dispenser, from the 'Bugz' series.

*2004* *6.5in (16.5cm) high*

**£1-2** **DMI**

A 'Boy' Pez dispenser, from the Pez Pals series, with applied caveman 'Body Parts'.

*In 1996 Pez released the Body Parts series of accessories and body parts that could be added to a standard dispenser to customise it. The themes included 'Caveman', 'Knight', 'Robin Hood', 'Skeleton' and 'Nurse'.*

*4.5in (11.5cm) high*

**£2-4** **DMI**

A Chinese Shelcore 'Peter Pez' in a car dispenser.

*When the rear of the car is pushed down, a slot behind the "PEZ" numberplate dispenses candy.*

*1999* *5in (12.5cm) long*

**30-50p** **DMI**

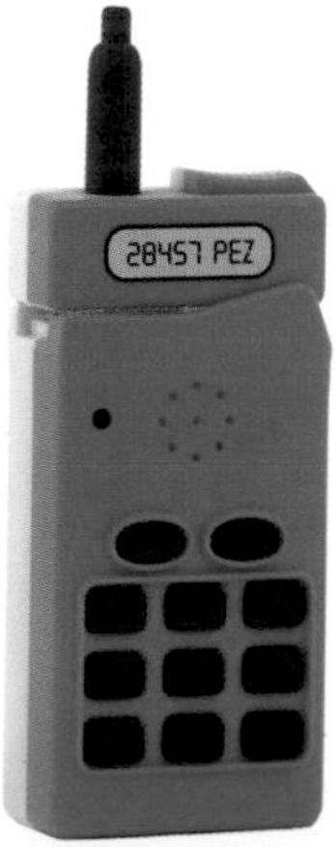


A European Pez dispenser, in the form of a walkie-talkie, with electronic ring tones.

*2003* *4.75in (12cm) high*

**£1-2** **DMI**

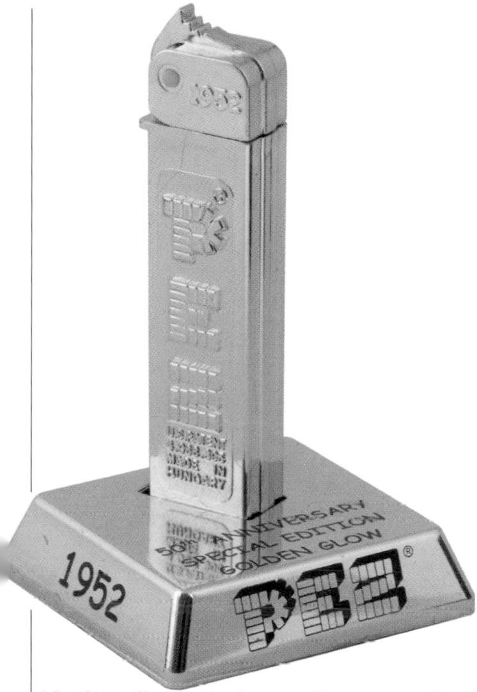

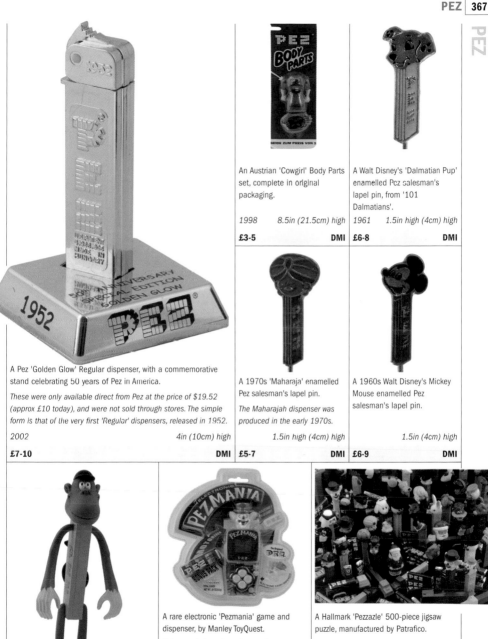

A Pez 'Golden Glow' Regular dispenser, with a commemorative stand celebrating 50 years of Pez in America.

*These were only available direct from Pez at the price of $19.52 (approx £10 today), and were not sold through stores. The simple form is that of the very first 'Regular' dispensers, released in 1952.*

*2002* *4in (10cm) high*

**£7-10** **DMI**

An Austrian 'Cowgirl' Body Parts set, complete in original packaging.

*1998* *8.5in (21.5cm) high*

**£3-5** **DMI**

A Walt Disney's 'Dalmatian Pup' enamelled Pez salesman's lapel pin, from '101 Dalmatians'.

*1961* *1.5in high (4cm) high*

**£6-8** **DMI**

A 1970s 'Maharaja' enamelled Pez salesman's lapel pin.

*The Maharajah dispenser was produced in the early 1970s.*

*1.5in high (4cm) high*

**£5-7** **DMI**

A 1960s Walt Disney's Mickey Mouse enamelled Pez salesman's lapel pin.

*1.5in (4cm) high*

**£6-9** **DMI**

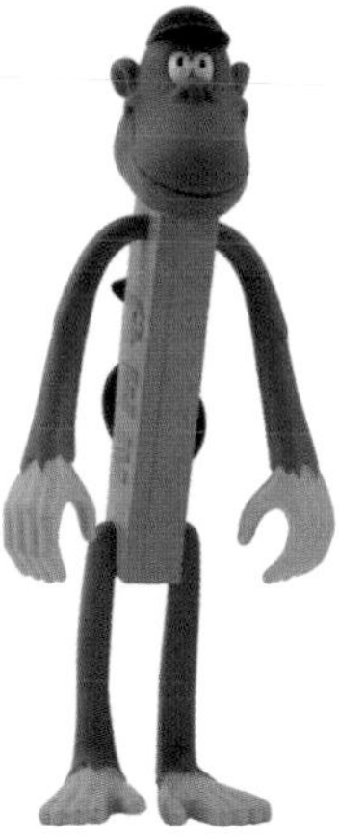

A Patrafico 'Bendables' Pez toy, with the head of Mimic the Monkey.

*2002* *6.5in (16.5cm) high*

**£2-3** **DMI**

A rare electronic 'Pezmania' game and dispenser, by Manley ToyQuest.

*This game is based on the popular computer game Tetris. To reward high scores, the head tilts back automatically and dispenses candy. This mechanism was considered hazardous and so the game was withdrawn from sale not long after it was launched.*

*2003* *8in (20.5cm) high*

**£5-8** **DMI**

A Hallmark 'Pezzazle' 500-piece jigsaw puzzle, manufactured by Patrafico.

*c1995* *Box 12in (30.5cm) wide*

**£8-12** **DMI**

## COLLECTORS' NOTES

- The first 'plastic' materials such as celluloid and vulcanised hard rubber were used in the late 19th century but Bakelite, developed in 1907 by Belgian chemist Dr Leo Baekeland, is considered by many to be the first truly synthetic plastic used in mass manufacture. Before this, pliable materials such as tortoiseshell and horn were bent into forms using heat.
- Dubbed the 'material of 1,000 uses', Bakelite is found primarily in darker colours such as brown and black, and occasionally in red, green and blue. Its development generated a boom in the plastics industry, and its success led to a vast number of different, often derivative, plastics being made. Thus, not all plastics are strictly 'Bakelite' although the term 'bakelite' is commonly applied to many early plastics.
- The 'golden age' lasted from c1910 to the 1950s, when cheaper injection moulded plastics took over. The adaptability of the material in terms of colour and form saw it being used for cost-effective mass production of many different objects from electrical insulators to kitchenware to decorative objects.
- Consider both colour and form when looking at a piece. Plastic allowed domestic pieces to break away from the dominance of dull woods and plain metals, so brighter colours are more desirable, particularly in strong tones such as cherry red. 'Catalin' was a phenolic resin made by the Catalin Corporation in the US, and is known particularly for its vibrant colours. Blue, red and green Bakelite is rare.
- The Art Deco style was dominant during this period and it is this that collectors seek out. Look for quintessential Deco designs, such as clean lines, stepped designs, streamlining and geometric forms. Condition is also all-important, with chips, crack and repairs affecting value considerably, particularly for more common pieces, and should be avoided. Some colours have faded, darkened or changed over time, but this does not affect value as seriously.

A Bakelite mottled dish, inset with a 1943 Canada cents coin, with moulded ball feet.

*5in (12.5cm) diam*

**£100-150** **MG**

An American Boontonware multicoloured dark green and orange bowl, made in Boonton NJ.

*7.5in (19cm) diam*

**£8-12** **BB**

An American Brookpark thick green mottled plastic bowl.

*8.25in (21cm) diam*

**£12-18** **BB**

A pair of mottled grey plastic mixing bowls, by Plastics In St Paul.

*5.25in (13.5cm) diam*

**£7-10** **BB**

A Prolon Ware mottled blue moulded plastic lunch tray, with indentations for matching plastic bowls and cups.

*14in (35.5cm) long*

**£15-25** **BB**

A King Life moulded plastic lunch tray, with indentations for matching for matching plastic bowls and cups.

*14in (35.5cm) long*

**£15-25** **BB**

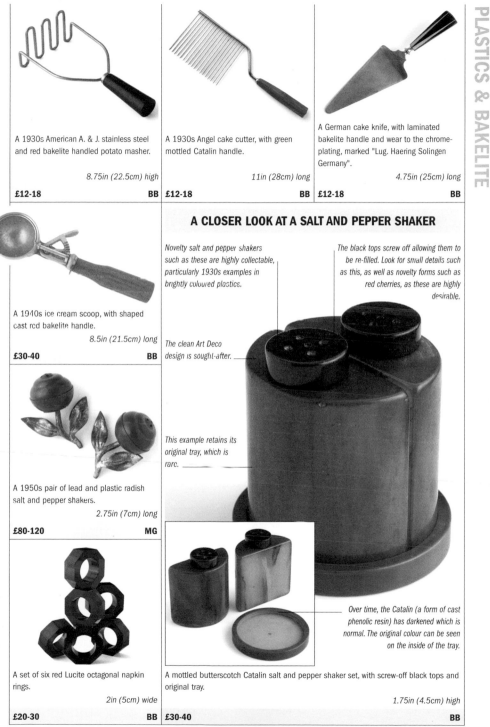

A 1930s American A. & J. stainless steel and red bakelite handled potato masher.

*8.75in (22.5cm) high*

**£12-18** **BB**

A 1930s Angel cake cutter, with green mottled Catalin handle.

*11in (28cm) long*

**£12-18** **BB**

A German cake knife, with laminated bakelite handle and wear to the chrome-plating, marked "Lug. Haering Solingen Germany".

*4.75in (25cm) long*

**£12-18** **BB**

A 1940s ice cream scoop, with shaped cast red bakelite handle.

*8.5in (21.5cm) long*

**£30-40** **BB**

A 1950s pair of lead and plastic radish salt and pepper shakers.

*2.75in (7cm) long*

**£80-120** **MG**

A set of six red Lucite octagonal napkin rings.

*2in (5cm) wide*

**£20-30** **BB**

## A CLOSER LOOK AT A SALT AND PEPPER SHAKER

*Novelty salt and pepper shakers such as these are highly collectable, particularly 1930s examples in brightly coloured plastics.*

*The black tops screw off allowing them to be re-filled. Look for small details such as this, as well as novelty forms such as red cherries, as these are highly desirable.*

*The clean Art Deco design is sought-after.*

*This example retains its original tray, which is rare.*

*Over time, the Catalin (a form of cast phenolic resin) has darkened which is normal. The original colour can be seen on the inside of the tray.*

A mottled butterscotch Catalin salt and pepper shaker set, with screw-off black tops and original tray.

*1.75in (4.5cm) high*

**£30-40** **BB**

PLASTICS & BAKELITE

A 1930s English brown mottled bakelite desk stand, with mounted timepiece and twin-lidded ink reservoirs, on an oblong stepped base.

**£30-50** **BIG**

An American green cast Catalin and chrome 'Bates Listfinder Cavalier' address and telephone directory, by Bates Mfg. Co. of Orange NJ.

*7.75in (19.5cm) long*

**£60-80** **MG**

A 1930s Telechron 'Selector Household Timer', with painted bars that can be pulled out to turn an appliance on or off, by plugging it in at the back.

*Warren Telechron Co. were a notable maker of clocks, an example of their most desirable design can be seen in the previous editions of this book.*

*5in (13cm) high*

**£25-40** **TM**

A green and black mottled clock-shaped pencil sharpener.

*The colour has also darkened with age, and originally would have been much brighter. The original colour can be brought back through skilled polishing.*

*2in (5cm) high*

**£50-70** **MG**

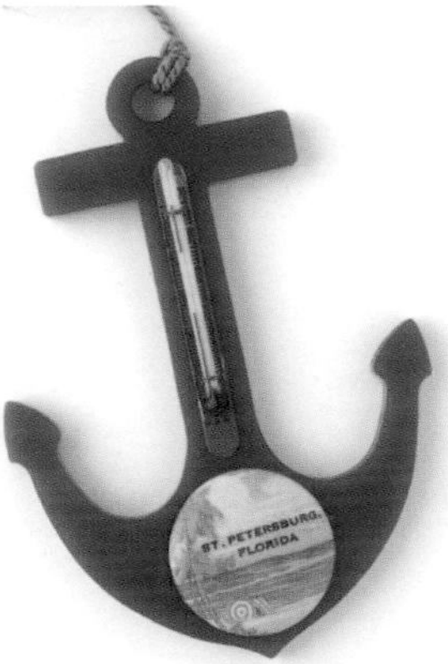


A green Catalin St Petersburg, Florida souvenir anchor, set with a thermometer and transfer-printed plaque.

*4.75in (12cm) diam*

**£30-50** **MG**

A pair of 1950s colourless Lucite curving 'knot' candlesticks, with metal candleholders.

*22.5in (57cm) high*

**£30-50** **MG**

A 1930s mottled yellow Catalin Catholic 'Christ on a Cross', inset with rhinestones and cast brass plaque.

*Religious pieces such as this have their own retro, kitsch appeal among some, and are loved by others for their period religious iconography.*

*8.25in (21cm) high*

**£50-80** **BB**

A 1930s French black and marbled cream and brown Lucite plant or flower holder, with no drainage holes.

*These were originally produced in sets and are scarce due to their fragility.*

*6in (15cm) high*

**£300-500** **MG**

PLASTICS & BAKELITE

A 1930s American wooden inlaid smoking box, with cedar interior, and red Bakelite accented chrome metal airplane and calendar.

*8.75in (22cm) high*

**£100-150** **MG**

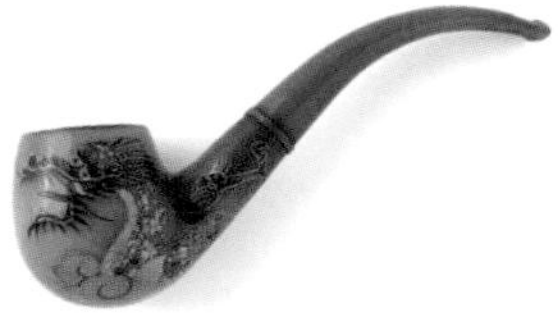

A 1930s cast Catalin pipe, hand-painted with a Chinese dragon design incorporating inlaid shell.

*The five-clawed dragon clutching the sacred tama (pearl) amid clouds is an enduring image in Chinese mythology.*

*5in (13cm) long*

**£70-100** **MG**

## A CLOSER LOOK AT A CIGARETTE BOX

*Pushing back the articulated roll-top lid pushes out five trays, each able to hold a cigarette, the other cigarettes are stored in the body.*

*It was designed by Maurice Robin (1912-82), who originally came up with the idea for the articulated lid for a pencil box, as he found wooden examples were hard to open.*

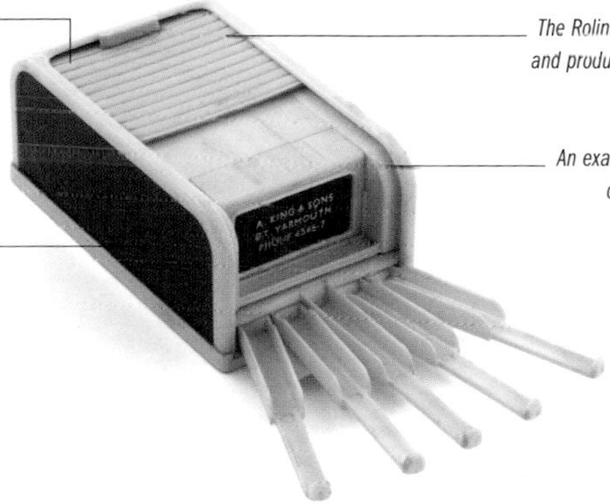

*The Rolinx company was founded in the late 1940s and produced a number of injection moulded plastic boxes, roof lights and even a dinghy.*

*An example of this ingenious 1950s box is in the collection of the Science Museum, London*

A 1950s English Rolinx Product cream Bakelite mechanical cigarette dispenser, Pat No. 593961 & 642536, with inset leather panels.

*5.75in (14.5cm) long*

**£20-30** **GROB**

A Stewart R. Browne brown mottled moulded Bakelite torch.

*8.25in (21cm) high*

**£60-80** **MG**

A green mottled Catalin egg-shaped sock darner.

*Carved lumps of Catalin such as this are sought-after, particularly in bright colours.*

*2.25in (6cm) high*

**£18-22** **BB**

A butterscotch Bakelite whistle.

*2.5in (6.5cm) long*

**£15-25** **MG**

### FIND OUT MORE...

**Bakelite Style,** *by Tessa Clark & Gad Sassower, published by Quintet Publishing, 1997.*

**Classic Plastics**, *by Sylvia Katz, published by Thames & Hudson, 1984.*

## COLLECTORS' NOTES

- As modes of travel expanded in variety from the turn of the century into the mid-20th century, and people became able to afford holidays away from home, travel posters increased in popularity. Examples were produced for railways, cruise liners, airlines and motoring, as well as general tourism. Most collectors tend to choose one particular area. Some also choose certain styles, such as Art Deco posters.
- The 'golden age' was arguably from the 1910s-30s, with television and other advertising taking over during the 1950s and '60s. Nevertheless, many appealing and collectable posters were produced during the post-war period, particularly for the boom in airline travel, and these can be valuable.
- A number of factors contribute towards value, including the visual appeal of the poster, its theme and the designer. As many posters are bought for display in homes, the overall design and theme play major roles in value, particularly if they express the excitement or romance of the mode of travel, or the destination shown. Bright colours and popular brand names can also make a poster more desirable.
- Notable designers such as Cassandre (Adolphe Mouron), Frank Brangwyn and Tom Purvis will add to the value, particularly if the design is typical of their work. Always consider condition. While folds and edge tears can be repaired professionally, damage or losses to the image will reduce value considerably.

'Largs, Ayrshire' railway poster, designed by Black, printed for BR by London Lithograph Co.

*40.25in (102cm) high*

**£150-200** **ON**

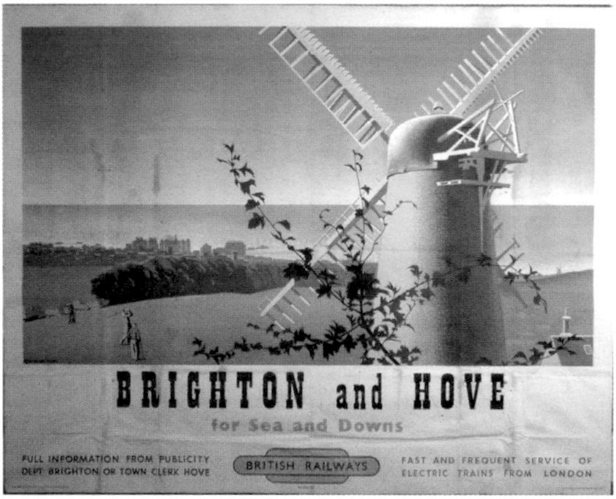


'Brighton and Hove for Sea and Downs', railway poster, designed by F.W. Wentworth-Shields, printed for the Railway Executive (SR) by The Baynard Press.

*1949* *50in (127cm) wide*

**£650-750** **ON**

'Bedford' railway poster, designed by Kerry Lee, printed by BR(LMR) by Waterlow and Sons Ltd, mounted on linen.

*1953* *40.25in (102cm) high*

**£40-60** **ON**

'Britain Land of Colour and Pageantry' railway poster, designed by Forster, printed for the B.T. & H.A. by Charles & Read.

*1954* *30in (76cm) high*

**£60-80** **ON**

'Cardiff Castle - Travel by Train' railway poster, designed by Ronald Lampitt, printed by BR(WR) by Jordison & Co Ltd, mounted on linen.

*50in (127cm) wide*

**£280-320** **ON**

'Chester' railway poster, designed by Kerry Lee, printed by BR (LMR) by Waterlow and Sons Ltd, mounted on linen.

*1953* *40.25in (102cm) high*

**£60-80** **ON**

'Dungeness By The Romney, Hythe and Dymchurch Railway' railway poster, designed by N. Cramer Roberts, printed by Vincent Brooks Day & Sons Ltd.

*The bright colours, superb condition and fabulous Art Deco styling of this poster, featuring a ship, make this desirable.*

*40.25in (102cm) high*

**£450-550** **ON**

## A CLOSER LOOK AT A RAILWAY POSTER

*Artist, designer and member of the Royal Academy, Frank Brangwyn (1867-1956) is noted for his prints and etchings, often produced for book illustrations.*

*Brangwyn shows the grandeur and scale of the bridge, almost suggesting a mountain range or cathedral, through the low angle of perspective and the light.*

*He was strongly influenced by Japanese prints, particularly single colour wood-cuts. This work also has similarities to that of Rembrandt and 18thC engraver Giovanni Piranesi.*

*It was designed for the London & North Eastern Railway, who employed a number of talented designers, and whose posters are highly collectable today.*

'The Forth-Bridge, LNER East Coast Route' railway poster, designed by Frank Brangwyn, printed for the LNER by Avenue Press, mounted on linen.

*50.5in (128cm) wide*

**£3,000-4,000** **ON**

'Edinburgh' railway poster, designed by Claude Buckle, printed for BR(SR) by Stafford and Co Ltd.

*40.25in (102cm) high*

**£150-200** **ON**

'North West England' railway poster, designed by Freda Marsden, printed for the LMS by Staffords.

*50in (127cm) wide*

**£550-650** **ON**

'Epping Forest' railway poster, designed by Walter E. Spradbery, printed for LNER by Vincent Brooks & Day Ltd.

*The flat areas of bright autumnal colours brings Clarice Cliff's designs to mind.*

*40.25in (102cm) high*

**£300-400** **ON**

'Fountains Abbey' railway poster, designed by Henry Rushbury, printed for the LNER by Ben Johnson & Co.

*50in (127cm) wide*

**£500-700** **ON**

'Callander & Oban Railway, In the Land of the Gael' railway poster, designed by an anonymous designer, printed by Dobson Molle & Co Ltd, mounted on linen with restoration.

*39.75in (101cm) high*

**£700-900** **ON**

## A CLOSER LOOK AT A RAILWAY POSTER

*This poster shows Bamburgh Castle. This range of posters aimed to promote rail travel to the east coast 'resorts' from Essex to Northumberland.*

*Flat, plain areas of colour are typical of Purvis' style, however the cooler colours are unusual.*

*Tom Purvis was an important artist for the LNER from 1923-45, helping to develop their recognisable style and producing over 100 designs for them.*

*It is undamaged, in excellent condition, and mounted on linen.*

'Northumberland' 1930s railway poster, designed by Tom Purvis, printed for LNER by S.C. Allan & Co Ltd.

*Tom Purvis became one of the first Royal Designers for Industry in 1936.*

*50in (127cm) wide*

**£2,200-2,800** **ON**

'Derwent Water, The Lake District' railway poster, designed by C. Baker, printed for LMS by Stafford & Co Ltd.

*Unsurprisingly, the picturesque Lake District featured in many LMS posters from the 1910s-40s. The calm waters, lack of people and the dramatic beauty of the hills and trees were offered as tantalising antidotes to busy city life.*

*40.25in (102cm) high*

**£500-600** **ON**

'Norwich' railway poster, designed by Claude Muncaster, printed for LNER by Gilmour & Dean Ltd, mounted on linen.

*39.75in (101cm) high*

**£400-500** **ON**

'King's Cross for Scotland' railway poster, designed by Freda Lingstrom, printed for LNER by The Avenue Press.

*40.25in (102cm) high*

**£200-300** **ON**

'Outings on the LNER' railway poster, designed by Gladys Peto, printed for the LNER by Vincent Brooks Day Co Ltd.

*c1928* *50in (127cm) high*

**£650-750** **ON**

'Rambles in the West Riding of Yorkshire' railway poster, designed by Schabelsky, printed for LNER by Vincent Brooks & Day Ltd.

*40.25in (102cm) high*

**£220-280** **ON**

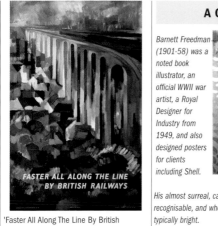

'Faster All Along The Line By British Railways' railway poster, designed by Myers, printed for BR(ER) by Waterlow & Sons Ltd, in excellent condition.

*40.25in (102cm) high*

**£350-450** **ON**

## A CLOSER LOOK AT A RAILWAY POSTER

*Barnett Freedman (1901-58) was a noted book illustrator, an official WWII war artist, a Royal Designer for Industry from 1949, and also designed posters for clients including Shell.*

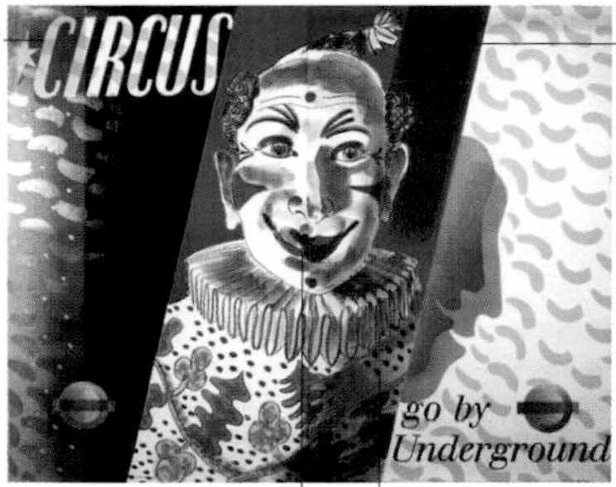


*This poster was produced over two separate sheets and used the best inks and lithographic techniques available at the time. Note the incredible toning and graduated colours.*

*His almost surreal, caricature-like style is highly recognisable, and where colour is used, it is typically bright.*

*This example is preserved on paper and came with an excellent provenance, having been owned by Freedman's son.*

'Circus – Go by Underground' two-sheet London Underground poster, designed by Barnett Freedman, printed by Curwen Press.

*1936* *40in (101.5cm) high (each sheet)*

**£600-700** **ON**

'Wales, Travel by Train' railway poster, designed by Frank Wootton, printed for BR(WR) by Waterlow & Sons Ltd, in excellent condition.

*Frank Wootton is best known for his renowned aviation pictures. Many of the much loved elements found in these paintings are also here, including a good rendering of the landscape and clouds and a certain 'mood' to the atmosphere.*

*50in (127cm) wide*

**£550-650** **ON**

'Pomifer Autumnus' London Underground poster, designed by John Burningham, printed by Waterlow and Sons Ltd, in excellent condition.

*1961* *40.25in (102cm) high*

**£150-200** **ON**

'For The Zoo' London Underground poster, designed by Maurice A. Miles, printed by The Baynard Press.

*This is an extremely desirable and rare poster due to the Art Deco, Cubist-style and powerful graphics. Miles designed two posters for the London Underground in the Cubist style, the other being for Kew Gardens, as well as one for Shell in 1933. He exhibited at the Royal Academy in 1931.*

*c1933* *40in (101.5cm) high*

**£1,800-2,200** **ON**

'South For Winter Sunshine' original poster paint design for a proposed BR(SR) poster, by Edmond Vaughan, signed.

*This recalls Alexander Alexieff's 1930 'The Night Scotsman' poster design for LNER, also featuring a train flying through the night clouds, which can be worth up to £12,000. This may be a reason why it was not put into production.*

*c1947* *25.25in (64cm) wide*

**£450-550** **ON**

'Paris Montmartre' French railway poster, designed by Maurice Utrillo, printed for SNCF by De Plas.

*Utrillo (1883-1955), was a painter living and working in Montmartre, Paris at around the same time as Picasso and Modigliani. He is famous today for his Parisian street scenes, as seen here.*

*1953* *39.75in (101cm) high*

**£120-180** **ON**

'Go to Paris' French railway poster, designed by Andre Planson, printed for SNCF by Hubert Baille & Cie.

*1953* *39.75in (101cm) high*

**£120-180** **ON**

'France Savoy' French railway poster, designed by Fontana Rosa, printed for SNCF by Draeger.

*1952* *39.75in (101cm) high*

**£120-180** **ON**

'The Munster Valley' French Alsace and Lorraine railway poster, printed by Serre & Cie.

*39.25in (100cm) high*

**£80-120** **ON**

'Auvergne – Visit France' French railway poster, designed by Gregoire, printed for SNCF by SNAP.

*1952* *39.75in (101cm) high*

**£120-180** **ON**

'Strasbourg, The Cathedral' Alsace and Lorraine Railways poster, designed by Ernest Schmitt, printed by Alsacienne.

*39.25in (100cm) high*

**£50-80** **ON**

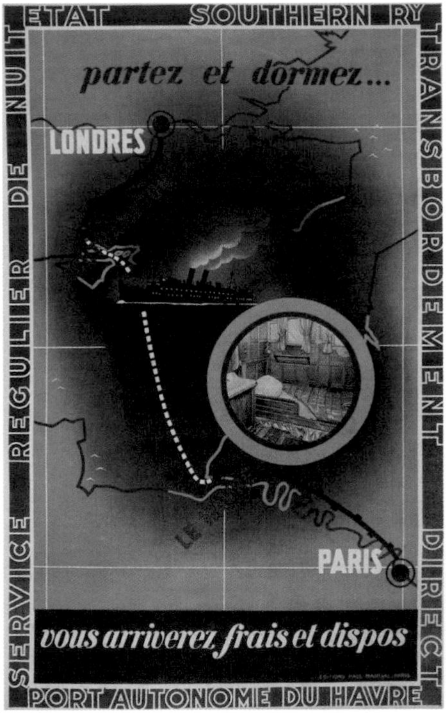


'Partez et Dormez... Londres, Paris' French railway poster, designed by Francis Bernard, printed by Paul-Martial, Paris.

*38.75in (97cm) high*

**£600-800** **SWA**

'Cannes' French railway poster, designed by Guy Derre, printed for the SNCF by Robaudy, Cannes.

*39.25in (100cm) high*

**£150-250** **LOZ**

'SNCF – Nice' French railway poster, printed for the Syndicat d'Initiative de Nice by L' Action Publicitaire of Monte Carlo.

*39.25in (99.5cm) high*

**£250-350** **LOZ**

'Paris-Lyon 4H.50 Automotrice Rapide Bugatti' French railway poster, designed by E.A. Schefer, printed for PLM by Chaix, mounted on linen.

*The famous name, sense of speed and the style of the train make this a desirable image.*

*1935* *37.5in (95cm) high*

**£500-600** **ON**

'Lötschberg, Bern-Lötschberg-Simplon' Swiss railway poster, designed by P. Colombi, printed by Kunstanstalt Brugger.

*This poster advertised the 14.6km long Lötschberg railway tunnel under the Alps. Construction began in 1906, and the tunnel opened in 1913 after a number of disasters caused serious setbacks.*

*1937* *40.25in (102cm) high*

**£250-350** **ON**

'Peaceful Switzerland' Swiss railway poster, designed by Emil Cardinaux, printed by Wolsberg-Druck.

*40.25in (102cm) high*

**£150-200** **ON**

'Pilatus Bahn' Swiss railway poster, designed by R. Winkler, printed by Frey & Conrad, folds.

*1902* *33.75in (86cm) high*

**£60-80** **ON**

'The Electric Simplon Line', Swiss railway poster, printed for Swiss Federal Railways by Fretz Bros Ltd, mounted on linen.

*40.25in (102cm) high*

**£120-180** **ON**

'Winter in Germany' German railway poster, designed by Werner von Axster-Heudtlass.

*1935* *39.75in (101cm) high*

**£120-180** **ON**

## A CLOSER LOOK AT A RAILROAD POSTER

*This ariel image of the famous dam was taken "at dedication ceremonies Sept 30, 1935" according to the poster, the dam itself was completed in 1936.*

*The dam was known as the Boulder Dam, as it spanned the Boulder Canyon. In 1947, Congress passed a resolution renaming it after President Herbert Hoover.*

*In terms of the colours, font and angular, collage-style composition, this poster subscribes more to avant-garde European poster styles of the 1930s than to US posters of the same period.*

*The use of the 'enroute to California' wording shows that the dam was a popular destination off the legendary route 66, near Kingman, as people drove west to Los Angeles.*

'See Boulder Dam Enroute To California', Amalgamated Lithographers, Chicago, with tears, wrinkles and slight paper loss at edges.

*c1936* *41in (104cm) high*

**£1,000-1,500** **SWA**

'Summer in Germany', German railway poster, designed by Werner von Axster-Heudtlass.

*c1935* *39.75in (101cm) high*

**£80-120** **ON**

'In a German Forest' German railway poster, designed by Otto Altenkird.

*c1935* *39.75in (101cm) high*

**£120-180** **ON**

'Norway, Land of the Midnight Sun' Norwegian photographic railway poster, printed for Norwegian State Railways by Grondahl & Son.

*1953* *40.25in (102cm) high*

**£60-80** **ON**

'We Shall Not Fail' American railroad poster, designed by Leslie Ragan, printed by Brett Lithographing Company restoration in margins, creases in image.

*This rare poster was produced during WWII to show the railroad's support of the war. The Statue of Liberty standing above the railroad toiling through the night makes a strongly propagandist statement.*

*1943* *41in (104cm) high*

**£3,500-4,500** **SWA**

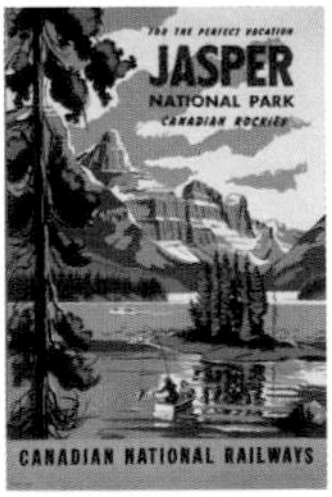


'Jasper National Park – Canadian Rockies' Canadian railway poster, by an unknown designer for Canadian National Railways.

*29.5in (75cm) high*

**£100-150** **ON**

## COLLECTORS' NOTES

- In general, the most desirable and collectable shipping and cruise liner posters were produced during the first few decades of the 20thC, when large, luxury cruise liners such as the Normandie, Titanic and Olympic were desirable modes of travel.
- Like railway posters, many posters advertised the destination, which often offered a sun-soaked countryside or water-born escape from every-day life. However, many of the more desirable and valuable examples show the ship itself, typically at sea.
- The name of the line or the ship, if well-known, will count towards value. Also look out for the work of notable artists, and dramatic artwork that summons up the romance and grandeur of the ship. Cruise liners declined in popularity from the 1950s onwards, when airlines offered a faster travel option.

'Bergen Line - The Shortest Sea Route to Norway' cruise liner poster, designed by Harry Rodmell, printed by Carew Wilson Massey Ltd.

*40.25in (102cm) high*

**£80-120** **ON**

'Arandora Star' cruise liner poster, printed for Blue Star Line.

*40.25in (102cm) high*

**£180-220** **ON**

'Great Britain and Ireland - T.S.S. Caledonian Princess via Stranraer and Larne' maritime poster, designed by Johnston, printed for Caledonian Steam Packet Co. by Waterlow & Sons Ltd, in excellent condition with folds.

*40.25in (127cm) wide*

**£180-220** **ON**

'Canadian Pacific The World's Greatest Travel System' Canadian shipping poster, by an unknown designer for Canadian Pacific.

*40.25in (102cm) high*

**£50-70** **ON**

'Belge Maritime du Congo', Belgian maritime poster, designed by Paul van Brempt, printed by E. Stockmans & Co.

*This poster advertises the Belgium to Congo route, aboard the Albertville. The Belgian hold on the Congo lasted from 1908-60.*

*1924* *39.75in (101cm) high*

**£700-800** **ON**

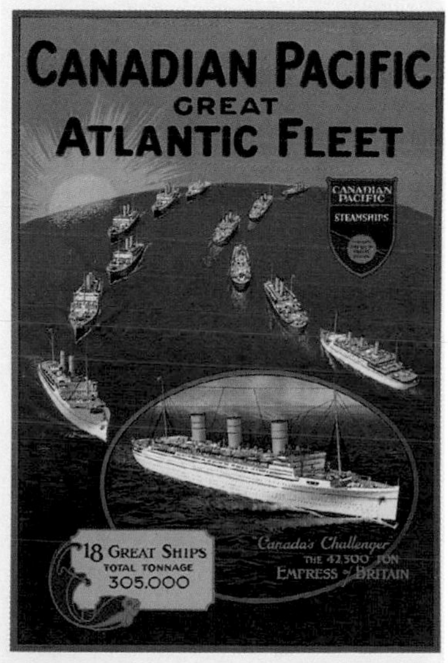


'Canadian Pacific Great Atlantic Fleet' Canadian shipping poster, by an unknown designer, restoration and repaired tear in image.

*This poster advertises the 42,500 ton 'Empress of Britain', which was launched in 1930 as the flagship of the Canadian Pacific Fleet. Renowned in the fleet for its luxury, it was hailed as the '5-Day Atlantic Giantess'.*

*c1932* *35.75in (91cm) high*

**£450-550** **SWA**

'Relax – Compagnie Maritime des Chargeurs Réunis' French cruise liner poster, designed by Rene Gruau, printed by Edition Bonches.

*Rene Gruau (1909-2004) was a famous fashion designer and illustrator. He worked for Dior amongst others, which explains the presence of the fashionably dressed lady.*

*38.5in (98cm) high*

**£300-500** **LOZ**

'Queen Mary – Queen Elizabeth – Fastest Ocean Service in the World' cruise liner poster, designed by Walter Thomas for Cunard White Star.

*38.75in (98.5cm) high*

**£400-600** **LOZ**

'Cunard to Canada' cruise liner poster, by Frank Newbould, printed by Thomas Forman & Sons, Nottingham, restoration and creases in corners and margins.

*40in (101.5cm) high*

**£250-300** **SWA**

'French Line Southampton to the West Indies' cruise liner poster, designed by Jean Walther, printed by Hill Siffken & Co.

*40.25in (102cm) high*

**£180-220** **ON**

'Messageries Maritimes - For a romantic trip to the south sea islands, travel by 'Polynésie' 1960s cruise liner poster, designed by C.M. Perrot.

*23.25in (59cm) high*

**£600-800** **LOZ**

'Cunard to Canada' 1950s cruise liner poster, designed by Charles Eddowes Turner, small loss and tears to the lower edge.

*This brightly coloured poster showing a ship sailing calmly into the sunset is bound to have tempted many. Turner (1893-1965) produced many maritime works, including those for Cunard, as well as landscape works exhibited at the Royal Academy.*

*40in (101.5cm) high*

**£500-800** **LOZ**

'Orient Line Cruises' cruise liner poster, designed by an unknown designer.

*40.25in (102cm) high*

**£300-400** **LOZ**

'Cruising with Orient Line' cruise liner poster, designed by Doris Dekk, printed by The Baynard Press.

*40.25in (102cm) high*

**£60-80** **ON**

'P&O Summer Cruises 1953' cruise liner poster, for the 28,000 ton 'Himalaya' and the 24,000 ton 'Chusan', printed by Nissen & Arnold Ltd.

*1953* *39in (99cm) high*

**£80-120** **ON**

'P&O Cruises' cruise liner poster, by an unknown designer, printed by Brown Knight & Truscott Ltd.

*The poster shows the Chusan, built in 1950. With the merger of P&O and Orient Lines in 1960, the new company held the largest fleet of cruise liners in the world.*

*39.75in (101cm) high*

**£120-180** **ON**

'Shaw Savill & Albion Co. Ltd' maritime calendar poster, by an unknown designer, printed by Purbrook & Eyres.

*1904* *14.25in (36cm) high*

**£180-220** **ON**

'Union-Castle Line, South Africa Land of Contrast' cruise liner poster, printed by Rotogravure.

*40.25In (102cm) high*

**£50-80** **ON**

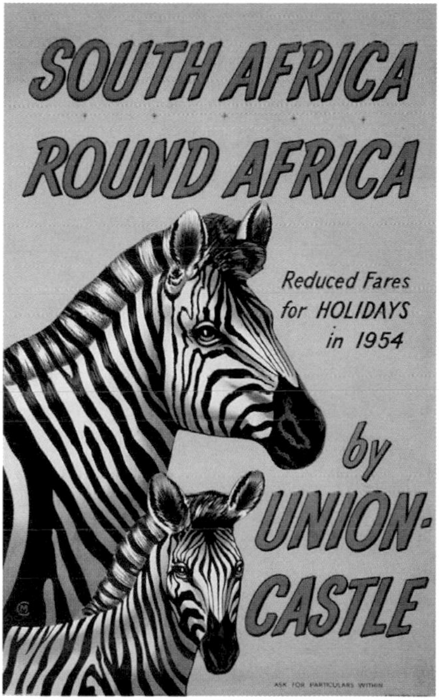


'South Africa Round Africa by Union Castle' cruise liner poster, designed by C.M., printed in England.

*Union Castle was a passenger and freight line operating from 1900-77. Liners were known for the 'Castle' suffix to their names, but more so for their lavender-painted hulls and black and red funnels.*

*1954* *40.25in (102cm) high*

**£40-70** **ON**

'Union-Castle to South Africa' cruise liner poster, printed by Baynard.

*1953* *40.25in (102cm) high*

**£60-80** **ON**

## A CLOSER LOOK AT A FERRY POSTER

*Leslie Carr is known for his architectural, marine and landscape scenes, and produced designs for the LNER, SR and British Railways.*

*This highly detailed poster would appeal to two markets: collectors of maritime and cruise posters, and also railway poster collectors.*

*The modern, almost watercolour-like style with flat area of colour is sought after as it is so decorative.*

*Not only is the style typical of the artist, it is also representative of one school of design of the period, and some of the work of the best designers of the period.*

'Drive Your Car Direct Onto The Train Ferry Boat', designed by Leslie Carr, printed for SR by Waterlow & Sons Ltd, mounted on linen with restoration.

*1936* *50in (127cm) wide*

**£1,800-2,200** **ON**

'Yeowood Line, An Ideal Holiday Cruise' cruise liner poster, designed by an unknown designer, printed by T. Forman & Sons.

*c1935* *40in (102cm) high*

**£400-500** **ON**

'Dover-Ostend Ferries' Belgian ferry poster, designed by F. Cheneval, printed for Belgian Marine by Marci, with damage.

*40.25in (102cm) high*

**£10-15** **ON**

'Fishguard-Rosslare' railway and maritime poster, designed by Arthur G. Mills, printed for Railway Executive (Western Region) by Waterlow & Sons.

*The dramatic design, where the ship looks ready to burst out from the poster's frame makes this poster desirable. Arthur Mills is also a recognised artist, known for his wartime design work for the Royal Society for the Prevention of Accidents.*

*40.25in (102cm) high*

**£350-450** **ON**

'Belgium via Harwich' railway and ferry poster, designed by Fred Taylor and Frank H. Mason, printed for LNER by Waterlow & Sons Ltd, mounted on linen.

*50in (127cm) wide*

**£800-1,200** **ON**

'Sealink' Italian language ferry poster, printed for BR Shipping Services by Waterlow Ltd.

*40.25in (102cm) high*

**£8-12** **ON**

## COLLECTORS' NOTES

- Air France was formed in 1933, when a number of smaller airlines were merged under one name. It was nationalised in 1946, and merged with Dutch airline KLM in 2003. Since the 1930s, it has had a strong tradition of producing superb advertising posters.
- The company employed leading poster designers, many of whom were French. These included Bernard Villemot, Vincent Guerra and Victor Vasarely. Designs typically combine the destination, a visual feel for the medium of travel and nearly always feature an aeroplane.
- Look for appealing, modern designs in bright colours that hint at the excitement and speed of air travel, or the romance and appeal of the destination. Notable destinations and modern, abstract designs can also add value.

'Air France - Amérique du Sud' airline poster, designed by Victor Vasarely, printed by the Perceval Studio.

*Artist and graphic designer Victor Vasarely (1908-97), is known for his 'Op Art' paintings and sculptures that utilise colour and geometric shapes to give optical and three-dimensional effects. Note how the treatment of the light on the sea on this poster reflects this.*

*1946* *19.75in (50cm) high*

**£200-400** **LOZ**

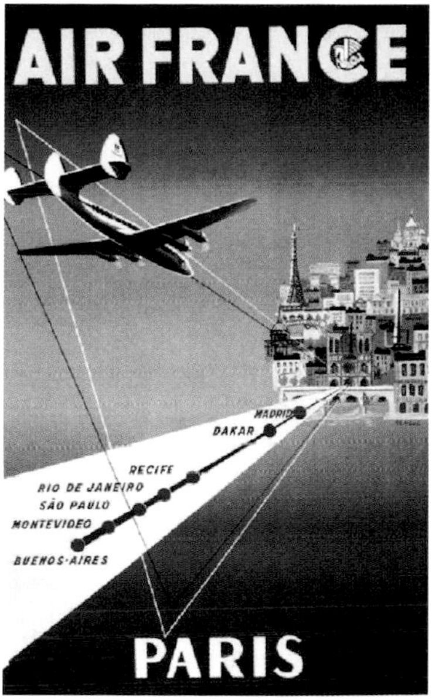


'Air France - Paris' airline poster, designed by Renluc, printed by Hubert Baille & Cie.

*1953* *42.25in (107.5cm) high*

**£600-1,000** **LOZ**

'Air France, Paris - New York' airline poster, designed by Bertrand & Perrier, printed by Alepee & Cie, Paris.

*39.25in (100cm) high*

**£600-800** **LOZ**

'Air France - Marseilles Iles Baléares - Alger' airline poster, designed by L. Solon, printed by France Affiches.

*19.75in (50cm) high*

**£200-300** **LOZ**

'Air France - Proche Orient' airline poster, designed by Vincent Guerra, printed by Alepee & Cie.

*19.75in (50cm) high*

**£200-300** **LOZ**

'Air France – Afrique Occidentale Française, Afrique Equatoriale Française' airline poster, designed by E. Maurus.

*The dizzying feeling of perspective, plane emerging from the sun and rich colours help make this example sought-after.*

*39.25in (100cm) high*

**£2,500-3,500** **LOZ**

'Air France, Afrique du Nord' airline poster, designed by Bernard Villemot.

*1950* *39.25in (100cm) high*

**£200-300** **LOZ**

## A CLOSER LOOK AT AN AIRLINE POSTER

*Air France is a popular airline who produced a good variety of posters that are popular with collectors today.*

*It is also the rarest of the series and has appealing artwork that is strongly suggestive of Africa, including the colours used.*

*Produced in 1946, this was the first design from a series of posters designed by Vincent Guerra for Air France.*

*Africa was, and continues to be, an important destination for Air France.*

'Air France – Afrique Occidentale – Afrique Equatoriale' airline poster, designed by Vincent Guerra, printed by Alépée & Cie, Paris.

*1946* *39.25in (100cm) high*

**£1,500-2,500** **LOZ**

'Air France, Côte d'Azur' airline poster, designed by Guy Georget, printed by Bedos & Cie à Paris.

*39.25in (100cm) high*

**£300-400** **LOZ**

'Air France, Californie' airline poster, designed by Guy Georget, and printed by S.A. Courbet.

*1963* *39.25in (100cm) high*

**£150-250** **LOZ**

'Air France, URSS' airline poster, designed by Mathieu, printed by Debrez et Butin, Monte-Carlo.

*39.25in (100cm) high*

**£80-120** **LOZ**

'Fly B.O.A.C. U.S.A' 1950s silk-screened airline poster, designed by Aldo Cosomati, 53/603, printed in Great Britain.

*30in (76cm) high*

**£120-180** **ON**

'Fly B.O.A.C. Britain', 1950s silk-screened airline poster, designed by Aldo Cosomati, 53/614, printed in Great Britain.

*30in (76cm) high*

**£200-300** **ON**

'Fly B.O.A.C. South Africa' 1950s silk-screened airline poster, designed by Aldo Cosomati, 53/606, printed in Great Britain.

*30in (76cm) high*

**£250-350** **ON**

'Fly B.O.A.C. India' 1950s silk-screened airline poster, designed by Aldo Cosomati, 53/6624, printed in Great Britain.

*30in (76cm) high*

**£220-280** **ON**

'Vuele por B.O.A.C. Japon', 1950s Spanish language airline poster, by Aldo Cosomati, 53/622, printed in Great Britain.

*30in (76cm) high*

**£220-280** **ON**

'Fly B.O.A.C. Pakistan' 1950s silk-screened airline poster, designed by Aldo Cosomati, 53/629, printed in Great Britain.

*These posters are part of a larger series that Cosomati designed for BOAC around the mid-1950s. They are sought-after for their striking collage-style imagery, with broad areas of bright colours. Exotic subjects and a touch of humour, such as the tiger's rather puzzled expression, tends to add to desirability.*

*30in (76cm) high*

**£250-350** **ON**

'Fly B.O.A.C. - It's a Smaller World by Speedbird' airline poster, designed by Beverley Pick.

*Beverley Pick is notable for his designs for Charing Cross railway station during WWII as well as for his post-war designs for airlines B.O.A.C. and BEA. During the mid-20thC, he ran his own design agency as well as being a director of a company producing designs for shop fittings, exhibition stands and even the Christmas lights on Regent Street in London.*

*1950* *39.75in (101cm) high*

**£300-400** **LOZ**

'New York World's Fair – American Airlines' airline poster, designed by Henry K. Bencathy.

*Here Bencathy use of the Fair's 'Unisphere' monument indicates both the fair, and American Airline's global reach.*

*1964* *40in (101.5cm) high*

**£300-400** **SWA**

'American Airlines to New York' airline poster, by Weimer Pursell.

*Pursell is notable for his Art Deco and Modernist designs for a number of companies including the 1933 Chicago World's Fair, Standard Oil, Coca-Cola and American Airlines. He also provided designs for Esquire and LIFE magazine.*

*c1950* *40in (101.5cm) high*

**£700-1,000** **SWA**

'AOA to USA' airline poster, designed by Jan Lewitt and George Him, printed by W.R. Royle.

*1948* *40.25in (102cm) high*

**£150-250** **ON**

'Aeromaritime Côte Occidentale d'Afrique' French airline poster, designed by Albert Brenet, printed by Mont Louis.

*1937* *39in (99cm) high*

**£100-150** **ON**

'Fly The President To London & Paris' airline poster, for Pan American World Airways.

*'The President' referred to a special transatlantic flight made to Europe by the double-decked Boeing Stratoclipper. Renowned for their size, speed, luxury and full sleeping accommodation, PanAm had the largest fleet of these planes in the world at the time.*

*39.25in (100cm) high*

**£300-400** **LOZ**

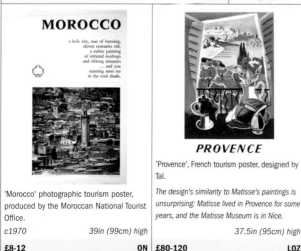

'Afrique Occidentale Française' tourism poster, designed by Paul Colin for the Office du Tourisme de l'A.O.F., printed by Diloutremer, with tear to top.

*Note how the artist has cleverly incorporated African imagery into the giraffe's markings.*

*39.25in (99.5cm) high*

**£800-1,200** **LOZ**

'Austria', tourism poster, designed by Kosel, printed by Alfred Wall.

*37.5in (95cm) high*

**£70-100** **ON**

'Belgium - Visit the Ardennes' tourism poster, designed by Poleff, printed by Protin et Vuidar for the Belgian and Luxembourgeois Tourism Board.

*1932* *39.25in (100cm) high*

**£70-100** **ON**

'Pau' French tourism poster, printed by Devambez, Paris.

*40.75in (103.5cm) high*

**£800-1,200** **LOZ**

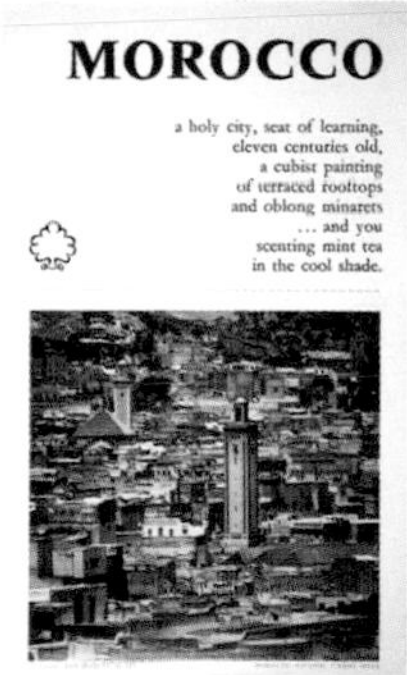
MOROCCO
a holy city, seat of learning,
eleven centuries old,
a cubist painting
of terraced rooftops
and oblong minarets
... and you
scenting mint tea
in the cool shade.

'Morocco' photographic tourism poster, produced by the Moroccan National Tourist Office.

*c1970* *39in (99cm) high*

**£8-12** **ON**

PROVENCE

'Provence', French tourism poster, designed by Tal.

*The design's similarity to Matisse's paintings is unsurprising: Matisse lived in Provence for some years, and the Matisse Museum is in Nice.*

*37.5in (95cm) high*

**£80-120** **LOZ**

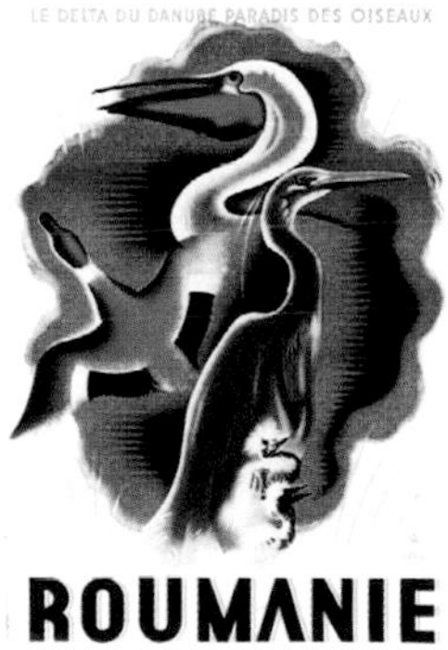


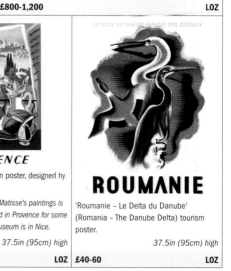

'Roumanie - Le Delta du Danube' (Romania - The Danube Delta) tourism poster.

*37.5in (95cm) high*

**£40-60** **LOZ**

'Scotland's Western Highlands and Islands' tourism poster, printed for David Macbrayne Ltd by John Horn Ltd.

*40.25in (102cm) high*

**£150-200** **ON**

'Switzerland - Alpine Postal Motor Coaches' tourism poster, designed by H.B. Wieland, printed by J.G. Muller.

*1939* *39.25in (100cm) high*

**£220-280** **ON**

## A CLOSER LOOK AT A TOURISM POSTER

*Dorothy Waugh was art production supervisor of the National Park Service and designed a number of posters for them.*

*She also taught typography and design, and managed the children's book department at publisher Alfred Knopf.*

*The colours chosen are highly patriotic. Many different aspects of America's political and social history that can be seen in the Parks are shown.*

*Many travel and tourism posters were produced under the Works Projects Administration's Federal Art Project from 1934-43, and are collectable today.*

'Historic National Parks and Monuments' US tourism poster, designed by Dorothy Waugh, printed by US Government Printing Office, with restoration to image and tears.

*c1934* *40in (101.5cm) high*

**£450-550** **SWA**

'See USSR - An Udarnik of the Magnitogorsk Steel Mills' 1950s Russian photographic tourism poster, by A. Skurikhin, printed for InTourist.

*Although a trip to Russia's premier steel works built under Stalin seems a somewhat depressing thought, Russia shows its pride in this mill by showing an Udarnik (super-productive worker) in a typical heroic social-realist pose.*

*33in (84cm) high*

**£180-220** **CL**

'Look What's Happening in Oklahoma!', US tourism poster, produced by Oklahoma Tourist Information, mounted on linen.

*c1960* *28in (71cm) high*

**£120-180** **ON**

'Bermuda' US tourism poster, designed by by Lesnon, printed by Mardon Son & Hall, Bristol, creases and tears in margins.

*38in (96.5cm) high*

**£700-800** **SWA**

## A CLOSER LOOK AT A SKIING POSTER

*Designed by Roger Broders, a notable French poster designer employed by the French Railways to promote tourism for a decade during the 1920s.*

*It is a 'snow train' poster, combining the popular subject of skiing with the collectable subject of railways.*

*His strong, stylized graphic compositions with bold colours are sympathetic to the subject - this is a typical example.*

*Broders also designed posters for the Cote D'Azur, which are highly collectable today. All his designs helped bring the Art Deco style to poster design.*

'Le Hohwald' French skiing poster, designed by Roger Broders, produced by the Railways of Alsace and Lorraine, printed by Lucien Serre & Cie in Paris.

*c1930*

*39.25in (100cm) high*

**£1,200-1,800** **LOZ**

'Le Markstein, La Nouvelle Station des Vosges', produced by the Railways of Alsace and Lorraine, printed by Lucien Serre & Cie in Paris.

*39.25in (100cm) high*

**£1,200-1,800** **LOZ**

'Chréa – Centenaire de l'Algérie' French Algerian skiing poster, printed by Baconnier, Algeria.

*Chréa was a popular skiing resort town south of Algiers until 1992 when the resort was abandoned due to military insurgency. Skiing posters have become enormously popular over recent years, typically with skiers. 1930s posters advertising resorts top the bill. Look out for bold, colourful and eye-catching designs that sum up the decorative style of the period or the glamour and fun of the sport.*

*1930* *39.25in (100cm) high*

**£500-800** **LOZ**

'Davos 1560m' Swiss skiing poster, designed by Herbert Leupin, printed in Switzerland.

*50in (127cm) high*

**£40-60** **ON**

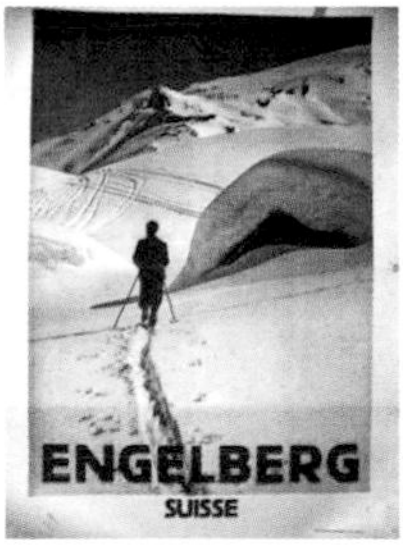


'Engelberg Suisse' Swiss photographic skiing poster, by an unknown photographer.

*39.25in (100cm) high*

**£300-400** **ON**

'Gstaad Saanenmöser Zweisimmen' Swiss skiing poster, designed by Hans Thoni, printed by Brugger Ltd.

*39.25in (100cm) high*

**£100-150** **ON**

'Harz' German photographic skiing poster, printed in Germany.

*1968* *29.25in (74cm) high*

**£28-32** **ON**

'Mürren Schweiz' Swiss skiing poster, designed by Helios, printed by Amstutz & Herdeg.

*40in (104cm) high*

**£100-150** **ON**

'Luchon-Superbagnères – Les Sports d'Hiver en France', designed by Roger Soubie for the International Skiing Contest, printed by Imprimeur Cornille & Serre in Paris.

*1923* *40.25in (102cm) high*

**£600-800** **LOZ**

'Winter Sports' skiing poster, designed by Ronald Brett, printed for Southern Railways by Baynard Press.

*1938* *40.25in (102cm) high*

**£250-350** **ON**

'Dean & Dawson Ltd To Winter Resorts' skiing poster, designed by Beytagh, folds.

*Dean & Dawson was an early pioneer of package tourism, which was begun by Thomas Cook in July 1941.*

*40.25in (102cm) high*

**£60-80** **ON**

'New Travel Allowance: £100 – Switzerland' Swiss skiing poster, designed by Schneider, printed for the Swiss National Tourist Office.

*40.25in (102cm) high*

**£40-60** **ON**

'Du Mont-Ventoux' skiing and tourism poster, printed by Rullière Freres.

*30in (76cm) high*

**£120-180** **ON**

## COLLECTORS' NOTES

- Shell posters are both product advertising and travel posters. The product never appears itself, but it is intrinsic to the posters, which aimed to show how one could use Shell oil to travel by car around Britain to see its rich heritage by visiting monuments and viewing nature. They also depicted animals and people, such as fishermen, who relied on Shell products. Again the product is nowhere to be seen.

- Cars and petrol stations are also intentionally not shown, meaning that the effects that oil production and use has on the 'picture perfect' landscape or the wildlife is further obscured. The series was initiated in 1932 by Jack Beddington (1893-1959), Shell's publicity manager, with the aim of encouraging people to travel for pleasure by car. He hired leading artists of the day including Graham Sutherland, Duncan Grant, Paul Nash and Edward McKnight Kauffer.

- Shell and BP formed a joint marketing venture in 1932, and grew to control the petrol market for the next 40 years, making their public image vitally important. Although petrol was rationed during WWII, another campaign during the 1950s continued to encourage people to use Shell's oil in their machinery or petrol to travel around Britain to sight see.

- The images were used on the side of delivery trucks and as posters and, today, these posters have become highly collectable. Although popular, scenes of wildlife from the 1950s tend to be less valuable than the starkly Modernist, abstract designs of the 1930s that some of these designers, such as Hans Scheleger or McKnight Kauffer produced. Modern renderings of landmarks fall somewhere in between the two categories, with value often depending on the fame of the artist and the visual appeal of the image.

'The Robin, A Friend to the Farmer Shell Tractor Oil' advertising poster no.24, designed by Harold Hussey, printed by John Waddington Ltd, signs of wear and tears.

*1952* *39.75in (101cm) wide*

**£80-120** **ON**

'The Barn Owl, A Friend to the Farmer Shell Tractor Oil' advertising poster no.19, designed by Peter Shepheard, printed by John Waddington Ltd, with damage.

*75in (101cm) wide*

**£60-90** **ON**

'Great Spotted Woodpecker, A Friend to the Farmer Shell Tractor Oil' advertising poster no.19, designed by Leonard Appelbee, printed by John Waddington Ltd.

*1952* *39.75in (101cm) wide*

**£80-120** **ON**

'The Blue Tit, A Friend to the Farmer Shell Tractor Oil' advertising poster no.30, designed by Harold Hussey, printed by John Waddington Ltd, some damage.

*1952* *39.75in (101cm) wide*

**£80-120** **ON**

'Ralph Allen's Sham Castle Near Bath' advertising poster no.461, from the Shell Landmark series, designed by Richard Guyatt, printed by Waterlow, in excellent condition.

*1936* *45.25in (115cm) wide*

**£280-320** **ON**

## A CLOSER LOOK AT A SHELL POSTER

*It was designed by Edward McKnight Kauffer, one of Britain's most renowned Modernist poster designers and artists, and among the best known designers for Shell.*

*It is in excellent condition, and is mounted on linen.*

*McKnight Kauffer takes the idea of art further than other designers in this poster, using an oil painting of Dinton Castle, indicating that the castle and landscape is a natural 'masterpiece'.*

*Look out for his more Modernist, abstract designs, which can fetch larger sums.*

'Dinton Castle Near Aylesbury' advertising poster, from the Shell Landmark series, designed by Edward McKnight Kauffer, printed by Waterlow, mounted on linen.

*44.5in (113cm) wide*

**£1,200-1,800** **ON**

'Llanthony Abbey Monmouthshire', advertising poster no.498, from the Shell Landmark series, designed by Denis Constanduros, printed by Waterlow, in excellent condition

*1937* *45.25in (115cm) wide*

**£250-350** **ON**

'The Tattingstone Wonder, Suffolk', advertising poster no.497, designed by W.J. Steggles, from the Shell Landmark series, printed by Waterlow, damaged and foxed.

*1937* *45.25in (115cm) wide*

**£180-220** **ON**

'Chanter's Folly and Dry Dock Appledore' advertising poster no.491, from the Shell Landmark series, designed by Clifford & Rosemary Ellis, printed by Waterlow, in excellent condition.

*1937* *45.25in (115cm) wide*

**£400-500** **ON**

'These Men Use Shell' advertising poster no.506, designed by Derek Sayer, printed by Waterlow, damaged.

*1937* *45in (114cm) wide*

**£180-220** **ON**

'These Men Use Shell' advertising poster no.509, designed by Edward Ardizzone, printed by Waterlow.

*1938* *45in (114cm) wide*

**£450-550** **ON**

'Grand Prix Automobile Pau' motor racing poster, designed by Ch. V. Surreau, printed by Havas Pau.

*1947* *43.25in (110cm) high*

**£350-450** **ON**

## A CLOSER LOOK AT AN AUTOMOBILIA POSTER

*O'Galop was the pseudonym of French poster artist and cartoonist Marius Rossillon (1867-1946), who designed the now famous Michelin man.*

*Devised in 1898 after the founders of Michelin noticed how human a stack of tyres looked, this was the first time the character ever appeared.*

*The phrases relate to how the tyres were meant to 'drink' obstacles, hence the Latin phrase which means 'Now is the time to drink!' or 'Cheers!'*

*Although this is a later (but original) printing, the fame of the poster and the popularity of the character ensures a high value.*

'Le Pneu Michelin Nunc est Bibendum' tyre advertising poster, designed by O'Galop and printed by Chaix Paris, mounted on linen, some folds and retouching.

*1913* *61in (155cm) high*

**£3,000-4,000** **ON**

'Jersey International Road Race' poster, promoting the race organised by the BARC and Jersey Motor Cycle & Light Car Club on Thursday April 28th 1949.

*This poster has many factors collectors look for: a sense of speed, an appealing vintage car, good stylisation and strong colours.*

*1949* *30in (76cm) high*

**£650-750** **ON**

A reproduction 1959 Sebring Grand Prix poster, showing the winning Aston-Martin DB3S driven by Shelby and Salvadori, signed with a thick blue pen by Roy Salvadori.

*40in (101.5cm) high*

**£50-70** **TCA**

A French language Monaco Grand Prix race advertising poster.

*Michael Schumacher finished in first place and Eddie Irvine in second. Both drove for Ferrari, whose car is shown here, although the brand name has been replaced with the location of the race.*

*1999* *24in (61cm) high*

**£40-60** **TCA**

A 1960s two-colour motor racing poster, advertising the Brands Hatch Lombank Trophy, on 31st January.

*30in (76cm) high*

**£40-60** **SAS**

A 1970s full-colour motor racing poster, advertising the Shell Sport 5000 race at Mallory Park.

*30in (76cm) high*

**£25-35** **SAS**

## COLLECTORS' NOTES

- Guinness first used advertising in 1928, when they employed agency S.H. Benson to produce a marketing and advertising campaign. They employed artist and designer John Gilroy (1898-1985), who went on to define Guinness' advertising into the 1950s. As the medium of television took over in the mid-1960s, the use of posters began to decline over the next 20 years.
- Gilroy's most famous campaign, launched in 1935, included zoo animals – most notably the toucan. The animals are mostly seen running away from their hapless zookeeper, having stolen his pint of Guinness. The caption 'My Goodness My Guinness' was used both to refer to the situation and hint at the alleged health benefits of the drink. Adding to this humour, he imbued what would be ferocious animals with friendly, comical expressions. Animals were used until 1961, when the last poster appeared.
- Two other themes were used, concurrently with and subsequent to the animal campaign. The first was that drinking Guinness gives you strength, a theme that continued to be used during WWII. The second was that a pint of Guinness was the ideal reward to relax with after work, typically for the working class man.
- Gilroy's classic animal posters with their green borders, plain backgrounds and red lettering tend to be the most desirable, particularly if they include gentle humour and a popular animal such as the seal or toucan. 'Guinness for Strength' posters tend to be more desirable when the subject does not involve the war, but generally, it is the most iconic and instantly recognisable designs that prove to the most desirable and valuable.

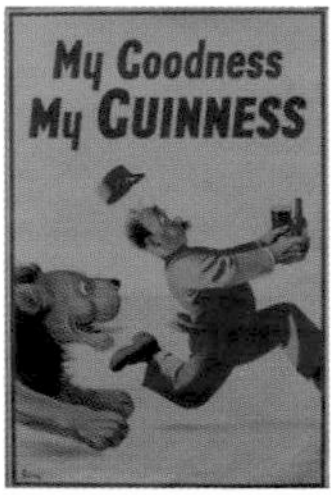


'My Goodness My Guinness' advertising poster, designed by John Gilroy, printed by Waddington.

*The lion was, surprisingly, Gilroy's least popular animal.*

*1937* *30in (76cm) high*

**£200-300** **ON**

'My Goodness My Guinness' advertising poster, designed by John Gilroy, printed by Waddington.

*When the public complained that if the ostrich has drunk the pint, then the glass would be the other way up, Gilroy explained that the ostrich was first balancing it on his beak.*

*1936* *40.25in (102cm) wide*

**£250-350** **ON**

'My Goodness My Guinness' advertising poster, designed by John Gilroy, printed by Sanders Phillips.

*1956* *40.25in (102cm) wide*

**£250-350** **ON**

'My Goodness Where's the Guinness' advertising poster, designed by Alfred Leete, printed by Sanders Phillips.

*1945* *59.75in (152cm) high*

**£220-280** **ON**

'Opening Time is Guinness Time' advertising poster, designed by John Gilroy, printed by Sanders Phillips.

*The presence of the famous toucan and bottle, and the excellent condition add to the value of this poster, even though it is relatively late in date.*

*1952* *40.25in (102cm) wide*

**£280-320** **ON**

'Lovely Day for a Guinness' advertising poster, designed by Tom Eckersley, printed by Mills & Rockleys.

*1956* *59.75in (152cm) high*

**£280-320** **ON**

'Guinness For Strength' advertising poster, designed by John Gilroy, printed by Waddington.

*1937* *30in (76cm) high*

**£150-200** **ON**

'Christmas Is Coming, Guinness For Strength' advertising poster, by an unknown designer, printed by Dangerfield.

*1934* *59.75in (152cm) high*

**£200-300** **ON**

'Guinness for Strength' advertising poster, designed by Edward Ardizzone, printed by John Waddington.

*Ardizzone (1900-79) was a writer and illustrator, especially of children's books, and also designed posters for Shell, among others.*

*1953* *59.75in (152cm) high*

**£280-320** **ON**

'Waterloo Bridge Is Coming Down – Guinness for Strength' two-sheet large advertising poster, designed by John Gilroy, printed by S.C. Allen & Co. Ltd, tears and folds.

*80.5in (204cm) wide*

**£120-180** **ON**

'My Goodness, My Guinness', watercolour design for the poster by John Gilroy, with pencil annotations by the artist, signed with initials and dated 1944.

*1944* *15.75in (40cm) wide*

**£650-750** **ON**

'After Work Guinness' advertising poster, designed by Tom Eckersley, printed by Mills & Rockley.

*1961* *59.75in (152cm) high*

**£300-400** **ON**

'Guinness After Work' photographic poster, by an unknown designer for S.H. Benson, printed by John Waddington Ltd.

*1961* *59.75in (152cm) high*

**£30-40** **ON**

'Guinness After Work' advertising poster, by an unknown design, printed by John Waddington.

*The reversal of the word 'Guinness' cleverly suggests a pub window, with the drinker sitting inside.*

*1961* *59.75in (152cm) high*

**£80-120** **ON**

## A CLOSER LOOK AT A GUINNESS POSTER

*It was designed by Abram Games, a highly respected poster designer who came to prominence designing posters for the Ministry of Information during WWII.*

*Through the large '5' and the simple wording, the message is conveyed simply and quickly, following Games' beliefs about poster advertising.*

*The style is eye-catching and its design is representative of the Modernist style that had taken hold of poster design during the 1930s.*

*The figure '5' is cleverly used upside down to represent the 'G' in Guinness, without losing any of its meaning.*

'5 Million Guinness daily', designed by Abram Games, printed by Mills & Rockleys.

*This new caption was devised to accompany a new advertising campaign including Guinness' first television commercials, in the early 1960s.*

*1960* *59.75in (152cm) wide*

**£120-180** **ON**

'5 Million Guinness Are Enjoyed Every Day' advertising poster, designed by an anonymous designer, printed by Mills & Rockleys.

*1960* *59.75in (152cm) high*

**£120-180** **ON**

'Clean Tasting Guinness' 1960s photographic poster, by an unknown designer for S.H. Benson, printed by Sanders Phillips & Co. Ltd.

*30in (76cm) high*

**£12-18** **ON**

'Opening Time is Guinness Time' poster, designed by Lander, printed by Mills & Rockleys.

*1956* *59.75in (152cm) high*

**£80-120** **ON**

'A Fistful of Guinness' and 'A Cold Guinness' advertising poster, by an unknown designer, printed by Clarkson New Press Ltd.

*This movie poster style poster was a departure for Guinness, and was a spoof of the 1964 Clint Eastwood film 'A Fistful of Dollars'.*

*1974* *59.75in (152cm) wide*

**£70-90** **ON**

'Give him a Guinness' advertising poster, by an unknown designer.

*30in (76cm) high*

**£15-20** **ON**

'Eat Australian Apples - British to the Core' fruit advertising poster, designed by F. Kenwood Giles, folds.

*30in (76cm) high*

**£120-180** **ON**

'Australian Fruit Is Here' food advertising poster, designed by A.H. Sands, folds.

*30in (76cm) high*

**£180-220** **ON**

'New Zealand Apples - The Finest The World Produces' fruit advertising poster, designed by Chas Shiers, folds.

*30in (76cm) high*

**£70-100** **ON**

'Vins de France', French advertising poster, printed by Bedos & Cie in Paris.

*1937* *63.75in (162cm) high*

**£600-800** **LOZ**

'Keep Baby Happy With Fennings' Children's Powders' baby food advertising poster, designed by Edward P. Lancaster.

*30in (76cm) high*

**£15-20** **ON**

'Thé de Chine Compagnie Coloniale', French tea advertising poster, designed by D'Ezy, printed by L. Martinet, Paris, mounted on linen.

*52.75in (134cm) high*

**£450-550** **ON**

'Rhum Négrita', French advertising poster, printed by A. Gué Fils in Poitiers, restored.

*35.25in (89.5cm) high*

**£350-550** **LOZ**

'Perrier New York Marathon 1983' advertising poster.

*Perrier was also a sponsor of the New York Marathon in 1979.*

*1983* *34.75in (88cm) high*

**£250-500** **LOZ**

'Player's Sun Valley', 1950s photographic American tobacco advertising poster.

*30in (76cm) high*

**£35-45** **ON**

'Royale' 1960s French cigarette advertising poster, by Gaillard, Paris.

*46.5in (118cm) wide*

**£200-400** **LOZ**

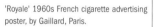

'Ribana – Benger's Badeanzüge', German bathing suit advertising poster, designed by Hans Neumann.

*49.25in (125cm) wide*

**£800-1,200** **LOZ**

'Kajak Bade-Dress' Austrian bathing suit, shoe and hat advertising poster, by the Otto Studio, Vienna.

*49.5in (126cm) wide*

**£400-500** **LOZ**

'John Church Shirtmaker', 1970s monochrome photographic poster.

*24.75in (63cm) high*

**£25-35** **ON**

'Bata Shoemakers to the World', 1970s advertising poster, for Lion Brand.

*30in (76cm) high*

**£25-35** **ON**

'Zig-Zag' La Super-Crème' French shoe polish advertising poster, by Dejke L. Luc, for the Société Industrielle de Produits d'Entretien et de Finissage, St Ouen.

*31.5in (80cm) high*

**£200-400** **LOZ**

'Slazengers' Lawn Tennis Balls - Wimblebon's Choice', British tennis ball advertising poster.

*The blank space on the bottom right corner could be printed with a retailer's address and details.*

*29.25in (74cm) high*

**£600-1,000** **LOZ**

## A CLOSER LOOK AT AN ADVERTISING POSTER

*This poster was designed by Raymond Savignac (1907-2002), perhaps the most famous post-war French poster designer, responsible for over 600 poster designs from the 1950s onwards.*

*The characters in his designs often have a form of 'resigned humour' and isolated comic nature to them, shown here in the cow's face.*

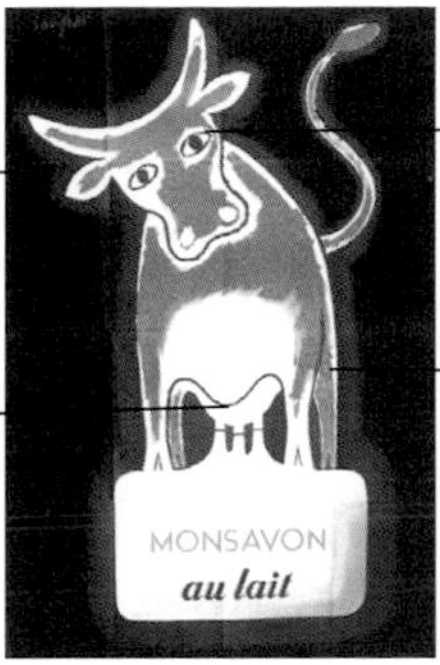


*It was this poster for Monsavon soap, designed in 1948, that launched his career - he cleverly uses the cow emptying its udder into the 'milk soap' to immediately suggest the product.*

*He worked with other legendary names like Cassandre and Bernard Villemot, and some of their influences can be seen in his minimal lines and blocks of colours.*

'Monsavon Au Lait' French soap advertising poster, designed by Raymond Savignac.

*1948* *58.25in (148cm) high*

**£2,000-3,000** **LOZ**

'Le Figaro', French newspaper advertising poster, designed by Raymond Savignac, printed by Bedos & Cie, Paris.

*61in (155cm) high*

**£800-1,200** **LOZ**

"You can now send Radiotelegrams to ships at sea' advertising poster, designed by Edward P. Lancaster HMSO GPO.

*1946* *30in (76cm) high*

**£45-55** **ON**

'Océanic, Radio - Télévision' French advertising poster, printed by Bedos & Cie of Paris.

*30.25in (77cm) wide*

**£100-200** **LOZ**

'Pneu Dunlop - Cycles le Globe', French bicycle tyre advertising poster, printed by Robaudy, Cannes.

*51.25in (130cm) high*

**£500-800** **LOZ**

## COLLECTORS' NOTES

- Posters produced in China during the last half of the 20th century give a fascinating social, political and economic insight into China after the take-over of Communism after the war, and with the 'Great Leap Forward' from 1958-60. The market for these items in the West is very new, and is still developing meaning that values may change as more is discovered and increasing attention is paid to the area by collectors.
- Earlier posters tended to be more traditional in design and imagery, focusing on ancient Chinese stories or characters, or beautiful landscapes. This aesthetic was swept away during the 1950s, and replaced by Communist propaganda, executed in a new 'modern' style using 'contemporary' imagery. Many were based on similar Russian propaganda posters, hence the Western appearance of some people.
- Mao Tse-Tung (1893-1976), Chairman of the Communist party of China from 1945-76 appears on a great many posters, progressing from a political leader to an almost god-like figure as time went on. He can also appear as a benevolent leader in touch with his people, and uniting them, and also as a military leader. He is also often shown as intrinsic to Communism, depicted with Stalin, Lenin and Marx.
- The military might of China was also a popular topic, with many citizens employed in the army or navy. The constant threat from the Capitalist West is apparent in many designs. One over-riding aim was to inspire the people to unite, build themselves up and work not only for their own personal good, but for the good of the Republic.
- Many thousands of most of these posters were printed, with many exact quantities not being known. Sizes of print-runs also varied enormously. The quality of paper used was poor, particularly early on, as they were not meant to last. The value depends largely on the message being conveyed, the imagery and the condition, among other factors such as date. Iconic or visually powerful imagery is likely to be more desirable, as are key messages. Beware of reproductions, which can often be identified from the printing methods used and the type of paper.

'Portrait Of Chairman Mao' Chinese propaganda poster, published by The Beijing Worker's Publishing House, Beijing, tears and repairs.

*This is believed to be the earliest official portrait of Chairman Mao after the foundation of the People's Republic of China on October 1st, 1949.*

*1949 30.75in (78cm) high*

**£1,000-1,500** **BLO**

'The East Is Red' Chinese propaganda poster, published by the People's Art Publishing House, Beijing, some tears.

*This image is based on a famous oil painting of Mao.*

*1954* *30in (76cm) high*

**£400-500** **BLO**

无限忠于毛主席

'Be Boundlessly Loyal to Chairman Mao' Chinese propaganda poster, published by Si Chuan Province People's Publishing House, loss to top left corner, tears.

*1968* *30in (76cm) high*

**£20-30** **BLO**

'United, We Stand' central panel of a 1970s three-sheet Chinese propaganda poster, rubber-stamped with a portrait of Mao Tse-Tung reading 'Highest Instruction. Never Forget Class Struggle' in the lower left margin.

*29.5in (75cm) wide*

**£800-1,200** **BLO**

中国人民解放军是毛主席亲自缔造、领导和指挥的人民军队

'The People's Liberation Army of China is a People's Army, Founded, Led and Directed by Chairman Mao' Chinese propaganda poster, published by The People's Art Publishing House, Beijing, damage and repairs.

*1977* *60.75in (154cm) wide*

**£450-550** **BLO**

伟大的马克思主义 列宁主义 毛泽东思想万岁

'Long Live the Great Marxism, Leninism and Mao Tse Tung's Thoughts' Chinese propaganda poster, with portraits of Stalin, Lenin, Engels and Marx on the flag, published by The Shan Xi People's Publishing House.

*1971* *42.25in (107cm) wide*

**£650-750** **BLO**

毛主席革命路线胜利万岁

'Long Live Chairman Mao's Revolutionary Direction' Chinese propaganda poster, published by People's Art Publishing House, Shanghai, damage and repairs.

*1967* *29.5in (75cm) wide*

**£100-150** **BLO**

'Chairman Mao is the Red Sun in the Hearts of the People All Over the World' Chinese propaganda poster, published by People's Art Publishing House, damaged.

*Here, as in many images, Mao appears like a spectral, benevolent and sun-like presence, guiding his people who rally beneath him.*

*1967* *29.5in (75cm) high*

**£120-180** **BLO**

毛主席是世界人民心中的红太阳

'Long Live Chairman Mao's Line on Literature and Art' 1960s Chinese propaganda poster, unknown artist, a model worker holds a white book of Mao's writings aloft, a horizontal repair across the centre of the image, minor loss to the bottom right corner, several marginal tears, pin-holes in the corners.

*30.5in (77.5cm) high*

**£200-300** **BLO**

敬祝毛主席万寿无疆

'Wish Chairman Mao Boundless Longevity' Chinese propaganda poster, tear and repair to top edge, pin-holes in the corners.

*1976* *29.5in (75cm) wide*

**£220-280** **BLO**

毛泽东思想的光辉永远照耀着我们前进的道路

'The Glory of Chairman Mao's Thoughts Light Our Road to Advance Forever' Chinese propaganda poster, published by People's Publishing House, some damage.

*1976* *29.5in (75cm) wide*

**£150-200** **BLO**

大力支援农业

'Give Energetic Support to Agriculture' 1970s Chinese propaganda poster, published by the Revolutionary Committee Of Culture Department, Shen Yang City.

*This poster is desirable as it combines a number of popular themes, including the arrival of the tractor to rural China, factories, paddy fields and the enormity of China, a farmer and Mao's Little Red Book. It is also a comparatively appealing, upbeat image.*

*30in (76cm) high*

**£1,200-1,800** **BLO**

'Enhance Vigilance, Protect the Motherland, Be Prepared to Destroy the Invading Enemies at Anytime' Chinese propaganda poster, published by People's Publishing House, Hu Bei Province, some wear and damage.

*1969* *29.5in (75cm) wide*

**£400-500** **BLO**

'Enhance the Joint Defence by Army and Militia, be Prepared to Destroy the Invading Enemies at Anytime' Chinese propaganda poster, published by the War Preparedness Office, Tianjin.

*1971* *29.5in (75cm) wide*

**£60-80** **BLO**

'The People of the Three Indo-China Countries Must Win, American Imperialism Must Lose' Chinese propaganda poster, published by People's Publishing House, Beijing, some wear and damage.

*The Chinese soldiers are trampling on the wreckage of an American plane, with the People marching behind them.*

*1971* *30in (76cm) high*

**£40-60** **BLO**

'Enhance Vigilance and Protect the Motherland' Chinese propaganda poster, published by People's Art Publishing House, Shanghai, some damage.

*1970* *29.5in (75cm) high*

**£50-80** **BLO**

'Honour Belongs to our Chinese Communist Party' Chinese propaganda poster, published by People's Art Publishing House, Shanghai.

*1964* *29.5in (75cm) high*

**£220-280** **BLO**

'Be Strictly on Guard' Chinese propaganda poster, published by Lv Da City Revolutionary Committee, Chairman Mao's Works Publication Office, Liao Ning Province.

*1971* *30in (76cm) high*

**£20-30** **BLO**

'Train Hard to Enhance Physiques of Officers and Soldiers' Chinese propaganda poster, published by The Pictorial Of The People's Liberation Army Of China, Beijing.

*This not only demonstrates China's military technical achievements, but also indicates the dedication of an army trained since a young age.*

*1960* *30in (76cm) high*

**£280-320** **BLO**

'Long Live the Friendship of the People and Army Between China and the Soviet Union' Chinese propaganda poster, depicting a Russian and a Chinese sailor, published by The People's Liberation Army Pictorial, Beijing.

*c1950* *30.75in (78cm) wide*

**£250-350** **BLO**

## A CLOSER LOOK AT A CHINESE POSTER

*This rare and desirable poster shows protests about the Vietnam war, and depicts Americans protesting outside the Senate House in the background.*

*It is very rare to find Chinese posters, made for display only in China, using English wording.*

*The use of English wording shows that the design was based on TV images and photographs of the time.*

*As well as an African-American and other Americans, the crowd includes a man who looks strangely like Stalin and a Russian worker.*

'Firmly Support the American People's Opposition to the US Imperialist Invasion of Vietnam' Chinese propaganda poster, published by The Shanghai People's Art Publishing House, Shanghai.

*The Vietnam War theme adds desirability.*

*1966* *41.25in (105cm) high*

**£2,500-3,500** **BLO**

'Enhance Combat Preparedness, Practice Military Skills to Kill the Enemy' Chinese propaganda poster, published by People's Art Publishing House, Beijing.

*This image of a young girl throwing a grenades with a rifle on her back is somewhat shocking, even today.*

*1976* *30.25in (77cm) high*

**£22-28** **BLO**

'Great Stalin Is The Saviour Of World Peace', 1950s Chinese propaganda poster, with some staining and creases.

*25.5in (65cm) high*

**£200-300** **BLO**

'Soviet Union - Friend of the Working People of the World' Chinese propaganda poster, published by The Chao Hua Art Publishing House, Beijing.

*Published in October 1957, this poster commemorates the 40th anniversary of the Russian Revolution.*

*1957* *29.5in (75cm) high*

**£350-450** **BLO**

'Revolutionary Friendship' Chinese propaganda poster, published by Shanghai People's Art Publishing House, printed by Three One Printing Factory, Shanghai.

*Showing the international reach of Communism and China's important part in it, Communist world leaders including Fidel Castro and Egypt's near-Communist leader Gamil Nasser, are shown visiting China.*

*1964* *30in (76cm) high*

**£60-80** **BLO**

'The American Imperialist Vainly Hopes to Follow the Invasion Route of Japan' Chinese propaganda poster, designed by Jue Min, some loss and repairs.

*Here a skeletal 'Japan' and a portly Truman-like 'US' compare notes on how to invade Communist China and spread Capitalism.*

*c1951* *21in (53.5cm) high*

**£120-180** **BLO**

'Thousands of Miles of Camping Melts Red Hearts' Chinese propaganda poster, published by People's Publishing House, Shanghai.

*These marching young people include 'Barefoot Doctors', farmers who were given basic medical training so they could provide care in remote villages where doctors would not settle. After a speech by Mao in 1965, the system became a formalised part of the Cultural Revolution, and ended in 1981. Their names comes from the fact that many were paddy field farmers, so hence worked barefoot.*

*1971* *29.5in (75cm) wide*

**£350-450** **BLO**

'Welcome The 1970s With New Success of Revolution and Production' Chinese propaganda poster, published by People's Art Publishing House, Shanghai.

*1970* *30in (76cm) wide*

**£350-450** **BLO**

'The Whole Nation Gets Mobilised and Works Energetically – Realise the General Task of the New Period' Chinese propaganda poster, published by Tianjin People's Art Publishing House.

*1978* *30in (76cm) high*

**£40-60** **BLO**

'Promote Physical Culture and Build Up the People's Health' Chinese propaganda poster, published by People's Publishing House, He Bei Province.

*1972* *30in (76cm) high*

**£250-350** **BLO**

'Be Good Sons and Daughters Of The Party' Chinese poster, published by People's Art Publishing House, Shanghai, some damage, tears and staining.

*1960* *30in (76cm) wide*

**£60-80** **BLO**

'Young People Are Like The Rising Sun For Our Country, All Our Hopes Are Placed On Them', published by Beijing People's Art Publishing House, printed by Beijing Five Three Five Printing Factory, some tears.

*1958* *30in (76cm) wide*

**£350-450** **BLO**

'Going All Out, Aiming Quickly, Getting Complete Success' Chinese poster, first printed by Shanghai First Printing Factory.

*1959* *30in (76cm) wide*

**£280-320** **BLO**

A 1960s Dong Feng 'People Who Help Themselves' promotional poster.

*Dong Feng is a car manufacturing company, and now also an importer, founded in 1969. The poster shows how working for them helps not only country, but the workers themselves.*

*30in (76cm) high*

**£100-150** **BLO**

'Follow The Party's Instruction, Be A New Generation Of Educated, Build the New Countryside Of Socialism' Chinese propaganda poster, published by People's Art Publishing House, He Bei.

*1960* *30in (76cm) high*

**£350-450** **BLO**

'Busy With Great Harvest' Chinese propaganda poster, published by People's Publishing House, Beijing, some damage.

*This traditional looking poster was produced a decade after the 1958-61 famine, when an estimated 20-30 million people died.*

*1972* *30in (76cm) high*

**£80-120** **BLO**

'Long Live the People's Republic of China' Chinese two-sheet propaganda poster, published by The People's Art Publishing House, Beijing.

*This huge poster, dominated by the seal of the People's Republic of China, shows a vision of the Republic of the future. The promised technologies include a (very American looking) space shuttle, rockets, helicopters, jet planes, monorails, huge cruise liners, tractors, industry, clear roads and communications, all based in a highly futuristic cityscape.*

*1979* *41.5in (105.5cm) wide*

**£2,000-3,000** **BLO**

'Try to Overtake Each Other in Friendly Emulation' Chinese propaganda poster, Zhe Jiang Province People's Art Publishing House, creases and tears.

*1964* *30in (76cm) high*

**£70-100** **BLO**

**FIND OUT MORE...**

**The International Institute of Social History**, *http://www.iisg.nl/~landsberger/*

'Travel Through Space on a Spaceship' Chinese propaganda poster, first printed by He Bei People's Art Publishing House in 1962, then by State-Owned Shanghai Tobacco Industry Printing Factory.

*This rather fantastical poster promotes China's entry into the Space Race, two years after Comrade Gagarin became the first man to go into space. The rocket, which looks like a 1950s tinplate toy, is probably the least bizarre element in this mix of different themes.*

*1963* *30in (76cm) high*

**£350-450** **BLO**

'A Brace of Partridges by Robert Ganthony' theatre poster, designed by John Hassall, printed by David Allen, losses to margin.

*1898* *30in (76cm) high*

**£35-45** **ON**

'Mr. Louis Mann & Miss Clara Lipman' American theatrical poster, marked "managed by Rich & Harris".

*Mann and Lipman were a husband and wife team who starred in many theatrical productions, many on Broadway, from the early 1900s to the 1920s.*

*c1910* *80.75in (205cm) high*

**£650-750** **CL**

'Love & A [Country] Cottage by Keble Howard' theatre poster, designed by John Hassall, printed by Thos. Storer.

*John Hassell (1868-1948) studied art in Antwerp, Belgium, and at the Academie Julien, Paris in 1894. This would have meant he was exposed to French Art Nouveau poster design, explaining the clear influence that can be seen in his designs. Japanese prints were also being considered by artists, and again their influence can be seen on his style. He was also a children's book illustrator and designed posters for other companies including the G.N.E.R.*

*30in (76cm) high*

**£350-450** **ON**

'A Country Girl' theatre poster, designed by an unknown designer.

*c1910* *25in (63cm) high*

**£70-90** **CL**

'Miss Dorothy Arnold' theatre poster, by an unknown designer.

*Arnold (1917-82) began her career in the theatre aged 12, and then moved into film, starring in 15 films between 1937-39. She is perhaps most famous for her 'on-off' marriage to Joe DiMaggio, which finally ended in 1954 when the baseball star married Marilyn Monroe.*

*c1938* *30in (76cm) high*

**£80-120** **CL**

'Captains Courageous' American theatrical poster, designed by Blanche McManus for The Century Co.

*17in (43cm) high*

**£400-500** **CL**

'Red Riding Hood' theatrical poster, by an unknown designer, printed by Taylors Printers Wombwell.

*Although this poster is in excellent condition, the rather risqué choice of artwork for a children's story may have been the real reason for the high price.*

*39.75in (101cm) wide*

**£200-300** **ON**

'Mame' Broadway musical poster, without text, designed by Berta.

*c1966* *39.5in (100cm) high*

**£60-80** **CL**

'Hair' French musical poster, for the Théâtre de la Porte St Martin, designed by Michael Butler.

*23.5in (60cm) high*

**£200-300** **LOZ**

'Indiana in Lewiston' exhibition poster, designed by Robert Indiana, printed by Brand X Editions.

*The design is based on Indiana's The Hartley Elegies: The Berlin Series'.*

*1991* *46.5in (116cm) high*

**£500-600** **SWA**

'British Industries Fair 1947' exhibition poster, designed by Abram Games, printed for HMSO by Board of Trade.

*The use of a Modernist style motif or graphic against a graduated coloured background is typical of Abram Games's style. His work has been gradually increasing in value over the past few years as interest grows. If you like them and haven't got one yet, time is running out.*

*1947* *19.75in (50cm) high*

**£280-320** **ON**

'Model Railway Exhibition Central Hall Westminster' exhibition poster, by an anonymous designer.

*1939* *30in (76cm) high*

**£40-60** **ON**

'International Exhibition Paris 1937', exhibition poster, designed by Jean Carlu, printed by Bedos & Cie.

*Jean Carlu (1900-97) is one of the most famous poster designers of the 20thC, particularly notable for his Art Deco posters and brightly coloured 1960s designs. He acted as chairman of the Graphic Publicity Section for this exhibition.*

*47.25in (120cm) high*

**£180-220** **ON**

'Salon du Cycle et de l'Automobile 1897', French car and bicycle exhibition advertising poster, designed by Pal (Jean de Palcologne), printed by Caby & Chardin, mounted on linen.

*1897* *51.25in (130cm) high*

**£800-1,200** **ON**

A Fish Design moulded silicone rubber wine cooler, designed by Gaetano Pesce in 1996, with Fish Design label.

*12in (30.5cm) high*

**£300-400** **GM**

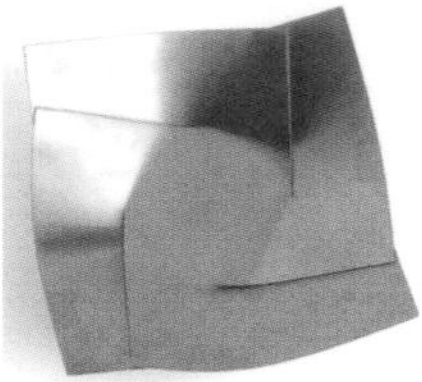

An Italian Danese 'Maldive 2019' steel dish, designed by Bruno Munari, with shiny exterior and brushed interior.

*7.25in (18.5cm) wide*

**£150-250** **GM**

An Italian Museo Alchimia 'Vassoio Oriented' black lacquered metal tray, designed by Alessandro Mendini in 1988.

*An early and influential champion of the Postmodern design movement, Mendini was a leading light of the Alchimia group founded in Italy in 1976.*

*19.5in (49cm) wide*

**£300-400** **GM**

A rubber picture frame, designed by Gaetano Pesce in 1996, metal stand to back.

*Pesce always tried to incorporate a face in these objects – note the shape of the yellow and red designs, particularly on the left.*

*9.75in (24.5cm) high*

**£150-200** **GM**

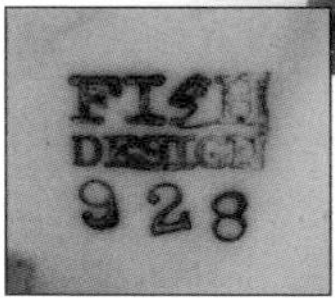


A 1990s American Fish Design rubber '928' vase, designed by Gaetano Pesce.

*Each piece is uniquely formed and coloured due to the way it is produced, using randomly shaped sections of different rubber, selected at random. Fish Design, a pun on the designer's name, was Pesce's 'diffusion' range and was less expensive than his limited 'personal' production. Many designs have been re-introduced recently.*

*10.75in (27.5cm) high*

**£200-300** **GM**

## A CLOSER LOOK AT A PEPPER GRINDER

*The handle is like a wing-nut, but is also like Mickey Mouse's ears. Pop culture was an important influence on many Postmodern designers.*

*The clean lines and use of chrome plated metal hark back to Modernism and the Art Deco era – historical influences can often be seen in many Postmodern designs.*

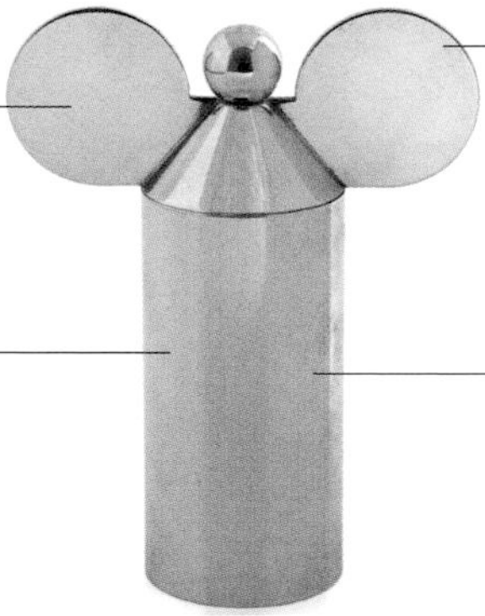

*Swid Powell was founded in 1983 and produced many high quality Postmodern designs by many eminent designers, most notably functional ceramic tableware.*

*Swiss husband and wife team Robert and Trix Haussmann are noted architects, who have also designed furniture for Knoll Associates.*

An American Swid Powell pepper grinder, designed by Robert and Trix Haussmann in 1986.

*5.25in (13.5cm) high*

**£150-250** **GM**

## COLLECTORS' NOTES

- First appearing in the early 19thC, pot lids are one of the earliest types of visually appealing packaging. Products include bear's grease (a hair product), toothpaste, and meat or fish paste. Blue or black and white printed pot lids were introduced in the 1820s, with coloured examples appearing in the mid-1840s. Makers include F.R. Pratt, T.J. & J. Mayer and Brown-Westhead & Moore.
- Over 350 images are known, many taken from watercolours by Jesse Austin. As so many were produced over large periods of time and records have not survived, it is not possible to date pot lids exactly. Events depicted, registration marks and some makers' marks can help to date certain pot lids to a smaller period, as can the form.
- Earlier lids, from before 1860, are usually flat and light in weight, with fine quality prints, and often have a screw thread. Lids from 1860 to 1875 are heavier and have a convex top. Later lids are even heavier in weight. Handle as many as possible to gain experience of weights and appearances.
- Look for lids with good, strong colours as faded, weak examples are worth considerably less. Chips to the flange and rim do not affect value seriously. Chips to the image, or restoration, can lower values by up to 50-75 per cent, even if well restored. Variations in colour, design or borders can affect value and complex or coloured borders usually add value. Non-circular lids usually date from after the late 1870s.
- Some collectors choose to collect by type: two of the most popular being for bear's grease, or those that show scenes of Pegwell Bay. Beware of reproductions – run your finger over a lid and if you can feel the transfer, it is likely to be a later reproduction. Numbers given here relate to lid reference numbers in Mortimer's pot lid reference book.

A Staffordshire 'Pegwell Bay, Lobster Fishing' pot lid, no.31.

*4.25in (10.5cm) diam*

**£100-150** **SAS**

A Staffordshire 'Pegwell Bay Shrimpers' pot lid, no.39, restored.

*A version can be found with boats in the top right, which is generally more valuable.*

*5.25in (13cm) diam*

**£40-60** **SAS**

A Pratt 'Herring Fishing: Landing the Catch' pot lid, no.62.

*4.25in (10.5cm) diam*

**£45-55** **SAS**

A Pratt 'Foreign River Scene' pot lid, no.82, with a hairline crack.

*4.75in (12cm) diam*

**£45-55** **SAS**

A Staffordshire 'Vue de la Ville de Strasbourg, Prise du Port' pot lid, no.84.

*4.75in (12cm) diam*

**£22-28** **SAS**

A Pratt 'Dangerous Skating' pot lid, no.296.

*This example has five steps on the right, the version with six is worth around the same.*

*2.75in (7cm) diam*

**£150-200** **SAS**

A Mayer 'Pheasant Shooting' pot lid, no.288, with mottled border and flange.

*The version without the border is worth around half as much. This lid was also from the notable Ball Collection.*

*5.25in (13cm) diam*

**£180-220** **SAS**

A Pratt 'The Sportsman' pot lid, no.305, with title.

*4.25in (10.5cm) diam*

**£22-28** **SAS**

A Pratt 'The Game Bag' pot lid, no.306.

*This is one of a pair, with 'The Sportsman', shown above.*

*4.5in (11cm) diam*

**£45-55** **SAS**

A Staffordshire 'Master of the Hounds' pot lid, no.295, gold banded border complete with purple base.

**£70-100** **SAS**

A Pratt 'The Swing' pot lid, no.327, with pointed leaf border.

*The version with a seaweed edge and flange can be worth twice as much.*

*4.5in (11cm) diam*

**£70-100** **SAS**

A Pratt 'The Fisher-boy' pot lid, no.291.

*3in (7.5cm) diam*

**£80-120** **SAS**

A Bates, Elliot & Co. 'Injury' pot lid, no.58, the reverse with impressed registration mark.

*The impressed diamond registration mark allows this piece to be dated. The design was registered on 11th June 1873 and these types of marks were discontinued in early 1883.*

*1873-83* *4.25in (10.5cm) diam*

**£100-150** **SAS**

A Bates, Elliot & Co 'Revenge' pot lid, no.59, later version, with white border.

*This is paired with 'Injury' to the left and completes the short story.*

*4.5in (11cm) diam*

**£150-200** **SAS**

A Mayer 'The Bride' pot lid, no.97, with fancy border.

*The blue band and inside and outside white border make this example so valuable. It was also part of the Cashmore Collection of pot lids.*

*4in (10cm) diam*

**£300-400** **SAS**

A Mayer 'The Bride' pot lid, no.97.

*This is the more standard border format and colouring.*

*3.25in (8cm) diam*

**£80-120** **SAS**

A Pratt 'The Toilette' pot lid, no.102.

*Examples with a wide gold band and no title can fetch over £1,000. Also look out for examples spelt 'Tiolette' as these can be worth up to twice this value.*

*3.25in (8cm) diam*

**£120-180** **SAS**

A Pratt 'Lady Fastening Shoe' pot lid, no.110.

*2.75in (7cm) diam*

**£70-100** **SAS**

A Pratt 'The Mirror' pot lid, no.101.

*2.75in (7cm) diam*

**£70-100** **SAS**

A Staffordshire 'The Wooer' pot lid, no.112, possibly by J. Ridgway.

*The presence of advertising wording can increase the value up to tenfold.*

*2.75in (7cm) diam*

**£70-100** **SAS**

## A CLOSER LOOK AT A POT LID

*The design was taken from a painting of a bullfight by G. Herbert, showing a Spanish lady on a balcony watching the action - hence the name.*

*This example is restored, which reduces its value, but is from the Ball collection, which adds to its desirability.*

*Collectors and experts have attributed the lid to Pratt due to the the shape with a raised border, which also appears on another Pratt lid.*

*All examples of this lid are hard to find, with the gold-banded border being the rarest version.*

A Staffordshire 'The Spanish Lady' pot lid, no.79, mottled and gilded flange, complete with matching base.

*4in (10cm) diam*

**£350-450** **SAS**

A Staffordshire 'Lady with Guitar' pot lid, no107, with no border.

*2.5in (6.5cm) diam*

**£45-55** **SAS**

A Pratt 'Girl with Grapes' flat pot lid, no.132.

*3.5in (9cm) diam*

**£120-180** **SAS**

## A CLOSER LOOK AT A PRATT POT LID

*This design was taken from a painting by famous portrait painter Sir Joshua Reynolds, painted in 1773 and now in the Wallace Collection, London.*

*It is a rare lid, and has only been found in this design, with no variations known.*

*The design was originally produced for use on tablewares, such as plates.*

*This example was from the McKenzie Collection.*

A Pratt 'The Strawberry Girl' pot lid, no.312.

*4.75in (12cm) diam*

**£550-650** **SAS**

A Pratt 'The Begging Dog' pot lid, no.262.

*This design was adapted by Jesse Austin from a painting by Sir Edward Landseer. Variations in the colour of the boy's coat do not affect value.*

*3in (7.5cm) diam*

**£40-60** **SAS**

A Pratt 'On Guard' pot lid, no.334, with dog under seat.

*Introduced in 1860, this design was produced for a long period of time – earlier examples have a bucket under the seat instead.*

*4.25in (10.5cm) diam*

**£20-30** **SAS**

A Mayer 'A False Move' pot lid, no.308.

*Not only does this appeal to chess collectors, but also to historians as it refers to the work of Cardinal Wiseman (1802-65) in redeveloping Roman Catholicism in England. The version without a border is usually worth the most.*

*5in (13cm) diam*

**£150-200** **BLO**

A Pratt 'Blind Man's Buff' pot lid, no.292, with registration mark disguised in the chandelier, and minor hairline crack.

*1856-83 3.25in (8cm) diam*

**£45-55** **SAS**

A Pratt 'Philadelphia Exhibition 1876' pot lid, no.155, on a trefoil lid.

*Look out for the scarcer version without the coach and horses on the bottom right. Pratt produced a number of commemorative ceramics for this exhibition.*

*c1876*

**£150-200** **SAS**

A Staffordshire 'St. Paul's Cathedral' pot lid, no.238, attributed to Bates, Brown-Westhead, Moore & Co.

*4in (10cm) diam*

**£200-300** **SAS**

A Pratt 'Embarking for the East' (206) pot lid, no. 210, with chain-link pattern border.

*The version with this border is the most valuable. It depicts the Highland Regiment departing for the Crimea.*

*4.75in (12cm) diam*

**£250-300** **SAS**

A Mayer 'Funeral of the Late Duke of Wellington' pot lid, no. 189, with a four section ornate border.

*This is based on the Baxter print of the funeral. The border and early date make this valuable – it has been reproduced as recently as the 1960s.*

*5.5in (13.5cm) diam*

**£500-600** **SAS**

## A CLOSER LOOK AT A BEAR POT LID

*Bears are popular and highly collectable pot lids subjects, and were used on pots of bear's grease, a hair wax.*

*The bears are brown here, which is rare – they are more commonly found in black.*

*The gold band and flange is also a rare feature.*

*At 3.25in (8cm) in diameter, it is also the smallest size, which is again very rare.*

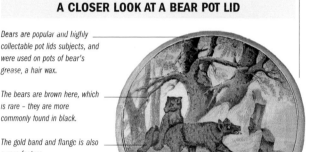

A Mayer 'Bears on Rock' pot lid, no. 10, with gold-banded border and flange, with matching base.

*3.25in (8cm) diam*

**£750-850** **SAS**

A Staffordshire 'Royal Coat of Arms' pot lid, no.173, with blank panel below.

*The version with the name 'J.N. Osborne' in the panel is more valuable.*

*4in (10cm) diam*

**£280-320** **SAS**

A Pratt 'The Bear Pit' pot lid, no.6, with no dome on the upper left.

*3in (7.5cm) diam*

**£70-90** **SAS**

### FIND OUT MORE...

**Pot lids and Other Coloured Printed Staffordshire Wares**, *by K.V. Mortimer, published by Antique Collectors' Club, 2003.*

## COLLECTORS' NOTES

- Powder compacts can be closely linked to the changing role, and appearance, of women in society. When they first appeared in the early 1920s, it was becoming more acceptable for women to apply make-up in public. As the decade went on, the rise of the 'Flapper' girl, and glamorous, exciting nights out in the city saw them become an essential accessory.
- After the war, the rise of the working woman meant that more disposable income was available for make-up and beauty products. Much of this needed to be, and was, portable. This growth was also promoted by Hollywood stars. However, by the 1960s, powder compacts had fallen from use due to the introduction of compressed powder and disposable cases.
- Most compacts came from the US, where names such as Elgin, Evans and Rex or Dorset are often highly sought-after. Desirable British makers include Stratton and Kigu.
- Powder compacts can be found in a variety of materials, primarily gold- or silver-coloured metal. As they were made to be seen, the designs can be elegant and eye-catching. Many represent the fashions of the day, with the Art Deco style of the late 1920s and '30s being one of the most desirable.
- The quality of the decoration and materials is an important indicator to value. Finely made enamelled cases, or the use of precious gems or metal, will usually indicate a valuable case. Combination cases that include other features, and novelty forms, are also usually sought after.
- As they were practical items, they were used, meaning many are in worn condition. Always try and buy in the best condition you can. Check that the mirror is intact, and look for the original puff or any packaging, as these are desirable features.

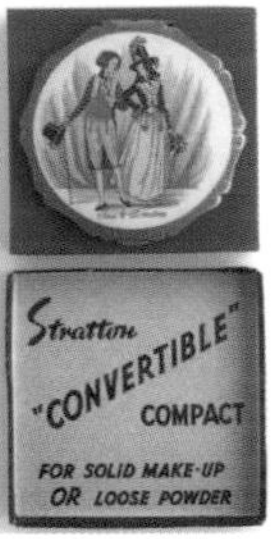


A 1950s Stratton courting couple 'Tous Le Directoire' Queen-shaped 'Convertible' powder compact, boxed.

*Box 4.25in (11cm) wide*

**£25-35** **SH**

A Stratton Queen-shaped 'Convertible' compact, depicting a courting couple.

*c1960* *3.5in (9cm) diam*

**£30-40** **MGT**

An early 1950s Vogue Vanities 'Transplanting Rice' compact.

*This scene is also found on ceramic pot lids, produced by leading factory Pratt. It was taken from a watercolour painted by Jesse Austin and inspired by Captain Stoddart's 'China Illustrated'.*

*3.75in (9.5cm) diam*

**£40-60** **MGT**

A 1930s Japanese cloisonne enamel compact, with chrysanthemum design and internal metal powder sifter.

*4in (10cm) diam*

**£80-100** **MGT**

A Stratton 'Petite' compact, with rose design by Suzy Seriau.

*French sounding names such as 'Seriau' were used to add a touch of Parisian glamour to an item.*

*c1960*

**£25-35** **MGT**

A 1950s Vogue Vanities fantasy bird powder compact, with original swan's down puff.

*3in (7.5cm) diam*

**£30-40** **SH**

A late 1930s Coty gilt base compact, from the Muguet range.

*Muguet des Bois is French for 'Lily of the Valley', the white flowers shown on the front of this compact. Coty also released a perfume under the same name.*

*2.5in (6.5cm) diam*

**£20-30** **MGT**

A Tosca 4711 small gilt base compact, with original 4711 satin pad, marked "Made in England".

*c1930* *2in (5cm) diam*

**£20-30** **MGT**

## A CLOSER LOOK AT A POWDER COMPACT

*Metal mesh detailing was popular during the 1920s and '30s, particularly for glittering evening handbags.*

*The butterfly and flower motif is an integral moulded part of the lid.*

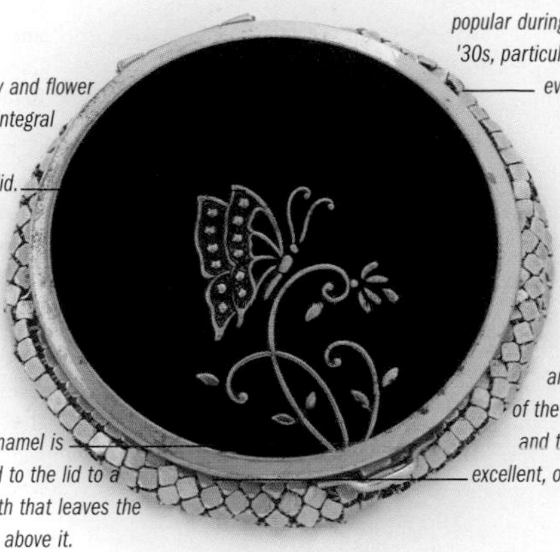

*Silver and black are typical colours of the Art Deco period, and the compact is in excellent, original condition.*

*The black enamel is then applied to the lid to a shallow depth that leaves the motif raised above it.*

A 1930s American Evans mesh-bottom black enamel and butterfly powder compact.

*2.5in (6.5cm) diam*

**£40-50** **SH**

A Estee Lauder Bermuda Blossom powder compact, with coloured rhinestone encrusted exterior, boxed.

*2004* *2in (5cm) diam*

**£80-100** **MGT**

A small Evans 'TalcSift', with scrolling guilloche white enamel and small roses to centre.

*2.25in (5.5cm) diam*

**£30-40** **NOR**

A small French compact, with guilloche enamelled rose to centre.

*2.25in (5.5cm) diam*

**£40-50** **NOR**

A Stratton red enamelled and flower compact.

*The flowers are cut through the enamel, into the gilt metal case.*

*3in (7.5cm) diam*

**£35-45** **NOR**

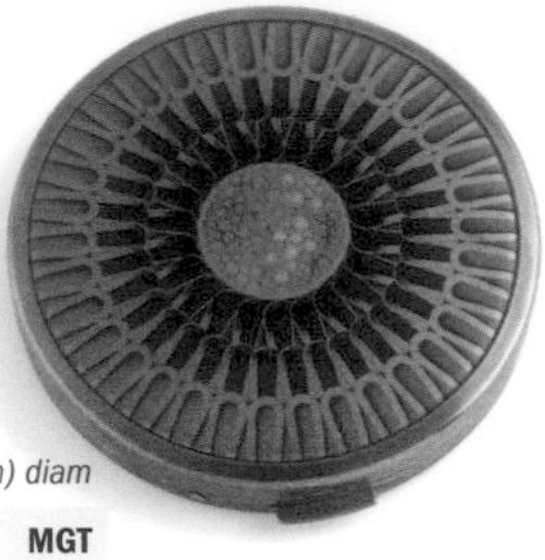

A 1930s Coty Art Deco 'Magnet Red' sunflower design powder compact, from their L'Aimant range, marked "New York".

*2.5in (6.5cm) diam*

**£25-35** **MGT**

A blue marble effect enamelled musical compact, with stepped form.

*This compact is worth more as not only is it musical, but the enamelling and stepped design are very appealing features. Many musical movements for such small items were made in Switzerland, often by Reuge or Thorens.*

*3in (7.5cm) diam*

**£80-120** **MGT**

A 1950s Evans white enamelled and gold-plated compact, with an embossed escutcheon motif to the centre.

*4in (10cm) diam*

**£25-35** **NOR**

A 1930s blue and brown cast phenolic compact, with mirror to back and woven leather toggle.

*The 1920s and '30s were the 'golden age' of plastics, and this piece will appeal as much to collectors of early plastics as to compact collectors.*

*3.25in (8.5cm) diam*

**£25-35** **NOR**

An un-named American silver circular compact, with beaded edges and central circular motif, stamped "Sterling".

*3.25in (8cm) diam*

**£60-90** **NOR**

An American Rex compact, with engraved central stylized foliate design, and circles of wavy lines.

*Rex Fifth Avenue is a popular brand, also known for its handbags.*

*4.25in (10.5cm) diam*

**£15-25** **NOR**

An American Rex of Fifth Avenue hand-engraved silver compact, with internal mirror and powder puff, stamped "Sterling".

*4in (10cm) wide*

**£50-80** **NOR**

A Novida compact, embossed with a design of an 18thC French lady picking flowers.

*2.25in (5.5cm) diam*

**£25-35** **NOR**

A 1920s unmarked silver dressing table powder box, with high relief applied four-leaf clover design, possibly from a dressing table set.

*2.25in (5.5cm) diam*

**£40-50** **NOR**

A Yardley of London bee design powder compact, sealed with original paper insert.

*c1951*

**£20-30** **MGT**

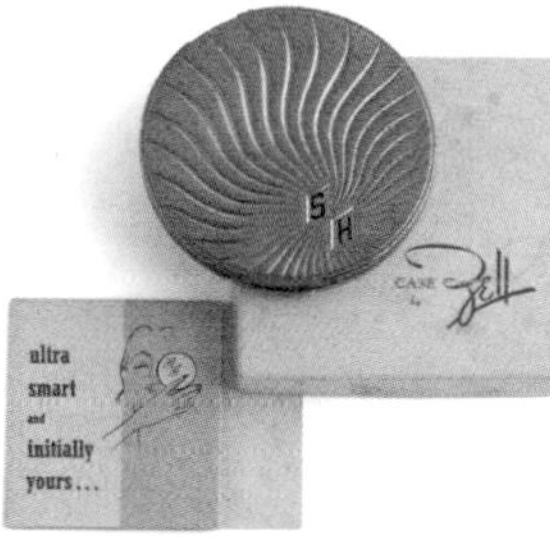


An American Zell 'Initially Yours' gold-tone powder compact, with interchangeable letters, boxed with original puffs and instructions.

*The letters could be changed to show the owner's initials. This compact is hard to find in complete, mint condition.*

*c1955* *3.75in (9.5cm) diam*

**£50-70** **SH**

## A CLOSER LOOK AT A POWDER COMPACT

*Evans used the brand name Le Rage during the 1950s for a small range of compacts.*

*They also produced a similar compact, with no indicator but charming scenes of well-known London landmarks.*

*The 'fun' aspect of the compact makes it all the more appealing - a '50s lady about town could remind herself of her activities by moving the arm and clock.*

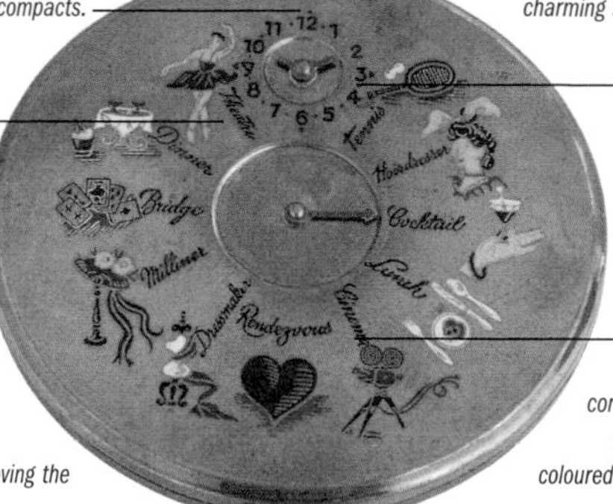


*It is large and in excellent condition, with no damage to the coloured enamel paint.*

A 1950s English Le Rage gold-plated and enamelled compact, with different times of the day, moving clock and activities.

*4.25in (10.5cm) diam*

**£60-90** **NOR**

A 1950s Kigu musical gold tone powder compact, with a leaf original box and instructions, boxed.

*Kigu is one of the most desirable and hotly collected names in compacts. They were first made in Hungary during the 1920s by Gustav Kiashek - the name being derived from the first two letters of his surname then forename. In 1939, his son George came to England and founded The Kigu Co. in 1947, advertising their wares as 'compacts of character'. They stopped making compacts in the late 1950s, moving over to costume jewellery.*

**£50-70** **SH**

A Rimmel boxed faux-jewelled powder compact set, with purple lipstick, mint and boxed.

*c1951*

**£35-45** **SH**

A 1950s Regent of London gold-tone metal powder compact and hand mirror, with hand-tooled inset burgundy leather panels, in clam-shaped case.

*This is in mint condition, and is a very unusual shape.*

*Case 6.5in (16.5cm) wide*

**£40-50** **SH**

An English Stratton black enamelled compact, with shaped edge and small cut steel/marcasite inset bow.

*2.75in (7cm) wide*

**£60-80** **NOR**

A 1940s American Lin Bren blue leather purse powder compact, with front press-stud opening, original puff and sifter slide catch.

*3.5in (9cm) wide*

**£35-45** **SH**

A 1930s un-named shaped square enamelled black compact, with Art Deco design to the circular flip-up lid.

*2.25in (5.5cm) diam*

**£30-50** **NOR**

A 1930s Art Deco style green and white enamelled gold-tone metal square compact.

*2.75in (7cm) wide*

**£40-60** **NOR**

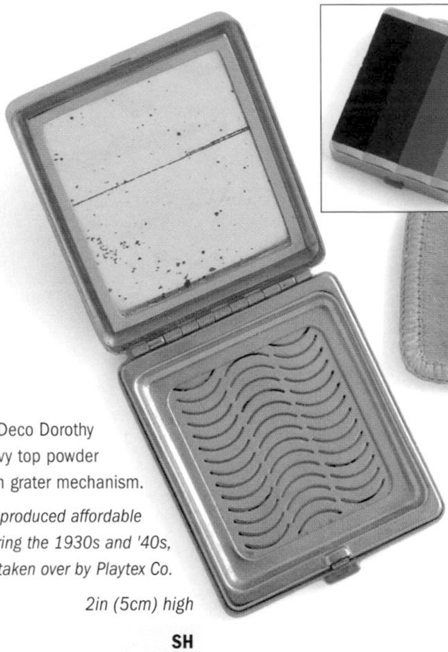

A 1930s Art Deco Dorothy Grey blue wavy top powder compact, with grater mechanism.

*Dorothy Gray produced affordable compacts during the 1930s and '40s, before being taken over by Playtex Co.*

*2in (5cm) high*

**£30-50** **SH**

A late 1940s-50s Dimopa powder compact, with lipstick, perfume and bullet eyeliner.

*As indicated by the title 'Brit Zone', this unusual compact shows a map of West Germany after the country was divided following WWII.*

*3.25in (8.5cm) wide*

**£70-90** **SH**

A 1940s English crinoline lady powder compact.

*2.75in (7cm) high*

**£30-35** **SH**

An American gold-tone square compact, inlaid with mother-of-pearl panels.

*2.75in (7cm) wide*

**£25-35** **NOR**

## A CLOSER LOOK AT A COMBINATION POWDER COMPACT

*Like many others, this example has all the features an elegant lady would require, including lipstick, cigarettes, a mirror, a comb, and of course a powder compact.*

*The strap was used to suspend the case from the wrist, freeing up both hands. They were typically used for evening events, hence the use of black.*

*It is in excellent, unused condition. Beware of examples that have missing, mismatched or badly re-glued mother-of-pearl panels.*

A gold-plated and mother-of-pearl pannier handle wrist hanging cigarette case and compact, with comb, lipstick holder.

*5.5in (13.5cm) long*

**£60-80** **NOR**

A 1950s reverse-carved Lucite square compact, with rose design.

*This is a desirable compact, and uses a technique that is commonly found with plastic costume jewellery of the period. The clear Lucite plastic is carved by hand in the desired pattern. The cavities are then injection-filled with coloured paste to give them colour and 'life', resulting in a three dimensional effect.*

*3in (7.5cm) wide*

**£30-50** **NOR**

An American Dorset Fifth Avenue hand-engraved silver compact, with diamond and rose motifs, stamped "Sterling".

*Another desirable name, Dorset made compacts from the 1930s-50s.*

*3.75in (9.5cm) wide*

**£60-90** **NOR**

A German Ciro silver-plated compact, set with blue stones in an 'S', and marked "Made in Baden".

*3.25in (8cm) wide*

**£40-60** **NOR**

An American Emrich gold-plated compact, with textured grid surface, the clasp inset square red rhinestones.

*3.25in (8.5cm) wide*

**£40-50** **NOR**

A 1950s American Weisner 'Trikettes' powder compact, with original puff and sifter and label, the exterior set with rhinestones, and with matching comb.

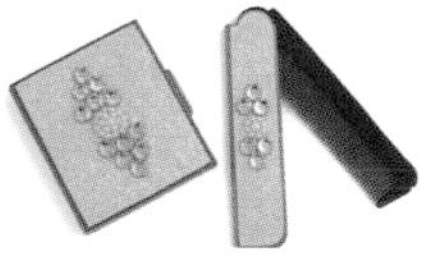

*The presence of the matching comb and the superb overall condition add much to the value of this compact. Weisner also made costume jewellery, which was typically inset with rhinestones.*

*Comb 4in (10cm) long*

**£60-70** **SH**

A 1920s cold-painted enamelled compact, with Art Deco style dog motif.

*Despite today's habits, the small ring does not indicate this is a key-ring – instead it was meant to be held on the finger.*

*2.5in (6.5cm) high*

**£100-150** **NOR**

A 1930s Divine 'Carol Singers' miniature compact, possibly American, with enamelled decoration.

*1.25in (3.25cm) wide*

**£60-80** **MGT**

A 1970s Faberge gold-plated triangular compact, with basketweave design, original box and refill.

*2.5in (6.5cm) high*

**£25-35** **NOR**

A 1970s Halston stylized heart-shaped silver compact, stamped "Sterling".

*Halston are a world-renowned fashion label, who were particularly popular during the 1970s. This is a late date for a compact, and it would probably have been expensive in its day.*

*2.5in (8cm) wide*

**£50-80** **NOR**

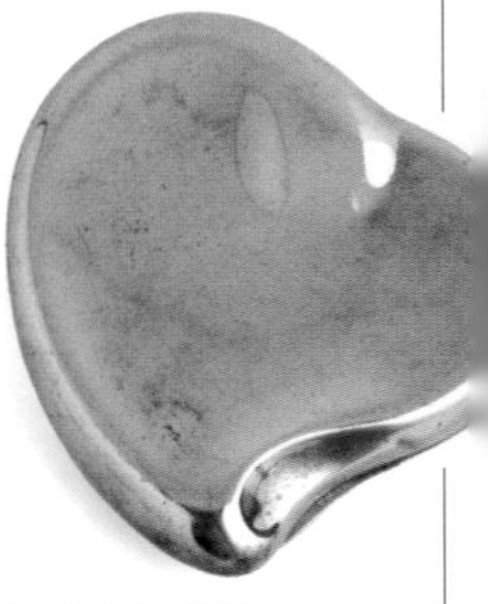

An American Elgin 'American' silver compact, with scrolling foliage, two-colour gold wash and engraved initials, stamped "Sterling".

*3in (7.5cm) high*

**£60-90** **NOR**

A Goodrich Drug Co. Drug Co 'Velvetina' face powder tin.

*Full and unopened tins are rare, and could be worth up to £100.*

*c1906* *3.5in (9cm) high*

**£35-45** **SH**

A 1950s Pygmalion engraved gold-tone ball powder compact, with original puff and sifter.

*2.5in (6.5cm) diam*

**£50-70** **SH**

A Colgate 'All the Witchery of Youth captured in Seventeen' card powder box.

*Despite the wonderfully eccentric name, this is a desirable object, due in part to the superb Art Deco design. There is also a compact that matches the box.*

*c1932*

**£20-30** **SH**

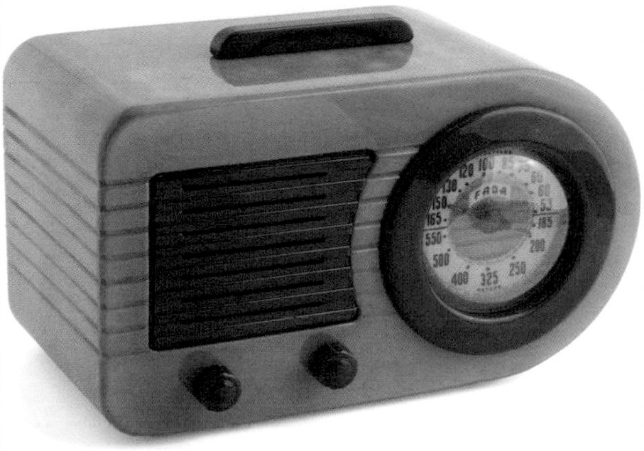


A late 1940s Fada yellow and red Catalin Model 100 Streamliner/Bullet, with inserted grille and ribbed knobs in excellent condition.

*The Fada 'Bullet' is one of the most recognisable vintage plastic radios. The inset red grille is a rare feature. If it was integral to and the same colour as the case, it would be worth around £500-750 in this condition. Pre-war tuning and volume knobs were smooth.*

*10.25in (26cm) wide*

**£1,800-2,200** **CAT**

A late 1940s Fada butterscotch Catalin model 1000 'Bullet' radio, in need of renovation.

*10.25in (26cm) wide*

**£350-450** **SDR**

A Murphy Type SAD 94S radio, in shaped Bakelite case, with original knobs and tuning sheet.

*1940*

**£80-120** **ATK**

A 1930s Bakelite 'Sparkling Champagne Music' champagne bottle-shaped radio, with 'crackle-finish' neck and cork/knob decals and chart on bottom.

*c1950* *23.5in (59.5cm) high*

**£60-80** **EG**

A German Telefunken 'Partner' AM transistor radio, with leather carrying case.

*This was the first Telefunken produced in a series.*

*1957*

**£40-60** **ATK**

A 1950s wooden cased Ferguson radio.

**£30-40** **TCM**

A 1970s Hitachi Solid State radio and alarm clock, with gold effect plastic casing and flip tune dial.

*7in (18cm) high*

**£15-20** **GAZE**

A 1970s Sarleen yellow plastic cased pocket radio, model no.38334, with original box.

**£6-8** **GAZE**

An uncommon British Railways (Southern) 'Sturry' dark green totem sign, in good overall condition.

*From an ex-South Eastern & Chatham Railway station between Canterbury West and Ramsgate.*

**£750-850** **GWRA**

A London Transport double-sided enamelled destination indicator for 'Barking – Bow Road', in good condition.

*24in (60cm) wide*

**£25-35** **GWRA**

A British Railway (North East) enamelled 'Gentlemen' sign, with black edged white lettering, in extremely good condition.

*36in (90cm) wide*

**£60-80** **GWRA**

An alloy 'Trains Cross Here' road sign, with glass studs, in excellent condition.

*30in (75cm) wide*

**£20-30** **GWRA**

A British Rail Engineering Limited commemorative oval alloy worksplate, commemorating the first locomotive built at the Swindon factory for export (to Kenya Railways) reading 'Supplied By BRE-Metro Ltd. Built B.R.E.L. SWINDON 525 HP – No 9016 – 1979', the rear with the details of the engine, the double arrow mark and the African company's crest.

*11in (27.5cm) wide*

**£60-80** **GWRA**

A scarce '70E' oval shedplate, with restored face, original paint showing through rim.

*This number was used for Reading Southern until 1962, and then at Salisbury until 1967.*

**£450-550** **GWRA**

A Canadian Montreal Locomotive Works 65359 cast-iron worksplate.

*This was from the 4-6-2 Pacific Locomotive no.15, built in 1923 and belonging to the Toronto Hamilton and Buffalo Railway.*

**£450-550** **GWRA**

An American rectangular cast iron worksplate 'American Locomotive Company General Electric Co. Schenectady N.Y. number 77404, September 1949'.

*1949* *12in (30cm) wide*

**£120-180** **GWRA**

A Great Western Railway roundhead mahogany cased wall clock, the side with ivorine plate "G.W.R. 668", in working order with non-original key.

*12in (30cm) diam*

**£500-800** **GWRA**

A Great Northern Railway horse drawn cart rear lamp, a brass plate on the domed top,with red bullseye lens, small, rectangular red glass either side, complete with original GNR, double burner fixed reservoir, and clearly stamped GNR on the front.

**£350-450** **GWRA**

An American electric railway box lantern, with large convex Vaseline glass lens with slide cover on rear.

*12in (30.50cm) high*

**£15-20** **JDJ**

An American four bulls-eye lens and enamelled railroad lantern, the black steel body with two blue and two amber lenses, marked on the top "Dressel Arlington, N.J. U.S.A.", some minor rust and chipping to some of the enamel on lens frames.

*20.50in (52cm) high*

**£60-80** **JDJ**

An American cast brass train bell, with original cast iron mount, repainted green.

*18in (45.50cm) high*

**£200-300** **JDJ**

An American small brass train whistle, with fancy cat finials, marked "1 1/2" on handle and mounted on a wooden base.

*9in (23cm) high*

**£30-40** **JDJ**

A Great Western Railway alloy 'Llanuwchllyn - Bala Jct' key token, with traces of blue paint.

*Key tokens were given to train drivers to operate single tracks ensuring that two trains did not try to approach the same single track from opposite directions at the same time.*

**£220-280** **GWRA**

A bound programme from the Caledonian Railway, 6-17th July 1914.

*8.5in (21.5cm) high*

**£35-55** **RCC**

A rare blue and white transfer-printed pearlware mug, showing an early locomotive named 'Manchester' pulling a wagon with an open carriage named 'Victoria Coronation London Royal Mail Liverpool'.

*c1838* *4in (10cm) high*

**£450-550** **SAS**

## COLLECTORS' NOTES

- Memorabilia connected to big name performers and bands tends to be the most valuable, with names like The Beatles, Elvis Presley, Michael Jackson, Jimi Hendrix and The Grateful Dead still at the top of the collecting charts.
- As with film memorabilia, provenance is key, especially when it comes to items owned or used by the star in question, so ensure you by from a reputable source.
- The value of paper-based memorabilia such as posters, magazines, concert tickets and album covers depends greatly on condition. Examples from early in an artist's career are often hard to come by as fewer would have been produced and items such as concert posters would have been thrown away after the event.

An Elvis Presley "Love Me Tender" sheet music book, published by Elvis Presley Inc.

*c1956*

**£25-35** **NOR**

An Elvis Presley "Hound Dog" sheet music book, published by Elvis Presley Inc.

*c1956*

**£25-35** **NOR**

An Elvis Presley "Treat Me Nice" sheet music book, published by Elvis Presley Inc., from the film "Jailhouse Rock".

*c1957*

**£15-20** **NOR**

A 'Reville Special, Elvis Presley, as he appears in the MGM film "It Happened at the World's Fair"' colour photographic poster, with folds.

*59.75in (152cm) high*

**£30-50** **ON**

A Elvis Presley black and white picture, clip framed.

**£7-10** **GAZE**

A 1963 Star Pics Elvis Presley calendar, lacks 'September'.

*1963*

**£5-8** **GAZE**

A limited edition Halcyon Days commemorative enamel box, from an edition of 500, commemorating the 25th anniversary of Elvis Presley death, with Andy Warhol's portrait of Elvis.

*2002* *2in (5.5cm)*

**£70-100** **HD**

A 1950s Elvis necklace, with gold-plated pendant with photograph of Elvis Presley.

*Pendant 0.75in (2cm) high*

**£40-50** **CVS**

A Paul McCartney painted moulded composition shoulder-head doll, with painted features, black real hair wig, cloth body with painted rubber hands, wearing a black velvet suit, white shirt and black felt tie, black leather imitation boots.

*1963-64* *24.5in (62cm) high*

**£2,000-3,000** **BONC**

## A CLOSER LOOK AT A BEATLES ALBUM COVER

*This album was released in the US only and was a compilation of tracks that were dropped from US versions of "Help!" and "Rubber Soul".*

*The photograph of the Fab Four wearing butchers smocks and draped in dismembered plastic dolls and lumps of raw meat was originally taken for a different project but was apparently pushed as the cover of this album as a comment on how Captiol had 'butchered' the band's catalog in the US.*

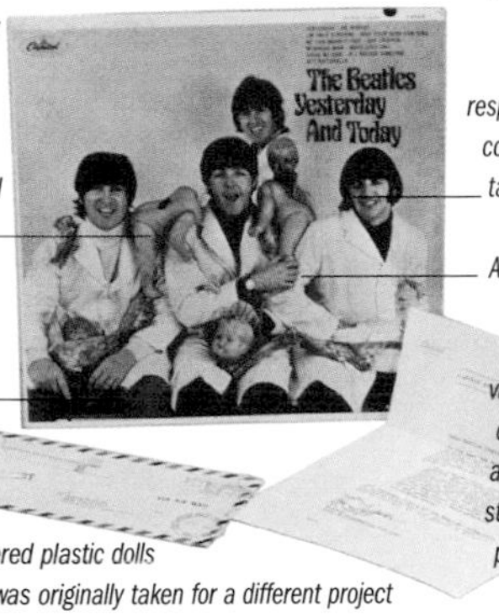


*Advanced copies to record store buyers and DJs garnered such negative responses that the 750,000 copies were recalled and a tamer cover was released.*

*A few were never returned and are known as 'first state' and are the most valuable. Some had a new cover pasted over the top and are known as 'second state' if the cover is still in place. 'Third state' covers are those with the cover removed and are the most commonly found.*

A rare Beatles 'butchers' album cover for "Yesterday and Today", together with a letter from Captiol Records detailing the recall of the cover.

*1966*

**£1,200-1,800** **DRA**

A set of four Beatles soft vinyl dolls, by Remco, with "The Beatles TM" stamp on back.

*4.75in (12cm) high*

**£250-350** **KNK**

A Beatles 'New Sound' cream and orange plastic toy guitar, by Selcol.

**£120-180** **CHEF**

John Lennon, 'The Hug', original numbered lithograph from an edition of 5,000, with chop mark, framed.

*c1988* *35.5in (90cm) high*

**£100-150** **DRA**

A 'Look' magazine poster of Ringo Starr photographed by Richard Avedon.

*1967* *31.5in (80cm) high*

**£40-60** **DRA**

Five pieces of Beatles memorabilia, including a rare Yellow Submarine pop-out decoration book, and four Beatles buttons with mirror backs, good condition.

*c1968*

**£350-450** **DRA**

Six pieces of Beatles memorabilia, including a Beatles metal tray, four souvenir buttons, gold metal commemorative coin, all in very good condition.

*c1964*

**£350-450** **DRA**

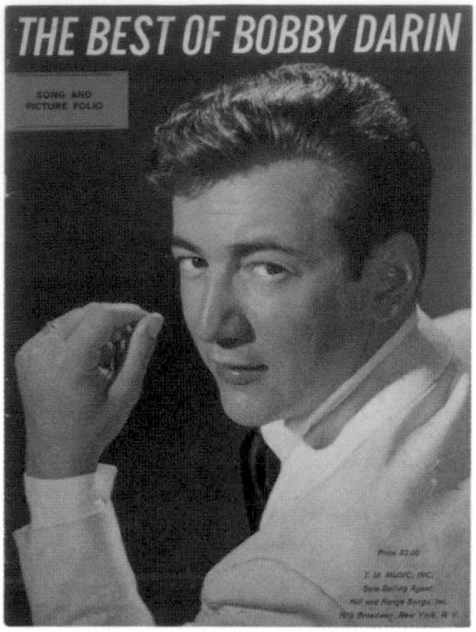


A 'The Best of Bobby Darin Song and Picture Portfolio', including song sheets.

*There has been a resurgence of interest in Bobby Darin since the release of the 2004 of the biopic 'Beyond the Sea', starring Kevin Spacey as Darin.*

*1963* *12in (30.5cm) high*

**£25-35** **NOR**

A The Andrews "Sisters Strip Polka" sheet music book, published by Edwin H. Morris & Company.

*Sheet music is usually collected for the cover artwork, particularly of stars in younger or typical appearance.*

*1942*

**£6-8** **NOR**

A rare promotional poster for The Doors self-titled debut album.

*1967* *28in (71cm) high*

**£500-800** **PC**

A The Elegants "Little Star" sheet music book, published by Keel Music Publ Co.

*1958*

**£10-15** **NOR**

A rare 'The Fabulous Fabian' Song and Picture Folio 1, with 17 photos candids, film and performance, and sheet music.

*1959*

**£20-30** **NOR**

A Led Zepplin "Stairway to Heaven" sheet music book, published by Warner Bros. Publications.

*1972*

**£8-12** **NOR**

A Ricky Nelson "Lonesome Town" sheet music book, published by Eric Music Inc.

*1958*

**£15-25** **NOR**

A 'Ladies & Gentlemen, The Rolling Stones' film concert poster, bearing signatures and with applied venue addendum.

*1974* *21in (53.5cm) high*

**£500-700** **PC**

A The Rays "Silhouettes" sheet music book, published by Regent Music Corporation.

*1957* *12in (30.5cm) high*

**£8-12** **NOR**

## COLLECTORS' NOTES

- Royal memorabilia has been popular since the early 19th century. Events connected to members of the Royal family were typically celebrated nationally and, with the advent of transfer-printing and the railways to act as a distribution network, these were often commemorated with specially produced ceramics. Although earlier examples are known, it was mainly during the reign of Queen Victoria (1837-1901) that the creation of commemorative ceramics began to boom.
- Most collectors choose one event or one monarch to focus on, as the range is so wide. Queen Victoria and the current Queen are often favoured by collectors, partly for the enormous range of pieces produced, which makes for a highly varied collection. Interest in the new generation of the Royal family is growing, as more events are commemorated as they grow up.
- There are a number of important general factors to consider when looking at commemorative ceramics. The first is the quality of the piece. Examples by well known high quality makers such as Royal Worcester, Royal Crown Derby and Doulton tend to be worth more, particularly if they are well decorated. Even if a piece is not by a major maker, if it is finely detailed and appealingly made, it will probably be of interest.
- The event too, is important. Fewer pieces were produced for the birth of Prince William than for Queen Victoria's Diamond Jubilee, for example. Some events also fall in and out of fashion and desirability. Look out for limited edition pieces, particularly those issued in very small editions of around 250 or less. If demand exceeds supply, then prices can rise dramatically. Keep all boxes and documents as these are important parts of the item and contribute towards its value.
- Condition is also very important. Damage or restoration will reduce the value considerably, especially for more modern pieces. However, some damage or restoration is acceptable on older, early 19th century pieces although a piece in truly mint condition will always command a premium.
- Also look for 'eye appeal', which can differ depending on the collector. Bright colours, and intricate designs tend to be universally popular, but some collectors prefer more sober and traditional coats-of-arms and 'etching' style portraits, with others preferring photographic portraits.

A Staffordshire Queen Victoria Coronation nursery plate, with a moulded floral and foliate border, and named and dated printed portrait, hairline crack.

*1838* *6.25in (16cm) diam*

**£220-280** **SAS**

A Staffordshire Queen Victoria Coronation nursery plate, with named and dated brown printed portrait enamelled in colours.

*This early plate, with its moulded daisy border, is also known with a black and white printed portrait without the hand enamelling, which is generally worth less.*

*1838* *6.75in (17cm) diam*

**£500-600** **SAS**

A Queen Victoria Coronation pearlware nursery plate, the border moulded with flower and foliage painted in coloured enamels, the centre printed in green with a named and dated portrait.

*1838* *5.5in (14cm) diam*

**£300-400** **SAS**

A Queen Victoria Coronation nursery plate, with flowerhead moulded border, the centre printed in blue with a named and dated portrait, restored.

*1838* *4.5in (11.5cm) diam*

**£180-220** **SAS**

A Queen Victoria Coronation earthenware plate, printed in blue with a dated design within a pink-banded border.

*1838* *7in (17.5cm) diam*

**£300-400** **SAS**

A Queen Victoria Coronation mug, printed with a named portrait flanked by flags and flowers, the reverse showing Britannia, the base named "Victoria R", rim and foot chipped.

*1838* *4in (10cm) high*

**£250-300** **SAS**

## A CLOSER LOOK AT A PROCLAMATION PLATE

*This portrait is based on the oil painting by Sir George Hayter (1792-1871), son of portrait miniature painter Charles Hayter.*

*This is a particularly well executed, decorative and high quality piece, hence the high price.*

*Hayter was appointed portrait and history painter to Victoria in 1837 and was responsible for a number of well-known portraits of her, becoming 'principal painter to the Queen' in 1841.*

*Here, she is shown in State dress with the wedding ring of England on her left hand, as she is officially proclaimed as Queen.*

A Continental Queen Victoria Proclamation porcelain plate, with printed full-length portrait and a cobalt blue ground highlighted in gilt including the 'VR' monogram, date and crown, restored.

*1837* *9.5in (24cm) diam*

**£650-750** **SAS**

A Queen Victoria Coronation earthenware jug, printed with portraits centred with names and dates, handle cracked.

*1838*

**£250-300** **SAS**

A Dimmock & Smith Queen Victoria Coronation earthenware plate, transfer-printed with an equestrian portrait with Windsor Castle in the background, the reverse with Coronation trophies, named Victoria.

*Kings, queens, emperors and other rulers have been shown on horseback for hundreds of years, and such portraits were used as a symbol of status, power and control. Many were based on Donatello's Renaissance bronze sculpture, the 'Gattamelata' of 1445-50, which itself was based on Ancient Roman examples.*

*1838* *7in (17.5cm) diam*

**£300-400** **SAS**

A Queen Victoria Proclamation earthenware jug, printed in black with portraits.

*1837* *7in (18cm) high*

**£250-300** **SAS**

A Queen Victoria Proclamation earthenware plate, with scalloped outline, with a printed design and ribboned wording reading "Hail Victoria", restored rim chips.

*1837* *8.75in (22cm) diam*

**£350-450** **SAS**

A Staffordshire Queen Victoria Proclamation pottery nursery plate, the border moulded with flower heads, the centre printed with a named and dated portrait, cracked.

*7.5in (19cm) diam*

**£180-220** **SAS**

A pair of Queen Victoria & Prince Albert Royal Wedding earthenware plates, the borders moulded with flowers and foliage, minor hairline crack.

*It is hard to find these vibrant and colourful plates together.*

*1840* *5in (13cm) diam*

**£350-450** **SAS**

A pair of Queen Victoria & Prince Albert Royal Wedding nursery plates, with flowerhead moulded border, the centre printed with named portraits, hairline crack and restored crack.

*1840* *6in (15cm) diam*

**£250-350** **SAS**

A Queen Victoria & Prince Albert Royal Wedding nursery plate, with flowerhead moulded border, the centre printed in black with named portraits.

*1840* *5.25in (13.5cm) diam*

**£80-120** **SAS**

A Queen Victoria & Prince Albert commemorative nursery plate, the border moulded with flowerheads, the centre printed and enamelled in colours with a portrait, restored.

*c1851* *6.5in (16.5cm) diam*

**£60-80** **SAS**

A Copeland & Garrett Queen Victoria & Prince Albert Royal Wedding earthenware plate, the reverse with printed and impressed marks.

*1840* *5.25in (13.5cm) diam*

**£80-120** **SAS**

A Queen Victoria & Prince Albert Royal Wedding earthenware plate, moulded with a coloured portrait of Prince Albert above a ribboned border of flowers lined in blue.

*1840* *7.25in (18.5cm) diam*

**£150-200** **SAS**

A Queen Victoria & Prince Albert Royal Wedding jug, moulded with colourful full-length portraits on a blue ground.

*4.75in (12cm) high*

**£120-180** **SAS**

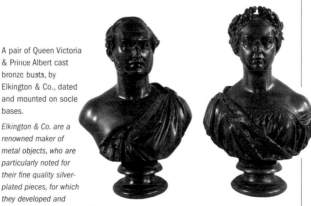

A pair of Queen Victoria & Prince Albert cast bronze busts, by Elkington & Co., dated and mounted on socle bases.

*Elkington & Co. are a renowned maker of metal objects, who are particularly noted for their fine quality silver-plated pieces, for which they developed and patented a process. These finely modelled and large bronze busts are based on examples by sculptor William Theed (1804-91) who was one of Victoria's favourite sculptors, and exhibited at the 1851 Great Exhibition as well as producing work for the Albert Memorial.*

*1864* *15.5in (39.5cm) high*

**£2,200-2,800** **SAS**

A Wallis Gimson & Co. Queen Victoria Golden Jubilee commemorative plate, with registered design number 41006 for 1886.

*This plate is no. 4 from the Portrait Series of monarchs, politicians and notable personalities produced by Wallis Gimson.*

*c1887* *11in (28cm) wide*

**£70-90** **RCC**

A Queen Victoria Golden Jubilee pottery plate, printed with a dated portrait, the rim lined in gilt.

*1887*

**£22-28** **SAS**

A Queen Victoria Golden Jubilee pottery plate, printed with a portrait, the border moulded with ribbons.

*The famous 'elbow on table' portrait was taken by the photographer Lafayette of Dublin in 1887.*

*1887*

**£22-28** **SAS**

A Hines Bros. Queen Victoria Golden Jubilee pottery plate, printed with young and old portraits and scenes from the Empire.

*1887*

**£5-8** **SAS**

A Doulton Lambeth Queen Victoria Diamond Jubilee blue glazed stoneware jug, moulded with young and old portraits in green.

*These are typical colours for Doulton stoneware.*

*1897* *7in (17.5cm) high*

**£80-120** **SAS**

A Doulton Lambeth Queen Victoria Golden Jubilee stoneware jug, with brown glaze and applied white moulded decoration of an enthroned Victoria flanked by figures emblematic of the Empire.

*1887* *4.5in (11.5cm) high*

**£70-90** **SAS**

A Copeland Queen Victoria Diamond Jubilee pottery jug, with white moulded portraits on a green ground, coat-of-arms and heraldic shield.

*1897* *7.75in (19.5cm) high*

**£40-50** **SAS**

A Doulton Lambeth Queen Victoria Diamond Jubilee glazed stoneware mug, moulded with a young and old profile portrait in green.

*1897*

**£50-80** **SAS**

A Doulton Lambeth Queen Victoria Diamond Jubilee stoneware beaker, with hallmarked silver collar and moulded young and old portraits.

*The addition of the hallmarked silver collar is both unusual and desirable, increasing the value of this beaker. Without it, it could be worth around half as much.*

*1897*

**£80-120** **SAS**

A Copeland Queen Victoria Diamond Jubilee pottery mug, glazed in green and with an applied moulded white portrait.

*1897*

**£70-100** **SAS**

A William Lowe Queen Victoria Diamond Jubilee pottery loving cup, printed with an inscription within a gilt jewelled cartouche flanked by flags and flowers.

*1897* *3.25in (8.5cm) high*

**£70-100** **SAS**

A Royal Worcester Queen Victoria Diamond Jubilee porcelain wall pocket, moulded with a portrait in profile and decorated in pale green and gilt.

*1897* *8.25in (21cm) high*

**£200-250** **SAS**

A Coalport Queen Victoria Diamond Jubilee plate, printed with a statue portrait within a boarder detailing the Empire, with gilt moulded rim.

*1897*

**£45-55** **SAS**

A Queen Victoria 'Longest Reign' commemorative pottery mug, for Whiteley, printed in pink with young and old portraits.

*1896*

**£70-100** **SAS**

A Doulton Lambeth Queen Victoria In Memoriam stoneware jug, glazed in green and moulded with a portrait and inscribed panels.

*To date, Queen Victoria ruled the United Kingdom for the longest time, being queen for 64 years.*

*1901* *8in (20cm) high*

**£200-300** **SAS**

A King Edward VII Royal Christening nursery plate, the border moulded with flowerheads, the centre printed in green with a scene.

*1842* *7.5in (19cm) diam*

**£70-100** **SAS**

A King Edward VII Royal Birth porcelain plate, printed in blue with infants at play among Prince of Wales feathers.

*1841* *8in (20cm) diam*

**£30-40** **SAS**

A Radford Edward VII Coronation bone china mug, with printed portraits flanked by flags and with named banner.

*1902* *3in (7.5cm) high*

**£60-80** **H&G**

A Bros Edward VII bone china mug, with coloured double portrait flanked by flags, the reverse with 'Teddington Festivities' printed wording and armorial shield.

*Most of these mugs are dated 26th June, the planned date for the coronation. Before this date, Edward was struck down with appendicitis and the coronation was delayed until August 9th. Those items that display both dates or the August postponement will usually command a premium.*

*3.25 (8.5cm) high*

**£100-150** **H&G**

A Doulton Lambeth King Edward VII Coronation stoneware beaker, moulded with green glazed portrait medallions and glazed in blue.

*1902*

**£70-100** **SAS**

A King Edward VII commemorative porcelain plate, marking the first year of the King's reign, printed with a design by Kepple and with a gilt decorated moulded border.

*1902*

**£25-35** **SAS**

A large Shelley Edward VIII Coronation loving cup, the waisted body with printed brown portrait flanked by coloured flags.

*1936* *4.5in (11.5cm) high*

**£80-120** **SAS**

A limited edition King Edward VIII Coronation large loving cup, by Paragon, from an edition of 1,000, set with twin gilt lion handles.

*1936* *6in (15cm) high*

**£120-180** **SAS**

A Royal Crown Derby Edward VIII Coronation loving cup, with sepia transfer-printed portrait, and decorated in gilt.

*As commemoratives are produced in advance of an event, more pieces commemorating Edward VIII's proposed coronation exist than many people think. This means that they are often not hard too find today at a variety of prices. However, this example fetched such a high price as it is by a very notable maker and is finely decorated and modelled. Loving cups are also popular shapes. It is worth looking out for pieces commemorating his abdication, as these are scarcer, partly as it was such an unpopular event and as there was a new coronation to be celebrated.*

*1936* *4.5in (11.5cm) high*

**£600-700** **SAS**

A Royal Crown Derby Edward VIII Coronation mug, with sepia transfer-printed portrait, and decorated in gilt.

*1936* *3in (7.5cm) high*

**£300-400** **SAS**

A Coalport King Edward VIII Coronation mug, the cobalt blue ground well-decorated in gilt, contained in a leatherette box.

*1936*

**£150-200** **SAS**

A Royal Doulton Edward VIII Coronation bone china mug, with with colour printed portrait and gilt highlights.

*Note the shaped handle, the gilt inset of which forms an 'E'. Doulton also produced a version for George VI.*

*1936* *3.25in (8.5cm) high*

**£200-250** **H&G**

A Crown Ducal Edward VIII Coronation earthenware mug, designed by Charlotte Rhead.

*Look out for ceramics by notable 1930s designers, such as Eric Ravillious, Laura Knight and Charlotte Rhead. If they have an Art Deco style form or decoration, this generally increases the desirability.*

*1936* *4.75in (12cm) high*

**£100-150** **H&G**

A Royal Doulton Edward VIII Coronation porcelain beaker, with printed profile portrait.

*1936*

**£200-300** **SAS**

## A CLOSER LOOK AT A COMMEMORATIVE GLOBE

*The globe show the British Empire, as it stood on Edward's planned accession, marked out in red.*

*The globe form is very unusual and adds variety to a collection of Royal commemorative ceramics.*

*The wording around the globe reads 'The Empire on Which the Sun Never Sets', and the foot bears printed wording commemorating the proposed coronation on May 12th 1937.*

*The reach of the British Empire is rarely so graphically shown on royal commemorative ceramics.*

A Melba Edward VIII Coronation globe, the base with wording around the foot.

*1936* *3.5in (9cm) high*

**£220-280** **SAS**

A limited edition King Edward VIII commemorative beaker, by Minton, from an edition of 2,000, decorated in colours and gilt.

*1936*

**£120-180** **SAS**

A Paragon Edward VIII coronation coffee cup and saucer, decorated in colours with gilt highlights.

*1936*

**£100-150** **SAS**

A Royal Crown Derby Edward VIII Coronation square dish, with shaped edges, decorated with a printed brown portrait and gilt rim.

*1936*

**£100-150** **SAS**

A Shelley King George VI and Queen Elizabeth Coronation Deluxe loving cup.

*1937* *3.5in (9cm) high*

**£120-150** **RCC**

A Shelley King George VI and Elizabeth Coronation porcelain loving cup, printed with sepia portraits amidst leaves, the reverse printed with portraits of the Princesses, with two gilt handles.

*1937* *4in (10cm) high*

**£100-150** **SAS**

A Royal Crown Derby King George VI and Elizabeth Coronation medium-sized mug, with printed sepia portraits on a blue ground and highlighted in gilt.

*1937* *3.5in (9cm) high*

**£250-350** **SAS**

## A CLOSER LOOK AT A LOVING CUP

*Royal Crown Derby are a notable factory, known for their fine quality ceramics and finely detailed decoration.*

*The handles are shaped as American eagles, which is an appealing feature that also reinforces the event commemorated.*

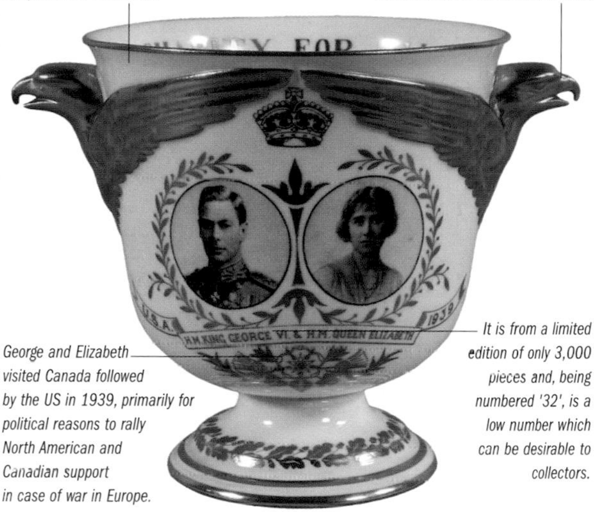

*George and Elizabeth visited Canada followed by the US in 1939, primarily for political reasons to rally North American and Canadian support in case of war in Europe.*

*It is from a limited edition of only 3,000 pieces and, being numbered '32', is a low number which can be desirable to collectors.*

A limited edition Royal Crown Derby chalice, commemorating a visit to the US by George VI, with printed sepia portraits on a light blue ground, the reverse decorated with the American eagle.

*4.5in (11.5cm) high*

**£280-320** **SAS**

A Crown Staffordshire King George VI and Elizabeth coronation mug, with printed brown portraits, and blue ground with gilt highlights.

*1937*

**£180-220** **SAS**

A Royal Doulton King George VI and Elizabeth Coronation beaker, with green ground.

*This was made in six different colours including ivory and pink. Blue is the rarest and can be worth £500. A similar beaker was produced for the cancelled coronation of George's brother Edward VIII.*

*1937* *3.75in (9.5cm) high*

**£285-320** **RCC**

A pair of King Edward VI in Memoriam pottery plates, one with named portrait of the King, one with younger named portrait of the Queen, hairline crack to the Queen.

*1910*

**£35-45** **SAS**

A limited edition Royal Crown Derby Queen Elizabeth II Coronation loving cup, from an edition of 250, printed in colours with a portrait oval of the Queen.

*This is a particularly appealing and evocative loving cup, from a strictly limited edition by a notable maker.*

*1953* *3.75in (9.5cm) high*

**£650-750** **SAS**

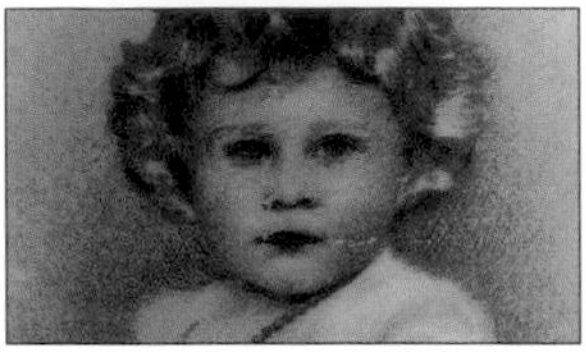

A Paragon Queen Elizabeth II Royal Birth mug, with transfer-printed brown portrait after Marcus Adams, lined in red and gilt.

*1926*

**£80-120** **SAS**

A limited edition Queen Elizabeth II Coronation loving cup, set with gilt lion handles and decorated in coloured enamels.

*1953* *4.5in (11.5cm) high*

**£180-220** **SAS**

A Royal Albert Queen Elizabeth II Coronation loving cup, with sepia portrait oval and red ground decorated with gilt highlights.

*1953* *4in (10.5cm) high*

**£500-600** **SAS**

An Aynsley Queen Elizabeth II Coronation Deluxe bone china plate, decorated in colours and gilt.

*1953* *10.25in (26cm) high*

**£220-280** **H&G**

An Aynsley Queen Elizabeth II Coronation cup and saucer, printed with a sepia portrait on a cobalt blue ground highlighted with gilt.

*1953*

**£30-40** **SAS**

A Burleigh ware Queen Elizabeth II Coronation earthenware mug, with sepia-toned printed portrait on a blue ground, flanked by flags.

*1953* *3.25in (8.5cm) high*

**£50-70** **H&G**

A Royal Doulton Queen Elizabeth II Coronation bone china beaker.

*1953* *4in (10cm) high*

**£40-60** **H&G**

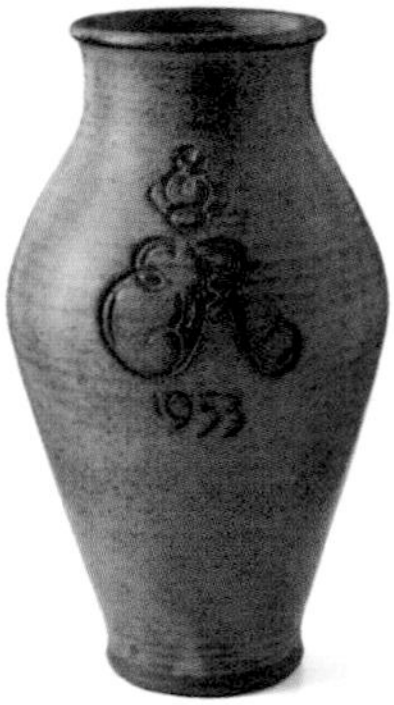


A Queen Elizabeth II Coronation studio pottery vase, by Alan Martin.

*1953*

**£35-45** **GAZE**

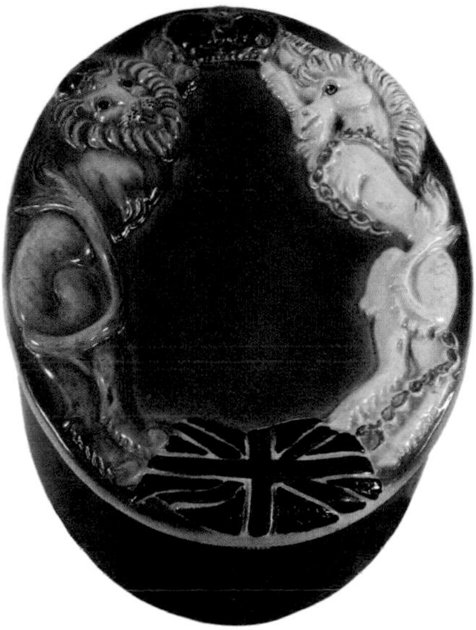

A Goldscheider Queen Elizabeth II Coronation pottery box and cover, moulded with a lion and unicorn supporting the crown.

*Austrian company Goldscheider are better known for their sought-after Art Deco style ceramic figurines of elegant ladies and dancers. Many 1940s-50s pieces were made by Myott & Sons in the UK.*

*1953* *6.75in (17cm) high*

**£80-120** **SAS**

A Spode Queen Elizabeth II Silver Jubilee bone china tankard.

*1977* *4in (10cm) high*

**£50-70** **H&G**

A Wedgwood Queen Elizabeth II Silver Jubilee large earthenware mug.

*1977* *4.5in (11.5cm) high*

**£30-40** **H&G**

A limited edition Paragon Queen Elizabeth II Silver Wedding loving cup, from an edition of 750, set with twin gilt lion handles, boxed.

*1972* *5in (13cm) high*

**£40-50** **SAS**

A pair of Lindon Cards novelty commemorative slippers, in the form of Queen Elizabeth II and Prince Philip, Duke of Edinburgh, in bed, marked "©1988".

*c1988* *11.5in (29cm) long*

**£30-50** **KCS**

A limited edition Prince Charles & Lady Diana Spencer Royal Wedding loving cup, from an edition of 750, set with twin gilt handles, with certificate.

*1981 5in (13cm) high*

**£70-100** **SAS**

A Spode Prince Charles & Lady Diana Spencer Royal Wedding bone china mug, with sepia portraits surrounded by a floral and foliate garland, including the flowers of England.

*1981 3.5in (9cm) high*

**£40-60** **H&G**

A Carlton Ware Prince Charles large twin-handled mug, designed by Luck & Flaw, together with four white pottery egg cups modelled as Queen Elizabeth II, the Duke of Edinburgh, Prince Charles, and Diana, Princess of Wales.

*Peter Fluck & Roger Law (also known as Luck & Flaw and Fluck & Law) were the creators of the 1980s-90s satirical 'Spitting Image' puppet series. These popular ceramics are based on the puppets they designed of members of the Royal family.*

**£40-60** **SAS**

A Carlton Ware Diana, Princess of Wales commemorative egg cup, designed by Fluck and Law, marked "©1982".

*c1982 4in (10cm) high*

**£50-60** **KCS**

A limited edition Chown Diana, Princess of Wales 35th Birthday mug, from an edition of 70, commissioned by Paul Wyton & Joe Spiteri.

*1996 3.75in (9.5cm) high*

**£40-60** **RCC**

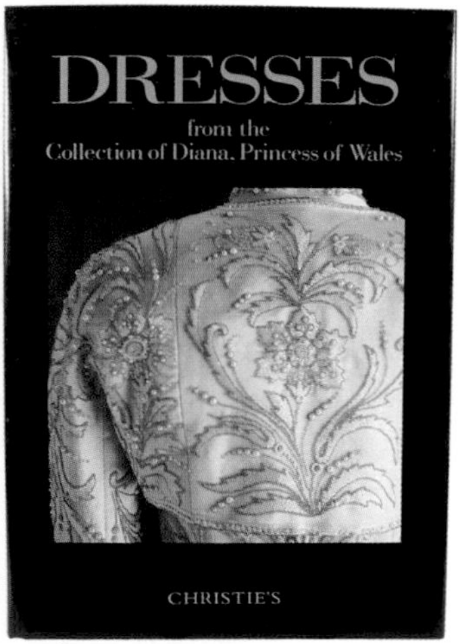


'Dresses from the Collection of Diana, Princess of Wales', presentation catalogue for the Christie's auction of 25th June 1997 complete with prices realised.

*1997*

**£180-220** **SAS**

A limited edition Aynsley Prince Charles & Diana, Princess of Wales Royal Divorce bone china mug.

*This mug was produced in a (comparatively large) limited edition of 5,000. Note how Diana and Charles are facing away from each other, even though the general format of the design is like most commemorative pieces. Compared to other events, few examples commemorating this unhappy event were produced making them rarer than many others.*

*1991 3.75in (9.5cm) high*

**£70-100** **H&G**

A limited edition Chown 'A Princess of the World' Diana, Princess of Wales commemorative plate, from an edition of 50, commissioned by Paul Wyton & Joe Spiteri.

*This plate was released one year after Diana's death.*

*1998 8.5in (21.5cm) diam*

**£50-70** **RCC**

A limited edition Caverswall Prince William Royal Birth bone china lion head beaker, from an edition of 1,000.

*1982* *4.5in (11.5cm) high*

**£60-80** **H&G**

## A CLOSER LOOK AT A LOVING CUP

*Items commemorating the young Princes William and Harry are rising in value, particularly as so few have been produced due to their youth and low number of events.*

*This is from a limited edition of only 50 pieces – competition for examples that come up for sale can be high.*

*Those celebrating William's life are particularly sought-after, as he is next in line to the throne.*

*It is by a noted maker, and is well decorated, with gilt highlights and a pastoral scene of the gardens at Highgrove.*

A limited edition J. & J. May Prince William Royal Birth loving cup, from an edition of 50 decorated with a scene of a pram in the gardens of Highgrove.

*1982* *4.25in (10.5cm) high*

**£400-500** **SAS**

A limited edition Chown Prince William 21th birthday mug, from an edition of 60, commissioned by Paul Wyton & Joe Spiteri.

*2003* *3.75in (9.5cm) high*

**£20-30** **RCC**

An Aynsley Prince Harry Royal Birth small bone china loving cup, with a transfer printed scene of Balmoral.

*1984* *2.25in (6cm) high*

**£60-80** **H&G**

A limited edition Chown Prince Harry 18th birthday mug, from an edition of 70, commissioned by Paul Wyton & Joe Spiteri.

*2002* *3.75in (9.5cm) high*

**£20-30** **RCC**

A Tsar Nicholas II of Russian 'Cup of Sorrows' enamelled beaker, some expected damage.

*1896* *4in (10cm) high*

**£150-200** **RCC**

A Prince Albert Edward & Princess Alexandra of Denmark Royal Wedding commemorative stoneware jug, moulded with heraldic shields, coats-of-arms and Prince of Wales feathers.

*1863* *6.75in (17cm) high*

**£22-28** **SAS**

A Queen Victoria 'The Royal Children' nursery plate, the border moulded with flowers and foliage, the centre printed with the Prince of Wales on a pony, with two of his sisters.

*c1846* *7in (17.5cm) diam*

**£200-250** **SAS**

A Prince Albert Edward & Princess Alexandra of Denmark, Royal Wedding pottery nursery plate, with moulded border, the centre printed with portrait, rim chips.

*1863* *7in (18cm) diam*

**£70-100** **SAS**

A Prince Albert Victor 'Visit to Burnley' commemorative pottery plate, by Wallis Gimson, the printed portrait flanked by flowers and lined in gilt.

*1886*

**£180-220** **SAS**

A Paragon limited edition Queen Elizabeth, the Queen Mother 80th Birthday commemorative large loving cup, from an edition of 750.

*1980* *5in (13cm) high*

**£22-28** **SAS**

A limited edition Princess Margaret In Memoriam bone china mug.

*Only a very small number of these mugs were commissioned.*

*2002* *3.5in (9cm) high*

**£30-40** **H&G**

A limited edition Princess Anne, Princess Royal & Captain Mark Phillips Royal Wedding large loving cup, by Paragon, from an edition of 500, set with twin gilt lion handles, with certificate.

*1973* *5in (13cm) high*

**£70-100** **SAS**

A limited edition Prince Edward and Sophie Rhys-Jones Royal Wedding plate, commissioned by Peter Jones China, from an edition of 2,500.

*8.5in (21.5cm) diam*

**£40-50** **RCC**

## COLLECTORS' NOTES

- Scottie dog memorabilia dates primarily from between the 1920s and '30s, and the 1950s, when the breed was at its most popular and fashionable. This was partly due to a number of famous personalities owning a Scottie. These included Shirley Temple and Presidents Eisenhower and Roosevelt. Roosevelt's dog was called 'Fala', and was the most famous White House dog. President Bush continues the tradition today, with 'Barney'.
- The jaunty and cheerful motif was used on many decorative and functional items around the home, but also appeared in fashion on handbags, pins, bangles and even clothing. Scotties have also featured heavily in advertising, and have helped sell a huge range of products. Some collectors concentrate solely on artwork showing Scotties. Look for 'Texaco' and 'Black & White Scottish Whisky' advertising pieces.
- Always consider the quality of a piece to determine its value. More finely made pieces will generally be worth more. However, as the appeal of Scotties is so wide, most pieces that have a 'cute' factor or have great visual appeal will be popular. Brightly coloured plastic items from the 1930s are very desirable, as is jewellery featuring Scottie dogs. Sculptural items such as doorstops, bookends and money banks are also popular with collectors.

A 1930s painted cast iron Scottie dog desk magnifier, with moveable lens.

*5in (13cm) high*

**£80-120** **DCC**

A 1930s Continental carved wood Scottie dog ashtray, with glass liner.

*6.25in (16cm) wide*

**£50-80** **DCC**

A 1930s wooden Scottie dog desk calendar, with paper calendar pages.

*4.5in (11.5cm) high*

**£30-40** **DCC**

A rare 1930s Scottie dog dice, with weighted revolving hexagonal wooden dice suspended between two painted metal dogs, on a wooden base.

*Base 5in (13cm) wide*

**£80-120** **DCC**

A 1930s painted cast metal matchholder, with a Scottie dog sitting on a book.

*2.5in (6.5cm) wide*

**£50-80** **DCC**

A very rare 1930s McClelland Barclay Art Company bronze box, with Scottie dog on lid.

*The McClelland Art Company was founded by McClelland Barclay (1891-1943) during the 1930s to produce a range of functional and decorative household objects. Barclay went missing in action during WWII, but had been a noted artist before the war, known for his paintings of beautiful women and his animal sculptures.*

*3.25in (8.5cm) wide*

**£150-200** **ROX**

A 1930s Japanese chrome-plated salt and pepper set, with Scottie dog and red plastic finials.

*These sorts of chrome-plated wares were produced to imitate the Art Deco styled copper and chrome homewares produced by the Chase Brass & Copper Co. in the US, see the example below.*

*5.75in (14.5cm) wide*

**£30-50** **ROX**

A 1930s Chase Brass & Copper Co. chrome-plated relish dish, with three cast and carved Catalin Scottie dogs.

*9.75in (25cm) wide*

**£40-60** **ROX**

A 1930s English carved pine wood Scottie dog corkscrew.

*Dog 5in (12.5cm) wide*

**£7-10** **CSA**

A 1950s hand-painted moulded ceramic Scottie dog teapot, with paw raised to form the spout.

*6.75in (17cm) high*

**£30-40** **ROX**

A 1950s black plastic Scottie dog wall-hanging clipboard, with painted red bow and brass clip.

*7in (18cm) high*

**£50-80** **MG**

A 1930s novelty wood and wire tie-rack, with applied moulded plastic Scottie dog motif.

*7.75in (20cm) high*

**£20-30** **ROX**

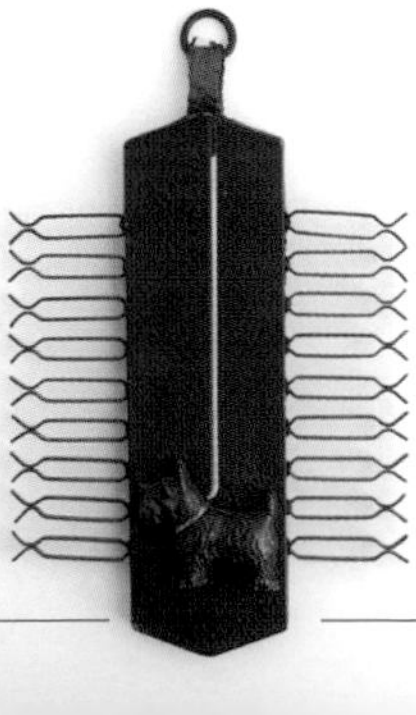

A 1930s painted metal Scottie dog money bank.

*Ideal for encouraging the thrifty Scot.*

*5in (13cm) high*

**£40-60** **ROX**

A 1930s-1940s painted metal Scottie dog money bank.

*3.5in (9cm) high*

**£50-70** **DCC**

A 1930s Continental carved wood seated Scottie dog egg timer, lacks tail.

*5in (12cm) high*

**£40-60** **DCC**

A small plush-covered Scottie dog toy, by an unknown maker.

*c1950* *3.25in (8cm) long*

**£20-30** **ROX**

A 1950s Marx Bros colour lithographed tinplate wind-up 'Wee Scottie' dog toy, with rubber tail and ears.

*5in (13cm) long*

**£40-60** **DCC**

A Wade Whimsie cast ceramic 'Jock' Scottie dog figurine, from Walt Disney's 'Lady & The Tramp'.

*Four characters from the Disney film were initially produced as Wade Whimsies in 1956, including Jock who was not wearing a coat. When Wade realised the character was wearing a coat in the film, they updated their design and released a second version wearing a blue tartan coat in early 1957. A third version was released in late 1957 with a green coat, as seen here.*

*c1957* *1.5in (4cm) high*

**£22-28** **LG**

A 1950s boxed set of playing cards showing Scottie dogs.

*3.5in (9cm) high*

**£30-50** **ROX**

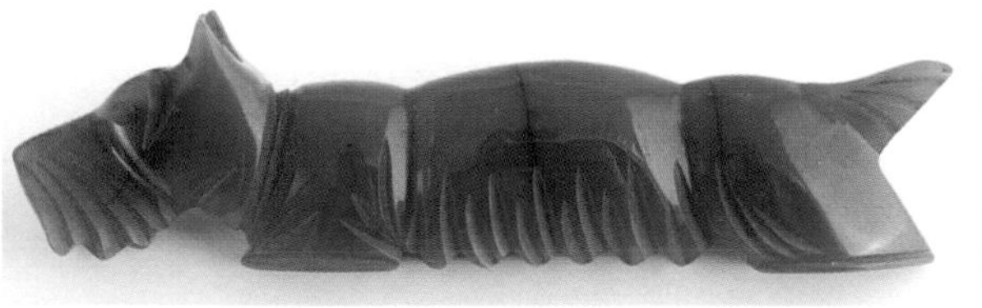

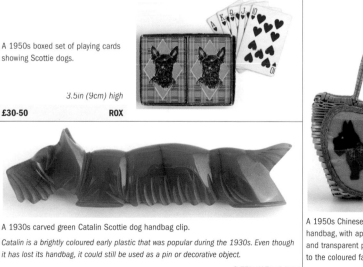

A 1930s carved green Catalin Scottie dog handbag clip.

*Catalin is a brightly coloured early plastic that was popular during the 1930s. Even though it has lost its handbag, it could still be used as a pin or decorative object.*

*6.75in (17cm) long*

**£100-150** **ROX**

A 1950s Chinese Mr Jonas woven wicker handbag, with applied cut-felt Scottie dogs and transparent plastic covering, with label to the coloured fabric interior.

*12.25in (31cm) wide*

**£60-90** **ROX**

An early 1930s seated Scottie dog pin, with a painted red collar and tongue.

*2in (5cm) wide*

**£25-35** **ABAA**

A 1940s French small orange ceramic Scottie dog pin, with hand-painted detail and metal mounts.

*1.5in (3.5cm) wide*

**£15-20** **ROX**

A 1940s red painted ceramic Scottie dog pin, with metal mounts and collar.

*2.75in (7cm) long*

**£30-40** **ROX**

A 1930s unsigned brass pin in the form of a Scottie dog's head smoking a pipe, with inset coloured diamanté and faux turquoise, the pipe topped with red diamante.

*2.5in (5cm) high*

**£20-25** **BY**

A late 1940s Japanese painted celluloid Scottie dog pin, marked "Occupied Japan".

*2.75in (7cm) wide*

**£70-100** **DCC**

A 1930s metal bracelet, with applied cast phenolic Scottie dogs, named 'Bill' and 'Bull', with hand-painted details.

*2.5in (6.5cm) wide*

**£80-120** **ROX**

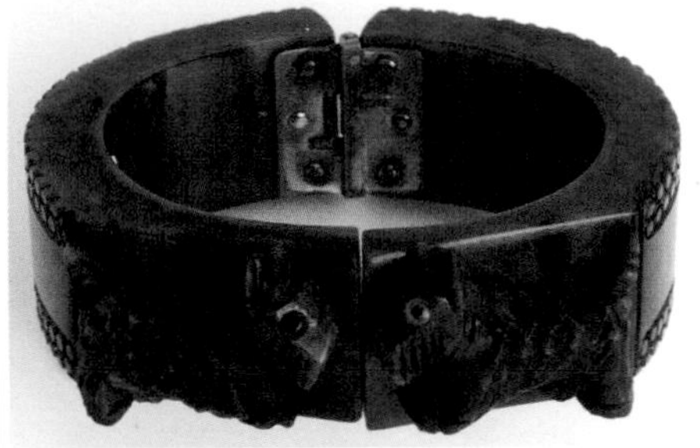

A 1930s green and yellow mottled cast phenolic hinged bracelet with two applied carved Scottie dogs.

*3in (7.5cm) wide*

**£120-180** **BY**

A 1930s red leather bracelet, with a gilt metal clasp and three applied hand-painted plastic Scottie dog heads.

*7in (18cm) long*

**£80-100** **ECLEC**

## FIND OUT MORE...

**Scottie Showcase**, *by Donna Newton, published by Country Scottie, 1988.*

**A Treasury of Scottie Dog Collectables**, *by Candace Sten Davies & Patricia Baugh, published by Collector Books, 1999.*

## COLLECTORS' NOTES

- Although sewing tools have been produced for centuries, the 19th century provides the largest market for collectors today due to the huge expansion in production and variety during this period. Sewing also became a popular and 'virtuous' hobby for the Victorian lady. Earlier examples are usually rare, partly as most were worn or damaged over time, or simply lost.
- Victorian tools were made from a variety of materials, including wood, metals such as silver and pressed brass, and even glass. Mother-of-pearl was very popular, with many sewing set components being carved from this material. Mauchlineware and Tartanware items are also commonly found. Silver tools were popular during the Edwardian era as the price of silver dropped.
- Many of the small, finely crafted pieces available today come from the complete, fitted sewing boxes that were available to the Victorian lady, and that have since been broken up. Many of these were French. Always examine all the pieces in a sewing box to ensure that they are original, although complete, original sets, particularly large ones, are scarce. Correctly sized and matching replacement tools can be challenging to find.
- Many homemade pieces can also be found, and can display a charm lacking in factory-made pieces. Thimble production boomed in the 19th century. Names such as James Horner, Charles Iles and James Fenton are sought-after, as is the steel-lined 'Dorcas' range. Thimbles made from precious metals, or that have been finely decorated are typically highly desirable.
- As inexpensive sewing machines and better quality factory made needlework became more readily available in the early decades of the 20th century, the demand for of sewing tools declined sharply. As the variety available is so diverse, collectors often focus on a single type of item, such as thimbles, compendia or needlecases. Look for finely crafted pieces in precious materials, as these will command the highest values.

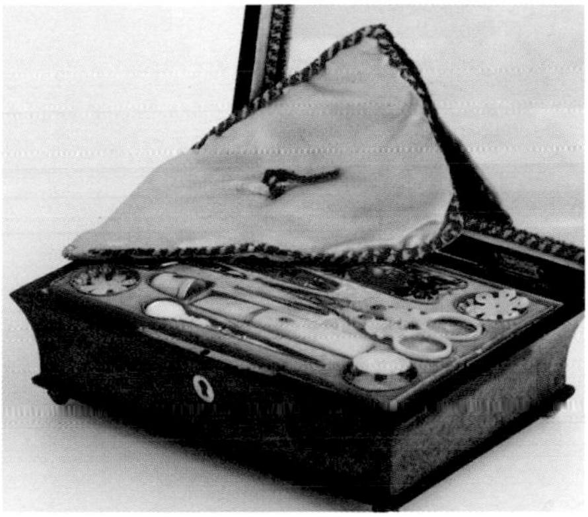

A French 'Palais Royal' amboyna wood sewing casket, with fitted interior holding sewing tools, the lid interior with mirror.

*The sewing tools all bear the flower insignia of the Palais Royal, which was a 19thC Parisian shopping arcade. The box and tools are all of fine quality, with many of the tools being made from carved mother-of-pearl. These are typical features of Palais Royal boxes which are the most desirable sewing tool boxes among collectors.*

*c1820* *7.5in (19cm) wide*

**£1,200-1,800** **RDR**

A late 19thC Swiss Alpineware carved pitch pine and beech wood sewing compendium.

*5in (13cm) high*

**£80-100** **JSC**

A 19thC rosewood sewing compendium, the turned handle with reel support, the top with a pair of pin cushions flanking a thimble, above a frieze drawer to hold further tools.

*5in (12.5cm) high*

**£150-200** **WW**

A turned wood 'The Voyage Sewing Necessaire' sewing kit, containing Sheffield steel folding scissors and other tools, with transfer-printed wording, patented in 1896.

*2.5in (6.5cm) high*

**£50-70** **BCAC**

A French miniature brown leather covered Gladstone bag sewing kit, opening to reveal a blue silk-lined compartment, the lid opening to reveal section for sewing tools, including gilt scissors, ivory thimble, pin holder, reel and cotton thread.

*c1880* *2in (5cm) high*

**£300-400** **BONC**

An early Tunbridgeware whitewood sewing clamp, the cylindrical body painted with stylized leaves and printed with a view of Brighton Pavilion.

*Tunbridgeware was a popular form of 19thC souvenir ware, produced in Tunbridge Wells, Kent, using small squares of wood in a mosaic pattern. Tape measures are frequently fitted into the cylinder of these clamps. They can be found with many different transfer-printed and hand-painted patterns typically including different town names.*

*7.5in (19cm) high*

**£350-450** **B**

An early 19thC white wood sewing clamp, the circular body painted with a laurel wreath and with a label reading 'A Trifle from Tunbridge Wells', the latter scratched but lettering clearly legible, some paint damage.

*6in (15cm) long*

**£250-350** **B**

A Tunbridgeware miniature sewing companion, with stickware collars, central recessed band for thread and red pin cushion.

*1.5in (4cm) high*

**£60-80** **B**

A Regency rosewood sewing clamp, with brown velvet-covered pincushion.

*The pincushion unscrews to reveal storage for a thimble.*

*8.25in (21cm) high*

**£120-160** **JSC**

A German needlecase, the Oriental-style doll's head with inset glass eyes and pierced ears, sewn onto a felt and fabric needlecase, woven with gold thread to look like an Oriental robe.

*c1910* *7.5in (19cm) long*

**£200-250** **MP**

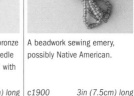

An American 19thC cast bronze hand and brown velvet needle case, the 'cuff and sleeve' with applied chainlink thread.

*4.5in (11.5cm) long*

**£200-250** **BCAC**

A beadwork sewing emery, possibly Native American.

*c1900* *3in (7.5cm) long*

**£40-50** **BCAC**

A Tunbridgeware whitewood sewing companion, the cylindrical body with internal tape measure and pin cushion to one side, the underside with coloured print of York Place, Tunbridge Wells, with green ribbon necklace.

*2in (5cm) diam*

**£180-220** **B**

A silver James Fenton thimble, with diamond shapes and punched dots, size 10, with Birmingham hallmark for 1899.

*1899*

**£30-40** **CBE**

An American Sterling 'Scenic' thimble, with hand-engraved scene of a village and punched dot design, with un-engraved cartouche.

*Thimbles with scenes of buildings are typical of American thimble design.*

*c1880s*

**£30-40** **CBE**

## A CLOSER LOOK AT A THIMBLE

*A John Piercy was listed in the 1818 edition of Wright's Triennial Directory as a manufacturer and patent holder of tortoiseshell thimbles, located at Snowhill, Birmingham.*

*Gold thimbles are much rarer than those in other metals, including silver, as their high original cost meant far fewer were made and sold.*

*In 1816, Piercy received patent no.4077 for thimbles made from tortoiseshell or horn and embellished with metal.*

*It is very finely made, particularly the filigree trellis area, but lacks its liner which was probably made from tortoiseshell. If it had retained it, its value may have risen over 50 per cent.*

An extremely rare George III 'Piercy's Patent' gold thimble, with a row of trellis piercing around the base, and an oval cartouche with script initials "EH", lacking liner.

*1815-20* *1.75in (2cm) high*

**£1,200-1,800** **WW**

A steel cored Charles Horner 'Dorcas' thimble, with plain band and repeated star design.

*This variation of the maker's mark indicates it was made after 1905.*

**£20-30** **CBE**

A 1930s German silver and enamel thimble, with rose motives, the crown inset with blue glass.

*This type of thimble was made until the 1970s, with quality of the enamelling and decoration becoming poorer later.*

**£40-60** **CBE**

A Scottish 'MacBeth' Tartanware hat-shaped thimble holder, unscrewing to reveal a metal thimble.

*c1870* *1.5in (3.5cm) high*

**£250-300** **RDR**

An early to mid-19thC beadwork on bone egg-shaped thimble case, with bone thimble.

*1.5in (4cm) high*

**£100-120** **JSC**

A German Gritzner 'Selecta R' sewing machine, mounted on a wooden stand, finished in black with transfer-printed gilt scrolling decoration.

*c1912*

**£40-60** **ATK**

A Canadian Wanzer & Co. of Hamilton small cast-iron sewing machine, with wear to gilt transfer decoration and original marble base.

*Wanzer was founded by Richard Wanzer in Hamilton, Ontario in 1858. By 1875, over 500,000 machines had been made. The company closed in 1892.*

*c1890*

**£80-120** **ATK**

## A CLOSER LOOK AT A SEWING MACHINE

*Grover & Baker was founded by tailors William C. Grover and William E. Baker. The company was active between 1851 and 1875 in Boston, Massachusetts.*

*In 1856 the company received a patent for a portable machine in a fitted case.*

*By the end of 1856, the company had reached serial number 7,000, meaning this this example was made in the first year of production.*

*The company was a founder of the US 'Sewing Machine Combination' syndicate that controlled the US sewing machine industry from 1856-77.*

An early Grover & Baker portable sewing machine, with original fitted wooden case, serial number 5,664.

*1856*

**£1,200-1,800** **ATK**

An English James Weir single-thread chain-stitch sewing machine, with cast iron base with moulded decoration.

*c1876*

**£120-180** **ATK**

A German Favorit colour transfer-printed tinplate child's sewing machine, marked "Made in Germany, British Zone".

*c1951*

**£80-120** **ATK**

A German 'Casige Nr. 1050' lithographed metal child's sewing machine, with rare line and eagle gilt transfer decoration, marked "British Zone".

*c1953*

**£60-80** **ATK**

An English toy sewing machine, wood-mounted, similar to the 'Singer 20', excellent condition.

*c1952*

**£50-80** **ATK**

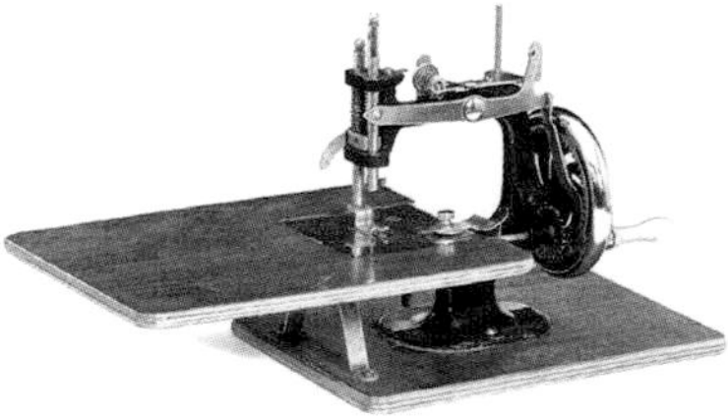

### FIND OUT MORE...

**Antique Needlework Tools and Embroideries**, *by Nerylla Taunton, published by Antique Collectors Club, 1997.*

**A Collector's Guide to Thimbles**, *by Bridget McConnel, published by Wellfleet Press, 1990.*

## COLLECTORS' NOTES

- With today's fad for all things 'retro' looking set to continue, the visual appeal and design of much 1960s and '70s memorabilia is usually the most important concern. Consider the form, colour, pattern and material. Bright, clashing colours, psychedelic patterns and futuristic 'space age' forms are typical. Some pieces followed the organic asymmetry of 1950s design, with plastic becoming increasingly important. Pop Art was an influential artistic movement and its effects can be seen across many areas.
- The work of leading designers is usually the most desirable and valuable, but even un-named designs can be desirable if they capture the look of the decades. Nostalgia is an important factor and products that inspire fond memories will typically find a ready market. As well as representing a 'new look' in post-war Britain, many pieces were aimed at convenience, with a new informality in many young homes. This was also backed up by a certain 'irreverence' for authority.
- Great Britain, and particularly 'Swinging London', was an important force, with Union Jacks and military themes adding to the growth in pop music and fashion that was finding fans across the world. Many pieces were not made to last, so always consider condition. A piece in truly mint condition will always be worth more than one with wear or damage.
- Always look for fine quality production and design as these factors are likely to lead to a higher value.

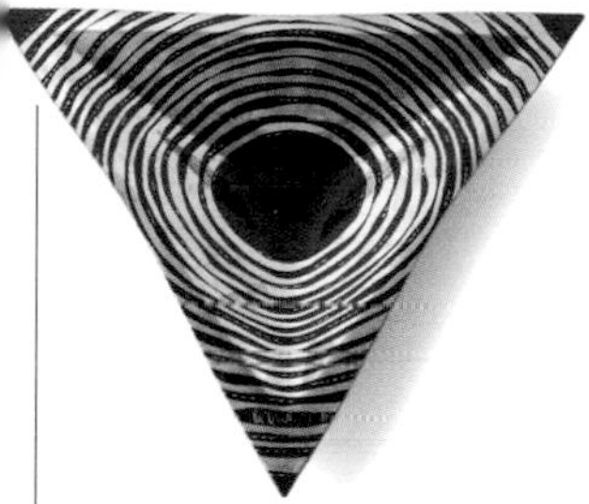

A 1970s Lu Martinson slump moulded triangular dish, with gold transfer-printed decoration.

*15.75in (40cm) wide*

**£10-15** **NOR**

A 1970s Lu Martinson slump moulded triangular dish, from the 'Dot' series, with gold transfer-printed decoration.

*11.75in (30cm) wide*

**£18-22** **NOR**

A set of transfer-printed tin drinks coasters, unmarked.

*These are very similar in design to the coasters designed by Ian Logan, but do not bear his name. See this section in the 2007 edition of this book for examples by Logan.*

*3.75in (9.5cm) diam*

**£10-15** **MTS**

A 1950s Pilkington's Royal Lancastrian ceramic free-form bowl, designed by Mitzi Cunliffe in c1950.

*Sculptor Mitzi Cunliffe (1918-2006) is best known for the face mask design of the BAFTA award, which she produced in 1955. She also designed numerous public sculptures and textiles for David Whitehead. Her strongly coloured asymmetric organic designs with black exteriors for Pilkington attempted to revive a company in serious decline after the war.*

*10.5in (26.5cm) diam*

**£150-200** **REN**

A 1950s Chinese 'bridge' themed cigarette lighter and ashtray.

*Transfer patterns of polka dots and playing card motifs were highly fashionable in the 1950s.*

*3.5in (9cm) high*

**£30-40** **MA**

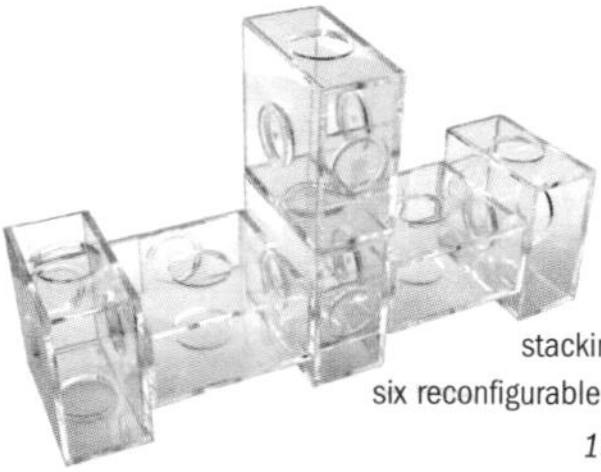

A 1970s Italian Guzzini clear, colourless plastic stacking unit, comprising six reconfigurable component parts.

*19.25in (49cm) wide*

**£18-22** **GAZE**

"Intro", issue no. 1, September 23rd 1967.

**£35-45** **GAZE**

## A CLOSER LOOK AT A BABE RAINBOW PRINT

*This image has become an icon of British Pop art, and is screen-printed on to tin, later editions are on paper.*

*It was commissioned in 1968 by Dodo Designs of London, who made many plaques printed with amusing designs and wording, which were sold in Carnaby St and other fashionable or tourist destinations.*

*Babe Rainbow was a fictional lady wrestler – the model's real name was Lucy Maloney, and the reverse bears her printed 'biography'.*

*It was produced in a limited edition of 10,000 and was intended to be sold for £1 each. This is from an un-numbered edition of 1,000.*

A 'Babe Rainbow' screenprint on tin, designed by by Peter Blake, commissioned and distributed by Dodo Designs.

*26in (66cm) high*

**£250-350** **DIM**

A late 1950s four-tier occasional table, with central column supporting four tiers on four turned legs.

*Both the shape of the tiers and the colours used are highly evocative of the 1950s, when such modern but affordable furniture quite unlike that of previous decades was extremely fashionable. This would have been bought as a 'flat-pack', for assembly at home.*

*23.5in (60cm) high*

**£100-150** **MA**

A late 1950s table lamp, with plastic shade.

*The shade and legs bring rockets, Sputnik and molecular design to mind – all were popular inspirations during the forward-looking 1950s and '60s.*

*39in (99cm) high*

**£50-80** **MA**

An American Howard Miller aluminium and walnut 'Starburst' clock, designed by George Nelson and Irving Harper in 1950, with Howard Miller label.

*This was from a series of clocks designed by Nelson. Since 2001, the design has been produced by Vitra.*

*18.5in (46cm) diam*

**£120-180** **FRE**

A 1960s Swiss Le Porte-Echappement Universel red plastic brass and metal 'P106 - Secticon' table clock, designed by Angelo Mangiarotti in 1956.

*9.5in (24cm) high*

**£80-120** **QU**

A Thomas Dam troll in a blue dress, marked "Th Dam 1979".

*Danish Dam trolls are the most desirable brand as well as being the original. This example is very large.*

*3in (33cm) high*

**£70-100** **MG**

SIXTIES & SEVENTIES

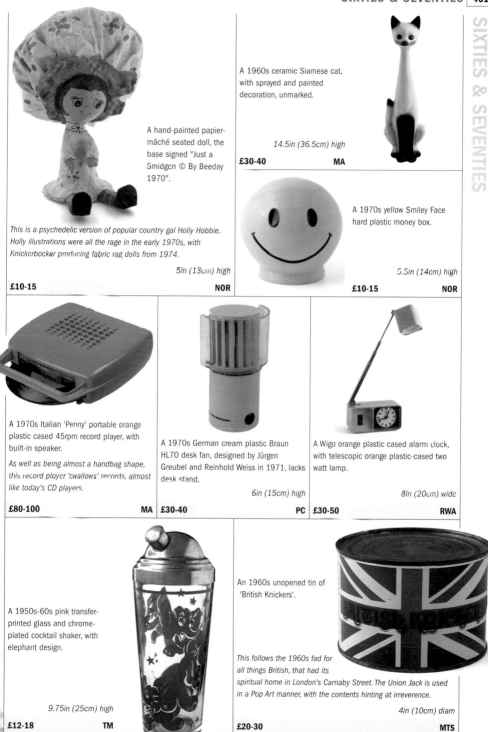

A hand-painted papier-mâché seated doll, the base signed "Just a Smidgen © By Beeday 1970".

*This is a psychedelic version of popular country gal Holly Hobbie. Holly illustrations were all the rage in the early 1970s, with Knickerbocker producing fabric rag dolls from 1974.*

*5in (13cm) high*

**£10-15** **NOR**

A 1960s ceramic Siamese cat, with sprayed and painted decoration, unmarked.

*14.5in (36.5cm) high*

**£30-40** **MA**

A 1970s yellow Smiley Face hard plastic money box.

*5.5in (14cm) high*

**£10-15** **NOR**

A 1970s Italian 'Penny' portable orange plastic cased 45rpm record player, with built-in speaker.

*As well as being almost a handbag shape, this record player 'swallows' records, almost like today's CD players.*

**£80-100** **MA**

A 1970s German cream plastic Braun HL70 desk fan, designed by Jürgen Greubel and Reinhold Weiss in 1971, lacks desk stand.

*6in (15cm) high*

**£30-40** **PC**

A Wigo orange plastic cased alarm clock, with telescopic orange plastic-cased two watt lamp.

*8in (20cm) wide*

**£30-50** **RWA**

A 1950s-60s pink transfer-printed glass and chrome-plated cocktail shaker, with elephant design.

*9.75in (25cm) high*

**£12-18** **TM**

An 1960s unopened tin of 'British Knickers'.

*This follows the 1960s fad for all things British, that had its spiritual home in London's Carnaby Street. The Union Jack is used in a Pop Art manner, with the contents hinting at irreverence.*

*4in (10cm) diam*

**£20-30** **MTS**

A 1950s English Dunhill 'Bumper' tankard-shaped table lighter, with polished chromium finish.

*3.5in (9cm) high*

**£30-50** **BLO**

A 1960s boxed Zippo pocket lighter, advertising the 'Hoover Electric Company', boxed.

*Lighter 2.25in (5.5cm) high*

**£35-45** **ML**

## A CLOSER LOOK AT A DUNHILL LIGHTER

*The patent for the design was applied for by Vernon Dunhill in 1938, just before the outbreak of WWII.*

*The lighter has a semi-automatic movement that strikes the flame when the cover of the book is opened.*

*Examples are rare, but those with the inner slipcase, and particularly the outer cover, are even rarer.*

*The spine of the book is usually worn through use, this example is in excellent, crisp condition.*

A rare English Dunhill 'The Light' book-shaped lighter, in burgundy morocco leather with gilt edges, with black card slipcase and red card outer cover with gilt lettering, in excellent condition.

*c1939* *4.25in (11cm) high*

**£400-500** **BLO**

An American Beauty Sterling cigarette case, hand-engraved with bird and foliage design.

*4in (10cm) high*

**£80-120** **NOR**

A 1930s-40s aluminium Machine Age pipe.

*Aluminium was a popular material after WWII as large supplies had been built up by the military during the war.*

*5.5in (14cm) long*

**£30-50** **BB**

An American Mayer China-Minners match holder and striker, designed by Alexander Girard for the La Fonda Del Sol restaurant in New York.

*The entire interior of this restaurant was designed by Girard, who is better known for his textiles for Herman Miller.*

*3.75in (9.5cm) high*

**£180-220** **HLM**

A European hand-painted majolica Native American tobacco jar.

*Many of these were made in Germany. As they were not airtight, their function was primarily decorative, rather than functional on a long-term basis.*

*c1900* *8in (20cm) high*

**£120-180** **TPF**

## COLLECTORS' NOTES

- The historical importance and inherent sense of danger and heroism associated with space travel has caused the market for space memorabilia to increase dramatically over recent years. There is also a limited supply of authentic pieces from certain flights, particularly earlier ones, with many of the best pieces already in private or public collections. Nevertheless, as the market for these early pieces dries up, collectors move on to later important flights.
- Items actually flown on space missions are at the peak of the market in terms of interest and value. Provenance is key, so always buy from a reputable source. Items such as flags, patches and personal items owned and used by astronauts tend to be the most desirable, as they are appealing to display and are only available in highly limited numbers. Some are sometimes unique. Wear and tear is expected and does not reduce value.
- Commemorative pieces are generally more affordable, with pieces produced around the time of the flight being the most desirable. Look for items that are evocative of the flight, and try to focus on important missions. Try to buy in as close to mint condition as possible as many items were mass-produced. If an item is signed, always ask for a certificate of authenticity.
- Russian memorabilia is usually less desirable and therefore more affordable than American items. This is due to the fact that cosmonauts were allowed to take items home after flights, and they have now reached the general market. Astronauts were not allowed to do this and had strict limits on what could be taken. Collectors are also generally less familiar with Russian missions, and language difficulties make it hard to learn more about a mission or piece.

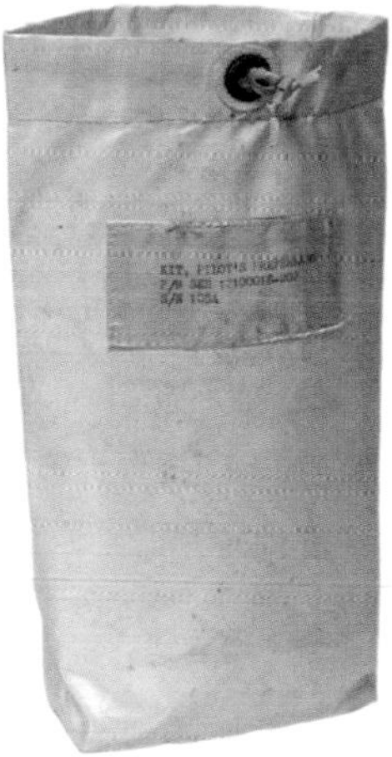

Pete Conrad's 'PPK', flown on Apollo 12, with printed label reading "Kit, Pilot's Preference / P/N SEB 12100018-202 / S/N 1054".

*Astronauts are only allowed to carry a limited number of mementos or personal possessions into space due to weight restrictions, hence the small size of this bag. They are known as 'Personal Preference Kits (PPK) or Official Flight Kits (OFK), and frequently contain flags or patches. Conrad was commander of this flight, which was the second to land on the moon.*

*1969* *9in (23cm) high*

**£1,400-1,800** **AGI**

A Goody aluminium comb, owned and used by Richard Gordon and flown on Apollo 12.

*1969*

**£1,400-1,800** **AGI**

A flown white Beta cloth and orange cellophane-covered Space Shuttle cushion, sewn and hand-stamped several times 'Scrap', with ID numbers and an inspection hand-stamp attached to the cellophane.

*18in (45.5cm) long*

**£70-90** **AGI**

A B.F. Goodrich right-hand inboard Space Shuttle tyre, used on Columbia on the STS 73 flight, showing the expected skid marks from a hard landing.

*1995* *40in (101.5cm) diam*

**£450-550** **AGI**

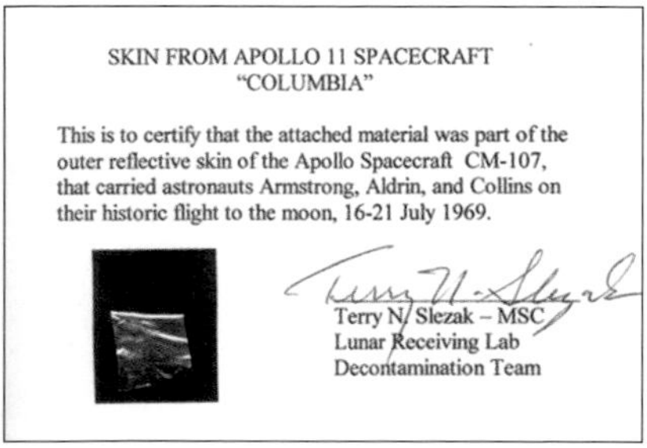

SKIN FROM APOLLO 11 SPACECRAFT
"COLUMBIA"

This is to certify that the attached material was part of the outer reflective skin of the Apollo Spacecraft CM-107, that carried astronauts Armstrong, Aldrin, and Collins on their historic flight to the moon, 16-21 July 1969.

Terry N. Slezak – MSC
Lunar Receiving Lab
Decontamination Team

A piece of Apollo 11 flown gold foil, mounted on a green 'Slezak' certificate of authenticity with commemorative wording relating to the moon landing.

*1969* *Foil 0.5in (1.5cm) high*

**£120-180** **AGI**

An American Apollo 11 colour printed commemorative poster

*1969* *40in (101cm) high*

**£120-180** **CL**

An Italian 'Gagarin U.R.S.S. Stazione Spaziale K9' two-sheet poster, promoting an Italian documentary, linen backed, minor defects.

*1966* *78.5in (199.5cm) wide*

**£500-600** **SWA**

An Italian 'Gli Eroi Della Stratosfera' film poster, for the Italian release of "On the Threshold of Space", printed by G. Scarpati, Naples, linen backed.

*1956* *55in (139.5cm) high*

**£220-280** **SWA**

A Czechoslovakian Oldrich Pelcak signed copy of his hardback book, with dust jacket, inscribed "To Colonel Demin, L.S. for memory about mutual work, from the author. Cosmonaut engineer Oldrich Pelcak. December 31, 1979".

*Pelcak (b.1943) flew on the Russian Soyuz 28 mission in 1978 and, along with Vladimír Remek, became the first cosmonauts who were neither American nor Russian.*

*c1979*

**£40-60** **AGI**

An American NASA Apollo 13 manned flight awareness poster, depicting the original crew of Lovell, Mattingly and Haise, marked "MSFC.MFA.P.13.69" in the lower right.

*1969* *11in (28cm) high*

**£15-25** **AGI**

'Life' magazine, July 16th 1966, containing a six-page pictorial of the first colour pictures of the lunar surface taken by Surveyor, modest edge faults.

*1966*

**£15-20** **AGI**

A Mercury MR-3 USAF colour negative, showing the launch of the Redstone rocket and Freedom 7 capsule piloted by Alan Shepard, in original sleeve.

*With this historic flight, Shepard became the first American, and the second human, to travel into space.*

*1961* *5in (12.5cm) high*

**£120-180** **AGI**

An English language Apollo-Soyuz Test Project (ASTP) enamelled 'Press' badge.

*This is the rarest of the badges produced for the mission due to the secret nature of the Soviet space program prior to this flight, which was the first human space flight jointly managed by two nations. This badge was also issued with Russian language wording, both are scarce and desirable.*

*1975* *2.5in (6.5cm) high*

**£100-150** **AGI**

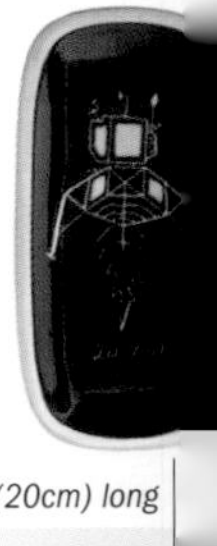

An English Jersey Pottery moon landing commemorative ceramic dish, with sgrafitto decoration of the Apollo landing module and date of the landing, the reverse painted "Jersey Pottery C.I.M."

*1969* *8in (20cm) long*

**£10-15** **GAZE**

## COLLECTORS' NOTES

- Cricket equipment has seen very few changes over the centuries, with the exception of cricket bats having been curved rather than straight before the mid-18thC. As a result, it is primarily the personal association or historical importance of a piece of equipment that dictates interest and value. Items bearing signatures of famous players, or that were used in or commemorate notable matches are typical.
- Most memorabilia dates from the mid-19thC onwards and ceramics, accessories, tickets, programmes and photographs are popular, adding variety to a collection. 'Wisden's Cricketers Almanac', published annually since 1864, continues to form the backbone of many collections. Early examples can be rare as few copies survive. Condition is also a key factor.
- In general, the more notable the player, or the more historically important the event, the greater the value. Notable players to look out for include Geoffrey Boycott (b.1940), Gary Sobers (b.1936), Don Bradman (1908-2001) and the legendary and instantly recognisable W.G. Grace (1848-1915), but even items connected to modern players or more recent events can still fetch high sums.
- When considering ceramics, metalware or other commemorative cricket themed items, consider the quality, maker and theme, as well as any player or match shown. The higher the quality, the more valuable it is likely to be. Early commemorative pieces from the mid-19th century can also be desirable. Eye appeal and how well a piece displays is also important.

A New Hall Pottery water jug, printed with a coloured portrait of Jack Hobbs walking out to bat and a facsimile signature, with a bat, ball and stump crest to the reverse, restored.

*c1930 6.5in (16cm) high*

**£300-400** **DN**

A New Hall Pottery water jug, printed with a portrait of Don Bradman batting and a facsimile signature, with a bat, ball and stump crest to reverse.

*New Hall Pottery, based in Hanley, Staffordshire produced fine quality ceramics from 1899-1956. During the 1930s, they produced a range of shapes, including jugs and plaques decorated with detailed and realistic lithographic transfers of notable players. At least six players are know to appear on a variety of shapes, and the range is popular with collectors.*

*c1930 6.5in (16cm) high*

**£60-700** **DN**

A New Hall Pottery water jug, decorated with a raised figure of Jack Hobbs playing a cut to one side and a head and shoulder profile study to the reverse.

*This piece is unrecorded and, with the exception of the handle, is unlike the normal style of New Hall jug. Perhaps this was a trial piece that was not put into production, a possibility that its undecorated nature would also support.*

*c1930 6in (15cm) high*

**£280-320** **DN**

A New Hall Pottery water jug, printed with an oval portrait of Herbert Sutcliffe going out to bat and a facsimile signature, with a bat, a ball and a stump crest to the reverse, restored.

*c1930 6.5in (16cm) high*

**£220-280** **DN**

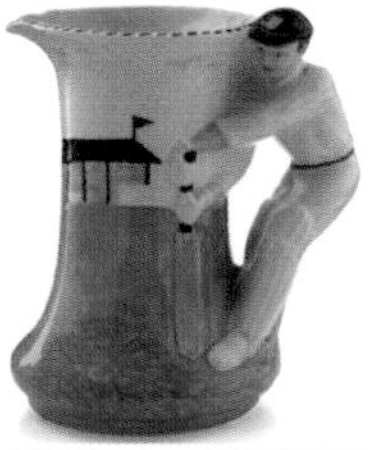

A 1960s Burleighware ironstone jug, the handle modelled in the form of a cricketer, moulded into a waisted jug, and Burleigh Ironstone stamp to the base.

*7.5in (18cm) high*

**£150-200** **DN**

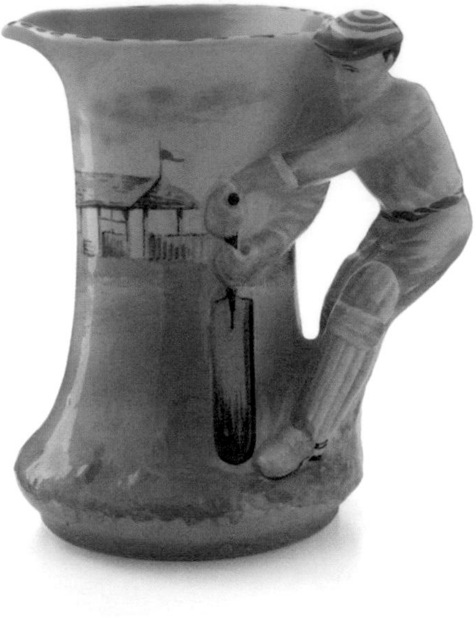

A Burleighware jug, the handle modelled in the form of a cricketer, moulded into a waisted jug, yellow and green background, and Beehive stamp to base.

*Burgess & Leigh are well-known for their yellow-bodied jugs with shaped, figural handles. Most are in the form of birds or other animals, making this cricketer rare. The sense of movement in his curving form is also notably different from the other, more static, designs. Also note how the painting is better in this example than the item on the previous page.*

*c1930* *7.5in (19cm) high*

**£1,000-1,500** **DN**

A Leeds creamware jug, moulded and decorated in relief with William Clark, Fuller Pilch, Charles Box, with their names beneath, the base faintly impressed "Leeds Pottery".

*These scarce jugs are copies of those made to commemorate a match between Nottinghamshire played Australia on May 20th-22nd 1878, which Nottinghamshire won.*

*c1920* *7in (17.5cm) high*

**£1,000-1,500** **DN**

A Royal Doulton 'The Boss' jug, printed with a boy wearing an umpire's coat with a cricket bat, crest 'The All Black Team', and Doulton backstamp and D2864 to base, repaired.

*7.5in (19cm) high*

**£450-550** **DN**

A Victorian Staffordshire loving cup, printed with two scenes of a cricket match, hand-coloured in yellow, green and burgundy.

*c1850* *4.5in (11.5cm) high*

**£180-220** **DN**

A Devonware loving jug, probably by Torquay Pottery, with a figure of W.G. Grace with raised bat and stumps, inscribed "He's The Man To Make The Pace So His Exploits We'll Sing. Here's To Thee Our Century Grace Who Better Would You Have".

*7.5in (19cm) high*

**£700-1,000** **DN**

A Yarmouth brown slipware jug, decorated with a scene of a batsman and wicket keeper, and the Isle of Wight and with grass-like motifs.

*5in (12.5cm) high*

**£50-70** **DN**

A Victorian Staffordshire jug, by Ford & Riley, printed with a cricket match and football scene, each of four players, with oval F. & R. Sports to base.

*c1882-93* *4in (10cm) high*

**£150-200** **DN**

A Royal Doulton 'Next Man In' coffee cup, printed with a boy sitting on a cricket bat, to the reverse the crest "The All Black Team", Royal Doulton backstamp and "E4336", vertical crack from rim.

*2in (5cm) diam*

**£350-450** **DN**

A Paragon nursery mug, decoration designed by Beatrice Mallett, printed with coloured figures of two boys playing cricket, and to the reverse "It's Tom's and Harry's fondest dream to be in their school cricket team", with Paragon stamp and "636".

*The colourway and style of the figures is similar to popular illustrator Mabel Lucie Attwell's designs for Shelley. Like Attwell, Mallett also produced illustrations of chubby children, which were reproduced on ceramics, in books and on postcards.*

*2.75in (7cm) high*

**£25-35** **DN**

A 1960s Sandland china mug, printed in green with a 19thC young boy cricketer, full-length holding a bat, Sandland stamp to base with impressed "1012".

*4in (10cm) high*

**£50-80** **DN**

A Victorian Staffordshire mug, printed and hand-coloured, with two scenes showing a cricket match in progress, and crossed bats and stumps to handle.

*3.25in (8cm) high*

**£150-200** **DN**

A Staffordshire mug, printed in claret with Victor Trumper of Australia and Archie MacLaren of England within an oval, "Australia and England 1905".

*This is a particularly rare and desirable mug, commemorating the 35 first class matches and five test matches played by Australia in England in 1905. Trumper (1877-1915) was a famous Australian batsman known for the stylishness of his batting, and was also Wisden cricketer of the year in 1903.*

*4in (10cm) high*

**£1,800-2,200** **DN**

A limited edition Wade Taunton Cider single-handled court mug, from an edition of 500, based on the original by Ford & Riley.

*5in (12.5cm) high*

**£40-60** **DN**

A Victorian Staffordshire jug, decorated in relief with figures of Box, Pilch and Clarke, hand-coloured and with floral motifs in lustre, with a strap handle.

*c1840* *3.5in (9cm) high*

**£60-80** **DN**

A Doulton Lambeth stoneware mug, moulded in relief with figures of Robert Abel, Sammy Woods and Gregor MacGregor, by John Broad, stamped to base "169", "O.P. & R.N." and "Rosetta Woods", restored.

*6in (15cm) high*

**£650-750** **DN**

A Victorian Staffordshire blue glazed mug, decorated in relief with three raised figures of Box, Pilch and Clarke, with a beaded rim.

*c1850-60* *3.5in (9cm) high*

**£80-120** **DN**

A Royal Worcester plate, with gilded facsimile signatures of the England and Australian teams for the 1953 Coronation Series, with a gilded date, the Ashes urn and a Worcester stamp to back.

*10in (25cm) diam*

**£350-450** **DN**

A Royal Worcester plate, with gilded facsimile signatures of the 1969 West Indies touring team, commemorating their visit to the Royal Worcester Porcelain Works, with "West Indies Cricket Team - 1969 Worcester May 5th", factory back stamp.

*10in (25cm) diam*

**£200-300** **DN**

A Royal Worcester plate, with a gilded rim, and gilded facsimile signatures of the 1938 Australians for their visit to the Royal Worcester porcelain works, 3rd May 1938.

*10in (25cm) diam*

**£450-550** **DN**

A Coalport commemorative plate, 'W.G. Grace Century Of Centuries', printed in puce with Grace's portrait to centre, Coalport stamp to back "In Commemoration of Dr. W.G. Grace's Century of Centuries 1866-1895", also in black "X1662".

*Grace is consistently popular with collectors, particularly in relation to well-made and decorated pieces that sum up his extraordinary career. This plate is rare in puce.*

*1895* *9in (23cm) diam*

**£1,200-1,800** **DN**

A limited edition Coalport 'W.G. Grace Century Of Centuries, 1895' commemorative plate, with Grace's portrait printed to the centre, the Coalport stamp to back "In commemoration of Dr. W.G. Grace's Century of Centuries 1866-1895", also in gold "X1662", in contemporary purpose made silk-lined red leather case, with gilt inscription "W.G. Grace Champion Cricketer".

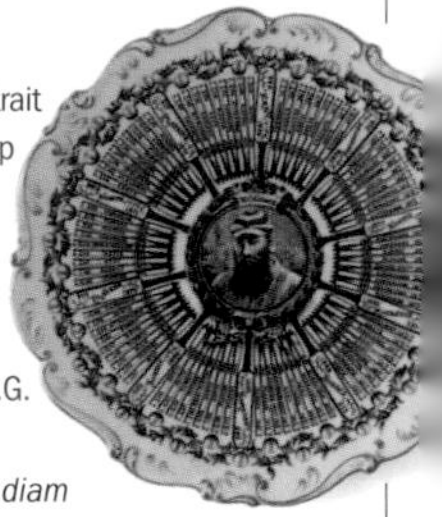

*9in (23cm) diam*

**£800-1,000** **DN**

A limited edition Coalport Century Of Centuries commemorative plate for Don Bradman, from an edition of 500, in a Coalport box.

*c1947* *9in (22.5cm) diam*

**£120-180** **DN**

A Windsor 'The Invincibles' commemorative plate, issued by the Bradford Exchange, to celebrate the 50th Anniversary of the 1948 Australian tour, with portraits of tourists to the rim and team celebrating to centre, with certificate, information pamphlet and original box.

*1998* *12in (30cm) diam*

**£250-350** **DN**

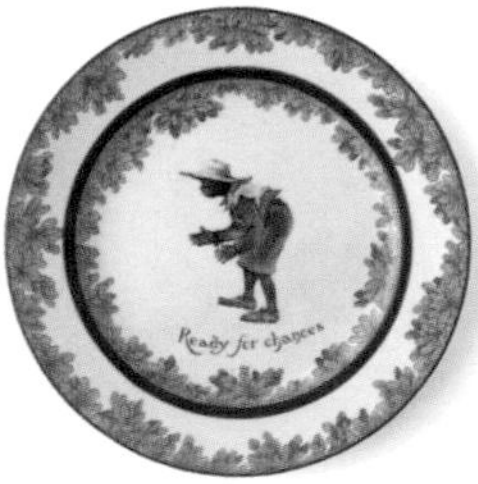


A Royal Doulton 'Ready For Chances' dessert plate, printed with a boy in a red polka dot shirt and a floppy hat, Doulton backstamp to base, repair to rim, small chips.

*8.5in (21.5cm) diam*

**£180-220** **DN**

A Devon Pottery 'Bodyline Series' studio pottery ashtray, inscribed "1933 Never Mind The Leg Theory, We Have The Ashes', impress mark to base "Devon Pottery & Bovey".

*3.5in (9cm) diam*

**£350-450** **DN**

A china crested model of cricket bag, printed with the arms of Wallasey.

*4in (10cm) wide*

**£22-28** **DN**

A china crested model of a cricket bag, printed with the arms of Paddington.

*4in (10cm) wide*

**£35-45** **DN**

An Arcadian bone china crested model of a submarine, printed with the arms of Lindfield, stamped "E4".

*3.5in (8.5cm) wide*

**£70-100** **DN**

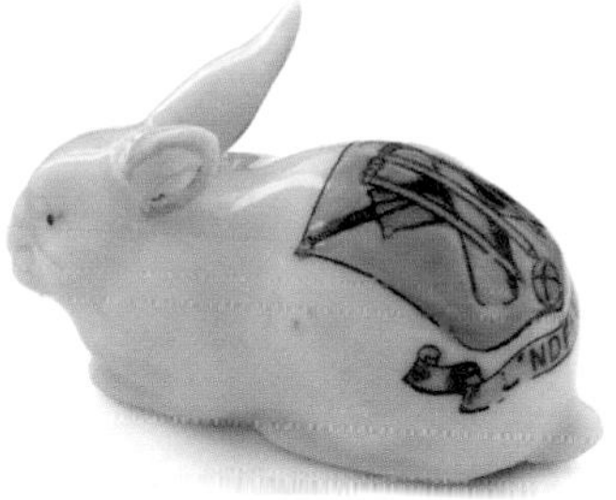

A Willow china crested model of a rabbit, printed with the arms of Lindfield, stamped to the base.

*c1900* *2.5in (6cm) high*

**£120-180** **DN**

A Swan china crested model of a cricket bat, printed with the arms of Torquay, various marks to the reverse.

*Crested ceramics were first made in the 1880s, and peaked in popularity between the 1900s and '20s. They were produced as souvenirs of towns and resorts by companies such as W.H. Goss. Arcadian and Grafton. A vast number of shapes, each decorated with a town's heraldic arms were issued, with the form or transfer on these examples being cricket themed.*

**£100-150** **DN**

A Willow Art china crested model of an elephant, printed with the arms of Lindfield, firing crack.

**£100-150** **DN**

A Carlton crested china figure of a batsman, walking with bat underarm, printed with the arms of the town of Chard for 1570, stamped to the base.

*4in (10cm) high*

**£150-200** **DN**

A Griffin china memorial cross, printed with the arms of Hambledon, 'The Cradle Of Cricket'.

*1900-09* *4.25in (11.5cm) high*

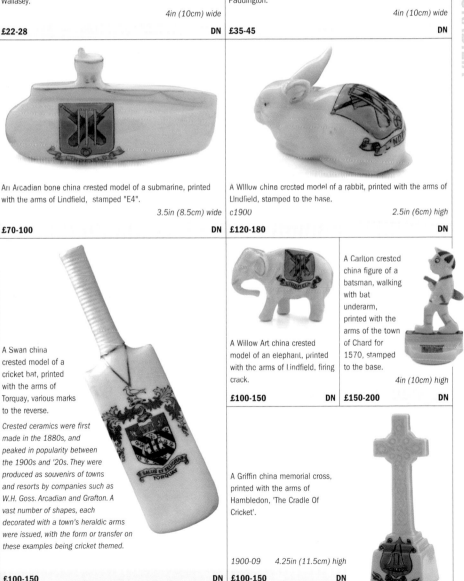

**£100-150** **DN**

A Victorian Staffordshire figure of a girl, modelled holding a cricket ball while leaning on stumps, restored.

*c1840* *5.25in (13cm) high*

**£100-150** **DN**

A Victorian Staffordshire figure of a young child holding a cricket bat, in smock-type dress and bloomers, with stumps, restored.

*6in (16cm) high*

**£120-180** **DN**

## A CLOSER LOOK AT A DOULTON FIGURINE

*George Tinworth (1843-1913) was the first designer employed by Doulton to produce art pottery, producing a series of plaques, figurines and vases from 1867 until his death.*

*This figurine is scarce and was produced in brown, as here, and coloured Doulton stoneware. The coloured version is usually of around the same value.*

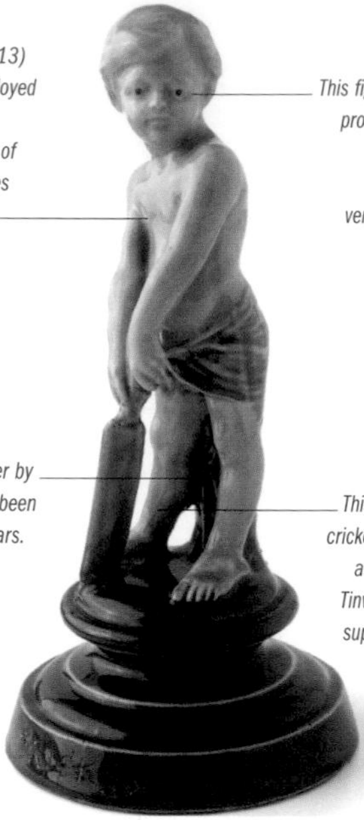

*His designs are sought-after by collectors and prices have been rising over the past few years.*

*This design would appeal to cricket memorabilia collectors as well as to collector's of Tinworth who appreciate his superb feeling for modelling the human form.*

A Doulton Lambeth boy cricketer, designed by George Tinworth, the boy dressed in a loin cloth, holding cricket bat, glazed in blue and cream, the plinth inscribed "Cricket" and with the monogram of George Tinworth, Doulton Lambeth impressed mark to base.

*c1890* *8.5in (21.5cm) high*

**£5,000-6,000** **DN**

A Minton porcelain figure of a young boy batsman, the base enamelled with the colours black, red and gold representing the motto of amateur cricket club 'I Zingari' 'Out of darkness, through fire, into light', with impressed marks for Minton and "2064".

*1880-90* *5in (12.5cm) high*

**£650-750** **DN**

A Victorian Staffordshire group of a batsman and wicket-keeper, with the batsman in a black hat and a yellow bat, the wicket-keeper with pink trousers, restored and repainted.

*6in (15cm) high*

**£650-750** **DN**

A Robinson & Leadbetter moulded parian figure of Dr. W.G. Grace, modelled full-length holding a bat, with a cap and a ball, stamped "R & L".

*This is a large and highly detailed, life-like figurine, by a notable maker who also made figurines of members of the Royal family and politicians.*

*c1880* *10.5in (27cm) high*

**£1,200-1,800** **DN**

A German bisque figure of Dr. W.G. Grace, the full-length figure wearing the M.C.C. cap.

*c1890* *9in (22.5cm) high*

**£150-200** **DN**

## A CLOSER LOOK AT A PAIR OF CRICKET FIGURINES

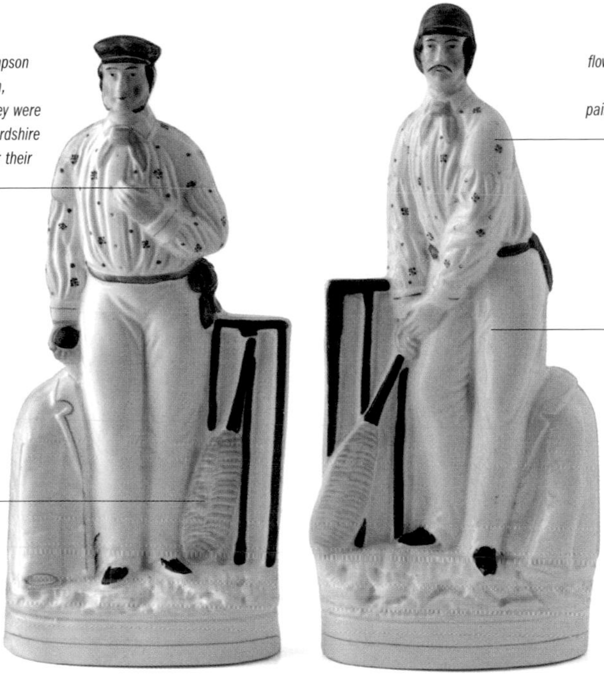

*They are probably by Sampson Smith, founded in Longton, Staffordshire in 1846. They were a notable maker of Staffordshire dogs and figures, however their work is rarely marked.*

*The figures are rarely found individually, but are even more scarce as a matched pair.*

*The faces and small flowers on their shirts are comparatively well-painted, unlike many later Staffordshire figures*

*As they are rare and early examples of Staffordshire figures, they appeal to collectors of Staffordshire figures as well as to collectors of cricket memorabilia, with competition driving the value higher.*

A pair of Staffordshire figures of a Julius Caesar and George Parr, with Caesar standing beside a set of stumps with a bat holding a ball, and with Parr standing before a wicket with a bat and his jacket to one side.

*c1865* *13in (32.5cm) high*

**£3,000-4,000** **DN**

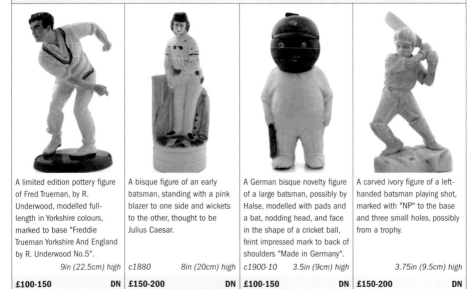

A limited edition pottery figure of Fred Trueman, by R. Underwood, modelled full-length in Yorkshire colours, marked to base "Freddie Trueman Yorkshire And England by R. Underwood No.5".

*9in (22.5cm) high*

**£100-150** **DN**

A bisque figure of an early batsman, standing with a pink blazer to one side and wickets to the other, thought to be Julius Caesar.

*c1880* *8in (20cm) high*

**£150-200** **DN**

A German bisque novelty figure of a large batsman, possibly by Halse, modelled with pads and a bat, nodding head, and face in the shape of a cricket ball, feint impressed mark to back of shoulders "Made in Germany".

*c1900-10* *3.5in (9cm) high*

**£100-150** **DN**

A carved ivory figure of a left-handed batsman playing shot, marked with "NP" to the base and three small holes, possibly from a trophy.

*3.75in (9.5cm) high*

**£150-200** **DN**

A New Hall Pottery oval plaque, printed with a portrait of George Duckworth keeping wicket, with a facsimile signature and a blue rim.

*c1930* *6.5in (16cm) high*

**£180-220** **DN**

A New Hall Pottery oval plaque, printed with a portrait of Don Bradman batting, with a facsimile signature and a brown rim with small firing crack.

*c1930* *6.5in (16cm) high*

**£350-450** **DN**

A Victorian porcelain stand, printed with a scene of a batsman and a wicket keeper, registered design mark no. 503470 for 1886.

*1886* *2.75in (7cm) diam*

**£70-100** **DN**

A Minton M.C.C. 50th anniversary commemorative ashtray, the rim decorated in the club's colours and with dated monogram to both sides, factory stamp to base.

*4.5in (11.5cm) diam*

**£300-400** **DN**

A Ford and Riley Victorian Staffordshire 'Sports Series' bowl, printed with a vignette of a cricket game to one side and football to the other, with Ford and Riley, Burslem backstamp, with the 'B' design.

*1882-93* *4in (10cm) diam*

**£400-450** **DN**

A Westerwald tapering blue stoneware jug, moulded in relief with eight figures of cricketers, the handle with boater and boots, three white rings to base probably from firing.

*c1890* *9.75in (24.5cm) high*

**£500-600** **DN**

A bisque spill vase, in the form of the Hambledon Stone on Broadhalfpenny Down, printed with the arms of Hambledon, "Hambledon Cricket Club circa 1750-1780".

*4in (10cm) high*

**£1,000-1,500** **DN**

A Lancaster & Sandland cake slice, printed with 'Old Father Time', with a gilded rim, stamped to back "Lancaster & Sandland, Hanley".

*1960s* *8in (20cm) long*

**£40-50** **DN**

A pack of De La Rue playing cards, each printed with a village cricket match in progress, still in original wrapper with duty stamp seal unbroken.

*c1946*

**£50-70** **DN**

A pack of Edwardian playing cards, each printed with a batsman, wicket keeper, fielder and a group of spectators to the reverse, complete with joker and blank card.

**£40-60** **DN**

A pack of De La Rue playing cards, each printed with an Edwardian cricketer batting, in original box, retailed by W.H. Raworth Stationers of Harrogate, damaged.

**£40-60** **DN**

A Victorian papier mâché rectangular snuff box, with a cricket match, chip to interior.

*This scene was taken from the 'The Cricket Match' painting of cricketers on the Artillery Ground, London. Painted by Francis Hayman R.A. in 1743, it now hangs at Lord's Cricket Ground.*

*3in (7.5cm) high*

**£300-400** **DN**

A black lacquered papier-mâché oval pill box, the hinged lid decorated with a scene of three Victorian style boys playing cricket, staining and marks to lid, sides repainted.

*2in (5cm) wide*

**£200-220** **DN**

A Victorian leather novelty inkwell in the form of a cricket ball, with a hinged lid and brass liners, and original glass ink bottle, decorated with simulated seam and stitching to the brown leather.

*2.5in (6.5cm) diam*

**£400-600** **DN**

An 1860s carved ivory walking stick handle in the form of a hand holding a cricket ball, realistically carved with a seam to the ball, marked "BM" to base.

*1.75in (4.5cm) diam*

**£150-200** **DN**

A rare Victorian copper wheel engraved glass goblet, the bowl with an etched scene of a cricketer bowling round arm to a batsman before a set of stumps, on a baluster stem and round star cut foot.

*This is a very well engraved scene, with a good sense of perspective. It must have been engraved by a skilled artist, and the inclusion of a Scottish thistle in the background is interesting.*

*c1850-60* *5.5in (14cm) diam*

**£5,000-6,000** **DN**

An unused Nottinghamshire cricket cap, awarded to Joe Hardstaff Jnr. and then passed to Bob Berry of Lancashire in 1952, together with a handwritten note from Berry confirming this.

*Considering the provenance attached to this piece, it is likely that it was acquired at one of the Lancashire player's benefit events.*

**£100-150** **DN**

An Edwardian silver and leather match holder and ashtray, by Edward Barnard & Sons, the holder in the form of a cricket ball with two strikes and a silver monogram, the ashtray with crossed stumps.

*1908* *8in (20cm) high*

**£180-220** **DN**

A Victorian gilt metal novelty propelling pencil, in the form of a cricket bat, with a ring holder, inscribed "Captain Henville Thresher Rifle Brigade" and "1901" to reverse.

*2.5in (6.5cm) long*

**£220-280** **DN**

An England navy blue cap, awarded to George Duckworth of Lancashire in the later period of his career, made by Hobbs Sports.

**£220-280** **DN**

A Victorian ivory M.C.C. token, with a 'Life Member No. 41' and M.C.C. monogram to the front, and 'Not Transferable' and the name "Arnold H. Butler" to the reverse.

*These tokens were issued from 1888-92, with only 200 members being elected at the then vast cost of £200 each. Rare at the time, these are even rarer today as so few remain in existence.*

**£500-600** **DN**

**FIND OUT MORE...**

**The Wisden Book of Cricket Memorabilia**, *by Marcus Williams, published by Seven Hills Books, 1990.*

## COLLECTORS' NOTES

- Golf developed during the 15th and 17th centuries on the scrubby grassland between farmland and the Scottish coasts, but has its origins in the ancient Roman game of paganica, in the Middle Ages France game jeu de mail and the Dutch game of ket holven.
- Clubs and balls form the basis of many a collection and, while examples from the 18th century or earlier are very rare, 19th century pieces are much more accessible to the collector.
- As most collectors also play, the many types of clubs and balls should be familiar terms, but make sure you are aware of the numerous more desirable manufacturers such as Thomas Dunn, Douglas McEwan, Tom Morris and Robert Forgan.
- Decorative memorabilia depicting the game of golf generally dates from the 1890s onwards. Ceramics by well-known manufactures such as Doulton and Shelley are always desirable. Prints, photographs and books are also popular collecting areas and add variety.

A John D. Wilson, 'Crolf' duplex club, with metal shaft.

*c1921*

**£350-450** L&T

An R.L. Urquhart Patent adjustable head iron, of conventional form, with marked face, hickory shaft, the wrapped leather grip, loose.

**£850-950** L&T

A rare Pro-swing practice club, with leaded brass ball head, hickory shaft and wrapped smooth leather grip.

**£800-1,200** L&T

A William Gibson 'Woodfaced Putter', the head stamped "Lillywhite's London Woodfaced Putter, Special" and with star mark, anti-shank, wry neck, hickory shaft with leather wrapped, square section grip.

*William Gibson was the largest manufacturer of golf clubs at one time.*

**£1,800-2,200** L&T

An R. Dickson long nose putter, the scared head stamped with maker's name, horn insert to sole and lead backweight, hickory shaft, replacement wrapped leather grip.

**£450-550** L&T

A Perwhit putter, with round profile face and hollowed back stamped "The Perwhit" patent no. 247116 and with the "Hendry and Bishop" mitre brand stamp.

*c1920*

**£350-450** L&T

An intermediate head putter, by H. Harris.

*c1890*

**£180-220** L&T

A long nose socket head putter, by A.H. Scott of Elie & Earlsferry, with greenheart shaft.

*c1895*

**£350-450** L&T

## A CLOSER LOOK AT A FEATHERY GOLF BALL

*Allan Robertson's grandfather set up a family business manufacturing golf clubs and balls, and his son (Allan's father) and Allan worked there. They were considered a premium brand.*

*Allan Robertson balls are considered desirable by collectors and the written provenance on the ball adds to this desirability.*

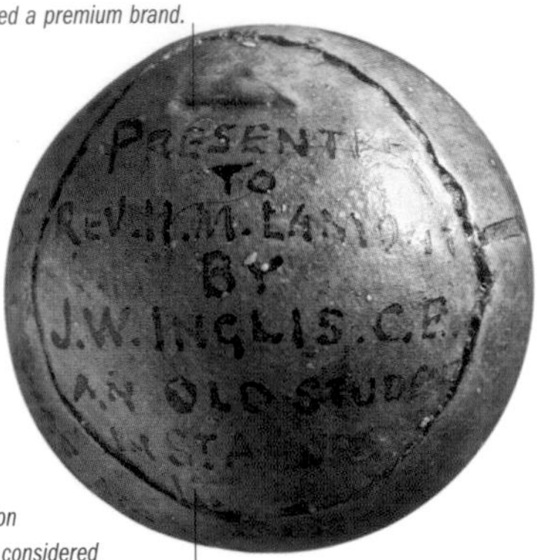

*Allan Robertson (1815-59) is considered one of the first professional golfers.*

*The writing is unclear, as it was Allan's uncle was called William Robertson not his father.*

A rare feather ball, of unusual proportions, inscribed in ink to the top "Presented to Rev. H.M. Lamont by J.W.. Inglis C.B (?), an old student in St. Andrews, 18**" and to the side bearing also in ink "This ball was made by Wil. Robertson, 1790, Father (?) of Allan , the famous golfer", with protected lacquer to ball.

**£25,000-30,000** **L&T**

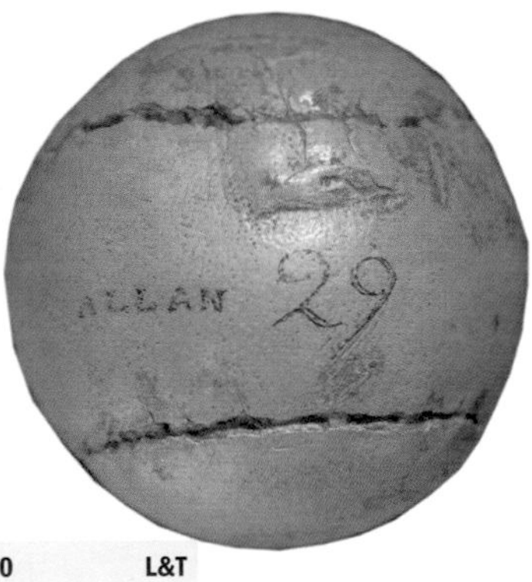

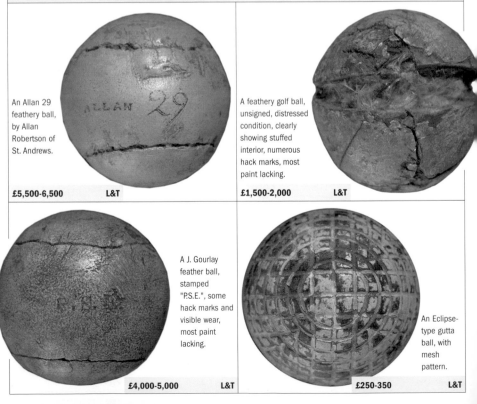

An Allan 29 feathery ball, by Allan Robertson of St. Andrews.

**£5,500-6,500** **L&T**

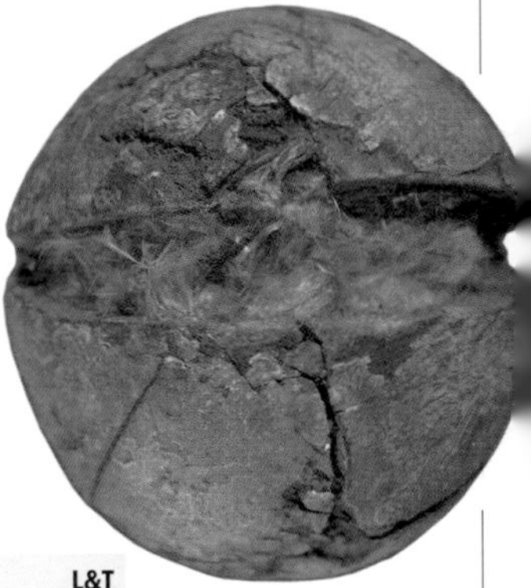

A feathery golf ball, unsigned, distressed condition, clearly showing stuffed interior, numerous hack marks, most paint lacking.

**£1,500-2,000** **L&T**

A J. Gourlay feather ball, stamped "P.S.E.", some hack marks and visible wear, most paint lacking.

**£4,000-5,000** **L&T**

An Eclipse-type gutta ball, with mesh pattern.

**£250-350** **L&T**

A 1920s large US vs Canada Kivani's International silver-plated golf trophy, with painted details to flags, mounted on a turned wooden stand.

*20.75in (53cm) high*

**£150-250** **TCF**

A 1930s Ladies amateur golf Championship silver-plated trophy, with four plaques around the base.

*15.25in (39cm) high*

**£500-600** **TCF**

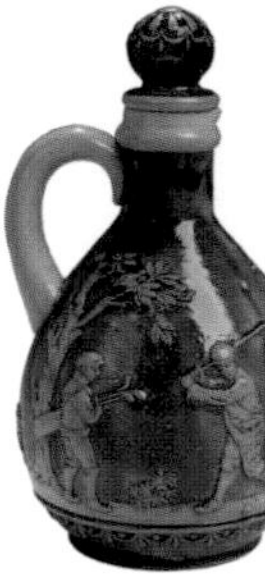

A Gerz salt-glazed stoneware jug and stopper, of ovoid form, relief moulded in the round with golfers and caddies in a landscape, loop handle to the neck, impressed marks to the underside.

*9in (23cm) high*

**£1,500-2,000** **L&T**

A Copeland Late Spode jug, with applied low relief images of golfers mid-swing and caddies, with printed and impressed marks and registered design number 345322.

*c1900*

**£450-550** **MSA**

A Lenox pottery tobacco humidor, hand-painted with a golfing scene in shades of green, printed mark to the underside, with rare Shreve & Co. sterling silver cover.

*6in (15.5cm) high*

**£4,000-5,000** **L&T**

A rare oversized Bobby Jones photograph, in original frame, with 'National Studios, NY' enlargement paper label on reverse, some general light soiling and few surface imperfections.

*c1930s* *41in (104cm) high*

**£600-800** **HA**

A 'Life Association of Scotland' lithographed advertising calendar, printed by Banks & Co., Edinburgh, with a golfing view of North Berwick, and with further golfing vignettes to the border.

*1893* *21.25in (54cm) wide*

**£2,000-3,000** **L&T**

Life Magazine, "Fore! Life's Book for Golfers", first edition, published by Life Publishing, New York, illustrated throughout, green cloth-backed pictorial boards with cover design of an enthusiastic female golfer, in the style of Charles Dana Gibson.

*1900*

**£600-700** **L&T**

W.W. Tulloch, "The Life of Tom Morris, with Glimpses of St. Andrews and its Golfing Celebrities", first edition published by T. Werner Laurie, London, illustrated from 27 photographs, frontispiece, original pictorial green cloth cover, spine lettered in gilt, front cover lettered in black.

*c1908*

**£800-1,000** **L&T**

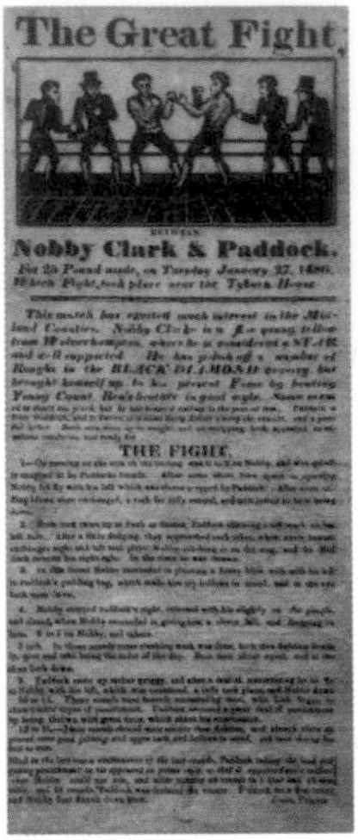


A rare printed handbill with an account of 'The Great Fight between Nobby Clark [sic] and Paddock, 27th January 1846 at Tyburn House.

**£600-800** **GBA**

A rare printed handbill with an account of the 'Great Battle' between Simpson & Brown 19th September 1831, near Doncaster.

**£600-800** **GBA**

An early photographic portrait of the prize fighter Tom Sayers.

*Thomas Sayers (1826-65) was a popular bare-knuckle fighter who was the first fighter to be declared World Heavyweight champion and was defeated only once in his career.*

**£450-550** **GBA**

A page autographed by Jack Dempsey, laid down to card, which reads "World Heavyweight Champion April 20th 1927", ink stain to top and bottom and central fold.

*5in (12.5cm) high*

**£70-90** **MM**

A limited edition 'Tuxedo' photographic print of Muhammad Ali, by Neil Leifer, signed by the photographer and Ali.

*30.75in (78cm) high*

**£800-1,200** **GBA**

A matchroom boxing top, worn by Nigel Benn.

**£150-200** **GBA**

A pair of boxing shorts worn by Eder Jofre, during his World Bantamweight Title fight against Katsutoshi Aoki in Tokyo on 4th April 1963.

**£350-450** **GBA**

An early 19thC silver lustre earthenware jug, the front with a printed design of the boxers Molineaux & Cribb, restored.

*Tom Molineaux (1784-1818), the son of a Virginian plantation slave, gained his freedom by winning his owner large sums of money through boxing matches. Although victorious against Rimmer in 1811, he was defeated in the same year by Tom Cribb (1781-1848) who remained Champion of England until 1824. In 1821 Cribb guarded the entrance to Westminster Abbey during the Coronation of George IV.*

*5in (12.5cm) high*

**£300-400** **SAS**

A tennis ball, signed by James Outram Anderson, Suzanne Lenglen, Charles Garland and Raymond J. Casey.

*Suzanne Lenglen (1899-1938) was a French tennis superstar and the first female tennis celebrity, who was referred to as "La Divine" by the French press. She won the Women's Singles title at Wimbledon six times and the French Championship six times also.*

*2.5in (6.5cm) diam*

**£900-1,200** **MSA**

## A CLOSER LOOK AT A TENNIS STEVENGRAPH

*Stevengraphs, invented c1836, are named after their inventor Thomas Stevens. The term has come to encompass silk pictures, bookmarks, postcards etc, made by a number of manufacturers.*

*This examples is in good, bright condition and retains its original mount, increasing the value.*

*Stevengraphs are collectable in their own right, making this doubly appealing.*

*This is one of many sporting themed stevengraphs, but is a scarce example.*

A rare 19thC 'The First Set' stevengraph, manufactured by Thomas Stevens, with original mount, framed and glazed, in excellent condition.

*Frame 8.75in (22cm) wide*

**£800-1,200** **MSA**

A rare Tunnicliffe painted ceramic match holder, decorated with a scene of a tennis match.

*3.5in (9cm) high*

**£650-750** **MSA**

A 1930s Shelley tureen and cover, with transfer of two young tennis players, the body with other scenes of young sportmen and women.

*11.5in (29cm) wide*

**£250-300** **MSA**

A 14oz tennis racket, with slightly bowed head, numbered "38" on label.

*26.75in (68cm) long*

**£700-800** **MSA**

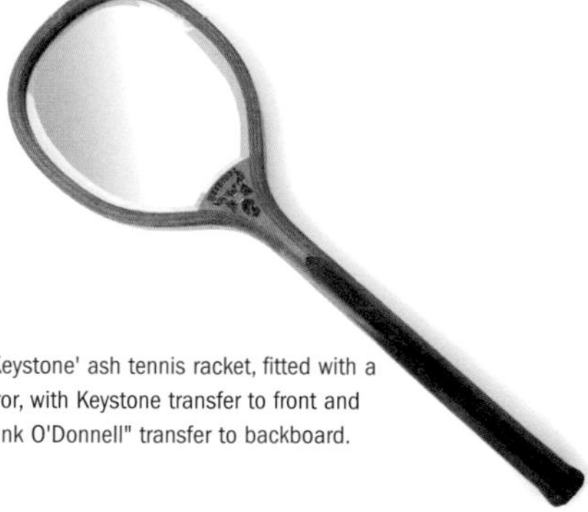

A 'Keystone' ash tennis racket, fitted with a mirror, with Keystone transfer to front and "Frank O'Donnell" transfer to backboard.

*c1900* *26.5in (67cm) high*

**£850-1,100** **MSA**

A faux leather-covered folding photograph frame, the front hand-painted with two frogs playing tennis on lily pads.

*7.5in (19cm) high*

**£200-300** **MSA**

A pair of French spelter tennis figures, each holding a racket, the lady about to serve, both mounted on turned wooden circular bases.

*c1900* *14.5in (37cm) high*

**£180-220** **WW**

A rare 19thC French mahogany and brass hand-held billiard scorer, marked "Decrette Paris".

*11.75in (30cm) high*

**£350-450** **MSA**

An 'International Table Croquet' boxed games set, by F.H. Ayres, comprising two small mallets, heads stamped "F.H. Ayres" coloured balls, fabric strips, metal hoops, with original box.

*Box 15.25in (38.5cm) wide*

**£250-300** **MSA**

## A CLOSER LOOK AT A TÔLEWARE TRAY

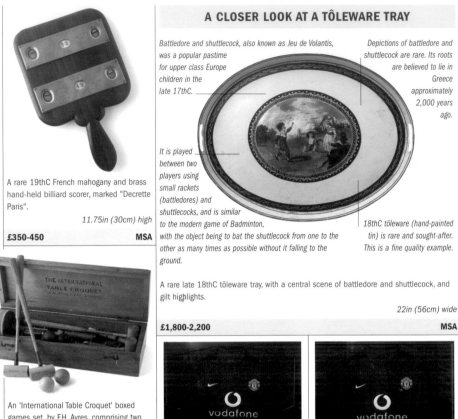

*Battledore and shuttlecock, also known as Jeu de Volantis, was a popular pastime for upper class Europe children in the late 17thC.*

*Depictions of battledore and shuttlecock are rare. Its roots are believed to lie in Greece approximately 2,000 years ago.*

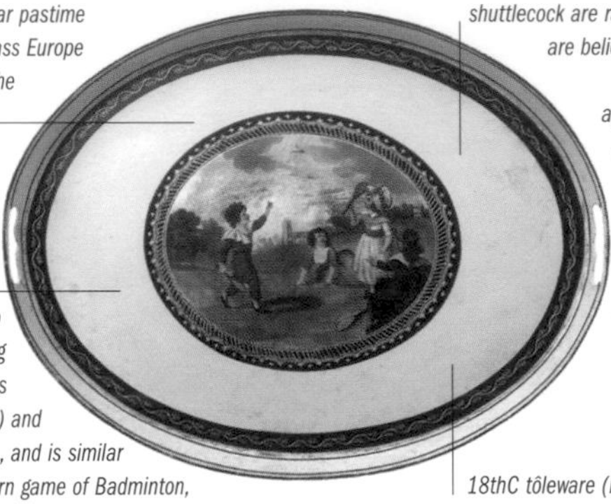

*It is played between two players using small rackets (battledores) and shuttlecocks, and is similar to the modern game of Badminton, with the object being to bat the shuttlecock from one to the other as many times as possible without it falling to the ground.*

*18thC tôleware (hand-painted tin) is rare and sought-after. This is a fine quality example.*

A rare late 18thC tôleware tray, with a central scene of battledore and shuttlecock, and gilt highlights.

*22in (56cm) wide*

**£1,800-2,200** **MSA**

A signed David Beckham Manchester United shirt, framed and with certificate.

**£200-300** **BRI**

A signed Roy Keane Manchester United shirt, framed and with certificate.

**£150-200** **BRI**

A signed photograph of David Beckham, clutching his England shirt after scoring against Argentina, framed with certificate.

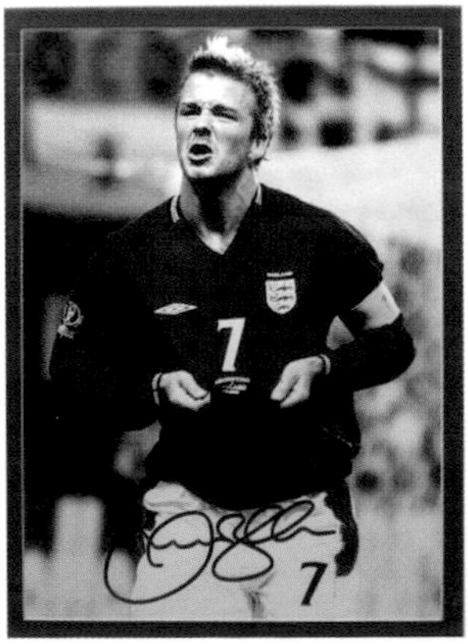

**£60-90** **BRI**

A framed photograph of David Beckham and Eric Cantona after scoring a goal for Manchester United, framed and mounted together with a ticket signed by Cantona, with certificate.

**£120-180** **BRI**

A signed photograph of the 1997/98 Season Arsenal Team, signed by 19 members of the team.

**£20-30** **BRI**

A group of Typhoo Tea Ltd collectors cards, showing famous football clubs, including Chelsea, Arsenal and Liverpool.

**£60-80 (set)** **BRI**

A large French Niagara no.2 wooden roulette wheel, with chrome metal and painted spinning wheel.

*c1900* *19.25in (49cm) diam*

**£850-1,200** **MSA**

A Beswick 'Morgan Stallion "Tarryall Maestro"' figure, designed by Graham Tongue, from the Connoisseur Horses series, with matte black finish, mounted on a polished wooden base set with a title plaque.

*1979-89* *11.75in (30cm) high*

**£350-450** **GBA**

A Beswick 'Arkle' figure, designed by Arthur Gredington, from the Connoisseur Horse series, with matte finish, mounted on a polished wooden base.

*1970-89* *12in (30.5cm) high*

**£120-180** **GBA**

A limited edition Albany Fine China model of a chestnut thoroughbred, modelled by David Lovegrove, from an edition of 250, set on a polished wooden plinth, in original fitted box, complete with original sales literature.

*11.5in (29.5cm) wide*

**£350-450** **GBA**

A limited edition Royal Worcester 'Red Rum' figure, designed by Doris Lindner, RW3955, from an edition of 250 from the Race Horses series.

*The popularity of the subject matter, the quality of the manufacture and the small size of the edition all add to the value of this handsome figure.*

*1975* *11in (28cm) high*

**£1,000-1,500** **GBA**

A Beswick 'Horse and Jockey' gloss figure, no.1862, designed by Arthur Gredington, style two.

*There is a very rare painted white version of this figure.*

*1963-83* *8in (20cm) high*

**£550-650** **GBA**

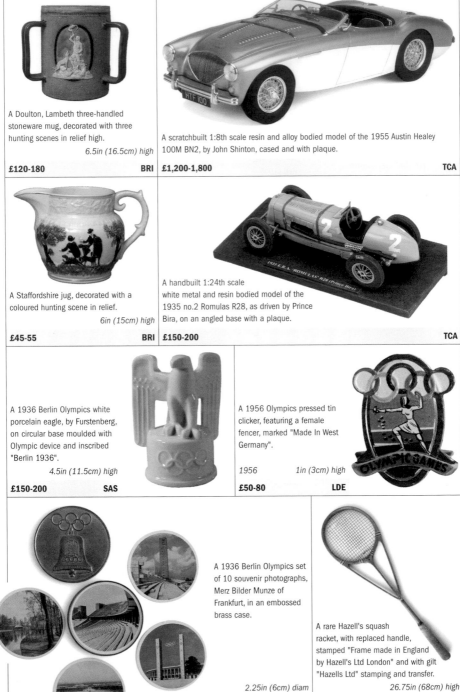

A Doulton, Lambeth three-handled stoneware mug, decorated with three hunting scenes in relief high.

*6.5in (16.5cm) high*

**£120-180** **BRI**

A scratchbuilt 1:8th scale resin and alloy bodied model of the 1955 Austin Healey 100M BN2, by John Shinton, cased and with plaque.

**£1,200-1,800** **TCA**

A Staffordshire jug, decorated with a coloured hunting scene in relief.

*6in (15cm) high*

**£45-55** **BRI**

A handbuilt 1:24th scale white metal and resin bodied model of the 1935 no.2 Romulas R28, as driven by Prince Bira, on an angled base with a plaque.

**£150-200** **TCA**

A 1936 Berlin Olympics white porcelain eagle, by Furstenberg, on circular base moulded with Olympic device and inscribed "Berlin 1936".

*4.5in (11.5cm) high*

**£150-200** **SAS**

A 1956 Olympics pressed tin clicker, featuring a female fencer, marked "Made In West Germany".

*1956* *1in (3cm) high*

**£50-80** **LDE**

A 1936 Berlin Olympics set of 10 souvenir photographs, Merz Bilder Munze of Frankfurt, in an embossed brass case.

*2.25in (6cm) diam*

**£80-120** **LDE**

A rare Hazell's squash racket, with replaced handle, stamped "Frame made in England by Hazell's Ltd London" and with gilt "Hazells Ltd" stamping and transfer.

*26.75in (68cm) high*

**£250-350** **MSA**

## COLLECTORS' NOTES

- When US President Theodore Roosevelt refused to shoot a bear on a hunting trip in 1902, and a cartoon covering the event was published, few realised how important it would become. Entrepreneur Morris Michtom then produced a bear to commemorate the event to sell in his Brooklyn store, and started a craze that is still with us today. Although the US produced the first bears, it was Germany that was the most prolific, and arguably produced the best bears.
- Germany's Steiff (founded 1886) are considered the finest maker, and bears made from 1902 to the 1930s are highly desirable and can be worth large sums. Bing, Hermann and Schuco (1921-1970s) are other notable German names. In the UK, Farnell (1908-1960s), Chad Valley (1915-78), Merrythought 1920-2006) and Chiltern (1915-1970s) are among the most collectable names. Dates ranges given refer only to years the factory produced bears.
- Learn typical forms by handling as many bears as possible and studying auction catalogues and reference books. This often gives the best indication to the maker and the period, particularly if a bear is not marked. For those looking to seek out bargains in a crowded market, learn how to recognise bears by smaller makers that others may not. Early American bears are scarce and can be hard to identify, but can have similarities to early German bears in form.
- Earlier, pre-WWII bears tend to have humped backs, long arms with upturned paws and pronounced snouts. Filling tends to be harder than modern bears and mohair was commonly used. Bears from the 1950s tend to be plumper, with rounder faces and bodies and shorter limbs. As sources of early desirable bears dry up and become more expensive, later bears from the 1950s onwards and by less famous makers are becoming more desirable.
- As well as the maker, date and form, the size, colour and condition are also important. Large bears or those in unusual colours will usually fetch more, as will those in better condition with intact fur. Beware of official replica bears, which look like older bears, and also the increasing number of fakes. If in doubt, smell a bear as the smell of age cannot yet be replicated. Another factor is eye appeal – the cute look of a bear can lead collectors to pay a higher price.

A Steiff teddy bear, with boot button eyes, stitched woollen nose and claws, blank "Steiff" button in ear.

*c1907* *10in (25.5cm) high*

**£1,000-1,500** **HGS**

A Steiff brown teddy bear, with boot button eyes, original pads, in excellent condition.

*c1910* *20in (51cm) high*

**£3,000-5,000** **TCT**

A Steiff white five-claw teddy bear, with blank button in his ear.

*Steiff produced very few white bears. All have light brown stitching, a colour used on white bears only. He is also an early, large and appealing bear, with full, even stuffing. This colour of blank button was only used between 1905 and 1909.*

*c1906* *20in (51cm) high*

**£5,000-6,000** **TCT**

A very rare Steiff white 'Muzzle Bear', with boot button eyes and original paw pads and stitching.

*Steiff bears with leather muzzles were made around 1910 to imitate the performing bears seen in streets and fairs. The muzzle is usually lost, and is exceptionally rare. He is also white, which adds further to his rarity and value.*

*c1912* *16in (40.5cm) high*

**£5,500-6,500** **TCT**

A Steiff Zotty bear, with growler.

*Zotty bears, from 'zottig' the German for shaggy, have shaved snouts and shaggy hair. They were introduced by Steiff in 1951 and were copied by other makers.*

*c1960* *16.5in (42cm) high*

**£50-80** **SAS**

A 1950s chocolate brown Steiff 'Teddy Baby', with sprayed-on claws and and stitched facial features, the ear with "ff" button.

*3.5in (9cm) high*

**£380-420** **HGS**

## A CLOSER LOOK AT A STEIFF BEAR

Petsy bears were introduced in 1928 and only produced for a few years, making them rare today.
Their heads have a distinctive seam that runs from the front to the back and across to the ears. The ears also contain wire making them poseable.
Also look out for the Petsy's blue eyes and cute, almost childish expression.
Unusually, they were soft-filled and had long, mohair tipped in a reddish-brown, giving them a shaggy, two-tone effect.
Do not confuse them with the later 'Zottig' bears or 1920s two-tone bears.

A very rare Steiff 'Petsy' bear, with "ff" button and blue glass eyes.

*1928* *17in (43cm) high*

**£7,000-9,000** **TCT**

A Steiff small brown mohair 'Strong Museum' replica bear, with original tags.

*c1983* *12.25in (31cm) high*

**£40-60** **TCT**

A Steiff large white mohair 'Strong Museum' replica bear, with original tags.

*These were made for the Margaret Woodbury Strong Museum of Juvenalia and Toys in Rochester, New York.*

*c1983* *19.75in (50cm) high*

**£200-300** **HGS**

A 1920s-30s Steiff brown mohair bear on wheels, with original red painted wooden wheels, cord and collar, in excellent condition

*25in (63.5cm) high*

**£600-800** **LHT**

A 1950s Steiff golden mohair 'Jungle' bear, complete with collar, button and tag, in excellent condition.

*'Jungle' bears stand on all-fours and have no frame and wheels, unlike the example to the left.*

*7in (18cm) long*

**£80-120** **LHT**

A large Chad Valley blonde mohair teddy bear, with black stitched snout, amber glass eyes and jointed body with rexine pads, label on right foot.

*c1953* *30in (76cm) high*

**£200-300** **HAMG**

A 1950s Chiltern Ting-a-Ling blonde mohair teddy bear, with orange and black glass eyes, black stitched nose, mouth and claws, and jointed limbs with rexine pads, general wear, damaged feet pads.

*14in (35.5cm) high*

**£120-180** **SAS**

A 1930s Chiltern light golden mohair teddy bear, with orange and black glass eyes, pronounced shaved muzzle, re-stitched nose and mouth, jointed limbs, general wear, muzzle repaired, pads recovered.

*24.5in (62cm) high*

**£120-180** **SAS**

A 1920s large red mohair bear, with shaved muzzle and original pads, probably by Chiltern.

*Red is a very rare colour.*

*27in (68.5cm) high*

**£1,200-1,800** **LHT**

An early 1930s Farnell white mohair 'Mascot' teddy bear, with bow and original card tag.

*These were made in the patriotic red, white and blue.*

**£200-300** **LHT**

A British Harwin & Co 'Old Mac' bear, with part re-created military uniform.

*Harwin was founded in 1914 and closed in 1930, and produced dolls and teddies designed by the founder's daughter. A number of dressed bears were also offered, but they are rarely found with all, or even any, of their original clothes.*

*c1914-18*

**£1,500-2,000** **LHT**

## A CLOSER LOOK AT A CHILTERN BEAR

*The Hugmee was one Chiltern's most popular ranges, and was made from the 1930s-50s - their popularity continues with collectors today.*

*He can be recognised as a later bear by his shorter limbs, plumper body and lack of two vertical nose stitches or shaved muzzle as many earlier 1930s Hugmee bears do.*

*The deep golden colour of this bear is unusual, and he is in absolutely mint condition.*

*This bear still retains his rare card tag. A similar bear in excellent condition but without the tag is worth £250-350.*

A 1940s-50s Chiltern large golden mohair 'Hugmee' teddy bear, with growler, bow and original card tag.

*20in (51cm) high*

**£500-700** **LHT**

A late 1950s Merrythought pink mohair Cheeky bear hand muff.

*For a child's functional item, this is in excellent condition. Pink is an unusual colour.*

*12in (30.5cm) high*

**£250-350** **LHT**

A 1920s British golden mohair teddy bear, possibly early Chad Valley, with black boot button eyes, black stitched nose and claws, jointed limbs and cloth pads.

*15in (38cm) high*

**£60-80** **SAS**

A 1950s British golden mohair teddy bear, possibly Chiltern with orange and black glass eyes, black stitched nose, mouth and remains of claws, jointed limbs, pads recovered.

*20.5in (52cm) high*

**£18-22** **SAS**

A British golden mohair teddy bear, with black boot button eyes, black stitched nose, mouth and claws, jointed limbs with brown felt pads and slight hump, general wear.

*11.5in (29cm) high*

**£17-20** **SAS**

A 1920s English large golden mohair teddy bear, by an unknown maker, the black stitched nose with two vertical stitches, glass eyes and felt pads.

*Although he shares many similarities with Farnell bears, and possibly early Merrythought, he is slightly different in terms of his form and type of mohair, and the maker cannot be identified.*

*24in (61cm) high*

**£400-600** **LHT**

A 1920s British black mohair teddy bear, with black boot button eyes, shaved muzzle, pink stitched nose, mouth and claws, jointed limbs with black cloth pads, worn.

*Associated with mourning events such as the sinking of the Titanic, black bears are rare.*

*15in (38cm) high*

**£180-220** **SAS**

## A CLOSER LOOK AT A FARNELL BEAR

*Founded in 1908, Farnell are known as the 'English Steiff' due to their high quality and the classic appearance of their bears.*

*The 'Alpha' range was Farnell's finest quality and highest priced range, and was introduced in 1925.*

*He is in extremely fine, almost mint, condition, with luxurious and deep fur which was a hallmark of Farnell bears.*

*He is a very large size. Christopher Robin's real 'Winnie The Pooh' was a similar 'Alpha' bear.*

A 1920s Farnell large golden mohair 'Alpha' teddy bear, with glass painted-back eyes, original stitching and paw pads.

*22in (53.5cm) high*

**£1,500-2,000** **LHT**

A 1920s-30s German light golden mohair teddy bear, with orange and black glass eyes, black stitched nose, mouth and remains of claws, slotted-in ears, jointed limbs, hump and growler, worn, pads recovered.

*18.75in (47.5cm) high*

**£22-28** **SAS**

A 1960s-70s German blonde mohair teddy bear, with black and clear eyes, brown stitched nose and mouth.

*20in (51cm) high*

**£12-18** **SAS**

A 1930s German composition teddy bear, with brown burlap covering, orange and black glass eyes and fur ears.

*9.5in (24cm) high*

**£12-18** **SAS**

An Eastern European bear, with clockwork mechanism and mohair covering.

*8.75in (22.5cm) high*

**£12-18** **SAS**

A golden mohair teddy bear purse, by an unknown German or English maker, with shoulder strap.

*A number of makers made 'functional' bears, with the most notable being Schreyer & Co, under the brandname 'Schuco'. However, the form and style of this bear does not allow identification of a maker.*

*c1918* *9.5in (24cm) high*

**£500-700** **LHT**

'The Travelling Bears in England', by Seymour Eaton, illustrated by V. Floyd Campbell, published by Barse & Hopkins, NY.

*10.75in (27.5cm) high*

**£40-60** **TCT**

'The Travelling Bears at Play', by Seymour Eaton, illustrated by V. Floyd Campbell, published by Barse & Hopkins, NY.

*10.75in (27.5cm) high*

**£40-60** **TCT**

### FIND OUT MORE...

**Bears**, *by Sue Pearson, published by De Agostini, 1995.*

**Teddy Bear Encyclopedia**, *by Pauline Cockrill, published by DK, 2001.*

## COLLECTORS' NOTES

- Soft toys can provide a more affordable, and more varied, alternative to collecting teddy bears. They also pre-date teddy bears, with the earliest well-known manufactured pieces being Margerete Steiff's elephants in the 1890s. Fabric kits were also made in the 19thC, which could be cut out, stuffed and sewn together at home.
- Consider the form and materials used to help identify the maker. Look at stitching and pads for labels or remains of labels as their position can also help.
- Steiff is, as ever, the most collectable name. Quality is high and cats and dogs in particular are eternally popular. Look out for unusual animals such as creatures and insects, as these can be surprisingly valuable. British company Merrythought is another desirable name. Pre-war examples tend to be more valuable than post war, although this is not always the case, if the character is rare, highly sought-after or in mint condition.
- However, if a vintage soft toy is well made and has an appealing, even cute and quirky, look it is likely to be collectable. Examine a toy carefully for damage – minor tears can be repaired, but major tears, fading and missing parts are more serious. Although dirty toys can be cleaned, this should be done professionally – never put one in a washing machine as this can damage the stuffing and the pile of the fur.

A 1950s Steiff plush and mohair bison soft toy, with card tag and fabric ear tag, in mint condition.

*12in (30.5cm) long*

**£180-220** **HGS**

A 1950s-60s Steiff 'Mockie' hippopotamus soft toy, with airbrushed features, wooden teeth and plastic eyes, lacks ear button.

*5in (13cm) high*

**£40-60** **PC**

An early 1950s Steiff rabbit on wheels pull-along soft toy, with "Made in US-Zone Germany" fabric tag.

*10in (25.5cm) long*

**£300-400** **TCT**

A Steiff rabbit on wheels rocking action pull-along soft toy, with large metal frame cycle, with ear button and yellow ear tag.

*9.5in (24cm) high*

**£400-600** **TCT**

A 1950s-60s Steiff small Koala soft toy, with card tag, in near mint condition.

**£80-100** **LHT**

A late 20thC Steiff miniature chimpanzee, with silver button and yellow fabric tag in ear.

*4.5in (11.5cm) high*

**£25-35** **F**

A late 1970s Steiff Studio life-sized hawk soft toy, with tag and button in ear.

*11in (28cm) high*

**£80-120** **LHT**

## A CLOSER LOOK AT A STEIFF SOFT TOY

*Eric is considered the rarest and most sought-after of Steiff's animals, as well as one of the most unusual.*

*He was very unpopular compared to other toys, such as dogs and cats, when originally released in two sizes the early 1960s, and few were sold.*

*Vintage examples have silver ear buttons with raised Steiff script, buttons on later re-issues from the 1990s onwards have an impressed Steiff script.*

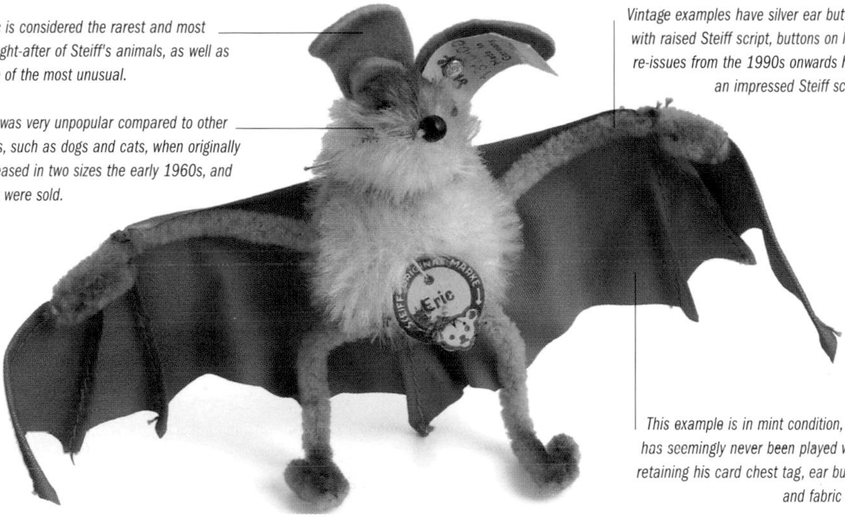

*This example is in mint condition, and has seemingly never been played with, retaining his card chest tag, ear button and fabric tag.*

A rare 1960s Steiff small 'Eric' bat, with pipe cleaner legs and plasticised fabric wings, no.1310.00.

*4.25in (10.5cm) high*

**£80-120** **NOR**

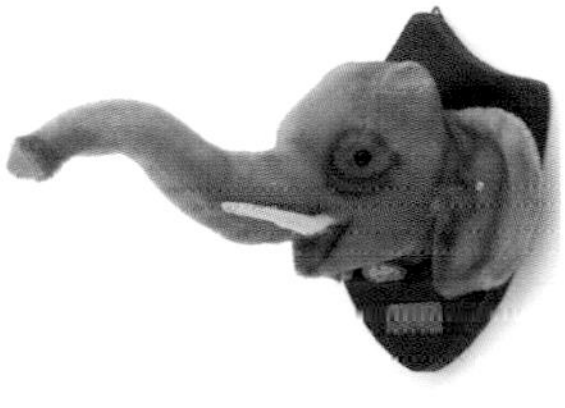

A 1950s Steiff elephant 'trophy' head, mounted on a shield-shaped wooden plaque.

*This rather gruesome Steiff object is, perhaps unsurprisingly, quite hard to find today.*

*10in (25.5cm) high*

**£200-300** **LHT**

A 1930s-50s Steiff grey wool 'pompom' mouse, with felt feet, ears and whiskers, leather tail.

*2in (5cm) long*

**£15-20** **TCT**

A 1950s Agnes Brush brushed felt 'Eeyore' soft toy.

*American maker Agnes Brush made a range of Winnie The Pooh characters, including the never-seen and terrifying 'Heffalump', which is rare and can fetch around £800.*

*11.5in (29cm) long*

**£350-450** **HGS**

A 1940s-50s Schuco grey mohair small 'Yes/No' donkey soft toy, in near mint condition.

*The 'Yes/No' mechanism was a hallmark of Schuco and was also used in its teddies and monkeys. Move the tail from side to side to make him shake his head, and up and down to make him nod.*

**£400-600** **LHT**

An Einco 'Our Tommy' soldier soft toy, with brushed felt military parade jacket, trousers, belt and original card label.

*This was produced early on in WWII as propaganda in an attempt to rally support. The tag reads 'Our Tommy - Are We Downhearted - No'.*

*c1940 7.5in (19cm) high*

**£80-120** **LHT**

## COLLECTORS' NOTES

- In the late 17th century changing tastes in interior decoration led to the need for the invention of new tools to create increasingly complex forms and patterns. As many new, often dedicated, tools were needed, specialist tool makers began to spring up. Beforehand, craftsmen had generally made the tools they needed themselves. The number of toolmakers increased dramatically during the 18th century, reaching a peak in the 19th century and fading during the 1930s-40s as ready-made furniture and components began to be produced commercially.

- Planes are one of the most popular items among today's collectors, with makers such as Norris in the UK and Stanley in the US being hotly sought-after. Specialist tools are another popular area, with those for barrel makers, watchmakers, musical instrument makers and goldsmiths being popular. Many are scarce, as fewer were made for such specialist purposes. A more generally used tool will be more common and thus generally less valuable.

- Most tools are mechanically extremely well engineered and made, and can be appreciated from that angle. Many tool collectors also focus on the design of a tool, and the skill that went into making it. As such, well-formed and highly decorative pieces can command large sums, particularly if early in date. A 'folk art' appeal also applies here, particularly with some early American items.

- The shape and purpose of a tool can help to date it, as can the material used and any decorative features. Consult specialist reference works to learn more. Always consider condition, as tools in mint and unused condition will fetch higher sums. Tools that are accompanied by their original packaging, which will usually date from the late 19th century into the early 20th century, are usually very rare. Look out for damaged or missing parts and examine wooden parts for signs of woodworm, as this reduces value considerably.

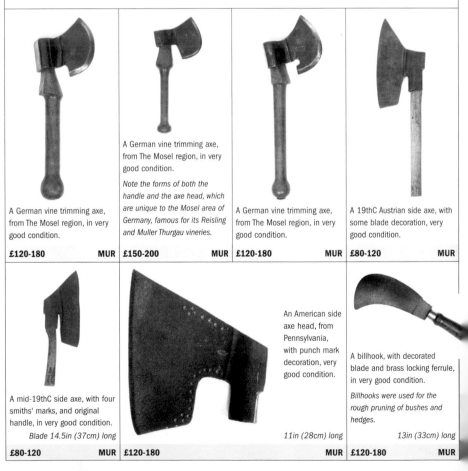

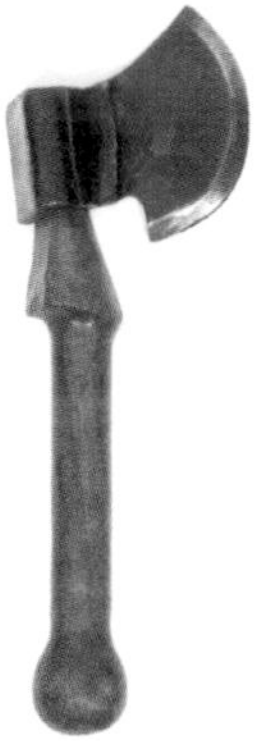

A German vine trimming axe, from The Mosel region, in very good condition.

**£120-180** **MUR**

A German vine trimming axe, from The Mosel region, in very good condition.

*Note the forms of both the handle and the axe head, which are unique to the Mosel area of Germany, famous for its Reisling and Muller Thurgau vineries.*

**£150-200** **MUR**

A German vine trimming axe, from The Mosel region, in very good condition.

**£120-180** **MUR**

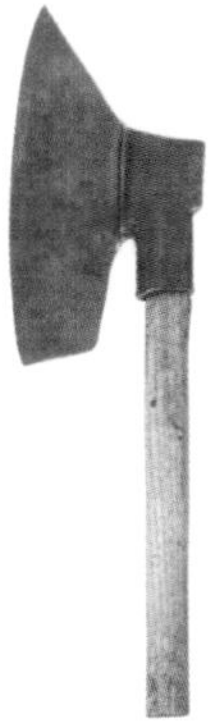

A 19thC Austrian side axe, with some blade decoration, very good condition.

**£80-120** **MUR**

A mid-19thC side axe, with four smiths' marks, and original handle, in very good condition.

*Blade 14.5in (37cm) long*

**£80-120** **MUR**

An American side axe head, from Pennsylvania, with punch mark decoration, very good condition.

*11in (28cm) long*

**£120-180** **MUR**

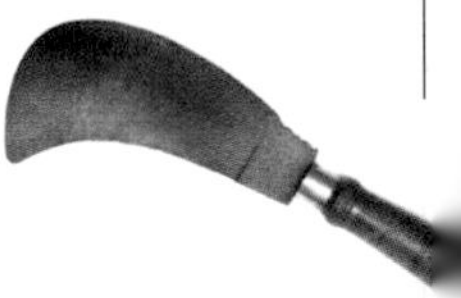

A billhook, with decorated blade and brass locking ferrule, in very good condition.

*Billhooks were used for the rough pruning of bushes and hedges.*

*13in (33cm) long*

**£120-180** **MUR**

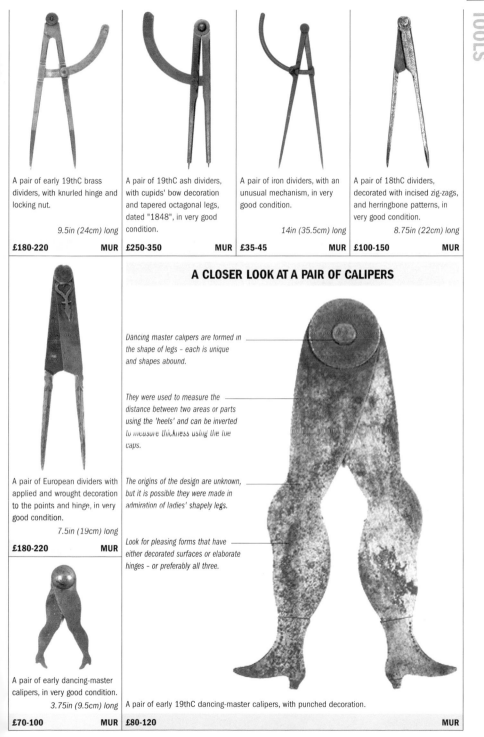

A pair of early 19thC brass dividers, with knurled hinge and locking nut.

*9.5in (24cm) long*

**£180-220** **MUR**

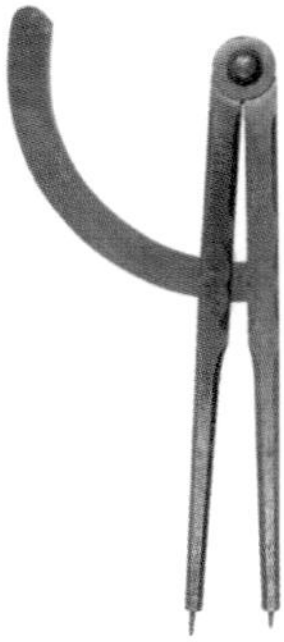

A pair of 19thC ash dividers, with cupids' bow decoration and tapered octagonal legs, dated "1848", in very good condition.

**£250-350** **MUR**

A pair of iron dividers, with an unusual mechanism, in very good condition.

*14in (35.5cm) long*

**£35-45** **MUR**

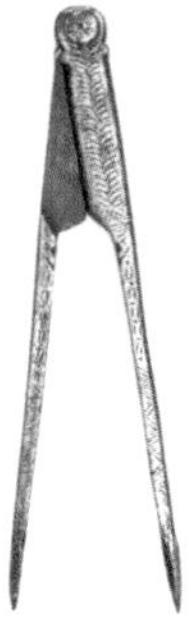

A pair of 18thC dividers, decorated with incised zig-zags, and herringbone patterns, in very good condition.

*8.75in (22cm) long*

**£100-150** **MUR**

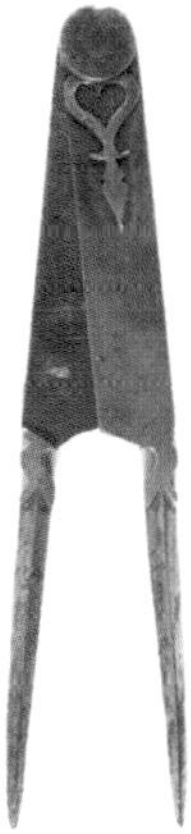

A pair of European dividers with applied and wrought decoration to the points and hinge, in very good condition.

*7.5in (19cm) long*

**£180-220** **MUR**

A pair of early dancing-master calipers, in very good condition.

*3.75in (9.5cm) long*

**£70-100** **MUR**

## A CLOSER LOOK AT A PAIR OF CALIPERS

*Dancing master calipers are formed in the shape of legs - each is unique and shapes abound.*

*They were used to measure the distance between two areas or parts using the 'heels' and can be inverted to measure thickness using the toe caps.*

*The origins of the design are unknown, but it is possible they were made in admiration of ladies' shapely legs.*

*Look for pleasing forms that have either decorated surfaces or elaborate hinges - or preferably all three.*

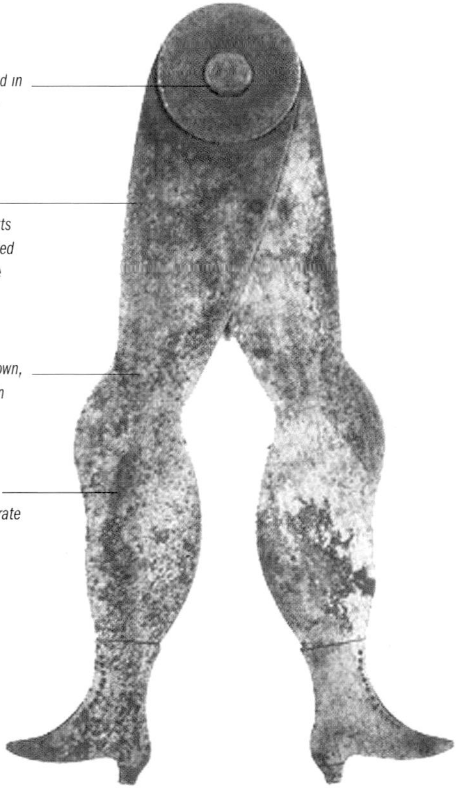

A pair of early 19thC dancing-master calipers, with punched decoration.

**£80-120** **MUR**

A pair of highly polished tailors' shears, by Wilkinson, Sheffield, in fine condition.

*These fine scissors were used for adjusting the length of a trouser or another garment. Sheffield is a renowned for its steel tools, instruments and cutlery.*

**£120-180** **MUR**

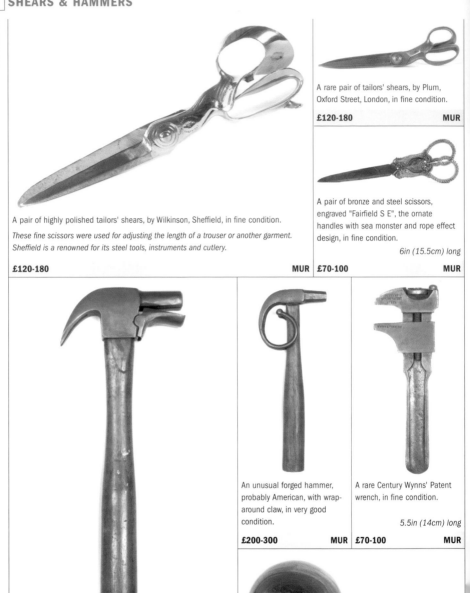

A rare pair of tailors' shears, by Plum, Oxford Street, London, in fine condition.

**£120-180** **MUR**

A pair of bronze and steel scissors, engraved "Fairfield S E", the ornate handles with sea monster and rope effect design, in fine condition.

*6in (15.5cm) long*

**£70-100** **MUR**

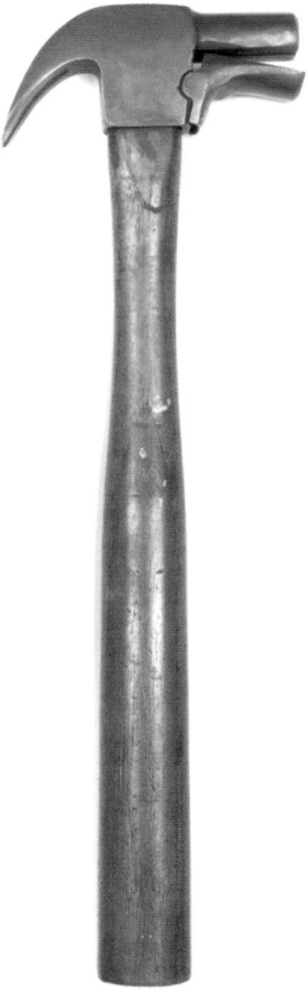

A rare and unusual American hammer, with small head split for removing nails.

**£120-180** **MUR**

An unusual forged hammer, probably American, with wrap-around claw, in very good condition.

**£200-300** **MUR**

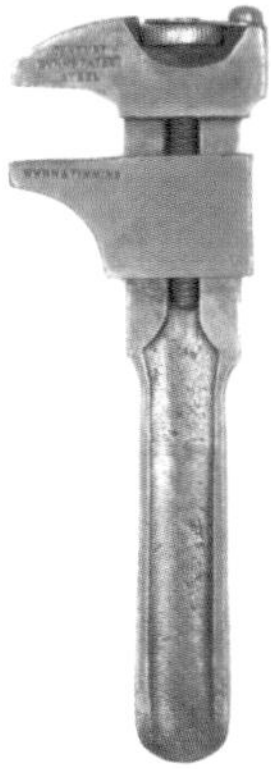

A rare Century Wynns' Patent wrench, in fine condition.

*5.5in (14cm) long*

**£70-100** **MUR**

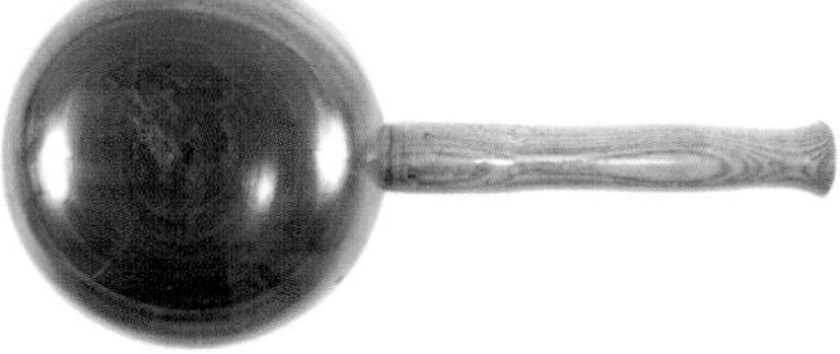

A Saddlers' lignum vitae collar mallet, with ash handle, in good condition.

*Lignum vitae, from the guayacan tree, is known for its strength and immense density, making it ideal for making a mallet.*

**£55-65** **MUR**

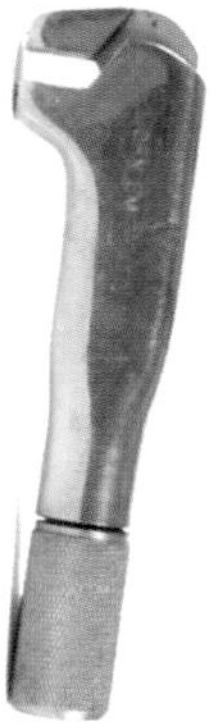

A nickle-plated wrench, marked "John Smith Ltd", in fine condition.

*3.5in (9cm) wide*

**£45-55** **MUR**

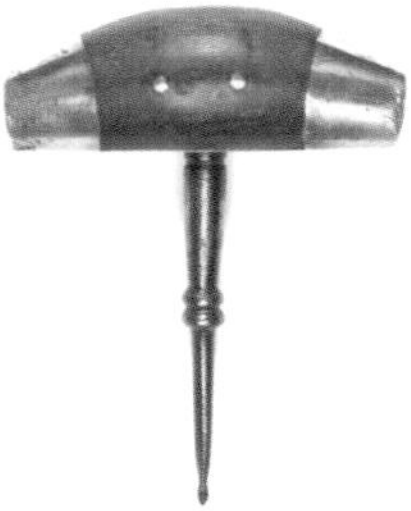

An 18thC European horn and brass gimlet, in very good condition.

*A gimlet is a tool for boring. It relies on the strength of the user to push the spike into the material to form a hole.*

**£80-120** **MUR**

A steel, with turned ebony, ivory and silver handle, in fine condition.

**£25-35** **MUR**

A very rare Georgian watchmakers' blueing pen, with rosewood handle, in very good condition.

**£150-200** **MUR**

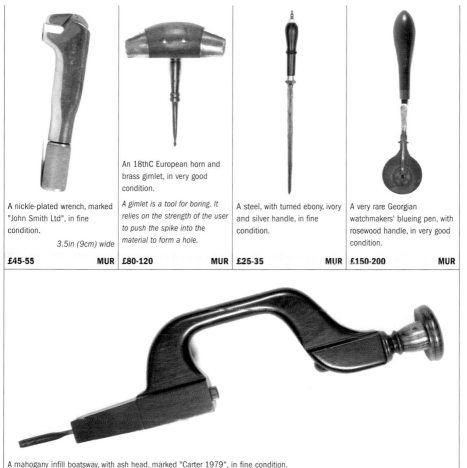

A mahogany infill boatsway, with ash head, marked "Carter 1979", in fine condition.

**£250-350** **MUR**

An early nickel-plated anvil on stand, in very good condition.

*4in (10cm) long*

**£50-80** **MUR**

A beam boring machine, minor treatment for woodworm, in very good condition.

**£80-120** **MUR**

A pair of large bank scales, in very good condition.

**£120-180** **MUR**

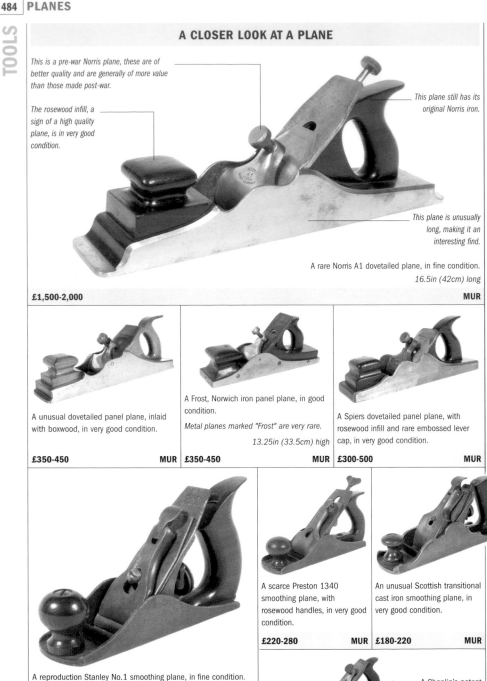

## A CLOSER LOOK AT A PLANE

*This is a pre-war Norris plane, these are of better quality and are generally of more value than those made post-war.*

*The rosewood infill, a sign of a high quality plane, is in very good condition.*

*This plane still has its original Norris iron.*

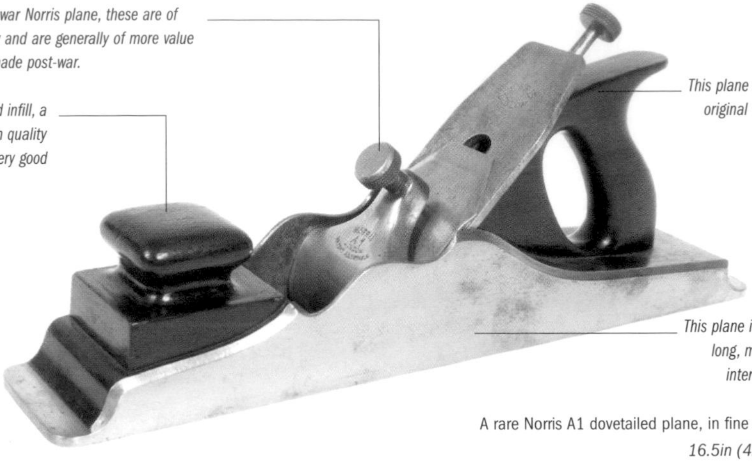

*This plane is unusually long, making it an interesting find.*

A rare Norris A1 dovetailed plane, in fine condition.

*16.5in (42cm) long*

**£1,500-2,000** **MUR**

A unusual dovetailed panel plane, inlaid with boxwood, in very good condition.

**£350-450** **MUR**

A Frost, Norwich iron panel plane, in good condition.

*Metal planes marked "Frost" are very rare.*

*13.25in (33.5cm) high*

**£350-450** **MUR**

A Spiers dovetailed panel plane, with rosewood infill and rare embossed lever cap, in very good condition.

**£300-500** **MUR**

A reproduction Stanley No.1 smoothing plane, in fine condition.

*In the early 1960s and 1970s there were about six different varieties of reproduction Stanley No.1's produced. Ironically, they are rarer than the originals and collectable in their own right.*

**£220-280** **MUR**

A scarce Preston 1340 smoothing plane, with rosewood handles, in very good condition.

**£220-280** **MUR**

An unusual Scottish transitional cast iron smoothing plane, in very good condition.

**£180-220** **MUR**

A Chaplin's patent fore plane.

**£80-120** **MUR**

A rare Cowell & Chapman styled rosewood and brass transitional plough plane, early replaced boxwood acorn finials to the stems, otherwise very good condition.

*This is an extremely rare plough plane, only a dozen or so of this model, made in Newcastle, have been discovered.*

**£1,800-2,200** **MUR**

A solid boxwood plough, by W. Denison, in very good condition.

**£200-300** **MUR**

A rare Mathieson bridle plough plane, with boxwood arms and full set of original planes, in very good condition.

**£220-280** **MUR**

A Mathieson screwstem plough, boxwood arms and nuts, in fine condition.

**£120-180** **MUR**

A Mathieson 9B screwstem plough, in fine condition.

**£120-180** **MUR**

A screwstem plough, by James Reid, Aberdeen, slight bruise to the wedge, otherwise very good condition.

**£70-100** **MUR**

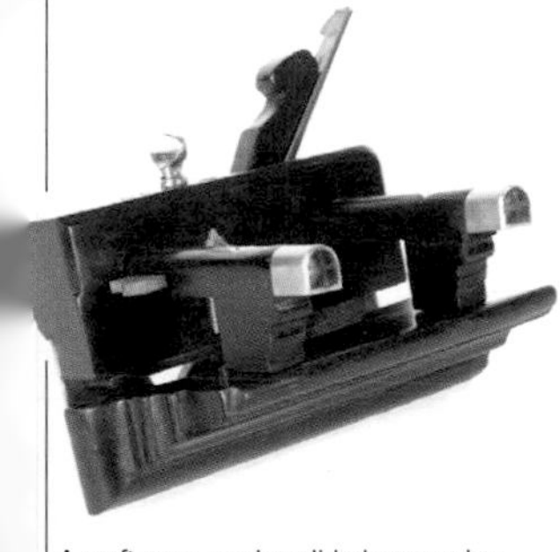

A craftsman-made solid ebony wedge stemmed plough plane, in very good condition.

**£200-250** **MUR**

A craftsman-made beech coachmakers' plough, with reduced compassed skate, in very good condition.

**£180-220** **MUR**

A craftsman-made coachmakers' plough, with boxwood body, beech arms and fence, stem wedges missing.

**£60-90** **MUR**

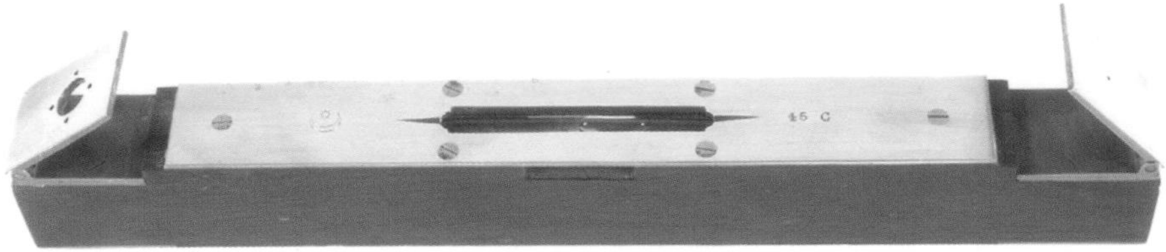

A rare Mathieson 45C sighting level, figured rosewood, in fine condition.

*This type of level was used by surveyors in their work, it is a rare tool.*

**£300-500** **MUR**

A very rare Mathieson ebony No.15D level, with moulded end cap feature, in very good condition.

*Mathieson made several very ornate levels, this is one of the rarest models, only a handful of this model have ever been found.*

*12in (30.5cm) long*

**£800-1,200** **MUR**

An ornate ebony inlaid spirit level, in very good condition.

*12in (30.5cm) long*

**£220-280** **MUR**

An ornate ebony inlaid spirit level, in very good condition.

*12in (30.5cm) long*

**£220-280** **MUR**

A very rare Preston ebony decorative level, in very good condition.

*10in (25.5cm) long*

**£200-300** **MUR**

A decorative spirit level, by Bennett & Burley, brass and ebony, in very good condition.

**£50-70** **MUR**

A unique Scottish rosewood level, with boxwood inlay mimicking the style of manufactured levels, in fine condition.

**£400-500** **MUR**

A Preston mahogany level, original trade label, in very good condition.

**£100-150** **MUR**

A 19thC oak plumb square, with moulded brass plates and iron plumb bob, in very good condition.

**£220-280** **MUR**

## COLLECTORS' NOTES

- Welsh toy company Mettoy released the first Corgi toys in 1956. They placed themselves in direct competition with Dinky's highly successful range of 'Supertoys', and became known as 'the ones with the windows' through their advertising campaigns. Their realistically glazed windows were an important innovation over Dinky. In addition, by 1959 they had developed exciting extra features such as opening doors, 'jewelled' headlights, and suspension known as 'Glidamatic'.
- They produced a hugely popular range of models from the 1960s and 1970s based on vehicles from TV programmes and films such as 'Batman', 'The Avengers' and 'Chitty Chitty Bang Bang'. Their success placed them ahead of the game in front of Dinky, and these models continue to demand high prices due to competition from other avid collectors, particularly of Bond and Beatles memorabilia.
- Versions and variations that are only available in limited numbers are desirable, so look out for unusual colours or features. For example, Batmobiles are rarer in matt black than gloss.
- Condition is a vitally important consideration. Collectors use a grading system to distinguish whether examples are in 'poor', 'fair', 'good', 'very good' or 'excellent' condition. Such a huge number of models were produced, many of which were damaged through play, that it is generally only those in excellent or mint condition that fetch high prices, unless very rare.
- 'Superdetailing' kits from the 1960s can lower the value if they have been applied to the model, as can repairs and repainting or other customisation. Original boxes in mint condition will add a substantial amount to the value and 'Whizzwheels' can also make a model more desirable.

A scarce Corgi 225 red Austin 7 (Mini) Saloon, with yellow seats and smooth spun wheelhubs, in very good condition and in yellow and blue all-card box.

**£40-60** **W&W**

A Corgi 201 turquoise Austin Cambridge Saloon, with flat spun hubs, in near mint condition and in all-carded blue box.

*The green and cream colour combination is rarer and is usually 50 per cent more valuable.*

*1956-61*

**£80-120** **VEC**

A Corgi 450 green Austin Mini Van, with red interior and painted silver grille, in mint condition and in yellow and blue all-carded box.

*The version with the unpainted grille is more desirable.*

*1964-67*

**£60-80** **W&W**

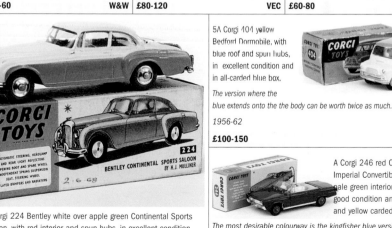

A Corgi 224 Bentley white over apple green Continental Sports Saloon, with red interior and spun hubs, in excellent condition and in blue and yellow carded box.

*1961-65*

**£120-180** **VEC**

A Corgi 404 yellow Bedford Dormobile, with blue roof and spun hubs, in excellent condition and in all-carded blue box.

*The version where the blue extends onto the the body can be worth twice as much.*

*1956-62*

**£100-150** **VEC**

A Corgi 246 red Chrysler Imperial Convertible, with pale green interior, in very good condition and in blue and yellow carded box.

*The most desirable colourway is the kingfisher blue version and can be worth up to four times the value of this version.*

*1965-68*

**£45-55** **VEC**

A Corgi 259 blue Le Dandy Coupé, with white roof and boot and wire wheels, in near mint condition and in blue and yellow carded box.

*1966-69*

**£150-200** **VEC**

A Corgi white 475 Citroen Safari 'Olympic Winter Sports', with red skis and sticks, figure, in near mint condition and in blue and yellow all-carded box.

*1964-65*

**£120-180** **VEC**

A Corgi 440 metallic dark blue Ford Consul Cortina Estate, with 'wood' panels to sides, complete with golfer, caddie, clubs and trolley, in mint condition with pictorial card box and display insert.

*1966-69*

**£120-180** **W&W**

A Corgi 233 orange Heinkel Economy Car, with lemon interior and cast hubs, in very good condition and in blue and yellow carded box with applied US retailers label for $1.00.

*1962-72*

**£70-100** **SAS**

A Corgi 438 metallic green Land Rover 109 WB, with grey plastic canopy and spun hubs, in excellent condition and in blue and yellow carded box.

*1963-77*

**£70-100** **VEC**

A Corgi 335 metallic dark red Jaguar 4.2 Litre 'E' type, with spoked wheels, in excellent condition and in bubble pack.

*1968-70*

**£45-55** **VEC**

A Corgi 262 metallic gold and black Lincoln Continental Executive Limousine, with spun hubs, in excellent condition and in blister card packet.

*1967-69*

**£70-100** **VEC**

A Corgi 230 red Mercedes-Benz 220 SE Coupé, with lemon interior and spun hubs, in excellent condition and in blue and yellow all-carded box.

*1962-64*

**£60-80** **VEC**

A Corgi 202 grey Morris Cowley, with flat spun hubs, in restored near mint condition and in blue all carded box.

*The value is reduced as this example has been restored.*

*1956-61*

**£45-55** **VEC**

A Corgi 226 dark red Morris Mini Minor, with yellow interior and cast hubs, in excellent condition and in yellow and blue carded box.

*1960-68*

**£100-150** **VEC**

A Corgi 249 black Morris Mini-Cooper, with red roof, lemon interior and deluxe wickerwork side panels, in yellow and blue all carded box.

*1965-69*

**£70-90** **CB**

A Corgi 205 red Riley Pathfinder, with flat spun hubs, in very good condition and in all carded blue box.

*1956-62*

**£60-80** **VEC**

A Corgi 281 lacquered purple Rover 2000 TC, with yellow interior and WhizzWheels, in near mint condition and in orange and yellow window box.

*This is the most desirable colourway for this model.*

*1971-72*

**£70-100** **VEC**

A Corgi 207 grey Standard Vanguard III, with red roof and flat spun hubs, in very good condition and in all-carded blue box.

*1957-62*

**£80-120** **VEC**

A Corgi 203 cream Vauxhall Velox, with flat spun hubs, in near mint condition, although slightly re-touched and in all-carded box.

*1956-61*

**£100-150** **VEC**

A Corgi 228 beige Volvo P-1800, with red interior and spun hubs, in near mint condition and in yellow and blue carded box.

*1962-65*

**£80-120** **VEC**

A Corgi 313 metallic blue Ford Cortina GXL, with Graham Hill figure, black roof, white interior and WhizzWheels, in mint condition and in orange and yellow window box.

*Look for the rare left-hand drive promotional variation with 'Cortina' number plate, which can be worth double the value of the standard model.*

*1970-73*

**£100-150** **VEC**

A Corgi 325 white Ford Mustang Competition, with red stripes and silver 'alloy' wheels, in blue and yellow carded box.

*1965-69*

**£50-70** **CB**

A Corgi 328 metallic dark blue Hillman Imp 'Monte Carlo 1966', with 107 racing number, in blue and yellow carded box.

*1966-67*

**£100-150** **WW**

A Corgi 321 red Mini Cooper 'S' Monte Carlo 1966, the white roof with facsimile "Timo Makinen" and "Paul Easter" signatures, in near mint condition and blue and yellow carded box with "1966 Monte Carlo Rally autographed Mini Cooper S" sticker.

*1966-67*

**£150-200** **WW**

A Corgi 150S red Vanwall 'Formula 1' Racing Car, numbered "25" and with white driver, in very good condition, in blue and yellow carded box.

*1961-65*

**£20-40** **CHEF**

A Corgi 515 blue Lotus Mark Eleven Le Mans Racing Car, with red seats, white driver and flat spun hubs, racing number 3, in excellent condition in blue and yellow carded box.

**£80-120** **VEC**

A Corgi Lotus Racing Team Gift Set 37, comprising three racing cars plus a VW Breakdown Truck with red trailer, lacks folding leaflet, in excellent condition and in blue and yellow window box with inner polystyrene tray.

**£250-300** **VEC**

A Corgi '1965 Monte Carlo Rally' Gift Set 38, comprising blue Citroen DS19, dark red Volvo 2000, and red Mini Cooper-S, in mixed condition and in blue and yellow picture box.

**£300-400** **VEC**

A Corgi 1144 Chipperfields Circus Crane and Cage with Rhino, in excellent condition and in blue and yellow window box.

*1969-72*

**£200-300** VEC

A Corgi 1121 Chipperfields Circus Crane Truck, with chrome jib, in excellent condition and in blue and yellow picture box.

*This is the second version with a chrome jib, which replaced the grey plastic jib in production from 1960-62. The prices for the two versions are the same.*

*1963-69*

**£120-180** VEC

A Corgi 503 Chipperfields Circus Giraffe Transporter, in mint condition and in blue and yellow pictorial carded.

*1964-70*

**£120-180** VEC

A Corgi 1130 Chipperfields Circus Horse Transporter, with six grey horses in original card and spun hubs, in excellent condition and in blue and yellow all-carded box with inner packing.

*1962-70*

**£180-220** VEC

A Corgi 1139 Chipperfields Circus Menagerie Transporter, with cast wheels, in excellent condition and in blue and yellow window box with inner polystyrene packing.

*1968-72*

**£200-300** VEC

A Corgi 487 Chipperfields Circus Parade Vehicle, with clown and chimpanzee figures, model club slip and two packing pieces, in blue and yellow carded box.

*1965-69*

**£150-200** SAS

A Corgi 426 Chipperfields Circus Mobile Booking Office, in excellent condition and in blue and yellow carded box.

*Capitalising on the popularity of circuses in the 1960s, Corgi released a range of ten Chipperfields models and four gift sets in co-operation with the circus. The range was discontinued in 1970 but was relaunched in 1994 with another 12 models. They are sought-after by collectors today.*

*1962-64*

**£350-450** VEC

A rare Corgi 511 Chipperfields Circus Poodle Truck, complete with four white and two black dogs and female trainer, in mint condition and in blue and yellow window box.

*The set should retain the plastic dome that sat over the poodles to obtain the best price.*

*1970-71*

**£80-120** W&W

A Corgi Chipperfields Circus Cage Gift Set 19, comprising a Land Rover with tin canopy and Elephant Cage on Trailer, in very good condition and with inner carded tray and packing and blue and yellow carded picture box.

*1962-68*

**£300-400** **VEC**

A Corgi Chipperfields Circus Gift Set 23, first version with Booking Office, Crane Truck, two Animal Cages and Gift Set 19, in excellent condition and in inner polystyrene tray and outer picture box.

*1962-66*

**£300-400** **VEC**

A Corgi Chipperfields Gift Set 23, second version with TK Giraffe Truck, Crane Truck, two Animal Cages and Gift Set 19, with corrugated packing sheet, in original pictorial box.

*The first version, issued between 1962 and 1966 was produced with the Booking Office rather than the Giraffe Truck. This version, produced for only one year, is more desirable.*

*1964*

**£320-380** **SAS**

## A CLOSER LOOK AT A CORGI GIFT SET

*Complete gift sets are hard to find as models and small accessories are easily lost, making complete sets like this hard to find.*

*Not only are the models and accessories in excellent condition, the packaging is also complete and in near mint condition.*

*Individually the Crane & Cage and Menagerie Transporter are both desirable, as are most toys from the Chipperfield range.*

*Gift Set 21 is one of the most sought-after gift sets made by Corgi.*

A Corgi Chipperfields Circus Gift Set 21, comprising Crane and Cage, Menagerie Transporter, in excellent condition and in complete inner and outer packaging in near mint condition.

*1969-71*

**£1,200-1,800** **VEC**

A Corgi 448 blue B.M.C. Police Mini Van, with red interior, aerial, spun hubs, police figure with tracker dog, in near mint condition and in inner carded tray with outer blue and yellow picture box.

*Complete examples of this model are hard to find as the figures were often lost through play.*

*1964-69*

**£150-200** **VEC**

A Corgi 351 blue RAF Land Rover, with tin rear canopy and flat spun hubs, in excellent condition and in blue carded box.

*1958-62*

**£70-100** **VEC**

A Corgi 352 blue RAF Vanguard Staff Car, with flat spun hubs, in near mint condition in blue carded box.

*1958-62*

**£45-55** **VEC**

A Corgi 209 black Riley Pathfinder Police Car, with flat spun hubs, aerial and roof box, in very good condition and in blue carded box.

*1958-61*

**£80-120** **VEC**

A Corgi green 405 Bedford Fire Tender, with black ladders, flat spun hubs, very slightly 'Superdetailed', in near mint condition in blue carded box.

*1956-60*

**£80-120** **VEC**

A Corgi 462 blue, green and white Commer Van 'Hammonds', with cast hubs, in near mint condition and in blue and yellow carded box.

*1971*

**£80-120** **VEC**

A Corgi 483 blue and white Dodge Tipper Truck, with cast hubs, in excellent condition and in blue and yellow carded box.

*1968-72*

**£45-55** **VEC**

A Corgi 64 red Forward Control Jeep, with working conveyor and farmhand figure, in very good condition and in blue and yellow pictorial carded box.

*1965-69*

**£60-80** **CHEF**

A Corgi 236 light blue Motor School Austin A60, with spun hubs, in mint condition and in blue and yellow carded box.

*1964-68*

**£55-65** **VEC**

A Corgi 255 dark blue Motor School Car, left hand-drive export issue, with spun hubs, in excellent condition and in blue and yellow carded box.

*The UK version is light blue and was issued under no. 236.*

*1964-68*

**£100-150** **VEC**

A rare Corgi 468 green, cream and brown Routemaster double decker bus, in the colours of the New South Wales Govt Transport Dept, with Naturally Corgi Toys Corgi Classics adverts, in blue and yellow carded box.

*1964*

**£50-80** **W&W**

A Corgi Agricultural Gift Set 5, comprising Livestock Transporter and pigs, Land Rover and other accessories and figures, generally in excellent condition and with inner polystyrene packing and outer blue and yellow window box.

*1967-75*

**£300-400** **VEC**

A Corgi Major 1110 red Bedford S Petrol Tanker, with flat spun hubs and 'Mobilgas' decal, in excellent condition and in blue and yellow carded box.

*1959-64*

**£180-220** **VEC**

A Corgi Major 1106 Karrier Decca Mobile Radar Van, complete rotating scanner and aerials, in very good condition and with blue an yellow carded box.

*Versions with four and five orange stripes were produced, the value is the same.*

*1959-61*

**£100-150** **W&W**

A Corgi light blue 435 Karrier Bantam Van, with white roof and 'Drive Safely on Milk' decals, in blue and yellow carded boxed.

*1962-63*

**£30-40** **W&W**

A Corgi 428 Karrier Ice-Cream Van, with 'Mr Softee' logo and swivelling salesman figure, in good condition and in blue and yellow carded box.

*1963-66*

**£150-200** **SAS**

A Corgi Major red 1111 Massey Ferguson 780 Combine Harvester, in excellent condition and in blue and yellow carded box together with original inner packing.

**£200-300** **VEC**

A Corgi Major 1126 dark blue Racing Car Transporter, with yellow 'Ecurie Ecosse' lettering and spun hubs, in excellent condition and in blue and yellow carded box including folded leaflet.

*Later versions had the lettering in orange, white and then raised light blue. This early version is more desirable by about 50 per cent.*

*1961-65*

**£250-350** **VEC**

A Corgi Major 1134 olive green 'US Army' Fuel Tanker, with spun hubs, in very good condition and in blue and yellow carded box.

*1965-66*

**£150-200** **VEC**

A Corgi blue and white Scammell 'Co-Op' Gift Set 1151, comprising of Commer Milk Float, Commer Van and Scammell Truck and Trailer, in mint condition and in correct plain mail-away carded outer packaging, not shown.

*1970*

**£350-450** **VEC**

A Corgi Ford 5000 Tractor & Conveyor Gift Set 47, comprising Ford Super Major Tractor with working Conveyor on Trailer, in near mint condition and with inner pictorial stand and blue and yellow picture box.

*1966-71*

**£250-350** **VEC**

A Corgi The Avengers Gift Set 40, comprising Steed's Bentley and Mrs Peel's Lotus Elan and two figures, in good condition and in blue and yellow pictorial box.

*1966-69*

**£200-300** **CHEF**

A Corgi 107 black Batboat on Trailer, with orange plastic fin, in excellent condition and in striped window box.

*The earlier version with a tin-plate fin cover was made from 1967-71 and is more desirable at about twice the value of this.*

*1974-81*

**£150-200** **VEC**

A Corgi 267 Batmobile, with Batman and Robin, lacking rockets, instructions and badge, fair condition, box lacking flap.

*A premium would be paid for a complete example. Matt black Batmobiles are about 50 per cent more valuable than gloss.*

*1966-67*

**£60-80** **CHEF**

A Corgi Batmobile & Batboat Gift Set 3, second version with plain cast wheels on Batmobile and two figures but lacking missiles, in mint condition and in inner polystyrene packing with outer window box.

*The first version was available between 1967-69 and had 'Bat' wheels on the Batmobile and four figures. It can be worth over twice as much as this later version.*

*1980*

**£250-350** **VEC**

A scare Corgi 803 The Beatles Yellow Submarine, with two red hatches and four Beatles figures, in excellent condition and in blue and yellow window box.

*Without the box and in average condition, these models are quite easy to find. The colour of the hatches, either side of the periscopes are the key to value. Examples with one white and one yellow hatch are worth about 25 per cent less, examples with one red and one white hatch are worth around 50 per cent more.*

*1970-71*

**£400-500** **W&W**

A Corgi 259 Penguinmobile, with Penguin figure holding a red and yellow umbrella, in very good condition and in striped window box.

*1979-80*

**£40-50** **SAS**

A Corgi 261 bright gold James Bond's Aston-Martin, with James Bond and bandit figure and with secret instructions, in very good condition and in diorama box.

*1965-69*

**£280-320** **CHEF**

A Corgi 269 white James Bond Lotus Esprit, with missiles still attached to sprue, in mint condition and with pictorial inner and outer film strip window box.

*1977-83*

**£50-80** **VEC**

A Corgi 811 blue and white James Bond Moon Buggy, in excellent condition and in window box with replaced cellophane.

*The roof-opening mechanism should be in working order to achieve the best price.*

*1972-74*

**£350-450** **VEC**

A Corgi white 336 James Bond's Toyota 2000 GT, with two figures, red aerial, two rockets on sprue and instructions, packet and diorama box, boot ajar.

*1967-69*

**£180-220** **SAS**

A Corgi 266 'Chitty Chitty Bang Bang', complete with four figures, in near mint condition and in blue and yellow window box, with replaced cellophane.

*1968-72*

**£120-180** **VEC**

A Corgi 268 The Green Hornet's 'Black Beauty', with cast wheels, sealed secret instructions pack containing leaflet, missiles and spinners, in virtually mint condition and with inner pictorial card and outer picture box.

*It is the superb condition of the model, the packaging and the accessories that make this example so valuable. Prices might rise more if the much mooted Hollywood film is ever made.*

*1967-72*

**£600-800** **VEC**

A Corgi 805 Hardy Boys Rolls-Royce, with bubble packed figures, in excellent condition and in blue and yellow picture box.

*1970-71*

**£80-120** **VEC**

A Corgi 277 red 'Monkees' Monkeemobile, with cast detailed wheels and four Monkee figures, in very good condition and in blue and yellow window box.

*1968-72*

**£250-350** **VEC**

A Corgi 258 white The Saint's Volvo P1800, with black logo on yellow decal, in very good condition and in blue and yellow carded box.

*Look for the very rare version with a white logo on blue label. The version with a white logo on red decal is worth about 10 per cent less.*

*1965-70*

**£150-200** **CHEF**

A Corgi 497 'The Man From U.N.C.L.E.'s Thrush Buster, with cast wheels, 'Waverley' ring, in mint condition and with inner pictorial stand and outer blue and yellow picture box.

*The white version is much more desirable and can be worth three times as much.*

*1966*

**£250-350** **VEC**

## COLLECTORS' NOTES

- Dinky toys were first released in 1931, under the name 'Modelled Miniatures'. They were intended as accessories for Hornby train sets, and only took on the name 'Dinky' in 1934, when the first cars were produced. The first car made was the 23a sports car.
- The newly renamed range proved popular and by 1935, over 200 models were available. These prewar toys, which mainly consisted of road vehicles but also included planes and ships, are the most valuable and desirable to collectors today.
- After a decline in production levels during the war, the slightly smaller scale 'Supertoys' range was released in 1947. In 1969, against growing competition from competitors such as Mattel's 'Hotwheels' and Corgi toys, the 'Speedwheels' range was introduced. The factory continued to produce toys until its closure in 1979. The name was then acquired by Matchbox in 1987, but has remained dormant since 2001.
- As well as date, condition and variations are two important factors to consider. Collectors prefer to buy examples in as close to mint condition as possible, with no signs of wear from play. The addition of an original box can increase the value by up to 40%.
- Variations can occur in terms of colour or detailing, such as wheels or transfers on the side of a van. Also look out for models made in France, or for export to countries like South Africa. Gift sets, with their original boxes, are also currently very popular.

A Dinky 448 turquoise Chevrolet El Camino Pick-Up with Trailers, in good condition and with box.

*1963-68*

**£100-150** **CHEF**

A Dinky 30c fawn Daimler, with black plain chassis and black ridged hubs, in excellent condition with slight mark to roof.

*1946-50*

**£70-100** **VEC**

A Dinky 2214 red Ford Capri Rally Car, with black bonnet and roof and '12' racing number, in mint condition and in damaged vacuform pack.

*1974-76*

**£100-150** **W&W**

A Dinky 212 white Ford Cortina Rally, with black bonnet, 'Castrol' and 'East African Safari' decals and '8' racing number, slight chipping and in original picture box.

*1965-70*

**£100-150** **W&W**

A Dinky 2161 metallic blue Ford Capri, with black roof, slight paint defect to roof, in original vacuform pack.

**£80-120** **W&W**

A Dinky 157 two-tone Jaguar XK120, in turquoise and dark pink, in associated box.

*1957-59*

**£150-200** **W&W**

A Dinky 214 dark blue Hillman Imp Rally, with 'Monte Carlo Rally' decals and '35' racing number, slight factory paint defect, in card picture box.

*1966-69*

**£70-100** **W&W**

A Dinky 38c green Lagonda Sports Coupé, with dark green interior, black ridged hubs and silvered windscreen, in excellent condition.

*1947-50*

**£100-150** **VEC**

A scarce French Dinky 512 dark blue Leskokart Midjet, with driver, in original box.

**£150-200** **W&W**

A Dinky 205 red and white Lotus Cortina Rally, with 'Monte Carlo Rally' decals and '7' racing number, in picture box.

**£100-150** **W&W**

A scarce pre-war Dinky 30b dark blue Rolls-Royce, with open chassis, black chassis and white tyres, minor chips to paint.

*1935-40*

**£120-180** **W&W**

A Dinky 172 cream and tan 'HighLine' Studebaker Land Cruiser, with cream ridged wheels, in excellent condition and with incorrectly labelled box.

*1956-58*

**£70-100** **VEC**

A pre-war French-made dark blue Dinky Super Streamline Saloon, with 13 bonnet louvres, red chassis and white Dunlop tyres and type one chassis and radiator grill, possibly repainted, unboxed.

*This is very similar to the British-issue model 24e made between 1934-40 but lacks the side window framing.*

**£150-200** **DN**

A Dinky 30d olive green Vauxhall, with black open chassis and black ridged wheels, in very good condition.

*c1946*

**£60-80** **VEC**

A rare Dinky Sports Car Gift Set 149, comprising a 109 Austin Healy, a 108 MG Midget, a 107 Sunbeam Alpine, a 110 Aston Martin and a 111 Triumph TR2, in competition finish and blue and white striped box.

*1958-61*

**£800-1,200** **W&W**

A Dinky 477 green and yellow Parsley's Car, from 'The Adventures of Parsley' TV series, in excellent condition and with uncut inner card and original picture box.

*1970-72*

**£70-100** SAS

A Dinky 112 yellow Purdey's TR7, from 'The Avengers' TV series, with black 'P' on the bonnet and Speedwheels, in excellent condition and with mint condition box.

*The version with a yellow 'P' within black can be worth up to twice as much.*

*1978-80*

**£60-80** VEC

A Dinky 105 white Maximum Security Vehicle, from the 'Captain Scarlet' TV series, with red interior, cast wheels and 'Radioactive' crate, in very good condition with card box, but lacks aerial.

*1968-75*

**£30-50** VEC

A Dinky 103 red Spectrum Patrol Car, from the 'Captain Scarlet' TV series, in very good condition and with card picture box.

*1968-75*

**£120-180** CHEF

A Dinky 104 Spectrum Pursuit Vehicle, from the 'Captain Scarlet' TV series, excellent condition, with stand, instructions, boxed

*This is the more valuable first version: the seated figure is not attached to the door.*

*1968-1972*

**£180-220** VEC

A Dinky 350 Tiny's Mini Moke, from 'The Enchanted House' TV series, with giraffe figure, in excellent condition and with inner pictorial stand and outer box.

*1970-71*

**£220-280** VEC

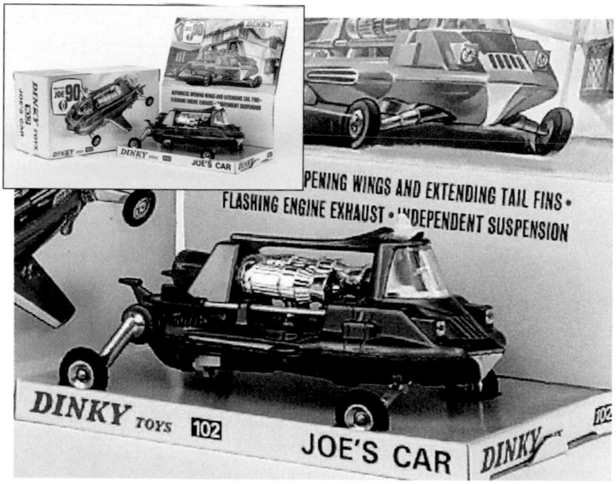


A Dinky 102 green Joe's Car, from the 'Joe 90' TV series, with figure, in excellent condition and with inner pictorial stand and outer picture box.

*1969-75*

**£250-350** VEC

A Dinky 108 powder blue Sam's Car, from the 'Joe 90' TV series, with lemon interior, red engine cover and cast wheels, in very good condition and with instruction sheet, inner pictorial stand and outer picture box.

*The silver version is the most common, look for the wine red colourway which can be worth about 20 per cent more.*

*1971-1975*

**£150-200** **VEC**

A Dinky 106 white 'The Prisoner' Mini-Moke, with flat spun hubs and silver-coloured windscreen, in excellent condition and with picture box.

*Spun hubs, as here, are slightly more desirable than cast hubs. Also look for examples with silver-coloured or black metal windscreens as they are more sought-after.*

*1967-70*

**£250-350** **VEC**

A Dinky 109 Gabriel's Model 'T' Ford, from 'The Secret Service' TV series, with figure, in near mint condition with box but lacking inner packaging.

*1969-71*

**£40-60** **VEC**

A Dinky 360 white Eagle Freighter, from the 'Space 1999' TV series, in near mint condition with unapplied decal sheet and with inner polystyrene moon display and outer window box, replaced cellophane.

*1975-79*

**£150-200** **VEC**

A Dinky 359 white Eagle Transporter, from the 'Space 1999' TV series, in near mint condition with unapplied decal sheet and with inner card tray and outer window box with replaced cellophane.

*1975-79*

**£150-200** **VEC**

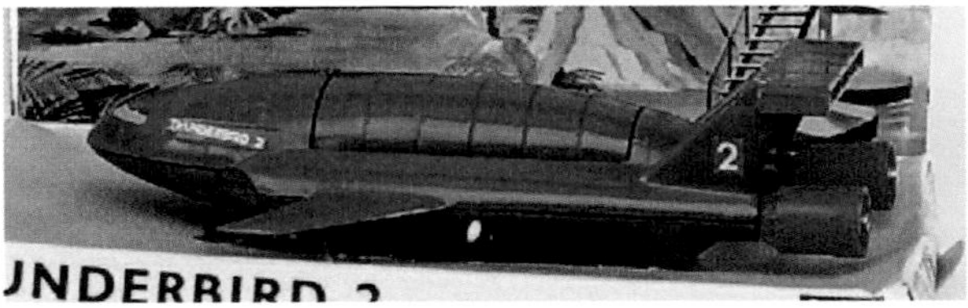

A Dinky 101 green Thunderbirds 2 & 4, with yellow plastic '4' inside, in excellent condition and with inner pictorial stand and outer picture box.

*Look out for the extremely rare metallic turquoise version, which could fetch over £1,000.*

*1967-73*

**£300-400** **VEC**

A Dinky 100 pink Lady Penelope's 'FAB 1', with Parker figure, in good condition and in damaged picture stand box.

*1967-75*

**£100-150** **CHEF**

A Dinky 352 yellow Ed Straker's Car, from the 'UFO' TV series, with white interior and cast spun hubs, in excellent condition and with original carded box.

*1971-75*

**£100-150** **VEC**

A Dinky 987 'ABC TV' Control room, complete with camera and camera man, in excellent condition and with original box.

*1962-67*

**£120-180** **W&W**

A Dinky 945 A.E.C. Fuel Tanker 'ESSO', in Lucas Oil livery with green cab and tank and white decals, in excellent condition and with original Lucas bubble pack.

*Without the Lucas livery, the model is worth about 30 per cent less.*

*1977*

**£120-180** **W&W**

## A CLOSER LOOK AT A FODEN TRUCK

*This example has the more desirable first-type cab, produced from 1947-52.*

*The second type cab does not have the flash on the side and has the radiator behind the grille. It was used from 1952-64.*

*As well as being a rare version, this example is in virtually mint condition and retains its box, also in fantastic condition, which is extremely rare.*

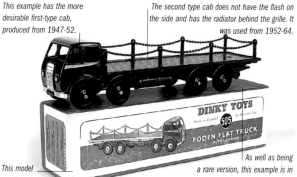

*This model was introduced in 1952 and so was only produced with this type cab for one year.*

A Dinky Supertoys 505 maroon Foden Flat Truck with Chains, with first type cab, silver flash, ridged hubs, in near mint condition and with blue box.

*A green version with a first-type cab was also produced and is worth about half this colourway.Foden trucks are a popular area with many collectors.*

*1952*

**£12,000-18,000** **VEC**

A Dinky Supertoys 960 orange Albion Lorry Concrete Mixer, with blue and yellow mixer, minor wear and chips, in striped box.

*1960-68*

**£60-80** **W&W**

A Dinky Supertoys 968 BBC TV Roving-Eye Vehicle, complete with cameraman, camera and aerial, in very good condition and with striped box.

*1959-64*

**£80-120** **W&W**

A Dinky 410 red Bedford Tipper Truck, with cream tipper body and unglazed windows, minor paint chip to body, in original box.

*The later version with glazed windows are worth about 30 per cent more.*

*1954-61*

**£150-200** **W&W**

A Dinky Supertoys 923 red and yellow Big Bedford Van 'Heinz', with 'Heinz 57 Varieties' wording and ketchup bottle logo, in mint condition and with striped box.

*The version with a tin of baked beans rather than a bottle of ketchup is usually worth only a third of this one.*

*1958-59*

**£1,500-2,000** **W&W**

A Dinky Supertoys 514 red Foden 14-ton Tanker, with first type cab flashed with silver, fawn tank and red hubs, some wear and minor chipping to tank, in original box.

*1948-52*

**£250-350** **W&W**

A Dinky Supertoys 901 red Foden eight-wheel Diesel Wagon, with second type cab, fawn flatbed body and Supertoy wheels, in excellent condition and with striped box.

*1954-57*

**£100-150** **VEC**

A Dinky Supertoys 903 dark blue Foden Flat Truck with Tailboard, with second type cab, orange flatbed and light blue hubs, in good condition but lacking box.

*All other colourways are worth double this version.*

*1954-57*

**£80-120** **DN**

A Dinky 905 maroon Foden Flat Truck with Chains, with second type cab, in striped box.

*c1956*

**£150-200** **CB**

A Dinky Supertoys 942 Foden 14-ton Tanker 'Regent', in dark blue cab and red, white and blue tank, in excellent condition and with striped box.

*1955-57*

**£300-400** **W&W**

A Dinky Supertoys 513 green Guy Flat Truck with Tailboard, first type cab with small hook and ridged wheels, slight chipping to paint, in blue box.

*The most valuable versions of this truck are the grey and blue colourway with first type cab, and the all-yellow version with the second type cab. Both of these can be worth between three and four times the value of this colourway.*

*1948-52*

**£250-350** **W&W**

A Dinky Supertoys 563 orange Blaw Knox Heavy Tractor, with driver, in good condition and with brown box with red and white printed label.

*The dark blue version with mid-blue roller is usually more valuable at over twice as much.*

*1948-54*

**£50-70** **CHEF**

A Dublo Dinky 073 bright green Land Rover and Horse Trailer, with orange trailer, black ramp and horse figure, in good condition and with yellow box.

*Dublo models were made to a scale of 1:76.*

*1960-64*

**£100-150** **DN**

A scarce Dinky Supertoy 935 dark blue Leyland Octopus Flat Truck with Chains, with yellow cab flash, pale grey flatbed and pale grey plastic hubs, in fair condition and with pictorial box.

*This is the most desirable colourway, all others are generally worth about a third of the value of this one.*

*1964-66*

**£500-700** **VEC**

A Dinky 917 blue Mercedes-Benz Truck and Trailer, with yellow and white trailers, minor wear and one door mirror missing, with pictorial inner stand and outer box.

*The two versions with company branding on the sides of the trailers can be worth up to four times as much.*

*1968-74*

**£70-100** **W&W**

A pre-war Dinky 28 dark blue 28b 'Pickfords' Delivery Van, with blue smooth hubs, in poor condition.

*1934-35*

**£150-200** **VEC**

A scarce 1960s French Dinky Supertoys 886 yellow 'Profileur 100 Richier' Grader (886), with red wheels and driver figure, slight age wear and minor paint chipping, in striped box.

**£150-200** **W&W**

A Dinky 982 mid-and light blue Pullmore Car Transporter, with loading ramp, in excellent condition and with striped box.

*The version with with glazed windows is usually worth about 20 per cent more.*

*1955-61*

**£120-180** **W&W**

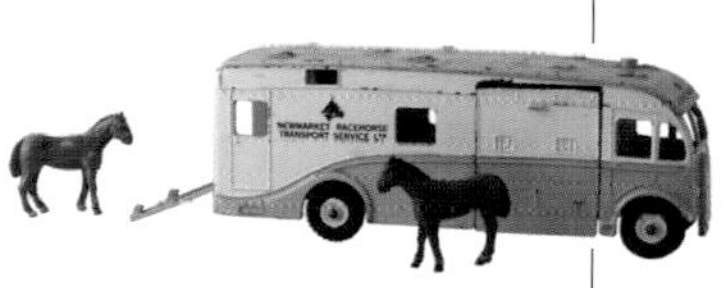

A Dinky Supertoys 979 Racehorse Transport, with two horse figures, in fair condition, with box lid only (not shown).

*1961-1964*

**£35-45** **CHEF**

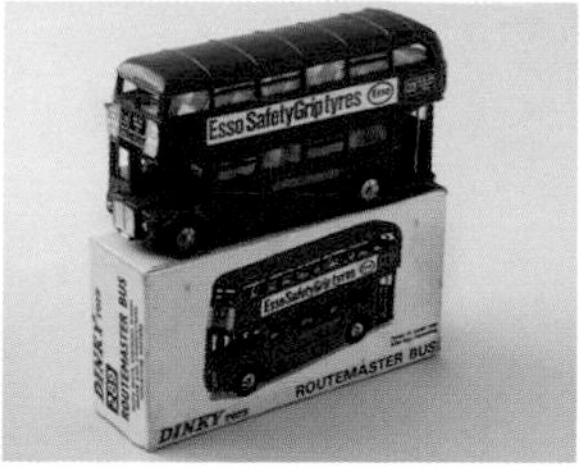


A Dinky 289 red Routemaster Bus, with 'ESSO Safety-Grip Tyres' label and driver figure, in yellow and white box.

*A rare deep purple version can be worth three times this traditional colourway.*

*1968-80*

**£40-60** **CB**

A Dinky Supertoys 975 Ruston-Bucyrus Excavator, in very good condition, exhaust pipe refitted, in original box with inner packaging and instructions.

*1963-67*

**£80-120** **W&W**

A Dinky Post Office Services Gift Set 299, comprising 260 Royal Mail Morris Van, 261 GPO Telephones Van, 750 Call Box, 011 Messenger, 012 Postman, in striped box.

*1957-59*

**£450-550** **W&W**

A French Dinky 884 Brockway Bridge Truck, with detachable bridge sections and two inflatables, in mint condition and with striped box, packing and paperwork.

*1962-64*

**£200-300** W&W

A 1960s French Dinky 808 'Camion G.M.C. Militaire Depannage' breakdown truck, complete with hook and cord, in excellent condition with box.

**£200-300** W&W

A 1960s French Dinky 809 'Camion G.M.C. Militaire Bache' truck, in excellent condition and with original box, inner packaging and USA decal transfers.

**£200-300** W&W

A Dinky 30f cream Ambulance, with black chassis and black ridged hubs, in very good condition.

*1947-1948*

**£55-65** VEC

A 1960s French Dinky 556 'Ambulance "ID19" Citroën', with minor wear, in original yellow card box.

**£70-100** W&W

A 1960s French Dinky 556 'Ambulance "ID19" Citroën', manufactured by Meccano, in original box.

**£120-180** CB

A Dinky 255 red Mersey Tunnel Police Van, the box missing one flap.

*1955-61*

**£30-50** CB

A Dinky 277 Superior Criterion Ambulance, in fair condition and with picture box.

*Examples with a 'gold' see-through box are slightly more desirable and can be worth about 20 per cent more.*

*1962-68*

**£22-28** CHEF

A 1960s French Dinky 823 'Camion G.M.C. Militaire Citerne Essence' tanker, complete with accessory road sign, in excellent condition and with original box, inner packaging and leaflet.

**£350-450** **W&W**

A French Dinky 822 Half-Track M3, complete with machine gun and rail, in mint condition and with yellow picture box.

*1962-64*

**£70-100** **W&W**

A 1960s French Dinky 825 'Camion Amphibie Militaire DUKW' amphibious vehicle, complete with driver, hatch cover and accessories, in mint condition and with box.

**£100-150** **W&W**

A 1960s French Dinky 'Camion Militaire de Dépannage Berliet' breakdown truck, with driver, in excellent condition and with box and instructions.

**£120-180** **W&W**

A 1960s French Dinky 883 'Char AMX Poseur de Pont' bridge laying tank, in mint condition and with original box and paperwork.

**£150-200** **W&W**

A Dinky 665 Honest John Missile Erector, complete with missile and instructions, in mint condition and with original box.

*1964-75*

**£100-150** **W&W**

A Dinky Supertoys 666 Missile Erector Vehicle and Corporal Missile Launcher, with black and white missile and metal erector gears, complete and probably unused but with some rusting, with striped box, packing and paperwork.

*1959-64*

**£200-300** **W&W**

A Dinky Supertoys 661 Recovery Tractor, with die-cast hubs and complete with hook and cord in working order, in excellent condition and in striped box.

*Examples with plastic hubs and a yellow picture box can be worth twice as much.*

*1957-65*

**£70-100** **W&W**

A Dinky Field Gun Set 697, comprising 688 Field Artillery Tractor, 687 Trailer and 686 25-pounder Field Gun, some damp damage to box.

*A scarce late example with a seldom-seen picture box.*

*1957-71*

**£120-180** **W&W**

A scarce pre-war Dinky 45 colour lithographed tinplate Garage, with minor discoloration and wear, in rare original card box.

*1935-40*

**£250-350** **W&W**

A scarce pre-war Dinky 48 tinplate Petrol Station, together with 'Power', 'Shell', 'Cleveland' and 'ESSO' petrol pumps and a Pratts motor oil bin, rust to staples, minor fatigue, four spots of rust to underside of base, one hose missing, in original card box with corrugated card packing piece.

*1935-41*

**£350-450** **W&W**

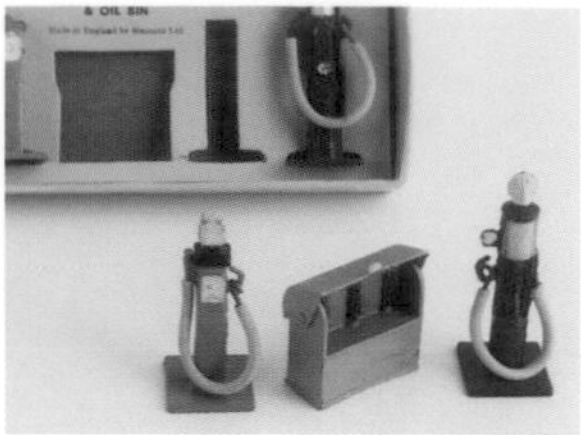

A Dinky Petrol Pumps Set 47, containing pumps 479a-49d with white rubber hoses and a plain yellow oil bin, in good condition, in yellow box with plain cardboard sleeve.

*1946-50*

**£120-180** **DN**

A pre-war Dinky A.A. Set 44, comprising of a 44a tinplate A.A. Box, post-war 44b A.A. Motor Cycle Patrol and 44c A.A. Guide directing and a 44d A.A. Guide saluting, all in very good condition and in pictorial box, split to one end of lid.

*1935-41*

**£200-300** **VEC**

A scarce pre-war Dinky Postal Set 12, comprising 12a GPO Pillar Box, 12b Air Mail Pillar Box, 12c Telephone Call Box, 12d Telephone Messanger, 12e Postman, 34b Royal Mail Van, together with another white call box, with original blue card box with yellow insert and blue string.

*1937-41*

**£450-550** **W&W**

A Dinky 005 Train and Hotel Staff set, in very good condition and in original box.

*1954-56*

**£70-100** **SAS**

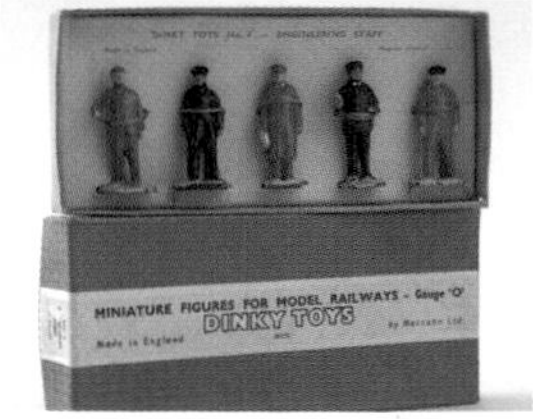


A Dinky Engineering Staff Gift Set 4, comprising two 4b Fitters, a 4c Storekeeper, a 4d Greaser and a 4e Engine-Room attendant, in green box.

*1946-54*

**£80-120** **F**

A pre-war Dinky Road Signs Set 47, complete with 12 signs, in excellent condition, in yellow box missing end label.

*1935-41*

**£70-100** **VEC**

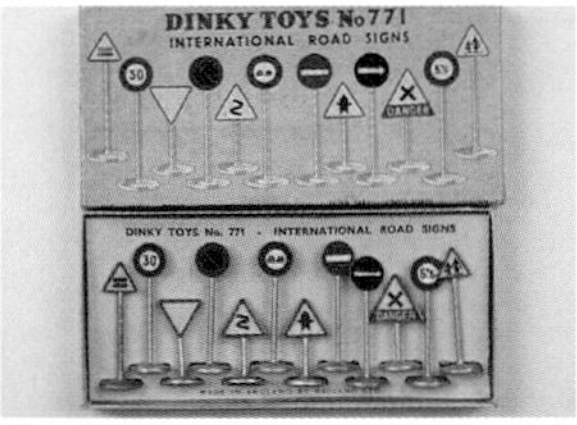


A Dinky International Road Signs Gift Set 771, complete with 12 signs, in near mint condition, in yellow pictorial card box.

*1953-65*

**£60-90** **VEC**

A Chad Valley wind-up scale model blue Fordson Major tractor, with orange wheels, complete with working steering and crank handle wind-up mechanism, in excellent condition, in good condition box with inner packaging.

*This model was only made for a year. The superb condition and box helps push the value upwards.*

*1952*

**£500-600** **VEC**

A rare Charbens model steamroller, green diecast body with red spoked wheels and roller, complete with smoke stack, canopy and steering wheel, in original box.

*4.5in (11.5cm) long*

**£350-450** **W&W**

A 1950s Leroy Cox 'Thimble Drome' Champion hand-painted diecast racer, painted in cream and black with 'Letelle', 'Johnny Rice' and '54' transfers.

*9.75in (25cm) long*

**£150-200** **AAC**

A 1950s Leroy Cox 'Thimble Drome' Champion hand-painted diecast racer, painted in yellow and red with 'Curtis', 'Chet Gibbons' and '5' transfers.

*Leroy Cox (1906-81) founded Cox Manufacturing in 1944, and made metal race cars from 1945. In 1947, he introduced the Thimble Drome Champion racecar, which could be propelled in circles by swinging it on a tether. He then began mounting a small fuel-powered engine and propeller on the back, so they could propel themselves. The business was successful and he diversified into aeroplanes during the 1950s. Examples are often found in poor condition, having been raced. The paintwork and transfers on these examples are particularly fine.*

*9.75in (25cm) long*

**£150-250** **AAC**

A 1950s Leroy Cox 'Thimble Drome' Champion hand-painted diecast racer, painted in blue and black with '36' transfers.

*9.75in (25cm) long*

**£150-200** **AAC**

A 1950s Leroy Cox 'Thimble Drome' Champion hand-painted diecast racer, painted in red and silver with '1' transfers.

*9.75in (25cm) long*

**£150-200** **AAC**

A Matchbox Series 22 Vauxhall Cresta, in pale grey with lilac side panels, boxed.

**£60-80** **W&W**

A Matchbox Superkings range Europa Caravelle caravan.

*c1978*

**£3-5** GAZE

A Mercury diecast light grey model Motor Scooter, with grey seat, ends of handle-bars worn.

**£50-70** SAS

A Mercury off-white and blue 216 model Lambretta 125 FC Triporteur Scooter, in very good condition.

**£70-100** SAS

A Morestone no.2 Foden Long-Distance Diesel Wagon, light beige cab and chassis, red back, beige wheels, near mint condition, with good condition box.

*1955-56*

**£120-180** VEC

A rare early 1900s Plank diecast two-seater open-topped car, painted in cream with red line detailing, louvered bonnet, cast spoked wheels, hole in the seat for a missing figure, some wear.

*2.5in (6.5cm) long*

**£50-70** W&W

A Tri-ang Spot-On 118 BMW Isetta, in pale blue with cream interior, in very good condition, with in poor condition box.

*1960*

**£45-55** VEC

A Tri-ang Spot-On 119 Meadows Frisky, in pale green with black roof and cream interior, in excellent condition, with excellent condition box.

*1960*

**£90-110** VEC

A Tri-ang Spot-On 118 BMW Isetta, in pink with cream interior, in near mint condition, with excellent condition box.

*1960*

**£70-100** VEC

A Tri-ang Spot-On 191 Sunbeam Alpine Convertible, in red with cream interior, in good condition, with fair condition box.

*1963*

**£80-120** **VEC**

A Tri-ang Spot-On 115 Bristol 406, in metallic green with red interior, in excellent condition, noting a slight casting flaw to roof, in good condition box.

*1960*

**£100-150** **VEC**

A Tri-ang Spot-On Austin A60, with roofrack, restored.

*1963* *4.25in (10.5cm) long*

**£25-35** **GAZE**

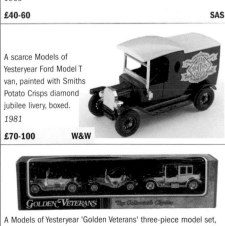

A Tri-ang Spot-On 266 red model Bull-Nose Morris, in original window box, with small paper tear to box and small fracture to cellophane.

*1965*

**£40-60** **SAS**

A scarce Models of Yesteryear Ford Model T van, in Arnotts Biscuits livery, boxed, minor wear.

*1982*

**£70-100** **W&W**

A scarce Models of Yesteryear Ford Model T van, painted with Smiths Potato Crisps diamond jubilee livery, boxed.

*1981*

**£70-100** **W&W**

A Models of Yesteryear 'Golden Veterans' three-piece model set, comprising a 1912 Rolls-Royce, 1911 Maxwell Roadster, and 1911 Daimler, in very good condition, with original window box.

**£35-45** **SAS**

An American slush-cast toy milk bottle truck, painted in silver, with embossed sides and rubber tires, in excellent condition.

*5.25in (13.5cm) long*

**£100-150** **BER**

A Hornby Series clockwork 0-4-0 LMS tank locomotive 516, repainted and restored.

**£70-100** SAS

A Hornby Series clockwork 0-4-0 GWR tank locomotive 5500, repainted and restored.

**£100-150** SAS

A Hornby Series clockwork 4-4-2 Nord locomotive and eight-wheeler tender 31801, repainted and restored.

**£150-200** SAS

A Hornby Series electric 4-4-2 Southern tank locomotive 2091, repainted and restored.

**£180-220** SAS

A Hornby Series electric LNER 0-4-0 locomotive 1368, with tender, in good condition, some retouching.

**£220-280** SAS

A Hornby O gauge no.3 E Caerphilly Castle, 2-4-2 locomotive and tender cab side, RN 2091, light to smoke box centre, 20-volt mechanism, minor damage.

**£200-300** W&W

A Hornby Series blue Cadbury's Chocolates Private Owners model van, restored.

**£40-50** SAS

A Hornby Series Seccotine Private Owners Wagon, in Service Dept. box "57370", repainted and restored.

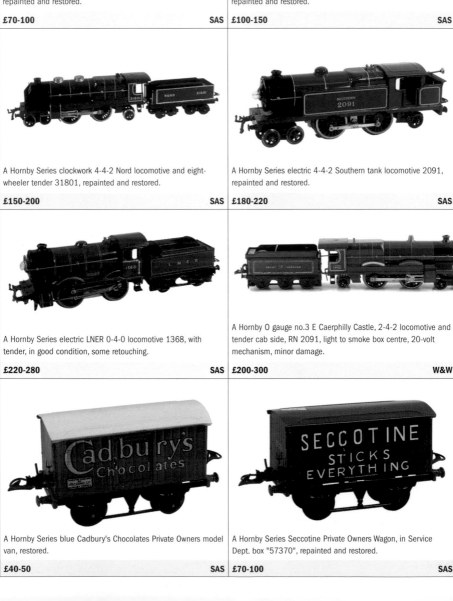

**£70-100** SAS

A Hornby Series No.2 LNER passenger 3rd brake, in original box, with some damage.

**£90-120** SAS

A Bassett Lowke 4-4-0 Southern electric locomotive and tender.

*16in (40.5cm) long*

**£180-220** GAZE

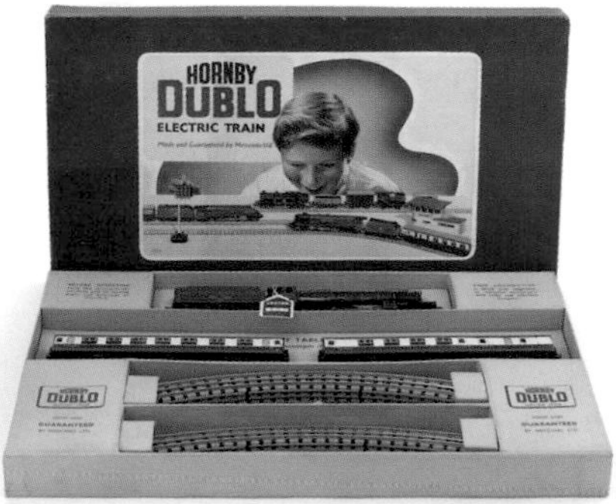

A Hornby Dublo EDP20 'Britolian' passenger train set, comprising 4-6-0 Bristol Castle engine and tender in BR green, RN7013 and two Western Region coaches in cream and brown livery, W15862 and W34881, complete with track and paperwork, boxed.

**£400-500** W&W

A rare early 1900s Tipp & Co. tinplate clockwork 4-4-4 carpet locomotive, with approx 1-gauge wheel spacing, boiler, smokebox and cab printed in maroon, black and yellow, towhook for tender, fixed key to clockwork for operation.

*13.5in (34.5cm) long*

**£250-350** W&W

A 1920s Märklin hand-painted train station no.2031, with storage shed to the side, luggage office and seats, one flight of stairs, chimneys brazed and renewed, some wear.

*20.75in (52cm) wide*

**£1,500-2,000** LAN

A Hornby Trains no.3 Station model, with end-ramps, with original box, one lid corner split.

**£70-100** SAS

A 1930s cream and red Meccano no.2 Constructor Plane toy, in good condition.

*Meccano, founded in 1901, initially called its self-build kits 'Mechanics Made Easy'. Nickel strips were introduced in 1908, with red and green sets being released in 1926. The Constructor range, widened from 1931 to include cars and planes, proved extremely popular. Boxes and catalogues are also collectable.*

*17.75in (45cm) long*

**£220-280** **SAS**

A cream and red Meccano no.1 Constructor Plane toy, with pilot, in good condition.

*10.25in (26cm) long*

**£150-200** **SAS**

A 1930s Meccano no.0 aircraft, complete with major parts including fuselage, four wings, fuselage base, tailplane, floats, wing struts, propeller, axle and two wheels, all finished in cream and red with RAF transfer roundels, minor assembly wear.

**£120-180** **W&W**

A 1930s cream and red Meccano no. 2 Constructor Car toy, with reproduction driver, side lights over-painted, and fatigue to wheels.

**£350-450** **SAS**

A Meccano no.2 construction car, finished in green and yellow with driver, long and short wheelbase parts, sport and normal mudguards, boat tail and short rear bodywork, clockwork motor with key and broken spring, paint chips and some losses.

**£450-550** **W&W**

A rare 1930s Spanish Meccano 'Aero' set box, containing the major parts of a cream red and blue kit including wings, fuselage, panels, engine mounts, floats, engine cowl, engines and propellers, wing and float struts, roundels and rudder, in original Spanish box with blue DC3 picture, some damage and loss.

**£220-280** **W&W**

A French 'Jouets Meccano' products catalogue, in very good condition.

*1936-37*

**£50-70** **SAS**

A French-made Meccano 'Le Livre Des Meilleurs Jouets' products catalogue, in very good condition.

*1938-39*

**£40-60** **SAS**

## COLLECTORS' NOTES

- During the mid-late 19th century, tinplated steel overtook wood as a material for making toys. It was less expensive to produce, more versatile and could be easily decorated with finer details. Germany became the centre of production, with now-legendary names arising, such as Marklin (founded 1856), Gebruder Bing (1863-1933), Schreyer & Co, known as 'Schuco' (1912-78) and Lehmann (founded 1881). From the late 19thC, companies such as Marx (1896-1982) and Ferdinand Strauss (c1914-42) were founded in the US, along with a few other more short-lived, smaller companies.
- 19thC tinplate tends to be hand painted, with colour lithographic transfers (a form of printing) taking over shortly after 1900. Lithography meant that even finer decorative details could be applied quickly and efficiently. Look closely at the surface of a piece. If it is hand painted, you will be able to see variation in the surface and also possibly brush marks. If the surface is shiny and totally flat, with tiny details, it is more likely to have lithographic decoration.
- After WWII, the centre of production moved to Japan, although West Germany was still a major producer. Toys became more novelty in format and theme, and were often battery powered. This also enabled them to have 'mystery actions' such as flashing lights, sparks and sounds. The fascination with outer space and the space race is reflected in the number of space-themed toys produced at this time. By the late 1960s, injection-moulded plastic had taken over.
- The type of toy, maker, size and date all count towards value. Toys by major names will always attract a strong following. If the toy is early and hand painted, it will usually be desirable. Large ships, early cars, zeppelins and planes are amongst the most valuable types. From the post-war period, large robots are generally the most desirable and valuable. Nevertheless, do not ignore the tiny tinplate penny toys, as these can fetch high sums too, depending on rarity and condition.
- Also consider the novelty toys such as clockwork moving figurines produced by those such as Gunthermann. Many have been reproduced today, so check colours against reference books and handle as much tinplate as possible to learn how to recognise originals. Extra details, such as opening doors on cars, will usually add desirability. Beware of rust and particularly scratched lithography, as this is nearly impossible to restore.

A 1920s Distler lithographed and hand-painted tinplate model Limousine, with red and black detailing, mudguards and running boards, chauffeur and spare wheel, registration plate "7673", replacements, and faint corrosion.

*1.5in (3.5cm) long*

**£200-300** **SAS**

A Louis Marx lithographed tinplate 'Electric Coupe', in red and yellow, with electric lights, rubber tyres, clockwork mechanism and electric drive.

*15in (38cm) long*

**£250-350** **BER**

A Louis Marx lithographed tinplate 'G-Man Pursuit Car', in blue and red, with seated figure holding gun inside and friction drive.

*14.25in (36cm) long*

**£300-400** **BER**

A Mettoy lithographed tinplate clockwork two door sedan, in red with yellow trim, with nickel grill and bumper.

*9in (23cm) long*

**£120-180** **BER**

A lithographed tinplate clockwork Phaeton, in brown with black trim, with seated driver and silver disc wheels.

*10in (25.5cm) long*

**£150-200** **BER**

A prototype Marx Lasalle roadster, with added horn and steering linkage, marked by factory on base, "Glendale Plant", in excellent condition.

*The superb styling, excellent condition and the fact that this is a, possibly unique, prototype make this highly desirable to collectors.*

c1940 *11in (28cm) long*

**£350-450** **BER**

## A CLOSER LOOK AT A TINPLATE ROADSTER

*The roadster is hand-painted rather than decorated with printed lithographs, indicating an earlier model that would have taken much longer to decorate.*

*It is well detailed, with headlamps, side lamps, a windscreen, realistically moulded, padded leather seat and even a handbrake to stop and start the motion.*

*At 11 inches long, it is also a rare, large size and this early type of car is highly desirable.*

*The wheels are well-made with spokes and rubber tyres, rather than just being single discs of tinplate, also indicating a high quality model.*

A Carette hand-painted tinplate Open Roadster, with embossed seating, nickel headlamps and side lanterns, hand brake to sides and clockwork mechanism.

*Although Carette closed in 1917, it was very prolific. Their large Limousines are particularly desirable.*

*c1906* *11in (28cm) long*

**£6,000-7,000** **BER**

A Schuco Wendeauto 1010, Maybach streamlined tinplate toy car, clockwork, working, missing key, the car runs without falling off the table.

*1950*

**£120-180** **TK**

A Distler Porsche Elextromatic 7500, restored with new bottom plate, some marks inside.

**£250-350** **LAN**

A Wüco No. 126-7 Volkswagen red chromolithographed Beetle, with friction drive, slight wear.

*5.25in (13cm) long*

**£70-100** **LAN**

A PN chromolithographed sheet metal limosine 320, with fly wheel mechanism, original box.

*5.5in (14.5cm) long*

**£30-50** **LAN**

A 1950s Schuco lithographed tinplate 'Tacho-Examico 4002' car, the movement in working order, with US-zone markings, with original box.

**£300-400** **LAN**

A 1960s Japanese W-Toy lithographed tinplate friction-powered red and cream Donald Duck 'Duckmobile', with original box.

*The Disney theme and good box artwork increase the value of this Japanese tinplate car.*

*6.5in (16.5cm) long*

**£150-200** **SAS**

A Japanese Masudaya 3575 metallic blue battery operated lithographed tinplate Volkswagen 'Beetle', in original box.

*5in (13cm) long*

**£22-28** **SAS**

A Distler Electromatic toy petrol station, plastic and tinplate with lithographed decoration and original box.

**£100-150** **ATK**

A Schuco lithographed tinplate 'Studio 1050' Mercedes racing car, complete with tools, box, leaflet and instructions.

*c1935*

**£100-150** **ATK**

A French Joustra lithographed and painted tinplate garage and a friction-powered Renault Dauphine, some wear.

*Joustra was founded in 1935 in Strasbourg by Guillaume Marx, who was previously a director of notable German tinplate toy maker Gebruder Bing of Nuremburg.*

*5.5in (14cm) long*

**£25-35** **LAN**

A 'Spiel Nutz' tinplate clockwork 'Micro-Racer', model 1041, with brake, key and original box for model 1042.

*3.5in (8.5cm) long*

**£50-80** **WDL**

A Louis Marx lithographed tinplate clockwork 'Racer', with checkerboard pattern in grill and seated driver, in excellent condition.

*13.5in (34.5cm) long*

**£280-320** **NB**

A Japanese Taiyo lithographed tinplate and plastic battery-operated GT racing car.

*9.5in (24cm) long*

**£10-15** **GAZE**

## A CLOSER LOOK AT A MARX CAR

*Milton Berle (1908-2002) was a famous US radio and television star from 1948 into the 1950s, known to millions as 'Uncle Miltie', and responsible for an early peak in television sales and viewing.*

*The lithographed design includes many of his most famous trademark phrases and slogans.*

*Look out for complete examples with their original box, which can raise the value to £150-250, although look for signs of age and wear as reproduction boxes are being made.*

*This example lacks Milton's plastic cowboy hat, which can be found in a light beige or red - both are worth roughly the same.*

A 1950s Louis Marx lithographed tinplate clockwork Milton Berle 'Crazy Car'.

*5.5in (14cm) long*

**£100-150** **AAC**

A 1950s German US Zone lithographed tinplate clockwork race game, the six-piece roadway with pit-stop shed, two cars and key.

**£40-60** **SAS**

A Louis Marx lithographed tinplate clockwork 'Uncle Wiggly' car, with seated Uncle Wiggly and egg basket and grass designs to side.

*7.5in (19cm) long*

**£250-350** **BER**

A Louis Marx lithographed tinplate clockwork 'Joy Rider' car, with comical graphics, lacks windshield and brief case.

*c1929* *7.5in (19cm) long*

**£60-80** **BER**

A rare Tipp & Co lithographed tinplate clockwork military radio truck 915, with accessories, headlights missing.

*Quality manufacturer Tipp & Co. used the initial 'TCO' on its toys.*

**£550-650** **LAN**

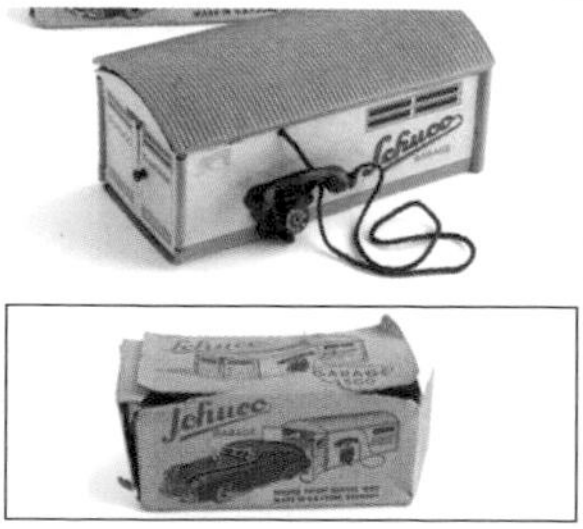

A Schuco lithographed tinplate 1500 garage, complete with original box.

*Original boxes for such toys are hard to find - this one is in relatively poor condition.*

*c1940*

**£30-40** **GAZE**

A 1960s Japanese Horikawa lithographed tinplate battery-operated fire engine, with a plastic ladder and decals to sides, marked "SH".

**£25-35** **WDL**

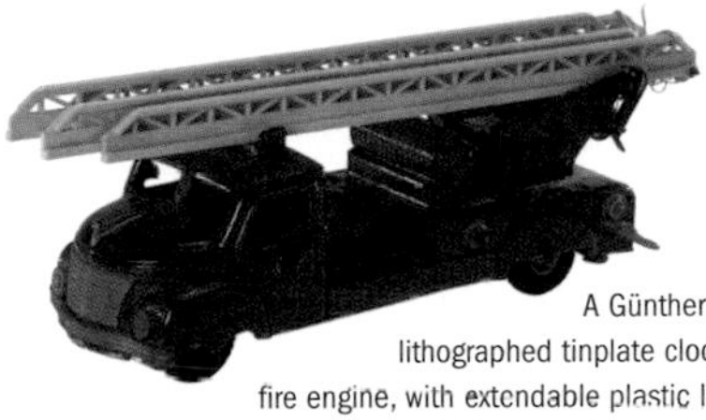

A Günthermann lithographed tinplate clockwork fire engine, with extendable plastic ladder, with two sheet metal figures, marked "Western Germany".

*Fire engines are popular vehicles in any metal material, particularly in the US. This example is large, complete and by a well-known maker, even though it is late in date.*

*12.75in (32cm) long*

**£55-65** **WDL**

A Russian lithographed tinplate Crane Truck, with hopper bucket, grey-blue jib and green and yellow bucket, in good condition, in fair condition box.

*12in (30cm) long*

**£70-100** **VEC**

A 1950s Gescha (Gebruder Schmidt) lithographed tinplate friction action building site truck, with rubber wheels, open tilting bed, shuffle to the front, marked "Made in Western Germany".

*12in (30cm) long*

**£40-60** **WDL**

An American Courtland lithographed tinplate clockwork 'Ice Cream' truck, with open bed, rubber tyres and decals to side.

*8.5in (21.5cm) long*

**£30-50** **BER**

An American Courtland lithographed tinplate Road Roller, the closed cab pulling a roller printed with animal graphics.

*This is a rare model, and is in very good to excellent condition.*

*9in (23cm) long*

**£60-80** **BER**

A German lithographed tinplate military truck and field gun, with diecast gun barrel, opening driver's door and hinged shell box, modelled in the style of a Magirus Deutz truck.

*12in (30.5cm) long*

**£70-100** **W&W**

A 1930s large painted tinplate doll carriage, with three wheels, with steerable front wheel, cast iron wheels, marked "DC Made in Germany".

*8.5in (21.5cm) long*

**£30-50** **WDL**

A German lithographed tinplate clockwork German airforce biplane, with bakelite propeller, ejector seat, plastic figure, marked "Made in Germany".

*c1937* *10in (25cm) long*

**£250-350** **WDL**

A Tipp & Co. painted and transfer-decorated propeller type '1424' biplane, with two wheels, removable wings, two small lights, and decorative foil stripes.

*14.75in (37cm) long*

**£40-60** **WDL**

A Bayer/Leverkusen lithographed tinplate advertising model of a Junkers JU 52 airplane, with interior decoration, three opening doors, 'D-AOHU' markings and the HK-emblem, with signs of wear.

*15.5in (38.5cm) long*

**£1,200-1,800** **LAN**

A Girard lithographed tinplate 'Airmail Monocoupe', with red wings, blue fuselage, seated pilot, disc wheels and clockwork mechanism.

**£100-150** **BER**

A French J.E.P. lithographed tinplate 270C Stuka Dive Bomber constructor plane with French roundels painted in splinter camouflage, with instructions, original box.

**£350-450** **SAS**

An Arnold lithographed tinplate wind-up inertia motor powered ocean liner, with detailed upper deck cabin, pilot's house, four stacks, two masts and lifeboats.

*Tin cruise liners such as this are popular, with large and well detailed examples by notable makers such as Marklin often fetching well over £10,000.*

*14in (35.5cm) long*

**£850-950** **BER**

A Fleischmann lithographed tinplate clockwork Oil Tanker, with good scale and detail, red and black hull, upper deck with narrow catwalk from pilot's cabin to rear cabin, single stack, lacks masts and some corrosion to upper deck.

*21in (53.5cm) long*

**£250-350** **BER**

A Tri-ang 4015 clockwork Motor Lifeboat navy blue, maroon and white toy, in original box, and in very good condition.

**£70-100** **SAS**

A 1950s Arnold tinplate motor boat, complete with original box and key.

*6.75in (17cm) long*

**£25-35** **GAZE**

A Girard lithographed tinplate 'Long Distance Bus', the yellow body with green roof and luggage rack, red wheels, driver and seated driver.

*This is a rare example with good detailing, in excellent overall condition.*

*13in (33cm) long*

**£850-950** **BER**

A Strauss lithographed tinplate clockwork 'Imperial Bus Lines' bus, in red and yellow with green running boards, seated driver and disc wheels.

*9.5in (24cm) long*

**£150-200** **BER**

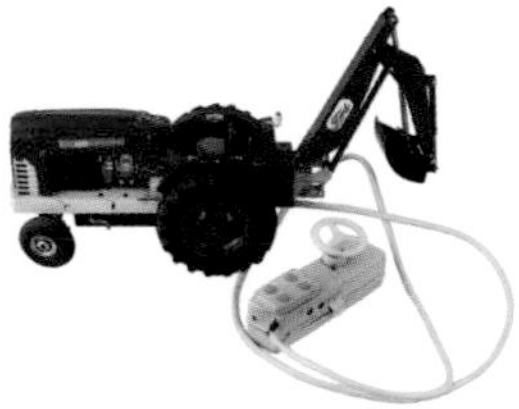

A Cragstan 1/12 scale lithographed tinplate Ford 4000 Industrial tractor, with backhoe and battery-operated remote control unit.

**£20-30** **CHEF**

A Schuco lithographed tinplate clockwork Go-Kart 1055 with driver, movement stalled.

*6in (15cm) long*

**£120-180** **LAN**

An Arnold lithographed tinplate clockwork motorbike no. 643, with chert headlights.

*7.5in (19cm) wide*

**£400-600** **LAN**

A Lineol lithographed tinplate German car and field gun, with three composition figures and various working details including a clockwork motor and electric lights, some losses.

*Along with Hausser and Elastolin, Lineol are well known for its composition soldiers. This large and well made set would appeal to tinplate and toy soldier collectors.*

*15.75in (40cm) long*

**£650-750** **ROS**

A Japanese Masudaya 'TM Modern Toy's lithographed tinplate tank, with clockwork mechanism.

*10.75in (27.5cm) long*

**£20-30** **GAZE**

A Wyandotte lithographed tinplate clockwork 'Hoky Poky' clowns on a railway pump truck, in excellent condition.

*5.5in (14cm) long*

**£100-150** **AAC**

A Noguchi-style 'Mechanical Space Man' blue, orange and red lithographed tinplate clockwork 'walking' robot.

*5.75in (14.5cm) high*

**£12-18** **SAS**

A Japanese Louis Marx painted tinplate battery operated 'Colonel Haphazard' spaceman, with black boots, NASA transfer, flex arms, plastic rockets on back and plastic gloves.

*11.5in (29cm) high*

**£60-80** **BER**

## A CLOSER LOOK AT A ROBOT

*This was made by notable Japanese company Horikawa, who used the trademark 'SH Toys'.*

*The finish and way it is made show this example is a 1980s reproduction of the original toy from 1966 - reproduction boxes are also made and sold.*

*The actions are excellent - the robot 'walks' forward with swinging arms, stops, doors on his chest open to reveal guns which spark and make sounds, the doors then close and he 'walks' on.*

*Look out for originals finished in silver, which is rare, and a variation with an astronaut's face in the head - these can fetch to £300-400 or more.*

A 1980s Japanese Horikawa lithographed tinplate battery powered 'Attacking Martian' robot, in excellent condition, in colour-printed card box.

**£80-120** **W&W**

A Japanese Yoshiya brown painted clockwork walking 'Action Planet Robot', with red boots and hands, celluloid inserts, and sparking mechanism in head, some splits to celluloid.

*c1960* *8.75in (22cm) high*

**£180-220** **BER**

A 1960s Japanese Marx lithographed tinplate and plastic battery operated remote control 'Mr Mercury' Robot, with sponge type pads to hands, light wear.

*123in (33cm) high*

**£250-350** **VEC**

A Japanese Masudaya 'Robot YM-3', with original box.

*Despite its vintage appearance, this robot was produced to commemorate the 20th anniversary of airing of the first "Lost in Space" episode on September 15th, 1965.*

*1985*

**£15-25** **TH**

A 1960s Japanese Yanoman battery-operated 5883 'Space Travelling Monkey' toy, with two plastic suitcases, in original box and in very good condition.

*This rather unusual toy was doubtlessly inspired by the test space flights containing monkeys that began in 1948 and rose in frequency during the 1950s. In May 1959, the monkeys Able and Baker became the first living beings to travel in space and return to Earth safely. Note the NASA logo on his chest.*

*8.25in (21cm) high*

**£150-200** **SAS**

A Japanese Nomura lithographed tinplate and plastic battery powered 'Mini Robo Tank', with 'Mystery Action' and original box.

*4.75in (12cm) high*

**£80-120** **SAS**

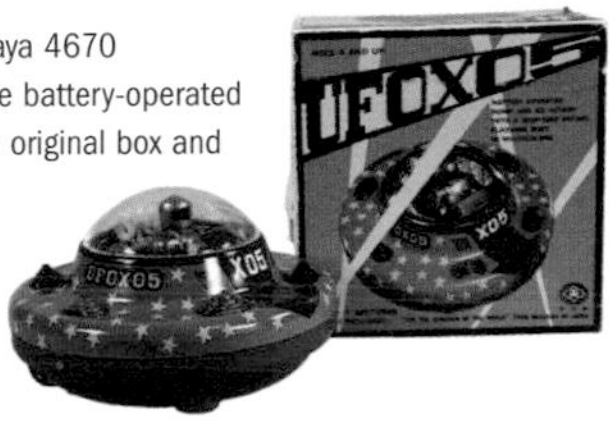


A Japanese Masudaya 4670 lithographed tinplate battery-operated 'U.F.O. X05' toy, with original box and packaging, in very good condition.

*The name of this toy was obviously inspired by the hit-TV show 'Fireball XL5', produced by Jerry Anderson of Thunderbirds fame, which aired from 1962-63.*

*7in (18cm) wide*

**£45-55** **SAS**

A Japanese Modern Toys lithographed tinplate battery-powered 'Apollo Space Capsule', with plastic lenses on nose, the astronaut 'floating' above the capsule, some fading to transfers.

*10.5in (26.5cm) long*

**£30-50** **BER**

A Japanese Linemar lithographed tinplate clockwork 'Two Stage Earth Satellite', that propels itself off its landing station.

*9.75in (25cm) long*

**£60-80** **BER**

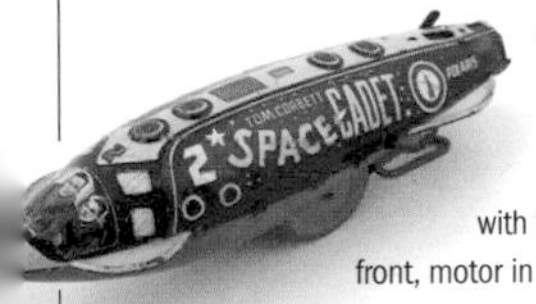


A scarce 1950s Marx lithographed tinplate clockwork 'Tom Corbett Space Cadet 2' space ship, with three astronauts printed on the front, motor in working order.

*12.5in (32cm) high*

**£70-100** **W&W**

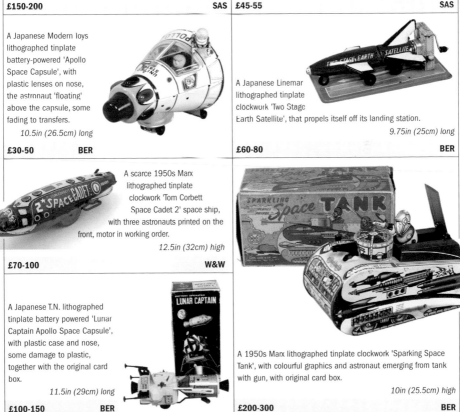

A Japanese T.N. lithographed tinplate battery powered 'Lunar Captain Apollo Space Capsule', with plastic case and nose, some damage to plastic, together with the original card box.

*11.5in (29cm) long*

**£100-150** **BER**

A 1950s Marx lithographed tinplate clockwork 'Sparking Space Tank', with colourful graphics and astronaut emerging from tank with gun, with original card box.

*10in (25.5cm) high*

**£200-300** **BER**

A Lehmann lithographed tinplate and fabric clockwork somersaulting 'Ajax' acrobat clown, in excellent condition.

*c1920* *9in (23cm) high*

**£1,000-1,500** **BER**

A Distler lithographed tinplate clown with saxophone, with mechanical musical and moving mechanism, some wear.

*8.75in (22cm) high*

**£200-250** **LAN**

A 1950s West German US-Zone Beck lithographed tinplate clockwork dancing clown, with moving head eyes and body.

*5.5in (14cm) high*

**£60-80** **LAN**

A Günthermann painted tinplate clockwork gymnast on horizontal bar, movement in working order, losses to paint.

*Günthermann (1887-1965) are known for their high quality whimsical, figural toys, which tend to be less common than Lehmann's. This is a scarce and desirable example.*

*7.25in (18cm) high*

**£700-900** **LAN**

A 1920s Lehmann lithographed and hand-painted tin husband and wife, with wind-up fly wheel action, the handbag and man's hand replaced.

*6.5in (16cm) high*

**£400-600** **LAN**

A Lehmann lithographed tinplate flat, hanging 'Minstrel man', made for the US market.

*c1906* *7.75in (19.5cm) long*

**£450-550** **BER**

A 1920s German KiCu lithographed tinplate wind-up billiard player with table, with original box.

*6.5in (16cm) wide*

**£600-800** **LAN**

A 1950s German Gescha (Gebruder Schmidt) lithographed tinplate clockwork 'Express Porter', with original finish and 2nd type box, with some restoration.

*3.25in (8.2cm) long*

**£45-55** **SAS**

A 1960s Japanese Alps plastic, lithographed tinplate and fabric battery powered 'Big John the Chimpee Chief', with original box.

*13in (33cm) high*

**£8-12** **GAZE**

A 1950s Japanese Nomura (TN) vinyl and lithographed tinplate 'Miss Friday The Typist' battery powered secretary at a desk, with moving hands, head, typewriter carriage and working bell, good condition.

**£30-40** **ATK**

A 1960s Japanese Alps lithographed tinplate and plush battery-operated 'Bubble Blowing Monkey' novelty toy, in original box.

*Box 11in (28cm) high*

**£50-70** **F**

A Japanese Linemar lithographed tinplate Fred Flintstone on Dino toy, walks when turned on, Fred with soft vinyl head, in excellent condition.

*Links to popular cartoon characters like Fred Flintstone generally make a toy more appealing and valuable, particularly if they are humorous like this one.*

*8.25in (21cm) long*

**£80-120** **TM**

A 1960s Kohler tinplate, felt and plastic pecking cockerel, with key, marked "Made in US Zone Germany", in excellent condition.

*4.25in (11cm) long*

**£25-35** **BB**

A 1920s Lehmann lithographed tinplate clockwork 'Performing Sea Lion', with paddling action and moving tail, in excellent condition.

*7in (18cm) long*

**£100-150** **BER**

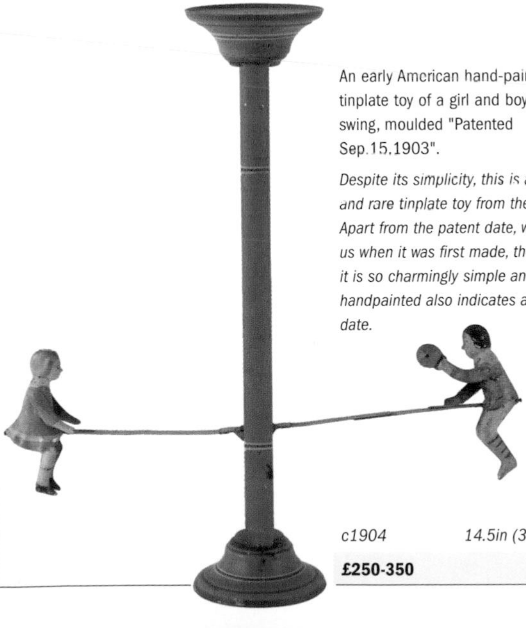

An early American hand-painted tinplate toy of a girl and boy on a swing, moulded "Patented Sep.15.1903".

*Despite its simplicity, this is an early and rare tinplate toy from the US. Apart from the patent date, which tells us when it was first made, the fact that it is so charmingly simple and handpainted also indicates an early date.*

*c1904* *14.5in (37cm) high*

**£250-350** **AAC**

A Japanese J. Chien lithographed tinplate merry-go-round, with four space rocket gondolas, in excellent condition.

*This seems more like a space station than a merry-go-round at a fair.*

*7in (18cm) high*

**£60-90** **AAC**

A Chien lithographed tinplate clockwork merry-go-round with colourful graphics, four gondolas and flag.

*The flag is often lost.*

*12in (30.5cm) high*

**£120-180** **AAC**

A large 1930s J. Chien lithographed tinplate clockwork 'Hercules' Ferris wheel.

*16.5in (42cm) high*

**£200-300** **AAC**

## A CLOSER LOOK AT A TINPLATE RAILWAY

*Karl Bub (1851-1966) was a prolific manufacturer of tin toys, many of which were exported to the US - they are particularly known for their clockwork transportation toys.*

*This example retains the box with commemorative label and the rare pictorial card base, printed with German scenes - it is all in overall excellent condition.*

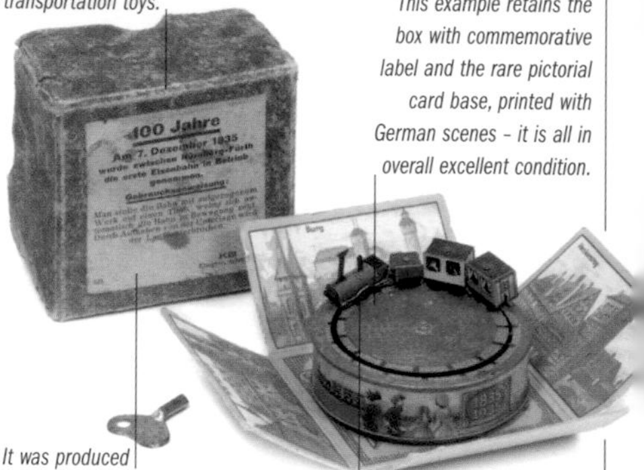


*It was produced in 1935 to commemorate the centenary of Germany's first railway, which ran from Nuremburg to Fürth, and which was opened in 1935.*

*At 3 inches in diameter, this is said to be the smallest clockwork-driven railway set ever produced.*

A German Karl Bub miniature lithographed tinplate railway, commemorating the 100th anniversary of Germany's first railway from Nuremburg to Fürth in 1835, in original box, spring driven, with instruction manual.

*1935* *3in (7.5cm) diam*

**£120-180** **ATK**

A Lehmann lithographed tinplate 'Rigi' model no.900 aerial passenger line, lacks station, in damaged original box with instructions.

*8in (20cm) high*

**£30-40** **WDL**

A 1930s lithographed tinplate water well and pump, decorated with storks, with tap and three buckets, probably German.

*8.75in (22cm) diam*

**£70-100** **WDL**

A 1920s French lithographed tin sand shovel, marked "S.I.F. J.P".

*3in (7.5cm) wide*

**£25-35** **DH**

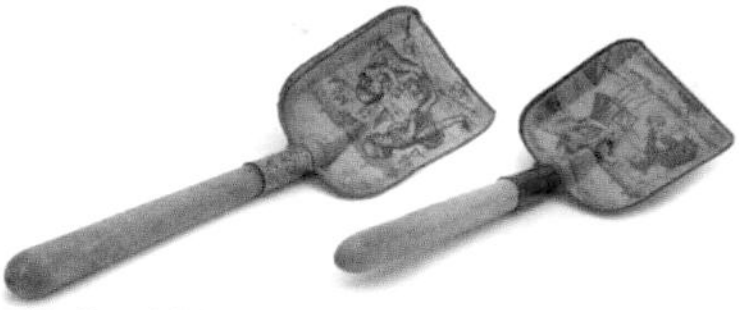

Two 1920s French lithographed tinplate child's sand shovels.

*Items like this and pail on this page are usually found in very worn condition, with the transfer worn through use in the abrasive sand.*

*3in (7.5cm) wide*

**£25-35** **DH**

### FIND OUT MORE...

**Art of the Tin Toy,** *and* **Pressland's Great Book of Tin Toys,** *both by David Pressland, 1976, www.artofthetintoy.com.*

## COLLECTORS' NOTES

- The highly popular and collectable range of merchandising licensed by Lucasfilms from 1977 has changed the way films are marketed.
- Although the first collectable was the Star Wars novelization, published in 1976, it was the action figures that every child wanted to collect. Kenner were the license holders in the US, after Mego turned down the opportunity, with Palitoy in the UK, Harbert in the Italy and Takara in Japan, among others.
- The small affordable figures were a huge hit with children and parents alike and over 100 figures from the first trilogy, together with accessories, monsters and vehicles, were produced by Kenner over eight years. As with similar ranges, early versions, rare variations and examples in mint condition are the most desirable.
- Given the huge range of items available, including stationery, cereal boxes, roller skates and toiletries, there is something to suit every pocket. Items such as lunch boxes and first edition books have cross-market appeal and can push the values up.
- Given the popularity of the original films and toys, it is not surprising that a vast array of merchandising has also been produced for the new prequel trilogy. However prices have remained low so far and it is likely that many mint and boxed examples have been kept in the hope of a rise in values in the future.

A Star Wars 'Luke Skywalker' carded action figure, by Kenner, on a 12-back card, the plastic bubble cut open.

*This is the second most valuable Luke Skywalker figure. The early version with a telescoping lightsaber is rarer and can double in price. As a result, fakes are known, so only buy from reputable sources.*

*1978*

**£100-150** **NOR**

A Star Wars 'Death Squad Commander' carded action figure, by Palitoy, in a 12-back card.

*When this figure was re-issued on an Empire Strikes Back card, it was renamed 'Star Destroyer Commander. This earlier version is more desirable.*

*c1978*

**£400-500** **KF**

A Star Wars - The Empire Strikes Back 'AT-AT Commander' carded action figure, by Palitoy.

*c1982*

**£70-100** **KF**

A Star Wars - The Empire Strikes Back Imperial TIE Fighter Pilot carded action figure, by Palitoy.

*c1982* *9in (22.5cm) high*

**£70-100** **KF**

## A CLOSER LOOK AT A STAR WARS FIGURE

*Chewbacca appears in a number of different guises, but this is the most sought-after.*

*This example has a black blaster rifle. Those released as part of the 'Early Bird' package had green blaster rifles and are slightly more desirable.*

*Chewbacca was one of the original 12 figures released in 1978 and so is found on the desirable '12-back' card as here.*

*When more figures were added to the range, the original 12 were re-issued on new '20/21 back' cards. These reissues are less valuable.*

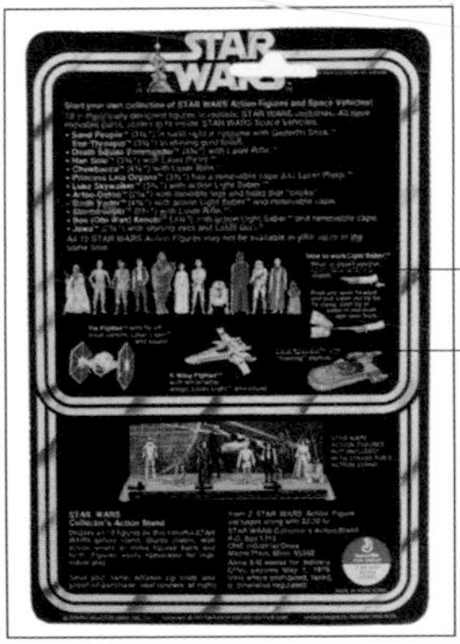


A Star Wars 'Chewbacca' carded action figure, by Kenner, on a 12-back card.

1978

**£100-150** **NOR**

A Star Wars - Return of the Jedi 'Lando Calrissian (Skiff Guard Disguise)' carded action figure, by Kenner.

*1983*

**£22-28** NOR

A Star Wars - Return of the Jedi 'Jawa' carded action figure, by Kenner, on Emperor figure offer card.

*This was a reissue of the Star Wars Jawa figure, and comes with the less valuable cloth cape.*

*1983*

**£15-25** NOR

A Star Wars - The Power of the Force (I) 'Artoo-Detoo (R2-D2) with pop-up lightsaber' carded action figure, by Kenner, with collectors coin, plastic yellowing slightly.

*1985*

**£80-120** NOR

A Star Wars - The Power of the Force (I) 'EV-9D9' carded action figure, by Kenner, with collectors coin.

*1985*

**£70-100** NOR

A Star Wars - The Power of the Force (I) 'Luke Skywalker (Imperial Stormtrooper Outfit) carded action figure, by Kenner, with collectors coin.

*Kenner introduced the Power of the Force range to revive interest in the figures after the first trilogy was released. Unfortunately the ploy did not work and the range was discontinued. 15 of the 37 figures were new, Anakin Skywalker and Yak-Face are the most desirable.*

*1985*

**£200-240** NOR

A Star Wars - The Power of the Force (I) 'A-Wing Pilot' carded action figure, by Kenner, with collectors coin.

*1985*

**£70-100** NOR

A Star Wars - Power of the Force (II) 'R2-D2' carded action figure, by Kenner, on multi-language red header card.

*c1995*

**£7-9** NOR

A Star Wars - Return of the Jedi 'Luke Skywalker (Jedi Knight Outfit) carded action figure, with 'tri-logo' card.

*Tri-logo cards were designed to reduce production cost for a number of international distributors including Palitoy in the UK. No new figures were introduced but a number of variations are of interest to collectors. However the majority are of little interest.*

*c1984*

**£60-80** KF

A Star Wars – The Empire Strikes Back 'MTV-7 Multi-Terrain Vehicle' mini-rig, by Kenner.

*c1982* *9in (22.5cm) wide*

**£15-25** **KF**

A Canadian Star Wars – Return of the Jedi 'Endor Forest Ranger Vehicle' mini-rig vehicle, by Kenner, sealed in the box.

*Mini-rigs were a range of small vehicles or appliances, designed by Kenner rather than Lucasfilms, that were never seen on screen.*

*c1984* *9in (22.5cm) wide*

**£60-80** **KF**

A Star Wars – The Empire Strikes Back 'Tri-Pod Laser Cannon' mini-rig, by Kenner.

*c1982* *4.5in (11.5cm) high*

**£7-10** **KF**

A Star Wars – The Empire Strikes Back 'Cloud City Playset', by Kenner, sealed in box.

*This playset was made exclusively for Sears.*

*c1978* *12in (30.5cm) wide*

**£220-280** **KF**

A Micromachines Star Wars 'Galaxy Battle Collector's Set', by Galoob, produced exclusively for K-Mart, collectors' number "024748".

*1994* *9.5in (24cm) high*

**£6-8** **KNK**

A Micromachines Star Wars cast plastic 'Rebel B-Wing Starfighter', by Galoob.

*These small vehicles were not sold individually and were only available as part of sets.*

*2in (5cm) high*

**£1-2** **KNK**

A Don Post Studios licensed replica 'Boba Fett' moulded plastic helmet, marked "1997 Lucasfilm Ltd, Made in China".

*Don Post Studios held a license to produce replica helmets and masks from the Star Wars film from 1977 until around the release of The Phantom Menace. A deluxe version of Boba Fett's helmet was also produced in fibreglass. They are sought-after on the second-hand market.*

*10.25in (26cm) high*

**£40-50** **BB**

A Hasbro Star Wars: Episode One Collector Edition Monopoly game, in sealed outer wrap.

*c1999*

**£18-22** **SAS**

A limited edition Illusive Concept 'Boba Fett' hand-painted latex bust, from an edition of 1,000, modelled by Mario Chiodo from the original costume, made in Mexico.

*15in (38cm) high*

**£150-200** **BB**

A rare Canadian Kelloggs cereal C-3PO coupon.

*1984* *5.5in (14cm) wide*

**£4-6** **KNK**

L. Neil Smith, "Lando Calrissian and the Mindharp of Sharu", published by Ballatine-Del Ray, with cover artwork William Schmidt, signed in silver pen by Billy Dee Williams (Lando Calrissian).

*1983*

**£15-25** **NOR**

A Star Wars reel-to-reel original soundtrack.

*1977* *7.25in (18.5cm) wide*

**£15-25** **NOR**

A Star Wars - Return of the Jedi vinyl wallet, produced by Adam Joseph, featuring Darth Vader and his Imperial Guard.

*c1983* *3.25in (8.5cm) wide*

**£8-12** **NOR**

A King Seely-Thermos Star Wars lunchbox and Thermos flask (not shown).

*Values for Star Wars lunchboxes are higher than other similar items as they appeal to lunchbox collectors as well.*

*1978* *8.75in (22cm) wide*

**£100-150 (set)** **STC**

## A CLOSER LOOK AT A STAR WARS NOVEL

*The novelization of Star Wars was released nearly a year before the film, with the first print run being only 10,000 copies. These were sent to out to bookshops, colleges and libraries in the US but around 8,000 were returned.*

*Ralph McQuarrie produced the concept artwork for the first Star Wars film, working on designs for many of the characters and vehicles in the original trilogy. This cover features early designs for the characters Darth Vader, Luke Skywalker, Chewbacca, R2-D2 and C-3PO which differ from the final look in the films.*

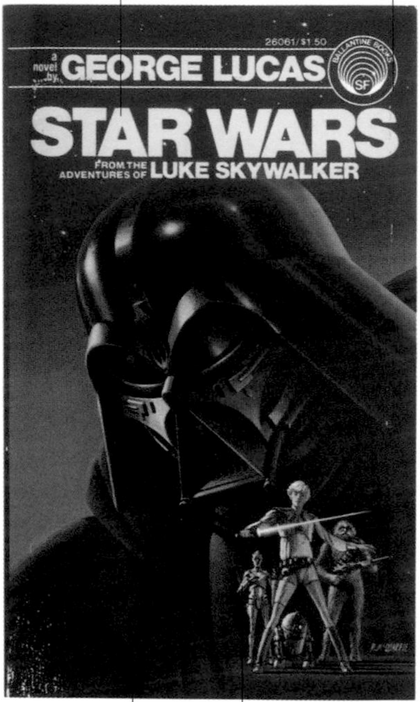


*When the film proved a massive success, the novel was reprinted in large numbers and with a different cover more in line with the film poster. These later editions are worth significantly less. The first hardback version, published a year later is also desirable at slightly more than this version.*

*The novel was ghost-written by popular genre author Alan Dean Foster from Lucas' original script. Foster went onto write two more Star Wars novels; Splinter of the Mind's Eye (1978) and The Approaching Storm (2002).*

George Lucas [Alan Dean Foster], 'Star Wars', published by Ballantine Del Ray, first paperback edition with cover artwork by Ralph McQuarrie.

*1976*

**£40-50** **NOR**

## COLLECTORS' NOTES

- Transformers began as a range of transforming action figures resulting from a collaboration between Japanese toy company Takara and US company Hasbro. The majority of the toys are manufactured by Takara and distributed by Hasbro. The initial designs based on existing Takara toy lines such as Diaclone and Micro Change, which were repackaged by Hasbro. Today, the majority of designs and character development is done by Hasbro.
- The first toys were released in 1984, with additional figures released every year until c1992, and while they were not initially popular in the US, they found many fans in the UK, Japan and Canada. Toys from this period are known as 'Generation 1' by collectors today.
- Hasbro attempted to relaunch a consolidated range in 1992 using the same moulds but with different colours and accessories but they were poorly received and were fazed out by 1995. These are known as 'Generation 2'.
- In 1995 the Beast Wars line was released with figures that transformed into realistic animals. Together with a complimentary CGI animated series, these proved a great success. This was followed up the the Robots in Disguise range (2001-02), which was a modest success and Transformers: Cybertron (2005-06). The upcoming live action Transformers film will also have a range of tie-in figure, toys and mechanising.
- With the various animated series, films, comics and video games connected to the Transformers brand, there can be a mind-boggling range of toys for each character. Examples that were produced for short periods of time and those in mint condition with the original packaging will be worth a premium.

A Transformers 'Cloudraker' Autobot Clone transforming action figure, by Takara/Hasbro, Generation 1, first released in 1987.

*Cloudraker can transform into a jet plane. The figure was sold in a two-pack with his 'brother' 'Fastlane', who was very similar in robot form, but transformed into a dragster racing car.*

*1987-92 4.25in (11cm) high*

**£6-8** **NOR**

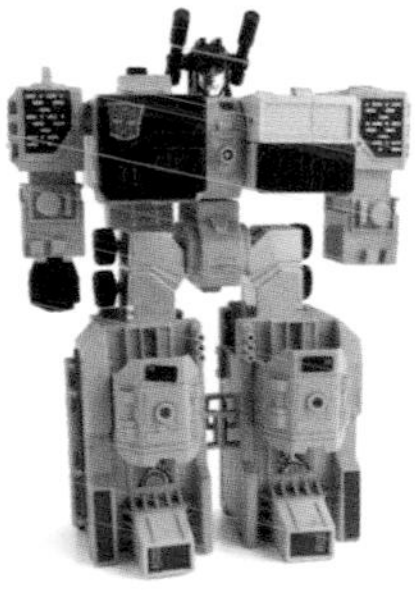

A Transformers 'Metroplex' Autobot transforming action figure, by Takara/Hasbro, from Generation 1, first released in 1985.

*Metroplex can transform into a city or battle station as part of Autobot City.*

*1985-92 10.5in (27cm) high*

**£35-45** **NOR**

## A CLOSER LOOK AT OPTIMUS PRIME

*Optimus Prime is leader of the heroic Autobots and battles to save his planet Cybertron from the evil Decepticons.*

*This toy is based on Takara's Diaclone figure 'Battle Convoy', designed by Hiroyuki Obara and Shoji Kawamori.*

*There have been various incarnations of the character and many variations on the original design, but most retain his iconic face mask. He will play a starring role in the upcoming live-action Transformers movie.*

*In his initial form, he could transform into a cab-over-engine semi-trailer truck and parts could be removed to form smaller figures such as 'Roller', a mobile scout buggy and 'Combat Deck'. He has become the most recognisable of all Transformer figures.*

A Transformers 'Optimus Prime' Autobot transforming action figure, by Takara/Hasbro, first released in 1984.

*9.75in (24.5cm) high*

**£20-30** **NOR**

A Transformers 'Cosmos' Autobot Minibot transforming action figure, by Takara/Hasbro, from Generation 1, first released in 1985.

*1985-92 2in (5cm) diam*

**£15-20** **NOR**

A Transformers 'Topspin' Autobot transforming action figure, by Takara/Hasbro, from Generation 1, first released in 1985.

*Topspin can transform into an open-cockpit aircraft.*

*1985-92* *4in (10cm) high*

**£2-3** **NOR**

A Transformers 'Twin Twist' Autobot transforming action figure, by Takara/Hasbro, from Generation 1, first released 1985.

*Twin Twist can transform into a Cybertronian Drill Tank.*

*1985-92* *4in (10cm) high*

**£2-3** **NOR**

A Transformers 'Grimlock' Autobot Dinobot transforming action figure, by Takara/Hasbro, from Generation 1, first released in 1985.

*Grimlock is team leader of the Dinobots and can transform into a T-Rex. Dinobots are firm fan favourites.*

*1985-992* *4.75in (12cm) high*

**£30-50** **NOR**

A Transformers 'Slag' Autobot Dinobot transforming action figure, by Takara/Hasbro, from Generation 1, first released in 1985.

*1985-92* *6.5in (16.5cm) long*

**£20-30** **NOR**

A Transformers 'Sludge' Autobot Dinobot transforming action figure, by Takara/Hasbro, from Generation 1, first released in 1985.

*1985-92* *8in (20.5cm) long*

**£25-35** **NOR**

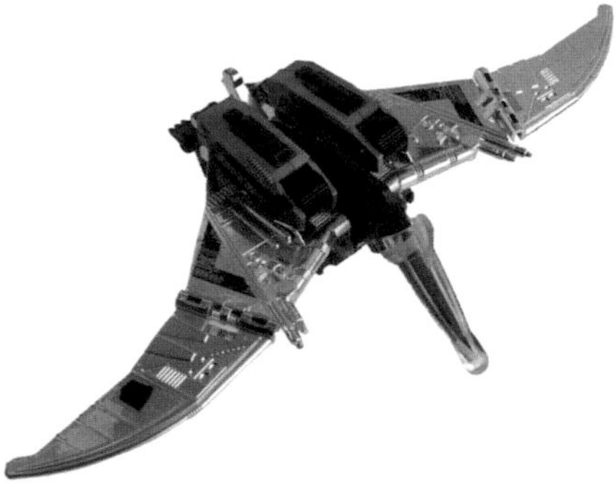

A Transformers 'Swoop' Autobot Dinobot transforming action figure, by Takara/Hasbro, from Generation 1, first released in 1985.

*1985-92* *9in (23cm) long*

**£40-60** **NOR**

A Transformers 'Snarl' Autobot Dinobot transforming action figure, by Takara/Hasbro, from Generation 1, first released in 1985.

*1985-92* *6in (15cm) long*

**£15-25** **NOR**

A Transformers 'Chop Shop' Decepticon Insecticon transforming action figure, by Bandai for Hasbro, from Generation 1, first released in 1985.

*Chop Shop was one of four Deluxe Insecticons made by Bandai and distributed by Hasbro in the US as part of the short-lived Beetras toyline. Due the arrangement between Hasbro and Takara, the Deluxe Insecticons comprising Venom, Barrage, Chopshop and Ransack never appeared in any Transformers TV shows although they did feature in Marvel UK and then later Dreamwave comics.*

*1985-92* *5.25in (13.5cm) long*

**£15-20** **NOR**

A Transformer 'Cutthroat' Decepticon Terracon transforming action figure, by Takara/Hasbro, from Generation 1, first released in 1987.

*Cutthroat transforms into a pterodactyl-like flying creature.*

*3.5in (9cm) high*

**£4-6** **NOR**

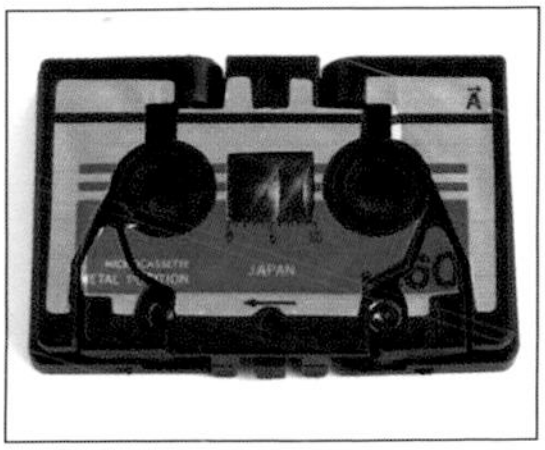

A Transformers 'Laserbeak' Decepticon transforming action figure, by Takara/Hasbro, from Generation 1, first released in 1984.

*Laserbeak transformed into a condor, a cassette and an eagle. He normally worked with Shockwave and was sold in a two-pack with Frenzy.*

*1984-92* *2in (5cm) wide*

**£3-5** **NOR**

A rare Transformers 'Soundwave' Decepticon transforming action figure, by Takara/Hasbro, from Generation 1, first released in 1984.

*Soundwave transforms into a stereo cassette player, making him a rare example of Transformer that does not transform into a vehicle or animal. He is a firm fan favourite and is teamed with a total of 10 different Decepticon cassettes. He is also one of the largest Transformers figures.*

*1984-9* *Stereo 4.25in (10.5cm) wide*

**£40-60** **NOR**

A Transformers 'Ravage' Decepticon transforming action figure, by Takara/Hasbro, from Generation 1, first released in 1986.

*Ravage transforms into a cassette tape, and worked with Soundwave. He was sold in a two-pack with fellow mini-cassette Rumble.*

*1986-92* *2in (5cm) wide*

**£3-5** **NOR**

A Transformers 'Shrapnel' Decepticon Insecticon transforming action figure, by Takara/Hasbro, from Generation 1, first released in 1985.

*Shrapnel transforms into a mechanical stag beetle.*

*1985-92* *5.25in (13.5cm) long*

**£3-5** **NOR**

## COLLECTORS' NOTES

- Mattel's Shogun Warrior range of toys was licensed from Japanese manufacturer Popy Toys and was released in 1979. The characters in turn were based on a number of popular Japanese giant robot manga and anime series including Go Nagai's "Mazinger Z", "Great Mazinger" and "Getter Robo". These series were the genesis of the popular 'mecha' genre, which features giant robots controlled by human pilots.
- Mattel introduced the range with four 21in-24in action figures comprising Raydeen, Dragun and The Great Mazinga, together with the rather incongruous Godzilla. A feature of these figures was their spring-loaded weapons. The range was popular enough for Mattel to add further characters, plus two die-cast ranges at 3in and 5ins and a range of action vehicles.
- Under pressure from regulators who were concerned with the safety aspect of the spring-loaded small missiles, and with declining sales, the line was dropped by Mattel by 1980.
- Being a short-lived line, these figures can be hard to find today, and examples with the original packaging as highly sought-after. The original Japanese Popy Toy versions are also very desirable.

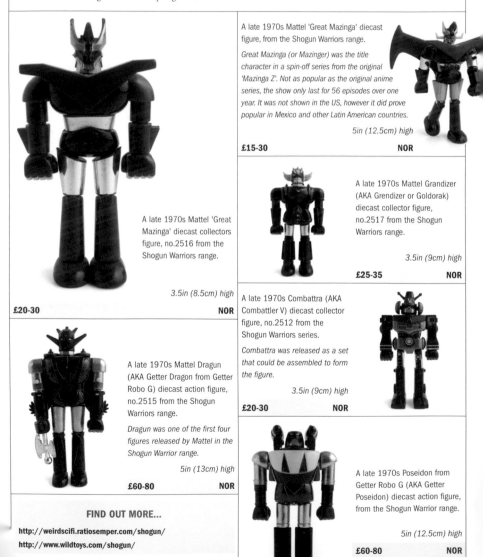

A late 1970s Mattel 'Great Mazinga' diecast collectors figure, no.2516 from the Shogun Warriors range.

*3.5in (8.5cm) high*

**£20-30** **NOR**

A late 1970s Mattel 'Great Mazinga' diecast figure, from the Shogun Warriors range.

*Great Mazinga (or Mazinger) was the title character in a spin-off series from the original 'Mazinga Z'. Not as popular as the original anime series, the show only last for 56 episodes over one year. It was not shown in the US, however it did prove popular in Mexico and other Latin American countries.*

*5in (12.5cm) high*

**£15-30** **NOR**

A late 1970s Mattel Grandizer (AKA Grendizer or Goldorak) diecast collector figure, no.2517 from the Shogun Warriors range.

*3.5in (9cm) high*

**£25-35** **NOR**

A late 1970s Combattra (AKA Combattler V) diecast collector figure, no.2512 from the Shogun Warriors series.

*Combattra was released as a set that could be assembled to form the figure.*

*3.5in (9cm) high*

**£20-30** **NOR**

A late 1970s Mattel Dragun (AKA Getter Dragon from Getter Robo G) diecast action figure, no.2515 from the Shogun Warriors range.

*Dragun was one of the first four figures released by Mattel in the Shogun Warrior range.*

*5in (13cm) high*

**£60-80** **NOR**

A late 1970s Poseidon from Getter Robo G (AKA Getter Poseidon) diecast action figure, from the Shogun Warrior range.

*5in (12.5cm) high*

**£60-80** **NOR**

**FIND OUT MORE...**

**http://weirdscifi.ratiosemper.com/shogun/**

**http://www.wildtoys.com/shogun/**

A Japanese 'Atragon SuperSub' submarine model kit, by Otaki.

*'Atragon', meaning undersea battleship was the English language title of a 1963 special effects film from the Toho Studio. The story was taken from a 1899 novel by Shunro Oshikawa, who is considered a pioneer of the science fiction genre. The Atragon submarine appeared in a number of other Toho Studio films including Godzilla: Final Wars.*

*c1963* *11.5in (29cm) high*

**£25-35** **NOR**

A Battle of the Planets 'The G-1 SP' model kit, by Entex.

*Battle of the Planets was the Western adaptation of the 1972 Japanese animated series 'Kagaku ninja tai Gatchaman'. While the adaptation was reasonably faithful, a number of additions and reductions were made to make the series more suitable to the young US market. Turner Entertainment released a second version known as G-Force: Guardians of Space, which was more in line with Japanese original. Such is the popularity of the series, that new toys and figures are being produced today, however original Gatchaman and Battle of the Planets toys are very rare.*

*1978* *Box 10.5in (26.5cm) wide*

**£35-45** **NOR**

A recent set of five 'Kagakuninjatai Gatchaman' PVC figures, by Unifive, in original packaging.

*Box 9in (23cm) wide*

**£5-10** **NOR**

A 'Galaxy Express 1999' flying train model kit, by Bandai.

*Galaxy Express started as a manga released in 1981 by Leiji Matsumoto. It spun off into an anime series produced by Toei Animation, and a number of movies.*

*Box 11.5in (29.5cm) wide*

**£25-35** **NOR**

A 1970s 'Frau Baw' 1:20 scale model figure kit, by Bandai, from the mecha anime series "Mobile Suit Gundam".

*6in (15.5cm) high*

**£6-8** **NOR**

A Super Dimension Fortress Macross 'VF-1 Valkyrie' robot/fighter plane, by Bandai, boxed.

*c1985* *Box 8.75in (22cm) high*

**£12-18** **NOR**

A Super Dimension Fortress Macross Robotech 'VF-1S Super Valkyrie Fighter' robot/fighter plane, with Transformer Jetfire applied decal.

*The Macross figures have 'transforming' capabilities, and generally had three forms; Fighter mode as a fighter plane, Battroid mode as a robot (as above) and GERWALK mode, which was somewhere in between. Initially Transformers were based on existing Japanese toys including Diaclone and Microman. Jetfire was based on the VF-1S and due to legal concerns was renamed Skyfire in the TV series.*

*9.75in (24.5cm) high*

**£60-80** **NOR**

## A CLOSER LOOK AT A MEGA MAN FIGURE

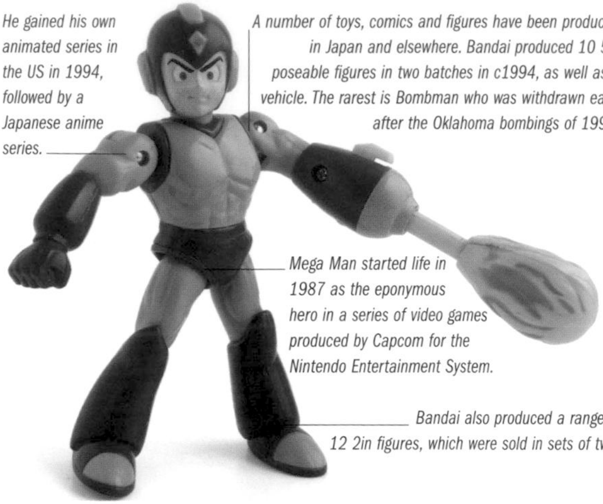

*He gained his own animated series in the US in 1994, followed by a Japanese anime series.*

*A number of toys, comics and figures have been produced in Japan and elsewhere. Bandai produced 10 5in poseable figures in two batches in c1994, as well as a vehicle. The rarest is Bombman who was withdrawn early after the Oklahoma bombings of 1995.*

*Mega Man started life in 1987 as the eponymous hero in a series of video games produced by Capcom for the Nintendo Entertainment System.*

*Bandai also produced a range of 12 2in figures, which were sold in sets of two.*

A 'Mega Man' poseable action figure, by Bandai, from the Mega Man range.

*c1994* *5in (12.5cm) high*

**£8-12** **NOR**

A 1980s bootleg "Macres" VF-1S Battroid Valkyrie robot/fighter plane.

*8.5in (21.5cm) high*

**£25-35** **NOR**

A 'Proto Man' poseable action figure, by Bandai, from the Megaman range.

*c1994* *5in (12.5cm) high*

**£5-10** **NOR**

A 'Guts Man' poseable action figure, by Bandai, from the Mega Man range.

*c1994* *5.25in (13.5cm) high*

**£5-10** **NOR**

A Micronauts 'Force Commander' interchangeable action figure, by Mego Corp., second series, boxed.

*Mego released Micronauts in 1976, based on the Japanese Microman range by Takara. They proved a huge success and in 1979 Mego introduced new characters not produced by Takara.*

*c1977 Box 9.5in (18.5cm) high*

**£30-50** **NOR**

A Micronauts 'Oberon' interchangeable action figure, by Mego Corp, from the second series, boxed.

*Oberon was "The Galactic Stallion with Magno Power Action and missiles, Vehicle for the Leader of the Micronauts".*

*c1977 7.25in (18.5cm) high*

**£35-45** **NOR**

A Micronauts 'Baron Karza' interchangeable action figure, by Mego Corp., from the second series, boxed.

*This figure was also produced as Captain Magno by the Hourtoy Co.*

*c1977* *Box 9.5in (18.5cm)*

**£40-60** **NOR**

A Micronauts 'Andromeda' interchangeable action figure, by Mego Corp., from the second series, boxed.

*Andromeda was "With magno power action, firing missiles, Baron Karza's star stallion"*

*c1977* *Box 9.5in (18.5cm)*

**£30-50** **NOR**

A Space Battleship Yamato (Star Blazers) 'Wildstar's SuperStar' model kit, by Bandai, Japan, boxed.

*Star Blazers is the English language title of Space Battleship Yamato, a mid-1970s Japanese animated science fiction series. As with Battle of the Planets, the English language version was dubbed and partly edited for the Western audience, although all the main themes and character developments are kept. The concept was used in two other original series as well as five movies and a number of video games. Disney currently own the rights to a live-action version of Yamato and are supposedly working on a script.*

*Box 10.75in (27cm) wide*

**£15-25** **NOR**

A Mini-Collection Series 'Wildstar's SuperStar' model kit, from the Star Blazers series.

*c1985* *Box 6in (15.5cm) wide*

**£6-8** **NOR**

A Star Blazers original soundtrack picture disc, released by Nippon Columbia Ltd, featuring the Space Battleship Yamato, in original bag.

*7in (17.5cm) diam*

**£25-35** **NOR**

A Star Blazers soundtrack picture disc, released by Nippon Columbia Ltd, featuring Derek Wildstar (Susumu Kodai) and Nova (Yuki Mori), in original bag.

*7in (17.5cm) diam*

**£25-35** **NOR**

## COLLECTORS' NOTES

- The game that is now known as chess is thought to have originated in India in the 6th century, and is known as 'Chaturanga'. However, a similar game evolved in China in the 2nd century BC. The game as played today uses rules set down in 15th century Italy. During the 18th and 19th centuries, the game boomed in popularity, leading to many sets being made.
- The majority of sets found in today's market date from the late 18th century onwards, with earlier examples being rarer and often very valuable. As chess is such an international game, sets were made in many different countries, with the Eastern export markets of China and India being particularly strong. European countries such as Britain, Germany and France also made sets.
- The style and design of sets varies from country to country and have changed over time. Learning these changes can help identify when and where a set was made. Many are made from carved and turned wood, but ivory, bone and tusks were also used. Most are stained with colours to differentiate sides. The 'Staunton' set, designed in 1849 by Nathaniel Cook was endorsed by the famous player Howard Staunton, and is one of the more popular styles to collect today, being the official set of the World Chess Federation.
- Sets should be complete and undamaged. The date, size, and quality and intricacy of the carving are also very important factors for value. The inclusion of a chess board is not too important as most chess collectors only desire one or two, and sets were not originally sold together with boards. Boxes can add value, particularly if they are of the period.
- The market is comparatively strong, with lively trade over the internet. Older, good quality sets are becoming harder to find and, as a result, more standard and commonplace sets are rising in value, in particular Staunton sets. Be aware of any national limitations on the transport of ivory and materials from endangered species, particularly for more modern sets using these materials.

A 19thC Jacques Staunton ivory chess set, with white king stamped "Jacques London", in a mahogany box.

*King 3.25in (8cm) high*

**£2,500-3,000** **BLO**

A 19thC English 'Staunton' pattern ivory chess set, one side stained red, the other natural, in mahogany box with sliding lid.

*King 2.75in (7cm) high*

**£180-220** **BLO**

An unweighted Jacques Staunton boxwood and ebony chess set.

*King 3.5in (9cm) high*

**£400-500** **BLO**

A late 19thC English Staunton-style boxwood and ebony chess set.

*King 4in (10cm) high*

**£60-80** **BLO**

A 19thC Jacques Staunton ivory chess set, by Fisher of London, one side stained red, one left natural, white king signed "Fisher, 188 Strand" and "Jacques London", in mahogany box.

*Fisher, based on the Strand in London, was a well-known maker and retailer of chess sets. This set can be dated more precisely to between 1860 and 1862 as Jacques' son joined Fisher in 1860, and the company moved to nearby Fleet Street in 1863.*

*c1861* *King 3.25in (8cm) high*

**£2,200-2,800** **BLO**

An English 'Barleycorn' pattern bone chess set, one side stained red, the other natural, together with a 19thC 'History of England' leather board/box.

*King 4.25in (11cm) high*

**£40-60** **BLO**

An English 'Washington' pattern ivory chess set, one side stained red, the other natural, in a wooden box with sliding lid.

*These sets are so called as George Washington is said to have owned a set in this pattern.*

*c1790* *King 3.5in (9cm) high*

**£500-600** **BLO**

## A CLOSER LOOK AT A CHESS SET

The solid, stocky charm of the form is appealing to many.
Irish sets have similarities in form to Scottish sets of the period.
This set is both rare and desirable.
The king and queen are particularly unusually carved.

A 19thC Irish boxwood and ebony chess set, with urn-shaped finials on kings, queens with large ball finials, bishops with tulip-shaped mitres, knights as horses' heads, rooks as concave turrets, pawns with ball finials topped with small spikes, in mahogany box with sliding lid.

*King 4.25in (11cm) high*

**£1,500-2,000** **BLO**

An English John Calvert ivory chess set, one side stained red, the other natural, kings surmounted with Maltese crosses, the queens with fleur-de-lys over reeded ball finials, the white king signed, "Calvert Maker, 189 Fleet Strt London".

*c1810*

**£1,500-2,000** **BLO**

An English ivory chess set, kings surmounted with Maltese crosses, queens with flame finials, bishops as mitres but with vertical reeded decoration, knights as carved horses' heads, rooks as turrets with flags, pawns with baluster knops and ball finials, in wooden box.

*This set is similar in style to the Calvert pattern also shown on this page, but has some interesting differences.*

*c1840* *King 4in (10cm) high*

**£1,800-2,200** **BLO**

A large size 19thC 'Dublin' pattern boxwood and ebony chess set, with twisted screw-like finials on kings, queens with ball finials, bishops with split mitres, knights as horses' heads raised on pedestals, rooks as turrets, pawns with ball finials.

*King 5in (13cm) high*

**£3,000-4,000** **BLO**

A 19thC Scottish ivory 'Edinburgh Upright' chess set, one side stained red, the other white.

*This style was the precursor to, and is thought to have inspired, the popular Staunton style.*

*King 3.25in (8cm) high*

**£1,000-1,500** **BLO**

## A CLOSER LOOK AT A CHESS SET

*This ches set can be dated, like many, by looking at sets that appear in paintings of contemporary interiors from the period.*

*The term 'monobloc' relates to the piece being made from a single piece of material, rather than a number of assembled pieces - these were more expensive to produce.*

*The form of the pieces is very tall, slim and elegant, which is desirable.*

*The size is comparatively small, which is another desirable feature.*

An 18thC boxwood and ebony chess set, with one side in boxwood, the other ebony, kings with double galleries, queens with single crowns, bishops with cleft mitres, knights as carved horses' heads, rooks as monobloc turrets, pawn with ball finials.

*King 2.75in (7cm) high*

**£1,500-2,000** **BLO**

A French 'Lyon' pattern ebony and bone chess set, the kings with cogged crowns, queens with petal knops and bishops with flat caped tops.

*The contrasting bone or ebony crests on the knights are unusual, as are their Grecian soldier-style helmets. This style of helmet was worn by many European armies at the beginning of the 19thC.*

*c1800* *King 2.75in (7cm) high*

**£5,000-6,000** **BLO**

A 19thC French 'Règence' pattern boxwood and ebony chess set, with rosewood, boxwood and mahogany edged chess board.

*King 3.5in (9cm) high*

**£200-300** **BLO**

A 19thC French ivory playing chess set, one side stained brown, the other natural, kings with baluster knops and cogged crowns and queens with baluster knops and ball finials, cased in a red leather mounted casket of the same period.

*King 3.25in (8cm) high*

**£800-1,200** **BLO**

A 19thC French 'Règence' pattern boxwood and ebony chess set, in mahogany box with sliding lid.

*King 3.25in (8cm) high*

**£200-300** **BLO**

A 19thC German Nuremberg bone bust chess set, one side stained brown, the other natural, bishops in military uniforms with high collars and polychrome decoration, knights as sea horses, rooks as turrets raised on columns.

*King 3.25in (8cm) high*

**£4,000-5,000** **BLO**

An 18thC collection of 'Spanish Pulpit' bone chess men including two bishops and two knights.

*The origins of these sets remains a mystery. Many have thought them to originate from the Russian village Kholmogory famous for its walrus and mammoth tusk carving, but the lack of walrus ivory as a material on this set suggests that this is highly unlikely. They are more likely to have come from England.*

*2.25in (6cm) high*

**£150-200** **BLO**

A Cantonese 'Burmese' pattern ivory chess set, one side stained red, the other natural, with carved decoration, bishops with mitres, knights as horses' heads, rooks as turrets with flags.

*c1810* *King 4.25in (11cm) high*

**£1,500-2,000** **BLO**

An early 19thC Cantonese 'Burmese' pattern ivory chess set, one side stained red, the other natural, with intricately carved foliate decoration, kings with foliate finials, queens with bud finials, bishops as mitres with crosses, knights as horses' heads, rooks as turrets with flags, the white rook with Union flag.

*King 4in (10cm) high*

**£450-550** **BLO**

An early to mid-19thC Cantonese 'Burmese' pattern ivory chess set, one side stained red, the other natural, with extensively carved foliate decoration, kings with floral knops, queens with bud finials, bishops with mitres surmounted with crosses, knights as horses' heads, rooks as turrets with flags, the white rooks with Union flag.

*King 3.5in (9cm) high*

**£250-350** **BLO**

An early 19thC Chinese export 'Bust' ivory chess set one side stained red, the other natural, the king and queen as monarchs' heads, bishops as mandarins or counsellors, knights as horses' heads.

*King 3.5in (9cm) high*

**£1,200-1,800** **BLO**

A Macao export 'Burmese' ivory chess set, one side stained a light red, the other natural, the pieces finely carved, kings and queens with monarch's faces carved in relief, bishops surmounted with crosses and clerics' faces carved in relief, knights as horses' heads with reins nicely carved, rooks as raised turrets with flags.

*This is a very nice example of a well-carved ivory set from the Portuguese trading colony of Macao.*

*c1810* *King 5in (13cm) high*

**£1,000-1,500** **BLO**

An early 19thC Cantonese 'Burmese' pattern ivory chess set, one side stained red, the other natural, with intricately carved foliate decoration, knights as horses' heads, rooks as turrets with flags, the white rook with Union flag.

*King 3.25in (8cm) high*

**£400-500** **BLO**

An early 19thC Cantonese 'Burmese' pattern ivory export chess set, one side stained pink-ish red, the other natural, the bishops with mitres and carved bishops' faces, knights as horses' heads, rooks as turrets with flags, pawns carved with elaborate floral decoration in wooden box with sliding lid.

*Cantonese sets are typically elaborately carved – this example is extremely detailed showing extra attention to worksmanship.*

*King 4.75in (12cm) high*

**£2,000-3,000** **BLO**

A 19thC Cambodian ivory chess set, one side stained light red, the other natural, kings with spiked finials, queens similar, knights as arched horses' heads, rooks of dome shape, pawns, smaller of domed shape.

*King 2.25in (6cm) high*

**£2,800-3,200** **BLO**

## A CLOSER LOOK AT A CHESS SET

*Rooks are always ships in Russian sets, due to a mis-translation of the Russian word for rook.*

*18thC Russian sets as finely carved as this are comparatively rare. The Russians vs the Turks is a popular theme.*

*It is carved from walrus ivory, a material taken from the tusks of walruses and traditionally used in Russia folk carvings from the Middle Ages.*

*The material is closely associated with the town of Kholmogory, which housed many bone and tusk carvers, where this set was made.*

A late 18thC Russian walrus ivory chess set with Russians vs Turks, the Turkish side with painted highlights, the Russian side left natural, Russian king wearing crown, holding a sceptre, seated on throne, Russian queen as vizier in Roman dress holding a spear, Russian bishop as elephant with tusks, Russian knight as horsemen in Roman dress, Russian rook as galleon bearing painted flag; Turkish king wearing a turban and seated on a throne, Turkish queen as a vizier, wearing a turban and holding a spear, Turkish bishops as elephants with tusks, Turkish knights as horsemen, Turkish rooks as felucca.

*King 3.5in (9cm) high*

**£12,000-18,000** **BLO**

A 19thC Indian export ivory chess set, one side stained green, other natural, kings with foliate spray finials, queens with pierced turrets and bud finials, bishops as mitres, knights as horses' heads.

*King 3.25in (8cm) high*

**£280-320** **BLO**

A mid-19thC Indian export ivory chess set, one side stained red, the other natural, kings with foliate sprays, queens with bud finials, bishops with leaf type decoration, knights as horses' heads, rooks as turrets with spires, pawns with baluster knops.

*King 3.25in (8cm) high*

**£350-450** **BLO**

A Vizagapatnam Indian export ivory chess set, one side stained green, the other natural, kings and queens with foliate knops, bishops as mitres, knights as horses' heads, rooks as foot soldiers bearing flags, raised on turrets, pawns decorated.

*Vizagapatam is a town in south-east India that produced and exported furniture and small pieces made from, or inlaid with, ivory. Styles often fused Indian and English.*

*King 4.75in (12cm) high*

**£2,000-2,500** **BLO**

An early 19thC Indian ivory chess set, probably Vizagapatnam, one side stained red, the other ^ natural, kings with large reeded ball finials over castellated galleries, queens similar with small size, bishops with unusually shaped mitres.

*King 3.25in (8cm) high*

**£1,000-1,500** **BLO**

A South American painted wood and bone mounted chess set with one side painted red and black, the other side left natural.

*c1950* *King 3.25in (8cm) high*

**£80-120** **BLO**

A 20thC German painted 'Nutcracker' wooden chess set, one side predominantly green, the other side predominantly red, kings as St. Nicholas, queens wearing cloaks, bishops as toy soldiers, knights as horses' heads, rooks as fairy castles, pawns as Christmas elves smoking pipes.

*King 4in (10cm) high*

**£120-180** **BLO**

A late 20thC Murano hot-worked glass 'sea life' chess set, the kings as Neptune with trident, queens as mermaids, bishops as octopi, knights as seahorses, rooks as jelly fish, pawns as starfish.

*Well-detailed sets such as these are time-consuming to make and require great skill. The more detailed and well formed they are, the more value they are likely to have. Examine all extremities closely for damage.*

*King 6.25in (16cm) high*

**£1,200-1,800** **BLO**

A 'Napoleonic' composition figural chess set, with British vs French, British king as Wellington, French king as Napoleon, British queen as Duchess of Wellington, French queen as Marie-Louise, bishops as infantrymen holding regimental colours, knights as horses' heads, rooks as wall sections, pawns as infantry.

*c1960* *King 4.25in (11cm) high*

**£150-200** **BLO**

A 20thC Indonesian painted wooden figural chess set, one side painted with yellow bases, the other painted with black bases, the chessmen as figures from Balinese mythology.

*King 5in (13cm) high*

**£700-900** **BLO**

A 20thC Ashanti tribal figural chess set, with metal chessmen painted in primary colours, one side predominately gilt, kings as chieftains, bishops as tribal elders, knights as rearing horses, rooks as tribal huts, pawns as foot soldiers.

*King 3.25in (8cm) high*

**£70-90** **BLO**

A late 18thC Indian Rajhastan ivory elephant chess king, with polychrome decoration and gilt highlights, showing two princes in an open howdah, raised on a gadrooned base.

*3.25in (8cm) high*

**£220-280** **BLO**

A rare Wedgwood Jasperware chess pawn, after a design by Joseph Flaxman, in the form of a bowman, raised on light mauve-coloured base, stamped "Wedgwood" on underside of base.

*John Flaxman (1755-1826), was a notable sculptor and draughtsman who was elected to the Royal Academy in 1800.*

*2.75in (7cm) high*

**£800-1,000** **BLO**

**FIND OUT MORE...**

**Master Pieces: The Architecture of Chess**, *by Gareth Williams, published by Viking Press and Apple Press, 2000.*

## COLLECTORS' NOTES

- Wood was one of the first materials used to make toys, with the majority being made at home or by independent craftsmen. Germany dominated the market during the 18th century and first half of the 19th century, with the centre of production based in Saxony. After lithographic printing was developed in 1797, and colour lithography in 1870, decorated paper could be added to the surfaces of wood that was die-cut or jigsaw-cut into shapes. Educational Noah's Arks were expensive, yet popular, toys.
- In the US, Albert Schoenhut (1850-1934) is one of the best-known names, and founded his factory in 1872. His wood and composition toys were sold all over the US and exported to Europe. Hand-painted circus toys with glass eyes are among the most popular. R. Bliss Manufacturing Co. of Rhode Island, was established in 1832 and grew to be a major manufacturer of paper covered wooden toys. They are particularly known for their doll's houses, which are much sought-after.
- In the UK, companies such as Chad Valley and Lines Brothers were known for their wooden toys. The industry was severely affected by the introduction of tinplated metal in the late 19th century. By the early 20th century, the decline had set in and during the 1950s, the more flexible and economical plastic took over from both materials.
- Always consider the condition, inspecting pieces all over. Large losses or damage to printed paper surfaces will reduce the value, as will flaked paint, repainted surfaces or chipped wood. Schoenhut figures often need restringing as the rubber cords have often perished, but this does not reduce value.

A Schoenhut jointed wooden donkey figure, with glass eyes and red felt blanket, in excellent condition.

*9in (23cm) long*

**£120-180** **BER**

A Schoenhut jointed wooden horse figure, with glass eyes and painted dappled decoration, in excellent condition.

*9in (23cm) long*

**£120-180** **BER**

A Schoenhut jointed wooden giraffe, with painted eyes, leather ears and hand-painted yellow and brown spotted effect, re-strung, with split to neck.

*The version with glass eyes is usually more desirable.*

*11in (28cm) high*

**£60-80** **BER**

A Schoenhut jointed wooden circus elephant, painted grey, with leather tusks and ears, stitched blanket and head piece and string tail.

*8in (20cm) long*

**£250-300** **BER**

A Schoenhut jointed wooden buffalo, with leather horns and string tail.

*8in (20cm) long*

**£100-150** **BER**

A Schoenhut's 'Humpty Dumpty Circus' set, containing strung wooden figures of a horse, an elephant, ringmaster, clown and dancer, together with ladder, chair and drum, and remnants of instruction booklet, in original box.

*This is one of Schoenhut's best known toys. Often single animals originated as part of a Circus set. It was made from 1903-1935.*

*c1930* *Elephant 8in (20cm) long*

**£400-500** **DN**

A rare Schoenhut jointed wooden 'Chinese Acrobat', with hand-painted features, redressed in white trousers and blue jacket, with rope cue.

*8in (20cm) high*

**£180-220** **BER**

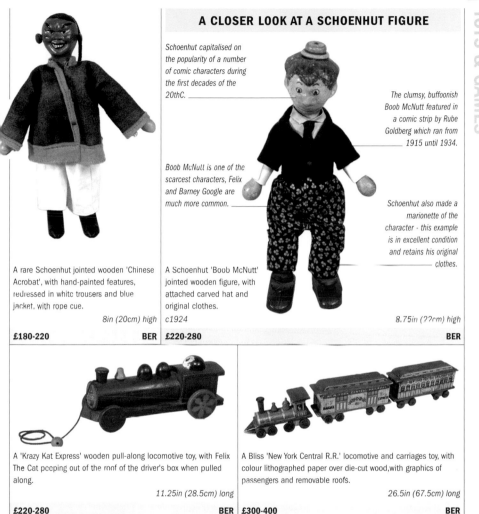

## A CLOSER LOOK AT A SCHOENHUT FIGURE

*Schoenhut capitalised on the popularity of a number of comic characters during the first decades of the 20thC.*

*The clumsy, buffoonish Boob McNutt featured in a comic strip by Rube Goldberg which ran from 1915 until 1934.*

*Boob McNutt is one of the scarcest characters, Felix and Barney Google are much more common.*

*Schoenhut also made a marionette of the character - this example is in excellent condition and retains his original clothes.*

A Schoenhut 'Boob McNutt' jointed wooden figure, with attached carved hat and original clothes.

*c1924* *8.75in (22cm) high*

**£220-280** **BER**

A 'Krazy Kat Express' wooden pull-along locomotive toy, with Felix The Cat peeping out of the roof of the driver's box when pulled along.

*11.25in (28.5cm) long*

**£220-280** **BER**

A Bliss 'New York Central R.R.' locomotive and carriages toy, with colour lithographed paper over die-cut wood,with graphics of passengers and removable roofs.

*26.5in (67.5cm) long*

**£300-400** **BER**

A pair of Bliss 'Grandma & Grandpa' rocking chair toys, with colour lithographed paper over wood, with die-cut legs hanging below the seats, some loss of paper and wear.

*12.5in (32cm) high*

**£220-280** **BER**

A rare Bliss 'Mother Goose' pull-along toy, with colour lithographed paper on die-cut wood, with a goose pulling Mother Goose along in her cart, the goose's legs revolving as the wheel, paper aged.

*13.75in (35cm) long*

**£280-320** **BER**

A Reed 'Twilight' paddlesteamer pull-along toy, with colour lithographed paper on die cut wood, wear to wood, two wheels repaired and replaced stacks.

*19.5in (49.5cm) long*

**£70-100** **BER**

## A CLOSER LOOK AT A TAROT DECK

*Etteilla (Jean-Baptiste Alliette, 1738-91) designed this tarot deck in 1788 for divinatory uses, rather than for use as a parlour game, as tarot had become in Europe.*

*The deck was also known as the 'Egyptian Gypsies Tarot', indicating its authenticity as Etteilla claimed tarot originated in Egypt.*

*The pack retains its card box and instructions and is in bright, clean condition.*

*Publisher Grimaud often used different keywords to Etteilla's original deck, but they were based on the work undertaken by Etteilla's school and students.*

A French B.P. Grimaud 'Grand Etteilla I' colour lithograph printed tarot deck, comprising 78 cards, together with original box and instructions.

*c1890*

**£400-500** **BLO**

A French B.P. Grimaud 'Grand Jeu De Mlle. Normand' colour lithograph printed tarot deck, comprising 53 cards, with original box and 'Grand Jeu de Société et Pràctiques Secrètes' instruction book, three pictorial cards shown.

*c1900*

**£300-400** **BLO**

An early 19thC French Classical stencil coloured mythology pack, with Arabic numerals numbered 1-25, comprising 25 cards with square corners, some wear.

**£250-350** **BLO**

A 19thC Italian pack of Florentine Adami pattern playing cards, comprising 52 square-cornered cards with stencil-coloured wood engravings, the backs with light blue floral design, with tax stamp of the Grand Duchy of Tuscany.

**£200-300** **BLO**

A French pack of 58 LeFebvre 'Grand Jeu Des Lignes De La Main' stencil coloured cards, with square corners and instruction pamphlet.

*c1890*

**£220-280** **BLO**

Six Persian 'As Nas' cards, with hand-painted tempera designs on papier-mâché.

*Poker may have derived from this 16thC Persian game.*

*c1860* *2.25in (6cm) high*

**£22-28** **BLO**

A 19thC Indian Mughal 'Ganijifa' pack of cards, with 52 hand-painted and lacquered papier-mâché cards in a painted wooden box with sliding lid.

**£180-220** **BLO**

A pig skin and silver mounted Bezique case, by Mudie & Sons of Piccadilly, London, in the form of miniature valise, silver marked with hallmarks for London, two ivory mounted "Rubicon Bezique Markers", two packs of playing cards by U.S. Playing Card Co. of Cincinnati, Ohio.

*c1930*

**£220-280** BLO

A tooled leather Bezique box, by Dreyfous, with red leather, gilt tooling, two hardwood and ivory whist markers, two packs of playing cards by Goodall & Son, London, interior with decorative fabric.

*c1890* *6.75in (17cm) wide*

**£150-250** BLO

A late 19thC "Marlborough" mahogany games box, by Goodall & Sons, with two wooden whist markers, two leather mounted Bezique markers, instruction booklet for Bezique, Rubicon Bezique, Solo Whist, Bridge and Progressive Whist Bridge, Hearts and Euchre.

*9.5in (24cm) wide*

**£250-350** BLO

An Austrian walnut and brass mounted games compendium, with set of 30 games counters, Austrian tarock playing cards, domino set, halma board with later 20thC games and cards.

*c1870* *12.25in (31cm) wide*

**£30-40** BLO

A 1920's Chinese Tsing Kee Ma-Jong Co. bone mah jong set, with bone tiles in ebonized box, and original instructions.

*Box 10.5in (27cm) long*

**£180-220** BLO

A Chad Valley mah-jong set, complete with instructions, card counters, and original card box.

*c1925* *Box 12.25in (31cm) wide*

**£100-150** BLO

A German 'Zeppelin' domino set, with carved wooden domino pieces, in original oblong card box.

*c1920* *8in (20cm) long*

**£100-150** BLO

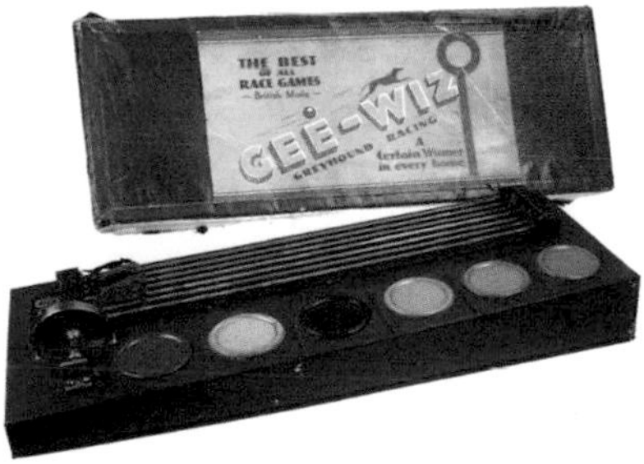


A British 'Gee-Wiz' tinplate greyhound racing game, with six greyhounds on slides in cardboard box.

*c1930* *15.25in (39cm) long*

**£12-18** BLO

## A CLOSER LOOK AT A SUTCLIFFE SUBMARINE

*Sutcliffe, founded in 1885, made boats from 1920. They were available with either nine or 12inch hulls and were made from a single piece, therefore removing the need to solder the two parts together.*

*The same form was used from 1955-74 for a licensed 'Nautilus' submarine from the Disney film '20,000 Leagues Under The Sea', which tends to be more valuable, often fetching up to £200 in the same condition with its box.*

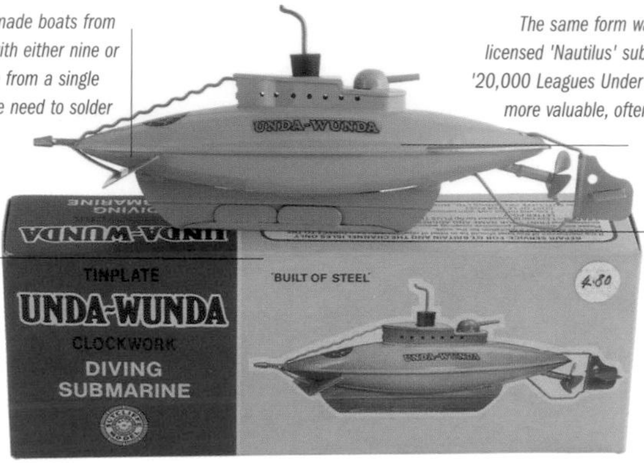


*These submarines had strong motors, allowing them to submerge and resurface, and it is rare to find examples which do not have extensive water damage and rust.*

*The submarine was produced from 1934-40 in grey and red with a shorter, deeper keel – it was re-introduced in 1946 with the keel shown here and produced in blue from 1976-81 only.*

A Sutcliffe Unda-Wunda clockwork pressed steel diving submarine, with rubber bung and periscope, mint in original box and with key.

*Sutcliffe, based in Leeds, closed down in 1984, partly due to competition from Far Eastern imports.*

*1976-81* *9.5in (24cm) long*

**£80-120** **W&W**

A Sutcliffe Commodore Cruiser clockwork powered pressed steel boat, with key, in original box.

*1977-81* *9in (23cm) long*

**£40-60** **W&W**

A Sutcliffe 'Jupiter' Ocean Pilot clockwork-powered pressed steel boat, with key and mast, original box, minor damage.

*1963-81* *9in (23cm) long*

**£50-70** **W&W**

A Sutcliffe pressed steel Victor Motor Torpedo Boat, with a clockwork motor, fore deck gun and torpedo tubes, in original box with key.

*1971-75* *9in (23cm) long*

**£60-90** **W&W**

A Sutcliffe Sprite Day Cruiser clockwork motor powered pressed steel boat, with key, in original box.

*1967-81* *9.5in (24cm) long*

**£100-150** **W&W**

A Sutcliffe Valiant clockwork powered pressed steel battle ship, with key, in original box.

*The Valiant Battleship was the first boat to be produced by Sutcliffe, in 1920. Early examples use a methylated spirit heated boiler, with clockwork being introduced after 1928. It was reproduced from 1978-80 and the rarest variation used an electric motor – only six are known.*

*12in (30.5cm) long*

**£120-180** **W&W**

A Victory Industries black plastic Vauxhall Velox saloon car, with red pressed metal interior, cream steering wheel and aluminium brightwork trim, in original box.

*c1950*

**£100-150** **W&W**

A Mego 'Batman's Batcycle' toy, with Batman and Robin figures, marked "©National Periodical Publications Inc 1974".

*Box 10.25in (26cm) wide*

**£25-35** **GAZE**

A 1930s scratch built model bi-plane, with turned wood body and silvered effect.

*15in (38cm) wide*

**£18-22** **GAZE**

A scarce large scale battery powered aluminium Astra Searchlight, with a rotating and tilting reflector lamp, glass cracked.

*12.5in (32cm) wide*

**£80-120** **W&W**

A post-WWII scarce Cragstan friction-powered American Army Artillery Jeep and field gun no.1000, in early utility box, with some wear.

**£80-120** **W&W**

An early 20thC Marklin cast iron and brass field cannon, with opening breech spring firing mechanism, one winder for angle adjustment and spoke metal wheels.

*12in (30.5cm) long*

**£100-150** **W&W**

A West German 'Bully Gladiator' Smurf figure, licensed by Schleich Peyo.

*2.75in (7cm) high*

**£2-3** **NOR**

A 'Washing' Smurf figure, licensed by Schleich Peyo.

*1979* *2in (5cm) high*

**£2-3** **NOR**

An Irwin 'Papa Smurf' carded Smurf figure, licensed by Schleich Peyo.

*1995* *7.75in (19.5cm) high*

**£6-8** **NOR**

A 1950s Japanese clockwork plush, fabric and tinplate rabbit toy, reading a farmyard animal book.

*8in (20cm) high*

**£40-60** **NOR**

A cold-painted bronze Beatrix Potter figure of a mouse.

*This used to be part of a game, and would have been used as a playing counter.*

*c1910* *1in (2.5cm) high*

**£100-150** **DG**

An American moulded celluloid wind-up 'Girl in a Mexican Hat' toy, the spinning hat with bakelite ball.

*Most of these celluloid dolls were produced in postwar Japan. They are very delicate, particularly today, so always looks out for cracks, dents and holes.*

*9.75in (24.5cm) high*

**£150-250** **MG**

A 1960s Japanese plush, fabric and tinplate clockwork cymbal-playing dog.

*7in (17.5cm) high*

**£40-60** **NOR**

A composition-headed drinking figure, with hand-painted features and sprung cloth and wooden body, marked "Foreign".

*6.5in (16.5cm) high*

**£8-12** **GAZE**

An early 20thC American cast iron model of a French bull dog.

*11in (28cm) high*

**£180-220** **ROS**

A View-Master picture disc of 'Historic St. Augustine Florida', by GAF Corp., packet no. A891.

*4.5in (11.5cm) wide*

**£3-5** **BH**

## COLLECTORS' NOTES

- Small pocket watches were first attached to wrists using a band in the late 16th century, and Girard Perregaux said it made wristwatches for the German Navy in the early 1880s. However, it was not until shortly after WW1 that they began to proliferate. The first few decades of the 20th century saw a boom in the manufacture of wristwatches, with both traditional clock and pocket watch makers turning to the new style and new companies springing up.
- The style of a watch can help to date it, although vintage styles are popular with today's makers. Small, round 'pocket watch' like shapes with wire lugs are usually early 20th century. Rectangular watches, or simple circular watches with clean-lined designs are usually from the 1930s. From the late 1940s onwards, watches started to become highly stylized and more innovative in shape, often taking on the styles of contemporary jewellery.
- The past two years have seen a popular revival in wristwatches, led by fashion magazines and TV programmes promoting a smarter look for men. This has prompted many to invest in a good quality watch, and even build collections. Contemporary examples by traditional top quality makers, and vintage examples by the same companies form the body of most collections, but 'fashion' watches that are sought-after mainly for their immediate visual appeal and period style have also recently grown in popularity.
- Watches from the 1950s are amongst the most popular today due to their simple, yet classic styling. Fine quality watches by names such as Rolex or Longines can often be found at lower prices than contemporary examples, sometimes even in precious metals. 1960s-'70s watches are particularly in vogue at present, with many of today's watchmakers copying these styles. Cases tend to be large and heavy, with futuristic designs and the use of colour, plastic and stainless steel.
- The brand, movement, materials and functions of a watch will help to indicate its value. Leading brands, such as Patek Philippe, are highly sought-after and within a brand certain 'iconic' models will be more desirable, such as Cartier's 'Tank'. The quality of the movement is important and should be correct for that watch. The more complex the watch is, the more valuable it is likely to be. Most prices given here are taken from the World Wide Traders Mark Room Floor.

A rare Breitling wristwatch, with a gold-plated case, the 'seconds' hand indicating the date on a dial on the outside, two windows showing the day and month in French, and a secondary dial at six o'clock showing the seconds.

*c1950*

**£600-900** **RSS**

A Breitling mechanical chronograph, with stainless steel case and two secondary dials.

*c1940*

**£300-500** **RSS**

A Breitling 'Chromatic' automatic chronograph watch, with stainless steel case, with left-handed calibre 12 movement.

*Breitling was founded in 1884 in St Imier, Switzerland and has built up a reputation for its precision chronographs. This movement was designed by Breitling, Heuer and Hamilton/Buren.*

*c1970*

**£1,000-1,500** **RSS**

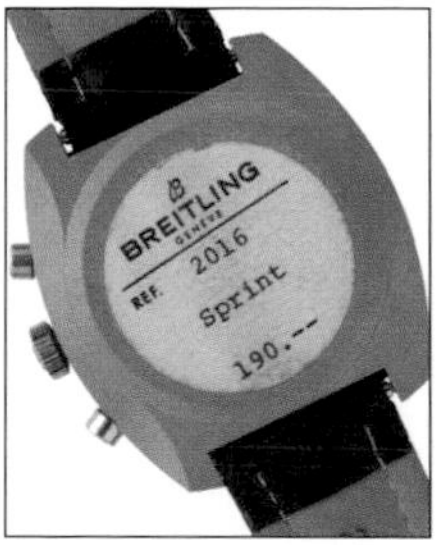


A new-old-stock, unused Breitling Sprint chronograph, with fibreglass case and original sticker, ref no. 2016.

*In worn condition, this watch would be worth around 40 per cent less.*

*1972*

**£350-500** **ML**

A new-old stock, unused Breitling three-register Long Playing chronograph, in fibreglass case, with original sticker, ref. 7103.3.

*1969*

**£400-600** **ML**

A 1930s American Hamilton wristwatch, with white gold-filled, engraved 'Square' cut-corner case, with Hamilton 17-jewel 987F movement.

**£80-120** **ML**

A 1930s Hamilton wristwatch, with white gold-filled 'Square B' engraved case, with Hamilton 987 17-jewel movement.

**£100-150** **ML**

A 1930s Hamilton wristwatch, with yellow gold-filled 'Square Plain' side engraved case, with Hamilton 17-jewel 987 movement.

*This yellow gold-filled finish is the rarer case variation.*

**£90-120** **ML**

A 1940s Hamilton wristwatch, with solid 14ct gold curved case, diamond-set dial and hidden lugs.

**£400-600** **ML**

A 1940s Hamilton wristwatch, with diamond-set dial, 14ct solid white gold case with stepped bezel, and Hamilton 982 19-jewel movement.

*Hamilton was founded in 1892 and produced its first pocket watches in 1894. Its high point was during the 1930s, and although it fell in prominence during the postwar period, it produced the first electric watch in 1957 and the first digital watch, the 'Pulsar', in 1972.*

**£400-600** **ML**

A 1930s American Hamilton Raleigh Plain white gold-filled wristwatch, with some brassing to the case.

*In unworn condition, this watch would be worth £100-150.*

**£70-90** **ML**

A 1930s Hamilton Perry wristwatch, with white gold-filled case and Hamilton 987 17-jewel movement.

**£120-180** **ML**

A 1960s Hamilton chronograph, with stainless steel case, bright red dial, and Valjoue 7750 movement.

**£100-150** **ML**

A 1970s Hamilton Self-winding automatic wristwatch, with large yellow gold-filled egg-shaped case, burgundy dial and Hamilton 679A 17-jewel movement.

**£70-100** **ML**

A 1950s LeCoultre 'Memovox' automatic large wristwatch, stainless steel case, with 17-jewel K911 Vacheron & Constantin movement signed "LeCoultre" and "VXN".

*Founded in 1833 in Switzerland, LeCoultre made ébauches, or near-finished movements. In 1925, it merged with Jaeger to form Jaeger LeCoultre, best known for its 'Reverso' watch, 1931.*

**£300-500** **ML**

## A CLOSER LOOK AT A LECOULTRE WATCH

*LeCoultre watches with movements marked 'VXN' indicate the movements were made for Vacheron & Constantin by Jaeger LeCoultre - many were used for LeCoultre watches in the US.*

*This example has its rare original glass, which is cut and shaped to fit around the lugs.*

*Usually, the glass has been replaced with plastic, which is easier to cut - a plastic replacement reduces the value to around £150-180.*

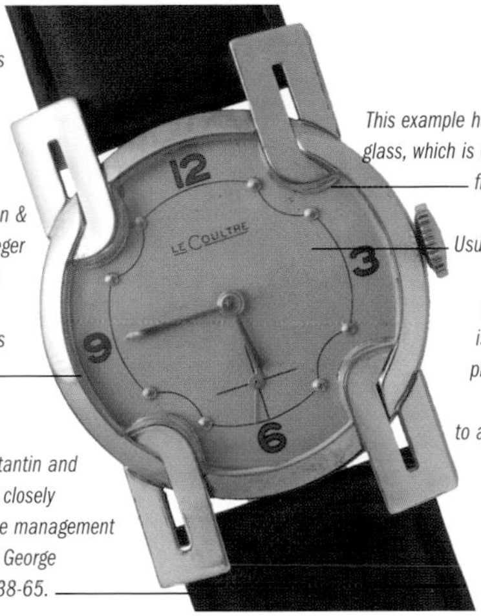

*Vacheron & Constantin and LeCoultre worked closely together under the management and ownership of George Ketterer from 1938-65.*

A rare 1950s LeCoultre 'Coronet' wristwatch, the gold-filled case with fancy lugs, the VXN 17-jewel movement signed "LeCoultre".

**£250-300** **ML**

A LeCoultre 'Memovox' automatic wristwatch, with yellow gold-filled case, full-sounding alarm, with 17-jewel 487 Vacheron & Constantin movement signed "LeCoultre" and "VXN".

*LeCoultre's watches, particularly in this simple 1950s style, are very popular at present. Stainless steel variations are generally worth more as less were made, making them rarer today.*

**£380-420** **ML**

A 1950s LeCoultre 'Futurematic' automatic wristwatch, with yellow gold-filled case, back-set mechanism and 17-jewel Vacheron & Constantin movement signed "LeCoultre" and "VXN".

*This watch is set using a wheel on the back, rather than on the side, of the case. An inscription above says "DO NOT PULL" as Piaget offered a similar mechanism at the same time that needed to be pulled to operate it.*

**£400-500** **ML**

A LeCoultre 'Futurematic' automatic wristwatch, with gold-filled case, two-tone dial, two-tone power reserve indicator and 17-jewel Vacheron & Constantin movement signed "LeCoultre" and "VXN".

*The stainless steel version of this watch was sold for $95 (about £50) in 1950.*

**£500-600** **ML**

A 1950s LeCoultre 'Beau Brummel' wristwatch, with solid 14ct gold case and exterior dot markers.

*Beau Brummel was a famous 18thC British 'Dandy' known for his sense of fashion, and a one-time friend and advisor to the Prince of Wales.*

**£250-300** **ML**

A 1970s LeCoultre Alarm wristwatch, with rare jumbo stainless steel case, two-tone dial-date window, Calibre 916 movement.

*The Memovox and Alarm are amongst LeCoultre's most desirable mid-late 20thC models.*

**£400-500** **ML**

A rare 1970s LeCoultre 'Memovox' wristwatch, with egg-shaped stainless steel case, alarm, two-tone dial signed "Memovox" and "HPG", and LeCoultre 916 movement.

*This watch is rare as it was expensive in its day and was only bought by 'progressive' people who followed up-to-the-minute fashions for large-cased watches. As such, parts are very hard to find. 'HPG' stands for 'High Precision Guaranteed', denoting a fine movement.*

**£400-500** **ML**

A rare 1970s Jumbo LeCoultre 'Memovox' automatic wristwatch, with egg-shaped stainless steel case with moveable bezel, two-tone dial and LeCoultre 916 movement.

*The back has a rare 'snowflake' design panel, and the dial is faded, as is expected with this model.*

**£600-900** **ML**

A 1940s Jaeger LeCoultre mechanical military-type wristwatch, with stainless steel case, black dial and seconds dial at six o'clock.

*c1940*

**£70-90** **RSS**

A 1950s Jaeger LeCoultre 18ct gold automatic wristwatch, with round case.

**£1,000-1,500** **RSS**

A 1950s Jaeger LeCoultre manual wind wristwatch, Swiss for the French market, with a round stainless steel case and seconds dial at six o'clock.

**£320-420** **RSS**

A Jaeger Automatic wristwatch, with gold-filled case, white dial, date window and 17-jewel movement.

*c1960*

**£500-600** **RSS**

A Jaeger LeCoultre automatic wristwatch, with round solid gold case, white dial and seconds dial at six o'clock.

*c1960*

**£500-600** **RSS**

A 1990s Jaeger LeCoultre 'Master Control' series 'Memovox' automatic wristwatch, numbered "3913" on the back, with a rare alarm using a striking hammer system.

*Introduced in 1992, the Master Control series undergoes 1,000 hours of assembly and testing. Styled to look like LeCoultre's most popular 1950s watches, many of its 1950s range names were also used.*

**£2,200-2,800** **ML**

A 1940s Omega wristwatch, with stainless steel case, black dial and painted Art Deco style numbers.

**£200-250** **RSS**

A 1940s Omega small railway-style wristwatch, with stainless steel case, black dial and seconds dial at six o'clock.

**£250-350** **RSS**

## A CLOSER LOOK AT AN OMEGA WATCH

*The shaped dial, with its distinctive faceted sections is known as a 'pie pan' dial and is a desirable feature.*

*The Constellation range was introduced in 1952, and was one of Omega's two main post-war ranges, alongside the Seamaster.*

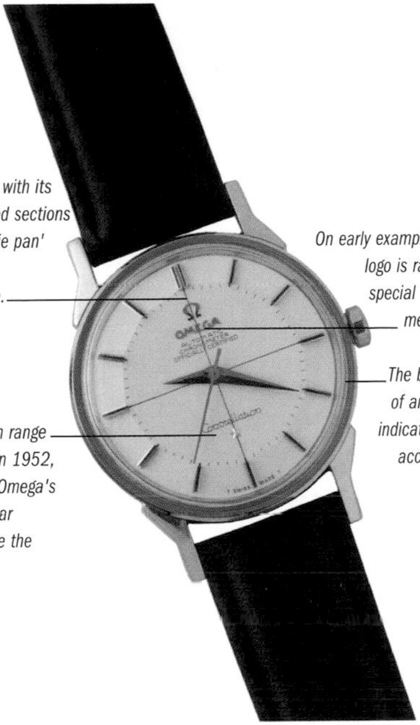


*On early examples, only the Omega logo is raised in relief and a special 'bumper' automatic mechanism was used.*

*The back bears a design of an observatory tower, indicating its chronometer accuracy and very high quality movement.*

A 1960s Omega 'Constellation' automatic chronometer wristwatch, with a stainless steel case, 'pie pan' dial, baton markers, Observatory back, and a Calibre 561b 24-jewel movement adjusted to five positions.

*Look out for gold cased examples with an original gold 'block' strap as these are scarce and valuable.*

**£300-500** **ML**

A 1940s Omega lady's wristwatch, with stainless steel case, white dial with luminous numbers, centre seconds and luminous hands.

**£220-280** **RSS**

A 1960s Omega 'Seamaster 30' manual winding wristwatch, with stainless steel case and white dial, and Omega Calibre 269 movement.

*This style of watch is currently very popular.*

**£100-150** **RSS**

An 1960s Omega gentleman's watch, with 18ct gold case, worn gold dial with centre seconds and date window, and Calibre no.600 17-jewel movement.

**£400-600** **BLO**

A 1960s-70s Omega 'Seamaster 30', with stainless steel case, black dial with luminous markers and hands, and seconds dial at six o'clock.

*Omega was founded in 1848 by Louis Brandt and had adopted the 'Omega' name by 1903. It has become renowned for its reliable and accurate Seamaster range, the popularity of which has been boosted by a recent connection to James Bond.*

**£300-500** **RSS**

An Omega 'Seamaster Memomatic' alarm wristwatch, with stainless steel case, silvered dial with baton markers, alarm indicator and date aperture, with Calibre 980 19-jewel movement, numbered "30017014".

*1.5in (4cm) diam*

**£200-250** **GHOU**

A 1970s Omega 'Constellation Electronic' wristwatch, with stainless steel case, black dial and date window.

*After 1970, Omega began to use electronic movements by Bulova for much of their Constellation series.*

**£120-180** **RSS**

## A CLOSER LOOK AT AN OMEGA SPEEDMASTER

*This limited edition watch was produced to commemorate the 25th anniversary of the Apollo XI space flight and moon landing in July 1969.*

*The back is engraved with a commemorative inscription and the fact that it is 'Flight Qualified By NASA For All Manned Space Missions'.*

*The Omega Speedmaster was worn on that flight, and became the only model of watch ever worn on the Moon.*

*Omega have released a number of space flight and moon landing commemorative watches. Check the wording on the back to identify and date the right model.*

A limited edition Omega 'Speedmaster Professional' manual winding chronograph, with a stainless steel case, black dial with three registers, from an edition of 2,500, and with original box, mission badge and papers.

*The Speedmaster gained its 'Professional' suffix in 1966 after astronaut Edward White wore a Speedmaster for the first American space walk in 1965.*

*1994*

**£1,500-2,000** **RSS**

A 1970s new-old stock Omega 'Chronostop' driver's wristwatch, with shaped stainless steel case, and black dial.

*The face has been turned by 45 degrees to allow it to be read easily when the driver is holding a steering wheel.*

**£500-700** **RSS**

A 1980s Omega 'Seamaster Lady Dynamic' lady's wristwatch, with stainless steel shaped case and bracelet, two-tone dial with date at six o'clock, red hands and markers.

**£250-300** **RSS**

A 1980s Omega 'Seamaster Dynamic' wristwatch, with stainless steel shaped case and bracelet, two-colour dial with red markers, date window at six o'clock, red and luminous hands, and Calibre 1430 quartz movement.

*This is the second generation of the 'Dynamic', which was first used in 1969 on watches with horizontal egg-shaped cases. This second range was released in 1985 and was produced only for a few years using very slim quartz movements.*

**£300-400** **RSS**

A limited edition Omega 'Speedmaster' automatic wristwatch, produced for the Winter Olympic Games in Albertville in 1992, from an edition of 500, with original strap.

*1992*

**£1,000-1,500** **RSS**

A 1950s Rolex 'Oyster' watch, with stainless steel case, white dial with seconds dial at six o'clock, and Rolex movement.

**£600-900** **BLO**

A Rolex 'Precision' lady's wristwatch, with 18ct gold case, gilt dial with centre seconds and baton markers, with Rolex 17-jewel movement.

*75in (2cm) diam*

**£180-220** **GHOU**

A 1960s Rolex 'Oyster Precision' junior-sized wristwatch, with stainless steel case and white 'textured' dial with baton markers.

**£500-750** **RSS**

A Rolex 'Oyster Precision' automatic wristwatch, with stainless steel case, black dial with hours and seconds markers, in excellent condition.

**£700-900** **RSS**

A Rolex 'Oyster Precision' wristwatch, with stainless steel case, champagne dial, centre seconds and Rolex 17-jewel movement.

**£700-900** **RSS**

A Rolex 'Oysterdate Precision' automatic wristwatch, with stainless steel case, white dial and magnified date aperture.

*Rolex was founded by Hans Wilsdorf in 1905, and introduced the world's first waterproof case, the Oyster, in 1926. In 1931, it developed the first reliable self-winding 'perpetual' watch. The name Tudor was used as a sub-brand from 1945.*

**£700-1,000** **RSS**

A Rolex 'Oyster Precision' automatic wristwatch, with stainless steel case and bracelet, silvered dial with baton markers and centre seconds, and Rolex 17-jewel movement.

*1.25in (3.5cm) diam*

**£280-320** **GHOU**

A 1960s Rolex 'Oyster Perpetual Air King' automatic wristwatch, with stainless steel case and bracelet.

**£400-600** **ML**

## A CLOSER LOOK AT A ROLEX

*Rolex initially concentrated on its Oyster-cased watches, not producing a chronograph until 1937 and naming it the 'Cosmograph' in 1960.*

*The Cosmograph Daytona is one of the most desirable Rolex models, becoming particularly sought-after during the mid-1980s after Paul Newman was photographed wearing one on the cover of Italian magazine Moda.*

*This is from the first series of Cosmographs delivered with a Rolex automatic mechanism. Before 1999 various, often manual wind, mechanisms by Valjoux and later Zenith, were used.*

*Look out for the Daytona models with 'exotic' 'Paul Newman' dials that have contrasting black and white dials and subsidiary dials and a red outer scale, as these are highly prized.*

A rare Rolex 'Oyster Perpetual Cosmograph Daytona' chronograph automatic wristwatch, with stainless steel case, white three register dial, with original papers.

*There can be a long waiting list for these watches, forcing values up on the secondary market.*

*c2002*

**£3,000-3,500** **RSS**

A Rolex 'Oyster Perpetual Datejust' automatic wristwatch, with stainless steel case and bracelet, silvered dial with baton markers, sweep centre seconds and date aperture at 3 o'clock, and Rolex 27-jewel movement.

*1.25in (3.5cm) diam*

**£500-700** **GHOU**

A Rolex 'Oyster Perpetual' lady's automatic wristwatch, the stainless steel case with gold bezel, winder and centre band of strap, and black dial with magnified date aperture.

**£600-900** **BLO**

A Rolex 'Oyster Perpetual Day-Date' certified chronometer automatic wristwatch, with yellow gold case and 'President bracelet', the matching gilt face with English day aperture and magnified date aperture.

**£3,200-3,800** **RSS**

A rare 1950s Tudor 'Prince Oysterdate' automatic wristwatch, with round solid gold case, matching gilt dial with Tudor rose logo and magnified date aperture.

**£350-550** **RSS**

A 1960s Tudor 'Ranger' automatic wristwatch, with stainless steel case and bracelet, black face and magnified date aperture.

*This was Tudor's version of the Rolex Explorer and, despite having a military look with the black dial, isn't a military watch.*

**£220-320** **ML**

A 1970s Airin chronograph wristwatch, with gold-filled 'TV' shaped case, dial with two subsidiary dials and 17-jewel movement.

**£100-150** **RSS**

## A CLOSER LOOK AT A CHRONOGRAPH

*A Quantieme Perpetual Calendar mechanical movement is highly complex and uses over 100 more components than a standard chronograph.*

*Often known as a 'QPC' movement, it reflects different days in each month and leap years without need for manual adjustment.*

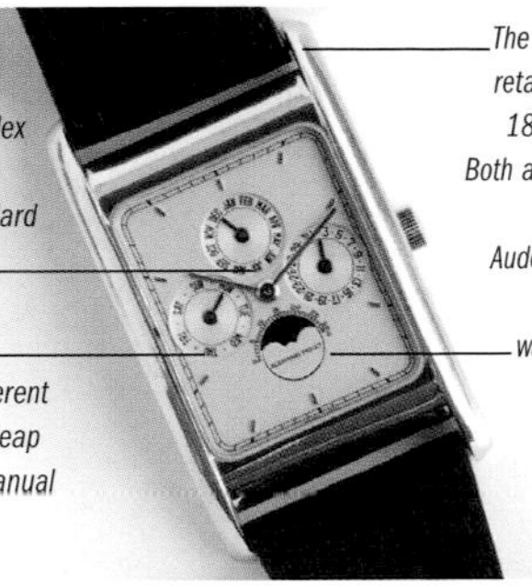

*The case is solid gold, and it retains its original strap and 18ct gold buckle and case. Both are in excellent condition.*

*Audemars Piguet, founded in 1875, is one of the top watchmakers in the world.*

An Audemars Piguet 'Quantieme Perpetual Calendar' automatic wristwatch, with 18ct gold rectangular case, silver dial with baton markers, moon phase and subsidiary day, month and date dials.

*1.75in (4.5cm) long 1in (2.5cm) wide*

**£6,000-9,000** **GHOU**

A 1980s Auricoste 'Professional' diver's automatic wristwatch, with stainless steel case, black finished bezel, as used by the French navy.

**£300-400** **RSS**

A 1950s Benrus 'jump hour' or 'direct read' watch, with yellow gold-filled case, stainless steel back and 17-jewel Swiss made movement, with original Benrus airlines box.

*Benrus was founded in 1921 by Benjamin Lazrus, with the name taken from the first three letters of his forename and last three letters of his surname. They initially produced cases which were fitted with Swiss movements. The late 1940s and 1950s were arguably their most innovative and successful period, with their 'alarm' and 'jump hour' watches being the most popular. From the 1970s they marketed, often fashionable, quartz watches produced by other makers, and are still active today.*

**£100-150** **ML**

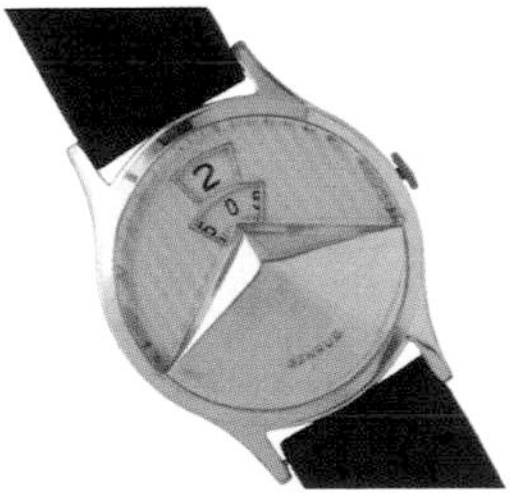

A Benrus 'jump hour' or 'direct read' watch, with chevron design gold filled case, and 17-jewel Swiss made movement.

**£100-150** **ML**

A Benrus 'direct read' or 'jump hour' watch, with white gold filled case and 17-jewel Swiss made movement

**£100-150** **ML**

A Bulova quartz watch, with gold-plate case, bezel engraved with roman numerals, and black face with gilt seconds dial at six o'clock.

**£20-30** **RSS**

A 1960s Cartier 'Tank Louis' wristwatch, with solid 18ct gold case, white dial with Roman numerals and cabochon set winder.

*Fakes of this highly desirable watch are commonly found. One indication of authenticity is that one arm of the 'V' on the 'VII' marker is made up of the word 'Cartier'.*

**£800-1,200** **ML**

A 1980s Cartier 'Must de Cartier' 'Tank' wristwatch, with 18ct gold vermeil case, cabochon set winder, white dial with Roman numeral markers.

*Vermeil is the word used to describe gold-plated sterling silver.*

**£400-600** **ML**

## A CLOSER LOOK AT A GRUEN WATCH

*The duo-dial version is more desirable than the centre seconds version. The centre seconds version was also less expensive.*

*The seconds dial is oversized compared to other similar watches so that a doctor could use it to measure bodily functions such as a pulse.*

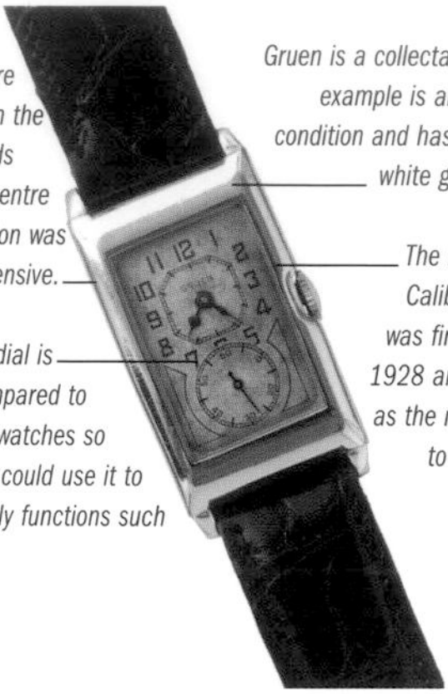

*Gruen is a collectable name. This example is also in excellent condition and has a rectangular white gold-filled case.*

*The movement is a Calibre 877, which was first produced in 1928 and is the same as the movement sold to Rolex for their notable and prized 'Prince' watches.*

A 1930s Gruen Duo-Dial Doctor's wristwatch, with a white gold filled case with engraved sides, and Gruen Calibre 877a movement.

**£800-1,200** **ML**

A 1980s Cartier 'Santos' lady's automatic wristwatch, with stainless steel and gold-set square case and articulated bracelet marked "Cartier", and cream coloured dial with painted Roman numerals.

**£600-700** **RSS**

A 1990s Cartier 'Pasha' automatic wristwatch, with stainless steel round case, turning bezel, sapphire cabochon-set winder, cream dial with painted Roman numerals and blued steel hands.

**£1,000-1,500** **RSS**

A 1970s Eterna 'Kontiki 20' sports wristwatch, with stainless steel case, original stainless steel articulated strap and black dial with baton markers and some fading from the sun.

**£180-220** **RSS**

A 1920s Gubelin manual wind watch, with a silver elongated case stamped '935', the silvered dial with exploding numerals.

*Rectangular watches are currently very popular, particularly if they display unusual features such as the 'exploding' numerals, or Art Deco styling.*

**£200-300** **ML**

A Heuer 'Regatta' sports automatic 134.600 series wristwatch, with a khaki-finished Autavia style case and articulated bracelet.

*Introduced in 1964, the Regatta underwent a transformation c1983, resulting in the 134.600 series. The series of blue and red discs acted as a countdown for yachtsmen.*

*c1985*

**£500-600** RSS

## A CLOSER LOOK AT A HEUER WATCH

*The Monaco is one of Heuer's most desirable and collectable models and has been produced in a number of variations since the 1960s.*

*It shot to fame when Steve McQueen wore a two register date version in the 1971 film 'Le Mans'.*

*It was one of the first waterproof automatic chronographs produced.*

*The instantly recognisable case is large, allowing it to be read easily when driving.*

A 1970s Heuer 'Monaco' automatic chronograph, with a gold-filled square case, polished blue dial with three registers, blue leather strap.

**£1,200-£1,800** RSS

A Heuer chronograph, with solid gold case and white dial with three registers.

*This is a re-edition of a model produced around 1964.*

*c1999*

**£800-1,200** RSS

A 1930s Illinois 'Manhattan' wristwatch, with engraved yellow gold-filled case, two-tone dial with seconds at 9 o'clock, and 17-jewel Illinois Springfield movement.

**£200-250** ML

A 1930s Illinois wristwatch, with engraved yellow gold-filled case, white dial with radium numbers and seconds dial at six o'clock.

**£120-180** ML

A 1970s Jenny 'Caribbean 1000' diver's automatic wristwatch, with stainless steel square case waterproof to 1,000 metres, black and yellow finished bezel, black face and date window, and 25-jewel movement.

**£320-380** RSS

A 1950s-60s Lip 'Dauphine Electric' wristwatch, with stainless steel case and silvered dial with baton markers and date window.

**£180-220** RSS

A 1970s Lip 'Nautic Ski' electric sports wristwatch, with silver-plated case and black revolving bezel and dial, with date window.

**£200-250** **RSS**

A 1930s Longines manual winding wristwatch, with rectangular platinum case, the dial set with diamonds and subsidiary seconds dial, and with Longines 17-jewel 9L movement.

**£800-1,000** **ML**

A 1950s Longines 'Galaxy' mystery dial wristwatch, the 18ct white gold case with faceted edge and diamond set 'Mystery' dial with full diamond markers.

*Mystery dials, popular in the 1950s and '60s, use a system of revolving rings, or discs, to move the 'hands'.*

**£400-600** **ML**

A Lord Elgin wristwatch, with gold-filled case, engraved oval hour marker and minutes hand, with Lord Elgin 21-jewel movement.

**£90-120** **ML**

## A CLOSER LOOK AT A LONGINES WRISTWATCH

*The watch has a 'mystery' face - with the minutes indicated by the white dot on the outer dial, and the hours by the arrow.*

*This watch is very rare as few were produced, with the space age style and theme being deemed too avant garde for most buyers.*

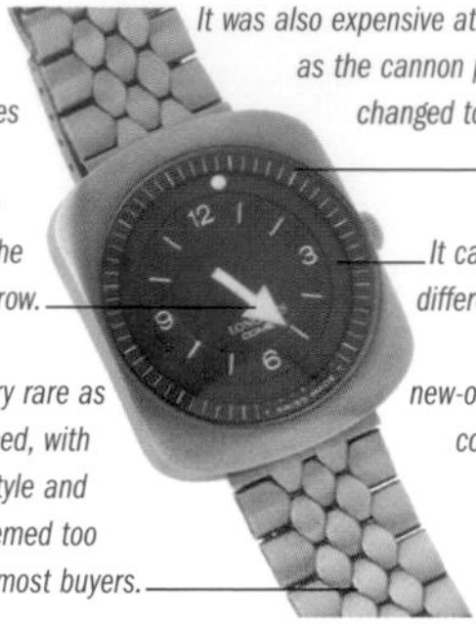

*It was also expensive at the time, partly as the cannon pinion had to be changed to allow the large dial to move.*

*It can be found with different dial colours. This example is new-old stock, in mint condition and has its original bracelet.*

A Longines 'Comet' manual winding wristwatch, with gold-filled cushion-shaped case and matching original Longines signed flip-lock bracelet, 'mystery dial' with arrow marker and 17-jewel Swiss-made signed Longines movement.

*c1972*

**£400-500** **ML**

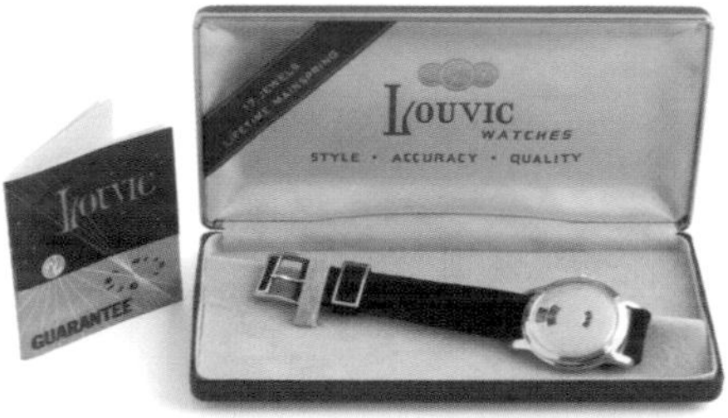


A 1950s Louvic 'DirectTime' direct-read wristwatch, with waterproof and shock resistant stainless steel case, 'jump hour' type face, original black velvet faced strap, and original box, instructions and ribbon.

*This example is in mint condition, together with its box and label. Both factors are extremely rare - in used condition without the box, the value would be around £50-80.*

**£100-150** **ML**

A 1960s new-old stock Merit chronograph wristwatch, with stainless steel case, two registers, silvered face, and Swiss-made 17-jewel movement.

**£120-180** **ML**

An Omega lady's cocktail back-wound wristwatch, with 18ct solid white gold case set with diamonds, with silvered dial and matching bracelet.

*75in (1.5cm) diam*

**£300-500** **GHOU**

A 1980s Orfina 'Ferrari' quartz wristwatch, with stainless steel case and matching articulated bracelet, designed by the Pininfarina Design Studio.

*Founded in 1973, Orfina's name is better known in connection with Porsche Design, for whom it manufactured watches for a period of time.*

**£250-350** **RSS**

An Orfina 'Lotus Swiss Fan Club' quartz wristwatch, with stainless steel case and bracelet, the yellow face with date window.

*c1982*

**£180-220** **RSS**

An Orfina for Porsche Design 'Military' chronograph, the black face with three subsidiary dials, and Lemania 5100 movement.

**£700-900** **RSS**

A Patek Philippe manual winding wristwatch, the solid 18ct gold case by Dennison of England, with black leather strap with 14ct gold buckle.

**£300-500** **BLO**

A 1960s Patek Philippe ladies wristwatch, with solid 18ct gold case and band, signed five times including on the Patek Philippe movement.

**£1,000-1,500** **ML**

A fine 1930s Patek Philippe manual winding wristwatch, ref no. 425, with solid gold curved rectangular case, silver dial with applied gold batons, faceted crystal, seconds dial at six o'clock and leather strap with gold buckle signed "Paul & Co."

*c1936*

**£7,000-9,000** **RSS**

An Alain Silberstein limited edition 'Krono 2' chronograph automatic wristwatch, stainless steel case, subsidiary dials showing 24-hour indication, triple date and moon phases, from edition of 999.

*Alain Silberstein is a noted French architect who started his own watch company. His unusual, often Bauhaus inspired watches were released in the 1980s, at a time when designer watches were growing in prominence.*

*1993*

**£1,500-2,000** **RSS**

A 1980s-90s Alain Silberstein quartz wristwatch, with stainless steel case, black face with geometric design and geometric coloured hands.

**£250-300** **RSS**

A 1960s Tissot 'Visodate' automatic wristwatch, with gold-filled square case, and 17-jewel movement.

*The Visodate is a well-known model, more commonly found in round cases from the 1950s-60s.*

**£100-150** **RSS**

## A CLOSER LOOK AT A VACHERON & CONSTANTIN WATCH

*The case is made from platinum, which is a very rare feature. This watch would have been extremely expensive originally.*

*The inside of the case is marked 'VF' for French master goldsmiths, silversmiths, jewellers and watchmakers Verger Frères who also worked for Van Cleef & Arpels and many leading watchmakers.*

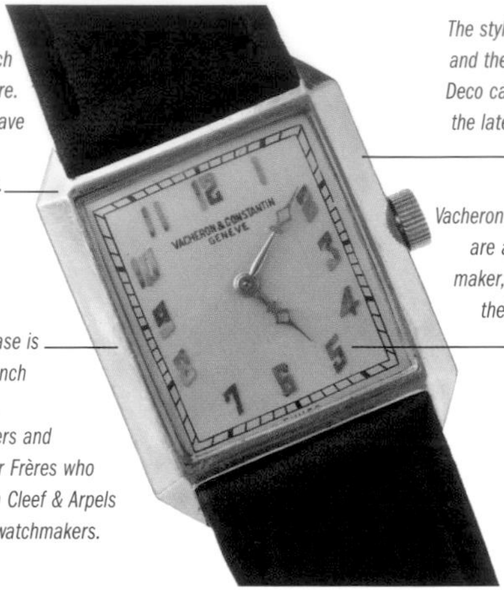


*The style of the mark and the desirable Art Deco case dates it to the late 1920s-early 1930s.*

*Vacheron & Constantin are a sought-after maker, renowned for their high quality watches.*

A 1920s Vacheron & Constantin manual winding wristwatch, with shaped platinum case with Verger mark and French dog's head platinum control mark, signed on the face, case and movement.

**£2,500-3,000** **ML**

A 1970s Tressa Lux 'Spaceman' automatic wristwatch, with chrome-plated stainless steel case, black face with day and date window and original DuPont 'Corfam' plastic strap.

*This watch was designed by Andre Le Marquand, who was inspired by the astronauts' helmets worn in July 1969 when man first landed on the moon. It was part of a range of space age design watches and has been exhibited at the Museum of Modern Art in New York. It was made in a number of different colours, all worth roughly the same.*

**£80-120** **RSS**

A Swiss Universal Geneva wristwatch, with stainless steel case, white dial and Swiss-made 17-jewel movement, probably made for United Nations military service.

**£70-100** **ML**

A 1940s Universal 'TriCompax' chronograph manual winding wristwatch, with stainless steel case, original discoloured dial with three registers.

*More affordable, mass-produced chronographs began to be made during the 1940s, with the Compax by Universal being a good example. Despite being hit by the affordability of quartz movements in the 1980s, the company has been relaunched and is even producing the Compax once again.*

**£300-500** **RSS**

A 1990s Universal 'Compax' chronograph wristwatch, with stainless steel case, two-colour dial with three subsidiary dials, and burgundy leather strap.

**£700-1,000** **RSS**

A late 1930s Vacheron & Constantin manual winding watch, with solid 14K gold case with hooded lugs, dial with seconds dial at six o'clock, and signed movement.

*Face 1.5in (3.5cm) high*

**£1,000-1,500** **ML**

A 1950s Vacheron & Constantin manual winding wristwatch, with round yellow gold case with 'cow horn' curving lugs, engraved wavy line dial with applied gold numerals, the back engraved "to Robert W. Findall Commemorating 31 years of association with Blanchard Press Inc. October 16, 1953".

**£2,200-2,800** RSS

## A CLOSER LOOK AT A VIXA WATCH

*The 'Type 20' was manufactured by six different makers during the 1950s and '60s, including Vixa.*

*It has a 'flyback' or 'Taylor' system, which allowed pilots to stop, reset and restart the chronograph with one push of a button, which is useful for aviation timing.*

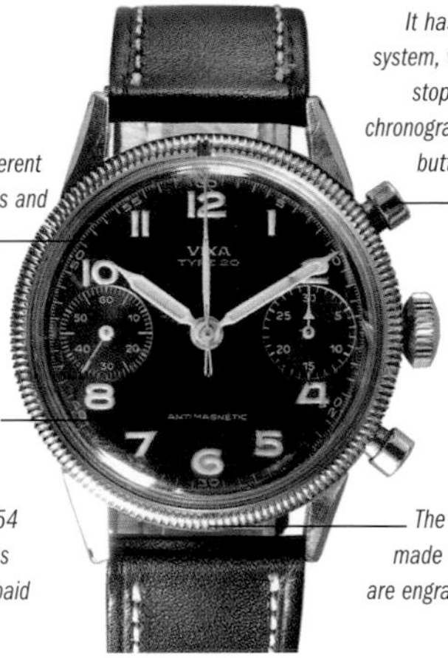


*Around 4,500 examples were made by German watch and stopwatch maker Hanhart from 1954 under the 'Vixa' name, as part of war reparations paid to France by Germany.*

*The cases of the Type 20s made for the French military are engraved '5100/54' before the serial numbers.*

A mid-1950s Vixa 'Type 20' antimagnetic chronograph military wristwatch, with stainless steel case, black dial with two subsidiary dials and luminous hands and Arabic numerals.

**£1,200-1,600** RCC

A Zenith 'Surf' automatic sports wristwatch, with stainless steel case and dark blue face.

*The blue dial is harder to find, it is said that only around 2,400 blue dial examples were made.*

**£150-200** RSS

A mid-1960s Gucci lady's Perspex cased wristwatch, with original strap.

**£180-220** PC

A 1960s Zodiac 'Olympos' automatic wristwatch, with asymmetric stainless steel case, two-tone dial with standard minute hand and 'floating' hour indicator, and 17-jewel Swiss movement.

*Along with the Seawolf, which was introduced in 1953, this is one of Zodiac's most recognised watches.*

**£80-120** ML

A limited edition TinTin chronograph wristwatch, with the Moon and Earth as hands on two of the three dials, complete with original rocket shaped box and card outer.

**£150-250** RSS

## COLLECTORS' NOTES

- Pocket watches were first made in the second half of the 16thC, and became the most convenient and reliable method of telling the time for the next four and a half centuries, until wristwatches took over after WW1.
- The 19thC saw a rapid rise in the number of watch factories, particularly after the Industrial Revolution, and a steady but considerable reduction in prices, making watches more accessible to the lower and growing middle classes. Railroad watches had to be reliable and affordable, and form a popular collecting area today, but the best and most valuable watches were typically made in Switzerland.
- The majority of pocket watches found today that date from the late 19thC to the early 20thC will usually be worth between £30 and £200, particularly if the case is base metal or gold-plated, the maker is not a renowned Swiss maker and the movement is basic and simply tells the time.
- Values today are indicated by a combination of factors including the maker, the quality and complexity of the movement, the quality of the materials used, the date of manufacture and rarity. A pocket watch with a solid flip lid is known as a 'hunter', and one with a flip lid with a viewing window is a 'half hunter'.

A gentleman's 14ct gold fob watch, with engraved hallmarked case and face, in original retailer's case by J. Mellanby, Stockton-on-Tees, with key.

**£220-280** **BLO**

## A CLOSER LOOK AT A POCKET WATCH

*It is by the oldest notable Swiss watchmaker Vacheron & Constantin, founded by Jean-Marc Vacheron in 1775. The combined name was used from 1819.*

*The case is in solid 18ct gold, and would have been highly expensive at the time. This means fewer would have been sold, making this example comparatively rare.*

*The back of the case is appealingly decorated and in excellent condition with no damage - surprising for such a high carat gold which is typically 'soft'.*

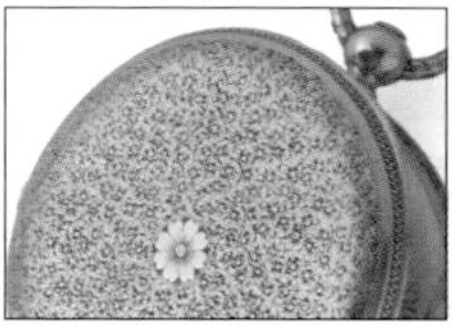

*The serial number engraved on the inside of the back dates its manufacture to between 1860-65 and probably around 1861, but it may have been sold later.*

A late 19thC key set Vacheron & Constantin 'hunter' pocket watch, with solid 18ct gold case, No.112346, white enamel dial with Roman numerals and signed movement.

*c1861* *1.5in (3.5cm) diam*

**£400-600** **ML**

A Swiss for the French military J. Auricoste 'Aural' chronograph pocket watch, with gold-filled case and Lemania 19-jewel movement, the back of the case with French military marks and numbered "5516".

*c1930*

**£200-300** **RSS**

A 1940s Zenith manual winding pocket watch, with chrome-plated steel case and large seconds dial at six o'clock, in mint condition.

**£80-120** **RSS**

A Charles Frodsham hunter pocket watch, with engine-turned London hallmarked silver case, the key wound movement signed "84 Strand, London", number "16870".

*Charles Frodsham was founded in the early 19thC and is a renowned maker of marine chronometers, clocks and watches.*

*1868*

**£180-200** **GHOU**

A 1970s Swiss for the South American market Breitling sports chronograph pocket watch, with chrome-plated stainless steel case, two subsidiary dials and original yellow sticker to back.

*This type of watch is used at sporting events to record the official times.*

**£150-200** **RSS**

A 1940s Lip 'Dauphine' pocket watch, with stainless steel case and large seconds dial, in mint condition.

*The Dauphine was a medium quality range, which included wristwatches.*

**£80-90** **RSS**

A Jaeger 'Chronoscope' sports chronograph pocket watch, measuring intervals of up to 1/5 of a second, with original box in mint condition.

**£80-120** **RSS**

A 1920s-30s Elgin travelling watch, in engraved sterling silver case, with shaped ring, blue cabochon set catch, and flip watch, the inside of the case marked "Illinois W.C. Co Elgin Sterling 2620483".

*2in (5cm) long*

**£100-150** **BB**

A 1920s-30s MAY-LO travelling purse watch, in flip-open sterling silver case engraved with alternating panels of plain and lines designs, with decal with three initials and blue cabochon set winder.

*1.5in (4cm) high*

**£100-150** **ML**

A "The Book of Time Vol II" novelty desk or travel watch, with green faux leather cover and brass 'pages', the front cover opening to reveal a flip-up, spring loaded first page with inset Defender Swiss Made watch.

*2.25in (6cm) high*

**£50-80** **ML**

## COLLECTORS' NOTES

- The cowboy has been an American icon since his origins in 1930s popular culture. The romantic appeal of fighting for justice combined with the excitement of fast horses, guns and battles, and the allure of the Wild West placed the many characters that represented him right at the heart of America's youth. This popularity boomed during the 1950s, with radio, comic strips and films already in full swing, and the new phenomenon of the television. Countrywide, boys and girls were captivated by the adventures of these new all-American heroes and heroines.
- The fictional 'Hopalong Cassidy' was one of the most important characters. The creation of Clarence E. Mulford, he appeared in a number of stories and novels from 1904. In 1935, William Boyd was asked to portray him, and the rude, hard-drinking, limping original character was transformed into a clean-cut, honest and polite hero. In June 1949, Hopalong Cassidy became the first network television series, on NBC. Sixty-six films were also made and he entered the lexicon of American heroes.
- Other important names include Gene Autry, 'The Singing Cowboy' and 'The Lone Ranger'. This, otherwise nameless, hero was devised by George Trendle and first appeared on radio in January 1933. Over 2,900 episodes were made until 1954, and he appeared on television from 1949-57. He and 'Hopalong Cassidy' were perhaps the two most influential cowboy characters, becoming deeply popular with children across the States, and invoking strong nostalgia today. This popularity was reinforced with large amounts of merchandise and memorabilia.
- Look out for items that exemplify a character, or else show him prominently. Well-known catchphrases and colourful representations will add appeal. As most of the memorabilia was aimed at children and often played with heavily, items are usually worn or damaged. As such, a premium will be paid for items in truly mint condition, particularly if they are hard to find. Quality also varied greatly, and many mass-produced, poor quality items were made. Look for well-designed, licensed items, as these are likely to be popular. Many items can be found for under £25, meaning a collection can be built affordably.

A Hopalong Cassidy 'My Horse Topper' record and sleeve.

*10in (25.5cm) high*

**£10-15** **BH**

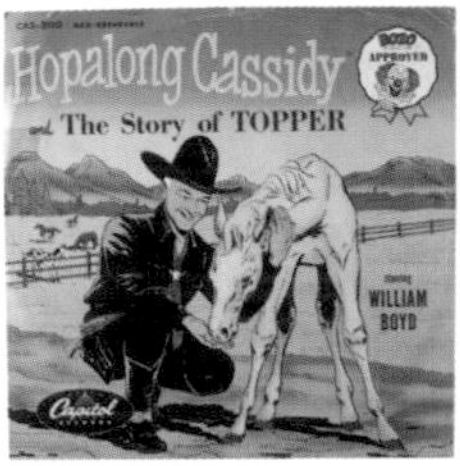


A Capitol Records 'Hopalong Cassidy and The Story of Topper' record, approved by Bozo The Clown.

*10in (25.5cm) high*

**£10-15** **BH**

A Popular Melodies Inc 'Take Me Back To Those Wide Open Spaces' sheet music.

*12in (30.5cm) high*

**£15-20** **BH**

An Australian Fawcett Publications 'Six-Gun Heroes' comic, No.2, with Hopalong Cassidy cover.

*1949* *12.25in (31cm)*

**£8-12** **BH**

An Australian Fawcett Publications 'Six-Gun Heroes' comic, No.3.

*Hopalong Cassidy appeared in 'Six-Gun Heroes' from 1950 and he appeared on the cover of the first three editions. By late 1953, Fawcett Publications had sold the title to Charlton.*

*1950* *12.25in (31cm) long*

**£10-15** **BH**

An original Hopalong Cassidy savings club postcard.

*In order to encourage children to save, Hoppy would visit banks around the US promoting his own bank account, which gave children a certificate and a Hoppy-shaped money box – plus the chance to meet Hoppy!*

*5.5in (14cm) wide*

**£3-5** **BH**

A Hopalong Cassidy 'Hoppy's Favorite Bond Bread' newspaper advertisement, from The Sunday Sun, Baltimore, on Sun Sept 30th 1951.

*14.75in (37.5cm) high*

**£8-12** **BH**

A Victory All Star half-gallon ice cream box, endorsed by Hopalong Cassidy, with 'Hoppy's Favorite' wording.

*7in (17.5cm) wide*

**£30-40** **BH**

## A CLOSER LOOK AT A HOPALONG CASSIDY MILK BOTTLE

*Large bottles such as this are rare.*

*William Boyd loved milk and was keen to promote it by visiting and endorsing dairies. Of course, it also helped to promote the show directly into homes.*

*The term 'Hoppy's Favorite' was frequently used to endorse milk and other products.*

*It retains its original cap, which is extremely hard to find as they were usually thrown away or damaged.*

A rare Country Club Dairy 'Cloverdale Milk' bottle, with transfer print of Hopalong Cassidy and original cap.

*This bottle is filled with polystyrene balls to show the printed design clearly.*

*8.75in (22cm) high*

**£40-60** **BH**

An Associated Brands Inc bottle of 'Hopalong Cassidy' hair trainer.

*5.25in (13.5cm) high*

**£10-15** **BH**

A transfer-printed 'Hopalong Cassidy' ceramic mug, the base moulded "Made in England".

*3.75in (9.5cm) high*

**£12-18** **BH**

A Hopalong Cassidy transfer-printed milk glass Lunch Milk Glass, with text reading 'Hoppy says "What Does Milk at Lunchtime do? Makes You Strong and healthy too!", moulded "Hoppy 11" on base.

*5in (12.5cm) high*

**£15-25** **BB**

A 1980s 'Topper' and 'Hopalong Cassidy' pocket knife.

*3.25in (8.5cm) long*

**£8-12** **BH**

## A CLOSER LOOK AT A HOPALONG CASSIDY HAT

*Bailey of Hollywood owned the rights to produce the official Hopalong Cassidy hat.*

*The retailer, Knox Hats of New York, is one the US' best known hat makers, with customers including F.D. Roosevelt, John D. Rockefeller and Enrico Caruso.*

*William Boyd himself wore Bailey's hats when playing Hoppy.*

*The quality is very fine and the condition of the hat and the box is excellent.*

A Bailey of Hollywood 'Genuine Hopalong Cassidy' hat, with silk lining and original Knox of New York card hat box.

*Hat 13.25in (33.5cm) wide*

**£80-120** **BH**

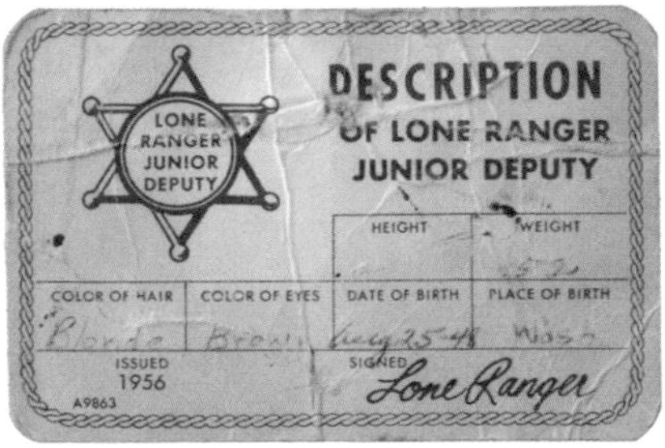


A Lone Ranger Junior Deputy card, issued in 1956.

*3.75in (9.5cm) long*

**£3-4** **BH**

A Princess Pat Hopalong Cassidy printed top, size 6.

*13in (33cm) high*

**£20-30** **BH**

"The Champ of Hollywood Hopalong Cassidy" shirt, size 10.

*20.75in (53cm) high*

**£30-40** **BH**

A 1950s vinyl Hopalong Cassidy school book bag, with wear.

*14.25in (36cm) wide*

**£40-60** **BH**

A 1980s Hopalong Cassidy printed yellow cotton handkerchief, marked "Copyright 1950 William Boyd".

*14.25in (36.5cm) wide*

**£3-5** **BH**

A Lone Ranger Bond Bread advertising ink blotter.

*8in (20cm) wide*

**£3-5** **BH**

A 1950s 'US Savings Bond Peace Patrol' Lone Ranger's members card.

*Launched from 1958-59, the 'Peace Patrol' aimed to make children put their allowances into special Hopalong Cassidy savings stamps, which could then be converted into US National savings bonds. The scheme featured as a storyline in TV's popular 'Lassie' series, aired on May 19th 1959, with Timmy aiming to win a certificate by signing up all his classmates to the Peace Patrol.*

*4in (10cm) long*

**£4-6** **BH**

A 1950s Lone Ranger postcard, with a printed message acknowledging a 1951 painting competition submission to the reverse.

*5.5in (14cm) long*

**£3-4** **BH**

A Dell 'Gene Autry and Champion' magazine, July-Aug 1956.

*1956* *10.25in (26cm) high*

**£5-8** **BH**

A Dell Comics 'Gene Autry Comics', March 1948.

*10.25in (26cm) high*

**£5-10** **BH**

A Columbia Records and Gene Autry 'Here Comes Santa Claus' record and sleeve.

*1950* *10in (25.5cm) high*

**£3-5** **BH**

A 1950s Gene Autry Sunbeam Bread advertising pin.

*1.25in (3cm) diam*

**£10-12** **BB**

A lobby card for Clint Eastwood in 'Coogan's Bluff'.

*1968* *14in (35.5cm) wide*

**£3-5** **BH**

A 'Bobby Benson' red opaque glass cereal bowl.

*Herbert C. Rice's 'H-Bar-O Rangers' show starring Bobby Benson was first aired on radio in 1932, in conjunction with H-O Oats cereal, and lasted until 1936. It was then revived in 1949 and over 350 episodes were aired until its demise in mid-1955. This bowl was probably a mail-in promotion.*

*6.5in (16.5cm) diam*

**£10-15** **BH**

A rare Wild Bill & Jingles transfer-printed plastic beaker.

*4.75in (12cm) high*

**£20-30** **BH**

A Cisco Kid and Sugardale Meats advertising red felt child's cowboy hat, the band printed "The Cisco Kid and Pancho Like Sugardale Meats" band.

*13.25in (33.5cm) long*

**£30-50** **BH**

A Tom Knapp cast bronze Butch Cassidy figurine, marked "CC 1981 TOM KNAPP".

*Painter and sculptor Tom Knapp lives in the Hondo Valley, New Mexico. He studied at the California College of Arts & Crafts, and was an artist with Walt Disney. He is listed in the 'Who's Who in American Art' and uses the lost wax technique to create Native Americans and related Westerner figures.*

*1981* *4.5in (11.5cm) high*

**£30-50** **BB**

A Voco Inc 'Polly Wolly Doodle' and 'Johnny Do Good' Wild West themed child's picture disc.

*1948* *7in (17.5cm) diam*

**£12-18** **BB**

A 1950s-60s Hero cast iron toy gun, with plastic handle insert.

*5.25in (13.5cm) long*

**£15-20** **BH**

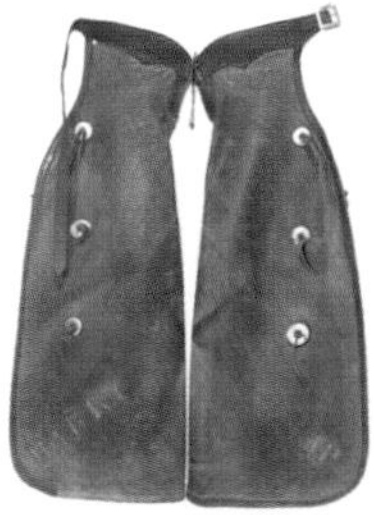

A pair of early 1900s Western leather chaps, with tooled latigo belt and trim and German silver conchos, marked "Harry" and "HP".

*39in (99cm) long*

**£75-100** **ALL**

## COLLECTORS' NOTES

- Corkscrews form the backbone of many wine and drinking collections. Of the two different groups, mechanical examples tend to be more valuable, with the 19th century being a hotbed of invention. Those employing ingenious methods, such as the Thomason type and the 'King's Rack' tend to be the most desirable. Simpler 'straight pull' examples are generally more affordable, with those made from precious metals, or early, rare patented examples worth higher sums.
- Other collectable items include wine labels, funnels and coaster and cocktail shakers. Well-made items produced from fine materials during the 18th, 19th and early 20th centuries tend to be more valuable. However, novelty pieces made during the 1920s, '30s, and '50s, can be desirable if they are amusing and fun. Most were bought to be used, and their value lies primarily in their novelty appeal.

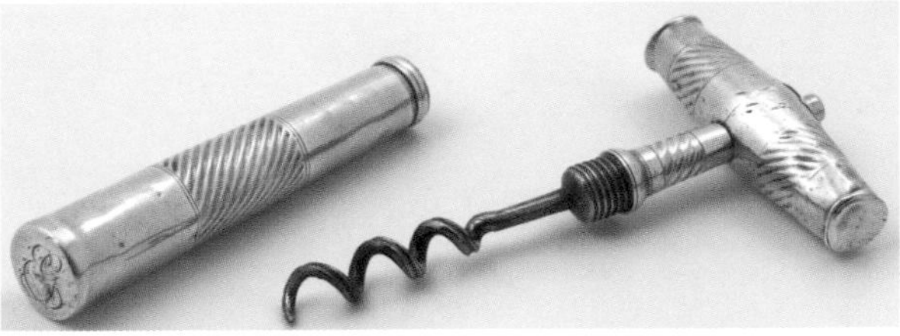

An English silver pocket corkscrew, by Samuel Pemberton, with screw-off sheath, stamped "SP".

*Pemberton is also known for making pencil holders and other small silver goods.*

*c1780* *3.5in (9cm) long*

**£220-280** **CSA**

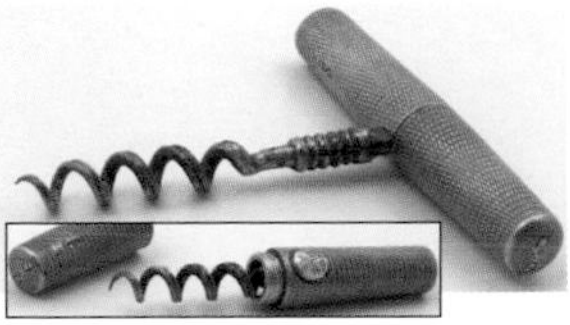

A rare English silver roundlet corkscrew, by Thomas Johnson, with baluster stem folding into case, fluted steel worm, stamped "TJ" and with Birmingham hallmarks.

*1862* *3in (8cm) long*

**£150-200** **CSA**

A French steel bladed straight-pull corkscrew, with rivetted cow horn handle and corkscrew helix.

*c1890* *3in (8cm) long*

**£12-18** **CSA**

An English six-tool steel folding bow, with horse hoof pick, button hook, corkscrew, screwdriver, gimlet and spike.

*The more accessories, the wider the piece and the higher the value.*

*c1850* *2.75in (7cm) long*

**£120-180** **CSA**

A 1920s cast brass straight pull novelty corkscrew, in the form of a kilted Scotsman holding a bottle of Scotch and leaning on a walking stick, with registration number.

*4.5in (11.5cm) long*

**£10-15** **CSA**

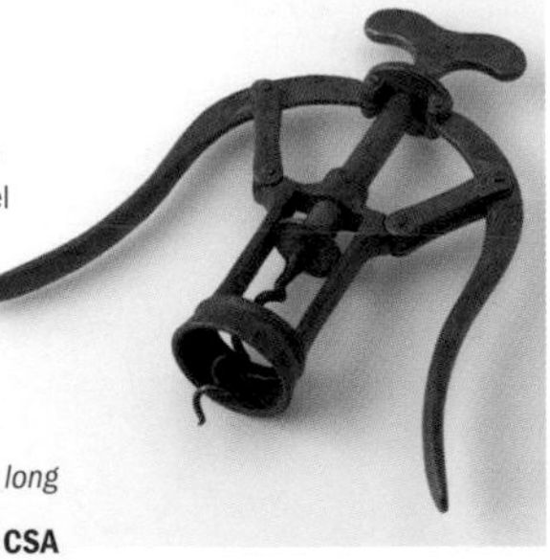

An A1 Heeley's Double Lever double-lever steel corkscrew, with copper finish, patented in 1880 and 1888.

*c1910* *7in (18cm) long*

**£60-80** **CSA**

An English 19thC narrow rack 'King's Screw' corkscrew, with brass barrel, wire helix, shaped bone handle complete with brush, hanging ring, and turned steel side handle

*c1830* *8in (20cm) long*

**£350-450** **DN**

## A CLOSER LOOK AT A DRINKING ACCESSORY

*This multifunction tool incorporates a spirit measure in the cup, a bottle opener in the sheath and a corkscrew inside.*

*Clever novelty combinations such as this were popular during the 1920s and '30s, and also the 1950s, but the chrome-plating and style of this example suggests the earlier period.*

*One side of the cup shows a miserable face representing the morning after and the other a happy face representing the night before.*

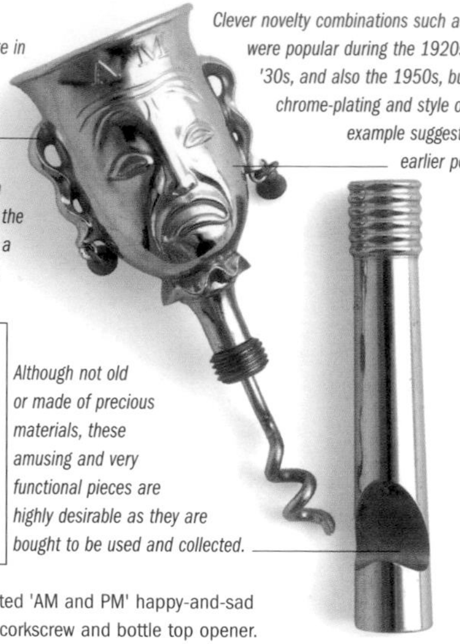

*Although not old or made of precious materials, these amusing and very functional pieces are highly desirable as they are bought to be used and collected.*

A 1920s-30s chrome-plated 'AM and PM' happy-and-sad combined shot measure, corkscrew and bottle top opener.

*5.5in (14cm) high*

**£40-50** **TM**

A chrome-plated bell cocktail shaker, engraved "Searoma" in Gothic script, with turned wooden handle, some scratches.

*10.75in (27.5cm) high*

**£30-40** **DWG**

A Victorian 'stamped out' Bacchanalian wine label, by C. Rawlings & W. Summers, London, with a shaped scroll border interspersed by grape bunches and surmounted by a mask pierced.

*c1860*

**£150-200** **WW**

A pair of British Airways 'Bourbon' and 'Rye' silver wine labels, commemorating the 10th Anniversary of British Airways Concorde, and given to passengers as flight souvenirs, with Birmingham hallmarks, in fitted box.

*1986*

**£300-400** **WW**

A British Airways 'Port' silver wine label, presented to passengers to commemorate their flight on Concorde by British Airways, with Birmingham hallmarks, boxed.

*1999*

**£30-40** **WW**

A Sherdley 'Cocktail Party' transfer-printed shot glass, designed by Alexander Hardie Williamson.

*Hardie Williamson was responsible for over 1,700 transfer-printed designs during the 1950s and '60s. Cocktails and drinking were popular motifs during this period.*

*3.25in (8.5cm) high*

**£7-8** **EWC**

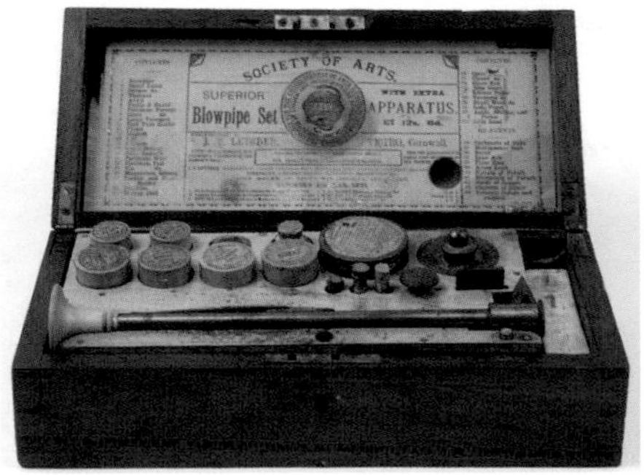


A J.T. Letcher of Truro, Cornwall 'Blowpipe Set', in a fitted wooden case, the lid with printed 'Society of Arts' label and list of contents.

*Blowpipe sets were used for analysing 'mineral substances'. Letcher, founded in 1878, made three types of which this is the middle in terms of complexity and cost, priced at one pound, six shillings and six pence in around 1900. The cheapest, simple box cost one guinea, while the top quality box cost double the cost of this example, and had a drawer full of crushed mineral samples for analysis.*

*c1900* *Case 10.75in (27.5cm) wide*

**£300-400** **BA**

A T. Eddington of Manchester cupping set, contained in a fitted, green velvet-lined mahogany box, with ivory maker's label, brass scarificator, two handblown glass cups, brass syringe and bottle.

*Cupping sets were used for the medical practice of 'bloodletting' in the early 19thC. Said to relieve 'vascular tension', cuts would be made in a vein with the scarificator, and a jar placed over the wound. The syringe would be mounted on top of the jar and extended to create a vacuum inside to help draw the blood out.*

*c1820* *9in (23cm) wide*

**£1,000-1,500** **BA**

A Coralee Smith hand-rolled and hand-painted ceramic 'Dester Landscape' sphere, signed "CS 03".

*2.75in (7cm) diam*

**£40-50** **BGL**

A Vienna cold-painted bronze 'The Cat Photographer' figure, with camera on tripod.

*Austrian cold-painted bronzes are finely modelled and painted, and hotly sought-after. They are frequently found in the form of animals taking unusual roles. This one would also appeal to collectors of photographica.*

*2.5in (6.5cm) high*

**£550-650** **ATK**

An 'Explosives A' metal sign, used on the sides of vehicles carrying hazardous materials.

**£15-20** **AGI**

An ornate colour printed and hand-coloured testimonial, awarded with a purse of money (not included) to William Broadbent by Thomas Power O'Connor, MP, father of the House of Commons, as a token of esteem for his services as King's Messenger over 46 years from 1874-1920, with views of Parliament, MP's names and floral border.

*1920* *41in (104cm) high*

**£220-280** **BLO**

A cast bronze porthole key, for use opening and sealing shut portholes on a ship.

*6.25in (16cm) high*

**£22-28** **COB**

# GLOSSARY

## A

**Acid etching** A technique using acid to decorate glass to produce a matt or frosted appearance.

**Albumen print** Photographic paper is treated with egg white (albumen) to enable it to hold more light-sensitive chemicals. After being exposed to a negative, the resulting image is richer with more tonal variation.

**Applied** Refers to a separate part that has been attached to an object, such as a handle.

## B

**Baluster** A curved form with a bulbous base and a slender neck.

**Base metal** A term describing common metals such as copper, tin and lead, or metal alloys, that were usually plated in gold or silver to imitate more expensive and luxurious metals. In the US, the term 'pot metal' is more commonly used.

**Bisque** A type of unglazed porcelain used for making dolls from c1860 to c1925.

**Boards** The hard covers of a book.

**Brassing** On plated items, where the plating has worn off to reveal the underlying base metal.

## C

**Cabochon** A large, protruding, polished, but not faceted, stone.

**Cameo** Hardstone, coral or shell that has been carved in relief to show a design in a contrasting colour.

**Cameo glass** Decorative glass made from two or more layers of differently coloured glass, which are then carved or etched to reveal the colour beneath.

**Cartouche** A framed panel, often in the shape of a shield or paper scroll, which can be inscribed.

**Cased** Where a piece of glass is covered with a further layer of glass, sometimes of a contrasting colour, or clear and colourless. In some cases the casing will be further worked with cutting or etching to reveal the layer beneath.

**Charger** A large plate or platter, often for display, but also for serving.

**Chromolithography** A later development of 'lithography', where a number of printing stones are used in succession, each with a different colour, to build up a multi-coloured image.

**Composition** A mixture including wood pulp, plaster and glue used as a cheap alternative to bisque in the production of dolls' heads and bodies.

**Compote** A dish, usually on a stem or foot, to hold fruit for the dessert course.

**Craze/Crazed/Crazing** A network of fine cracks in the glaze caused by uneven shrinking during firing. It also describes plastic that is slowly degrading and has the same surface patterning.

**Cuenca** A technique used for decorating tiles where moulded ridges separate the coloured glazes, like the 'cloisonne' enamelling technique.

**Cultured pearl** A pearl formed when an irritant is artificially introduced to the mollusc.

## D

**Damascened** Metal ornamented with inlaid gold or silver, often in wavy lines. Commonly found on weapons or armour.

**Dichroic** Glass treated with chemicals or metals that cause it to appear differently coloured depending on how it is viewed in the light.

**Diecast** Objects made by pouring molten metal into a closed metal die or mould.

**Ding** A very small dent in metal.

## E

**Earthenware** A type of porous pottery that requires a glaze to make it waterproof.

**Ebonized** Wood that has been blackened with dye to resemble ebony.

**E.P.N.S.** Found on metal objects and standing for 'electroplated nickel silver', meaning the object is made from nickel which is then electroplated with silver.

## F

**Faience** Earthenware that is treated with an impervious tin glaze. Popular in France from the 16th century and reaching its peak during the 18th century.

**Faceted** A form of decoration where a number of flat surfaces are cut into the surface of an object such as a gem or glass.

**Faux** A French word for 'false'. The intention is not to deceive fraudulently but to imitate a more costly material.

**Finial** A decorative knob at the end of a terminal, or on a lid.

**Foliate** Leaf and vine motifs.

## G

**Guilloché** An engraved pattern of interlaced lines or other decorative motifs, sometimes enamelled over with translucent enamels.

## H

**Hallmark** The series of small stamps found on gold or silver that can identify the maker, the standard of the metal and the city and year of manufacture. Hallmarks differ for each country and can consist only of a maker's or a city mark. All English silver made after 1544 was required to be fully marked.

# IJKL

**Incised** Applied to surface decoration or a maker's mark that has been scratched into the surface of an object with a sharp instrument.

**Inclusions** Used to describe all types of small particles of decorative materials embedded in glass.

**Iridescent** A lustrous finish that subtly changes colour depending on how light hits it. Often used to describe the finish on ceramics and glass.

**Lithography** A printing technique developed in 1798 and employing the use of a stone upon which a pattern or picture has been drawn with a grease crayon. The ink adheres to the grease and is transferred to the paper when pressed against it

# MNO

**Millefiori** An Italian term meaning 'thousand flowers' and used to describe cut, multi-coloured glass canes which are arranged and cased in clear glass. When arranged with the cut side facing the exterior, each circular disc (or short cane) resembles a small flower.

**Mint** A term used to describe an object in unused condition with no signs of wear and derived from coinage. Truly 'mint' objects will command a premium.

**Mount** A metal part applied to an object made of ceramic, glass or another material, with a decorative or functional use.

**Nappy** A shallow dish or bowl with a handle used for drinking.

**Opalescent** An opal-like, milky glass with subtle gradations of colour between thinner more translucent areas and thicker, more opaque areas.

# P

**Paisley** A stylized design based on pinecones and foliage, often with added intricate decoration. It originated in India and is most often found on fabrics, such as shawls.

**Paste (jewellery)** A hard, bright glass cut the same way as a diamond and made and set to resemble them.

**Patera** An oval or circular decorative motif often with a fluted or floral centre. The plural is 'paterae'.

**Piqué** A decorative technique where small strips or studs of gold are inlaid onto ivory or tortoiseshell on a pattern and secured in place by heating.

**Pontil** A metal rod to which a glass vessel is attached when it is being worked. When it is removed it leaves a raised disc-shaped 'pontil mark'.

**Pot metal** Please see 'Base metal'.

**Pounce pot** A small pot made of wood (treen), silver or ceramic. Found on inkwells or designed to stand alone, it held a gum dust that was sprinkled over parchment to prevent ink from spreading. Used until the late 18th century.

**Pressed (Press moulded)** Ceramics formed by pressing clay into a mould. Pressed glass is made by pouring molten glass into a mould and pressing it with a plunger.

# R

**Reeded** A type of decoration with thin raised, convex vertical lines. Derived from the decoration of classical columns.

**Relief** A form of moulded, pressed or carved decoration that protrudes above the surface of an object. Usually in the form of figures of foliate and foliage designs, it ranges in height from 'low' to 'high'.

**Repoussé** A French term for the raised, 'embossed' decoration on metals such as silver. The metal is forced into a form from one side causing it to bulge.

# S

**Sgraffito** An Italian word for 'little scratch' and used to describe a decorative technique where the outer surface of an object, usually in glazed or coloured ceramic, is scratched away in a pattern to reveal the contrasting coloured underlying surface.

**Sommerso** Technique developed in Murano in the 1930s. Translates as 'submerged' and involves casing one or more layers of transparent coloured glass within a layer of thick, clear, colourless glass.

**Stoneware** A type of ceramic similar to earthenware and made of high-fired clay mixed with stone, such as feldspar, which makes it non-porous.

# T

**Tazza** A shallow cup with a wide bowl, which is raised up on a single pedestal foot.

**Tooled** Collective description for a number of decorative techniques applied to a surface. Includes engraving, stamping, punching and incising.

# V

**Vermeil** Gold-plated silver.

**Vesta case** A small case or box, usually made from silver, for carrying matches.

# W

**White metal** Precious metal that is possibly silver, but not officially marked as such.

# Y

**Yellow metal** Precious metal that is possibly gold, but not officially marked as such.

# INDEX TO ADVERTISERS

| CLIENT | PAGE NO. | | |
|---|---|---|---|
| Dorling Kindersley | 95 | DMG Antiques & Collectables Fairs | 299 |
| KCS Ceramics | 125 | | |

# KEY TO ILLUSTRATIONS

Every collectable illustrated in the DK Collectables Price Guide 2008 by Judith Miller & Mark Hill has a letter code that identifies the dealer or auction house that sold it. The list below is a key to these codes. In the list, auction houses are shown by the letter A and dealers by the letter D. Some items may have come from a private collection, in which case the code in the list is accompanied by the letter P. Inclusion in this book in no way constitutes or implies a contract or a binding offer on the part of any of our contributors to supply or sell the goods illustrated, or similar items, at the prices stated.

**AAB (D)**
**Ashmore & Burgess**
Mob: 07702 355122
info@ashmoreandburgess.com
www.ashmoreandburgess.com

**AAC (A)**
**Alderfer Auction Company**
501 Fairground Road,
Hatfield, PA 19440 USA
Tel: 001 215 393 3000
info@alderferauction.com
www.alderferauction.com

**AB (A) (D)**
**Auction Blocks**
P.O. Box 241 Shelton
CT 06484, USA
blockschip@yahoo.com

**ABAA (D)**
Abacus Antiques
No longer trading

**ADE (D)**
**Art Deco Etc**
73 Upper Gloucester Road,
Brighton, Sussex BN1 3LQ
Tel: 01273 329 268
Mob: 07971 268 302
johnclark@artdecoetc.co.uk

**AG (D)**
**Antique Glass at Frank Dux Antiques**
33 Belvedere
Bath BA1 5HR
Tel: 01225 312 367
m.hopkins@antique-glass.co.uk
www.antique-glass.co.uk

**AGI (A)**
**Aurora Galleries International**
30 Hackamore Lane, Suite 2,
Bell Canyon, CA 91307, USA
Tel: 001 818 884 6468
vcampbell@auroraauctions.com
www.auroragalleriesonline.com

**AGR (D)**
**Adrian Grater**
25-26 Admiral Vernon Antiques Arcade
141-149 Portobello Road
London W11 2DY
Tel: 020 8579 0357
Mob: 07814 286 624
adriangrater@tiscali.co.uk

**ALL (A)**
**Allard Auctions**
P.O. Box 1030,
419 Flathead St., 4, St Ignatius
MT 59865 USA
Tel: 001 460 745 0500
info@allardauctions.com
www.allardauctions.com

**ANF (D)**
**Anfora Glass Factory**
Contact through:
Vetro & Arte Gallery
Calle del Cappeller 3212,
Dorsoduro, Venice 30123,
Italy
Tel: 0039 41 522 8525
www.venicewebgallery.com

**AOY (D)**
**All Our Yesterdays**
6 Park Road, Kelvinbridge,
Glasgow G4 9JG
Tel: 0141 334 7788

**ART (D)**
**Artius Glass**
Street, Somerset BA16 0AN
Tel: 01458 443694
Mob: 07860 822666
wheeler.ron@ic24.net
www.artiusglass.co.uk

**AS&S (A)**
**Andrew Smith & Son**
The Auction Rooms, Manor Farm, Itchen Stoke
Winchester, Hampshire
SO24 0QT
Tel: 01962 735 988
www.andrewsmithandson.com

**ATK (A)**
**Auction Team Köln**
Postfach 50 11 19, Bonner Str.
528-530, D-50971 Cologne,
Germany
Tel: 00 49 221 38 70 49
auction@breker.com
www.breker.com

**ATL (D)**
**Antique Textiles & Lighting**
34 Belvedere, Lansdowne Road,
Bath BA1 5HR
Tel: 01225 310 795
joannaproops@aol.com

**B (A)**
**Dreweatt Neate, Tunbridge Wells**
Auction Hall, The Pantiles,
Tunbridge Wells,
Kent TN2 5QL
Tel: 01892 544 500
tunbridgewells@dnfa.com
www.dnfa.com

**BA (D)**
**Branksome Antiques**
370 Poole Road, Branksome,
Poole, Dorset BH1 1AW
Tel: 01202 763 324/679 932

**BAD (D)**
**Beth Adams**
Unit G043/4, Alfies Antique Market, 13 Church Street,
Marylebone, London NW8 8DT
Mob: 07776 136 003
www.alfiesantiques.com

**BB (D)**
**Barbara Blau**
South Street Antiques Market
615 South 6th Street,
Philadelphia,
PA 19147-2128 USA
Tel: 001 215 592 0256
bbjools@msn.com

**BCAC (D)**
**Bucks County Antiques Center**
Route 202, Lahaska,
PA 18931 USA
Tel: 001 215 794 9180

**BEJ (D)**
**Bébés et Jouets**
c/o Lochend Post Office,
165 Restalrig Road,
Edinburgh EH7 6HW
Tel: 0131 332 5650
bebesjouets@tiscali.co.uk

**BEL (A)**
**Belhorn Auction Services**
PO Box 20211, Columbus,
OH 43220 USA
Tel: 001 614 921 9441
auctions@belhorn.com
www.belhorn.com

**BER (A)**
**Bertoia Auctions**
2141 De Marco Drive
Vineland, NJ 08360 USA
Tel: 001 856 692 1881
toys@bertoiaauctions.com
www.bertoiaauctions.com

**BGL (D)**
**Block Glass Ltd**
blockglss@aol.com
www.blockglass.com

**BIG (A)**
**Bigwood Auctioneers**
The Old School, Tiddington
Stratford-upon-Avon,
Warwickshire CV37 7AW
Tel: 01789 269 415
www.bigwoodauctioneers.co.uk

**BH (D)**
**Black Horse Antiques Showcase**
2180 North Reading Road
Denver, PA 17517, USA
Tel: 001 717 335 3300
info@antiques-showcase.com
www.antiques-showcase.com

**BLO (A)**
**Bloomsbury Auctions**
Bloomsbury House,
24 Maddox St, London W1S 1PP
Tel: 020 7495 9494
info@bloomsburyauctions.com
www.bloomsburyauctions.com

**BMN (A)**
**Auktionshaus Bergmann**
Mohrendorfer Str.4,
91056, Erlangen, Germany
Tel: 00 49 9131 45 06 66
www.auction-bergmann.de

**BONS/BONC/BONBAY (A)**
**Bonhams**
101 New Bond Street,
London W1S 1SR
Tel: 020 7629 6602
info@bonhams.com
www.bonhams.com

**BPAL (A) (D)**
**The Book Palace**
Jubilee House, Bedwardine Rd,
Crystal Palace
London SE19 3AP
Tel: 020 8768 0022
orders@bookpalace.com
www.bookpalace.com

**BR (D)**
**Beyond Retro**
110-112 Cheshire Street,
London E2 6EJ
Tel: 020 7613 3636
sales@beyondretro.com
www.beyondretro.com

**BRI (A)**
**Brightwells**
Easters Court, Leominster
Herefordshire, HR6 0DE
Tel: 01568 611 166
www.brightwells.com

**BY (D)**
**Bonny Yankauer**
Tel: 001 201 825 7697
bonnyy@aol.com

**C (A)**
**Cottees**
The Market, East Street,
Wareham, Dorset BH20 4NR
Tel: 01929 552 826
auctions@cottees.fsnet.co.uk
www.auctionsatcottees.co.uk

**CA (A)**
**Chiswick Auctions**
1 Colville Road,
London W3 8BL
Tel: 020 8992 4442
sales@chiswickauctions.co.uk
www.chiswickauctions.co.uk

**CB (D)**
**Colin Baddiel**
Stand B25,
Gray's Antiques Market,
South Molten Lane,
London W1Y 2LP
Tel: 020 7408 1239

**CAT (D)**
**CatalinRadio.com**
Tel: 001 419 824 2469
steve@catalinradio.com
www.catalinradio.com

**CB (P)**
**Christina Bertrand**
tineke@rcn.com

**CGPC (D)**
**Cheryl Grandfield Private Collection**

**CHA (D)**
**Charlotte Marler**
Booth 14, 1528 West 25th St
New York, NY 10010 USA
Tel: 001 212 367 8808
char_marler@hotmail.com

**CHEF (A)**
**Cheffins**
Clifton House, 1 & 2 Clifton
Road, Cambridge CB1 7EA
Tel: 01223 213 343
fine.art@cheffins.co.uk
www.cheffins.co.uk

**CHS (D)**
**China Search**
P.O. Box 1202, Kenilworth,
Warwickshire CV8 2WW
Tel: 01926 512 402
helen@chinasearch.co.uk
www.chinasearch.co.uk

**CL (D)**
**Chisholm Larsson**
45 8th Avenue, New York
NY 10011 USA
Tel: 001 212 741 1703
info@chisholm-poster.com
www.chisholm-poster.com

**CLV (A)**
**Clevedon Salerooms**
The Auction Centre,
Kenn Road, Kenn, Clevedon,
Bristol BS21 6TT
Tel: 01934 830 111
Fax: 01934 832 538
info@clevedonsalerooms.co.uk
www.clevedon-salerooms.com

**COB (D)**
**Cobwebs**
78 Old Northam Road,
Southampton SO14 0PB
Tel: 02380 227 458
www.cobwebs.uk.com

**COLC (D)**
**Collectors Cameras**
P.O. Box 16, Pinner,
Middlesex HA5 4HN
Tel: 020 8421 3537

**CRIS (D)**
**Cristobal**
26 Church Street,
London NW8 8EP
Tel: 020 7724 7230
steven@cristobal.co.uk
www.cristobal.co.uk

**CSA (D)**
**Christopher Sykes Antiques**
The Old Parsonage, Woburn,
Milton Keynes MK17 9QL
Tel: 01525 290 259
www.sykes-corkscrews.co.uk

**CVS (D)**
**Cad Van Swankster at The Girl Can't Help It**
Alfies Antiques Market,
Stand G100 & G90 & G80,
13-25 Church Street,
Marylebone, London NW8 8DT
Tel: 020 7724 8984
cad@sparklemoore.com

**D (A)**
**Dickens Auctioneers**
The Claydon Saleroom
Calvert Road, Middle Claydon
Buckingham, Bucks MK18 2EZ
Tel: 01296 714434
info@dickinsauctioneers.com
www.dickinsauctioneers.com

**DAW (A)**
**Dawson's**
Now trading as Dawson & Nye
www.dawsonandnye.com

**DCC (P)**
**Dee Carlton Collection**
qnoscots@aol.com

**DETC (D)**
**Deco Etc**
122 West 25th Street
New York, NY 10001 USA
Tel: 001 212 675 3326
deco_etc@msn.com
www.decoetc.net

**DF (D)**
**Dad's Follies**
moreinfo@dadsfollies.com
www.dadsfollies.com

**DG (D)**
**Donay Games**
Tel: 01444 416 412
www.donaygames.com

**DH (D)**
**Huxtins**
david@huxtins.com
www.huxtins.com

**DIM (D)**
**Dimech**
Stand F46-49
Alfies Antiques Market
13-25 Church Street,
London NW8 8DT
Mob: 07787 130 955

**DMI (P)**
**David Midgley**
dgmidgley@yahoo.co.uk

**DN (A)**
**Dreweatt Neate**
Donnington Priory Salerooms,
Donnington, Newbury,
Berkshire RG14 2JE
Tel: 01635 553 553
donnington@dnfa.com
www.dnfa.com/donnington

**DRA (A)**
**David Rago Auctions**
333 North Main Street,
Lambertville, NJ 08530 USA
Tel: 001 609 397 9374
info@ragoarts.com
www.ragoarts.com

**DSC (P)**
**British Doll Showcase**
squibbit@ukonline.co.uk
www.britishdollshowcase.co.uk

**DWG (D)**
South Street Antiques Market
615 South 6th Street,
Philadelphia,
PA 19147-2128 USA
Tel: 001 215 592 0256

**ECLEC (D)**
**Eclectica**
2 Charlton Place, Islington,
London N1
Tel: 020 7226 5625
liz@eclectica.biz
www.eclectica.biz

**EG (A)**
**Edison Gallery**
Tel: 001 617 359 4678
glastris@edisongallery.com
www.edisongallery.com

**ELI (D)**
**Eve Lickver**
P.O. Box 1778 San Marcos
CA 92079 USA
Tel: 001 760 761 0868

**EWC (P)**
**Emma Wilson Collection**
Tel: 07989 493 831

**F (A)**
**Fellows & Sons**
Augusta House, 19 Augusta
Street, Hockley,
Birmingham B18 6JA
Tel: 0121 212 2131
info@fellows.co.uk
www.fellows.co.uk

**FAN (D)**
**Fantiques**
Tel: 020 8840 4761
Mob: 07956 242450
paula.raven@ntlworld.com

**FD (D)**
**Fragile Design**
14-15 The Custard Factory,
Digbeth, Birmingham B9 4AA
Tel: 0121 224 7378
info@fragiledesign.com
www.fragiledesign.com

**FFM (D)**
**Festival For Midwinter**
No longer trading

**FIS (A)**
**Auktionshaus Dr Fischer**
Trappensee-Schlosschen
74074 Heilbronn, Germany
Tel: 00 49 7131 15 55 70
www.auctions-fischer.de

**FRE (A)**
**Freeman's**
1808 Chestnut Street,
Philadelphia, PA 19103 USA
Tel: 001 215 563 9275
info@freemansauction.com
www.freemansauction.com

**GA (D)**
**Gentry Antiques**
Rod & Lino Shop,
Little Green, Polperro,
Cornwall PL13 2RF
Tel: 07974 221 343
www.cornishwarecollector.co.uk

**GAZE (A)**
**Thos. Wm. Gaze & Son**
Diss Auction Rooms, Roydon Rd,
Diss, Norfolk IP22 4LN
Tel: 01379 650 306
sales@dissauctionrooms.co.uk
www.twgaze.com

**GBA (A)**
**Graham Budd Auctions**
P.O. Box 47519,
London N14 6XD
Tel: 020 8366 2525
gb@grahambuddauctions.co.uk
www.grahambuddauctions.co.uk

**GC (P)**
**Graham Cooley Collection**
Mob: 07968 722 269
graham.cooley@metalysis.com

**GCA (D)**
**Griffin Cooper Antiques**
South Street Antiques Market
615 South 6th Street,
Philadelphia,
PA 19147-2128 USA
Tel: 001 215 592 0256

**GGRT (D)**
**Gary Grant Choice Pieces**
18 Arlington Way,
London EC1R 1UY
Tel: 020 7713 1122
garyjamesgrant@btinternet.com

**GHOU (A)**
**Gardiner Houlgate**
Bath Auction Rooms,
9 Leafield Way, Corsham,
Nr Bath SN13 9SW
Tel: 01225 812 912
www.gardinerhoulgate.co.uk

**GL (D)**
**Gary Lickver**
P.O. Box 1778,
San Marcos, CA 92079, USA
Tel: 001 760 744 5686

**GM (D)**
**Galerie Maurer**
Kurfürstenstrasse 17
D-80799 Munich, Germany
Tel: 0049 89 271 13 45
info@galeriemaurer.de
www.galerie-objekte-maurer.de

**GORL (A)**
**Gorringes, Lewes**
15 North Street, Lewes, East
Sussex, BN7 2PD
Tel: 01273 472 503
clientservices@gorringes.co.uk
www.gorringes.co.uk

**GOR (A)**
**Gorringes, Worthing**
44-46 High Street, Worthing,
West Sussex BN11 1LL
Tel: 01903 238 999
clientservices@gorringes.co.uk
www.gorringes.co.uk

**GROB (D)**
**Geoffrey Robinson**
Stand GO77-78 & GO91-92,
Alfies Antiques Market,
13-25 Church Street,
London NW8 8DT
Tel: 020 7723 0449
www.alfiesantiques.com

**GWRA (A)**
**Gloucestershire Worcestershire Railway Auctions**
Tel: 01684 773 487 /
01386 760 109
www.gwra.co.uk

**H&G (D)**
**Hope and Glory**
131A Kensington Church St,
London W8 7LP
Tel: 020 7727 8424

**HA (A)**
**Hunt Auctions**
256 Welsh Pool Road,
Exton, PA 19341 USA
Tel: 001 610 524 0822
www.huntauctions.com

**HAMG (A)**
**Dreweatt Neate (Godalming)**
Baverstock House, 93 High St,
Godalming, Surrey GU7 1AL
Tel: 01483 423 567
godalming@dnfa.com
www.dnfa.com

**HD (D)**
**Halcyon Days**
14 Brook Street,
London W1S 1BD
Tel: 020 7629 8811
www.halcyondays.co.uk

**HERR (A)**
**Auktionshaus W.G. Herr**
Friesenwall 35
D-50672, Cologne, Germany
Tel: 0049 221 25 45 48
kunst@herr-auktionen.de
www.herr-auktionen.de

**HGS (D)**
**Harper General Store**
Tel: 001 717 964 3453
lauver5@comcast.com
www.harpergeneralstore.com

**HLM (D)**
**Hi & Lo Modern**
161 Montclair Avenue
Montclair NJ 07042 USA
sales@hiandlomodern.com
www.hiandlomodern.com

**JBC (P)**
**James Bridges Collection**
james@jdbridges.fsnet.co.uk

**JDJ (A)**
**James D Julia Inc**
P.O. Box 830, Fairfield,
Maine 04937 USA
Tel: 001 207 453 7125
jjulia@juliaauctions.com
www.juliaauctions.com

**JH (D)**
**Jeanette Hayhurst Fine Glass**
32A Kensington Church Street
London W8 4HA
Tel: 020 7938 1539

**JN (A)**
**John Nicholson Auctioneers**
The Auction Rooms, 'Longfield',
Midhurst Road, Fernhurst,
Haslemere, Surrey GU27 3HA
Tel: 01428 653727
sales@johnnicholsons.com
www.johnnicholsons.com

**JSC (P)**
**Jean Scott Collection**
www.stanhopes.info
jean@stanhopes.info

**KCS (D)**
**KCS Ceramics**
Tel: 020 8384 8981
karen@kcsceramics.co.uk
www.kcsceramics.co.uk

**KF (D)**
**Karl Flaherty Collectables**
Tel: 01476 445 627
kfckarl@aol.com

**KNK (D)**
**Kitsch-N-Kaboodle**
South Street Antiques Market,
615 South 6th Street,
Philadelphia,
PA 19147-2128 USA
Tel: 001 215 382 1354
kitschnkaboodle@yahoo.com

**L (D)**
**Luna**
139 Lower Parliament Street
Nottingham NG1 1EE
Tel: 0115 924 3267
info@luna-online.co.uk
www.luna-online.co.uk

**L&T (A)**
**Lyon and Turnbull Ltd.**
33 Broughton Place,
Edinburgh EH1 3RR
Tel: 0131 557 8844
info@lyonandturnbull.com
www.lyonandturnbull.com

**LAN (A)**
**Lankes**
Triftfeldstrasse 1, 95182,
Döhlau Germany
Tel: +49 (0)928 69 50 50
info@lankes-auktionen.de
www.lankes-auktionen.de

**LB (D)**
**Linda Bee**
Stand L18-21, Grays Antique
Market, 58 Davies Street,
London W1Y 2LP
Tel: 020 7629 5921
lindabee@grays.clara.net
www.graysantiques.com

**LC (A)**
**Lawrence's Fine Art Auctioneers**
The Old Linen Yard, South St,
Crewkerne, Somerset TA18 8AB
Tel:01460 73041
www.lawrences.co.uk

**LDE (D)**
**Larry & Diana Elman**
P.O. Box 415, Woodland Hills
California CA 91365 USA

**LFA (A)**
**Law Fine Art**
www.lawfineart.co.uk

**LG (D)**
**Legacy**
No longer trading

**LHT (D)**
**Leanda Harwood**
Tel: 01529 300 737
leanda.harwood@virgin.net
www.leandaharwood.co.uk

**LOZ (A)**
**Frederic Lozada Enterprises**
10, rue de Pomereu,
75116 Paris, France
Tel: 0033 1 53 70 23 70
www.fredericlozada.com

**MA (D)**
**Manic Attic**
Alfies Antiques Market, Stand
S48/49, 13 Church Street,
London NW8 8DT
Tel: 020 7723 6105
ianbroughton@hotmail.com

**MAC (D)**
**Mary Ann's Collectibles**
South Street Antiques Center
615 South 6th Street,
Philadelphia,
PA 19147-2128 USA
Tel: 001 215 592 0256
Tel: 001 215 923 3247

**MAX (A)**
**Maxwells Auctioneers**
133a Woodford Road
Woodford Cheshire SK7 1QD
Tel: 0161 439 5182
info@maxwells-auctioneers.co.uk
www.maxwells-auctioneers.co.uk

**MBO (D)**
**Mori Books**
Amherst Book Center
141 Route 101A, Amherst,
NH 03031 USA
Tel: 001 603 882 2665
moribook@bit-net.com
www.moribooks.com

**MEM (D)**
**Memory Lane**
45-40 Bell Blvd, Suite 109,
Bayside, NY 11361 USA
Tel: 001 718 428 8181
memlnny@aol.com
www.tias.com/stores/memlnny

**MC (D)**
**Metropolis Collectibles, Inc.**
873 Broadway, Suite 201, New
York, NY 10003, USA
Tel: 001 212 260 4147
orders@metropoliscomics.com
www.metropoliscomics.com

**MCOL (P)**
**Mick Collins Collection**
www.sylvacclub.com
admin@sylvacclub.com

**MG (D)**
**Mod Girl**
South Street Antiques Market
615 South 6th Street,
Philadelphia,
PA 19147-2128 USA
Tel: 001 215 592 0256
modgirljill@comcast.net

**MGL (D)**
**Mix Gallery**
17 South Main Street,
Lambertville NJ, USA
Tel: 001 609 773 0777
mixgallery1@aol.com
www.mixgallery.com

**MGT (D)**
**Mary & Geoff Turvil**
Vintage Compacts, Small
Antiques & Collectables
Tel: 01730 260 730
mary.turvil@virgin.net

**MH (D)**
**Mad Hatter Antiques**
No longer trading

**MHC (P)**
**Mark Hill Collection**
Mob: 07798 915 474
books@markhillpublishing.com
www.markhillpublishing.com

**MHT (D)**
**Mum Had That**
info@mumhadthat.com
www.mumhadthat.com

**MILLB (D)**
**Million Dollar Babies**
Tel: 001 518 885 7397

**ML (D)**
**Mark Laino**
Mark of Time
132 South 8th Street,
Philadelphia, PA 19107 USA
Tel: 001 215 922 1551
lecoultre@verizon.net

**MM (A)**
**Mullock Madeley**
The Old Shippon, Wall-under-
Heywood, Church Stretton,
Shropshire SY6 7DS
Tel: 0169 477 1771
info@mullockmadeley.co.uk
www.mullockmadeley.co.uk

**MP (P)**
**Marie Penman**
Private Collector

**MSA (D)**
**Manfred Schotten Antiques**
109 Burford High Street,
Burford, Oxfordshire OX18 4RH
Tel: 01993 822 302
enquiries@schotten.com
www.schotten.com

**MTS (D)**
**The Multicoloured Time Slip**
eBay Store: multicoloured
timeslip
eBay ID: dave65330
Mob: 07971 410 563
dave_a_cameron@hotmail.com

**MUR (A)**
**Tony Murland Auctions**
78 High Street, Needham
Market, Suffolk IP6 8AW
Tel: 01449 722 992
tony@antiquetools.co.uk
www.antiquetools.co.uk

**NA (A)**
**Northeast Auctions**
93 Pleasant Street
Portsmouth, NH 03801, USA
Tel: 001 603 433 8400
www.northeastauctions.com

**NAI (D)**
**Nick Ainge**
Tel: 01832 731 063
Mob: 07745 902 343
nick@ainge1930.fsnet.co.uk

**NB (A)**
**Noel Barrett Auctions Ltd**
P.O. Box 300, Carversville,
PA 18913 USA
Tel: 001 215 297 5109
www.noelbarrett.com

**NEA (A)**
**Neales of Nottingham**
192 Mansfield Road,
Nottingham NG1 3HU
Tel: 0115 962 4141
nottingham@dnfa.com
www.dnfa.com/nottingham

**NOR (D)**
**Neet-O-Rama**
14 Division Street, Somerville,
NJ 08876 USA
Tel: 001 908 722 4600
www.neetstuff.com

**NPC (D)**
**No Pink Carpet**
Tel: 01785 249 802
www.nopinkcarpet.com

**OACC (D)**
**Otford Antiques & Collectables Centre**
28 High Street, Otford,
Kent TN15 9DF
Tel: 01959 522 025
www.otfordantiques.co.uk

**ON (A)**
**Onslows**
The Coach House, Manor Road,
Stourpaine, Dorset DT11 8TQ
Tel: 01258 488 838
enquiries@onslows.co.uk
www.onslows.co.uk

**OUT (D)**
**Outernational**
info@outernational.info
www.outernational.info

**PB (D)**
**Petersham Books**
C/O Biblion
1-7 Davies Mews,
London W1K 5AB
Tel: 020 7629 1374
info@biblion.com
www.biblion.com

**PC (P)**
**Private Collection**

**PCC (P)**
**Peter Chapman Collection**
pgcbal1@supanet.com

**PCOM (D)**
**Phil's Comics**
P.O. Box 3433, Brighton
Sussex BN50 9JA
Tel: 01273 673 462
phil@phil-comics.com
www.phil-comics.com

**PL (D)**
**Peter Layton**
London Glassblowing
7 The Leather Market
Weston Street,
London SE1 3ER
Tel: 020 7403 2800
info@londonglassblowing.co.uk
www.londonglassblowing.com

**POOK (A)**
**Pook and Pook**
463 East Lancaster Avenue,
Downington, PA 19335, USA
Tel: 001 610 269 4040/0695
www.pookandpook.com

**PSA (A)**
**Potteries Specialist Auctions**
271 Waterloo Road, Cobridge,
Stoke-on-Trent ST6 3HR
Tel: 01782 286 622
enquiries@potteriesauctions.com
www.potteriesauctions.com

**PWE (A)**
**Philip Weiss Auction Galleries**
1 Neil Court, Oceanside,
NY 11572 USA
Tel: 001 516 594 073
info@philipweissauctions.com
ww.philipweissauctions.com

**QU (A)**
**Quittenbaum Kunstauktionen**
Hohenstaufenstrasse 1,
D-80801 Munich, Germany
Tel: 0049 89 33 00 756
info@quittenbaum.de
www.quittenbaum.de

**RAON (D)**
**R.A. O'Neill**
No longer trading

**RBC (D)**
**Reasons To Be Cheerful**
Mob: 07708 025 579

**RBRG (D)**
**RBR Group at Gray's**
158-168 Gray's Antiques
Market, 58 Davies St,
London W1Y 5LP
Tel: 020 7629 4769
www.graysantiques.com

**RCC (D)**
**Royal Commemorative China**
Paul Wynton & Joe Spiteri
Tel: 020 8863 0625
Mob: 07930 303 358
royalcommemoratives
@hotmail.com

**RDR (D)**
**Rogers de Rin**
76 Royal Hospital Road
Paradise Walk, Chelsea,
London SW3 4HN
Tel: 020 7352 9007
www.rogersderin.co.uk

**REN (D)**
**Rennies**
47 The Old High Street
Folkestone,
Kent CT20 1RN
Tel: 01303 242427
www.rennart.co.uk

**RG (D)**
**Richard Gibbon**
34-34a Islington Green
London N1 8DU
Tel: 020 7354 2852
neljeweluk@aol.com

**RH (D)**
**Rick Hubbard Art Deco**
Tel. 01794 513 133
www.rickhubbard-artdeco.co.uk

**RITZ (D)**
**Ritzy**
7 The Mall Antiques Arcade,
359 Upper Street,
London N1 0PD
Tel: 020 7704 0127

**ROS (A)**
**Rosebery's**
74-76 Knight's Hill, West
Norwood, London SE27 0JD
Tel: 020 8761 2522
auctions@roseberys.co.uk
www.roseberys.co.uk

**ROX (D)**
**Roxanne Stuart**
Tel: 001 888 750 8869
Tel: 001 215 750 8868
gemfairy@aol.com

**RSS (A)**
**Rossini SA**
7 Rue Drouot
75009 Paris, France
Tel: 00 33 1 53 34 55 00
www.rossini.fr

**RWA (D)**
**Richard Wallis Antiks**
Tel: 020 8529 1749
info@richardwallisantiks.co.uk
www.richardwallisantiks.com

**S&T (D)**
**Steinberg & Tolkien**
193 King's Road
London SW3 5ED
Tel: 020 7376 3660

**SAS (A)**
**Special Auction Services**
Kennetholme, Midgham,
Nr. Reading, Berkshire RG7 5UX
Tel: 0118 971 2949
mail@specialauctionservices.com
www.specialauctionservices.com

**SCG (D)**
**Gallery 1930 Susie Cooper**
18 Church Street, Marylebone,
London NW8 8EP
Tel: 020 7723 1555
gallery1930@aol.com
www.susiecooperceramics.com

**SDR (A)**
**Sollo:Rago Modern Auctions**
333 North Main Street,
Lambertville, NJ 08530 USA
Tel: 001 609 397 9374
info@ragoarts.com
www.ragoarts.com

**SH (D)**
**Sara Hughes Vintage Compacts, Antiques & Collectables**
Mob: 0775 9697 108
sara@sneak.freeserve.co.uk
http://mysite.wanadoo-members.co.uk/sara_compacts/

**SM (D)**
**Sparkle Moore at The Girl Can't Help It**
Alfies Antiques Market, Stand
G14-22, 13-25 Church Street,
Marylebone, London NW8 8DT
Tel: 020 7724 8984
sparkle@sparklemoore.com
www.sparklemoore.com

**SOTT (D)**
**Sign of the Tymes**
Mill Antiques Center,
12 Morris Farm Road,
Lafayette, NJ 07848 USA
Tel: 001 973 383 6028
jhap@nac.net
www.millantiques.com

**SS (D)**
**Spencer Swaffer Antiques**
30 High Street, Arundel
West Sussex BN18 9AB
Tel: 01903 882 132
spencerswaffer@btconnect.com
www.spencerswaffer.com

**STC (D)**
**Seaside Toy Center**
Joseph Soucy
179 Main St, Westerly
RO 02891 USA
Tel: 001 401 596 0962

**SWA (A)**
**Swann Galleries Image Library**
104 East 25th Street, New York,
NY 10010 USA
Tel: 001 212 254 4710
swann@swanngalleries.com
www.swanngalleries.com

**SWO (A)**
**Sworders**
14 Cambridge Road, Stansted
Mountfitchet, Essex CM24 8BZ
Tel: 01279 817 778
auctions@sworder.co.uk
www.sworder.co.uk

**TCA (A)**
**Transport Car Auctions**
14 The Green, Richmond,
Surrey TW9 1PX
Tel: 020 8940 2022
oliver@tc-auctions.com
www.tc-auctions.com

**TCF (D)**
**Cynthia Findlay**
Toronto Antiques on King
276 King Street West, Toronto,
Ontario M5V 1J2 Canada
Tel: 001 416 260 9057
www.torontoantiquesonking.com

**TCM (D)**
**Twentieth Century Marks**
Whitegates, Rectory Road,
Little Burstead, Nr Billericay,
Essex CM12 9TR
Tel: 01268 411 000
Mob: 07831 778 992 /
07788 455 006
info@20thcenturymarks.co.uk
www.20thcenturymarks.co.uk

**TCS (D)**
**The Country Seat**
Huntercombe Manor Barn,
Nr Henley on Thames,
Oxon RG9 5RY
Tel: 01491 641349
info@whitefriarsglass.com
www.whitefriarsglass.com

**TCT (D)**
**The Calico Teddy**
Tel: 001 410 433 9202
calicteddy@aol.com
www.calicoteddy.com

**TFR (D)**
**Floyd & Rita's Antiques & Collectibles**
Tel: 001 416 200 2761
antiques@floydrita.com
www.floydrita.com

**TGM (D)**
**The Glass Merchant**
Tel: 07775 683 961
Tel: 0208 668 2701
glassmerchant@yahoo.co.uk

**TH (D)**
**Toy Heroes**
42 Westway, Caterham-On-The-Hill, Surrey CR3 5TP
Tel: 01883 348 001
www.toyheroes.co.uk

**TM (D)**
**Tony Moran**
South Street Antiques Market,
615 South 6th Street,
Philadelphia,
PA 19147-2128 USA
Tel: 001 215 592 0256

**TOA (D)**
**The Occupied Attic**
Tel: 001 518 899 5030
occattic@aol.com
seguin12@aol.com

**TOJ (D)**
**These Old Jugs**
Susan L. Tillipman
Tel: 001 410 626 0770
susan@theseoldjugs.com
www.theseoldjugs.com

**TP (D)**
**Tenth Planet**
Unit 37a, Vicarage Field
Shopping Centre, Ripple Road,
Barking, Essex IG11 8DQ
Tel: 020 8591 5357
sales@tenthplanet.co.uk
www.tenthplanet.co.uk

**TR (D)**
**Terry Rodgers & Melody**
1050 2nd Avenue,
New York, NY 10022 USA
Tel: 001 212 758 3164
melodyjewelnyc@aol.com

**TSIS (D)**
**Three Sisters**
South Street Antiques Market,
615 South 6th Street,
Philadelphia,
PA 19147-2128 USA
Tel: 001 215 592 0256

**VET (D)**
**Vetro & Arte Gallery**
Calle del Cappeller 3212,
Dorsoduro, Venice 30123,
Italy
Tel: 0039 41 522 8525
www.venicewebgallery.com

**VV (D)**
**Vintage To Vogue**
28 Milsom Street
Bath BA1 1DG
Tel: 01225 337 323
www.vintagetovoguebath.com

**VEC (A)**
**Vectis Auctions Ltd**
Fleck Way, Thornaby,
Stockton on Tees TS17 9JZ
Tel: 01642 750 616
admin@vectis.co.uk
www.vectis.co.uk

**VM (D)**
**VinMag Co.**
39-43 Brewer Street,
London W1R 9UD
Tel: 020 7439 9525
sales@vinmag.com
www.vinmag.com

**VZ (A)**
**Von Zezschwitz**
Friedrichstrasse 1a,
80801 Munich, Germany
Tel: 00 49 89 38 98 930
www.von-zezschwitz.de

**WAD (A)**
**Waddington's Auctioneers**
111 Bathurst Street, Toronto,
Ontario, Canada M5V 2R1
Tel: 001 416 504 9100
www.waddingtons.ca

**W&W (A)**
**Wallis & Wallis**
West Steet Auction Galleries,
Lewes, East Sussex BN7 2NJ
Tel: 01273 480 208
auctions@wallisandwallis.co.uk
www.wallisandwallis.co.uk

**WDL (A)**
**Kunst-Auktionshaus Martin Wendl**
August-Bebel-Straße 4, 07407
Rudolstadt, Germany
Tel: 0049 3672 424 350
www.auktionshaus-wendl.de

**WHP (A)**
**W. H. Peacock**
26 Newnham Street,
Bedford MK40 3JR
Tel: 01234 266 366
www.peacockauction.co.uk

**WW (A)**
**Woolley & Wallis**
51-61 Castle Street, Salisbury,
Wiltshire SP1 3SU
Tel: 01722 424 500
www.woolleyandwallis.co.uk

**ZDB (D)**
**Zardoz Books**
20 Whitecroft, Dilton Marsh,
Westbury, Somerset BA13 4DJ
Tel: 01373 865 371
www.zardozbooks.co.uk

# DIRECTORY OF SPECIALISTS

If you wish to have any item valued, it is advisable to contact the dealer or specialist in advance to check that they will carry out this service and whether there is a charge. While most dealers will be happy to help you with an enquiry, do remember that they are busy people. Telephone valuations are not possible. Please mention the DK Collectables Price Guide 2008 by Judith Miller & Mark Hill when making an enquiry.

## ADVERTISING

**Huxtins**
david@huxtins.com
www.huxtins.com

## ANIMATION ART

**Animation Art Gallery**
13-14 Great Castle St, London W1W 8LS
Tel: 020 7255 1456
Fax: 0207 436 1256
gallery@animaart.com
www.animaart.com

## ART DECO

**Art Deco Etc**
73 Gloucester Road, Brighton, Sussex, BN1 3LQ
Tel: 01273 329 268
johnclark@artdecoetc.co.uk

## AUTOGRAPHS

**Lights, Camera Action**
6 Western Gardens, Western Boulevard, Aspley, Nottingham, HG8 5GP
Tel: 0115 913 1116
Mob: 07970 342 363
nick.straw@lca-autographs.co.uk
www.lca-autographs.co.uk

## AUTOMOBILIA

**C.A.R.S. of Brighton**
The White Lion Garage
Clarendon Place,
Kemp Town, Brighton Sussex
Tel: 01273 622 722
Fax: 01273 622 722
whiteliongarage@fsmail.net
www.carsofbrighton.co.uk

## BOOKS

**Biblion**
1-7 Davies Mews, London W1K 5AB
Tel: 020 7629 1374
info@biblion.com
www.biblion.com

**Zardoz Books**
20 Whitecroft, Dilton Marsh, Westbury, Somerset BA13 4DJ
Tel: 01373 865 371
www.zardozbooks.co.uk

## BONDS & SHARES

**Intercol**
43 Templar's Crescent, Finchley, London N3 3QR
Tel: 020 8349 2207
sales@intercol.co.uk
www.intercol.co.uk

## CERAMICS

**Beth Adams**
Unit GO43/4, Alfies Antique Market, 13 Church Street, Marylebone, London NW8 8DT
Mob: 07776 136 003
www.alfiesantiques.com

**Nick Ainge**
Tel: 01832 731 063
Mob: 07745 902 343
nick@ainge1930.fastnet.co.uk
decoseek.decoware.co.uk

**Beverley**
30 Church Street, London NW8 8EP, UK
Tel: 020 7262 1576
www.alfiesantiques.com

**China Search**
P.O. Box 1202, Kenilworth, Warwickshire CV8 2WW
Tel: 01926 512 402
Fax. 01926 859 311
helen@chinasearch.uk.com
www.chinasearch.uk.com

**Eastgate Antiques**
S007/009, Alfies Antique Market, 13 Church St, Marylebone, London NW8 8DT
Tel: 0207 258 0312
info@alfiesantiques.com
www.alfiesantiques.com

**Feljoy Antiques**
Shop 3, Angel Arcade, Camden Passage, London N1 8EA
Tel: 020 7354 5336
Fax: 020 7831 3485
joy@feljoy-antiques.demon.co.uk
www.chintznet.com/feljoy

**Adrian Grater**
Georgian Village, Camden Passage,London N1
Tel: 020 8579 0357
adriangrater@tiscali.co.uk

**Susie Cooper at Gallery 1930**
18 Church St, London NW88EP
Tel: 020 7723 1555
Fax: 020 7735 8309
gallery1930@aol.com
www.susiecooperceramics.com

**Gary Grant Choice Pieces**
18 Arlington Way, London EC1R1UY
Tel: 020 7713 1122

**Gillian Neale Antiques**
P.O. Box 247, Aylesbury HP201JZ
Tel: 01296 423754
Fax: 01296-334601
gillianneale@aol.com
www.gillianneale antiques.co.uk

**Louis O'Brien**
Tel: 01276 32907

**Rick Hubbard Art Deco**
Tel: 01794 513133
www.rickhubbard-artdeco.co.uk

**Geoffrey Robinson**
Stand GO77-78 & GO91-92, Alfies Antiques Market, 13-25 Church Street, London, NW8 8DT
Tel: 020 7723 0449
unknown@unknown.com
www.alfiesantiques.com

**Rogers de Rin**
76 Royal Hospital Rd, Paradise Walk, London SW34HN
Tel: 020 7352 9007
Fax: 020 7351 9407
rogersderin@rogersderin.co.uk
www.rogersderin.co.uk

**Sue Norman**
Antiquarius, Stand L4, 135 King's Rd, London SW34PW
Tel: 020 7352 7217
sue@sue-norman.demon.co.uk
www.sue-norman.demon.co.uk

## CIGARETTE CARDS

**Carlton Antiques**
43 Worcester Road, Malvern, Worcestershire WR14 4RB
Tel: 01684 573 092
dave@carlton-antiques.com
www.carlton-antiques.com

## COINS

**Intercol**
43 Templar's Crescent, Finchley, London N3 3QR
Tel: 020 8349 2207
sales@intercol.co.uk
www.intercol.co.uk

## COMICS

**Phil's Comics**
P.O. Box 3433, Brighton Sussex BN50 9JA
Tel: 01273 673 462
phil@phil-comics.com
www.phil-comics.com

**The Book Palace**
Bedwardine Road, Crystal Palace, London SE19 3AP
Tel: 020 8768 0022
Fax: 020 8768 0563
www.bookpalace.com

## COMMEMORATIVE WARE

**Hope & Glory**
131a Kensington Church St, London W87LP
Tel: 020 7727 8424

**Recollections**
5 Royal Arcade, Boscombe, Bournemouth, Dorset BH14BT
Tel: 01202 304 441

**Royal Commemorative China**
Paul Wynton & Joe Spiteri
Tel: 020 8863 0625
Mob: 07930 303 358
royalcommemoratives@hotmail.com

## COSTUME & ACCESSORIES

**Beyond Retro**
110-112 Cheshire St, London E2 0EJ
Tel: 020 7613 3636
sales@beyondretro.com
www.beyondretro.com

**Cad van Swankster at The Girl Can't Help It**
Alfies Antiques Market, Stand G100 & G90 & G80, 13-25 Church St, London NW88DT
Tel: 020 7724 8984
cad@sparklemoore.com

**Cloud Cuckoo Land**
6 Charlton Place, London, N1
Tel: 020 7354 3141

**Decades**
20 Lord St West, Blackburn BB2 1JX
Tel: 01254 693320

**Fantiques**
Tel: 020 8840 4761
paula.raven@ntlworld.com

**Linda Bee**
Grays Antiques Market, 1-7 Davies Street, London, W1Y 2LP
Tel/Fax: 020 7629 5921
www.graysantiques.com

**Old Hat**
66 Fulham High St, London SW63LQ
Tel: 020 7610 6558

**Sparkle Moore at The Girl Can't Help It**
Alfie's Antiques Market, Shop G100 & G90 & G80, 13-25 Church St, London NW8 8DT
Tel: 020 7724 8984
sparkle.moore@virgin.net
www.sparklemoore.com

**Vintage Modes**
Grays Antiques Market, 1-7 Davies Mews, London W1Y 5AB
Tel: 020 7409 0400
info@vintagemodes.co.uk
www.vintagemodes.co.uk

**Vintage to Vogue**
28 Milsom Street, Bath, Avon BA1 1DG
Tel: 01225 337 323

## COSTUME JEWELLERY

**Cristobal**
26 Church St, London NW8 8EP
Tel: 020 7724 7230
steven@cristobal.co.uk
www.cristobal.co.uk

**Eclectica**
2 Charlton Place, Islington, London N1
Tel/Fax: 020 7226 5625
liz@eclectica.biz
www.eclectica.biz

**Richard Gibbon**
34/34a Islington Green, London N1 8DU
Tel: 020 7354 2852
neljeweluk@aol.com

**Ritzy**
7 The Mall Antiques Arcade, 359 Upper Street, London N1 0PD
Tel: 020 7704 0127

**William Wain at Antiquarius**
Stand J6, Antiquarius, 135 King's Road, London SW3 4PW
Tel: 020 7351 4905
w.wain@btopenworld.com

## DOLLS

**Bébés & Jouets**
c/o Lochend Post Office, 165 Restalrig Road, Edinburgh EH7 6HW, UK
Tel: 0131 332 5650
bebesjouets@tiscali.co.uk

**British Doll Showcase**
squibbit@ukonline.co.uk
www.britishdollshowcase.co.uk

**Sandra Fellner**
A18-A19 and MB026, Grays Antique Market
Tel: 020 8946 5613
sandrafellner@blueyonder.co.uk
www.graysantiques.com

**Victoriana Dolls**
101 Portobello Rd, London W112BQ
Tel: 01737 249 525
Fax: 01737 226 254
heather.bond@totalserve.co.uk

## FIFTIES, SIXTIES & SEVENTIES

**Twentieth Century Marks**
Whitegates, Rectory Road, Little Burstead, Nr Billericay, Essex CM12 9TR
Tel: 01268 411 000
info@20thcenturymarks.co.uk
www.20thcenturymarks.co.uk

**Design20c**
Tel: 01276 512329 / 0794 609 2138
sales@design20c.co.uk
www.design20c.co.uk

**Fragile Design**
14-15 The Custard Factory, Digbeth, Birmingham B9 4AA
Tel: 0121 224 7378
info@fragiledesign.com
www.fragiledesign.com

**Luna**
139 Lower Parliament Street Nottingham NG1 1EE
Tel: 0115 924 3267
info@luna-online.co.uk
www.luna-online.co.uk

**Manic Attic**
Alfie's Antiques Market, Stand S48/49, 13-25 Church St, London NW8 8DT
Tel: 020 7723 6105
ianbroughton@hotmail.com

**The Multicoloured Timeslip**
eBay Store: multicoloured timeslip
eBay ID: dave65330
Mob: 07971 410 563
dave_a_cameron@hotmail.com

**Retro Etc**
13-14 Market Walk, Market Square, Old Amersham, Bucks HP7 ODF
Tel: 07810 482900
info@retroetc.com
www.retroetc.com

## FILM & TV

**The Prop Store of London**
Great House Farm, Chenies, Rickmansworth, Herts WD3 6EP
Tel: 01494 766 485
steve.lane@propstore.co.uk
www.propstore.co.uk

## GENERAL

**Alfie's Antiques Market**
13-25 Church St, London NW88DT
Tel: 020 7723 6066
info@alfiesantiques.com
www.alfiesantiques.com

**Bartlett St Antiques Centre**
5-10 Bartlett St, Bath BA12QZ
Tel: 01225 466689
Monday to Saturday (excluding Wednesday)

**Bermondsey Market**
Crossing of Long Lane & Bermondsey St, London SE1
Tel: 020 7351 5353
Every Friday morning from 5am

**Brackley Antique Cellar**
Drayman's Walk, Brackley, Northamptonshire NN13 6BE
Tel: 01280 841 841

**The Ginnel Antiques Centre**
Off Parliment St, Harrogate, North Yorkshire HG1 2RB
Tel: 01423 508 857
info@theginnel.com
www.redhouseyork.co.uk

**Great Grooms at Hungerford**
Riverside House, Charnham St, Hungerford, Berkshire RG17 0EP
Tel: 01488 682 314
Fax: 01488 686677
antiques@great-grooms.co.uk
www.great-grooms.co.uk

**Heanor Antiques Centre**
11-3 Ilkeston Rd, Heanor, Derbyshire
Tel: 01773 531 181
sales@heanorantiquescentre.co.uk
www.heanorantiquescentre.co.uk

**Heskin Hall Antiques**
Heskin Hall, Wood Lane, Heskin, Chorley, Lancashire PR7 5PA
Tel: 01257 452 044

**Otford Antiques and Collectors Centre**
26-28 High St, Otford, Kent TN15 9DF
Tel: 01959 522 025
Fax: 01959 525858
info@otfordantiques.co.uk
www.otfordantiques.co.uk

**Past Caring**
76 Essex Road London N1 8LT

**Portobello Rd Market**
Portobello Rd, London W11
Every Saturday from 6am

**Potteries Antique Centre**
271 Waterloo Rd, Cobridge, Stoke-on-Trent ST6 3HR
Tel: 01782 201 455
Fax: 01782 201518
www.potteriesantiquecentre.com

**The Swan Antiques Centre**
High Street Tetsworth, nr Thame, Oxfordshire OX9 7AB
Tel: 01844 281777
Fax: 01844 281770
antiques@theswan.co.uk
www.theswan.co.uk

**Woburn Abbey Antiques Centre**
Woburn Abbey, Woburn, Bedfordshire MK179WA
Tel: 01525 290 333
www.woburnantiques.co.uk

## GLASS

**Andrew Lineham Fine Glass**
Tel/Fax: 01243 576 241
Mob: 07767 702 722
andrew@antiquecolouredglass.com
www.antiquecolouredglass.com

**Antique Glass at Frank Dux Antiques**
33 Belvedere, Lansdown Road, Bath, Avon BA1 5HR
Tel/Fax: 01225 312 367
www.antique-glass.co.uk

**Francesca Martire**
Stand F131-137, First Floor, 13-25 Alfies Antiques Market, 13 Church St, London NW8ORH
Tel: 020 7724 4802
www.francescamartire.com

**Jeanette Hayhurst Fine Glass**
32A Kensington Church St., London W8 4HA
Tel: 020 7938 1539

**Mum Had That**
info@mumhadthat.com
www.mumhadthat.com

**Nigel Benson 20th Century Glass**
Mob: 07971 859 848
nigel@20thcentury-glass.com
www.20thcentury-glass.com

**No Pink Carpet**
Tel: 01785 249 802
www.nopinkcarpet.com

**Cloud Glass**
info@cloudglass.com
www.cloudglass.com

## KITCHENALIA

**Appleby Antiques**
Geoffrey Vans' Arcade, Stand 18, 105-107 Portobello Rd, London W11
Tel/Fax: 01453 753 126
mike@applebyantiques.net
www.applebyantiques.net

**Below Stairs of Hungerford**
103 High Street, Hungerford, Berkshire,RG17 0NB
Tel: 01488 682 317
Fax: 01488 684294
hofgartner@belowstairs.co.uk
www.belowstairs.co.uk

**Ken Grant**
F109-111 Alfies Antiques Market, 13-25 Church Street, Marylebone, London NW8 8DT
Tel: 020 7723 1370
k-grant@alfies.clara.net

**Ann Lingard**
18-22 Rope Walk, Rye, Sussex TN31 7NA
Tel: 01797 233 486

## MECHANICAL MUSIC

**Terry & Daphne France**
Tel: 01243 265 946
Fax: 01243 779 582

**The Talking Machine**
30 Watford Way, London NW4 3AL
Tel: 020 8202 3473
Mob: 07774 103 139
talkingmachine@gramophones.ndirect.co.uk
www.gramophones.ndirect.co.uk

## PAPERWEIGHTS

**Sweetbriar Gallery Ltd**
**56 Watergate Street**
Chester, Cheshire, CH1 2LA
Tel: 01244 329249
sales@sweetbriar.co.uk
www.sweetbriar.co.uk

## PENS & WRITING

**Battersea Pen Home**
PO Box 6128,
Epping CM16 4CG
Tel: 01992 578 885
Fax: 01992 578 485
orders@penhome.com
www.penhome.com

**Henry The Pen Man**
Admiral Vernon Antiques
Market, 141-149 Portobello Rd,
London W11
Tel: 020 8530 3277
Saturdays only

## PLASTICS

**Paola & Iaia**
Unit S057-58, Alfies Antiques
Market, 13-25 Church Street,
London NW8 8DT, UK
Tel: 07751 084 135
paolaelaialondon@hotmail.com

## POSTERS

**At The Movies**
info@atthemovies.co.uk
www.atthemovies.co.uk

**Barclay Samson**
By appointment only
Tel: 020 7731 8012
richard@barclaysamson.com
www.barclaysamson.com

**DODO**
Stand F073/83/84,13-25
Church Street, Marylebone,
London NW8 8DT
Tel: 020 7706 1545
www.dodoposters.com

**The Reelposter Gallery**
72 Westbourne Grove,
London W2 5SH
Tel: 020 7727 4488
Fax: 020 7727 4499
info@reelposter.com
www.reelposter.com

**Rennies**
47 The Old High Street,
Folkestone, Kent CT20 2RN
Tel: 01303 242427
info@rennart.co.uk
www.rennart.co.uk

## POWDER COMPACTS

**Sara Hughes Vintage Compacts, Antiques & Collectables**
Mob: 0775 9697 108
sara@sneak.freeserve.co.uk
http://mysite.wanadoo-members.co.uk/sara_compacts/

**Mary & Geoff Turvil**
Vintage Compacts, Small
Antiques & Collectables
Tel: 01730 260 730
mary.turvil@virgin.net

## RADIOS

**On the Air Ltd**
The Vintage Technology Centre,
Hawarden, Deeside CH5 3DN
Tel/Fax: 01244 530 300
info@vintageradio.co.uk
www.vintageradio.co.uk

## ROCK & POP

**Beatcity**
PO Box 229, Chatham,
Kent ME5 8WA
Tel/Fax: 01634 200 444
www.beatcity.co.uk

**More Than Music**
PO Box 2809,
Eastbourne,
East Sussex BN21 2EA
Tel: 01323 649 778
morethnmus@aol.com
www.mtmglobal.com

**Tracks**
PO Box 117, Chorley,
Lancashire PR6 0UU
Tel: 01257 269 726
Fax: 01257 231340
sales@tracks.co.uk
www.tracks.co.uk

## SCIENTIFIC & TECHNICAL, INCLUDING OFFICE, OPTICAL

**Arthur Middleton Antiques**
Tel: 020 7281 8445
Mob: 07887 481 102
www.antique-globes.com

**Branksome Antiques**
370 Poole Rd, Branksome,
Dorset BH12 1AW
Tel: 01202 763 324

**Cobwebs**
78 Old Northam Rd,
Southampton SO14 0PB
Tel/Fax: 02380 227 458
www.cobwebs.uk.com

**Early Technology**
Monkton House, Old
Craighall,Musselburgh,
Midlothian EH21 8SF
Tel: 0131 665 5753
michael.bennett-levy@virgin.net
www.earlytech.com

**Stuart Talbot**
PO Box 31525,
London W11 2XY
Tel: 020 8969 7011
talbot.stuart@talk21.com

## SMOKING

**Richard Ball**
richard@lighter.co.uk

**Tagore Ltd**
c/o The Silver Fund, 1 Duke of
York Street, London SW1Y 6JP
Tel: 07989 953 452
tagore@grays.clara.net

**Tom Clarke**
Admiral Vernon Antiques
Centre, Unit 36,
Portobello Rd, London W11
Tel: 020 8802 8936

## SPORTING MEMORABILIA

**Manfred Schotten**
109 High Street,
Burford,
Oxfordshire OX18 4RH
Tel: 01993 822 302
Fax: 0 1993 822055
enquiries@schotten.com
www.schotten.com

**Old Troon Sporting Antiques**
49 Ayr St,
Troon KA10 6EB
Tel: 01292 311 822

**Simon Brett**
Creswyke House,
Moreton-in-Marsh GL56 0LH
Tel: 01608 650 751

**Warboys Antiques**
St. Ives, Cambridgeshire
Tel: 01480 463891
Mob: 07831 274774
johnlambden@sportingantiques
co.uk
www.sportingantiques.co.uk

## TOYS & GAMES

**Automatomania**
Logie Steading, Forres, Moray
IV36 2QN, Scotland
Tel: 01309 694 828
Mob: 07790 71 90 97
www.automatomania.com

**Collectors Old Toy Shop & Antiques**
89 Northgate, Halifax, West
Yorkshire HX1 1XF
Tel: 01422 360 434
collectorsoldtoy@aol.com

**Colin Baddiel**
B24-B25, Grays Antique
Market, 1-7 Davies Mews,
London W1K 5AB
Tel: 020 7408 1239
Fax: 020 7493 9344
toychemcol@hotmail.com
www.colinsantiquetoys.com

**Donay Games**
Tel: 01444 416 412
info@donaygames.co.uk
www.donaygames.com

**Garrick Coleman**
75 Portobello Rd,
London W11
Tel: 020 7937 5524
Fax: 0207 937 5530
www.antiquechess.co.uk

**Hugo Lee-Jones**
Tel: 01227 375 375
Mob: 07941 187 2027
electroniccollectables@hotmail.com

**Intercol**
43 Templars Crescent, Finchley,
London N3 3QR
Tel: 020 8349 2207
Mob: 077 68 292 066
sales@intercol.co.uk
www.intercol.co.uk

**Karl Flaherty Collectables**
Tel: 02476 445 627
kfcollectables@aol.com
www.kfcollectables.com

**Sue Pearson Dolls & Teddy Bear**
18 Brighton Square, 'The
Lanes', Brighton, East Sussex
BN1 1HD
Tel: 01273 774851
info@suepearson.co.uk
www.suepearson.co.uk

**The Vintage Toy & Train Shop**
Sidmouth Antiques &
Collectors' Centre,
All Saints' Rd,
Sidmouth EX10 8ES
Tel: 01395 512 588

**Wheels of Steel (Trains)**
Gray's Mews Antiques Market,
B10-B11, 58 Davies St,
London W1K 5LP
Tel: 020 7629 2813
wheelsofsteel@grays.clara.net
www.graysantiques.com

**Pauline Parkes**
Windsor House
Tel: 01608 650 993

**Polly de Courcy-Ireland**
PO Box 29,
Alresford,
Hampshire SO249WP
Tel: 01962 733 131

**Susan Shaw Period Pieces**
Saffron Walden, Essex
Tel: 01799 599217

## WATCHES

**Kleanthous Antiques**
144 Portobello Rd,
London W11 2DZ
Tel: 020 7727 3649
antiques@kleanthous.com
www.kleanthous.com

**70s Watches**
graham@gettya.freeserve.co.uk
www.70s-watches.com

**The Watch Gallery**
1129 Fulham Road, London
SW3 6RT
Tel: 020 7581 3239

# DIRECTORY OF AUCTIONEERS

This is a list of auctioneers that conduct regular sales. Auctioneers who wish to be listed in this directory for our next edition, space permitting, are requested to email info@thepriceguidecompany.com by 1st February 2008.

## LONDON

**Bloomsbury Auctions**
Bloomsbury House, 24 Maddox Street, London W1 S1PP
Tel: 020 7495 9494
Fax: 020 7495 9499
www.bloomsbury-book-auct.com

**Bonhams**
101 New Bond St, London W1S 1SR
Tel: 020 7629 6602
Fax: 020 7629 8876
www.bonhams.com

**Christies (South Kensington)**
85 Old Brompton Rd, London SW7 3LD
Tel: 020 7581 7611
Fax: 020 7321 3311
info@christies.com
www.christies.com

**Rosebery's**
74-76 Knights Hill, West Norwood, London SE27 0JD
Tel: 020 8761 2522
Fax: 020 8761 2524

**Sotheby's (Olympia)**
Hammersmith Rd, London W14 8UX
Tel: 020 7293 5555
Fax: 020 7293 6939
www.sothebys.com

## BEDFORDSHIRE

**W. & H. Peacock**
The Auction Centre, 26 Newnham St, Bedford MK40 3JR
Tel: 01234 266366
Fax: 01234 269082
www.peacockauction.co.uk
info@peacockauction.co.uk

## BERKSHIRE

**Dreweatt Neate**
Donnington Priory, Donnington, Nr. Newbury, Berkshire RG14 2JE
Tel: 01635 553553
Fax: 01635 553599
donnington@dnfa.com
www.dnfa.com

**Law Fine Art Ltd**
Firs Cottage, Church Lane, Brimpton, Berkshire RG7 4TJ
Tel: 0118 971 0353
Fax: 0118 971 3741
info@lawfineart.co.uk
www.lawfineart.co.uk

**Special Auction Services**
The Coach House, Midgham Park, Reading, Berkshire RG7 5UG
Tel: 01189 712 949
Fax: 01189 712 420
commemorative@aol.com

## BUCKINGHAMSHIRE

**Amersham Auction Rooms**
125 Station Rd, Amersham, Buckinghamshire HP7 0AH
Tel: 08700 460606
Fax: 08700 460607
info@amershamauctionrooms.co.uk
www.amershamauctionrooms.co.uk

## CAMBRIDGESHIRE

**Cheffins**
Clifton House, 1&2 Clifton Road, Cambridge CB1 7EA
Tel: 01223 213 343
Fax: 01223 271 949
fine.art@cheffins.co.uk
www.cheffins.co.uk

## CHANNEL ISLANDS

**Martel Maides Ltd.**
The Old Bank, 29 High Street, Channel Islands GY1 2JX
Tel: 01481 713463
Fax: 01481 700337
sales@martelmaides.co.uk
www.martelmaides.co.uk

## CHESHIRE

**Bonhams (Chester)**
New House, 150 Christleton Road, Chester, Cheshire CH3 5TD
Tel: 01244 313 936
Fax: 01244 340 028
www.bonhams.com

**Bob Gowland International Golf Auctions**
The Stables, Claim Farm, Manley Rd Frodsham, Cheshire WA6 6HT
Tel/Fax: 01928 740668
bob@internationalgolfauctions.com
www.internationalgolfauctions.com

## CLEVELAND

**Vectis Auctioneers**
Fleck Way Thornaby, Stockton-on-Tees, Cleveland TS17 9JZ
Tel: 01642 750616
Fax: 01642 769478
www.vectis.co.uk

## CORNWALL

**W. H. Lane & Son**
Jubilee House, Queen Street, Penzance TR18 4DF
Tel: 01736 361447
Fax: 01736 350097
info@whlane.co.uk

**David Lay FRICS**
The Penzance Auction House Alverton, Penzance TR18 4RE
Tel: 01736 361414
Fax: 01736 360035
david.lays@btopenworld.com

## CUMBRIA

**Mitchells Fine Art**
Auctioneers, Station Road, Cockermouth, Cumbria CA13 9PZ
Tel: 01900 827800
Fax: 01900 828073
info@mitchellsfineart.com
www.mitchellsfineart.com

**Penrith Farmers' & Kidds**
Skirsgill Saleroom, Skirsgill, Penrith, Cumbria CA11 0DN
Tel: 01768 890781
Fax: 01768 895058
info@pfkauctions.co.uk
www.pfandk.co.uk

## DERBYSHIRE

**Bamfords Ltd**
The Old Picture Palace, 133 Dale Road, Matlock, Derbyshire DE4 3LT
Tel: 01629 574460
www.bamfords-auctions.co.uk

## DEVON

**Bearne's**
St Edmund's Court, Okehampton St, Exeter, Devon EX4 1LX
Tel: 01392 207000
Fax: 01392 207007
enquiries@bearnes.co.uk
www.bearnes.co.uk

**Bonhams**
Dowell St, Honiton, Devon EX14 1LX
Tel: 01404 41872
Fax: 01404 43137
honiton@bonhams.com
www.bonhams.com

**Charterhouse**
The Long Street Salerooms, Sherborne, Dorset DT9 3BS
Tel: 01935 812277
Fax: 01935 389387
enquiry@charterhouse-auctions.co.uk
www.charterhouse-auctions.co.uk

**HY Duke & Sons**
Weymouth Avenue, Dorchester, Dorset DT11QS
Tel: 01305 265080
Fax: 01305 260101
enquiries@dukes-auctions.com
www.dukes-auctions.com

**Onslows**
The Coach House, Manor Road, Stourpaine DT11 8TQ
Tel/Fax: 01258 488 838
www.onslows.co.uk

**Semley Auctioneers**
Station Rd, Semley, Nr Shaftesbury, Dorset SP7 9AN
Tel: 01747 855122
Fax: 01747 855222
semley.auctioneers@btinternet.com
www.semleyauctioneers.com

## ESSEX

**Ambrose**
Ambrose House, Old Station Rd, Loughton, Essex IG10 4PE
Tel: 020 8502 3951
Fax: 020 8532 0833
info@ambroseauction.co.uk
www.ambroseauction.co.uk

**Sworder & Sons**
14 Cambridge Rd, Stansted Mountfitchet, Essex CM24 8DE
Tel: 01279 817778
Fax: 01279 817779
auctions@sworder.co.uk
www.sworder.co.uk

## GLOUCESTERSHIRE

**Bruton Knowles**
The Tithe Barn, Southam, Cheltenham, Gloucestershire GL52 3NY
Tel: 01242 573904
Fax: 01242 224463
www.bkonline.co.uk

**Dreweatt Neate (Formerly Bristol Auction Rooms)**
Bristol Salerooms, St. John's Place, Apsley Road, Clifton, Bristol BS8 2ST
Tel: 0117 973 7201
Fax: 0117 973 5671
bristol@dnfa.com
www.dnfa.com/bristol

**Cotswold Auction Co.**
Chapel Walk Saleroom, Chapel Walk, Cheltenham, Gloucestershire GL50 3DS
Tel: 01242 256363
Fax: 01242 571734
info@cotswoldauction.co.uk
www.cotswoldauction.co.uk

**Mallams Fine Art Auctioneers and Valuers**
26 Grosvenor Street, Cheltenham GL52 2SG
Tel: 01242 235712
Fax: 01242 241943
cheltenham@mallams.co.uk
www.mallams.co.uk/fineart

**Moore, Allen & Innocent**
The Norcote Salerooms, Burford Road, Norcote, Nr Cirencester, Glos GL7 5RH
Tel: 01285 646 050
fineart@mooreallen.co.uk
www.mooreallen.co.uk

## HAMPSHIRE

**Andrew Smith & Son**
The Auction Rooms, Manor Farm, Itchen Stoke, nr. Winchester SO24 0QT
Tel: 01962 735988
Fax: 01962 738879
auctions@andrewsmithandson.com

**Jacobs & Hunt Fine Art Auctioneers**
Lavant Street,
Petersfield GU32 3EF
Tel: 01730 233 933
Fax: 01730 262 323
auctions@jacobsandhunt.com
www.jacobsandhunt.com

## HEREFORDSHIRE

**Brightwells**
The Fine Art Saleroom,
Ryelands Rd, Leominster,
Herefordshire HR68NZ
Tel: 01568 611122
Fax: 01568 610519
fineart@brightwells.com
www.brightwells.com

## HERTFORDSHIRE

**Tring Market Auctions**
Brook Street, Tring HP23 5EF
Tel: 01442 826 446
Fax: 01442 890 927
sales@tringmarketauctions.co.uk
www.tringmarketauctions.co.uk

## ISLE OF WIGHT

**Ways, The Auction House,**
Garfield Rd, Ryde,
Isle of Wight PO33 2PT
Tel: 01983 562255
Fax: 01983 565108
www.waysauctionrooms
.fsbusiness.co.uk

## KENT

**Dreweatt Neate**
Tunbridge Wells Saleroom,
The Auction Hall, The Pantiles,
Tunbridge Wells, Kent TN2 5QL
Tel: 01892 544500
Fax: 01892 515191
tunbridgewells@dnfa.com
www.dnfa.com/tunbridgewells

**Gorringes**
15 The Pantiles,
Tunbridge Wells TN2 5TD
Tel: 01892 619 670
Fax: 01892 619 671
auctions@gorringes.co.uk
www.gorringes.co.uk

## LANCASHIRE

**Capes Dunn & Co.**
The Auction Galleries,
38 Charles St,
Manchester, M1 7DB
Tel: 0161 273 1911
Fax: 0161 273 3474

## LEICESTERSHIRE

**Gilding's**
Roman Way Market,
Harborough, LE16 7PQ
Tel: 01858 410414
Fax: 01858 432956
sales@gildings.co.uk
www.gildings.co.uk

**Tennants Co.**
Millhouse, South Street,
Oakham, Rutland LE15 6BG
Tel: 01572 724 66
Fax: 01572 72 4422
oakham@tennants-ltd.co.uk
www.tennants.co.uk

## LINCOLNSHIRE

**Golding Young & Co.**
Old Wharf Rd, Grantham,
Lincolnshire NG31 7AA
Tel: 01476 565118
Fax: 01476 561475
enquiries@goldingyoung.com
www.goldingyoung.com

## MERSEYSIDE

**Cato, Crane & Co**
6 Stanhope St,
Liverpool L8 5RE
Tel: 0151 709 5559
Fax: 0151 707 2454
www.cato-crane.co.uk

## NORFOLK

**Gaze and Son**
Diss Auction Rooms, Roydon
Road, Diss IP22 4LN
Tel: 01379 650306
Fax: 01379 644313
sales@dissauctionrooms.co.uk
www.twgaze.com

**Keys Auctioneers & Valuers**
Aylsham Salerooms, Palmers
Lane, Aylsham, Norfolk NR11
6JA
Tel: 01263 733195
www.keysauctions.co.uk

**Knights Sporting Auctions**
The Thatched Gallery,
The Green, Aldborough,
Norwich, Norfolk NR11 7AA
Tel: 01263 768488
Fax: 01263 768788
www.knights.co.uk

## NOTTINGHAMSHIRE

**Mellors & Kirk Fine Art Auctioneers**
Gregory Street, Nottingham,
Nottinghamshire NG7 2NL
Tel: 0115 9790000
Fax: 0115 9781111
enquiries@mellors-kirk.com
www.mellors-kirk.co.uk

**Neales of Nottingham**
The Nottingham Salerooms,
192 Mansfield Road,
Nottingham NG1 3HU
Tel: 0115 962 4141
Fax: 0115 969 3450
nottingham@dnfa.com
www.dnfa.com/neales

**T Vennett-Smith Auctioneers and Valuers**
11 Nottingham Road, Gotham,
Nottingham NG11 0HE
Tel: 0115 9830541
Fax: 0115 9830114
info@vennett-smith.com
www.vennett-smith.com

## OXFORDSHIRE

**Mallams**
Pevensey House, 27 Sheep St,
Bicester, Oxfordshire OX6 7JF
Tel: 01869 252901
Fax: 01869 320283
bicester@mallams.co.uk
www.mallams.co.uk

**Mallams (Oxford)**
Bocardo House, 24a St.
Michaels Street, Oxford,
OX1 2EB
Tel: 01865 241358
Fax: 01865 725483
oxford@mallams.co.uk
www.mallams.co.uk

**Soames Country Auctions**
Pinnocks Farm Estate,
Northmoor, Witney OX8 1AY
Tel: 01865 300626
soame@email.msn.com
www.soamesauctioneers.co.uk

## SHROPSHIRE

**Halls Fine Art**
Welsh Bridge,
Shrewsbury SY3 8LA
Tel: 01743 231 212
Fax: 01743 271 014
FineArt@halls.to
www.hallsgb.com

**Walker Barnett & Hill**
Cosford Auction Rooms,
Long Lane, Cosford,
Shropshire TF11 8PJ
Tel: 01902 375555
Fax: 01902375566
www.walker-barnett-hill.co.uk

**Mullock Madeley**
The Old Shippon,
Wall under-Heywood,
Nr Church Stretton,
Shropshire SY6 7DS
Tel: 01694 771771
Fax: 01694 771772
info@mullockmadeley.co.uk
www.mullock-madeley.co.uk

## SOMERSET

**Clevedon Salerooms**
The Auction Centre, Kenn Road,
Kenn, Clevedon, North
Somerset BS21 6TT
Tel: 01934 830 111
Fax: 01934 832 538
info@clevedon-salerooms.com
www.clevedon-salerooms.com

**Gardiner Houlgate**
The Bath Auction Rooms,
9 Leafield Way,
Corsham, Bath,
Somerset SN139SW
Tel: 01225 812912
Fax: 01225 811777
auctions@gardiner-houlgate. co.uk
www.invaluable.com/gardiner-houlgate

**Lawrence's Fine Art Auctioneers Ltd**
South St, Crewkerne,
Somerset TA18 8AB
Tel: 01460 73041
Fax: 01460 74627
enquiries@lawrences.co.uk
www.lawrences.co.uk

## STAFFORDSHIRE

**Potteries Specialist Auctions**
271 Waterloo Rd, Cobridge,
Stoke-on-Trent,
Staffordshire ST6 3HR
Tel: 01782 286622
Fax: 01782 213777
www.potteriesauctions.com

**Richard Winterton**
School House Auction Rooms,
Hawkins Lane, Burton-on-Trent,
Staffordshire DE14 1PT
Tel: 01283 511224

**Wintertons**
Lichfield Auction Centre
Fradley, Lichfield, WS13 8NF
Tel: 01543 263256
Fax: 01543 415348
enquiries@wintertons.co.uk
www.wintertons.co.uk

## SUFFOLK

**Diamond Mills**
Orwell Hall, Orwell Rd,
Felixstowe, Suffolk IP11 7BL
Tel:01473 218 600
diamondmills@btconnect.com
www.diamondmills.co.uk

**Neal Sons & Fletcher**
26 Church St,
Woodbridge,
Suffolk IP12 1DP
Tel: 01394 382263
Fax: 01394 383030
enquiries@nsf.co.uk
www.nsf.co.uk

## SURREY

**Barbers**
The Mayford Centre,
Smarts Heath Rd,
Woking, Surrey GU22 0PP
Tel: 01483 728939
Fax: 01483 762552
www.thesaurus.co.uk/barbers

**Clark Gammon**
The Guildford Auction Rooms,
Bedford Road, Guildford, Surrey
GU1 4SJTel: 01483 880915
Fax: 01483 880918
fine.art@clarkegammon.co.uk
www.clarkegammon.co.uk

**Ewbank Auctioneers**
The Burnt Common Auction
Rooms, London Rd,
Send, Woking,
Surrey GU23 7LN
Tel: 01483 223101
Fax: 01483 222171
www.ewbankauctions.co.uk

**Dreweatt Neate (Formerly Hamptons)**
Baverstock House, 93 High
Street, Godalming GU7 1AL
Tel: 01483 423 567
Fax: 01483 426 392
godalming@dnfa.com
www.dnfa.com/godalming

## EAST SUSSEX

**Burstow & Hewett**
Lower Lake, Battle,
East Sussex TN33 0AT
Tel: 01424 772 374
www.burstowandhewett.co.uk

**Dreweatt Neate (Eastbourne)**
46-50 South St,
Eastbourne,
East Sussex BN214XB,
Tel: 01323 410419
Fax: 01323 416540
eastbourne@dnfa.com
www.dnfa.com

**Gorringes**
Terminus Rd, Bexhill-on-Sea,
East Sussex TN39 3LR
Tel: 01424 212994
Fax: 01424 224035
www.gorringes.co.uk

**Gorringes**
15 North St, Lewes,
East Sussex BN7 2PD
Tel: 01273 472503
Fax: 01273 479559
www.gorringes.co.uk

**Raymond P. Inman**
The Auction Galleries, 98A
Coleridge Street,
Hove BN3 5 AA
Tel: 01273 774777
Fax: 01273 735660
r.p.inman@talk21.com
www.invaluable.com/raymondinman

**Wallis & Wallis**
West St Auction Galleries,
Lewes, East Sussex BN72NJ
Tel: 01273 480208
Fax: 01273 476562
auctions@wallisandwallis.co.uk
www.wallisandwallis.co.uk

## TYNE & WEAR

**Anderson and Garland**
Anderson House, Crispin Court,
Newbiggin Lane, Westerhope,
Newcastle upon Tyne NE5 1BF
Tel: 0191 430 3000
andersongarland@aol.com
www.andersonandgarland.com

**Corbitts**
5 Mosley St, Newcastle-upon-Tyne, Tyne and Wear NE1 1YE
Tel: 0191 232 7268
Fax: 0191 261 4130
collectors@corbitts.com
www.corbitts.com

## WARWICKSHIRE

**Locke & England**
18 Guy Street,
Leamington Spa CV32 4RT
Tel: 01926 889100
Fax: 01926 470608
valuers@leauction.co.uk
www.leauction.co.uk

## WEST MIDLANDS

**Bonhams, Knowle**
The Old House,
Station Rd, Knowle,
Solihull, B930HT
Tel: 01564 776151
Fax: 01564 778069
knowle@bonhams.com
www.bonhams.com

**Fellows & Sons**
Augusta House,
19 Augusta St, Hockley,
Birmingham,
West Midlands B186JA
Tel: 0121 212 2131
Fax: 0121 212 1249
info@fellows.co.uk
www.fellows.co.uk

## WEST SUSSEX

**John Bellman**
New Pound Wisborough Green,
Billingshurst,
West Sussex RH14 0AZ
Tel: 01403 700858
Fax: 01403 700059
enquiries@bellmans.comuk
www.bellmans.co.uk

**Denhams**
The Auction Galleries,
Warnham, Nr Horsham,
West Sussex RH123RZ
Tel: 01403 255699
Fax: 01403 253837
enquiries@denhams.com
www.denhams.com

**Rupert Toovey**
Spring Gardens, Washington,
West Sussex, RH20 3BS,
Tel: 01903 891955
auctions@rupert-toovey.com
www.rupert-toovey.com

## WILTSHIRE

**Finan & Co**
The Square, Mere,
Wiltshire BA12 6DJ
Tel: 01747 861411
Fax: 01747 861944
post@finanandco.co.uk
www.finanandco.co.uk

**Henry Aldridge & Sons**
The Devizes Auctioneers,
Unit 1, Bath Rd Business
Centre, Devizes,
Wiltshire SN10 1XA
Tel: 01380 729199
Fax: 01380 730073
www.henry-aldridge.co.uk

**Woolley & Wallis**
51-61 Castle St,
Salisbury,
Wiltshire SP1 3SU
Tel: 01722 424500
Fax: 01722 424508
enquiries@woolleyandwallis.co.uk
www.woolleyandwallis.co.uk

## WORCESTERSHIRE

**Andrew Grant**
St Mark's House,
St Mark's Close,
Cherry Orchard,
Worcester WR5 3DJ
Tel: 01905 357547
Fax: 01905 763942
fine.art@andrew-grant.co.uk
www.andrew-grant.co.uk

**Gloucestershire Worcestershire Railwayana Auctions**
'The Willows',
Badsey Rd, Evesham,
Worcestershire WR117PA
Tel: 01386 760109
www.gwra.co.uk

**Phillip Serrell**
The Malvern Saleroom,
Barnards Green Rd, Malvern,
Worcestershire WR143LW
Tel: 01684 892314
Fax: 01684 569832
www.serrell.com

## EAST YORKSHIRE

**Dee, Atkinson & Harrison**
The Exchange Saleroom,
Driffield,
East Yorkshire YO25 6LD
Tel: 01377 253151
Fax: 01377 241041
exchange@dee-atkinson-harrison.co.uk
www.dahauctions.com

## NORTH YORKSHIRE

**David Duggleby**
The Vine St Salerooms,
Scarborough,
North Yorkshire YO11 1XN
Tel: 01723 507111
Fax: 01723 507222
www.davidduggleby.com

**Tennants**
The Auction Centre, Leyburn,
North Yorkshire DL8 5SG
Tel: 01969 623780
Fax: 01969 624281
enquiry@tennants-ltd.co.uk
www.tennants.co.uk

## SOUTH YORKSHIRE

**A. E. Dowse & Sons**
Cornwall Galleries, Scotland
Street, Sheffield S3 7DE
Tel: 0114 2725858
Fax: 0114 2490550
aedowes@aol.com
www.aedowseandson.com

**BBR Auctions**
Elsecar Heritage Centre,
5 Ironworks Row, Wath Rd,
Elsecar, Barnsley,
South Yorkshire S748HJ
Tel: 01226 745156
Fax: 01226 361561
www.onlinebbr.com

**Sheffield Railwayana**
43 Little Norton Lane,
Sheffield, S8 8GA
Tel: 0114 274 5085
ian@sheffrail.freeserve.co.uk
www.sheffieldrailwayana.co.uk

## WEST YORKSHIRE

**Andrew Hartley Fine Arts**
Victoria Hall Salerooms, Little
Lane, Ilkle,
West Yorkshire, LS29 8EA
Tel: 01943 816363
info@andrewhartleyfinearts.co.uk
www.andrewhartleyfinearts.co.uk

## SCOTLAND

**Bonhams Edinburgh**
65 George St,
Edinburgh EH2 2JL
Tel: 0131 225 2266
Fax: 0131 220 2547
edinburgh@bonhams.com
www.bonhams.com

**Loves Auction Rooms**
52-54 Canal St, Perth,
Perthshire, PH2 8LF
Tel: 01738 633337
Fax: 01738 629830

**Lyon & Turnbull**
33 Broughton Place,
Edinburgh EH1 3RR
Tel: 0131 557 8844
Fax: 0131 557 8668
info@lyonandturnbull.com
www.lyonandturnbull.com

**Lyon & Turnbull**
4 Woodside Place,
Glasgow G3 7QF
Tel: 0141 353 5070
Fax: 0141 332 2928
info@lyonandturnbull.com
www.lyonandturnbull.com

**Thomson, Roddick & Medcalf Ltd.**
44/3 Hardengreen Business
Park, Eskbank, Edinburgh,
Midlothian EH22 3NX
Tel: 0131 454 9090
Fax: 0131 454 9191
www.thomsonroddick.com

## WALES

**Bonhams Cardiff**
7-8 Park Place, Cardiff,
Glamorgan CF10 3DP
Tel: 02920 727 980
Fax: 02920 727 989
cardiff@bonhams.com
www.bonhams.com

**Peter Francis**
Curiosity Salerooms, 19 King
St, Carmarthen, South Wales
Tel: 01267 233456
Fax: 01267 233458
www.peterfrancis.co.uk

**Welsh Country Auctions**
2 Carmarthen Road, Cross
Hands, Llanelli,
Carmarthenshire SA14 6SP
Tel: 01269 844428
Fax: 01269 844428
enquiries@welshcountryauctions.com
www.welshcountryauctions.com

## IRELAND

**HOK Fine Art**
4 Main St, Blackrock, Co
Dublin, Ireland
Tel: 00 353 1 2881000
fineart@hok.ie
www.hokfineart.com

**Mealy's**
The Square, Castlecomer,
County Kilkenny, Ireland
Tel: 00 353 56 41229
/41413
Fax: 00 353 56 41627
info@mealys.com
www.mealys.com

# CLUBS, SOCIETIES & ORGANISATIONS

## ADVERTISING

**Antique Advertising Signs**
The Street Jewellery Society, 11 Bowsden Ter, South Gosford, Newcastle-Upon-Tyne NE3 1RX

## AUTOGRAPHS

Autograph Club of GB
gregson@blueyonder.co.uk
www.acogb.co.uk

## BAXTER PRINTS

**The New Baxter Society**
c/o Reading Museum & Art Gallery, Blagrave St, Reading, Berkshire RG1 1QH
baxter@rpsfamily.demon.co.uk
www.rpsfamily.demon.co.uk

## BANK NOTES

**International Bank Note Society**
43 Templars Crescent, London, N3 3QR

## BOOKS

**The Enid Blyton Society**
93 Milford Hill, Salisbury, Wiltshire SP1 2QL
Tel: 01722 331937
www.enidblytonsociety.co.uk

**The Followers of Rupert**
www.see.ed.ac.uk/~afm/followers

## BOTTLES

**Old Bottle Club of Great Britain**
2 Strafford Avenue, Elsecar, Nr Barnsley, South Yorkshire S74 18AA
Tel: 01226 745 156

## CERAMICS

**Carlton Ware Collectors' International**
The Carlton Factory Shop, Copeland St, Stoke-upon-Trent, Staffordshire ST4 1PU
Tel: 01782 410 504
cwciclub@aol.com
www.lattimore.co.uk/deco/carlton.htm

**Chintz World International**
Tel: 01525 220272
Fax: 01525 222442
www.chintzworld-intl.com

**Clarice Cliff Collectors' Club**
Fantasque House, Tennis Drive, The Park, Nottingham NG7 1AE
www.claricecliff.com

**Goss Collectors' Club**
Tel: 01159 300 441
www.gosschina.com

**Hornsea Pottery Collectors' & Research Society**
128 Devonshire St, Keighley, West Yorkshire BD21 2QJ
hornsea@pdtennant.fsnet.co.uk
www.easyontheeye.net/hornsea/society.htm

**M.I. Hummel Club (Goebel)**
Porzellanfabrik, GmbH & Co. KG, Coburger Str.7, D-96472 Rodental, Germany
Tel: +49 (0) 95 63 72 18 03
Fax: +49 (0) 95 63 9 25 92

**Keith Murray Collectors' Club**
Fantasque House, Tennis Drive, The Park, Nottingham NG7 1AE
www.keithmurray.com

**Lorna Bailey Collectors' Club**
Newcastle Street, Dalehall, Burslem, Stoke-on-Trent ST6 3QF
Tel: 01782 837 341

**Mabel Lucie Attwell**
Abbey Antiques, 63 Great Whyte, Ramsey, Huntingdon PE26 1HL
Tel: 01487 814753

**Moorcroft Collectors' Club**
Sandbach Rd, Burslem, Stoke-on-Trent, Staffordshire ST6 2DQ
Tel: 01782 820500
Fax: 01782 820501
cclub@moorcroft.com
www.moorcroft.com

**Pendelfin Family Circle**
Cameron Mill, Howsin St, Burnley, Lancashire BB10 1PP
Tel: 01282 432 301
www.pendelfin.co.uk

**Poole Pottery Collectors' Club**
The Quay, Poole, Dorset BH15 1RF
Tel: 01202 666200
Fax: 01202 682894
www.poolepottery.co.uk

**Potteries of Rye Collectors' Society**
22 Redyear Cottages, Kennington Rd, Ashford, Kent TN24 0TF
barry.buckton@tesco.net
www.potteries-of-rye-society.co.uk

**Royal Doulton International Collectors' Club**
Minton House, London Rd, Stoke-on-Trent, Staffordshire ST47QD
Tel: 01782 292292
Fax: 01782 292099
enquiries@royal-doulton.com
www.royal-doulton.com/collectables

**Royal Winton International Collectors' Club**
Dancers End, Northall, Bedfordshire LU6 2EU
Tel: 01525 220 272
Fax: 01525 222 442

**The Shelley Group**
38 Bowman Road, Norfolk, Norwich NR4 6LS
shelley.group@shelley.co.uk
www.shelley.co.uk

**Susie Cooper Collectors' Group**
Panorama House, 18 Oaklea Mews, Aycliffe Village, County Durham DL5 6JP
www.susiecooper.co.uk

**The Sylvac Collectors' Circle**
174 Portsmouth Rd, Horndean, Waterlooville, Hampshire
admin@sylvacclub.com
www.sylvacclub.com

**Novelty Teapot Collectors' Club**
Tel: 01257 450 366
vince@totallyteapots.com
www.totallyteapots.com

**Official International Wade Collectors' Club**
Royal Works, Westport Rd, Stoke-on-Trent, Staffs ST6 4AP
Tel: 01782 255255
Fax: 01782 575195
club@wade.co.uk
www.wade.co.uk

**Royal Worcester Collectors' Society**
Severn Street, Worcester, WR1 2NE
Tel: 01905 746 000
sinden@royal-worcester.co.uk
www.royal-worcester.co.uk

## CIGARETTE CARDS

**Cartopulic Society of GB**
7 Alderham Avenue, Radlett, Herts WD7 8HL

## COINS

**British Numismatic Society**
c/o The Warburg Institute, Woburn Square, London WC1H 0AB
www.britnumsoc.org

**Royal Numismatic Society**
c/o The British Museum, Dept of Coins and Medals, Great Russell Street, London WC1B 3DG
Tel: 020 7636 1555
RNS@dircon.co.uk
www.users.dircon.co.uk/~rns

## COMMEMORATIVE WARE

**Commemorative Collectors' Society**
The Gardens, Gainsborough Rd, Winthorpe, nr Newark NG24 2NR
Tel: 01636 671377
chris@royalcoll.fsnet.co.uk

## COMICS

**Association of Comic Enthusiasts**
L'Hopiteau, St Martin du Fouilloux 79420, France
Tel: 00 33 549 702 114

**Comic Enthusiasts Society**
80 Silverdale, Sydenham, London SE26 4SJ

**Beano & Dandy Collectors' Club**
www.philcomics.com/collectors_club.html

## COSTUME & ACCESSORIES

**British Compact Collectors' Club**
PO Box 131, Woking, Surrey GU24 9YR

**Costume Society**
St. Paul's House, Warwick Lane, London EC4P 4BN
www.costumesociety.org.uk

**Hat Pin Society of GB**
PO Box 74, Bozeat, Northamptonshire NN29 7UD

## DISNEYANA

**Walt Disney Collectors' Society**
c/o Enesco, Brunthill Road, Kingstown Industrial Estate, Carlisle CA3 0EN
Tel: 01228 404 062
www.wdccduckman.com

## DOLLS

**Barbie Collectors' Club of GB**
117 Rosemount Avenue, Acton, London W3 9LU
wdl@nipcus.co.uk'

**British Doll Collectors Club**
'The Anchorage', Wrotham Rd, Culverstone Green, Meopham, Kent DA13 0QW
www.britishdollcollectors.com

**Doll Club of Great Britain**
PO Box 154, Cobham, Surrey KT11 2YE

**The Fashion Doll Collectors' Club of GB**
PO Box 133, Lowestoft, Suffolk NR32 1WA
Tel: 07940 248127
voden@supanet.com

## FILM & TV

**James Bond 007 Fan Club**
PO Box 007, Surrey KT15 IDY
Tel: 01483 756007

**Fanderson - The Official Gerry Anderson Appreciation Society**
2 Romney Road, Willesborough, Ashford, Kent TN24 0RW

## GLASS

**The Carnival Glass Society**
P.O. Box 14, Hayes, Middlesex UB3 5NU
www.carnivalglasssociety.co.uk

**The Glass Association**
John Greenham, High Trees, Dean Lane, Merstham, Surrey, RH1 3AH,
www.glassassociation.org.uk

**Isle of Wight Studio Glass**
Old Park, St Lawrence, Isle of Wight, PO38 1XR
www.isleofwightstudioglass.co.uk

**Pressed Glass Collectors' Club**
4 Bowshot Close, Castle Bromwich B36 9UH
Tel: 0121 681 4872
www.webspawner.com/users/pressedglass

## KITCHENALIA

**National Horse Brass Society**
2 Blue Barn Cottage,
Blue Barn Lane,
Weybridge,
Surrey KT13 0NH
Tel: 01932 354 193

**The British Novelty Salt & Pepper Collectors Club**
Coleshill,
Clayton Road, Mold,
Flintshire CH7 15X

## MARBLES

**Marble Collectors Unlimited**
P.O. Box 206
Northborough,
MA 01532-0206 USA
marblesbev@aol.com

## MECHANICAL MUSIC

**Musical Box Society of Great Britain**
PO Box 299,
Waterbeach,
Cambridge CB4 4PJ

**The City of London Phonograph and Gramophone Society**
2 Kirklands Park,
Fyfe KY15 4EP
Tel: 01334 654 390

## METALWARE

**Antique Metalware Society**
PO Box 63, Honiton,
Devon EX14 1HP
amsmemsec@yahoo.co.uk

## MILITARIA

**Military – Crown Imperial**
37 Wolsey Close, Southall,
Middlesex UB2 4NQ

**Military Historical Society**
National Army Museum,
Royal Hospital Rd,
London SW3 4HT

**Orders & Medals Research Society**
123 Turnpike Link,
Croydon CR0 5NU

## PAPERWEIGHTS

**Paperweight Collectors Circle**
P.O. Box 941,
Comberton,
Cambridgeshire CB3 7GQ
Tel: 02476 386 172

## PENS & WRITING

**The Writing Equipment Society**
wes.membershipsec@virgin.net
www.wesoc.co.uk

## PERFUME BOTTLES

**International Perfume Bottle Association**
396 Croton Road, Wayne,
PA 19087 USA
www.ipba-uk.co.uk

## PLASTICS

**Plastics Historical Society**
31a Maylands Drive,
Sidcup, Kent DA14 4SB
mail@plastiquarian.com
www.plastiquarian.com

## POSTCARDS

**The Postcard Club of Great Britain**
34 Harper House,
St. James' Crescent,
London SW9 7LW

## POTLIDS

**The Pot Lid Circle**
Keith Mortimer
Tel: 01295 722 032

## QUILTS

**The Quilters' Guild of the British Isles**
Room 190,
Dean Clough, Halifax,
West Yorks 3HX 5AX
Tel: 01422 347 669
Fax: 01422 345 017
info@quiltersguild.org.uk
www.quiltersguild.org.uk

## RADIOS

**The British Vintage Wireless Society**
59 Dunsford Close,
Swindon,
Wiltshire SN1 4PW
Tel: 01793 541 634
www.bvws.org.uk

## RAILWAYANA

**Railwayana Collectors Journal**
7 Ascot Rd, Moseley,
Birmingham B13 9EN

## SEWING

**International Sewing Machine Collectors' Society**
www.ismacs.net

**The Thimble Society**
1107 Portobello Rd,
London W11 2QB
antiques@thimblesociety.co.uk
www.thimblesociety.co.uk

## SMOKING

**Lighter Club of Great Britain**
Richard Ball
richard@lighter.co.uk

## SPORTING

**International Football Hall of Fame**
info@ifhof.com,
www.ifhof.com

**British Golf Collectors Society**
anthonythorpe@ntlworld.com
www.britgolfcollectors.wyenet.co.uk

## STAMPS

**Postal History Society**
60 Tachbrook Street,
London SW1V 2NA
Tel: 020 7545 7773
john.scott@db.com

**Royal Mail Collectors' Club**
Freepost, NEA1431,
Sunderland, SR9 9XN

## STANHOPES

**The Stanhope Collectors' Club**
jean@stanhopes.info
www.stanhopes.info

## STAINLESS STEEL

**The Old Hall Club**
Sandford House, Levedale,
Stafford ST18 9AH
Tel: 01785 780 376
oht@gnwiggin.freeserve.co.uk
www.oldhallclub.co.uk

## TEDDY BEARS & SOFT TOYS

**British Teddy Bear Association**
PO Box 290
Brighton, Sussex
Tel: 01273 697 974

**Merrythought International Collectors' Club**
Ironbridge, Telford,
Shropshire TF8 7NJ
Tel: 01952 433 116

**Steiff Club Office**
Margaret Steiff GmbH,
Alleen Strasse 2, D-89537
Giengen/Brenz, Germany

## TOYS

**Action Man Club**
PO Box 142,
Horsham, RH13 5FJ

**The British Model Soldier Society**
44 Danemead, Hoddesdon,
Hertfordshire EN119LU
www.model.soldiers.btinternet.co.uk

**Corgi Collectors' Club**
PO Box 323, Swansea, Wales
SA1 1BJ

**Hornby Collectors Club**
PO Box 35, Royston,
Hertfordshire SG8 5XR
Tel/Fax: 01223 208 308
hsclubs.demon.co.uk
www.hornby.co.uk

**The Matchbox Toys International Collectors' Association**
P.O. Box 120, Deeside,
Flintshire CH5 3HE
kevin@matchboxclub.com
www.matchboxclub.com

**Historical Model Railway Society**
59 Woodberry Way,
London E4 7DY

**The English Playing Card Society**
11 Pierrepont St, Bath,
Somerset BA1 1LA
Tel: 01225 465 218

**Train Collectors' Society**
P.O. Box 20340,
London NW11 6ZE
Tel: 020 8209 1589
tcsinformation@btinternet.com
www.traincollectors.org.uk

**William Britain Collectors Club**
P.O. Box 32,
Wokingham RG40 4XZ
Tel: 01189 737080
Fax: 01189 733947
ales@wbritaincollectorsclub.com
www.britaincollectorsclub.com

## WATCHES

**British Watch & Clock Collectors' Association**
5 Cathedral Lane, Truro,
Cornwall TR1 2QS
Tel 01872 264010
Fax 01872 241953
tonybwcca@cs.com
www.timecap.com

# COLLECTING ON THE INTERNET

- The internet has revolutionised the trading of collectables. Compared to a piece of furniture, most collectables are easily defined, described and photographed. Shipping is also comparatively easy, due to average size and weight. Prices are also generally more affordable and accessible than for antiques and the Internet has provided a cost effective way of buying and selling, away from the overheads of shops and auction rooms. Many millions of collectables are offered for sale and traded daily, with sites varying from global online marketplaces, such as eBay, to specialist dealers' websites.
- When searching online, remember that some people may not know how to accurately describe their item. General category searches, even though more time consuming, and even purposefully misspelling a name, can yield results. Also, if something looks too good to be true, it probably is. Using this book to get to know your market visually, so that you can tell the difference between a real bargain and something that sounds like one, is a good start.
- As you will understand from buying this book, colour photography is vital – look for online listings that include as many images as possible and check them carefully. Beware that colours can appear differently, even between computer screens.
- Always ask the vendor questions about the object, particularly regarding condition. If there is no image, or you want to see another aspect of the object – ask. Most sellers (private or trade) will want to realise the best price for their items so will be more than happy to help – if approached politely and sensibly.
- As well as the 'e-hammer' price, you will probably have to pay additional transactional fees such as packing, shipping and possibly regional or national taxes. It is always best to ask for an estimate for these additional costs before leaving a bid. This will also help you tailor your bid as you will have an idea of the maximum price the item will cost if you are successful.
- In addition to well-known online auction sites, such as eBay, there are a host of other online resources for buying and selling, such as fair and auction date listings.

# INTERNET RESOURCES

### Live Auctioneers
**www.liveauctioneers.com**
**info@liveauctioneers.com**
A free service which allows users to search catalogues from selected auction houses in Europe, the USA and the United Kingdom. Through its connection with eBay, users can bid live via the Internet into salerooms as auctions happen. Registered users can also search through an archive of past catalogues and receive a free newsletter by email.

### invaluable.com
**www.invaluable.com**
**sales@invaluable.com**
A subscription service which allows users to search selected auction house catalogues from the United Kingdom and Europe. Also offers an extensive archive for appraisal uses.

### The Antiques Trade Gazette
**www.atg-online.com**
The online version of the UK trade newspaper, comprising British auction and fair listings, news and events.

### Maine Antique Digest
**www.maineantiquedigest.com**
The online version of America's trade newspaper including news, articles, fair and auction listings and more.

### La Gazette du Drouot
**www.drouot.com**
The online home of the magazine listing all auctions to be held in France at the Hotel de Drouot in Paris and beyond. An online subscription enables you to download the magazine online.

### AuctionBytes
**www.auctionbytes.com**
Auction resource with community forum, news, events, tips and a weekly newsletter.

### Auction.fr
**www.auction.fr**
Online database of auctions at French auction houses. A subscription allows users to search past catalogues and prices realised.

### Auctiontalk
**www.internetauctionlist.com**
Auction news, online and offline auction search engines and live chat forums.

### Go Antiques/Antiqnet
**www.goantiques.com**
**www.antiqnet.com**
An online global aggregator for art, antiques and collectables dealers who showcase their stock online, allowing users to browse and buy.

### eBay
**www.ebay.com**
Undoubtedly the largest and most diverse of the online auction sites, allowing users to buy and sell in an online marketplace with over 52 million registered users. Collectors should also view eBay Live Auctions (www.ebayliveauctions.com) where traditional auctions are combined with realtime, online bidding allowing users to interact with the saleroom as the auction takes place.

# INDEX

## A



## B

# D

# E



# F

# W



# Y



# Z